THE AMERICAN ALPINE JOURNAL
2004

Above: Josh Helling on an unnamed peak in the Orvin Fjella, Queen Maud Land, Antarctica. *Mike Libecki*
Cover: The stunning southeast face of Jirishanca, home of three new routes in 2003. Jeremy Frimer

Zion's Red Awakening (above). *Brian McCray*
Gambo flying past growlers in the Gerlache Strait, Antarctica. *Peter Lane Taylor*
Last Cry of the Butterfly on the Citadel, Kichatna Spires, Alaska (below). *David Kaszlikowski/StudioWspin.com.pl*
The Hand of Fatima, Mali (below, right). *Jimmy Chin*

Alexander Huber on the Open Book pitch of Zodiac, Yosemite. *Heinz Zak*

Corporate Friends
of the
AMERICAN ALPINE JOURNAL

We thank the following for their generous financial support of the 2004 American Alpine Journal

Title Sponsor

Marko Prezelj on the rappel-traverse, the Jones-Lowe route of North Twin, Alberta. *Steve House*
Mark Jenkins unaware of the coming storm while attempting a new route on the Inominata Ridge, Mont Blanc, Italy. *John Harlin II*

Friends
OF THE
AMERICAN ALPINE JOURNAL
We thank the following for their generous financial support:

BENEFACTORS:
The H. Adams Carter Endowment Fund for the American Alpine Journal
Yvon Chouinard

PATRONS:
Ann Carter, Peter D. McGann, M.D.
Gregory Miller, AAC New York Section
Louis F. Reichardt, Steve Schwartz

SUPPORTERS:
James Ansara, Mark A. Richey

SPECIAL THANKS TO:

Cascade Climbers
Neale E. Creamer
Jeff Cunningham
David W. Davidge III
David J. Harden
Richard E. Hoffman, M.D.
Neil Gehrels
Z. Wayne Griffin, Jr.
Dennis J. Meister
Tamotsu Nakamura
Royal Shannon Robbins
Robert B. Schoene, M.D.
William R. Stall
Dag Wilkinson
Charles R. Wilson
Michael Yokell

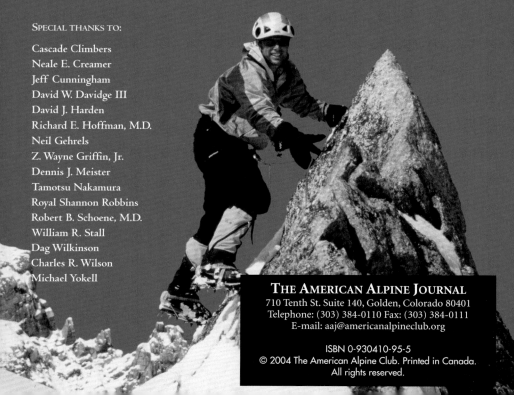

THE AMERICAN ALPINE JOURNAL
710 Tenth St. Suite 140, Golden, Colorado 80401
Telephone: (303) 384-0110 Fax: (303) 384-0111
E-mail: aaj@americanalpineclub.org

ISBN 0-930410-95-5

THE AMERICAN ALPINE JOURNAL
2004

VOLUME 46 ISSUE 78
CONTENTS

CLIMBS AND EXPEDITIONS

Khumbu Climbing School, *by Conrad Anker;* Climber Impacts and Access in Peru's Cordillera Blanca, *by Adam French;* Mt. Everest Alpine Conservation and Restoration Project, *by Alton Byers;* Update on the Himalayan Cataract Project, *by Geoffrey Tabin;* Mountain Hut Competition, *by Jay Wiener.*

Including: Everest: 50 Years on Top of the World, *by George Band;* Everest: Summit of Achievement, *by Stephen Venables;* Chris Bonington's Everest, *by Chris Bonington;* Tenzing, *by Ed Douglas;* Mountains of the Mind, *by Robert Macfarlane;* Imperial Ascent, *by Peter L. Bayers;* Where the Mountain Casts Its Shadow, *by Maria Coffey;* The Naked Mountain, *by Reinhold Messner;* The Beckoning Silence, *by Joe Simpson;* Dougal Haston, *by Jeff Connor;* Himalayan Vignettes, *by Kekoo Naoriji;* Range of Glaciers, *by Fred Beckey;* The Six Alpine/Himalayan Climbing Books, *by Frank Smythe;* Mountaineering: The Freedom of the Hills, *by The Mountaineers;* The Stettner Way, *by Jack Gorby;* Mount McKinley's West Buttress, *by Brad Washburn;* Yosemite, *by Alexander Huber and Heinz Zak;* Ordeal By Piton, *edited by Steve Roper;* Under a Sheltering Sky, *by Colin Monteath;* Southeastern Rock, *by Harrison Shull.*

Remembering Guy Edwards, Andrew Embick, Bill Mosconi, and George Senner.

The American Alpine Journal

John Harlin III, *Editor*

Advisory Board
James Frush, *Managing Editor*
Rolando Garibotti, Steve Hutchins, Mark Jenkins
Chris Jones, Dougald MacDonald, Mark Richey

Assistant Editor
Kelly Cordes

Art Director
Adele Hammond

Production and Editorial Assistants
Lili Henzler, Roger May

Contributing Editors
Steve Roper, *Features*
Lindsay Griffin, *Climbs & Expeditions*
Joe Kelsey, *Climbs & Expeditions*
David Stevenson, *Book Reviews*
Frederick O. Johnson, *Club Activities*

Cartographer
Martin Gamache, Alpine Mapping Guild

Translators
Christiane Leitinger
Molly Loomis
Henry Pickford

Indexers
Ralph Ferrara, Eve Tallman

Regional Contacts
Danny Kost, *Wrangell-St. Elias*; Drew Brayshaw & Don
Serl, *Coast Mountains, BC*; Colin Haley & Gordy Skoog,
Washington Cascades; Raphael Slawinski, *Canadian
Rockies*; Bill Wright, *Yosemite*; Antonio Gómez
Bohórquez, Jeremy Frimer and Richard Hidalgo, *Peru*
Rolando Garibotti, Patagonia; Damien Gildea,
Antarctica; Harish Kapadia, *India*; Nazir Sabir, *Pakistan*;
Elizabeth Hawley, *Nepal*; Tamotsu Nakamura,
Japanese expeditions; Lindsay Griffin, *Earth*

With additional thanks to
Alaska Mountaineering School, Bruce Andrews
Rodulfo Araujo, Chris Belczynski, Chris Benway and
Café Andino, Eric Bjørnstad, Peter Carse, Casa de Zarela
Jonny Copp, Alex & Nathalie Catlin, Jim Earl
Kris Erickson, Alex Fidi, Grzegorz Glazek, Dave Hart
Jeff Hollenbaugh, Sean Isaac, Brad Johnson
David Jones, Bronson MacDonald, Daryl Miller
Julian Neumayer, Marc Piché, Red Point Creative
Joe Reichert & Nancy Juergens, Marcelo Scanu
Rick Staley, Mike Strassman, Jack Tackle, Mark Twight
Talkeetna Ranger Station, Josh Wharton

Jonny Copp on a failed attempt at a new line on Mt. Hunter's north buttress. *Ke...*

THE AMERICAN ALPINE CLUB

PREFACE

By coincidence I took over the editorship of the *American Alpine Journal* the year the American Alpine Club turned 100. To commemorate the occasion, we devoted 60-some pages in the 2002 *AAJ* to looking back on AAC history and on events in American climbing during that period. Now, just two years later, it's another big anniversary: the *AAJ* turns 75. But instead of devoting a chunk of the *AAJ* to hindsight when there's so much happening today, we've decided to celebrate the occasion by republishing every *AAJ* ever printed. This being 2004, the republishing will be electronic: we're putting all 75 years of the *AAJ* online and on DVD/CD, thus serving history while also helping climbers worldwide who are researching tomorrow's objectives. But I'll get back to that. First, since this is the only place you'll get to read about it, let me reflect briefly on the last 75 years of the *American Alpine Journal*.

The *AAJ* didn't spring to life at the Club's founding. Our gestation period lasted 27 years, during which time Boston's Appalachian Mountain Club allowed our outings to be published in a section of their journal, *Appalachia*. Not until 1929 did Volume I, Number 1 of the *American Alpine Journal* find its way into the mailboxes of our 193 members. From this time forward the Journal became the Club's chief production and one of its largest single expenditures, perpetually in need of—and receiving—subsidies to meet costs. But there was never a doubt about its importance. The new publication was the primary tool fulfilling our charter to "promote and disseminate knowledge" of the high mountains. The book rapidly became a focal point where members shared their enthusiasm and their climbing experiences.

It's a delight to look at the early issues of the *AAJ*. The intelligence and knowledge revealed in the articles, as well as their relaxed frankness—the confiding voices of kindred spirits—all have great charm. So too the crisp black letterpress type on creamy wove paper, the wide margins, the glossy black and white photographs. Such pleasing results did not come about by accident. The *AAJ* was fortunate to have been guided in its first four decades by a stellar group of scholar-mountaineers. Allen Carpé (editor of the first issue), Howard Palmer, J. Monroe Thorington, Bob Bates, David Robertson, and Francis Farquhar, to name six of them, applied their considerable talents to the Journal during these years. Their wide-ranging knowledge of mountains and much else, their discerning taste, and their literate prose, set a lofty mark. Thorington in particular stands out—not only for his lengthy tenure as editor (1934-1946), but for his wide-ranging interests and delight in all things mountainous, his literary inclinations, and his irrepressible joie de vivre. Under Thorington the Journal brimmed with fascinating new material on alpinism and worldwide alpine culture.

There are gems scattered about these early issues that have as much potential to charm and educate us now as they did the day they were printed. In 1956 Dr. Charles Houston offered words on how to select expedition teams: "Good health is imperative, but over and above these qualities is a sense of humor, strength of character, courage in the face of adversity, ingenuity, and consideration for one's fellows. …rock acrobats and entrepreneurs do not belong in the Himalaya."

We come now to the man who, more than anyone else, is identified with the *American Alpine Journal*, H. Adams Carter, editor for 35 of the 75 years we commemorate. This multilingual, multi-tasking, one-man editing phenomenon took the helm in 1959. At the time of his passing in 1995, the *AAJ* had evolved into the climbing world's journal of record, the place where each year the most significant climbs are officially set down in writing.

In the year Ad's first issue was published, the American Alpine Club had 518 members. The last issue he edited was mailed to a membership nearly five times that size; it is now over 7,000. Ad Carter's legacy to the American Alpine Club and to the climbing community was a superb mountain journal, reporting the deeds of new-route climbers from all countries, in all ranges: the only thing of its kind in the world. He said in a *Himalayan Journal* article 11 years ago that he did not know what the *AAJ* would be like after he left it, only that it would be different. It's a tribute to his vision that in the nine years since Ad's death it has *not* become that much different.

While we'd all like to cherish the *AAJ*'s legacy by owning a complete collection, the $3,500-and-up pricetag on the used book market is a bit steep, especially if we need to have them shipped to, say, Bulgaria, home of climbers who put up one of 2003's great routes on Thalay Sagar (a feature story in this Journal). The next best thing is to slip a disc into your computer and pull up every page as you want it. This is coming soon, so stay tuned through your membership in the AAC or by periodically checking the AAC's website. The *AAJ* will also come online this year, which will allow you to do your research wherever you live, from Alaska to Zanskar.

In the meantime, we've compiled a comprehensive index to all 75 years of the *AAJ* and placed it on the Web, free to download (www.AmericanAlpineClub.org). This is without doubt the most comprehensive list of mountain accomplishments ever assembled: the ultimate research foundation for the digital *AAJ* library to come. But inevitably there will be flaws, and we invite you to help us in improving the index's accuracy and depth. Instructions are published with the index.

While there, you might want to download the *AAJ* International Grade Comparison Chart, which digests the international alphabet-soup of ratings found in our climbing reports into something intelligible across various borders and ponds. American Alpine Club members received a printed copy in the mail last winter.

Finally, a note about soul. The Climbs & Expeditions section of this *AAJ* (the heart of the book) expanded by over 40 pages from last year's, and yet the book's total page count had to remain the same. Sacrifices came by scrapping two feature articles, already written, and scrimping elsewhere, too. I bemoaned to Darío Bracali—a correspondent in Argentina—about needing to cut back on publishing some of the exploratory non-technical ascents of virgin peaks in his country, and he chided me with wise words that remind me of why I love this Journal: "A humble opinion from a reader/climber: Technical climbing is the exploration of difficulty. Before that, there must be the exploration of the world, the world that allows difficulty to exist. I believe both are parts of mountaineering, and that the journal would loose half its magic if it devotes itself only to technical stuff. I love them both, and I don't like to lose either. Your journal is one of the few today that shows us the always-broadening world. It gives us the information we need to go climbing!"

We welcome your feedback on where you think the *American Alpine Journal* should go in the next years. Please address your comments to aaj@AmericanAlpineClub.org. Or better yet, catch me in the hills.

JOHN HARLIN III

THE CRYSTAL SNAKE

*Overlooking the Everest circus and yet a world away, a rivulet
of water ice plunges down the huge north face of Nuptse, Nepal.*

WILLIE BENEGAS

The Everest-Nuptse base camp, with the north buttress of Nuptse in the background. *Damian Benegas*

One phone call changed our lives. It came from a guiding company in January 2003, with an offer
to guide Everest in the upcoming spring. It was the fiftieth anniversary of the first ascent, and for
me this was an offer that evoked mixed feelings. I knew that this year could be the biggest nightmare in the mountain's history. There were going to be too many expeditions, too much press,
and too many ego-trippers. And, having personally guided this Big Mama, I knew that when it
comes to "Sagarmatha," people have far too much ego.

From my experience, a mix of poorly run private expeditions meeting in base camp is a formula for disaster. In the spring of 2002, after summiting and arriving back at the South Col, I had to go back up the mountain to rescue a Hungarian in trouble. It seems his "friends" had decided that in some mystical way he would manage to return safely to camp, even though he had collapsed at 8,200 meters. The rescue excursion could have cost me my fingers, and the bottom line in 2003 was that I refused the offer.

When that phone call came in January, I decided that it was time for Damian, my twin brother, and I to embark on our own quest in the search for the ultimate art of suffering. We would pursue one of my deepest dreams: "Fatai Sarpa Nuptse," the Crystal Snake of Nuptse. My introduction to the Snake came in the spring of 1999 during my first trip to Everest. I will never forget that day when I arrived at Camp I, at the top of the infamous Khumbu Icefall. A layer of clouds covered the entire Western Cwm, but suddenly the sky partially cleared, showing the Crystal Snake through the mist. I was

Willie Benegas in the Khumbu Ice Fall approaching Nuptse, with The Crystal Snake glistening in the back ground. Two thousand feet of "The Tail of the Snake" isn't visible. *Damian Benegas*

looking at the most impressive and beautiful line that my eyes had ever seen. A couloir of perfect ice, faultless and clear as crystal, ran from bottom to top.

During my next two journeys to Sargamatha, I studied Nuptse, becoming almost obsessed. We climbers are really good at imagining lines up a mountain, our little brains connecting couloirs, ramps, and chimneys. Imagining myself on that route seemed easy because everything looked like it made perfect sense.

The Crystal Snake is on the flank of the imposing north buttress of Nuptse, whose main summit rises to 7,855 meters. The name Nuptse is Tibetan for "west peak." When you enter the Western Cwm you are looking directly up at Nuptse. While the prime objective of most climbers on this planet is Sagarmatha, consider this: Everest has had more than 1,000 summiters, while its neighboring peak, Nuptse, has seen only six ascents since it was first climbed in 1961.

The following is the account of our expedition.

March 21. We managed to escape Kathmandu at long last, flying to the village of Lukla, and decided to take our time reaching base; not having many responsibilities there seemed no point in arriving early. The trek went perfectly. At every tea house we met hordes of climbers on their way to Everest, and endured the endless question: "So, you're climbing Everest?" To which we tirelessly responded, "No, we're trying a new route on the north face of Nuptse." It seemed that our answer wasn't interesting, because few people wanted to know more.

April 4. The moment we had arrived at base camp, an Irish-American expedition invited us to their puja. It was a good excuse to drink a lot of rakshi, and, of course, to meet some of my dearest friends, Phenden, Nima Sheri, Nima Undy, and Pemba Gelgen. Each of us had managed to set our feet on the top of the world two or three times. After settling into camp our friend Lama Jambu offered to do a personal puja for us in order to ask permission of the mountain to allow us to enter and have a safe journey. It was a big honor. We have known Lama for almost five years and shared many expeditions and adventures together. A retired monk with seven climbs of Everest, he's a world-class climbing Sherpa. We had an amazing puja with our friends, just a small group of people who got together to enjoy a good time in the pursuit of a Himalayan mountain. While the party and laughter were growing, Sherpas from other expeditions came to wish us good luck on our adventure. The other Westerners had come to reach the top of the world, but we were different. We were the weirdoes of Everest Base Camp.

For nearly two weeks we had been working on our acclimatization, going up to Camp II on Everest and helping to fix ropes toward the South Col. There were soon to be crowds of climbers heading up, including those who simply dreamed of being climbers. For me, this trip was a culture shock. For the last three years, I had come to this base camp as a guide in charge of big expeditions. This involved lots of decision-making for other people. Now, it was so different: my brother, myself, and Edurne Pasaban with her Lhotse team were the only members of the team. The contrast of the two styles was astonishing. Big expeditions aren't bad—after all, I'm a guide and such expeditions bring bread to my table—but yes, they are certainly different.

There were about 500 Westerners in base camp, with a total of over 1,000 people, counting the local staff. An internet café with four computers offered remarkably fast connection for $1 per minute—Sherpas from Namche had decided to take advantage of the small town of Everest BC. There was also a clinic and a small store that sold yak meat from the previous season. Oh, and don't forget the French massage guy. Yes, this was Everest Base Camp, where everybody was more interested in the top of the world than in its majestic surroundings.

The first weeks of our acclimatization proceeded without problems other than the classic issues that arise from discussions with other teams. Expedition Sherpas had a habit of running up the mountain, all the way to Camp II, without harnesses or crampons. I found this tremendously disturbing, especially when a South African team told me that it was none of my business. It soon became my business when I rappelled into a crevasse looking for the body of a Sherpa.

But it's time to stop complaining and to start the climbing story.

May 6. The bergschrund looked like a gigantic fence, ready to protect the Snake from intruders. I got the first pitch, and as I started climbing a huge, overhanging, steel-hard and cave-like wall, I imagined I was an insect biting at the tail of this gigantic snake. It seemed she was irritated.

I tried to think of every position I could use to help me to set ice screws. The first 45 feet went okay, but the last 15 feet went over a lip. Damian, across from me, sent words of encouragement.

He kept telling me to place more gear, but of course that was too much to ask. I was hardly able to hold myself, much less spend precious time trying to set a Russian titanium screw in the ice. Slowly but surely, I managed to go over the overhang and then climb 80 feet of steep ice. I finally set the anchors, and the first lead of the climb became history. While we still had at least 40 more pitches to go, it was a good introduction. For the moment, our Snake had tolerated a pair of mosquitoes on her back with a minimum of complaint. We rappelled and headed back to camp.

But the Snake was not going to let us get away that easily. When I arrived at the tent, Damian was about 40 feet behind me. I dropped my tools and backpack, turned around, and looked back. Surprise! All I could see of Damian was his head. The rest had vanished into the glacier. "I don't understand," he said. "I followed your steps!" Perhaps he had eaten more cookies than I.

After carefully studying our route, we realized that the climb would be divided into many sections. The first step, the Snake's tail, was about 2,000 feet of hard ice and mixed climbing.

Damian Benegas at the top of the rock band enjoying the best 55° hockey field in the world. Pith 3, day 3, ca 6,800m. *Willie Benegas*

There appeared to be no possibilities for bivvies, and it seemed to be the crux of the route. The main body of the Snake was about 2,000 additional feet. One rock step in particular looked directly at us and seemed to be whispering, "If you prick me with your sharp tools I will shake you off!" Finally, there was the neck and the head. It was clear that we would have to be fully determined to once again embrace the art of suffering.

May 15. We were acclimatized and ready to go. I will never forget looking up and seeing only an endless snake of ice. The morning sun gave her a terrifying shine, an aura of impossible ice surrounded by reckless rock towers. Everything looked way too steep. The ice was so brittle that

Willie enjoying another Nuptse open bivy with "the mean meals" of 6 days: frozen Clif Bars. Day 2, ca 6,700m. *Damian Benegas*

it reminded me of all the wine glasses I had broken at home. We quickly reached a little cave visible from below. Looking at it from the glacier we fantasized that it could hold a set of twins. In fact it was barely big enough to fit one of us. At least now we had a good belay station that did a fine job of protecting Damian from all the dinnerplate-sized shards of ice that I sent straight down at him each time I struck the ice with my tools.

We climbed nine more pitches, each hard. There was nothing less than M3 WI4 with a couple of 5.9 M4 WI5 pitches thrown in. Let's just say that I was in need of adult diapers. At 6,100 meters my lungs were bursting in the constant search for any and all tiny molecules of oxygen. Time passed and the sun began to leave us. Every belay became an endless search for bivy spots. We were beginning to think that we had more chance of winning a lottery than finding decent bivvies.

The day at last came to a close. We were now at the bottom of the snake's main body and it was getting dark and chilly. Not able to find a decent bivy spot, we hung in our harnesses—our bed for the night. It ended up being a sleepless night where every 20 minutes or so we needed to move in order to keep the circulation moving in our legs. Time passed slowly.

We both complained a lot. Melting snow became the most serious business at hand. Since we couldn't sleep, hydration was the next priority. At 2 a.m. we decided to start melting snow again, but I screamed when I looked at the stove. Surprise! I saw a burner but no gas canister. I screamed again, and then Damian started screaming with me. Our simultaneous screams were probably loud enough to create an avalanche in the Khumbu. Our main tool—the only thing that would keep us alive in this environment—had, for some mysterious reason, broken without any explanation. (Note to self: next time stick with an MSR.)

I found the canister 10 feet below us, stuck in a crack. When finally I was able to retrieve it, the valve broke in half, probably from the cold. I couldn't believe it. After so many years of

Willie on lead pitch 1, day 3, ca 6,900m, solving the first rock band. *Damian Benegas*

dreaming and preparing for this climb, were we going to fail because of this damned stove? Damian, who is really good at fixing things, thought it might be possible to repair it. With not much of my brain functioning, I said we should drop 90 percent of the gear and give the route a single-push try. Damian spent an hour working with his knife and duct tape. He tried hard to fix the thing, but to no avail. We suffered out the rest of the night.

May 16. In the morning, as the sun reached our stiff joints, we came to a decision. We would leave all our gear and head down. This was a good way to blackmail ourselves, because we would have to return, if for nothing else than to retrieve it. The thought of re-leading all the previous pitches brought chills to the back of my neck, but 10 rappels later we arrived at the base. Looking up, I swore that we would not allow ourselves to let this failure discourage us. We would be back!

We decided to drop into our friends's camp, where we reloaded our tummies with dhal bhat (food of champions). We realized that we were going to be short of ice screws, and set about begging some from other teams. But the only screws we could find were cheap Russian ones. The last time I tried to use one of these it ended up as a twisted piece of metal ready to be dumped into a recycling container. The ice we were going to encounter on this route was way too hard for these screws. Finally, an obliging Indian team agreed to send up two screws from base camp. It was a good excuse to rest while we waited in camp for one more day.

May 17. We spent our rest day organizing gear and discussing final preparations for the journey up the Snake. In the name of super-light alpine style, we agreed to take only enough food for four days. We also decided to take a rack of six pins, a handful of stoppers, a half-dozen cams, six ice screws, and two 60-meter ropes.

May 18. We departed early in the morning. Damian had cracked a rib as a result of the classic "Khumbu Cough," and he was in a tremendous amount of pain. As a result, we agreed that I would lead the hard sections. I was personally okay with this because it meant I would be safe from the big rockets one normally sends down while leading. Damian deserves way more credit than I do, considering he was climbing this hard, at this altitude, on top of feeling bad already; he definitely deserved the medal for the Art of Suffering.

It was a nerve-wracking time, leading with marginal gear. The weather was unstable and delivered a constant spindrift that attacked me from all directions. We arrived back at our precious gear stash and had no other choice than to bivy again at the same spot. At least this time we had a little more time to get situated, and we managed a better bivy. Though still hanging in our harnesses, we were at least protected from the spindrift.

May 19. Entering the main body of the Snake put us in a most extraordinary couloir, surrounded by orange granite with a perfect streak of smooth green and blue ice stretching above and below. The climb had become mostly hard ice, and the plates I was sending down onto Damian grew in size. Safe belays for my brother proved almost impossible to find. The ice would bounce all over and finally strike him without mercy.

As we approached the first rock band, the spindrifts became an annoyance; I found myself wishing I had scuba gear. After four pitches we saw that the weather had become so bad that we decided to look for a safe bivy spot. Once again we were dreamers—there was no such thing as a good bivy. After some digging we managed to make a small ledge that was agreeable to both of us since we were able to escape from the harness torture. Unfortunately, we were forced to spoon each other and to spend the night getting hit by spindrift and being pushed off the ledge. By morning our sleeping bags were totally wet.

May 20. We realized that if this weather was not going to change, we were going to be in a world of pain and trouble. Continuing the climb with frozen, wet gear was a bad, bad idea. We hoped that the next bivy would be better. As it turned out, it was a great day of climbing, but we were still plagued by our ever-present companion: spindrift. We entered the first rock band, a hard, mixed section. Luckily for us, another perfect couloir ran through the middle, followed by the most amazing ice-skating field. It was a 55-degree face, smooth and shiny as a mirror.

Halfway through the rock band, it was time to bivy again. Now we were really high on this gigantic face, with little gear left to get back down. Our sleeping bags were once again totally frozen, and melting snow on the stove proved extremely difficult. We had no choice but to close our bivy bags as much as possible and put positive energy into our thoughts. I fell asleep thinking, "Please do not let the next avalanche be big enough to pull us off this face."

May 21. You know you've had a cold night when both you and the sleeping bag are covered with a layer of ice.

We now followed the neck of the Snake. Steep ice, followed by mixed climbing, finally brought us to the head. We were entering the final part of the journey. But what a big surprise the Snake had for us! She turned out to be a cobra, with poison in her fangs. The terrain had turned easy enough for us to climb simultaneously, but soon I realized that the 55-degree slope was poised to avalanche. It was impossible to turn back, so we had no choice but to continue. With every step I sank to my thighs, wondering when she would strike. Looking back at Damian, I realized that at

Willie on the summit of Nuptse after climbing The Crystal Snake. Everest and Lhotse are in the background.
Damian Benegas

any moment he could be swept away. I screamed down to him, "This thing is going to slide at any moment. I'll let the rope loose and try to get over to the right!" He replied, "No way will I let you do that!" Since the ropes where frozen and I had big gloves on, I decided to use my knife to cut the ropes close to my harness.

I waited for Damian at a single rock in the middle of this huge bowl of snow, where we rested for a few minutes feeling like castaway sailors not wanting to let go of a tiny island. With no idea how the snow was still holding in place, we stepped onto the face and continued climbing for about 300 meters more until we were finally in the clear.

Fortunately, the weather was the best of the climb. After a few hours we arrived at the base of the first rock band on the ridge. Here, at last, we found a great bivy site!

May 22. The morning weather was dreadful. With tremendous winds and heavy spindrift, visibility was almost zero. We were having a hard time reading the route—and there was no room for mistakes, as we were exhausted from too many days of hard climbing at high altitude with little sleep. Our theory that 400 calories a day would be sufficient turned out to be far from realistic.

I began a one-pitch traverse to the right, but the rock became crappy; combine that with fresh snow, and I had a hard time finding even psychological protection. Somehow I managed to create a psychological belay, and soon enough Damien came traversing. He is a good climber and I knew he was in a lot of pain. I looked at him with admiration as he passed the crux without a single problem.

And so we continued, with more puzzling climbing, always guessing where to go next. At least it was easy terrain at this point, with only an occasional hard section. The weather was turning horrendous, and we desperately looked for a bivy site. The only safe place we could find

Willie on the descent at ca 7,500, with 900 meters of rappelling and down-climbing to Everest's Camp 2. *Damian Benegas*

was at the base of a rock step. Damian started digging a platform while I began climbing another pitch, looking for a better spot. My pitch started with a mixed section, nothing really hard. Gigantic spindrifts threatened, and once, if I hadn't decided to move to the side, I would have been back next to Damian in an unconventional way. Finding the climbing too dangerous to continue, I decided to return to my brother while I could still do it under control. Once there, I managed to find the best spot to sleep. Damian had the worst place, and I knew he would spend all night moving back and forth. At least I was cozy.

May 23. We woke up early and started climbing into a very bad day. We knew that there was only one way off Nuptse, and that was to traverse to the other side of the main north buttress. High winds and the constant spindrift attacked us from all directions. After a couple of hours we found ourselves at the top of the buttress. At around 7,575 meters we saw the summit was so close that it gave us new energy and enough excitement to say, "Let's do it!"

And so, after six days of constant battle with spindrift, wind, and hard climbing, the Snake granted us permission to reach the summit. The wind ceased and the clouds cleared, and soon it was so warm that we even removed our down jackets. I reached the summit at one o'clock and Damian arrived 20 minutes later. The view was one of the most amazing that we had ever seen: Everest, Lhotse, Pumori—yes, life was good.

As with any summit, the top is only the halfway point, and we still needed to get down. We started rappelling the 1979 British route, and after endless downclimbing we arrived at Everest's Camp II at 10 p.m. There, the crew from Alpine Ascents was waiting for us with warm food and a beautiful dry sleeping bag for me. Damian shared his girlfriend's bag, and we both had a fine night.

Epilogue:

We've been told that climbing the Snake must have been one of the most difficult things we had ever done. In fact it wasn't the climb itself that was the most difficult, but what happened to us after the summit, when we spent 12 hours trying to save the life of Sherpa Karma. We called desperately over the radio for assistance, but it seemed everyone was too busy with his or her own tribulations. The only team who came to help us was the Alpine Ascents expedition and Manuel Luigi, an Italian climber. After 10 hours of continuous effort, Sherpa Karma sadly passed away at the beginning of the icefall, at 5,790 meters. As the Sherpas say, "The Gods of the mountains followed him in his journey to the after life."

Just a couple of days after this misfortune, a M17 helicopter with eight climbers aboard crashed into Everest Base Camp. Again, we found ourselves desperately trying to save lives. Yes, my friends, what was hard for us was not the climb. It was the continuous effort to save the lives of human beings, and not being able to achieve it.

Summary of Statistics:

Area: Khumbu Himal

Ascent: North face of Nuptse (7,861m), The Crystal Snake (1,500m, 42 pitches and much soloing, 5.9 M4 WI5). Six days in May, 2003. Willie and Damian Benegas.

A Note About the Author:

Born and raised in the wild heart of Patagonia, Willie Benegas (34) has pursued a long apprentice-ship in the mountains. Willie has pushed his craft on the big walls of Yosemite, the airy summits of South America, and the loftiest peaks of the Himalaya. Willie completed his first major ascent in the winter of 1989 with a route up Patagonia's west face of Pitriquitron (VI 5.9 A3 WI2/3), which is still unrepeated. In the following years, Willie made the first ascent of the north face of the Nameless Tower, record speed ascents in Yosemite Valley, and attempted major new routes on the north faces of Thalay Sagar and Jannu. In 2001, he set the world record speed ascent/descent of Aconcagua (22,831'), summited Everest for a second time, and ran the legendary Leadville Ultra 100-mile Race. In the spring of 2004, Willie reached the Top of the World a fourth time.

MOONLIGHT SONATA

On the oft-attempted southeast buttress, two Russians define commitment, deprivation, and triumph of the spirit while making the first ascent of 7,804-meter Nuptse East, Nepal.

YURI KOSHELENKO

One of the great lines of the Himalaya, the oft-attempted and finally climbed southeast buttress of Nuptse East rises 8,000 vertical feet to a (formerly) virgin summit. A chronology of attempts appears at the end of this article. *Valeri Babanov*

Most people find contentment living quietly within their own boundaries. Other personalities need to discover their breaking points. A climber takes this quest as his duty, and his pursuit of risk counterbalances the quiet lives of the majority.

Mountains, too, have their individual character. As we humans express ourselves in words, so the mountain talks in the language of its height, relief, and proportions. Nuptse East is not poster beautiful, like the Matterhorn. Its charm is in the naturalness of its climbing line. This great route is the southeast ridge, with its lower slopes of rock, ice, and snow, then huge seracs, and finally up the pyramidal tower's left side to the summit. The perfection of this line is more than enough to supply climbers with a pulse.

To breathe as clouds do, to see places unseen even by birds, to observe the Earth's interior raised almost eight kilometers high, to reach the unlawful: that's what attempting such a route means.

Our small expedition arrived at base camp near the pedestal of Nuptse's southern wall at the end of September, when the monsoon leaves. Billy and Fabrizio, two American climbers also wishing to try their luck on this wall, were already there. On September 21 we joined them at base camp; and the next day we were on our routes. They were attempting a new line on a buttress to the right of ours. These two days Nuptse was misty and obscured most of time by the last monsoon clouds. Then, suddenly in the evening, we had an exciting vision: Nuptse, appearing from behind the clouds almost in zenith. Oh, my Lord. Such a mountain is a climb to high Heaven. Fabrizio and Bill never tired of repeating "Crazy!" meaning not just the view, but also our excitement. When the base of a mountain is veiled by clouds and only the battlement can be seen soaring so very high in the sky, a vision like that may delight, confuse, or both.

The bottom part of the southeast ridge is, overall, a large mass built of magnificent light granite filled with ice and covered by snow. The first bastion is precarious with falling stones, but higher up monoliths cut by ice streams provide complex and aesthetic freeclimbing. We named the tower at the top part of an edge "The Tower of God," as it represents the most perfect granite construction we have ever seen, and was no doubt raised with the help of the Creator's hand.

The ridge's edge was crowned with crests of an "empty snow" alternating with abrupt masses of ice. Here we faced complex "snow mushrooms" (a mass of snow hanging vertically with no firm foundation). The climbing was technically quite difficult, but at least there was still oxygen. This passage was just one necessary part of the whole route, and was far from being a deciding moment. The complex technical job was expected to come higher, at 7,000 meters.

We reached 6,900 meters only on October 15, after periods of rough weather had twice kept us from reaching this height. Thus far we were fixing ropes. However, from this point on we moved in alpine style. We had used the lower section for our acclimatizing period, before rushing to the summit. We chose our tactics based on what we had learned from all the previous attempts, beginning in 1986. It allowed us to use short periods of favorable weather, while saving ourselves for the final leap to the top.

The first summit attempt came on October 20, but we failed. The wind above 6,500 meters proved too strong, so again we turned back at 6,900 meters, realizing that in such wind frostbite is inevitable. We descended to base camp and then proceeded to the Deboche wood zone. After a month at high altitude, it's necessary to breathe the middle level's air, filled with the scent of rhododendrons.

During this time our friends Billy and Fabrizio finished their own expedition. Strong snow-fall during these days stopped them, still at a height of 6,100 meters. Our decision to go down had

Valeri Babanov at 6300m on the 250 vertical meters of rock at the Diamond Tower. *Vladimir Suviga*

proven correct, and I found this to be a good sign.

Base camp was covered with snow when we returned on October 27. Two days later we underwent a psychological ordeal. Moving up the rope with ascenders and a heavy backpack, I suddenly discovered that my rope had frayed on a projecting block three meters above me, and I was hanging from only two thin strings. Hypnotized by these last two threads, I freeclimbed past them. But the very moment the job was done, I noticed (suddenly, again!) a big stone falling fast directly to where Valeri should be now! I was still in shock, with heavy pulsing blood from my own experience; and now the stone. It disappeared with a frightening singing and soon an acute sound of impact came from somewhere below. Then I heard Valeri shouting something I couldn't understand—but the shout meant that he was alive! The boulder had passed quite near to him, releasing the energy of casual and savage danger. It was the classic example of what we call the law of pairs. The impression of such a beginning accompanied me for a long time. The mountain was playing with us.

The next day we reached 6,900 meters for the third time. The southeast ridge fades into a wide crest, smoothly turning into a slope of snow and ice below the topmost tower. We had to make a

Vladimir Suviga on the Diamond Tower traverse during the spring 2003 attempt. *Valeri Babanov*

decision about tactics. The route above 7,000 meters was expected to be technically difficult, requiring equipment. To be able to move quickly, we would have to leave something behind. We had abandoned our down overalls far below. Now we abandoned our sleeping bags, spare socks and mittens, one pad, and the larger part of our food. We believed that at heights above 7,000 meters a meal brings no pleasure.

Here is what we took higher: the tent, one pad, two gas-cylinders with a burner, tea, medical kit, sugar, four snow stakes, five ice screws, seven pitons, five cams, some nuts, about 10 carabiners, and two 60m ropes, one 8.6mm and one 5.5mm.

We attained 7,450 meters in a day and a half. This passage was a snow and ice slope, with a number of bergschrunds. The first night without sleeping bags (approximately at 7,225 meters) proved to be a much harder test than I would ever have presumed despite all our readiness for deprivation. Both Valeri and I were on the only pad, which was half a meter wide; we were like a pair of sardines in a can. We tried to warm our feet with down jackets. Our gas stove suffocated in the absence of oxygen so its flame was unstable and weak, much like the tiny light of a spirit-lamp. We did not slumber, nor even become drowsy, but always felt the cold penetrating through our clothes, gradually seizing our vital space. Just before dawn I began to make respiratory exercises, warming myself a little bit and producing a faster bloodstream in my lungs.

The next night, November 2, at 7,450 meters, just before the final storm, was even harder than the previous one. During the day Valeri, having replaced me in the lead, passed two of the first difficult pitches at the bottom of the topmost tower. Viewed from the outside, it looked like an easy job for him. But internally—I don't think so. In addition to our continuous struggle with cold, Valeri had a sudden attack of the fever. Medical measures had to be taken quickly; I lay beside him and covered his feet with a parka. Soon he felt much better, feeling warmed, and he even could fall asleep for a short time. To brighten up the night some way, I tried to turn on our gas stove from time to time, but it gave no warmth at all.

In such a situation we sensed our friendship as special, that we were kindred souls. We depended on each other, and accordingly we fully trusted each other. Without this, it would be useless to even to think of reaching the summit.

At 6 o'clock in the morning we started to prepare for the coming out. Despite the fact that two sleepless nights had taken much of our vital strengths, we were ready for the fight. We had something helping us in our assault: the moral certainty that our reaching the summit had been predetermined from above.

At 8:40, when we began climbing the ropes fixed the previous day, my brain clicked and said: at 6 p.m. we'll reach the top, but not earlier. This was realistic. But then the mind game began; using cunning and counting, a certain part of me, less realistic, wanted the hope of an earlier summit. Finally, we agreed with 3 p.m.

The tent at 7,450m, taken on the summit day. In 10 hours they reached the summit of Nuptse East, 7,804m. *Valeri Babanov*

All through the day I had the sensation that actually there were three of us. This third was a certain Presence, "Kun-Dun," as they say in Tibet.

At the beginning Valeri and I were switching places, but then Valeri went three pitches one after another without a break. We reasoned as one individual, each doing our own part in order to reach a common result. At one belay station Valeri decided to leave his backpack; so I placed some of his items into my own sack.

Orienting on the route proved difficult, sometimes requiring traverses across couloirs with mixed firn and ice and direct passages over M4-M5 rock. We had to find a passage leading onto the crest. The photograph I had seen in Valeri's magazine was stamped in my memory. There wass a way to the crest along a narrow ledge of snow, in the opposite direction to the basic line of our movement. Yet we were seeing rocks and nothing more. There was nothing similar to that ledge. Evening approached while we were still far from the top; it was not clear how far. Meanwhile we had already reached about 7,700 meters, and the other tops of Nuptse were clearly visible almost on the same level we

Valeri Babanov on the Diamond Tower traverse during the spring attempt.
Vladimir Suviga

were. It was the critical moment of the rise, and we both had doubts. We were high, but the top was still inaccessible. Moving further upward meant night climbing and the descent after, with all possible consequences, from frostbite to an increasing probability of making a fatal mistake.

The wind and cold were powerful, fingers did not warm up any longer, and it was clear that night would increase these torments.

"Do we continue?" Valeri asked.

Hard mixed climbing at 7,700 meters. The summit was reached at 7:20 p.m. in the moonlight. *Yuri Koshelenko*

"You can't go back without the summit, can you?"

He was silent. My question was also his answer.

We looked into each other's eyes for a while and then all the doubts faded away. We calmed down at once.

I had the feeling that our decision did not involve the physical mind, that it came from above. There was still a Presence, even in this decision.

After that I moved forward until options led in two directions. One was definitely a dead end; the other went to the left, against the basic line of movement, and I had no doubt it was the way to the crest. Again Valeri moved ahead. The sun disappeared behind the horizon. He went behind the bend and the rope tensioned, so we climbed simultaneously for some time, moving by touch in the abrupt snow couloirs. It got dark quickly. I knew we were going to the top; my whole body worked automatically, using all the skills and experience of 20 years in mountaineering. Consciousness had separated, conceiving the world independently, and the part of the route we had already done became a separate climb for me.

Some time later I found Valeri above. He was standing on the crest and looked like a big black bird with waving wings, while the night sky served as background. As I approached the belay, he asked, "would you come till the very crest? There are 15 or 20 meters to go." But there were 60. After we arrived on the crest, the wind penetrated my body as if I were only in my underwear and the cold was outer space. But behind the bulge we could see the pyramid of Everest; so we were near our goal. The top seemed just a few steps away, maybe five meters or ten, not more. While Valeri moved upward, I began freezing; my body persistently reminded me it wanted to go down. But we moved further, Valeri first, with me following.

The summit view shook me. Though the moon was not full, its light was more than enough to see the supernatural beauty of that vast expanse. Directly below us lay the Western Cwm, with the giants Everest and Lhotse trailing long snow plumes into Tibet. "Om Mani Padme Hum"— these were the words written there, I'm sure.

As it is impossible to measure mentally the whole empty breadth of space, so it would be impossible to analyze the beauty before us. We both stood as bewitched, soaking in this scene, and finally we embraced. Such embraces express many things: brotherhood, pride, silent joy of fulfillment. Our bodies had suffered hard, but the overcoming spirit was pleased. We stood on the uppermost point at 8:30 p.m. It was time now to think about going downward as we both were seriously overcooled, with all reserves exhausted.

We led the first pitches alternately, and later rappelled. During the descent we missed Valeri's pack, so it still is hanging on a rock somewhere close to the top. It was November 3 (about 12:30 a.m.) when we came to the tent at 7,450 meters; we were almost fully exhausted. Moving downward the last rope length, I lost a flashlight. It fell down a steep ice couloir, sparkling last signals of farewell. And at that very moment a blurry comprehension found its way through my tiredness; I realized that we had climbed the mountain.

One more night without sleeping bags, without sleeping a second, in a small tent, together on the only pad, and with all thoughts focused on tomorrow's descent. In the morning, at once after rising, we continued the descent. We reached the sleeping bags at 6,900 meters at 2 p.m. We put up the tent, drank some tea, and finally went to bed. Our slumber was deep, but when we awoke on November 4 we both felt a kind of collapse; we had not yet reached the elevation where the organism can be restored.

We could barely get out of our sleeping bags. Nevertheless, at 5:30 p.m. we were back at base camp. I do not find that "happiness" is a suitable word to describe our state after the mountain. For some time we stayed lost between reality and daydreaming. The requirements of our bodies were real; at the same time our consciousness was always somewhere near, but aside. Our emotions had a sense that we had been beyond the limit for a while. A kind of division had happened, and the result was a blurry vision of the future, along with a strong fixed sense of the universe acquired at the summit.

A night ascent of an unknown, nearly 8,000-meter, summit is always full of uncertainty, especially about coming back. We had made a decision comparable to a high meditation level, when in the last outward breath the possibility of no return becomes real. For us, the climb was not simply an achievement. It was a check of our capabilities, but first of all it was the recognized harmony between the spirit's direction and its embodiment in the physical world. We reached this virgin summit because of our mutual consent, and thanks to the mental denial we each accomplished.

A NOTE ON THE AUTHOR:

Widely considered one of Russia's best climbers, Yuri Koshelenko has contributed lead articles to the *AAJ* about his routes on Bhagirathi in the Garhwal (*AAJ* 1999), the Great Trango in the Karkorum (*AAJ* 2000), Lhotse Middle (*AAJ* 2002), and other climbs. His first hard route was on the north face of Ak Su in 1988, and he has barely rested since then. He is with a Russian team attempting a new route on the north face of Mt. Everest as we go to press.

Yuri Koshelenko (left) and Valeri Babanov at the Nuptse south face base camp, 5,200m. Valeri captioned this: "We are so happy."

SUMMARY OF STATISTICS:

AREA: Khumbu Himal, Nepal

ASCENT: First ascent of Nuptse East (7,804m), via southeast buttress (2,500m vertical, ED 5.8 M5 WI3 90°), by Valeri Babanov and Yuri Koshelenko. Fixed ropes to 6,400m over two weeks in October. Three days alpine style to summit from 6,900m camp, and two days descent to base camp.

CHRONOLOGY OF ATTEMPTS:

For reference, note that the British (Bonington) Route followed the south ridge to reach the main summit of Nuptse (7,861m) in the spring of 1961 using siege-style tactics (see *AAJ* 1962, p. 99). The following chronology is for the southeast ridge (also known as the south pillar and south spur) and nearby south face alternatives attempting to reach Nuptse East (7,804m). It was compiled using various published records (*AAJ, Climbing, Rock & Ice*), Elizabeth Hawley's records, and information supplied by Valeri Babanov and Mark Twight.

1986, May: Jeff Lowe and Mark Twight (U.S.A.). Highpoint: 6,400m. 8 days continuous alpine style. Stopped by bad weather. See *AAJ* 1987, p. 232.

1987, January: Jeff Lowe and Mark Twight. 6,500m. Alpine style. See *AAJ* 1987 p. 232.

1987, October: Fabrizio Manoni and Enrico Rossi (Italy). 6,700m. Four bivouacs. Stopped by snow conditions. See *AAJ* 1988, p. 206.

1987, October: Rob Newsom and Jim Yoder (U.S.A.). 400m above base camp at 5,640m. Continuous blizzard. See *AAJ* 1988, p. 206.

1989, May: Peter Arbic and Jim Elzinga (Canada), and Enrico Rossi and Kurt Walde (Italy), in overlapping but semi-independent teams. 6,900m (Italians) and 7,500m (Canada). Alpine style for 15 days. Stopped by storms. See *AAJ* 1990, p. 228.

1994, October: Michel Fauquet, Christophe Moulin, and Gérard Vionnet (France). 7,500m. Fixed ropes on first 1,000m. Stopped by wind. See *AAJ* 1995, p.238.

1995, October: Eight-member team led by Wolfgang Pohl (Germany). 7,050m. Fixed 1,900m of rope. Stopped by wind. See *AAJ* 1996, p. 272.

1997, October: Hans Kammerlander and Maurizio Lutzenberger (Italy). Southwest ridge attempt to reach still-virgin Nuptse East. 6,600m. Alpine style. Stopped by deep snow. See *AAJ* 1998, p. 312.

1999, May: Italian-French trio led by Giancarlo Ruffino. 6,050m. Alpine style.

2002, May: Barry Blanchard (Canada), Steve House (U.S.A.), Marko Prezelj (Slovenia).

The southeast face of Nuptse East. Moonlight Sonata (Babanov-Koshelenko) ascends the southeast buttress to the summit of Nuptse East (7,804m). This has been the most-attempted line. The Blanchard-House-Prezelj attempt is left of the buttress and reached 7,300m. The far left route is the original British Route to Nuptse Main (7,861m; Bonington et. al.). *Valeri Babanov*

Route left of SE buttress. 7,300m. Alpine style. Stopped by wind. See *AAJ* 2003, p. 388.

2002, October: Valeri Babanov solo. 6,250m. Fixed 1,000m of ropes. Stopped by wind. See *AAJ* 2003, p. 396.

2003, April: Valeri Babanov and Vladimir Suviga. 7,450m. Fixed ropes to 6,400m. Stopped by storm.

2003, April: Hans Kammerlander (Italy) and five companions. Route near Slo-Can-Am (Blanchard-House-Prezelj) attempt. 6,900m. Fixed to 6,700m. Stopped by strong winds.

2003, October: Billy Pierson and Fabrizio Zangrilli. Attempted route was right of SE buttress. Some fixed rope. Stopped by knee injury.

2003, October: Valeri Babanov and Yuri Koshelenko. Reached summit via SE buttress. Fixed rope to 6,400m. Alpine style from there to summit.

WALKING THE FENCE

The Southern Picket enchainment, Washington

WAYNE WALLACE

The South Picket Group from the north. *Wayne Wallace*

Let's face it: we don't live in the Himalaya or Antarctica. So, I wondered: is it possible to find a world-class climbing adventure here in the lower 48—specifically, in my own backyard, the North Cascades? I decided the trick was to be creative, pursuing link-ups, traverses, and other variations on the enchainment theme. It's a wonderful trend that's happening across the country and indeed the world, enabling grand tours along summits all day—or all week. There is no limit to what can be accomplished by approaching the heights this way, especially with the new light gear and a strong set of legs.

Traversing the entire Southern Picket Range in a single push might seem an unlikely goal. These peaks are steeper and more jagged than any other ridge around. Glaciers cling to both sides of the east-west wedge of gneiss and granite. It rises out of deep valleys 7,000 vertical feet and spans more than four miles. To many climbers, just one of its elusive summits is a prize on a long weekend trip. Let us now quote from the Book of Beckey: "In the Southern Picket Group, the steep escarpment of the N. faces, with several extremely steep and badly crevassed glaciers that divide individual peaks, competes as one of the grandest scenes in the North Cascades. Because of the rugged terrain, the Picket Range has remained the wildest and most unexplored region in the North Cascades." This range arouses our deepest fires of adventure. Just ask aspiring Northwest mountaineers about the Pickets and observe the look in their eyes.

Wayne Wallace on the summit of East Twin Needle. *Colin Haley*

The idea for the traverse began with a trip I carried out with two teams climbing Mt. Challenger from opposite directions. Each team met at the summit of this North Cascades wilderness classic, swapped car keys, then descended via the other teams' route. This enabled all involved to traverse this amazing peak and see new ground the whole way. After five long days of travel and climbing, we met in Seattle to party and swap cars.

With all the great fun we had, I began thinking about other possibilities. Sometime in the year 2000, the Southern Pickets came to mind. But had Peter Croft already bagged every summit along this ridge? Apparently not.

The complete traverse of the South Picket Group goes from right to left across the skyline. *(1) Little McMillan Spire, (2) East McMillan Spire, (3) West McMillan Spire, (4) East Towers traverse, (5) Inspiration Peak, (6) Pyramid Peak, (7) Mt. Degenhardt, (8) Mt. Terror, (9) The Rake, (10) The Blip, (11) East Twin Needle, (12) West Twin Needle, (13) The Himmelhorn, (14) The Ottohorn, (15) The Frenzelspitz, (16) The Chopping Block.* Gregg Brickner

Colin Haley on the SE face of West MacMillan Spire. *Wayne Wallace*

The traverse seemed preposterous, but I began setting out to recruit partners anyway. I found one person who was so enthusiastic that he tried it without me! In July of 2002 Colin Haley (only 17 at the time) and Mark Bunker made their way across seven of the summits before being turned away by typical Pickets weather. As they talked of returning for another go, my obsessive dream turned to a raging and all-consuming passion.

Never having been in the range, I then did my own reconnaissance with Lane Brown. We managed to climb West McMillan and traverse over to the east ridge of Inspiration. It now seemed doable—but it would be a very long and unknown trek.

In June of 2003 I tried it with Jens Klubberud, only to get rained off after only four peaks. We left a cache that later turned out to be quite helpful on the trip I was to organize later. As a rare high pressure system set in during July, I discovered I had no partner. In desperation I approached Colin only to be told that he felt loyal to his first partner. Eventually he agreed to go. Mark, at risk of losing his employment, wanted to join in as well, and so our team was set.

Under blue skies we slogged in—my third time in a year. We thought going as far as possible, as soon as possible, was the way to go, so we hiked in and traversed over the three McMillan Spires on the first day. We were working well together as a team, even though Mark and I had never climbed together. All three routes go at about 5.6 to 5.8 and, individually, are wonderful climbs on their own.

The second day we rolled through the 5.9 cracks on Inspiration Peak, of early Beckey fame. To our joy we found my cache intact; it guaranteed us ample food and fuel for the rest of the journey. The Pyramid (II 5.8) looked bad, but we found surprisingly beautiful rock on its cliffs. After Degenhardt (class 4), Mt. Terror (II 5.6) lived up to its name with unsound blocky sections. Lingering on the summit, I couldn't help thinking of the pioneering efforts of those who came before. I could just see Ed Cooper, Mike Swayne, Dave Hiser, and Charles Bell negotiating their way up the last gendarmes to finish the great north buttress of Terror. It is a route that intimidates bold climbers even today. The voices of Fred Beckey and Silas Wilde seemed to echo along these steep, glaciated walls.

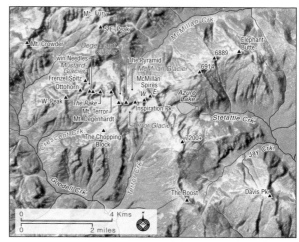

The Southern Picket Range. *Martin Gamache, Alpine Mapping Guild*

At the next col we saw that the Rake (IV 5.9) was not going to give in easily. I climbed on vertical to overhanging rock on pitons to avoid a loose gully below. From there the route was a half-mile of pure ecstasy, classic alpine ridge climbing. On and on it went, and at times we rode the ridge like a horse. We found ourselves pressed to find water and a flat place to sleep near sunset. After rappelling from the Rake's summit, the west peak felt accommodating for our last night on the ridge. But it didn't help our sleep to view the next peak, East Twin Needle, in the fading light.

On the morning of the third day we saw how difficult it would be to stay directly on the

Wayne Wallace and Colin Haley on the east ridge of The Rake. *Mark Bunker*

The Three Picketeers on The Rake summit bivy. *Mark Bunker*

ridgecrest. I have never quite understood the argument differentiating a traverse from enchainment, but I believe a pure traverse stays on direct line from summit to summit, whereas an enchainment can vary and wind around. We found it necessary to traverse around a bit on the East Twin Needle (II 5.10a), but it was still very difficult ascending the tremendously exposed east arête.

After dealing with these difficulties, I had hopes of completing this audacious undertaking. However, after wandering over the West Twin (class 3), we found it was not over in the least. We paused to discuss how we should approach and climb the steep, daunting Himmelhorn (III 5.10+). There were two options: traverse across the north face or attack the steep ridge directly. We eventually agreed to let me have a go at the true ridgecrest. It turned out to be one of the hardest new-route leads I have done in the alpine arena. Delicate 5.10+ moves led me up to the amazing ridgecrest, at which point Colin led a razor-sharp edge to the summit. Tottering on this remote mountaintop, we found great joy.

The Ottohorn (class 3) was next and proved to be only the third summit that wasn't fifth class. The Frenzlespitz (II 5.6) was a fine ending to this stupendous traverse.

On the way out the next day, not wanting our trip to end, we went up the Chopping Block (III 5.5). It provided a great view of the range as well as ending our journey on a luckier number of summits, 14 in all. We estimated we did 50 or more technical pitches, many of which we simul-climbed with gear between us. The whole trip was done in a four-day period.

We were amazed at the quality of the climbing we had encountered, and it left us with an overwhelming sense of accomplishment not usually available in the lower 48 states. Each day held magic that I hope all climbers can experience at some point. As one of the Three Picketeers, Mark, said later, "the only problem is this smile I can't seem to get off my face. It's starting to freak out everyone at the office!"

SUMMARY OF STATISTICS:

Area: Washington State, North Cascades National Park, The Picket Range

ASCENTS: The Complete Southern Pickets Traverse (VI 5.10+), Mark Bunker, Colin Haley, and Wayne Wallace. East to west traverse, ascending 14 summits. Three routes were first ascents: The Rake, East Twin Needle, and Himmelhorn. A total of about 50 technical pitches in all.

Peaks as follows: July 25: Little McMillan Spire, southeast face, III 5.8; East McMillan Spire, east ridge, II 5.6; West McMillan Spire, east ridge/face, III 5.8. July 26: Inspiration Peak, east ridge, III 5.9; Pyramid Peak, east ridge/face, II 5.8; Mt. Degenhart, east ridge, class 4; Mt. Terror, east ridge, II 5.6; The Rake, east ridge, IV 5.9. July 27: East Twin Needle, southeast ridge/face, II 5.10a; West Twin Needle, east ridge, class 3; Himmelhorn, east ridge/north face, II 5.10+; Ottohorn, east ridge, class 4; Frenzlespitz, southeast ridge/face, II 5.6. July 28: Chopping Block, northeast face, II 5.6.

A NOTE ON THE AUTHOR:

Wayne Wallace has enjoyed adventurous climbing for over 30 years. His two children and a high-rise carpentry job keep him on his toes. Wayne spends his available time chasing after the classic climbs in the western states and a particularly hard-to-get girlfriend. His main goal is not to be placed in the very back of the AAJ *too soon.*

Thirteen summits, but who's counting? The Three Picketeers, left to right: Wayne Wallace, Mark Bunker, and Colin Haley.
Mark Bunker

Non C'é Due Senza Tre

The great line on Nalumasortoq goes free, Greenland.

Micah Dash

The Central and Third pillars of Nalumasortoq, showing the exquisite dihedral of Non C'é Due Senza Tre at the far right. *Nathan Martin*

Sitting in the Camp 4 parking lot, I felt my anxiety building to a crescendo. I was freaking out, which often happens. My partner was injured, our project was over, and I was just informed that some Brits were heading off to Greenland in a few weeks. Surely they were going to free the route that I had been obsessing about for a year. I was fatalistic; my season was totally over. I should change my plans to climb in Greenland, forget about free-climbing Half Dome, sell my rack, and take up scuba diving.

But instead I headed to Copenhagen and eventually the Tasermiut Fjord of southeastern Greenland. This would be my second trip to the island in just under a year. In August of 2002, as I bade farewell to the granite walls of Tasermiut, I had a feeling I would be back. For the next seven months I obsessed over the possibility of free-climbing the 850-meter aid route on the right pillar of Nalumasortoq, the route known as Non C'é Due Senza Tre, first done in 2000. This was an amazing line that I might have sent in 2002 had things been a bit more optimal. It was my version of the fisherman's tale about the big one that got away. Climbers often lament about heading off to the greater ranges and getting completely shut down—then returning for another attempt at the climb of their lives. My tale would be charting no new ground.

I was not exactly sure how I was going to come up with the money to visit Greenland for the second time. But with a bit of luck, a bit of hard work, and a generous grant from the American Alpine Club, all turned out well. For this expedition my new friend Thad Friday, a mechanical engineering student at the University of Colorado, would be my climbing partner. Thad, with his savings from his job at the campus library, came up with the money for his part of the expedition. We set off toward what we both hoped would be the best free climb either of us had ever experienced. Our style and objective were very specific: the right pillar of Nalumasortoq, ground up, without fixed lines, swinging leads, and in 24 hours.

The relationship between Thad and myself was strictly business and we worked well as a team. Where I was weak he was strong, and vice versa. Early in his climbing career Thad had racked up an impressive tick list of solo aid climbs. He told me that he had "put his aiders on the back burner," or maybe he said he "burnt his aiders." I am not sure what he said because he has a tendency to be very soft spoken. So, having burnt his aiders, he had no other choice but to free climb in Greenland. Now a dedicated free-climber, his ethics, dedication, and passion for climbing drive him. When I first met him, I could see he put a tremendous amount of energy into every pitch, especially for an on-sight. Unlike me, he is methodical and calculating. Overconfidence, most likely mine, led us to think that we would have the route in the bag and done within a week—this was an idea that would eventually become the joke of our expedition.

After a five-hour boat ride from the coastal town of Nanortalik, we were dropped off on the shores of Tasermiut Fjord. Quickly, we secured some of our supplies in a nearby cave and began the trek toward Nalumasortoq. Strolling into our base camp after a three-hour hike, we were graced with the presence of several middle-aged, half-naked Russian climbers washing themselves and their clothes in the river. Immediately, we questioned the quality of the water that we had consumed moments before, downstream. In front of us stood a fully naked Russian, as proud and stoic as the statue David. With mug in hand he asked us, from what we could gather, if we wanted some Turkish coffee. Refusal was not an option. The sun was out, the bugs were horrendous, and Thad was getting sick of my constant monologue (I have never been able to keep silent). So we sat for a few awkward moments with our new naked Russian friends and sipped some coffee.

They informed us of their plans to climb the central pillar of Nalumasortoq, then "jump." Jump, what the heck were they talking about? I assumed that I had lost something in

Micah Dash and Thad Friday having another go at Non C'é Due Senza Tre.
Nathan Martin

the translation. With a bit more charade-like antics we figured out that they were intending to establish a new route on the central pillar. Then their fearless leader, Valery Rozov, would BASE jump from the summit while wearing a special suit. Great, I thought to myself, jump, fly, sail, all in a fricking clown suit for all I care. As long as they were not climbing the route that I had been agonizing over for the past seven months, they could do whatever they wanted. Thad and I, however, were there to send our route, and of course I did not hesitate in letting them know. My mouth opened—which it often does at inopportune times—and spewed out our plans. We would hike up in the morning, free every pitch, and be back to camp in 24 hours, having bagged the first alpine-style free ascent of Nalum-asortoq. With that we gathered our gear, spit out the coffee grounds, and headed off to find a place to sleep.

We decided to begin at dawn. Torn between nervous anxiety and sheer excitement, I lay in the tent twisting and turning, trying my best to fall asleep. After a few minutes or hours my internal monologue woke me up. It was time to go. I shook Thad awake believing it was dawn. Staggering out of the tent like prairie dogs emerging from their underground burrows, we stood gazing into the sky, trying to decipher if it was dusk or dawn. Following a few moments of bewilderment, we determined that we had been asleep only for a few hours (we had forgotten to bring a clock). Thad glared at me with a mixture of frustration for being woken up and sympathy for his climbing partner who was too crazy to sleep. I felt bad tainting Thad's Zen-like demeanor. A few hours later, confident that it was dawn, we headed down to our dank cooking hovel, shoved coffee and food into our faces, and headed to the cliff.

Thad Friday following pitch 9 on Non C'é Due Senza Tre. *Micah Dash*

It took us a lot more work, effort, commitment, and persistence than originally calculated to free the route. We faced a multitude of obstacles: wet rock, weather, the internal plumbing of the wall, and every other factor that comes into play when you are trying to climb at your best in an alpine environment. Not only did we both need to be having a good day, on the same day, but objective hazards played a large part inhibiting our success. Water that flowed over lichen left the granite un-free-climbable. Once the top stopped seeping, the bottom would start a few hours or even days later. Instead of concluding early in the expedition that until the snow melted from the summit a free ascent would be unlikely (this would have saved us three attempts), we threw ourselves at the route with wild abandon.

Several attempts come to mind that exemplify our haste. Once we made it to the base of the seventh pitch, where we stared intently across the fjord at a menacing, incoming storm. We went down, and in a few hours the heavens unleashed a fury that lasted nine days. On another attempt only 200 meters from the ground, Thad backed off a wet pitch. Annoyed and anxious, I tried to lead it. After a few desperate feet of what had been easy 5.10, I swallowed my pride and had to agree. We bailed. Thad was trying to tell me to relax, but I could not hear him. Not because he was not speaking loud enough, but because I did not want to.

After every attempt we would rappel to the base, pull our ropes, and walk back to camp. The trail thus created meandered through glacial moraines, talus, and, worst of all, Camp Moscow. Bailing off a route time after time means that frustration is incurred when explaining one's efforts, struggles, and defeats. With every failure came questions and comments from the multinational community, which now included a wild team of four outstanding Spaniards and

Thad Friday doing the happy cowboy ride on the summit of Nalumasortoq's Third Pillar. *Micah Dash*

the American duo Nathan Martin and Timmy O'Neill.

The latter two had come to Greenland after my endless commentary about how good the climbing was. But for the first nine days after their arrival we sat in a dank cave and had circular conversations about climbing ethics, professional climbers, girls, and our dwindling supply of tobacco. Sometimes I would ask about their epic alpine ascent of Fitz Roy, but I backed off when I realized that maybe they had not forgotten the pain. Thad and I could see that they were questioning their decision to visit Greenland. It took them a while to decide that they wanted to be there. Or, maybe it took them a while to realize that they were totally committed.

Meanwhile, we sat in the rain and snow, hyper-caffeinated and bored. Sometimes we would venture over to the Spaniard's camp and sit for hours sipping maté and munching on chocolate. Their generosity and kindness was a tremendous bonus to our experience. Nathan and Thad were amazingly quiet; if they spoke at the same time you could still hear a mouse fart. This was in contrast to Timmy and me, who stopped talking only to breathe, eat, or sleep.

Team Russia was now fixed two-thirds of the way up the central pillar. They had stuck to classic siege tactics and seemed closer to success than Thad and me. The Spaniards, having climbed a new line on the left pillar, also in big-wall style, were nearing the top. I began to question our strategy and thought maybe we should either fix lines or have the second jumar. Either of these two plans would be more than legitimate and would speed up the ascent significantly. My frustration was reaching a climax, but Thad wanted nothing to do with jumars, aiders, or fixed lines. We agreed that a true free ascent meant that at the very least one climber would have to lead and follow every pitch cleanly. Every hard pitch needed to be freed on lead. If one of us were to jumar, then no one person would have freed the climb entirely. If we approached it from the very highest of our personal standards, then we would be happy. This was not the standard at which free climbs were established in this area. In technical difficulty and in overall effort required, our route could be most closely compared to stacking Yosemite's Rostrum on top of Astroman. Timmy dubbed our style—that of alternating leads—the "Huberization" of Greenland. This is not that farfetched since Thomas and Alex Huber strongly inspired our style.

We gave it another go. After 18 hours we had passed our previous high point. The wall was dry and the surroundings breathtaking. Four more pitches of steep jamming, liebacking, and run-out stemming brought us to a large ledge that looked to be only 50 feet below the summit. With the sun low in the sky and our hands sore and dry from climbing in the cold arctic air we decided to take a break. We pushed a few rocks around to make a temporary bivy spot. Then came the biggest mistake of our trip. Having left behind all but a light rack and some Snickers bars, we stopped moving. Within a few minutes we were frozen stiff as the arctic wind blew straight through our climbing pants. But after about three hours the sun had come back around the wall and we thought about heading for the summit. Unfortunately, the chilling wind and the cold rock had stripped us of our motivation. By climbing light and fast, or "light and lucky," we had left behind the minimum requirements for a successful ascent. We were simply too cold to continue and had to be content with our efforts in reaching the top of the original line. Reluctant to descend but too cold to climb, we threw the ropes over the edge and rappelled.

After 17 rappels my feet hit the glacier and simultaneously I screamed, "We fucked up!" Easy to yell this while safe and warm, but truly we had made a major mistake. Five attempts had brought us to within spitting distance of the summit. I had come to Greenland for the second time to bag this amazing route only to rappel without standing on the summit. I wondered how many times in our climbing lives we would get the opportunity to get the first free ascent of such an amazing line. Stumbling exhausted into camp, we evaded our friends and went to sleep.

Rationalizations of an almost-successful ascent began the next day. I believe that in alpine climbing you should stop only after standing on the summit—and we had not. The last 50 feet, or whatever it may be, counts. Thoughts and contradictions swirled around in our minds. The pit of my stomach felt empty. I wondered how Thad felt, but he remained reticent, contented with his own personal effort, at least for the time being. Deep within, I believed that we had lost our chance of completing the line that had tormented and inspired me at the same time.

Timmy and Nathan were up on the wall. This was their third attempt and I knew that they had it in the bag. Their style was different from ours; they had opted to use ascenders for the second and led in blocks. If we had used the same methods maybe we would have sent our route. We talked it over but came to the same conclusion: we had decided on a style and would do our best with it. The next morning Timmy and Nathan strode into camp. The gleam in their eyes was unmistakable—they had succeeded. The four of us gathered our gear and headed down to the lower camp to celebrate and to drink the rest of the alcohol. The fire grew larger with every swallow of gin and tonic. Laughter turned into screaming which metamorphosed into howling; soon our bodies were strewn around the fire as a drunken sleep consumed us.

More days passed and more bad weather rolled into the fjord. With this weather came the same boring, repetitive conversations covering all of the same topics that we had expounded upon over and over. Thad started making crazy meals, generally consisting of fat and grease. His fried cheese sandwiches were making me sick. But Tim and Nathan loved them.

Thirty days had gone by and Thad and I had yet to stand on a summit. It was time to shift our focus. After a little recon we had decided on a new objective, the north face of the "Dome." Once again the style was to swing leads, free climb, and not drill. The route unfolded before our eyes. Every new pitch seemed to be the last. We would set up a belay, grab the rack, and ever so timidly continue up. Again, we chose to leave behind everything but the most minimal amount of gear. But what would happen if Thad or I were to commit into the unknown and find no protection at all? Or, more importantly, how the hell were we going to get down, having brought only a few hexes to leave behind? Finally gaining the summit, Thad gazed across the vast expanse of land and directly toward our previous objective, the right pillar. He had been feeling its presence all day. The summit that we now stood on seemed minuscule in comparison. I felt that someone was kicking me in the gut, beating me for coming so close to something that I wanted so badly. Of course nobody was kicking me but myself. Maybe Thad was feeling the same thing. I hoped he was. Gathering our gear, we snapped a few photos and began an epic descent once again into the unknown.

After a few days of rest, we noticed that the weather was still looking good. The walls surrounding us begged to be climbed, and the opportunity for new objectives were endless. But I wanted nothing of it. I felt unfulfilled and wanted to give our pillar another shot. Prior to our ascent of the Dome, the notion of attempting the pillar for the sixth time seemed unfathomable. How easily we forget the pain!

When we arrived in Greenland, spring was just showing its early stages. Winter snowdrifts had yet to melt and the glaciers appeared harmless. Now, 33 days later, the land had changed. The glaciers showed deep, foreboding crevasses, and water ran like torrents over the ice, creating marvelous rivers that flowed into one another and then down to the fjord's edge. It was time to try again.

Reaching the ledge atop pitch 17 just before midnight, we squeezed our bodies into the same bivy spot as before. This time we decided that less is not always more and hauled along a single sleeping bag that we both squeezed into. After a few puffs on a freshly rolled cigarette we drifted into a sleep-like state for several hours only to awake to see the northern lights circling above. A new day was emerging. It was time to climb.

I was eager to get started as soon as possible. Thad wanted nothing of it; he was committed to staying in the sleeping bag until it was warm enough to climb. He reminded me that if we had stayed put until it warmed up on our last attempt, maybe we would not be at this spot again. I rolled another cigarette. Like a small child I kept harassing him, asking if it was time to go. Finally he succumbed to my persistence, or maybe he simply thought it was warm enough to get up.

Several hundred feet of traversing led us to a small ledge perched beneath two pitches of wet, overhanging cracks. A feeling of impending doom crept into my soul. Certainly this would be our last attempt; soon we would be leaving for home. Climbing up here a seventh time seemed about as ridiculous as jumping off while wearing a flying clown suit. It was Thad's lead and after some strenuous handjamming he reached a small ledge one pitch from the summit and set a belay. My nervous anxieties, combined with my inability to control the uncontrollable, overcame me. Following the pitch I kept asking him what the next section looked like and felt even more nervous with every reply or lack thereof. I pressed my face against the cold wall as the world around me became increasingly dim. Nausea swept over me like a wave.

I reached the belay thankful that Thad had led the crack. One pitch to go! All of the previous 22 pitches had gone absolutely free—and neither of us had taken any falls. Thad was glad to hand me the rack. After a few feet I quickly realized that my constant fear of being committed high on a wall without sufficient gear was about to become real.

This was my moment of truth. Had we come all the way to Greenland to get shut down by my anxiety, or was this to be a story of success? Above us lurked a lichen-covered, slightly overhanging, off width. "Great. At least I can get in it," I thought to myself. Then came the quandary: how was I going to protect it? Aid climbing was not an option; I might have considered jumping off rather than pulling on gear after all of our efforts. Shaky as usual, I climbed farther and farther above Thad with only one piece of good protection between us. Looking down I could see my partner getting increasingly jittery with every foot I gained. I kept muscling my way up, one move from either total success or total disaster.

Micah Dash and Thad Friday cruising in to Tasermiut Fjord.

Out of breath, I reached the top and set up a belay. A few moments later, red faced and relieved, Thad worked his way up. It was all over and the relief was great. The weight I had felt since the summer of 2002 was lifted. We were not going to have our fisherman's tale of the big one that got away. Thad would not have to kill me and leave my body to rot in the cave. He was not going to go home with the same lack of fulfillment that I had experienced in 2002. We sat for a few moments on the summit, snapped the usual photos, and pondered our efforts. All of my internal frustrations, anxieties, and monologues vanished as we sat there in the most beautiful place we had ever been, totally happy and content, and finding for a few moments the kind of internal calm and silence that can be felt only while climbing.

SUMMARY OF STATISTICS:

ASCENTS: Greenland, Tasermiut Fjord, Nalumasortoq. First free ascent of the Third Pillar, Non C'é Due Senza Tre (850m, 21 pitches, V 5.11+R). Micah Dash and Thad Friday.

The Dome, first ascent of The Pillar (15 pitches, IV 5.10X). Micah Dash and Thad Friday. (For details on The Pillar, see Climbs & Expeditions in this Journal.)

A NOTE ON THE AUTHOR:

Micah Dash is a native of Lancaster, California. He started climbing in 1998 at Squamish, British Columbia. Soon climbing took over his life. In 1999 he moved to Yosemite Valley and didn't leave for almost three and a half years. Currently he is finishing his undergraduate studies at the University of Colorado, Boulder.

JIRISHANCA

A climbing history of the Hummingbird Peak's southeast face, Peru.

JEREMY FRIMER

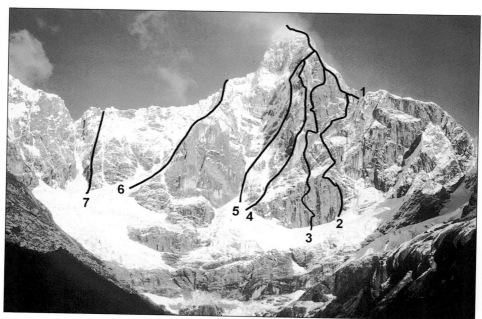

The southeast aspect of Jirishanca (6,094m): (1) East Buttress (800m, ED1, Egger-Jungmair, 1957). (2) Suerte (700m, ED2, 6c+ A2 WI5+, DeLuca-Piccini-Stoppini, 2003) (no summit). (3) Tambo, Churros y Amigos (1,100m, ED3/4, 7a A2 95° M4, Clouet-Jourdain, 2003). (4) Japanese Route (1,100m, ED2, Nakatsuka-Okada-Sato-Shinohara-Yoshiga, 1973). (5) Fear and Loathing (1,050m, ED3/4, A2 WI6+, Bullock-Powell, 2003) (no summit). (6) Peruvian-Slovenian attempt (Monasterio-Kovac-Kozjek, 2000). (7) Austrian attempt (Angreiter-Coleselli-Erdenkaufer-Gerin-Gumpold-Murg-Oppurg-Schoisswohl-E Wurm-G Wurm-Wurzer, 1974). *Jeremy Frimer*

No range is more identified by a single event than Peru's Cordillera Huayhuash. In the shadow of *Touching the Void* lies a spectacular group of mountains, complete with a rich, 68-year history of committed alpinism. The crown jewel of the Amazon Basin, Yerupajá (6,617m) was the focus of Reinhold Messner and Peter Habeler's first international expedition (1969); José Luis Fonrouge and Carlos Comesaña also opened a route on Yerupajá six months before their first ascent of Fitz Roy's Supercanaleta. Others who have visited the Huayhuash include Walter Bonatti, Joe Brown, Alan Rouse, and, more recently, Mick Fowler, Lionel Daudet, and Jeff Lowe.

Just north of Yerupajá is the sharp, delicate summit of Jirishanca, the "Hummingbird

Peak" (6,094m). The name could be a comparison between the summit and a hummingbird's bill. Alternatively, it could be referring to the hummingbird's speedy heart rate, much like that of climbers awed by Jirishanca's southeast face. I had plans to try the west face of Yerupajá on my inaugural expedition to the Huayhuash. But when I laid eyes on Jirishanca, I quivered in my plastic boots. Thoughts of Yerupajá fluttered into the wind as I assiduously attended to a personal fascination with the Hummingbird Peak. Since that awestruck moment, Jirishanca's specter has lived within me. My two attempts, one thwarted by illness (2000) and one by weather (2002), have left my reverence for this alpine masterpiece untouched.

The mountain first gained notoriety when a Peruvian Army transport plane crashed into its southeast face in 1954. Surprisingly, this is the only known incident resulting in fatalities on the mountain. Austrian Alpine Club expeditions in 1936 and 1954, along with an American expedition in 1950, resulted in the first ascents of many Huayhuash peaks—but not Jirishanca. The Austrians returned in 1957 after recruiting some "heavy artillery," including the Dolomite guide Toni Egger, who 18 months later would meet his end on Cerro Torre.

The Austrians decided not to attempt Jirishanca's west face, which, "high and formed of fluted ice flanks and steep walls, would have been impossible." In light of the equipment of the day, perhaps this assessment was justified. The 60-degree ice sheets of the 900-meter west face have since allowed six quality routes of predominantly TD difficulty, the first established in 1969 by an eight-man Italian team led by Riccardo Cassin. After cutting steps and fixing ropes, they reached the summit ridgeline. "They had to surmount an ice mushroom on unstable, precarious ice, spongy and fluffy on the surface. The axe cracked everything, their feet gave way and it was hard to make the next move. The delicate icy skull-cap was the final defense of the virginity of the face of this 20,099-foot colossus." Their West Rib Route follows an aesthetic, bending ice arête and is now a classic. (This and other quotes come from *Mountain World 1958-59* and *AAJ 1970*; for routes on the west and southwest faces, see *AAJ 2003*, page 308.)

The 1957 team of Austrians also ruled out the snowy north ridge, in spite of it offering the easiest route to a Jirishanca summit (the lower north peak). To traverse from the north summit to the true summit would involve a treacherous "advance along [the connecting] knife edge, not unlike a cockscomb of ice." The first ascent of the north ridge came seven years later (1964), by Americans Gary Colliver and Glen Denny. Incidentally, this is the only route to date that reaches the north summit of Jirishanca; the route has yet to be linked to the true summit.

The Egger team also dismissed the "gruesome" southeast face and set out on the east buttress, approaching it from the north. Towering rock and ice cliffs adorned by icicle fringes earn this route an ED1 rating by modern standards. Climbing in expedition style, the Austrians fixed ropes on the lower rock pillar to reach the snowy, icicle-fringed section at mid-height, where they tunneled behind an ice cliff. After placing a high camp, they launched onto the upper rock pillar. "The difficulties of this brittle rock nose above the abyss demanded a supreme effort from my certainly hardened men." A summit attempt was stifled by deep snow on the final ridge, where "one could have gained height only in swimming fashion." They retreated.

After making the first ascent of Yerupajá Chico, Jirishanca's southern neighbor, the Austrians returned to Jirishanca. With the end of the dry season fast approaching, they decided to attempt the summit with an "extreme personal effort," skimping on food and sans tent. "This is the hardest tactic one can imagine on such a difficult and high mountain—and in times of peace, nobody could be ordered to pursue such an action. But Egger and Jungmair went voluntarily." Aided by fixed ropes still in place, they reached their previous high point early on their second day and began

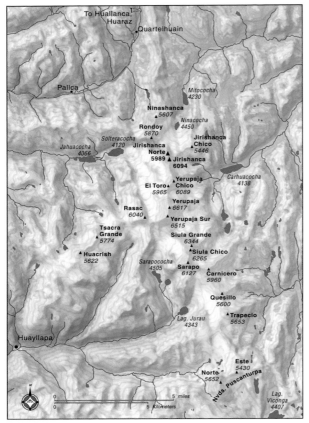

The Jirishanca region of the Cordillera Huayhuash. *Martin Gamache/Alpine Mapping Guild*

a bold traverse of the summit ridge. On July 12, 1957, Toni Egger and Siegfried Jungmair stood on the summit of Peru's last unclimbed 6,000-meter peak. Their ascent was "probably one of the boldest climbing feats ever performed in the Cordillera."

As all the major peaks of the Huayhuash had been climbed, expeditions began focusing on the remaining unclimbed faces. A wave of expeditions advanced on the southeast face of Jirishanca during the early 1970s. First to arrive was a Japanese team from the Moji Alpine Club in 1972. They retreated from a highpoint 300 meters up the face but did discover the long-sought wreck-age of the airplane that had crashed 18 years earlier. The fol-lowing year, a Japanese team of 15 led by Masayuki Shinohara approached the southeast face ready for a prolonged siege. Over the course of 49 days they succeeded in making the first ascent of the southeast face, having forced a route up the left edge of the right-side rock wall and joining the East Buttress below the upper rock pillar and continuing to the summit. They had faced sustained steep rock and ice, including an eight-meter rock overhang as well as overhanging ice cliffs, which they aid climbed on ice screws.

Jirishanca's southeast face quickly attracted a third expedition, this time a group of Austrians in 1974. This team of eleven climbers led by Jürgen Gumpold tackled the far left side of the face, requiring six days to reach Jirishanca's south ridge near the Jirishanca-Yerupajá Chico Col. The rock buttress leading to the south ridge involved rock to 5.10a on the lower parts and ice-cliff dodging higher up. The weather then deteriorated and they retreated. In descent, they watched an avalanche emanating from Yerupajá Chico overwhelm the route they had traveled that day.

This early period of exploration ended with the 1974 expedition and the southeast face faded from the limelight for 26 years. A second wave of interest, which persists to this day, began in 2000 when Pavle Kozjek, Marjan Kovac (both from Slovenia), and Aritza Monasterio (Peru) teamed up for the first alpine-style attempt on the face. In seven hours they tackled the unclimbed south-southeast spur—an ascending, narrow edge, stacked with ice mushrooms—to reach the south ridge, where the difficulties intensified. Having floundered in deep snow to that point, the team opted for descent and reached base camp 23 hours after departing.

This Peruvian-Slovenian team was also the first group of brave souls to talk seriously about an attempt on the Direttissima: straight up the fall line to the tip of Jirshanca's pointed summit. After climbing the bombarded funnel, it would ascend through mixed ground, passing a semi-circular overhanging rock cliff at mid-height to reach the snow bowl below the final challenge: a steep, mixed headwall 200 meters in height, capped by overhanging icicle-fringed ice cliffs. Fitting of such a supreme mountain, the most direct route would also have the distinction of being the most difficult. Needless to say, they have not been the last to dream of this still unclimbed jewel. Alun Powell, while on Fear and Loathing in 2003, watched the formidable line sustain regular bombardments. Upon returning to civilization, Powell made a standing offer of a bouquet of roses for the first to climb the Direttissima.

High Mountain Sports published an article on the Huayhuash in 2001, including an image of the southeast face of Jirishanca. This sparked a flood of interest, beginning with three visits in 2002. Alun Powell and Nick Bullock (U.K.) were the first. In May they began climbing the center of the face, only to be caught by an avalanche that promptly deposited them back at the base, partially injured. Yanik Bérubé (Canada) and I arrived in July just as a storm rolled in. We sat in base camp for 12 days, "doing time" as the storm outside gradually abated and an intestinal storm in Yanik stole center stage. As we packed it in, I wondered if I would ever again be willing to psych myself up enough to try the Direttissima. Finally, Slovenians Rok Zalokar and Urban Azman attempted a line beginning in the center of the face that would traverse a sloping snow ledge rightward before striking upward along the line that the French would climb in 2003. Zalokar was soaked while aiding through a dripping overhang, and his clothes and boots froze overnight. Instead of risking cold injury, the strong, young team retreated.

The word was out on Jirishanca; six teams visited the Huayhuash in 2003 with the southeast face as their primary objective. Tragedy and triumph marked the beginning of the season as Austrians Alexander Fidi and Julian Neumayer perished on the southwest face of the neighboring Jirishanca Chico while acclimatizing. Soon thereafter, Alun Powell and Nick Bullock, ready for a rematch with the Hummingbird, made the first alpine-style ascent of the southeast face by their bold new line, Fear and Loathing. The season was far from over; Aymeric Clouet and Didier Jourdain of France showed up and finessed their way up the center of the right-side rock face, resulting in their challenging new route, Tambo, Churros, y Amigos. (See adjoining articles.)

The 2003 climbing season included a strange twist. Italians Stefano DeLuca, Paolo Stoppini, and Piccini Alessandro, with a power drill in hand, forged a line up the right side of the right-side rock face, connecting with the base of the East Buttress after 18 pitches of climbing to 5.11+ and A2. Their new route, Suerte ("Luck"), follows a wandering line of over 40 bolts (see Climbs & Expeditions). For a bolted line to connect with a route first climbed by none other than Toni Egger is either a blunt statement on bolting ethics or a profound coincidence.

Jirishanca's southeast face is by no means climbed out. The far left side of the face is still wide open. Just left of center, another possible line could primarily climb ice to reach the south ridge just before it kicks back. And then there's that bouquet of roses....

Jeremy Frimer is the author of the upcoming guidebook, Cordillera Huayhuash: Select Treks and Climbs *(2005, Elaho Publishing, Squamish, Canada). See www.elaho.ca for more information.*

FEAR AND LOATHING

Alpine-style suffering on Jirishanca's great southeast face.

NICK BULLOCK

Al Powell at 6,000 meters on Jirishanca. *Nick Bullock*

We started to climb at one in the morning and I felt terrible. Approaching the start of an evil chimney—the drain for anything falling from Jirishanca's massive southeast face—we well remembered that this was the place where we had nearly died in 2002 during an avalanche. Our breathing grew labored. Was it the altitude? Or were we psyching up for the sprint ahead? But our decision was made. We would solo for a while. Speed was safety.

As we entered the dark confines, the sense of menace was overpowering. Fighting the desire to quit, we began our sprint. The climbing was not too difficult, but I desperately wanted to escape this sinister place. It took an age to break loose from the clutches of the chimney, then I aimed for a large, overhanging buttress to the right, silhouetted in the eerie half-light of the moon. I could sense the massive gargoyles of snow and ice stuck to the soaring towers directly above. Why had Al Powell talked about earthquakes the day before? Where was he? I turned to look below. Yes, he was there, a pinprick of light still in the confines, plugging away as quick as his body would allow. Our partnership had started in Peru three years earlier. My aggressive, impatient character was tempered by his steady, laid-back approach. We were in this together now, gnarled and knotted like old oaks.

Dawn arrived and high-lighted our spectacular setting. We

Al Powell on the endless ice of Fear and Loathing. *Nick Bullock*

clung to life in the middle of a great, concave amphitheater. Upside down organ-pipes hung all around us in this cold cathedral, some as thick as tree trunks. The mountains behind woke for another day, lit with a deep red glow as the sun lifted its head above the horizon. Immediately, the warmth made its presence felt. A large serac broke from the wall above and crashed down, scattering into a thousand pieces. Minutes later a second one followed. With every resounding crash we cowered, insects at the bottom of an egg timer.

Al cut across the rippled ice, moving right and aiming for the vertical ice towering above. I moved toward him, crossing runnels furrowed by falling debris. We were pitching the climbing now since the chance of something crashing from above and wiping us out was very real. Roped, the fall wouldn't kill us.

After a fantastic and sustained 60-meter pitch of vertical water ice, I belayed, casting a wary eye above. A runnel of rotten rock waited, covered by a thin skin of ice and topped with a bulbous overhang of icicles. This was not the type of ground for someone new to the fathering game, like Al.

My lead! I climbed straight up. Good ice gave way to a skin of rotten crud. Frantically I scratched and scraped, eventually managing to reach a large cluster of icicles drooling from the exit. The screw I had placed an eternity ago was 15 meters below and Al was another 10 meters below that. Placing three more screws into the crud, with one tied off and two wobbling, I made a move up, then another. Feet kicked, lumps of crud flew. Al dodged, I swore, an axe ripped. I lurched, I reversed. I tried two more times; both failed.

"Any ideas?" I yawped to Al, who hadn't made a sound the whole time I was swinging around trying to kill myself.

"Why don't you aid it?"

"On what? Everything is rotten."

"Just slap a sling on your top screw to stand in, then aid it on your axes."

The thought of aiding through rotten ice didn't appeal to me. "I don't do aid!"

After an hour Al realized I wasn't joking.

Groveling up unconsolidated snow at the top of the overhang, I vowed never to scoff again at aid climbers: I had succeeded by aiding on my axes. Al started to climb but quickly decided to jug one rope. I belayed him on the other while watching television-sized blocks of ice ring constantly down the steeple of rock opposite. Approaching me, Al stared at me and whispered, "you're a fucking nutter!" That pleased me.

Two pitches of unprotected powder-bashing placed us on a knife-edge arête of snow beneath a great tilting serac fringed with a massive mouth of sharp teeth. We dug out a ledge for a bivy and ate our evening meal while sitting out a storm.

Through the night the clouds swarmed, but later, to my great relief, the sky cleared. Easing the stiffness from our aching bodies on the first pitch, we saw the sunrise and the mountain begin its morning song. Six pitches of weaving and groveling followed. Climbing vertical, unprotected mush ate into the time, and it was with joy that I tunneled through the second wafer-thin cornice of the day onto the ridge. Celebration took the form of a whole Mars Bar each.

At last the foreboding face was left behind. We were now on the East Buttress, first climbed by Egger and Jungmair in 1957. A panoramic vista opened out in front of me: new valleys, intense blue lakes, new mountains. I felt alive.

Dropping down from the cornice, I traversed to belay at the side of a large ice overhang. Al swam past then crawled beneath a wild umbrella of ice, where he fixed a belay. "You're going to love this!" As I climbed to meet him, I didn't think I was. Sitting at the rear of the cave, he reminded me of a fly in the jaws of a Venus flytrap, but this fly was attached to ice screws and sitting at the edge of a hole looking directly down the face. As I traversed the wall of thin snow surrounding the hole, Al yelled quite loudly, "Careful, you haven't seen how far that overhangs!" I hadn't, but as I minced around the hole to join him it became obvious.

"Why is nothing on this mountain normal?" I moaned. Al ignored my moaning and set about digging a bivy ledge, making a pulpit overlooking a congregation of fine mountains.

The third day followed in a similar fashion to the second. The climbing was never as hard as the first day but it just kept coming. We cut slots, carefully crawled over crumbling rock, pulled overhanging ice. Having squirmed up more bottomless powder, I basked in the sun and checked the buttress above. The rock was the same as lower down: a pile of crumbling corn-flakes. Rusty pegs sprouted from lumps of congealed mud, and rotting ropes swung forlornly in the wind.

I pointed out a line I had spotted to my left. It looked more in keeping with everything we had already done and would be more new climbing. Al set off around the corner to check it out.

"It looks like it'll go," he mumbled. "It looks okay as long as the ice isn't rotten."

A very sustained 55 meters later he escaped the confines of the runnel, pulling through an ice overhang and belaying at the base of a tottering dollop of snow. On the next section—the third, vertical, unprotected excavation pitch of the climb—I surprised myself by digging through it easily; it must have been all the practice I was getting.

Leading onto the steep summit ridge, every step kicked into rotten, sun-bleached snow gave me reason for rejoicing. A long traverse left found me burrowing through Joe Simpsonesque flutings of death and led me to thoughts of hanging over the headwall. I didn't fancy emulating the epic that occurred on Siula Grande, and so we belayed.

Following my weaving steps, Al joined me at my confined spot. Continuing directly up the runnel, he chopped through the top of the fluting and continued up a steep, icy slope. The afternoon bubble-up of clouds had started earlier than normal and soon it spitted hail. Spindrift poured down the runnel, hitting me. It continued to fall in great clouds, blowing across the hundreds of fringed icefalls covering the headwall to my left.

I became concerned. We had climbed all day, having eaten only one bar of chocolate each. I could feel my body eating away muscle for fuel and imagined returning to my job in the prison gymnasium emaciated. The drug-detox class would come into the gym fresh from the street, rattling and drug addled. They'd take one look at me, smile, and wink, recognising a fellow sufferer. Little did they know the drug of my choice didn't come in tablet form!

The lack of food and energy would make waiting on the ridge in this weather very risky. The line had dictated that we move light and quick. We couldn't slip down to the valley for a rest and food before our summit push. We had no ropes fixed, no stash of food, no place prepared to safely sit out a storm. This was the style of climbing we both preferred, but if we stayed up here I was going to make the worst crack addict look healthy.

Our passage across the corniced ridge in near white-out conditions was a tad disconcerting. I guessed that the towering pile of crud swirling in and out of the mist half a pitch away was the summit. Al appeared out of the driving snow, fighting his way along the ridge. With no food and unable to see what we would be climbing into, we hung around praying for the weather to clear. But after waiting half an hour our prayers were not answered. It didn't feel fair, but a lesson learned long ago that life isn't fair turned us around to start the long and scary journey home.

SUMMARY OF STATISTICS:

AREA: Peru, Cordillera Huayhuash

ASCENT: Jirishanca's southeast face to very near the summit, Fear and Loathing (900m to merger with East Buttress route and approximately 150m beyond, 25 pitches, ED 3/4, A2 WI6+ 90°+). Al Powell and Nick Bullock. June 15-18, 2003.

Nick Bullock would like to thank the B.M.C., the M.E.F., Mammut, and D.M.M. for their support.

Tambo, Churros y Amigos

One crazy adventure on the southeast face of Jirishanca.

DIDIER JOURDAIN

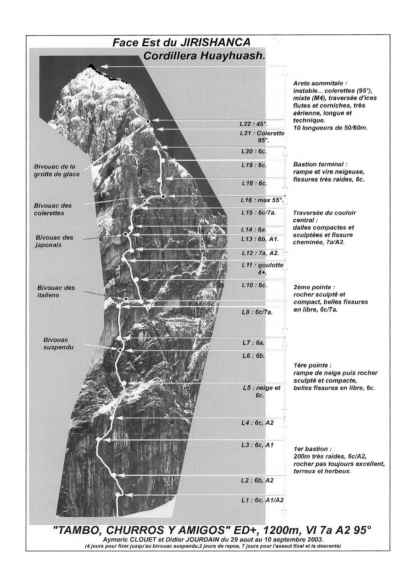

Face Est du JIRISHANCA
Cordillera Huayhuash.

Arete sommitale :
instable... colerettes (95°),
mixte (M4), traversée d'ices
flutes et corniches, très
aérienne, longue et
technique.
10 longueurs de 50/60m.

L22 : 45°.
L21 : Colerette 95°.
L20 : 6c.
L19 : 6c.

Bastion terminal :
rampe et vire neigeuse,
fissures très raides, 6c.

L18 : 6c.
L16 : max 55°.
L15 : 6c/7a.

Traversée du couloir
central :
dalles compactes et
sculptées et fissure
cheminée, 7a/A2.

L14 : 6a.
L13 : 6b, A1.
L12 : 7a, A2.
L11 : goulotte 4+.
L10 : 6c.

2ème pointe :
rocher sculpté et
compact, belles fissures
en libre, 6c/7a.

L8 : 6c/7a.
L7 : 6a.
L6 : 6b.

1ère pointe :
rampe de neige puis rocher
sculpté et compacte,
belles fissures en libre, 6c.

L5 : neige et 6c.
L4 : 6c, A2.
L3 : 6c, A1.

1er bastion :
200m très raides, 6c/A2,
rocher pas toujours excellent,
terreux et herbeux.

L2 : 6b, A2.
L1 : 6c, A1/A2.

Bivouac de la grotte de glace

Bivouac des colerettes

Bivouac des japonais

Bivouac des italiens

Bivouac suspendu

"TAMBO, CHURROS Y AMIGOS" ED+, 1200m, VI 7a A2 95°
Aymeric CLOUET et Didier JOURDAIN du 29 aout au 10 septembre 2003.
(4 jours pour fixer jusqu'au bivouac suspendu, 2 jours de repos, 7 jours pour l'assaut final et la descente)

One of the early aid pitches on Tambo, Churros Y Amigos. *Didier Jourdain*

After a last long night in El Tambo, we took the bus directly the Cordillera Huayhuash. We had with us three weeks of food, which amounted to seven bags of 30 kilos each. After about 10 hours of the collectivo bus, we arrived at Queropalca in the night, a little town lost at the end of the Peruvian mountain pampas. Already it felt like an adventure. Then a long day of walking with mules took us past the pretty Carhuacocha (Lake) to the foot of Jirishanca, at 4,500 meters. Along the way the mules took a little bath in the river, and when it started to snow, we faced the hard fact that our gear was totally soaked. Then we realized something even worse: "Oh my god! The toilet paper!" It, too, was soaked. We managed to save eight napkins—how many days would they have to last? And then the weather turned really miserable.

Edgar, a 14-year-old shepherd, visited to exchange some trout for rope after the climb. He became the only person we would see in 22 days. Only Christophe, the two-kilo

Aymeric Clouet running it out on his new route on Jirishanca. *Didier Jourdain*

The Ice Spider section of Clouet and Jourdain's difficult new route on Chacraraju Este, climbed just before Jirishanca. *Didier Jourdain*

chicken, kept our morale up. But she was losing weight too quickly. Eventually we left camp for four days of climbing. Aymeric attacked the first pitch at the lowest, most overhanging part of the face. It snowed every day. We climbed slowly in the mud and grass, half aid and half free, having to clean the cracks to place protection. A pitch a day for the first two days, spiced by a fall from a sky hook. What a start.

The next day, two pitches took us through very steep, dirty, poor rock to the top of the first bastion. Then we crossed a snow ramp, where we found an odd dropped bolt (of Italian origin). Now the free climbing could begin, as the rock was much better here. One more 80-meter pitch in crazy sculptured limestone, and then a new storm. Back to the bivouac, with 300 meters of fixed rope above and finally high-quality rock.

The next day we returned to the base camp for two days of rest and eating, and of course to save on toilet paper. Six big trout awaited us, along with a thinner chicken. We looked at our supplies and realized that only eight days of food remained. It was time for the final push, which looked like it would provide aesthetic free climbing.

A day took us up the fixed ropes, where we learned the old lesson that there is always something that doesn't work on an ascent; this time it was the stove: two hours to heat soup. Another great start.

The crux of the second day was a steep freeclimbing crack to reach a good ledge: no portaledge this night. But Aymeric lost his mind over the stove. The next pitch had a ridiculously good belay: two 10mm bolts! Why a bolt when there were such good cracks? We had left our own bolts behind so as not be tempted. Then snow began falling again.

The third day we diagonaled left up a dihedral with an icy pitch and met the Japanese route, with its old fixed ropes, pitons, and bolts. We used three of those bolts to cross a slab, and climbed two hard pitches on the right with a bit of aid climbing on poor rock, using a skyhook. We placed the bivouac on a poor ledge.

The fourth day, we crossed some gray slabs on the right to reach the central chimney gully; a long mixed pitch took us to the ledge under the final bastion. We were free climbing again, but now under a friendly sun. We went to sleep to the rhythm of the stove. That night the sky brightened from storms far below to the east, over the Amazon Basin. Impressive.

We left the portaledge there, on the fifth day. Three splendid pitches in cracks and slabs were steeper than expected; it was a gas at 5,800 meters. Then Aymeric played with his ice-axes in the large ice roof ringing the entire top of the mountain, a roof that had frightened us since the first day we saw them. He climbed it free, which was amazing. We played at being tightrope walkers on the snow arête that glided into the sky. As night fell, we discovered a cave under a icy roof. Nine technical pitches through icy roofs, bad rock, ice-flutes, and cornices eventually took us to the summit the sixth day. It was a magic moment.

Another night in the ice cave, and then a long day brought us back to the ground. We removed our fixed ropes, and on the last abseil down, in the night, another storm hit us. Snow had returned, but for us it was "la buena suerte" (good luck). The following day, over-tired, sick, and beyond any feelings, we shuttled back the last of our gear. Edgar came to give us some potatoes and to take us back to civilization. We gave him the rope. It had been a crazy adventure, which wouldn't end until the first meal, the first beer in El Tambo.

SUMMARY OF STATISTICS

AREA: Peru, Cordillera Huayhuash

ASCENT: Southeast face of Jirishanca, Tambo, Churros Y Amigos (1,100m, ED3/4, 7a A2 95° M4). Aymeric Clouet and Didier Jourdain. August 29–September 10, 2003.

Clouet and Jourdain also climbed a major new route on Chacraraju during their visit to Peru. See Climbs & Expeditions.

The spec on the ice roof is not a fly, it's Aymeric Clouet climbing free. *Didier Jourdain*

Topping out on Tambo, Churros Y Amigos, with SW face of Jirishanca Chico behind. *Didier Jourdain*

THE ENDLESS SUMMER
EXPEDITION

A quest to lose oneself between Alaska and Antarctica.

ALUN HUBBARD

Sailing vessel *Gambo, hard-reefed and* close-hauled in breezy conditions in the Gerlache Strait, Antarctic Peninsula.
Peter Lane Taylor

In 1999 Dave Hildes and I scraped our pennies together and bought a 47-foot steel ketch called *Gambo*, which, over the next four years—with the help of a scratch crew of climbing misfits, barflies, and dumpster-divers—we bobbed our way up to Alaska, down to Hawaii, on to New Zealand, and then hung a left to Cape Horn, Antarctica, and South Georgia Island. Ostensibly, our purpose was to bag loads of remote mountains in a hard-assed, Tilmanesque manner, but the trip more likely resembled a low-budget floating gypsy/eco-tourist operation. During this time I made many new friends, lost some, learned how to sail, shout loudly, and inflict significant liver damage upon myself. I also pretty much forgot how to climb.

For the excessively pedantic, we covered about 25,000 miles and attempted about 40 mountains, of which we succeeded on about half. Notable named ascents include Cook (St. Elias Range), Persson (near Cook); Baird, Aspiring, Cook (NZ); Luigi, 1st & 2nd Sisters of Fief, Hoegh, Britannia (Antarctica); and an attempt on Paget (South Georgia).

I served a full sentence. Dave Hildes, Tobyn Ross, Chris Barnet, Bernard (Casanova) Eyrhart, Greg Brown, Jeff Martin, Chris (Jabba) Nelson, Paul Dumfy, Peter (Pedro) Taylor, John (Jonkim) Millar, Grant Redvers, Davide Fasel, Elliot Robertson, Andy Mitchell, Lena Rowat, Hamish Millar, Tim Hall, Martin Stuart, Davie Robinson, and Stuart Holmes all did suspended time.

Space and the impaired attention span of the modern reader preclude a full chronological account of this enterprise, so herein I've rendered the high- and low-lights in all their unadulterated glory into a series of user-friendly vignettes.

Early May, 1999, Vancouver, British Columbia. Hildes and I are in a fix. We've got head-splitting hangovers, two free months, and an abundance of bad news. The body of Davide Persson, our good friend and our most experienced climber, has just been recovered after he caught an edge and fell while telemarking down Mt. Rainier's Liberty Ridge. Andy Grey, owner and skipper of Loki, recruited to sail us up to Disenchantment Bay, Alaska, and back, has bailed us for his pregnant girlfriend. Bertrand has woman troubles (actually we've all got woman troubles, but thankfully we're not all French). So we've no team, no transport, no women, and I'm not feeling so hot either.

However, it's one of those balmy spring British Columbia days, and we head downtown to meet Andy for a conciliatory voyagette around False Creek before lining up more illicit activities for the evening ahead. During the festivities I spot a red dragon painted on the bow of a sailboat moored at a nearby marina. Later, Hildes and I scramble over a gate to check her out. The boat is big, green, and built like a brick shithouse. A gruff voice hails us from below. I explain my Welsh roots and our plight. One salty sea-dog, Dai Neale, invites us aboard and cracks the seal on a bottle of Mount Gay. We compliment him on a fine boat; he enquires as to how much we've got in the bank.

Ten days later, the day the registration papers are signed, we weigh *Gambo*'s hefty anchor and head north with our new acquaintances, Chris and Tobyn, both shanghaied from a local pub. We're to pick-up Greg (who's just returned from Mt. Logan's east ridge) and Casanova on the way. The boat's skookum and we haven't a care in the world, apart from where to put fuel, how to sail, decode a tide-table, etc.

Four weeks later, St. Elias Range. After an uncomfortable bivy forced by an unwelcome blizzard that sprang up 15 hours earlier, leaving us wandering blindly like lost sheep looking for the top of Mt. Cook, we stumble out of sleeping bags to a clear dawn and a stunning post-storm skyscape. Bertrand's toes are frostbitten and we're into the last rations, but the wind has dropped and the dream team is back in action. Everything is plastered in rime ice, and in the 20-minute slog to the now-visible summit, Mt. Logan starts to glow and is then brilliantly silhouetted against the rising sun. On top we shake hands, take photos, smile, and stamp about a lot. It's a fantastic moment and I innocently ask if anyone's up for a little jaunt to Antarctica.

Somewhere between Hawaii and New Zealand, October, 2000. I lie listlessly across my bunk as the last puff of wind dies and the blocks and booms start banging again and the sails flog themselves to death. Soon the racket will be drowned by the monotonous drone of the diesel, which may put me to sleep. We left the women and Tonga, an idyllic but now dreamlike Eden, five days ago, along with Greg whose somewhat unexpected ritual of tears, loathing, and Prozac was getting out of hand. All is well now, but the equinoctial gales predicted from New Zealand have failed to materialize. Sailing *Gambo* about the tropics in light breezes is a bit like using a Hagland Polar Terrain Vehicle for a Californian road trip. *Gambo* has bobbed and wobbled its way across the Pacific for as long as I can remember, and the ocean has become my view, toilet, bath, sun-bed, compost-heap, source of nutrition, Sunday matinee, late-night thriller, and psychological nightmare. Dead Calm is the film that springs to mind. With no wind and not much fuel left, soon the ocean may become my mistress.

The decent booze ran out yesterday and Jabba-the-Hut (Chris) has slowly but systematically pulled *Gambo*'s interior apart in search of tedium-relieving distractions. I've hidden the analgesics. Suddenly he gives out a yelp and his grime-covered bulk emerges from the fo'c's'le victorious with two trays of forgotten Budweiser under each arm. We tuck into the warm, gaseous fluid.

Six hours later, just after midnight, Jabba and I are on watch. The beer is finished but we've made a sizeable dent in the synthetic gin picked up in Samoa. It's also Jeff's birthday, and we've been celebrating by chucking Chinese firecrackers stuffed into pickled eggs and mouldy vegetables down below hoping to provoke some response, any response. Jeff and Dumfy know better, so miffed and clutching the remains of the gin, Jabba and I attempt "Follow the Leader" from one end of the boat to the other without touching the deck. Tangled in the rigging somewhere, I lose consciousness and land on deck with a thud.

I wake in the same position, blistering under the heat and sweating alcohol. It is another perfect cloudless tropical day with no wind, and I have a parched throat, a tongue stuck to the roof of my mouth, and a jackhammer is pounding my head. Jeff, the fresh-faced birthday-boy, beams me a smile as he hauls in a tuna. I squint empathetically at the suffocating fish as it quivers before Jeff smacks it over the head with a spanner.

Later, taking down our daily position, I realize we are within yards of the international date line. In a spontaneous surge of euphoria, we stop the engine, strip, and jump in. We're five days from the nearest civilization and, impulsively, somewhat mysteriously, all four of us start swimming away from the boat. The film has now switched to Picnic at Hanging Rock. After five minutes we stop, tread water, and look back and marvel at this surreal little green and white bobbing thing that has carried us mere mortals such vast distances. Then a ripple crosses the water. I feel a whiff cross my face and in stunned terror we watch *Gambo*'s sails ruffle. The headache's gone and Jeff's 10-hour birthday is also up.

Mid-October, 2001, Lyttelton Boat Yard, New Zealand. Grant's back, all fresh faced and keen from a week's pre-med emergency course at Wanaka. He's got a bunch of Kiwi guiding mates in tow. They look hard and surly and dubiously poke around what's left of *Gambo*. "When you planning to leave?" one of them asks innocently enough. I disentangle myself from a spaghetti of wiring and my response even sounds ludicrous to my own ears. "Er, end of the month?" *Gambo* equals chaos and sits on the hard surrounded by her own intimate innards. As we speak, Jonkim is grinding out ominously large chunks of the bow and stem, while Garry is drilling apparently random holes in the boat, shaking his head in a not entirely encouraging fashion. It's been non-stop for the last fortnight and I haven't showered in this time, falling unconscious each night in the same filthy clothes in a hastily cleared space below. But there's progress. The new engine is in, the rigging's good, and the hull's been blasted, welded, and painted half a dozen times.

Gambo's tribulations as she's been dismembered and deconstructed have provided the mainstay entertainment for all the other boat owners in the yard, who fine tune and polish their cherished beauties for the racing season. But the lack of pretension of our motley crew have endeared us to all and not an hour goes by without someone waltzing over to offer a beer, old paint, advice, or the like. Garry, our hired, weather-beaten Kiwi of indeterminate age who subsists entirely on a diet of Nescafé and Rothman's, has become an oracle in all things nautical. At first I was too bashful to inform him of our true intentions, but now that he's got wind of it, he's taken up the crusade with gusto. "Na, mate, ya gonna wan' nothin' less than inch plate up front to take on those bergs. Don' wan'er goin' daaan like the Titanic, eh?" During a bleak moment, I consult the Oracle. "Ah, na worries, she's a bit of Maori job, but she's a goer." I'm reassured but still have to find money, skis, anti-fowling, obscure charts, depth sounder, medical kit, outboard, inflatable, a year's provisions, more money, and the instructions for putting the wiring back together. Jonkim walks up, hand over his eye. He's got a shard of steel in it.

Six weeks later, around 57 degrees south in the Southern Ocean. We're well south of the Antarctic convergence zone now, and again the ocean has become our world. But this time there's no shortage of wind and it's pretty cold too. The batteries no longer hold charge and the diesel fuel's gone waxy. More significantly, the wind has picked up to 70 mph north-westerly, gusting force 12. To anyone well versed in "How to Sail" textbooks that's "Air filled with foam, waves over 45 feet, sea completely white with driving spray, visibility greatly reduced." Under such conditions these books will also inform one to employ "storm survival tactics," jargon for pulling the sails down, which seems eminently sensible. Progress is definitely on the up though, and in a week we've covered 1,500 miles under bare poles. Cape Horn looms about five days off.

Outside, it's pretty breezy and the waves are phenomenal. Estimating wave height is much like estimating ice-climb angles; both are prone to embellishment. I am mesmerized by these gray-bearded monsters, stacked up, wave upon wave upon wave, and get a distant, out-of-body feeling marveling at the surreal mass of water that emerges out of the gloom. Our mast, 50-feet high, is dwarfed by them. But they have a long wave-length and *Gambo* surfs nicely and feels in control. I'm just concerned for any further deterioration and icebergs, of which I'd spotted one.

It is primeval below: the dank, semi-frozen interior is like a bombed World War I dugout. We flinch as the biggest waves break on deck, shuddering the steel frames and squeezing high-pressure jets of freezing water through the hatch seals. Everything drips and virtually all time not on watch is spent in salt-sodden sleeping bags keeping warm. Morale is high, though. We're exhilarated by the sheer scale of the waves and isolation, and therein lies the beauty of going to sea with a bunch of mountaineers. It's a marginal improvement on snow-holing, and there's plenty of music, literature, and food.

On December 3 the pressure bottoms out and the cold front passes through, accompanied by a savage wind shift and a sea that in nautical-speak is termed "lumpy." I hastily re-read the "storm" chapter in the textbook, and it informs me to throw all manner of junk off the stern attached to 300-foot loops of one-inch nylon hawser to reduce boat speed. We do this but it has no effect, so we then deploy a 20-foot water-parachute from the bow that comes mighty close to ripping my arm off. This works better, though, bringing our bow up into the 100-mph gusts. The real problem is there's no prevailing swell though; the sudden wind shift has sent the whole lot into a random towering maelstrom and there's little to do other than sit tight. After 18 hours the wind slackens, so the storm sail is hoisted, and on we go.

That night we get knocked down. Grant's on watch, the rest of us are sleeping, and suddenly the boat is thrown over about 130 degrees to starboard and back up, all within 10 seconds. After the initial shock of coming to on the cabin floor, surrounded by utter chaos (topped off with a vat of lovingly prepared veggie chili), it's pretty obvious from the motion that the boat's okay. I call out to each of the crew. Jonkim and Peter, who have also been flung across the cabin, are fine. Grant, who'd been doing the chili justice at the chart table, sat in horror as the galley rained upon him. Cutlery, pressure cooker, and the entire set of "unbreakable" crockery had dispersed around the cabin in a zillion pieces. There's a knife embedded in the woodwork next to his head. We sit there in a mass of books, pots, clothes, broken glass, and food, dazed and confused. As the adrenaline hit subsides, I stifle a giggle and a lighter side to the bedlam prevails. It's not at all unlike the feeling after surviving one's first whanger.

January 2002, Weincke Island, Antarctica. With the additional ballast of Hildes, Elliot, and Davide Fasel picked up in Ushuaia (along with a ton of kit/stores and a couple of skinned sheep), now we are the Magnificent Seven and the Endless Summer Antarctic Expedition is a reality. We've been based along the west coast of the Peninsula (a.k.a. the Banana Belt) for almost a week and we're having a hoot. The infamous Drake Passage was a doddle (even to complete sailing novices) and New Year's Day was appropriately celebrated in a haze of single malt and a stupidly entertaining, if not outright vicious, snowball fight with the crew of a French charter boat.

Apparently though, the Antarctic summer season is not going well-the weather is uncharacteristically unstable and sea ice completely jams Crystal Sound, our intended climbing destination 200 miles farther south. Nonetheless, we are stunned by the magical scenery, wildlife, and the wealth of mountains and gorgeous routes. An easy decision is made to focus our efforts on the Wall and Fief Ranges of Wiencke Island until conditions south ameliorate. Within minutes of mooring up against the fast-ice in Port Lockroy, our skis and climbing kit are unloaded. Jonkim, Davide, Hildes, and Elliot camp in the midnight twilight for a three a.m. start to check out the first of the unclimbed Seven Sisters of Fief. I awake early, and am pleased to see that only ski tracks remain. Later, Grant, Peter, and I sail *Gambo* round to a safer haven in Dorian Cove, where numerous shorelines can be set up to hold the boat steady in the 90-mph williwaws that sweep down from the icecap. A shallow reef across the entrance also bars the bigger bergs from wreaking havoc. We are quickly learning the perils of Antarctic yachting, but Dorian Cove provides the perfect haven, complete with an operations hut built by the British Navy during WWII and equipped with bunks, Primus stoves, and 1940s pin-ups.

By early evening, getting anxious, we spot two figures skiing across Thunder Glacier. Within minutes Jonkim and Davide schuss the last slopes down into the cove. As they arrive, Hildes and Elliot come into view. They are knackered but elated, and I am chuffed as hell, badgering them with countless questions. They succeeded on a difficult mixed route up chossy rock, with some

The *Gambo* flying past growlers in the Gerlache Strait. *Peter Lane Taylor*

taxing pitches. But the indefatigable Jonkim is up for more and with the weather not going one way or t'other, tentative plans are made for an attempt on Mt. Luigi, the highest peak on the island.

At four a.m. the weather is perfect. Unfortunately, I cannot say the same for myself. Three months with only the odd argument to raise the pulse has taken its toll, and now, sweating hard, I labor along on my rusted skis with Peter and Grant, all of us in Jonkim's trail. The lad is unstoppable. Despite my ailing physique, conditions are ideal. The route up and onto the east shoulder is straightforward, and soon I am psyched and breaking trail up to the base of the summit pyramid. Skis are dumped and Grant takes the lead. All of a sudden I'm hit by that odd sensation that comes from being reacquainted with steep places with good views. Grant puts on a spurt. He weaves in and about a number of hanging seracs, traverses onto steepening ground, and after a final strenuous pitch it's an easy slope to the summit and we're shaking hands, all smiles, slapping each other on the back with all of Antarctica spread out at our feet. A life's savings, three oddball years, a few hundred gray hairs, 1,000 petty arguments, 20,000 miles—but it's been worth it.

Danco Island, February 2002. A month on and morale is no longer high. Despite notable success-es—a stunning midnight ascent of Mt. Hoegh with Davide, Jonkim, and the British Army in tow, and a fantastic first ascent and yahoo descent of Mt. Britannia—generally we've been frustrated by unremitting conditions. What did we expect? Thick sea ice has thwarted attempts to get farther south, and the unstable weather has stalled our more committed mountain projects. Even the Gentoo colonies are suffering: there's little snow-free ground about the rookeries and no sign of life from the eggs that should have hatched months ago. The Antarctic summer is short, and the winter night is drawing in.

The 'Shroom, Wall Range, Wiencke Island. The team's route follows the gully right of the relatively snow free rock band, into the splodge of cloud and up into rimed cornices above. *Peter Lane Taylor*

The team is restive and dysfunctional; the original crew have been in close proximity for almost half a year now and is beginning to crack. Interaction is at an all-time low, and Jonkim, the expedition mainstay, has bailed, ostensibly due to worries back home. However, there's also the fact that our relationship has hit rock bottom, his proud self-reserve steam-rolled by my hot-headed, petulant outbursts. All the same, I'm gutted and at least get a private moment to tell him so before he leaves. So Jonkim, Elliot, and Hildes have sailed back to Ushuaia for reprovisioning and a crew swap, leaving Grant, Peter, Davide, and me based at Danco Island with a month's provisions and grand ambitions for a 60-mile traverse and ascent of the highest unclimbed peak of the peninsula, Mt. Walker, via the appropriately named Downfall and Forbidden Plateau. Apart from climbing Mt. Britannia and a few other modest rock peaks, our climbing plans have been frustrated by the weather, which isn't exactly horrendous, just damp, unstable, and generally shite—the cloud hardly lifts, leaving us blind trying to weave torturous routes through a labyrinth of increasingly tenuous crevasses. It is maddening, and, apart from kayaking, knitting hats, carving whalebone, climbing icebergs, holding up the odd cruise ship, quibbling, and attempting to make homebrew out of jam, much time is passed in the horizontal angle of repose.

A fortnight after watching *Gambo* sail into the sunset, a mast and sail appear on the horizon to the north, but hopes are dashed when it is revealed that the hull is red, not green. Still, we take the Zodiac to indulge our curiosity and are welcomed aboard by a genial skipper and his mixed group of charter passengers.

Five hours and many beers later we are no longer so welcome; furthermore, it is dark, snowing hard, and the wind has picked up. We are about three miles from Danco Island, the GPS is buggered, and though two sheets to the wind, I vaguely comprehend the nuttiness of our situation. Peter's gone quiet, possibly to sleep, though more likely questioning his karma-debts as to how he ended up with such a bunch of losers. Davide has morphed into a drama queen and is arguing incomprehensibly with/at Grant who appears to be in a stupor. My head torch beams faintly into the dark, snowy gloom as I clutch a compass that appears to be stuck on west. Peter perks up though and we try to keep an ear out for the warning sounds of water breaking against rocks or icebergs. Before long, we are somewhere in the middle of Errara Channel, the sea is getting choppy and the Zodiac is taking on water. It is ridiculously wet and cold and quite absurd. Davide is now in full Wagnerian rant, setting the world to right and everyone to shame. Suddenly, out of the darkness he springs and jumps Grant. It's impossible to discern if it's a fight or a wrestle or an over-zealous hug—but for sure he's lost his marbles. It is pitch dark. Davide is standing in his Welly boots and Gore-Tex jacket in an 11-foot inflatable boat that is bucking wildly in ice-strewn water in the middle of a blizzard. He has Grant by the collar and is screaming at him. Both are on the brink of going overboard. Grant, with astonishing presence of mind, collapses to the bottom of the Zodiac, dragging Davide down with him. The freezing water sloshing about brings Davide round. He shakes off, sits upright, and moves back to his place, muttering. We get on our way, whatever way that is. Another idyllic night of the Endless Summer Expedition.

Back at Wiencke, early March 2002. Perched precariously on steep snow about nine pitches up the Grade IV gully of the 'Shroom, I am attached to Andy Mitchell, one of the new crew, who is trying to look confident and who in turn is attached to Peter, who is busy taking photographs. This is my third attempt at this route, and, although the wind has picked up and bits of cornice sweep down on us, ice conditions are splendid. It is going well and I am having a laugh. Andy, the expedition's eager water-quality scientist, also seems to be enjoying himself despite not having done this before. I am trying not to think of the consequences of a fall. We are nearing the crux of the route, where the headwall steepens into an overhanging cornice that I am psyching up to bore into. It is getting blustery and spindrift is whipping up. Furthermore, the good ice has given way to banked powder with the odd firn lens, and I place a dubious ice screw, then an even more dubious stake and tentatively move up some. I'm leaning right back now, feet high, and my left axe and arm shoved deep into the snowbank in front, the other digging into the cornice above. A table-sized chunk loosens, topples, and cascades downward. I am beginning to suffocate in the spindrift. With as much strength as I can muster, I thrust upward and forward in a desperate attempt to gain purchase in this powdery stuff surging about me. Next instant, I am ejected. With axes flailing, I topple backward, but before gaining too much downward momentum my crampons bite into firmer snow and I manage to hold steady. I plant both axes firmly, cough, splutter, wipe my eyes clear, and grin over toward Andy, who is no longer looking so cheerful.

I give it one more half-assed attempt, but after a piece of cornice smacks me in the face, I call it a day. Andy looks relieved, Peter disappointed, but the weather's breaking again and we've got to get off before it starts avalanching proper. Unfortunately, Andy takes twice the time descending as he did ascending. Toward the bottom of the gully where the angle eases, Peter and I, now well below Andy try to coax him to turn around, face outward, and plunge step. He turns but doesn't look too happy. Suddenly, irrationally gripped, he closes his eyes and takes a blind step into the void and loses it, accelerating headfirst. "Get your axes in!" we both yell as he shoots past, the rope snaking wildly behind. We have about enough time to swap manic grins before Andy disappears down a hidden bergschrund and the rope jerks both of us downward. It takes our combined weight and strength to bring him to a stop and eventually, after a lot of pulling, his head pops out. In his broad West-Country accent he asks if we can do some science now. I concur.

February 2003, the Scotia Sea. We're deep into the Southern Ocean again with a largely new crew. This time we're headed due east from Cape Horn toward the fabled island of South Georgia. There's a slight problem though: the engine is buggered, and South Georgia is sieged by whopping great tabular icebergs and detritus associated with the break-up of the Larsen-B ice shelf the previous year. The cause of the engine failure is a broken drive plate, mortally weakened when we ran into an unmarked mooring line in the Beagle Channel. Not until after three days and 500 miles is it apparent that something is seriously amiss, when all manner of unhealthy clanks and groans start emanating from the bell housing. Thankfully, I have on hand a mechanical wizard and am introduced to some of the more endearing eccentricities of the crew. Hamish Millar, Jonkim's older brother, in great earnestness enlightens me. It's my "bad karma" that has led to the diesel's demise. Somewhat piqued, I quiz his mechanical authority, Hamish replies that not only does he know a mechanic but, furthermore, has just read Zen and the Art of Motorcycle Maintenance.

However, we are unanimous in our decision to forge on since *Gambo* is a sailing vessel after all, and we are already halfway to South Georgia. Fighting talk, and, indeed, ignorance is truly bliss. A day later we cross the convergence zone and hit the ice. The tabular bergs are immense, and we spend a whole day skirting round one particular set of monsters, keeping a close eye out for the growlers and bergy-bits that have broken off. Without the engine or being able to sail to windward if a real howler blows up, I am very aware that the risk is now real. Furthermore, since we have no way to charge batteries to power the radar, this risk is multiplied by the fact that night is still seven hours long and, when it's not blowing hard, we're inevitably fogbound. Hence, we heave-to. I opt for the two till five a.m. "dog-watch" to get the boat underway as soon as dawn breaks.

It is cold, muggy, and eerie as hell during the night while the blocks and tackle creak and clank and the wind whistles through the rigging. Every quarter of an hour I try to penetrate the gloom with a spotlight. Coleridge was right: you can smell ice, and I am in a state of perpetual anxiety. On the third night of this, 50 miles off Shag Rocks, the wind drops to a gentle 15 mph and the boat starts rocking violently in the swell. As the gray hints of dawn materialize, I note that visibility is down to 80 feet in the thick fog that cocoons us. But within minutes it becomes calm; the swell and rocking ease. I squint into the gray gloom and discern a patch of darker gray. I don't know if the fog has thinned, or if my eyes are adjusting, but I can make out various shadows of gray all around. Suddenly, I realize that not only are we surrounded by ice; we are in the lee of a massive berg. Even as I start to unlash the tiller, I can make out cracks and detail in its face where it has calved, and with rising panic realize it is almost on top of us. It wouldn't likely sink us, but at best it would bring the masts down, which without the engine amounts to much the same thing in the long run. I release the jib furling and within seconds the boat is heading downwind, away from the looming face, but into a cluster of house-sized bergs. I close haul and beat, skimming within a few yards of one of them. Then we are free, away from immediate danger. I am tired of this; I want to make landfall and the next day we do just that, setting eyes on the highest peaks of South Georgia.

March 2003, Mt. Paget. A fortnight later, Stuart, Grant, Davie, and I are five miles up the Nordenskjold Glacier with a week of supplies, attempting to push a new route up South Georgia's highest peak, Mt. Paget, via its unclimbed east ridge. It's been a breezy 10 days and we have been acquainting ourselves with the island's captivating wildlife and rugged beauty along with the inhabitants of the BAS base at King Edward Point (KEP). While the team has been out on various forays generally pestering penguins, getting blown about, and being avalanched off mountains, I have been up to my eyeballs in grease pulling apart *Gambo*'s diesel and have recovered the buckled remains of the drive plate. With the help of a concerned girlfriend, a new drive plate has been ordered and dispatched from the U.K. It might arrive on a supply ship, but for now the air pressure is high, the forecast good, and we're making real progress on a route through to the 5,600-foot col that lies between Paget and Roots. I suggest halting near a buttress marking the start of a steep icefall. It is a crisp, clear evening, and we'll get an early start, taking advantage of the cold to get us over the snowbridges. We camp, eat, brew up, and settle in for the night.

At 4 a.m. I wake and check my altimeter; it must be on the blink since we've apparently gained 1,300 feet of elevation. I snooze some more, then Stuart quizzes me about the pressure. I work out that the barometer has dropped more than an inch as the first gust hits. Stuart is for moving, but I

Jonkim Millar hoofing up the start of the east flank of Mt. Luigi, Wiencke Island, with the Gerlache Strait and the Wall Range falling away behind. *Peter Lane Taylor*

reassure him that nothing measures up to Patagonian winds and we'll be just fine. I call out to the other tent and we decide to sit tight. Oh, dearie me. An hour later and I am bent painfully against the side of the tent trying to relieve the tension on the poles and seams. The tent is filled with a fine mist forced through the layers of fabric, and the interior guys that have been rigged have just popped their retaining loops. I am about to suggest collapsing the tent when nature obliges. The first pole goes, then a second and third crack in quick succession. As the flysheet shreds in a wild frenzy, I concede to Stuart that the last gust was perhaps worthy of Patagonia. We are, however, distinctly better off than the other two, who suddenly have no tent at all, and in a surreal running commentary inform us that their rucksacks, full of climbing gear and a week of food and fuel, have just ripped from their anchors and are flying off down the glacier. I snuggle deeper into my sleeping bag and resign myself that our attempt on Paget is to be delayed for a wee tad.

A week on and I'm being ferried in the Zodiac back to the Nordenskjold, this time with the two relative novices, Tim and Hamish, since Stuart has decided he doesn't like bad weather, Grant doesn't like the look of Paget, and Davie just thinks I'm a wanker. We leave them at Grytviken to mind the boat and their blossoming relationships with KEP. For a change though, we can at least see Paget, which is a promising start. After a night camped at edge of the glacier, we awake to a

Gentoos foraging at low tide in Dorian Bay, with Mt Luigi dominating the skyline above. The top of the east ridge is the left hand skyline. *Peter Lane Taylor*

cold and windy dawn, but with clear skies and after a long day, we set up the tent in a crevasse above the first icefall. Day two we thread our way through a second icefall, and after setting off a wind-slab avalanche, come to a halt in failing visibility below a series of seracs. After half an hour's deliberation, by which time it clags in completely, Hamish convinces us to ski into an icefall to find a sheltered spot to pitch the tent. Eventually we choose a snug little corner deep between two mammoth blocks. I am glad of this, since during the next five days it snows constantly, about twenty feet, and, while cocooned in our grumbling, rumbling icefall, we can hear the roar of large avalanches sweeping down to our left from the hanging seracs above. Although the icefall has a definitive ephemerality about it, we are undoubtedly better off. We doze in a state of perpetual hibernation, wisely concocting less painful methods for consuming porridge while maximizing our bladder capacities. On the third day, after tiring of getting my pants filled with spindrift and watching my turds fly off in incredible gusts, I dig the most elaborate shithouse in South Georgia. Thank heaven for small joys.

On the fifth night the blizzard moderates and the dawn is cloudless and windless. After a slow start digging out the tent, we are back on the planks and ski into a large basin, the back of which forms the east ridge proper. We hoof it up a 1,000-foot, 40-degree gully to the right and after a lot of puffing and swearing top out onto the crest of the east ridge. The view is phenomenal and I am in raptures. Although the summit is still almost three miles off, with over 4,000 feet of ascent, the route looks good with a couple of interesting sections. Conditions underfoot are excellent and the weather remains perfect.

Then Tim drops a bombshell and informs us that he won't go on. He mentions wife and family, and how exposed, committed, and short of food we are. There is no reasoning with him. Hamish also feels out of his depth and backs down. I am pissed off but defer an immediate retreat by announcing that I'll go it alone after lunch. We sit and eat, marveling at the tremendous views of the ridge, down the whole of the south coast, and at the peaks that surround us, rising straight out of an azure Southern Ocean dotted with bergs. Our meal is accompanied by my monotonous running commentary regarding the amazing, once-in-a-lifetime, never-to-be-repeated opportunity they are about to pass up. Tim is having none of it, but a suggestion that a little look-see, while practicing some ice axe arrests, provokes a thoughtful look from Hamish and then he bites. Despite the bad karma crap, I am beginning to really like him. He's turning out to be garrulous version of his rock-hard younger brother.

We potter along the ridge, fixing belays, and generally pratting about. Hamish is having a ball, and although the wind picks up the sky remains clear and by the time we return to our col, Tim is well into digging out a snow hole. I'm skeptical, but Tim retorts with a succinct "fuck you," and so we go with it, erring on the side of caution. Eventually it is finished and we enjoy a rare, perfect South Georgia sunset.

Snuggling down, I concede that the ice cavern is indeed much roomier and warmer than the tent (or the boat, for that matter). Then the drips commence and the roof starts to sag. Five hours later, after little sleep, we waste the first hour of dawn rescuing kit buried under a heap of mushy snow. By the time Hamish and I set off, an ominous lenticular cloud is already draped over Paget. The race is on and we push fast, making superb progress along the ridge, turning numerous cornices and ice pinnacles, and dealing efficiently with a couple of airy ice pitches.

After three hours the weather is definitely deteriorating; the wind has picked up, and a bank of cloud is sweeping in. At just over 8,500 feet, some 1,000 feet from the now completely obscured summit, the first gust hits us, and a series of surreal cloud tendrils sweep up from below. However, on the opposite side of the ridge, we have a completely unobscured view of the whole of Cumberland Bay and so call up KEP on the VHF radio. It is the first they've heard from us in nine days and Sarah Lurcock sounds relieved. After a few pleasantries, she informs us that the latest surface prognosis is good, but that there's a small system lingering to the south, the edge of which may be affecting us. I wholeheartedly agree, and, as a sustained gust knocks me off my feet, I express disbelief that it's a balmy, cloudless day down there, a mere five miles away. Before signing off, Sarah

Davie Robinson enjoying a spindrift breakfast in typical South Georgia style in the gully on the North Ridge of Quad 5. *Stuart Holmes*

asks if we can say a few words at our high point for one of the few previous Paget summiteers, who has become the latest fatality in the war in Iraq. With this somber news—and now completely engulfed by cloud and a snowstorm—it takes little for us to decide to retreat. After a quick hug, a photo, and a few words of tribute to Mark Stratford, we backtrack into the mounting maelstrom.

The voyage of doom, mid-April 2003, somewhere in the South Atlantic. We are at last within spitting distance of the east coast of Argentina, Mar del Plata to be exact. The last week's been purgatory, excruciatingly frustrating with either constant headwinds or no winds. We have wobbled back and forth across the Plata Estuary, failing to gain any westing against the strong easterly current. We are onto our last LPG bottle and water is low, too. The decent food ran out yonks ago, and the last of the veggies have retreated to inaccessible corners of the boat to die a malingering, rancid death. We have covered well over 3,000 miles since leaving South Georgia, though less than half of it in the right direction. The new drive plate never did arrive, and a temporary welding job on the old one was a tad too temporary. Stuart is a week late for work, and flights home are being missed by all, resulting in frayed tempers and a lot of whinging. I'm almost enjoying myself, not least due to others' frustration (bastard that I am), but also I've got an ominous feeling about landfall and am now learning how to actually sail; every degree closer to the wind that can be coaxed out of *Gambo* yields a meaningful reduction in our ETA. This has suddenly all changed. The glass has fallen, an easterly risen, and under full sail we gallop toward Mar del Plata at eight knots throughout the night. By mid-afternoon the next day we are within 15 miles, but the wind has now risen to gale force and is veering south. Stuart, who has been at the helm all day in a state of rapturous ecstasy at the thought of making landfall, is visibly gutted when I announce that we are going to heave-to and sit it out. I'm just not willing bring *Gambo* into an unknown port, in a gale and poor visibility without the engine.

Throughout the night we drift northeasterly and by midday Saturday the gale subsides, but we have lost over 40 miles and begin again the laborious process of beating into light headwinds. As darkness draws in, we can see the telltale orange glow of city lights, the first sign of civilization in almost three months. With a favorable wind shift to the northwest during the night, we have a sense of renewed excitement and anticipation come morning.

Easter Sunday is gorgeous and the oppressive atmosphere of the last weeks vanishes. We catch fish, lounge about on deck, and chat and joke happily while watching the city tower-blocks looming larger and larger as *Gambo* tacks back and forth in an ideal zephyr. By late afternoon we are within three miles of port, and though it's an undignified end to the trip, we are not willing to risk another calamity. We request a tow from the port. They are happy to oblige and within an hour we are ogling the evening strollers as we enter the harbor. We tie up and a friendly, curious local, Alfredo, greets us and passes over a bottle of chilled beer. We are a sight indeed, but the cold beer tastes magical.

A day or so later, after we are all stuffed and sated and almost normalized once again, I stop by an internet café to quickly whizz through e-mail. At the bottom of the pile is a short message from Lena stating that Jonkim Millar and Guy Edwards are 3 days overdue from an attempt on the northwest face of Devil's Thumb. The worst is presumed. My stomach knots up and I'm overcome. With a grief-laden heart, I go to find Hamish and the next day we pack up, say our goodbyes to *Gambo*, and head home to yet stormier seas. This story is dedicated to Jonkim. He was an exceptional individual and his memory lives strong with all of us who were fortunate enough to sail and climb with him.

SUMMARY OF STATISTICS

AREA: Antarctica, South Georgia, New Zealand, Alaska

ASCENTS:

Alaska: First ascent of Mt. Persson (NW Cook, 3880m) and second ascent of Mt. Cook (4,200m), via a new route–linked traverse from sea level.

Antarctica, Wiencke Island: Three ascents, two likely to be first ascents. 1) The First (or northernmost) of the Seven Sisters of the Fief Range above Port Lockroy—ca 1,200m by its northwest ridge. 2) The "Shroom," a ca 900m corniced summit on the Wall Range, climbed via "Crag Jones" gully (opposite Noble Peak) to ridge heading up left (north). 3) Mt. Luigi (1,400m) climbed by its east ridge via an exceptionally good ski route with a snow climb of 300m to the summit of up to 50°.

Peninsula first ascents: 1) Stolze Peak (ca 1,580m), on skis. 2) The westernmost peak of the Laussedat Heughts, and Mt Hoegh, on skis with short technical sections at the end. 3) Mt. Britannia (ca 1,500m) on Ronge Island, climbed via two routes: east ridge (directly opposite Danco Island), technical; southeast ridge, mostly on skis.

Peninsula Icecap Plateau: ski traverse from the Orel Ice Fringe to the Downfall. Weathered off the downfall at the crux, precluding an attempt at FA of Mt. Walker. Many other unnamed peaks (up to 1,400 m) were climbed along the Banana Belt of the Antarctic Peninsula, some of which had likely been climbed by unofficial BAS parties, but not all. South Georgia: Numerous attempts on Paulsen, Quad5, and Marikoppa Peaks. To within 300 m (& beyond difficulties) of the summit of Mt. Paget (ca 2,900m) via a new east ridge route.

A NOTE ABOUT THE AUTHOR

Alun Hubbard might be described as an unhinged Welshman with a penchant for high places and latitudes, typically approached by unorthodox means involving water. He is also passionate about frozen water, and works for the University of Edinburgh, School of Geosciences, as a glaciologist and ice sheet modeller. He is of no fixed abode, though occasionally consorts with an increasingly impatient girlfriend and has half a boat currently moored in Uruguay. He is looking for crew.

Grants: Gore, Polartec, the Royal Geographic Society with Neville Shulman, the British Mountaineering Council, and the Mount Everest Foundation provided invaluable support, without which this enterprise would never have been more than a dream.

Davide Fasel, Jonkim Millar, and Alun Hubbard tripping the midnight-light fantastic on the summit of Mt. Hoegh. *Alun Hubbard*

FENRIS

Notes from a dream fulfilled in Queen Maud Land, Antarctica.

MIKE LIBECKI

The first base camp location, with Ulvetanna in the back ground. The plane is an Antanov II bi-wing single engine from Poland. *Mike Libecki*

Dreams? Goals? Fantasies? These words may sound attractive but they mean absolutely nothing. Zilch. Nada. Zero. At least not without their most important ingredient: absolute, genuine belief. Just as mystery is the most important ingredient of any true adventure, absolute belief is the most important ingredient in fulfilling any real dream, goal, or fantasy.

My patience had wearied over a far-fetched dream that had teased me for many years, but finally last December I looked down from an airplane at the ice surrounding the coldest and windiest continent on earth: Antarctica. I was about to arrive in Queen Maud Land, which, to me, is the home of the most stunning and unique granite formations on the planet. My original partners had bailed on me, and all financial sources had left open wounds draining me into debt, yet I still would not take "no" for an answer. I knew a solution would present itself, as it always does. Finally, my laughter would echo among the fantastic towers I had dreamed about for so long.

Just a week before boarding the monstrous aircraft on its way to the frozen continent, on a flight I was prepared to take alone, Josh Helling, one of my best friends and climbing partners, finally bowed to the opportunity of a lifetime and acquiesced to the sacrifices required to join the expedition. My friendship and climbing partnership with Josh is unlike any other: respect for one another's techniques, absolute love of life, trust, safety; and most importantly, our dream to reminisce about our adventures when we get old and wrinkled.

Josh Helling skiing near Ulvetanna. *Mike Libecki*

The dove-gray morning sky cried with us as we drove our half-ton of haul bags and ski equipment to the Salt Lake City airport. It was the end of a cold November and winter had already painted the mountains white. Pain wrenched my heart over the coming two-month absence from my family. We said our sweet-sorrow goodbyes at the airport and held tight to the crutch of optimism.

Josh and I were headed for the Antarctic Logistics Center International, or ALCI, a Russian-owned and-operated company in Cape Town, South Africa. They were starting their third year of providing flights to the nearest coast of Antarctica, where Russia's officially claimed base, Novolazarevskaya, is located. The only communication we had had with ALCI involved necessary permits, finances, and logistics. We had no impression of what to expect from our Russian contact. We knew only that they were going to transport us to the walls we had dreamed of for so many years.

Spider-webbed red eyes—and limp hair oiled with jet lag—showed my haggardness from the flight from Atlanta to Cape Town, the world's longest commercial run (15 hours and 8,170 miles—a third of the way around the globe). One of the directors of ALCI, Vasily, met us with a firm handshake, a big, friendly grin under piercing blue eyes, and a polite, slightly accented

English. Less than an hour after arriving in Cape Town, Vasily was debriefing us on the Ilyushin-76 cargo plane we would take to Antarctica and what it would be like when we landed at Novolaz-erevskaya, better known as simply Novo. We provided our Environmental Protection Act permit and permits in cooperation with the Antarctic Treaty. Many countries have agreed upon such covenants in order to keep Antarctica as pure, preserved, and politically peaceful as possible.

At midnight on our second day in Cape Town we stood in front of the massive Ilyushin-76. It reminded me of Han-Solo's spaceship, the Millennium Falcon, because of the huge, bubble-like compartment under the nose. In mid-flight we changed into insulated clothing and double-boots for the subzero temperatures that awaited. After six and a half hours, we landed atop the glassy ice covering the tarmac. A frigid breeze and bright sunshine exploding out of the Antarctic azure welcomed us as we stepped onto clear-blue ice.

Novo base consisted of about 15 red, yellow, and blue insulated tarp-tent structures the size of my two-car garage. A much larger tent served as a kitchen. Strange wooden structures—fitted with sleigh bottoms—served as homes to the Russian crew who live here during the summer season. Diesel powered heaters ran 24 hours a day in all of the shelters.

We loaded our food, fuel, and gear into an Antonov-2, a small, single engine biplane from Poland. Though it was 30 years old, and somewhat slow, if the engine were to fail, the two-wing

The west wall of Fenris showing the line of ascent. *Mike Libecki*

technology would allow the plane to glide to a safe landing. As we rose into the perfect Velvia-blue sky and headed for the dream walls, the tents at Novo looked like candied sprinkles on a white frosting cake. Soon, all we could see were the distant peaks of the Wholthat Mountains and a vast ice desert. Less than half an hour later, enormous summits came into view, looking like gigantic teeth thrust out of the icy plains by the jaws of Mother Earth.

We landed near Ulvetanna, the highest peak in the area and one that proudly dominated the view. I imagined royal trumpets sounding off to announce the presence of the stunning granite towers. We gazed in awe at monumental sculptures crafted by God himself--He must have known how sweet life would be for a human to set eyes upon such fantastic summits.

We created our base camp by carving six-foot-tall ice-block walls that surrounded an area big enough for a sleep tent and a cook tent. We brought two 20-gallon airtight barrels to be used as toilets. To honor and respect Mother

Quality time at camp in Queen Maud Land. *Mike Libecki*

Earth's last hope of a pristine continent, we planned to remove most of our feces.

Once base camp was established, we set out to explore a specific group of towers in the Orvin Fjella area. This was comprised of steep fingers, fins, and walls of sharp granite in an area of about 140 square miles. Some of these spires rose well over 3,000 feet above the ice, and the individual monoliths appeared to be holding hands beneath the gums of ice that entwine them. We were super-psyched to do a ski circumnavigation of the area and investigate the walls in hopes of finding at least one beautiful crack system. We did not come here to climb a contrived route; we came to this pristine and gracious land to climb natural features and cracks that would make obsessed climbers find frozen drool below their mouths after seeing it.

As we skied past a huge tower called Fenris, it revealed its perfect, pyramidal west wall and pointy summit that pierced the brilliant blue sky. Not only was the wall itself astounding in its triangular shape, but a system of corners and cracks split the wall perfectly in half. It was an aesthetic, attractive objective for vertical pleasures.

As we progressed among the monumental granite, we were dumbfounded by the grandeur of the unrivaled rock formations. The walls exuded a feeling of holy magnitude. Ulvetanna's overhanging north and east faces sent shivers through my body. Kinntanna, a three-tiered group of spear-tipped summits, bound together like Siamese twins, reminded me of steep mountains found only in fairy tales and legends. The Holtanna massif is another true masterpiece, resembling a massive butterfly with its wings spread. Each wing was a 2,000-foot tower that almost mirrored the other one. The left wing resembled a proudly perched lion glowing with power; the right wing looked like a huge ship's prow with a perfect, vertical skyline. Snow petrels—dove-like birds with small, black onyx eyes—flew around the sharp summits. We continued our circumnavigation back to base camp. The west wall of Fenris and the aesthetic system of cracks that split its face impregnated me with an obsession to climb it. The thought of its luscious long corners teased me. The addicted climber inside me became aroused by the thought of

Snow petrel. *Mike Libecki*

my hands and fingers inside the virgin cracks.

We carved a new six-foot deep weather haven into the mile-thick ice cap near the west wall of Fenris. Several inches of snow fell, followed by high winds and gusts to 80 miles per hour. We started racking gear, sorting food and fuel, and getting ready for our attempt to live in the vertical world. We shuttled loads with skis and sleds to the base of the wall, two miles from our base camp.

The sky stayed true blue. The 24-hour sun and its ally—the earth's largest ozone hole—relentlessly battled our sunscreen. This day was relatively warm, about 20 degrees Fahrenheit. More snow petrels with their beady black eyes flew above us.

Josh was victorious on the two-out-of-three rock-paper-scissors for the first lead, and it looked beautiful: a hairline seam that slightly widened with elevation. Josh meandered up an easy ice slope, then delicately tooled his way over a deep cavern/crevasse to a short 70-degree section before he could touch the granite. The start of the paper-thin seam above Josh was several feet out of reach, leaving natural hooks his only option. Josh carefully equalized hook placements on small crystals—was he shivering from the cold or the whipper so close at hand? A fall here would have been serious, most likely throwing him into an ice-cavern's pit of despair. He delicately moved onto the hooks. Compromising with gravity instead of fighting it, he tapped in a few small copperheads, then some assuring bird beaks. Before long, he was in cruise control above the A4 crux. Just a couple days later, we had over 600 feet of rope fixed and were ready to commit to the wall.

A whiteout took over the camp on the first day of the new year. Rest day. We had packed enough supplies to live on the wall for three weeks—exactly when our Russian friends would pick us up. I yearned to be on the wall, to be cold, enjoying anything warm, and learning more about real appreciation in my fragile body. We packed our final loads of sleeping bags and the precious pee bottle and skied away from base camp toward Fenris.

While we were living on the wall the average temperature dropped to the single digits and below. The frozen onslaught made everything a chore. Every day we reluctantly unzipped our stagnant sleeping bags and started our routine: fire up the stove, melt ice, stir hot chocolate, stir oatmeal, take a shit, and lash on the battle armor for the day's subzero upward progress.

The pitch above our camp looked very wide, very hollow, and very rotten. I started off into off-width cracks. Fortunately, our portaledge camp was underneath an eight-foot roof as I threw off rotten flakes the size of couch cushions, followed by several pillow-sized flakes. I hung on nuts and cams in the back of crumbling off-width cracks. I am sure Josh cursed me with every

Looking out from the icebox bivy. *Mike Libecki*

Josh Helling climbing out of the second portaledge camp.
Mike Libecki

exploding crash of rock, and rightfully so. But it was fucking scary trying to send the huge flakes to the icy ground without slicing open my rope or flesh. Exploding fragments threatened the portaledge and Josh even under the overhang.

We swapped pitches through plenty of rotten cracks, switching from free to aid constantly. Changing into free climbing shoes from double plastic boots was not especially enjoyable, especially at minus five degrees. Having feeling in our toes and feet was just a fantasy (believe in the warmth…believe in the warmth…). We both got our share of frozen, run-out off-widths and squeezes. Challenges came often while trying to feel edges and features with numb feet, as eroding rocks showered the belayer.

Our first small storm on the wall hit us as we finished the last of our double hauls to a big snow and ice ledge halfway up the wall. It went from cold, to really fucking cold, very fast. The suffering freeze we had prepared for arrived just in time to catch us off guard. We shivered in minus 20 degrees. The snowstorm broke into the most amazing light show. Trillions of sparkling ice crystals glittered around us, and I felt like a wizard in a fairy tale too fantastic for this world. Thin black shadows from fang-tipped summits shot across the ice cap. Pink, orange, and yellow ribbons of sunlight gorgeously attacked.

Treacherous beauty: continuous, loose, and rotten. We agreed that if the leader decided it was too dangerous, the other would not question him. The detached and balanced blocks that looked like they should already have fallen concerned us. With patience and optimism we proceeded higher as the temperature got lower.

Soon we found ourselves hanging in a huge cave we called the Ice Box Bivy. I doubt if the temp ever went above the single digits at any given time inside this dark and dreary cave. It was so cold that our feet were numb as we left the portaledge in the morning.

Josh led the third-to-last pitch as I endured what became the coldest belay of my life. I spent the time jumping, dancing, kicking, and flinging my arms just trying to keep circulation flowing. I will never forget that day: the cartoon-style shivering and chattering teeth, as well as my crazy bargains with God for just a tiny bit of warmth (believe in the warmth…believe in the warmth…). My feet were completely numb for hours. I am not proud that I got my first spot of real frostbite.

My last lead had an awkward squeeze chimney that took everything I had left in me. I had to take off my helmet so I could fit inside before snaking over an overhanging roof to the summit ramp. Josh not only got the first pitch but also the last little summit pitch. The west wall's summit blob was only big enough to straddle like a horse. In contrast to the consistently unstable and frigid weather during the climb, we were blessed with a calm, blue-bird summit day. The sun was at its lowest point of the day, changing from sunset to sunrise as it rolled across the horizon, smiling in all its glory.

In my seven-year-old tradition of celebrating Chinese astrology on expeditions, we pulled out our plastic Ram and Sheep masks to celebrate the Year of the Ram on the top of the wall. I thought about my family, my friends, and how important people are in this life. I closed my eyes and digested deep thoughts of how much energy and sacrifice from so many people it took to make this expedition, this summit, and this ultimate reality possible. Appreciating appreciation ruled my psyche.

We spent the last few days on the icecap kite skiing and enjoying our surroundings. Our Russian friends showed up on time and flew us back to Novo. We spent a week there waiting for the 100-mile-per-hour winds to die down so the Ilyushin could land. Bonding with our Russian friends, we spent our last days laughing; eating delicious Russian wieners, cabbage, and kraut; playing board games; listening to traditional Russian music; and of course drinking way too much vodka. Tears fell when we left Novo, and I have a strong feeling that it won't be long before I meet my comrades again.

SUMMARY OF STATISTICS

Area: Queen Maud Land, Antarctica. Orvin Fjella region of prominent walls and towers.

Ascent: First ascent of the west face–west summit of Fenris. Helling-Libecki Route (2,150', VI 5.10 A4). Climbing dates: December 30, 2003 to January 14, 2004. Expedition dates: November 29, 2003 to February 3, 2004. Josh Helling and Mike Libecki.

A NOTE ABOUT THE AUTHOR

Mike Libecki strives to live in the "now" on ultimate expeditions around the world. He currently has 12 more expeditions planned into remote areas on the planet that are home to mysterious, untouched, large rock formations. When not on or planning expeditions, Libecki, 31, spends his time pursuing his passions of writing, photography, videography, presenting his adventures around the country, and spending time with his family. He lives through his belief in the need to follow true passion, and that a positive situation will always present itself while doing so. He often is heard singing, "The time is now, and life is sweet!"

Libecki would like to thank his major sponsor Mountain Hardwear, without which the expedition would not have taken place, and also Black Diamond, Clif Bar, MSR, and Sterling Ropes, as well as the support of his wife, family, and friends.

Josh Helling and Mike Libecki enjoying a Year of the Ram Celebration on the summit of the west wall of Fenris. *Mike Libecki*

BETWEEN THE LIGHT AND THE SHADOW

Struggling with wind and cold while putting up the Bulgarian route on the north face of Thalay Sagar, Garhwal, India.

NIKOLA LEVAKOV

The great north face of Thalay Sagar, 6,904m. The routes start on the glacier at about 5,400m.
Patrice Glairon-Rappaz

At our arrival at base camp I counted 25 tents. I hadn't expected such attendance, as I had heard of no more than two expeditions per season to Thalay Sagar. Now there were Korean, Dutch, and French climbers, and us: the Bulgarians.

The Koreans stood out with their Mountain Hardwear tent that looked like a spaceship with round portholes. They were sponsored by seven big companies and attempted the Australian route (the icy gully in the middle of the wall). Their team had rich experience, with most of its members having climbed above 8,000m. For one person in the group this was his fourth time on Thalay Sagar. I found it really strange that only two climbers would be trying for the summit. They told me that the ice was thin, the anchors for the fixed ropes were bad, and that it was very dangerous. They came back from 6,400m because one of the two climbers became ill.

The three Dutch climbers attempted the east face via a new route. During their final attack the weather was bad and it was snowing, but they managed to reach the top. They were wonderful people. This wasn't their first time in the region. One of them, Melvin, had climbed the neighboring peak, Bhrigupanth. The Dutch expedition chose a nice line: it was always sunny!

The French were a party of four. I think they were attempting to make a 400-meter variant of the normal route along the gully. Two of them made it, the other two didn't. It was quite difficult to communicate with them.

We Bulgarians were a great team. We had everything we needed. Our cook, Jenak, was wonderful. It

Nikola Levakov leading at about 6,200m on Between the Light and the Shadow. *Hristo Hristov*

was a real pleasure to talk with him. He didn't know any European languages or European meals, but he was so charming that everything turned out okay. Our liaison officer, Bra, was really helpful. There was no need for me to act as "the leader." We made our decisions together, as a group.

Everyone told us that our route was a beautiful project, but very dangerous and extremely difficult. We already knew that. The thing we didn't know was the drastic change of temperatures after the end of September. Most of the days were sunny, the weather was stable, but the temperatures dropped dramatically. That made us speed up the whole process. We had planned to work on the route from the 2nd till the 15th. We hadn't planned to sleep on the portaledge, which we had brought just for emergencies.

The moment we decided that we had had enough time for acclimatization we all moved up to the French advance base camp at about 5,400m. Together with Zheko and Hristo, we equipped with ropes the way from the normal route to the beginning of our rock-and-ice wall. We decided to fix about 550 meters of static rope on the wall and gradually move our portaledge

The north face of Thalay Sagar: (1) Northwest Couloir/West Ridge (1,400m, 5.8 A1 60°, Kligfield-Thackray-Thexton, 1979); (2) Between The Light and The Shadow (1,400m, VI 5.10 A2, Hristov-Levakov, 2003); (3) High Tension (1,400m, ABO 7b A3+, Bolotov-Davy-Klenov-Pershin, 1999); (4) Hungarian (1,400m, 5.8 85°, Dékány-Ozsváth, 1991); (5) Australian (1,400m, VII 5.9 WI5, Lindblade-Whimp, 1997); (6) One-Way Ticket (ED+, VII 5.8 M6 WI6, Benoist-Glairon-Rappaz, 2003); (7) Italian attempt (1,000m, ED, 5.11 80°, Rosso-Ruffino-Vanetti, 1994). *Patrice Glairon-Rappaz*

Hristo Hristov digging a snow cave on the shoulder at 6,700m the day before the summit. *Nikola Levakov*

upward, and afterward to go for the summit. With six nights spent on the portaledge we finally reached 6,400m. There were days in which we climbed only about 100 meters because of the great technical difficulties. On the sixth day, Zheko decided to climb down for a day or two of rest at "the green grass." He wished us luck and descended. Hristo and I took a backpack with a gas stove, a small pot, and very few clothes. On the previous day we had fixed 200 meters of rope above the portaledge—our last rope. We had a 60m dynamic rope and 60m 6mm static rope.

On October 11 we started early and after the end of the fixed rope we climbed 60 meters of ice, 70 meters of mixed terrain, 35 meters of ice, 50 meters of slate (awful belay stations), another 50 meters of slate, and 80 meters of snow and ice until the shoulder below the summit at 6,700m. I had thought that when I reached the shoulder I would go to the southern side and that there would be no wind and that from there I would belay Hristo. But the wind there was as strong as on the northwest face. Hristo climbed up and we discussed the situation. The only possible solution was to dig a snow cave. I belayed

Hristo as he started digging. I couldn't stand the cold, so I joined him to warm up. In about an hour we were ready to move into the cave. We had very little food and absolutely no bivouac equipment. We used everything we had to try to stay warm. We massaged each other's feet, trying to keep them warm. At some point we even managed to get some sleep.

At 8 a.m. we told ABC that we were heading for the summit. We walked along a rocky edge where we saw remains of old fixed ropes, but they were of no use. Suddenly we came to a vertical chimney, IV+, where the rock was, to put it mildly, friable. While I was climbing it I was thinking that this peak had saved some surprises for us till the very end. Hristo came and offered me the lead to the summit. It was very kind of him, but I let him go first. When one is at 6,904 meters there is absolutely no difference in who is first and who is second. Throughout the whole journey I was filming with my video camera. Hristo is one of the toughest men I've seen. We reached the summit at 12:47 p.m.

We tied the Bulgarian flag at the only possible place. We took pictures, sang the Bulgarian hymn, and I interviewed Hristo. We stayed at the summit for about half an hour. On the way down the most difficult section turned out to be the snow and ice slope under 6,700m and the band of slate, where there wasn't a single secure belay point. It took us many hours to reach the good anchors we had used on the way up. It was already dark and we had only one headlight at the abseils. The strong wind blew streams of snow powder over us. We reached the end of the fixed rope and sighed with relief. Hristo climbed one belay point ahead of me. I heard a cry. Hristo writhed with pain. He had fallen about 10 meters and had hurt his pelvis. Slowly and carefully we reached the portaledge.

Hristo said, "Everything is great!" But it wasn't like that. I tried to take off my shoes, but I couldn't. I cut the inner shoe and pulled out my feet, which no longer felt like mine. With Hristo's help we started to "work on them." After six nights on a portaledge and one night in a snow cave, the lack of sleep finally took its toll. In the morning we cut the sleeves off Hristo's turtleneck and used them for my socks. I put on his three-layer shoes and headed for ABC with no luggage. I left everything with the hope that somebody would use it during the second attempt and would bring it down. After a couple of hours Valia met me at the end of the fixed ropes with hot tea. In a while Hristo also came down, carrying quite a lot of luggage. I told Valia, "Meet him as a king!"

SUMMARY OF STATISTICS

AREA: India, Gahrwal Himalaya

ASCENT: North face of Thalay Sagar, Between the Light and the Shadow (1,400m, VI 5.10 A2). Hristo Hristov and Nikola Levakov. October 7-12, 2003.

Hristo Hristov died on May 20, 2004 during the descent after climbing Mt. Everest by north side without oxygen. His body was found and identified some days later above the Second Step.

Translation by Tcveta Misheva

Hristo Hristov at home on the north face of Thalay Sagar. *Zheko Vatev*

THE DUTCH ROUTE

The northeastern, sunnier side of Thalay Sagar yields its first complete route.

MIKE VAN BERKEL

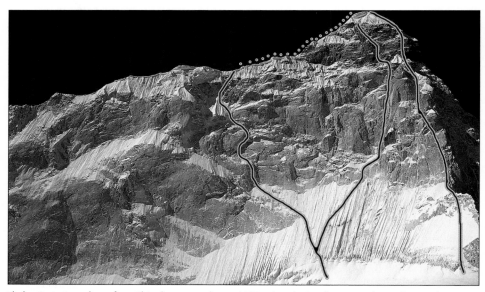

Thalay Sagar's northeast face. This photo was taken in 2001, when the Dutch team made an alpine style attempt. The face is in dry conditions compared to 2003. The Dutch route is on the left (800m, ED-, VI 5.8 A1 AI5, 2003). In the middle is the Polish attempt that failed due to a fall 150m below the summit (650m, 5.9 A1 55°, Kpys-Skierski, 1987). On the right is the Northeast Ridge (1,000m, VI 5.9 A1, Czok-Doseth-Guldal-Nesheim-Skorek, 1983). Further right on the arête above the north face is the Italian attempt, which reached the schist band (1,000m, ED, 5.11 80°, Rosso-Ruffino-Vanetti, 1994). *Melvin Redeker, www.melvinredeker.com*

The northeast face of Thalay Sagar had been on our minds since our 2001 trip to the Garhwal. We had climbed the south side of Bhrigupanth alpine style on October 12. By that time it was way too cold to consider climbing the northeast face of Thalay Sagar, where we had spotted a nice line going to the southeast ridge. In August 2003 Cas van de Gevel, Melvin Redeker, and I were back, well prepared, well trained, and with a plan. Inspired by the 1997 climb on the north face by Athol Whimp and Andrew Lindblade, we were carrying portaledges and some static rope. Our plan was simple: establish a camp near the glacier, fix the couloir leading to a col at 6,000 meters, bring all the gear to the foot of the face, bring up the rope, and start the climb. All of this took about three weeks, so by the time we actually started the climb we were well acclimatized and familiar with the approach.

The northeast face is about 1,500 meters wide and 800 meters high, with perfect granite smeared with ice. Amazingly, only the northeast pillar had been climbed to the summit, leaving a superb face open for exploration. One attempt had been made by a Polish team in 1987 to climb a direct route just left of the northeast pillar. They got high but missed the summit when their lead climber fell 150 meters short of the top.

On September 17 our portaledges hung under the bergschrund and we were ready for the ascent. Three days were spent fixing half of the face. The first day we climbed primarily 50-degree snow and ice. The advantage of the face's eastern aspect became clear, with sunshine all morning. This was also its downside since the sun would warm the face, allowing ice to come crashing down. Nothing too bad, but still quite painful when experienced head on.

On the second day the interesting climbing began: some hollow ice at the start, then two pitches of near-vertical ice in a Chamonix-like couloir, and then excellent ice higher up. On our third day a traverse to the left gave way to two more steep ice pitches underneath an overhanging corner. At the top of these pitches our nice line of ice was cut by a belt of overhanging granite.

After three days of climbing we were ready for a rest day, and we would have to

Cas van de Gevel just below the northeast face of Thalay Sagar. The Dutch team fixed rope up to 6,500 meters before launching for the summit. *Melvin Redeker*

decide if we would take the portaledges up the face or just make an early start, get up to the high point, and climb alpine style from there on. Not wanting to lose a good-weather day carrying portaledges, we opted for the latter option, although this meant getting up at two in the morning.

Doing just that, we were at our high point at sunrise, carrying sleeping bags and two days of food. As none of us were really into artificial climbing, it was left to Melvin to try the overhang, basically because he'd read a book about it. Getting better at it with every move, he moved upward and we were soon united on the ice above the overhang. That afternoon we climbed three more pitches on snow and ice with some steep bits, but also lower-angled terrain with icy flutes. As it began to get dark, we approached the steep mixed section that gave access to the southeast ridge.

We spent the night on a little ledge, looking at the moon and the reflections of lightning from the other side of the mountain. Harried by constant spindrift, we were happy to greet the

Melvin Redeker aiding the small roof because someone had to do it. *Cas van de Gevel*

sunshine the next morning. After we did two difficult mixed pitches, the granite gave way to metamorphic slate. Set at a slightly lower angle, this section was covered with powder snow and gave Cas two powder-burrowing pitches. As we arrived at the ridge the weather deteriorated, and so, hoping for better weather the next day, we decided to sleep a little lower in a cave we'd passed. This turned out to be much smaller than we had remembered and didn't give much protection from the snow that fell all night. Cas somehow managed to drop his sleeping bag, giving him a really miserable night.

Next day the snow was still falling but there was no wind. Not wanting to wait a day hoping for better weather and running out of food, we had to get to the summit. On the ridge a full-blown storm welcomed us, solving the wind riddle. Luckily the ridge was just wide enough between the cornices and the abyss of the south face. One pitch of slate—not as loose as we had expected—gave way to a nearly horizontal section leading to the summit cone. This we climbed by a 60-meter couloir, at the top of which the cornices from the left and right met. So, on September 23 at 11:30 a.m., we reached the top. Not in the mood to linger at the highest point in these stormy, white-out conditions, we radioed base camp of our success and took our summit pictures.

Conditions on the descent were dangerous, as the snow built up at a rapid pace, dislodging small avalanches on the ridge and covering us with spindrift while rappelling. Our descent picked up speed as we reached the upper fixed rope, and in the last light we searched for our camp under the bergschrund. Eventually we found it buried under a meter of fresh snow. We took the platforms and that night slept in a makeshift tent on the col a little lower down, away from the avalanches. Another long day finally took us to base camp, 10 days after setting out.

Cas van de Gevel just below the rock belt on the northeast face. *Melvin Redeker*

Our route is very interesting, with 17 pitches of vertical ice, artificial climbing, mixed V+, and a nice ridge as dessert, in some of the most spectacular mountain scenery in the Himalaya. We are grateful for the help we received from our cook, Heera, who besides providing us with wonderful meals also helped carry supplies. Completing the team was our liaison officer, Yogi, always helpful and with the latest weather data.

The post-monsoon season of 2003 on Thalay Sagar was a good one. A week after our climb two French climbers, Stéphane Benoist and Patrice Glairon-Rappaz, reached the summit after climbing a new route on the north face, left of the 1997 line. Later in October, a Bulgarian team climbed the couloir on the right side of the north face. Stable, but very cold weather at the end of September and beginning of October, together with excellent ice conditions, contributed to our successes.

SUMMARY OF STATISTICS

AREA: India, Garhwal Himalaya

ASCENT: East face of Thalay Sagar, The Dutch Route (800m + 400m approach, ED-, VI 5.8 A1 AI5). Mike van Berkel, Cas van de Gevel, and Melvin Redeker. September 17-23, 2003.

ONE-WAY TICKET

Surrealistic purity on the new French route up the north face of Thalay Sagar.

PATRICE GLAIRON-RAPPAZ

Stéphane Benoist leading one of the key ice pitches of One-Way Ticket, with 95-degree ice above.
Patrice Glairon-Rappaz

On the base of the face during the second day of climbing. *Patrice Glairon-Rappaz*

I emerge from the portaledge a zombie. A quick glance at my watch, not for the time, but for the barometric pressure: it's a bit better! It's 4 p.m. and it has already been more than three days since we were stopped by the bad weather at 6,000 meters in the heart of the north face of Thalay Sagar. This morning Patrick and Jérôme descended. It was too much for them. Too much snow, too much rime and humidity, too much waiting, uncertainty, and what's more, Patrick wasn't feeling well. During such times it is easy to become discouraged. While weighing the pros and the cons one wonders what one is doing in such a place, and whether it's really worth all the trouble. We all know this feeling.

Steph and I feel empty inside. Now we are just two after all these preparations together, these difficult carries, and these five days of sharing the route already.

I remember everything that brought us here, to India, to this face. First the photo in the book Himalaya Alpine Style, and then more photos by the Australian climbers; they planted a dream that we might leave our own imprint on this sumptuous face. And then there was all the preparation. But above all, I remember the shock of arriving and discovering the wall. The dreams and the reality merged suddenly in front of our eyes, and there had been no deception. This face! With a line of goulottes [bottleneck couloirs] in its center a line emerges that is improbable, unimaginable, surealistic, of rare purity. Such a line! It would be too terrible not to climb it; we must try to understand such purity. Ephemerality adds a dimension that only ice can bring to a route.

We passed days and days with our eyes riveted on the face scrutinizing its translucent sheets for the places where the passage of an alpinist could turn from dream to reality. And then we attacked this line, despite certain doubts among us.

Jérôme Thinières leaving the portaledge during a calm spell at 6,000m, where they were stopped for three days. *Patrice Glairon-Rappaz*

Now it is just Steph and me in the portaledge, being hammered by spindrift. But it is nice enough outside, and the clouds that imprisoned the summits have dissipated hour by hour. We will climb back up the 60 meters of rope fixed by Jérôme in bad weather at the foot of the big sheets of ice. But oulala, it's hard to move. We are stiff from these three days of waiting without moving in the portaledge. I exit first and follow the rope on the traverse. Little by little the route's first big question mark unveils itself: an immense sheet of steep ice. We had said it could be breached somewhere—but where?

Well, it seems it is passable everywhere. The ice feels good, and the flame that had been inside me rekindles. Steph joins me and seems also to be reassured and enthusiastic by seeing the ice thick and good. We return to our shelter happy from our little outing.

This morning, the sixth day on the route, is a new start. We prepare hastily because it was already late when we noticed that it was nice outside; we had been fooled again by strong flows of snow hitting our shelter, which left us thinking it was another day of bad weather.

Everything is frozen, the tubes of the portaledge are jammed, the cold is arctic, a strong wind beats against the face, and my feet are numb. We battle, all of our efforts united, to bring them back to life. What a fright!

Finally we can climb. It's 10 a.m. and the first ice sheets mark the start of the mountain's real difficulties, which won't let up until the summit. On the third pitch of the day, Steph makes it to the famous big ice sheet—this ecstasy of beauty: 85-90° for 70 meters with an exceptional quality of ice, a blend between styrofoam and sorbet thick enough to stick tools into comfortably. We hoist our gear and are forced to install ourselves on our ledge in the middle of a 90° goulotte.

Another night under the spindrift after a day where it was impossible to rewarm ourselves. It will always be like this. Inside it's tight and the stove fumes make us nauseous. We sleep drunk with fatigue, the altitude marking us little by little.

We wake late. It will always be like this, also. The cold is glacial: -12°C inside the portaledge.

This morning everything inside is covered in frost and every movement releases an ice shower. Numb and slow, we break camp and start again on a full menu where the sustained pitches link with frequent sections of 90°. It is a fabulous climb and we savor every moment. It's a game of tightrope walking on steep and fragile plates of ice that gives the name to the route, "One-Way Ticket."

Hauling the evil sack burns the last two or three calories in my body. I am tired of the work of hauling, and I don't want to cart this stuff any higher. We must try a new approach: fix a bit higher and then a light assault on the summit. I believe in our chances for success this way. Steph isn't programmed for this scenario and has doubts. But I insist I that I want nothing more to do with taking down and setting up this wretched portaledge that's stealing all of my energy. We finally agree to try it my way.

We install our camp at 6,500m tonight. Eat, drink. The soup with bacon doesn't work.

Patrice Glairon-Rappaz at the belay in the toboggan-goulotte high on the north face. *Stéphane Benoist*

We are cooked, and Steph vomits. I move to my side and don't rest well this night. We are exhausted.

Good news! We wake up feeling much better. Today we won't move the camp. The nearness of the summit is tempting, and so we'll fix all our rope and return to sleep here. Steph leads a hallucinogenic pitch that ends with 10 meters of an ice drip. When I join him at the belay with empty arms, we have both been worked by the pitch. Looking up we can see that it is not finished. We can't believe how beautiful it is. We link up two more pitches in a giant toboggan run. Amazing.

We have fixed three ropelengths, about 150m, that allow us to slide right into camp. This evening we must drink more than usual to recuperate well and to be in form for tomorrow because a hard day awaits us. Installed now comfortably in our ledge, we realize that we are making a crazy route! And we must savor it because we surely won't ever again climb a route like this again.

The wakeup alarm; it is 3 a.m. All is frosted inside the ledge; the cold numbs our slow movements. I sense that something isn't right, that I'm not well today. I suffer badly on the fixed ropes. Now that dawn has come, I climb in the lead and it's a clumsy torture. I make a long traversing pitch that takes us to the foot of the schist part of the face, where we meet the Australian route. Steph joins me then engages above in inobvious dry tooling and avoids falling with several close recoveries.

After that a length on evasive ice plates covered in snow. And then Steph takes a super hard pitch, a wormlike offwidth stuffed with snow and distant protection. Following this, my torture is like being transformed into a sausage; I am full of admiration when I join him at the belay. Here we are, at the foot of the big chimney that marks the end of the difficulties, we are at about 6,750m. We have done the line, but we are exhausted.

The summit holds out its hand across its cap of snow. A final effort to break through the cornice, and we are like magic on top!

It is always a big moment to find oneself on a mountain's summit, but this time even more so, because the climb was beautiful and hard and therefore we savor all the more the reward.

Hagard, we mechanically take some photos despite the icy wind. It is 17h15; we must think about the descent now. A final 360-degree look across the Garwhal that is bathed in clouds, and we depart for an acrobatic descent through the overhangs. We rejoin our camp at about 20h00 after a series of impressive rappels.

Filled with joy and drunk with fatigue, we don't even turn on the stove before plunging into dreams. The next day the descent is long and taxing, and we bring our heavy sacks back to advanced base camp in the night. I fall asleep almost with my eyes open and plunge directly into dreams. We wake feeling exploded, and we have trouble doing anything concrete. Our heads are still up high, while our tired bodies don't respond to our commands. Our feet and hands have been killed by the cold's assaults during the 10 days on the face.

Our friends join us in the morning to help us break the camp. That's it. We turn our backs to this wall that will haunt our dreams for a long time to come, and we steer toward other horizons in the world of civilization.

SUMMARY OF STATISTICS

AREA: India, Garhwal Himalaya

ASCENT: North face of Thalay Sagar, One-Way Ticket (1,200m, ED+, VII 5.8 WI6 M6). Stéphanie Benoist and Patrice Glairon-Rappaz. Ten days in September, 2003. The first five days (to 6,000m) included Patrick Pessi and Jérôme Thinières.

Translated by John Harlin III

HAJJI BRAKK & K7

Alone among the granite spires of the Charakusa Valley, Pakistan.

STEVE HOUSE

Hajji Brakk's tiny ca 6,000m summit joins a cluster of spires above the Charakusa Glacier. On the left is Fati Brakk, and on the right is Farhod Brakk. House reached the summit via the couloir above the arrow. *Steve House*

"Malo levo," Marko requested, and I obliged. With a step I triggered the sweet spot, and we watched in awe as a slab avalanche rumbled down our up-track in the couloir. It would have been a fatal ride for anyone below, but we reasoned that it will be safe now, and so with the conviction of the damned, we held our breath and gingerly climbed down the crown of the slide and cramponed toward base camp.

Avalanches had been the defining events of the 2003 Slovenian-American Masherbrum expedition. Each time we left base camp we had been confronted by dangerous snow. After seven frustrating weeks our final attempt on Masherbrum ended at just over 20,000 feet when we were faced with a large snowslope spanning the hugely corniced ridgecrest. By this point we were resigned to belaying pitches on even the simplest snowslopes. On my lead I set off the expedition's ninth human-triggered slab avalanche and it had traveled 200 feet and stopped at the feet of my belayers. Collectively, our idea of success had been evolving from climbing Masherbrum in alpine style to simply surviving the expedition and having the chance to return home. On this occasion it required little discussion to conclude that we were finished. But we lingered anyway. On a good day anyone could traverse this slope with a poodle, but on days like this the fact that alpinists reach any summits at all seemed like a distant and bizarre concept.

A week later, back in the oppressive heat of Islamabad I accompanied Marko Prezelj and Matic Jost to the airport for their flight home. And then I paid a visit to Pakistan's Ministry of Tourism in order to draw another permit and surrender myself, once again, to the Karakoram.

In North America we would never call the Karakoram Highway a "highway." Instead it reminds me of a windy logging road that I drive in my old Landcruiser. I go eight times a year and load a rickety wood trailer with rounds of lodgepole pine and Douglas fir to bank against the long North Cascadian winters. The Karakoram Highway makes even that road look good, and at home I can drive as slowly as I like. But not in Pakistan. Here I expect to be jarred from side to side, hour after hour, as the driver hurls his van around the famously narrow corners. It occurs to me that I have become numb to certain rigors of this place, which is to say that I have finally come to feel at home here, too. The thought gives me comfort. But 10 hours into the drive a sense of isolation finally sneaks up on me as it so often does through the clucking enunciations of an unfamiliar language. I listen to the Balti chatter and wonder what they are talking about and what would I be talking about had I company, which I don't. This makes me sad and homesick, and the feeling sits there in the bottom of my gut, sloshing heavily back and forth with each new change in the minivan's direction. We drive through the day's slow dawn and I skip breakfast and again skip lunch and later start to feel ill, much the same as the ache that had festered in my sloshing gut. Then I start to think about where I am and where I'm going, and the "where I'm going" part makes me feel less sorry for myself and eventually it makes me feel happy.

HAJJI BRAKK

My pack is built too lightly for this heavy load and it pulls me sideways and adds to the feeling of drunkenness as I weave across the rock-strewn surface of the Charakusa Glacier. This eventually brings me to a small feeder glacier where I add crampons to my clumsiness and hurry across underneath a serac that looms hugely from its position 2,000 feet above. I feel like a naked pawn running past a distracted queen.

At noon I reach the top of the glacier and scrape out a ledge in the snow, brew a large pot of sweet tea, and watch the sunlight cross the face of the unnamed peak above me. I've taken to calling this spire Hajji Brakk, after my good friend and cook, Ghulam Rasool, who became Hajji this past year. Hajji is the title given to those Muslims who have made the pilgrimages to the Muslim holy sites in Mecca and Medina. When I first saw the spire, a few weeks earlier, I had thought of Chamonix's Grand Charmoz standing sentinel over the Mer de Glace. The sweeping ice face starts wide and at first isn't too steep. But soon it looks to be plenty steep before it narrows

Looking up the ice runnel on Hajji Brakk after the crux rock section. *Steve House*

further and turns to rock. The rock is checkered with a few crack systems and chimneys, and some of these contain ice, which I could see during the approach. The face concludes on the mountain's northeast shoulder and is capped by a pyramid of granite rising to the point of a Karakoram needle. As soon as I saw it I knew I had to climb it, but at that time I had been hiking out from the successful (i.e., survived) Masherbrum expedition.

Now I'm back.

The sun sets early when you're bedded down at the base of an Asian north face, and I doze until 2 a.m. My watch alarm goes off inside my knit hat, and an hour later I find myself struggling with the bergschrund with one light on my helmet and one strapped to my thigh. Breathlessly, I clear the 'schrund and within 10 minutes I am forced to halt twice—gasping for breath each time—before I find exactly the right pace to steadily take me up the snow and ice and into the growing light of dawn.

By the time I switch the lights off, I'm on my frontpoints and being careful—the exposure has grown below me. The ice is good and hard and fractures into slabs like chunks of a shattered mirror that go skidding and then whirring down the face before I can see what is reflected there. When I do catch a glimpse I see possibilities unrealized: my own body sliding against the ice and making a nylon zipping sound and then going airborne in an unwitnessed blur of color; me here with another partner, climbing more slowly as a team of two, but without any sense of doubt; showing pictures to the Piolet d'Or committee on a distant and cold evening in France—and even while I stand in front of them, wondering if I need or even care about their approval. Then I see myself on a summit alone above the clouds and beyond all the noise.

Sometimes the climbing kicks up a notch before a mental movie finishes, and I focus as I should on the tools swinging from the shoulder-elbow-wrist-grip and pay attention to my frontpoints as I tune into any possible looseness in a crampon or unnoticed fracturing in the ice that holds me here.

I chop a step in the ice a few feet below the rock wall and move up to stand on it and start to place a screw. A powerful noise cracks the stillness and I realize that the biggest risk up here isn't falling off due to my own failing, but to be hit by even minor stone- or ice-fall. Before I can conclude the thought, the remains of a cornice have disintegrated 30 feet to my right, gravity pulverizing tons of frozen water into millions of harmless ice crystals. The cornice fell down a frozen waterfall I had considered climbing. I reverse the ice screw, tap out the core, return it to my harness, and climb further up and left. After 100 feet I stop, repeat the process with the step and the ice screw, add a second screw, and clip myself in.

I look up as I flake out the rope. It doesn't look too bad: a small chimney is choked by a snow mushroom and capped by a solid-looking chockstone. Sorting the rack, I rig a self-belay system and climb up to the mushroom and place a screw just beneath it. I don't touch the snow. The mushroom is big and I know from experience that it is much, much heavier than I am.

The chockstone's right side looks to be steep mixed climbing; I avoid it by moving up left. But after a little effort I can't get into any of the stemming positions I thought I saw from below, so I back slowly down to the top screw. The right side it is, then. A good pick torque for my right tool and a

Looking down the last difficult rock pitch. *Steve House*

shaky edge for my left, and then up with the feet; it feels as steep as it looked. Foot shuffling reveals a better stance, and I clean dry dirt out of a crack and place a small cam.

This climbing feels much harder than I want it to feel, which makes me stand cautiously with my back leaning against the mushroom. I look down at the anchor I am backroped to and wonder if I should descend. Should I give up now without demonstrating to myself that the climbing really is too hard for me, alone, so far away from anyone else that I might as well be on the moon?

"But what do I need?" I ask myself. "Do I need to fall off? Do I need to push right past what I can actually do in order to learn my limits? Isn't that why I have judgment?" It would be truly stupid to fall up here self-belayed to the clove hitch on an 8mm half rope. No matter how much I can live inside my own cerebellum right now and divorce myself from physical discomfort and exertion, I won't be able to divorce myself from the pain of actual injury. And once I've bounced to a stop on the end of this cord, my goose might be cooked. Of course I knew all this coming up here, so what has changed?

I don't have the answers.

I look up and study the moves ahead of me. I can't see more than 10 feet because the terrain

The perfect summit of Hajji Brakk, approximately 5,985m. *Steve House*

is so steep it blocks my view, but below the chockstone I can see some horizontal edges wider than my picks and a couple of discontinuous knifeblade cracks and some good dry-tools in the spaces alongside the chockstone itself. I look down again but this time I don't look past my feet. I whisper to myself: "Don't fall."

Above the chockstone the ground slackens a bit, but 20 feet further the business begins again. I slow down and take care to keep my cord straightened out and to use every opportunity to place gear. It isn't much, but what there is seems good. I break the pitch down into sections that my mind can understand—better to avoid a repeat of the earlier internal discussion. After a sloping ledge I come to a good horizontal crack and nest four pieces together to create an anchor. I try to rest on the narrow stance for a few minutes before going down to clean the pitch.

Standing by my second anchor, I scratch around the shallow cracks and corners above me like a dentist probing for flaws in enamel. I don't find anything, so I climb down five feet to a stem from which I can pull myself to the right into another crack system, and two hours later I emerge with my eyes encrusted in dirt and a torn pant leg and no more rock gear. Then it's past yet another chockstone and onto a fat runnel of ice. The dirt in my eyes reminds me of being 15 and working as a potato picker all day under the end-of-summer Oregon sun in a 40-acre field that was planted too deeply. For that I got 18 dollars and my own 50-pound sack of tubers, but for this I get an undignified pitch on less than perfect rock completely devoid of ice until the very top. Both experiences are the same in that I emerge feeling worn from self-abuse.

The way is clear to the shoulder but the climbing isn't over, just the hard stuff. I need to eat and drink now because it's been too long. For the first time since I had that talk with myself I am aware of time's rapid passage. I need to get going because it is already early afternoon and I still plan to get down tonight. The climbing is easier and I enjoy it. I also enjoy the climbing-induced tiredness that is starting to pull on my shoulders. Unfocused thoughts and made-up movies no

The view northwest from the summit of Hajji Brakk. Masherbrum is the big peak on the left, K2 the even bigger one on the right. The route shown is on Spansar Brakk, climbed by Conrad Anker and Peter Croft in 23 hours round trip in 1998 (5.11). It follows the obvious ridge between the arrows. *Steve House*

longer play in my head, and my mind has cracked open to where I feel the snow and ice and rock under my tools and crampons without having to search for the sensation. I concentrate on where to swing and where to kick and before I know it I'm at the end of my 75-meter rope and building a three-piece anchor of an ice screw, a piton, and a stopper.

I belay three more pitches, climb ropeless for a while, and then belay a short, 20-foot pitch and land myself on the near-flatness of the shoulder.

"Tick, tock, tick, tock," I whisper to myself.

"Why do I whisper to myself?" I say aloud and as the words come out I am taken back by the strangeness of imposing my full voice onto the stillness and I don't speak out loud again.

My crampons grate noisily on the rock as I hoist onto a ledge and use my knee to gather my feet underneath me and hold onto both sides of the rock fin while I slowly stand up. I touch the pinnacled summit and sit back down. Now I can look around to count all the eggs in my basket: K6, Link Sar, K7, Chogolisa, Broad Peak, K2, Mustang Tower, Masherbrum looking massive, and Nanga Parbat hanging like a dream on the southern horizon. I snap some photos and think that I'm being too quick about this part and take a last look at K6 and K7 and maneuver onto my belly to stretch my legs down, crampons scratching for the ledge that is there somewhere just below me.

K7

I am awakened at 5:30 on the morning of my thirty-third birthday by the ignoble bowel pressure of someone who has spent all summer in Pakistan. In the same moment I also register that it is raining in a determined, incessant way that means today will be another rest day. The first act of

Looking west from K7's basecamp. The pyramid is Nayser Brakk, first climbed in 1988 by a British team.
Steve House

my thirty-fourth year in the world is to squat in the cold rain and half-dawn and try to keep from spraying shit all over my shoes. It occurs to me that it can only get better from here.

The next day is full of sunshine. I am hiking up the glacier with a rucksack full of courage, which means I have too many ice screws and ropes and spare picks for my three tools. The clear sky reveals the full strength of the Karakoram sun, which has already been at work for hours on the ice of my next climbing objective. By the time I round the ridge and see the east face of K7, a big chunk of ice is gone. A long crucial section. The route is out of shape and no longer worth trying.

When alone I seem to be visited more easily by the blessings of equanimity, and now I wonder whether I am experiencing good or bad luck. Good luck that the route is so clearly out of condition that I won't waste my precious time in a futile attempt? So out of condition that I won't unknowingly climb underneath precariously bonded sheets of water ice? Or bad luck that I wasn't here a day or a week earlier and been up the route and safely back down by now?

I have to decide that it is good luck and that I have more to accomplish in my remaining time here, and so I return down-glacier, scouting for other weaknesses in K7's outer wall. Eventually I find a possibility to explore the next day.

It is early when I begin climbing K7's southwest face in crampons. I ascend frozen runnels of ice, stopping on ledges to haul my small pack. In the pack is a parka, a bivy sack, a stove, pot, a small amount of food, a light, and two pairs of gloves. For equipment I carry rock shoes, two slings, five nuts, nine titanium pitons, and a single ice screw. After several hundred feet I switch to my rock shoes and tie the boots to my harness. The morning light is still gray and the temperature is cool and I'm making great time for several hundred feet. But the next pitch is harder and I self-belay despite the dangerously skinny static rope, and I slow way, way down. I finish the pitch but the climbing was harder than I had been ready for: 5.10 moves a few feet above my gear. I clean the pitch on rappel and reclimb it with the pack and a skinny, jerry-rigged 6mm static rope that twangs over sharp crystals.

The next pitch looks harder and I climb a body length above my belay to a steep crack leading to a chimney and a chockstone. I make it there and look around the corner at more difficult climbing ahead. It is said that samurai warriors were able to make all decisions within the space of seven breaths, but it doesn't even take me five: I rig my rappel and leave. I have finally gone too light on gear and the climbing is too hard.

Back on the glacier it is just noon. I feel good having gotten up and down 1,000 feet of steep granite alone with my light gear and one skinny rappel rope in the space of a morning. Judgment had won out and I hadn't fallen. I might not be climbing, but I am learning. But now I have only five days before my porters arrive, and there isn't time to waste. I head back around the end of the southwest ridge and follow a hunch.

Three hours later I am 1,500 feet above the glacier. This time I have found a workable route. Also, the faded fixed ropes make it clear that others have found it before me. After climbing several hundred feet, I return to the glacier, confident that I have discovered the drawbridge that will allow me access to K7's watchtower.

Back at base camp Rasool, my cook, acts like the proverbial Italian mother, "Eat, Eat!" and the curry indeed is delicious. I declare a rest day and am not roused from my tent until the sun makes it unbearably hot. It doesn't take long to pack now after so many consecutive days of practice. I know precisely what I need, and more importantly, what I don't need. I take the essential 60 meters of 6mm static cord that I bought so many years ago from a shop in Chamonix the day before setting off on a memorable solo of the north face of the Dru. This climb cured me of hard soloing until this past year. I replenish a few wired nuts and pitons and this time bring two ice screws. I add a bivy sack and an old pair of down pants. In goes my favorite lime-green DAS parka, the titanium pot, a stove, energy food, and some soup mix. When I hang it all from my scale it measures 18 pounds, the traditional point where I dump it all back out on the ground and go through every item, checking that each has multiple uses, that all these uses are essential, and inspecting for things I can do to lighten the total load. But this time I break tradition and skip the gear dump—this is basically the kit I've carried the last two weeks, and I've made all the improvements I can.

In the morning the barometric pressure is low but steady, and a few clouds soften the light. I walk alone up the glacier feeling close to my full strength. Before noon I am again at the top of the initial rock barrier and climbing across a snowy ledge, into a short couloir, then onto an ice face. The climbing here is monotonous but I am tuned to my pace at altitude, and when I have to focus I focus on not stopping. The section is long, and as I reach the top of the ice face after a small battle with my own self-discipline, I stop to survey my options. There are two. One is a steep-looking waterfall that descends from a snowpatch to the upper right corner of my ice face. The ice is blue and shady and steep. From the other corner of the face leads a series of mixed steps that look less steep, but possibly threatened by an old serac. Since the climbing in these mountains seems always to be harder than it looks, and the right side looks quite hard, I elect to go left.

To properly judge the seracs I make a long traverse to the crest of the rib that bounds this face and look back at them from another angle. It has been a long time since those white and rounded seracs have calved down my route. I am happy for that and excavate a small stance to observe and eat and drink a little.

The perfect spire of K7 rising above the Charakusa Glacier, as seen from Hajji Brakk. All the other peaks seen in this photo are unclimbed. (1) House (x = highpoint). (2) Japanese original route. *Steve House*

The climbing winds wonderfully back and forth on runnels and across occasional ledges. One small chockstone is steep and strenuous enough that I start to lose proper form just when I need it most. But a good swing, a lucky stick, and a deliberate stem bring my torso back into line. I'm up the rocky stretch and it is beginning to snow.

Next is ice and I head up marveling at its ancientness and feeling a familiar shiver of discovery at the magnitude and dimension of this world. I resent the need to move my body with purpose and care, detracting from the emotion of my world view. But this is neither the time nor place for resentment. The ice is getting steep and I can see that it will soon be steeper and so I chop a step for one foot, climb up to it, and rest there. I simultaneously inspect the terrain above me and gather in all the components of my quietest mind, and when everything is already complete in my head I gently loosen one tool and start climbing.

The climbing is steep, as is often the case with seracs, and I head up into vertical ice. Where it begins to overhang and become chalky I traverse right. I struggle to set a solid right foot to stem and move onto, swinging my tools hard and starting to feel the first burn of a pump. Instinctively I loosen my grip and for the sin of overdriving my tools I curse and forgive myself.

At the top of the step I find myself on moderate 60-degree ice with incredible exposure. I see a jutting serac up and right and remember the landmark from my last real break earlier in this day that already feels like an indefinite time ago. The visibility has dropped and it is snowing like it means it.

I climb toward the serac and notice a hollow beneath its cantilevered roofline. A hundred feet further I confirm the onset of dusk with my wristwatch and downclimb back to the hollow.

A slip of spindrift hisses toward me and I step into the hollow as the snow slides past and becomes airborne. The wind lifts it toward me where it dances on the air in front of my bivy site. I place a screw in the back wall and clip to it and start scraping a flat hollow in the snow. I dress in my wonderfully green parka that is exactly like the one my friends Barry and Rolo wear, and I don the puffy pants I used to wear for cook duties back in my Denali-guide days. I slide into the five-ounce bivy sack that Todd made from lightweight fabric, promising it would last only five bivvies but that was already 30 bivvies ago. I settle my warm self onto the empty pack feeling that I am not alone.

After tea and soup and crackers and then more tea I have to pee, and this everyday act becomes a welcome confirmation that I am alive as I sit here under a roof of ice listening to it snow. A little time and snowfall and wind remind me of the unhuman and ultimately the inhuman aspects of life here on this face, and I begin to wonder if I would know it if I died up here. Would I notice if life gave out? Because there certainly isn't anyone else here who could, and outside of a few thin physical connections there is damn little to anchor me to the world I left behind. I don't know what death will be like, but I wouldn't be surprised right now if it was just like climbing, except that I wouldn't feel the pull of survival and so it wouldn't feel like anything at all once my curiosity about the terrain had been satisfied. I would lie down and stop because there was no reason whatsoever to do anything else. I think of soloing and of the will to live and for the first time I think I understand something about the will being essential to feeling alive.

I am awake in my bivy at five a.m. and it is snowing still harder and the tongues of spindrift have become avalanches. It is obvious that this place is becoming more and more inhospitable. I contemplate my options. Rappelling from here would be long and tedious and exposed to avalanches from the wide face above me. Climbing up means I must travel through them, but it would be quicker and I might have some ability to run to higher ribs and the occasional rock for cover. And then I could rappel the line of the waterfall ice on the right side, which did not hold a steep snowslope above it.

I wait because for the moment neither is a good option, and I am safe for the time being and can wait all day if necessary. I eat a bar and consider the summit for a moment, but it seems abstract. Surviving seems concrete and important, which I remember is something I learned more about last night.

Two hours later I am packed and my pack feels lighter because I'm rested or because I used so much fuel and food or both and I head out into a clearing morning. There are six to ten inches of snow stuck to the ice slope that starts out steep enough that I can use my tools and then begins to roll back. I trend to the right where the slope seems crested and drive the shafts of my ice tools in because I know there is a risk of the top layer avalanching and I feel the wanting tug of survival very, very strongly for each and every moment of the long hour that it takes me to get to the top of the slope. By now the clouds have come back as suddenly as they had left. The snow becomes deep and the slope flat and I can't see past the end of my arm.

I sit on my collapsed wet pack and stare at the gut of the cloud that shrouds this mountain and consider how I can't climb if I can't see. I get a brief clearing and see that I am immediately above the waterfall and only a few hundred feet short of the ridgecrest. There are crevasses between me and the ridgecrest, and cornices hang like Christmas lace over the other side of the ridge. It would be a 15-minute walk to the crest and then just a few hours up the ridge to the summit in good weather. But the weather is not good. Then the clouds close back in and I continue sitting until 9 a.m. I'm cold and damp and have nowhere to hide from the increasingly intense snowfall. I can admit now what I already knew before, and I stand up and begin flaking out my too-short rap line. Arranging hardware bits on my swami belt, I slowly plod my way across to the top of the waterfall.

I rappel methodically, looking for anchors that use the least of my small rack. The granite provides ample horns and the hard ice gives threads. A hundred feet at a time. On the twelfth rap I swear loudly to whatever creator is or isn't listening and promise that I'll never leave my leg-loops behind again. I continue and after 16 I loose track of how many rappels I've made.

The storm does not dissipate, but its strength does dissolve some as I lose elevation. I some-times stop to rest and when I stop I count to 10 and remind myself that there is nothing for me here and make myself get up and carry on. It is as if my legs are heavier in descent than in ascent, and I get to the ice face and downclimb carefully, trying to focus clearly through the fog of dissi-pating motivation and creeping fatigue.

Before dusk I reach the glacier and once again I sit and this time I drink from a meltwater stream that runs so clean that it looks as if it flows with ultra-liquid properties. The mountains above me are shrouded in quiet storm and it rains lightly. The cold water sits in my gut as if it doesn't know what to do with such abundance, and I feel a not-unfamiliar mix of disappointment and pride at looking up at where I have been. I count to 10 and stand up and sketch in my mind a picture of a glowing woodstove and a curled dog at my feet and the caress of 16-year-old Glen-morganie. I put one foot forward, back toward the direction of life.

SUMMARY OF STATISTICS

AREA: Pakistan Karakoram, Charakusa Valley.

ASCENTS: First ascent of Hajji Brakk (personal name, approximately 5,985m), (1,200m vertical, 5.9). Steve House, solo. July 31, 2003. Approximately 19 hours round trip.

Various attempts at new routes on K7 reaching a maximum altitude of 6,200m. Steve House, solo. August 2003.

A NOTE ON THE AUTHOR

Steve House guides private climbs in Washington's North Cascades and throughout the world. He is the training coordinator for North Cascades Mountain Guides's guide development and contin-uing education program and is also the National Coordinator of Alpine Guide Education for the American Mountain Guides Association (AMGA). He has put up standard-setting new routes on McKinley and other Alaska Range peaks and in the Canadian Rockies, and has climbed so often in Pakistan that he rents a room to keep his expedi-tion gear in the Karakoram.

Self portrait on K7. *Steve House*

ANNAPURNA III

*Expeditioning the British Way during the first ascent
of the southwest ridge, Nepal.*

BY KENTON COOL

Southwest ridge of Annapurna III. *Kenton Cool*

Slumped in my sleeping bag, I desperately tried to get the stove going. I looked across at Ian, who was shaking uncontrollably with cold. Beyond him lay John. I couldn't see him in the darkness, but I was reminded of his presence by his wracking cough. Tired and cold, the three of us lay on a tiny ledge at 6,800 meters on the southwest ridge of Annapurna III. As a new wave of coughing overcame John, I secretly prayed for a way off the peak, but no miracle came—this is, after all, the British way.

The southwest side of Annapurna III lies up a little valley mere hours from the bustle of the main Annapurna Sanctuary trek. Our trip began after my friend Sam visited Slovenians who had attempted the line in 2000. The pictures he brought back were powerful enough to convince me that this was the route to take my climbing onto a higher level.

Annapurna III lies to the east of its bigger brother. Standing at 7,555 meters, it dominates the head of the valley that it guards. The southwest ridge stands out from a large, complex face that boasted only one route, far to one side. Our line stood out due to its initial rock buttress and soaring, fluted ridge above. For us mere mortals, the line had two big attractions: it looked "doable" and it seemed safe. Two years passed before I set eyes on the line.

It's immediately worth clarifying the style we climbed in. I suppose it was a quasi-alpine style of sorts. The Slovenians, it turned out, had left the lower rock buttress fixed, but their ropes were not used for our upward progress except for one move high up, which was freed the second time around. In places their anchors were used. The Slovenian line was also used in our descent and also by John as a jug line the second time up. We found little in the area to acclimatize on, so we initially climbed the lower half of the route, spent a couple of nights at 6,000 meters, stashed food and gas, and returned to base camp. On our next try every pitch was freed, with the second climbing, not jugging. The third guy jugged the Slovenian line with a heavy load. A pure alpine ascent was the plan, but the use of existing anchors and the stashing of gear first time round does admittedly take away from this style, and I'm sure some will criticize us. We, however, had fun.

September of 2003 saw Ian Parnell, the American John Varco, Kiwi Sarah Adcock, and me all meet up in Kathmandu. In true British style the meeting had to be celebrated with a large consumption of different alcoholic drinks (including a cocktail named Annapurna Glory—who said the Brits are modest?). This resulted in three hours of sleep before a bone-shaking, nine-hour bus trip to Pokhara, stopping only briefly to eat and to pick up 12 rather shabby-looking porters.

The walk in traditionally takes five or six days through lush, dense forest, a far cry from the barren dustiness of the Khumbu region. Relaxed walking, combined with pleasant tea houses, made for an excellent way to de-stress from the rigors of western life. My three companions, never having been to Nepal, were surprised by how laid back and hospitable the Nepalese were; they are surely among the friendliest people in the world. The only problem in those first few days was the heat; we were all caught out by this. Expecting colder conditions, we had little in the way of cool clothing.

The first hint of trouble came on the morning of the last day before base camp. It wasn't so much a hint, but more like an out-and-out strike. Demanding more money, the porters dropped their loads and began walking down the valley. Only after the promise of an extra two days' pay would they consider carrying any farther. This form of blackmail is a personal gripe of mine. Having previously agreed to a price arranged by our sirdar, the porters waited until we were in a position with little option but to agree to the new terms. I've had similar problems all over the Himalaya, and while I sympathize with the problems of local people, there is no excuse for what amounts to robbery. This, combined with the theft of warm clothing loaned to the porters for the

Helmet? Who needs a helmet? Ian Parnell low on the route.
Kenton Cool

walk in, left a bitter taste to the otherwise jolly approach march.

That day's walk proved to be quite exciting, with two cold, scary river crossings and lowering the loads down a 12-meter cliff. Arriving at base camp in a light drizzle surrounded by mist lent an eerie feel to the desolate site. Quickly paying the now-happier porters, we started to put up the tents.

The good thing about being a British alpinist is that traditionally we're generally all unfit and we're always on shoestring budgets. This of course leads to a ghetto-style base camp with shitty food. Yet we have a good reputation for both epics and success! John Varco, our American friend, seemed totally mad for the concept of British alpinism, and this was lucky because there was a very British feel to this trip. Eating our first base-camp meal in the misty darkness with no mess tent didn't quell his enthusiasm.

I had a vague memory of Sam saying that the walk from base to Advanced Base Camp (ABC) was bad, and the view I soon looked at, from the top of a nearby moraine, confirmed my fears. An apocalyptic landscape of loose rock and dirt stretched upward. Now, due to a wee argument with the ground some years back (which I lost), my ankles and moraines aren't good friends. The sight horrified me. Five days of load ferrying later, Sarah and I stood at the site of ABC; the moraine had turned out to be a pussycat really, with distance being the only concern. But with Sarah's help ABC was established and stocked.

Returning to base camp, we found an Italian team, and, although we knew they were coming at some point, their presence made us uneasy. Thoughts of the stand-off between Don Whillans and the Italians in Patagonia in the 1960s flashed through my mind, along with Bonington's famous picture of Don suggesting that the rival team climb elsewhere. John seemed up to the task of telling them, and Ian, as ever, was keen to photograph the event. As it turned out, we had three warm, friendly guides from Courmayeur as neighbors who didn't have desires on our line.

During a rest day at base camp, in true Brit style we realized that either we hadn't packed a few items back in the UK or else we had left them in a beery haze in Kathmandu. This included all my thermal underwear, the spare stove, most of John's snow pickets, the shovel, and any decent hill food. But Sarah, leaving us to guide in the Khumbu, could buy goods in Pokhara with the last of our money and send them up. Thanks to my miscalculations, we now had about $100 left to buy all these goods and get back out. True British style. John loved it!

Climbing is a dangerous sport; there is the danger of serious injury or death even on a boulder problem. This danger is heightened a little by the time you get to the Himalaya, and although one of the reasons we selected this route was due to the fact it looked safe, objective dangers can manifest themselves in many ways. The icefall between ABC and the base of the wall was not so much objectively dangerous as just plain dangerous. The traditional method of travel underneath such huge tottering cliffs of death was a simple one...run! This proposal was from John, who took gold in the "icefall sprint." The prize was a smashed Slovenian helmet at the far end and the chance to duplicate the feat the following day. This sprint might lose its terror the more we passed, but it never lost its potential of creating instant death.

Finally, all three of us sat beneath the wall. Ian, keen as ever, wanted the first pitch, so while John and I sorted the kit into three loads,

Ian Parnell dispatching the Kitty Litter Pitch. *Kenton Cool*

Ian racked up. Then howls echoed off the rocky walls. "Shit, shit, shit." I looked up to see Ian hopping round in one shoe. Through the stream of obscenities, John and I established that Ian had dropped a rock shoe down the bergschrund. We also quickly worked out that he had only one pair on the trip. John turned a furious red. Ian looked distressed. I lit the stove and made tea. An hour and much tea drinking later, John emerged with the shoe held aloft. A pitch later saw us on the flat glacier beneath the main wall, but the lost time through shoes and tea-making meant

John Varco jugging the kitty litter with a double load. *Kenton Cool*

pitching the tent there and fixing a few pitches.

Waking late the next morning (another good Brit trait), we hastily packed and fired up the lines. The plan to climb with two big sacks had broken down to two big sacks and a haul bag. A mere four pitches took almost all day, with the pig being the big problem: we had never expected to haul and therefore had no kit to do so. We were, however, moving up and found a great ledge where we spent a good night losing to John at cards.

Following the Slovenian topo the next day, we expected 5.11 A2 climbing. Instead we found vertical kitty litter and very nasty R/X ground of generally moderate standards. Nepal is not known for its good rock, but this sandstone-shale was appalling, with exfoliating flakes and loose rock everywhere. It was horrific. Our secret weapon was Ian with his background of hard routes on appalling shale cliffs in the southwest of England. He rather enjoyed the experience, while John and I simply encouraged him and dodged the rocks he pulled off. We spent the second night on the wall in a bat cave, with Ian sleeping on my head and John half out the cave; not the best-ever night but it was safe. Day three saw us reach the top of the rock in 200 meters of easy mixed ground, with the afternoon lost to tea drinking and playing cards. Pitching the tent, we saw that the rest of the route looked enticing.

We spent the next few days camped at 6,000 meters. John, slow to acclimate, remained in the tent with a banging headache while Ian and I ferried a load to 6,250 meters on the snow arête. The evening was spent hydrating, losing to John at cards once again, and debating whether we shouldn't simply just go for the top right then.

Sense luckily always returns, and Day 6 saw us reversing the route to ABC and trudging back to base camp in the twilight. The rest period we had there saw the only real bad weather of the trip, with about four inches of snow. Although this quickly burned off, it was enough to persuade us to have an extra rest day.

The Italians, who had been on the hill during the bad weather, returned to base camp dejected; with only a week left, it seemed unlikely they would summit. Although I felt for them, I was secretly pleased that the mountain was ours and that there was no element of competition left (not that there ever was much).

It's amazing how quickly four days can pass, and it's amazing how slow six hours of moraine can seem. Our return to ABC seemed a massive chore, with Ian only just making it in the twilight. We therefore decided to rest another day. John was most pleased with another chance to introduce further new rules to "Alaskan Way," a version of gin that he kept winning.

The next plan was that Ian and I were to fire the lower rock buttress in a day with light loads while John jugged the Slovenian lines with a heavy load. This seemed to work well, with all pitches going free and in good time. Ian and I reunited with John at the end of the day with hot tea and a tent he had pitched for us—a pretty good setup, I thought.

The next day, however, was not as good; we made little progress up the snow for good reason: our sacks were simply too heavy. After three hours we were completely spent. I'm not sure how the others felt, but for me this was a physical and mental crash. (It's worth noting that Brits are always bad at expressing feelings; it's not the done thing. A group hug may have eased my burden, but the British Way states otherwise.) Doubts entered my mind: the altitude, my physical fitness, the weather. All the normal doubts, really, but they were amplified by the enormity of the mountain. Despite our ditching food and gas, the sacks felt heavy again the next day, when a slow plod up 45-degree slopes felt hard. To add to my doubt, swirling clouds enveloped us before it snowed, forcing us into another short day.

Three people in a tent little bigger than a Bibler doesn't make for a comfortable night, especially when the wind presses the fabric hard against your face. A sleepless night made way for a beautiful

The key "Door Hinge Pitch" on the second band. Varco leads with Annapurna South in the background. *Kenton Cool*

The redneck on easy ground above the first rock band. *Kenton Cool*

day and a short climb to the second rock band. Here we split again. Ian dug a snow hole and pitched the tent while John and I fixed a pitch. The following hours, to us, felt like true freedom; without a sack we could move fast, with the sea of clouds beneath us offering a stunning view. John rapidly secured the rope, and we zipped down to camp to be treated to a sunset that filled me with hope for the oncoming events.

The second rock band, an item of much debate, was solved only by climbing it. A long, funky lead by John over massive loose flakes put us on a snowpatch that ran to an exit gully. The Slovenians had perhaps gone farther left, but Ian confidently disappeared up a thin gully that seemed to be a little tricky if his swearing was to be believed. The line proved to be a winner, and soon John took over and quickly disappeared onto easier-angled ground as the light began to fade. Resigning ourselves to a poor bivy, we chopped into the night to produce a long, thin ledge to semi-lie on. The Ghetto, as it became known, was really the only poor bivy on the route. Neither stove would light, and John developed a bad cough that produced gooey blood. He was pretty incoherent. It was one of the few times all three of us got properly cold. Ian re-warmed hot-water bottles midway through the night in an attempt to keep us warm.

Dawn finally arrived. Our tired, cold, aching limbs barely worked as we packed the kit away, waiting for an elusive sun. John seemed much better, and although his cough was still bad, his chirpiness had returned. I kicked off the ledge and worked up toward the ridge; despite the poor night I had a certain confidence. At last we were on virgin ground, something we were all pleased about. A classic knife-edge ridge wandered its way up onto a plateau before a false summit. Looking back at the others, I was rewarded with a wonderful sight of two figures plastered onto the ridge with the hills and plains rolling away behind them.

Our plan was to establish a camp as high as possible and then push to the summit, though we were concerned about the distance we had to make across the summit plateau at 7,500 meters. But with a bitterly cold wind tugging at us, we later stopped to discuss our options. Ian's watch read 6,800 meters. A bivy here would leave one hell of a summit day, but soon our discovery of a huge ice cave was the clinching card. Crawling inside was like entering a Tolkien book: huge, thin ice flutes hung down in the blue, shimmering light, and the hole disappeared into a dark abyss where an icy beast must have lain in deep slumber. Twenty minutes of chopping allowed the tent to be pitched free from wind.

No one had much appetite. Trying to force down noodles was almost impossible and chocolate was as bad. John lamented about his high-energy carbo super-food sitting in my kitchen at home. I had always scoffed at those who wrote about altitude apathy, but now all three of us couldn't even be bothered to eat or drink. Fluids are the key but somehow doing nothing seemed to work better.

Deciding to take a stove and a shovel and little else, we emerged out of the cave into the harsh light of day to find a furiously cold wind. Unroped, we staggered off at our own pace. John stopped to adjust a crampon and fell behind, and after a while I looked back to see him some distance away. A wave of anger flushed through me. "He's not strong enough," I thought. "His pace is too slow and he'll never make it. But I can. Leave him and go on yourself." Ian soon stopped, saying, "Screw this." I pushed on at a quickening pace. "Just leave them, you're stronger." Climbing for me, luckily, is more than such selfishness. Climbing is about teamwork and friendship, a bond between partners. Looking back now, I'm disgusted with my thoughts. Maybe it was the fear of going alone or a realization that we were a team, but I stopped and waited. There was no doubt, of course, about the strength of John or Ian, both of whom could run rings

Ian Parnell at approximately 7,100m with the end in his sights. *Kenton Cool*

around me. So why was I so suddenly selfish?

Popping onto a false summit, we realized that the main summit was much closer than we had thought. Nothing was going to stop me or my friends from nailing this one. Two years of longing and five weeks of grueling effort were coming down to this. Tying into our 5.5-mm Spectra cord, I hammered off along the ridge, screaming into the biting wind. I felt like a god, with waves of adrenaline washing over me. John thrust his tools into the air; the battle charge had been sounded. The summit came abruptly, the ground dropping off all around. Yelling to the sky, I burst into tears. I'm sure I wasn't the only one.

Heading back, I had feelings that can't be explained. Somehow I knew that we'd be okay, and for the first time in days I was relaxed and calm. John led us back along the ridge in the freezing wind toward the shelter of the cave. Our cave was heaven, with the wind beaten and the mountain beaten. The stove purred. Hugging and slapping each other, we slumped down to a strange silence, each of us lost in thought.

We spent the afternoon in the cave, despite how early it was. We concluded either we were a lot higher than we thought or that the summit was 300 meters lower than stated. We joked that we'd ask for part of our peak fee back!

Leaving in the morning was hard, for we were more spent than we thought. Finally Ian left, forcing John and me to follow. Reversing the route was slow; soloing down the middle snow ridge was frightening, and the snow had a strange consistency that didn't inspire confidence. Our idea of reaching the Slovenian ropes this day slowly evaporated as our legs and minds tired. Three mentally exhausted people slept that night knowing that at least ABC would be reached the next day.

Although we used the Slovenian lines to rap the buttress, I believe it would have been possible to do this without their line. But in our state it seemed stupid not to use the fixed ropes. I can't condone the fact that the Slovenians left the lower rock in such a mess (with all the rope), but I have to say I'm glad they did. Rapping the three-year-old lines was nervewracking, and strange, groaning noises came from the ropes. John struggled down on a Munter hitch, having dropped his belay device, and spent 15 minutes at one stance trying to untangle the twists.

The icefall tried one last time to kill us. A swirling mist meant that we got lost among the tumbled blocks, and we spent much longer in the death zone than we should have. Our dulled senses after 10 days of effort left us not caring about the danger.

It's strange how distances get exaggerated. Stumbling down in the twilight to base camp, we found that everything took on huge proportions. The loads were heavy from trying to clear ABC in one carry, and we were tired from 10 days' work. The path, unclear at the best of times, seemed to have disappeared completely, leaving miles of unstable moraine. We had split up soon after leaving ABC, John leaving first. Ian and I simply looked and nodded at each other. Although Ian is my regular partner on trips (we live 10 minutes apart yet I rarely see him and never climb with him at home), he infuriates me sometimes—but I love him for it. As the light faded, we simply thanked each other. Why I don't know, but we both understood.

At one point, stumbling, I thrust out a pole to no avail. Twisting, I cartwheeled down the slope, finally pulling myself to a sitting position. I saw the dark figure of John close by, and this was the only reason I didn't cry through frustration. Instead I quietly got up and carried on. Ian passed me just before base camp, leaving me alone for the last short distance. Sitting on a boulder in the moonlight, I looked back up our route. I felt pleased and proud thinking what all three of us had just achieved. Now it was time to leave for home—but then I remembered we had no money. Still, wasn't that the British way?

SUMMARY OF STATISTICS:

AREA: Annapurna Massif, Nepal

ASCENT: First ascent of the southwest ridge of Annapurna III, 7,555m. Kenton Cool, Ian Parnell, and John Varco, October 2003. "A rating is not required as all had a great time and ratings simply add competition and bitterness to what should be a fun sport."

A NOTE ON THE AUTHOR:

Kenton Cool, 30, lives in Sheffield, England, with his girlfriend Sarah, who seems to be able to out-climb, out-ski, and out-party him. Every day he's climbing is great because it means he's not at work and therefore having fun. Kenton is part way though his international guides' ticket. He would like to thank Mountain Hardwear, the British Mountaineering Council, the Mount Everest Foundation, Urban Rock, DMM, Black Diamond, and Arc'teryx.

MIXED MESSAGES

Is hard M-sport-climbing influencing high-standard alpinism?

EDITED BY DAVID DORNIAN

"Chained," published with permission of Randy Rackliff. His prints are available at www.coldcold-worldpacks.com

In 2002 the American Alpine Journal *published a thought piece written by Raphael Slawinski. Raphael's thesis was that the enjoyable pastime created by climbing short, but physically difficult, sport-mixed routes, reassured by closely spaced protection in a low-commitment environment, might provide training that could be transferred directly to cutting edge alpine accomplishments. He held out the hope that standards of difficulty, safety, and speed on the big rigs of the world would improve as a result of all the practice being taken close to the road. Current "extremes" would become casual strolls for an increasing number of climbers as a result.*

That autumn, Steve House sent an e-mail to Raphael, which he cc'd to select friends and sparring partners. House objected to Slawinski's easy conclusions in the article, and he wanted to open further discussion. Of course, Raphael replied to Steve in some detail (Raph is an academic, and he's of Polish birth, too), and in a moment of fey humor, Raphael added even more climbers to the cc list.

The dialogue that ensued was massively entertaining. It spanned months, nations, generations, and in the end totaled more than 30,000 words. This demonstrated, if nothing else, that prolonged exposure to cold and high altitude tends to suppress cognitive ability. The exchanges started out dutifully examining the potential for sport-mixed practice to improve alpinism, but swerved at their end toward the soft shoulder of "What makes a hard alpine climb, anyway?" and, "Honey, what kind of an example are we setting for the kids?"

For better and worse, it all was saved. Now, after numerous requests for electronic copies of these archives, some of the principal correspondents are urging that key arguments be published.

Please, as you read, don't hold people over the fire on the finer points they make—these were "informal" exchanges, composed in odd moments. Dip in and browse these mixed messages like eavesdropping on a tavern table discussion—after all, a good deal of what follows was likely composed with a beer beside the keyboard.

I have gone back and stripped from the exchanges most of the personal slights, overt chest pounding, slack-jawed wandering, and nostalgic histories (in other words, thrown out all the good stuff), and corrected the bad punctuation and hysterical spelling, then winnowed the rest to get everything down to printable length. Though few of the original innuendos are reproduced here, rest assured that they have been retained on file for future blackmailing purposes....

Try reading the two articles that follow Mixed Messages—Robert Jasper's No Siesta and Steve House's North Twin—in the context of this discussion. You might also consider Slawinski's Mt. Temple reports in the Canadian Rockies section of Climbs & Expeditions. For that matter, factor in any number of recent articles and reports, and temper with your own experience.

David Dornian

Subject: *house on caffeine*
From: *"Steve House"*
To: *"Raphael Slawinski"*
Sent: *Saturday, October 26, 2002 8:30 AM*

Raphael,
I just read your *AAJ* article this morning (and drank a bunch of coffee). Cool, I like to see things put together that way. It is really helpful for everyone to think about the "big picture." I have cc'd this to some folks because I think it's a great discussion.

I must say I have problems with your logic (easy to be a Monday-morning quarterback, I know):

You make an assumption that sport (rock) climbing has improved overall standards in the mountains. I would disagree totally. I would argue that sport (rock) climbing has lowered standards. The Alps are an example of this. There were far more people climbing the harder (5.11 and up) routes in the Dolomites 15 years ago than there are currently. Also in Chamonix, the rock routes getting done are the ones that you rap from, not the big routes in the Ecrins. In Patagonia the people doing the big routes according to the alpine ethos aren't sport climbers, they're "from" the valley [Yosemite]...

You cite Beyond Good and Evil, but fail to mention that the belays (once part of the crux) are now two fat bolts each and you just rap whenever you want. Nobody has done the final pitches yet. That is not the same route it originally was!

I don't think you'd be able to prove that standards of any kind have been raised in the mountains (rock, ice, mixed) since around the 1980s.

Now that it is done, Rocket Man [a bolted mixed route in the Rockies] is a great alpine outing, one I'd like to do. But how many days did Dave [Thomson, the first ascensionist] work on it? How does that fulfill your alpine ideal? It doesn't—you can't even call it an alpine route. M-16 [on Howse Peak—Backes-Blanchard-House, 1999] should get climbed in a day. The crux is really short (80 feet) and the rest isn't harder than a normal top-end waterfall. But it goes unrepeated because of the psychological barrier. I wouldn't be surprised at all if it is technically easier than Rocket Man, but none try because of its alpine characteristics. And wasn't that part of the point in the name?

You gloss over risk too easily. The real issue is what allows you or me to make harder moves at the sport crag—the fact that I'll suffer no consequences for falling. Yours is the second article (the first was in the *Canadian Alpine Journal* [written by Scott Semple]) that claims sport, or "M" climbing is going to revolutionize standards in the mountains. In neither article is mention made of the presence or absence of risk in these differing approaches.

T - A = 0

[House's expression for "Talk minus Action equals Zero".]

Steve House has authored some of the most significant ascents in North America over the last 10 years, many of which have been lead articles in the AAJ.

*   *   *

On Tuesday, October 29, 2002, at 10:50 AM, Raphael Slawinski wrote back:

I have had sufficient caffeine this morning that I finally feel fit to answer you. I have no objection whatsoever to this discussion. Indeed, I am pleased that my article has not sunk into immediate obscurity.

I admit to being surprised that you should disagree so strongly with what I wrote. Allow me to quote verbatim from the conclusion of my article:

"In spite of the great advances in mixed climbing made over the last quarter of a century, one is struck by how slowly the technical standards in the mountains advance relative to standards at the crags. Whereas in the 1970s standards did not appreciably differ between crag and mountain routes, today the gap between them has grown to such an extent that they almost appear to be different disciplines. While on the one hand this points to the immense possibilities for applying M-climbing techniques to the mountains, it also underscores the degree to which the high standards of M-climbing rely on a controlled crag environment. While the gap between the two is only likely to grow, perhaps the rising standards at the crags will contribute to a corresponding rise in the alpine realm."

What is it precisely that you object to here? The suggestion that M-climbing might come to have an impact on alpinism? I admit that when I started writing the article, I thought I would be able to show that it has already had such an impact. As I researched the subject, I was inescapably forced to the conclusion that while there is a greater base of "hard" ice and mixed climbers today, this has not translated into higher standards in the mountains, certainly not above and beyond what has been accomplished in the '80s.

In my article I have already quoted specific examples of how M-climbing has translated into "hard" traditional mixed routes (like Stuck in the Middle on the Terminator Wall [of Mt. Rundle]). This past summer the A-Strain [The Andromeda Strain on Mt. Andromeda] (V, M5+) has seen multiple ascents, some taking as little as 15 hours car-to-car, by local climbers like Kim Csizmazia and Rob Owens—climbers with a strong background in traditional as well as M-climbing.

What is very obviously missing from this list is any mention of major new alpine routes, routes where skills acquired at the crags (like the ability to onsight, say, 5.12 and M8) are used to raise standards over what has been done in the '80s by climbers with much more modest technical abilities. So while I would argue that sport climbing has led to a consolidation of standards, I would also have to agree that it has not resulted in new and more difficult alpine routes. The examples I have used above are all from the Canadian Rockies, but I think the same holds true for other ranges.

I fully agree with you that the biggest stumbling block when transferring M-climbing skills from the crags to the mountains is the introduction of risk (I referred to it in my article somewhat euphemistically as reliance on a "controlled crag environment"). I fully acknowledge that what has made technically hard routes from Octopussy [Colorado Rockies] to Musashi [Canadian Rockies] possible is the elimination (or at least the minimization) of risk. But I also know that being able to onsight, say, 5.12 and M8 on bolts makes onsighting 5.11 and M7 on virgin ground a lot more palatable. Like rock climbing before it, mixed climbing has come to encompass a huge range of activities. One should not restrict oneself to only one facet of the game.

Raphael Slawinski has topped the competition at the Ouray Ice Festival, and climbed technical ice all over North America. Closer to his Calgary home he is a relentless alpine achiever, with a continual stream of first ascents and regular repeats of Rockies testpieces. He has put up some of the world's hardest bolted M-routes.

* * *

From: Steve House

I object to the assumption that sport climbing increased the level of rock climbing in the mountains:

I would agree it has lead to a consolidation of the level of rock climbing in the mountains and I concede to not being as educated as I might be on the recent history of rock. As comparison, I'd hold up routes like Divine Providence (hard 5.12 above 4,000 meters, on the Grand Pilier d'Angle [Mont Blanc]) with François Marsigny in the late '80s for alpine trad, or the 8b sport route on the Aig. du Midi (12,800', late '80s) in comparison to what has been done more recently. There are plenty of hard alpine rock routes in Europe where you have to onsight 5.12c or harder to do them. They were mostly done (at least begun) in the 1980s.

Huber's Bellavista (5.14, trad gear, but fixed/rehearsed as a sport route) or Bubu Bolle's Women and Chalk—in my book those are still in the rock climb category, not the alpine climb category. But that is just me and my Bonatti-reading ass. And after 20 years, is this such a great leap? I'd say that repeats are way, way different than first ascents.

To continue our heated agreement, and to further my idea that alpinism has only regressed since the 1980s, I would cite the north face of the Grandes Jorasses as representing nearly all the stages of technically-hard alpinism [see No Siesta in the following article—Ed.]. [Also] Andy Parkin's routes, some done solo, in the Chamonix Aiguilles. The Catalonians on the south face of Annapurna, west face of G4, Kukuczka/Piotrowsky in the "Hockey Stick Gully" on the south face of K2—all in the 80's—all alpine style.

Will sport-mixed climbing help us reach that level again? Everyone going out and climbing the Andromeda Strain in 15 hours car-to-car will bring us collectively much closer to that goal than M11 will.

In my conversations with [Scott] Semple and [Will] Gadd, I realized that my Alpine grail is a lot different than theirs. Their grail is closer to being a technically difficult route on an alpine face, altitude not being important, and style being less important than pure difficulty. Mine is the Sickle on the west face of K2; theirs is M12 on Kitchener/Howse/Logan. These aren't mutually exclusive, of course, but certainly different.

Show me, and I will believe.

* * *

From: Scott Semple:

As mentioned to Barry [Blanchard] months prior to the publication of the CAJ, "my article has nothing to do with alpine climbing." ("What article?" he replied.)

My thesis was (is) that the TECHNICAL skill level of ice and mixed climbers in the CANADIAN ROCKIES has risen since the mid-1990s and been criticized, downplayed or ignored by the "assessments of non-participants." More recent accomplishments remain largely unknown while visiting climbers lemming to do testpiece-now-trade-routes that locals lap.

P.S. Much more importantly, Steve, where's your article for my spoof mag? Your editor awaits...

Scott Semple lives in Canmore, Alberta. He is an accomplished sport-mixed climber, a promising alpinist, and editor of the parody magazine Falling.

* * *

From: Joe Josephson

I'm sincerely curious on just how many people are criticizing the bolted mixed climbs. I'm certain these issues exist but I have doubts about just how much.

I've not been around the Rockies as much as in the past, but aside from a few exceptions in a particular area or route, I've never heard any dissing of bolts that should be taken seriously.

Barry writes things like "NO BOLTS" for some of the routes they've done. In my mind, when a wild route is done with no bolts it is a significant achievement. No better or more valid than a wild route done with bolts—they are just different. Both have a place.

The thing that bugs me about the mixed revolution—far beyond the fact that it's not all that new—is Mixed climbers saying that it's the way forward, or that pure ice climbs are "easy" and "boring." This makes no more sense than any crusty alpinist holding onto traditional ethics.

I think a major dose of history needs to be prescribed for many of the climbers in both camps. Go and read the "Hot Flashes" and "Great Debate" articles of the mid '80s. Remember sport climbing versus traditional climbing? All that silly lycra spewing, etc? We all laugh at it now. I would hope we've learned to rise above it.

Joe Josephson wrote the guidebook Waterfall Ice Climbing in the Canadian Rockies. *He has climbed big alpine routes from Patagonia to Alaska, and is currently working on a guide to the Mt. Logan massif. He lives in Montana.*

* * *

From: Will Gadd

OK, I've been trying to keep out of this but I've had my morning Red Bull so here goes:
This whole debate is as "rational" as a Christian/Muslim/Atheist discussion. Steve believes in his style of alpine climbing. Raph has found a new Koran in mixed climbing. With that in mind, I'd like to proselytize in a friendly way about what I call Mountain Divinity. The church of Mountain Divinity is based on the idea that mountains are holy; I've decided to believe this after watching alpenglow, flying on thermals at sunset, and paddling down the Nahanni in the fog. Services to be held every day anywhere outside (failing that, bars will work).

While the above is meant only semi-seriously, it is a credo I'd like to live up to—the climbers I most admire are those who climbed lots, slandered little, and shared the mountains often before they died at a ripe old age. They had faith in what they did, and did it well.

Hugs and kisses.

Will Gadd has put up standard-defining sport-mixed climbs since the genre was invented, won the X-Games and the first season of the Ice World Cup competitions, and climbed difficult new alpine itineraries at home and abroad. He is author of Ice and Mixed Climbing: Modern Technique.

* * *

From: Jeff Lowe

Although what I've read is obviously only a part of a longer discussion, I get the general idea of the respective viewpoints. Personally I like Will's approach the best. Do your own thing with integrity, and communicate the things you've experienced and learned with honesty and humility, humor and enthusiasm, and you'll end up influencing new climbers more than if you beat them over the head with the rightness of "your" style and the "wimpiness" of their style. Climbing is evolving as always in multiple directions. There are some exceptionally strong and creative hands grabbing the rock and gripping the tools: who knows where they'll climb next, or how? I, for one, don't want my personal myopia to be passed on as some sort of gospel. Let's invite the sport climbers out into the mountains. Those few that come will teach us all a thing or two.

Jeff Lowe was five years ahead of the curve in U.S. climbing for three decades. He brought us waterfall ice climbing, sport mixed climbing, World Cup competitions, and extreme alpinism in the great ranges.

* * *

From: Bill Belcourt

Come on Will! Before busting with the "I'm OK, you're OK" hippie BS, think about what these guys are saying. It is certainly as legitimate as ratings, and when's the last time you didn't rate a route, or pick one based on what it had to offer?

We have not been good stewards of critical thinking among new climbers. The result is a bunch of bolts and press celebrating shit routes, with one type of climbing experience replacing others because there is no sense of history among the protagonists. It's not, "All good, braah." It's fairly [screwed] up. And all of us are somewhat responsible for not wanting to spend the time or energy to discuss the issues.

Talk it up as much as possible, whatever your views. Hopefully, the result will be thoughtfulness and restraint when it comes to new routes by younger climbers. Where do I stand on these important issues? Alpine climbing rules, and you sport-mixed climbers are just a bunch of pansies.

Bill Belcourt is an accomplished alpinist, now working in product development for Black Diamond.

* * *

From: Barry Blanchard

I think that here in the Rockies the winter alpinist is wise to resort to aid for some moves and indeed some passages because you're less likely to fall and die. Falling off and dying pushing winter free climbing for the sake of winter free climbing is worse style than resorting to aid. I'd love to free all the steep and hard stuff that I run into up there but hey, this isnt Cham', it ain't granite; it's limestone and it's serious and it's often blobbed up with meter-deep snow forms dripped from Satan's own 45-gallon candle. If aid keeps you alive it is cool (but bolts could do the same thing—keep you alive. So does retreat. I consider going down as succeeding in the covenant with those who created the game).

Barry Blanchard has painted more masterpieces on Rockies north faces than any other single climber. He has long been a student of climbing's history and techniques and enjoys thinking and writing about it.

* * *

From: Raphael Slawinski

Whether M-climbing is seen as having advanced alpinism (or as even having the potential to do so) depends to some extent on what one values in alpine climbing. As Steve pointed out, people have different alpine grails. That grail might be a huge objective, possibly at altitude, climbed with a bare minimum of means; technical difficulty would be important but not the principal consideration; and style would have more to do with speed than with any notions of free climbing. That grail might also be a smaller but more technical objective, with emphasis placed on elements of what constitutes good style: this might mean climbing free, possibly leashless, with no jugging and/or hauling.

In many ways the '80s marked the pinnacle of achievement in alpinism. It is likely that the technical standards of the Hungo Face of Kwangde or of the Golden Pillar of Spantik are still not far off the top standard attained on an alpine-style high mountain route. And arguably no alpine-style ascent has surpassed the commitment of Voytek Kurtyka's and Robert Schauer's first ascent of the Shining Wall of Gasherbrum IV. Even by today's standards Kurtyka was a brilliant technical climber (for instance, he soloed 13a at the crags, displaying a level of boldness and technical skill unmatched by most of today's leading alpinists or M-climbers). So where do we go after a climber of Kurtyka's caliber has pushed the alpine envelope?

More fundamentally it might be questioned whether high standards in the mountains should be equated with high technical standards. It is certainly easier to impress chicks and editors by climbing something with a big number on it. Somehow IV M10 sounds much more impressive than VI M4.... But is it really harder? How does one objectively compare the overall difficulty of a long "moderate" route to a shorter but technically more vicious one?

* * *

From: Mark Twight

I believe it was John Bouchard who originally said, "either the muscle is exercised or it returns to its original weak state." His declaration illustrates exactly why higher sport-mixed standards do not automatically raise technical standards in the mountains.

The human mind adapts to new conditions slowly enough that often, in the moment, man's mental capacity appears finite. Because modern man is used to achieving goals with a certain degree of speed he won't wait to naturally develop the improved mental capacities necessary to confront a new challenge. Instead man manipulates the challenge in order to successfully address a particular aspect of it.

Climbing routes at the highest level of gymnastic difficulty requires the use of bolts to minimize risk. Risk is the aspect of the problem most difficult to contend with, yet easiest to manipulate. It is not as easy to find shortcuts in the process of gaining movement skills, endurance, and strength. They require long-term attention and time.

And working out the hardest moves is likely impossible if a six-foot dirt nap is the result of falling short. Most minds are simply not strong enough to handle eating the whole elephant. It's digested with one bite at a time.

Once bolts excise risk and the mind grows accustomed to playing freely on the overhanging consequence-free crags the mental muscle that allows man to adapt to high-risk atrophies, returning to its original, weak state. A withered ability to deal with risk is inconsistent with alpinism. No matter what level of technical ability a climber achieves at the crag, without a resilient mind, able and accustomed to entertaining high risk, that climber won't be pushing any limits in the chaotic alpine environment. At least not until flaccid mental muscles are trained up to the task.

In this sense, Belcourt was right when he wrote that sport-mixed climbers are pansies.

Gymnastically hard (but risk-free) routes make men better monkeys but they certainly don't improve mental agility or resilience within the context of alpine chaos. Without being hunted every now and then a man cannot retain the skills required to stay at the top of the food chain. It's all a game until the other guy is shooting back.

"Direct Action, No Prisoners."

Mark Twight is a noted climber, writer, photographer, and commentator. His repeated attempts at self-immolation brought high-standard alpinism to the American consciousness during the '90s. With Andy Parkin, he put up the route Beyond Good and Evil, mentioned earlier in this article. He works for Grivel North America.

* * *

From: David Dornian

...and a cheery "Top o' the food chain" to you, too.

Careful, you could extend the metaphor a little too far on that "mental muscle" conceit. Press the issue and you'd have to acknowledge that real, physical muscle doesn't correlate that closely with climbing success at any level. Think about how heavy, directed training of a single type is typically associated with overweight thugs who gradually become a) inflexible, b) clumsy, c) egomaniacal, d) ill-humoured, e) indisposed to doing anything but more training, and f) bad dressers.

Smart people? Well, I think it's generally accepted that smart people anticipate possible outcomes, solve problems, manage risk, develop tools and techniques, get help, practice, and prepare. Even most cows have enough sense to feel the cold wind coming and turn their backs to a storm rather than face into its fury. "Mental muscle" might just be another way of saying "stubborn" or "too stupid to come in out of the rain."

Confront risk directly if you're a nihilist or a fatalist—then I suppose it just doesn't matter, by definition. Otherwise, confronting risk for its own sake can appear quite juvenile. It may count as "...being hunted every now and then," or as "developing the improved mental capacities," but it also may count as evolution in action.

Decide what you want to achieve, and then ask yourself WHY you want to achieve it. Only then should you choose HOW you want to achieve it, select tools, and decide on appropriate techniques. Mental atrophy only comes when you refuse to think.

I personally subscribe to the Blair Witch Project, or Halloween, or Stupid theories of alpinism, where with each climb I get all dressed up and grab the camera and initially set out to make—and then somehow inevitably become a player in—my own silly low-budget horror movie.

David Dornian is North American representative to the International Council for Competition Climbing, and the collector of this correspondence.

* * *

From: Abby Watkins

Same old pissing on the fire hydrant.

Good on ya, Will, for setting it straight. Anything other than the walk up is contrived. In fact, the summit is contrived, as there is nothing there we need for our daily lives. We climb because it feels so good. [We] can't leave a pin scar in the rock, but it's ok to mow down a forest to build our houses. We vote in governments who have no problem leveling a mountain range to find the evil terrorist, or destroying the habitat of the largest Caribou herd left in the wild to drill for oil. The true purists are those who live simply, whose efforts are spent wholly on feeding themselves and their family. Climbing itself is a luxury. Why get overheated about exactly how people are supposed to enjoy it? The [mountains] are big enough to house both sport and traditional mixed routes. Both exist in plenty. Most of us enjoy both types of adventures, and are glad that both exist.

Abby Watkins wins ice and mixed climbing competitions, climbs big walls by herself, and teaches women how to climb.

* * *

From: Barry Blanchard

We're climbers, not the sharpest tools in the shed. I think we're stuck trying to figure this out with lesser-evolved brains. But if no cow ever faces away from the herd how will greener pastures ever be discovered? If all cows went into the storm there would probably be no cows and no need of greener pastures.

I assume that Musashi perfected the two-sword technique in the dojo and did take it out to the battlefield to make a "cut" [Musashi is also the name of an M12 sport route in the Rockies]. Spend too much time engaging and you will probably get cut, though.

In my life the summit provides the point to turn around and I seem to need that as much as I need food. Don't know if I am helping, but this sure is fun. I'm in agreement....

* * *

From: Scott Johnston

Folks need to say what they mean or not say it. Sadly, I think that the salient point of the whole argument is being overlooked: "Where is climbing going and where will these various movements take climbing?"

[We] know very well what is entailed in alpine climbing and understand that sport climbing is but a sliver of the climbing continuum. But the bulk of the community is not participating in leading-edge breakthroughs and many participants lack perspective on the macrocosm of climbing. I'm seeing that the public has entered the sport in the last five years and that a 10-year vet is an old timer. I submit that these folks are in no way prepared to be handed the reins of climbing's future. Most haven't a clue as to its past. The closest they get to the full climbing spectrum is to thumb the pages of the rags. The direction climbing is going is being dictated by the media and newbies who [motivate] the marketing machine.

Sport climbing is a true sport in that it allows direct comparisons. [It] is easily packaged, with grades and cool photos. Average schmucks who read the magazines get their inspiration from what they believe the elite are doing. You can't take a photo of, or put a meaningful number on, commitment. So the true adventure, the soul expanding aspect of climbing becomes down-played. Do we really want climbing to become the sport of those who think adventure is defined by where they can drive their new Ford Explorer?

The next generation of climbers should be encouraged to discover challenges by seeking out commitment. What I fear is [regression] in climbing where the fixation is on numbers. [Numbers] can only truly affect a very small group of elite climbers. The rest of us slobs are stuck in the second, third, or 20th tier and we should be able to have defining moments even if we can't crank one-arm pull ups.

[We have] the opportunity to steer the direction climbing takes. Acknowledge a differentiation between Sport and Alpine, and make it clear in the media, [else] climbers will come to know climbing from a very narrow perspective, doomed to be seen as just an extreme sport. Don't sell climbing short, don't distill out the essence and present only that soulless message.

Scott Johnston has climbed on most continents since 1973, and is currently a climbing and backcountry ski guide for North Cascades Mountain Guides.

* * *

From: Valeri Babanov

When you are too high in the high mountains, you can't be one way. It is too dangerous. Speed is important for safety, and you have to be flexible, or you break. Style is of course very important and you try to climb in the best style always, but you also need to CLIMB. You need to understand you are real people—skill and experience are knowing your limits.

Hans Kammerlander and Reinhold Messner are also flexible in this way, knowing when to use what style. So, I'm a realist! Me, I prefer to finish my dreams. I don't want to be old and still have only the dreams.

Valeri Babanov has twice been awarded the world's most prestigious alpine recognition: the Piolet d'Or; this year it was for his ascent of Nuptse East (see Yuri Koshelenko's article Moonlight Sonata in this Journal).

* * *

From: Andy Kirkpatrick

I can't really comment personally as I haven't done any bolted M climbing. But as for non-bolted mixed, like we have in Scotland, well it's the foundation of all the big mountain stuff British climbers do, and so when it comes to mental strength and commitment, plus that important and often overlooked gnarl factor there is no better training, and that's maybe why the Brits seem to be leading the way in some areas of mountaineering.

Andy Kirkpatrick started from Hull and to date has made it as far as Sheffield, but he's done it the hard way – via an enchainment of the world's worst alpine terrain. An intense writer, he has claimed in print "Don't believe the hype. Winter climbing is 10 percent physical, 90 percent mental. If you're good at jigsaws you'd probably be good at mixed climbing. It's simply a frozen puzzle, your tools and crampons torquing and camming the pieces to fit. And like a jigsaw, the moves are easy. It's just finding them that's hard..."

* * *

From: Roger Payne

One really significant booster for climbing standards is international gatherings and meets. When you get an international group of high performance climbers in one place things happen. People want to quickly climb the classics, then the testpieces, and then the hardest route in the guidebook. Suddenly that climb everyone has been waiting 10 years for the second ascent of has a queue at the bottom, and improbable blank spaces are being filled with harder new routes. Then sitting around the bar people talk about other big climbing challenges, and start to make plans for trips to get them done. It was at an international climbing meet in Scotland, fully refreshed in the bar and high on the buzz of climbing mischief, that a discussion about the use of bolts in the mountains highlighted the idea of a free ascent of Cerro Torre's Egger-Maestri Route. Then sure enough, not long afterwards, three people from the meet (Leo Houlding, Alan Mullin, and Kevin Thaw) were packing their bags for Patagonia.

Roger Payne has climbed hard on gritstone and in the Himalaya, has run the British Mountaineering Council, and is presently steering the UIAA toward the Olympics.

* * *

From: Steve House

Admittedly, I had ulterior motives in stirring all of this up. I have tremendous respect for many of the M-routes that have gone up since I started waterfall climbing in the Rockies 10 years ago. There is an amazing pool of talent and experience and I would love to see that growth trend extend to alpinism.

The last of the new material should come from Andrej Stremfelj, of Slovenia: "The young people outgrew me in climbing a long time ago. All I can give them now is part of my rich experience. In the high mountains, such experience can be key to survival. Expeditions are my only opportunity to pass on some of my knowledge to the new generation. The young quickly acquire pure technical knowledge, but it is much more demanding to show them the essence of alpinism, which is in my opinion of capital importance for success. This is one of my future challenges."

"...not for difficulty alone, but for elegance and style..."

Climb fast and take chances.

* * *

No Siesta

The first free (dry tooling) ascent of perhaps the hardest mixed route in the Alps, on the north face of the Grandes Jorasses, France.

ROBERT JASPER

One of the great north walls of the Alps, the Grandes Jorasses has been the testpiece of generations. The steep snowfield on the left is the Shroud, the buttress to its right leading to the highest summit is the mega-classic Walker Spur, and No Siesta is illustrated. Many other routes spiderweb the face. *Markus Stofer*

No Siesta takes an ingenious and psychologically demanding line through one of the great walls of the Alps, the north face of the Grandes Jorasses. That Jan Porvaznik and Stan Glejdura managed to climb such a line in 1986, with the techniques and gear used 17 years ago, was truly outstanding. At that time high-standard ice climbing was still in its infancy in the Alps, and waterfall climbing was barely known in the alpine valleys. This was true even though photographs of Jeff Lowe on Bridalveil Falls (Colorado, 1974) fascinated the young generation in the Alps. A few Europeans

Markus Stofer following the tenth pitch of No Siesta. *Robert Jasper*

started to climb waterfall ice, but only as training for their Alpine routes on the difficult north faces.

In 1976 Nick Colton and Alex MacIntyre climbed the notorious north face couloir on the Grandes Jorasses, thereby opening the first of the modern extreme ice routes on alpine terrain. Ten years later the two Czechs Porvaznik and Glejdura climbed a new route they named No Siesta in three days, on ice up to 90 degrees and rock requiring 5.10 A2 climbing. It was a masterpiece, far ahead its time.

All efforts to repeat the route failed until 1997 when the Frenchmen François Marsigny and Olivier Larios climbed it, also taking three days. The route's reputation as a horror was confirmed.

Other hard mixed routes in the early nineties like Beyond Good And Evil (M5+ A1/2), on the Aiguille du Pélerins (Andy Parkin and Mark Twight), and my hardest solo first ascent, Knocking On Heaven's Door (M6 A2) on the Jungfrau, were typical for this period: displaying a high level of climbing but using aid techniques where necessary. Stevie Haston and Laurence Gouault opened Scotch On the Rocks (M7) on Mont Blanc du Tacul in 1995, one of the first hard all-free routes on a high peak in the Alps. This seems to be the first step into a new dimension. Until now, Vol de Nuit (M8-)—opened by my wife Daniele and me on the Tacul two years later—was the hardest all-free and boltless multipitch mixed route in the Alps.

The ascent of No Siesta

March 17, 2003: The reports had been for good conditions in Chamonix, but in fact only the Argentiere area was in good shape. While hiking across the Leschaux Glacier I blamed myself for not having called Jean Christophe, but I hadn't wanted to talk about my plans to anybody. I didn't even tell my climbing partner, Markus Stofer, about the route I had in mind until we were in

Stofer settling in for a snooze during the second night on No Siesta. *Robert Jasper*

the car heading toward Chamonix.

Day 1, March 18: After waking up at 2 a.m., we crossed the glacier and started up the initial 55-degree slope. In about 350 meters we encountered the first rocks and tied in to begin the climb proper. The difficulties began immediately. Using 70-meter ropes we climbed sections up to M7+, following thin slivers of ice and clean granite. My dream to free climb No Siesta was beginning to come true. When I reached the section that had looked difficult from the ground, I realized how much I relied on my mixed climbing experience of the previous years. Without it I would have certainly grabbed the old rusty pitons in the steep section. Instead I used the rotten stuff only as "protection," and I climbed by hooking my tools in the thin icy crack.

We reached the first bivy used by the Czechs with three hours of daylight remaining, so we continued to an extremely uncomfortable ledge just large enough for one person, where we spent the night.

Day 2, March 19: At first light it was snowing. But the Swiss weather forecast didn't get it wrong after all, because by 10 a.m. the clouds had lifted. We spent almost the entire day climbing the crux central section, originally graded 5.10b, A1/A2. When we reached the crux pitch a strange sound betrayed my efforts to imitate the friction of EBs with the front points of my crampons. Using a daring underhook ala the Canadian M-climbing testpiece Musashi, and a mantel push up, I dared to climb the crux and found myself ready to "take off" on a holdless slab too far above my last protection to change plans. There was only one option: climb it! In a trance I climbed on, then placed a few cams in the overhanging crack above.

I managed it on sight in the free mixed style. M8 in such a great alpine north face: unimaginable! On this pitch I again realized that without all the M-climbing training of the last years I would not have been able to free climb such hard moves on an 1,100-meter face. We then found the second bivouac used by the Czechs and decided to have a slightly more comfortable night, at least compared to the first.

Day 3, March 20: The third day arrived quickly and we climbed sections of M5/M6 at almost 4,000 meters. At 15:00, after a final corner, we reached the summit crest with its fantastic view of the Grand Paradiso and the Italian Valle d'Aosta. So Siesta had been my best alpine mixed climb ever.

Hard all-free alpine mixed climbing on the big faces in modern style is still in its infancy—by this I mean routes from M7 upward. There are many possibilities on the north faces, but most climbers still prefer dry-tooling using bolts for protection. The few existing hard mixed routes without bolts in the Alps don't get repeated. The trend is still "mixed sport climbing."

That there are so many different disciplines within climbing seems okay to me. In the last years the game was to push the grades searching for the impossible. Hard routes like Musashi (M12), The Game (M13), and No Limits (M12+/13) have gone up. I have a lot of fun on these routes, and for me they are the optimal training for big faces without bolts. Of course, this M-climbing must be combined with general alpine experience and hard free climbing.

My feelings were confirmed last December (2003) in Patagonia, when Stefan Glowacz and I made the first ascent of The Lost World (1,100m, 5.10d M8) on Murallon, on the Hielo Continental. We succeeded only because we put all of our effort into fast climbing without compromise—otherwise the weather conditions would not have given us a single chance during the two months we spent there. We climbed 26 hours non-stop in alpine style, with no bolts or breaks, and achieved our goal of climbing completely free in rock, ice, and mixed terrain.

Jasper testing his M-skills on a dry section of No Siesta. *Markus Stofer*

Robert Jasper enjoying relatively laid back terrain on No Siesta. *Markus Stofer*

We were also faster than we could have been with aid climbing. This was our recipe for success. (See Climbs & Expeditions in this Journal.)

I believe that in the next years more and more people will use the skills gained by modern bolted mixed climbing for real adventure on the big faces—the hard mountains of the world where there are no bolts and risk remains. So I'm certain that mixed climbing will change the top levels of alpinism. Even if it takes years before more routes like No Siesta get their first free ascents in winter, I think these routes will be the future of modern mixed climbing.

SUMMARY OF STATISTICS

AREA: France, Mont Blanc Range

ASCENT: Grandes Jorasses, north face, first free (M-climbing) ascent of No Siesta (1,100m, VI M8 E5). Robert Jasper (Germany) and Markus Stofer (Switzerland), March 17-19, 2003. The "E" grade is a new "risk" grade being developed by Robert Jasper for mixed, alpine, and waterfall climbs; the current top-end is E6.

A NOTE ABOUT THE AUTHOR

Robert Jasper was born in 1968 in the Black Forrest area of Germany. He now lives under the Eiger's north face, his favorite wall, which he has climbed by 11 different routes, including the first ascent of Symphonie de Liberte (5.13a/b) with his wife Daniela. He is a professional climber and has soloed more than 100 of the hardest north face routes in the Alps, including various first ascents. In the sport world, he has climbed Europe's hardest mixed sport climb, No Limits (M12+/13), as well onsighting rock routes to 5.13b and redpointing to 5.14a. He has also climbed in Patagonia and Nepal. Robert and Daniela have a 17-month old son, Stefan.

NORTH TWIN REVISITED

Pursuing the adventure attitude on Canada's greatest wall.

STEVE HOUSE

The great north wall of the Rockies. Routes from left to right: Jones-Lowe (1974), House-Prezelj variation (2004), and Blanchard-Cheesmond (1985) are on the north face; Abrons-Carman-Millikan (1965). The summit immediately above the face is Twins Tower; the snow summit to the left is North Twin itself. None of the north face routes have been repeated. *Steve House*

Prezelj starting the crux pitch on the second day. The steep headwall above and right has never been attempted. *Steve House*

Among North American alpinists, the north face of North Twin is as steeped in climbing mythology as the most famous faces in the world. Before last April, it had seen only two ascents, by two different routes, each of which is known in the collective consciousness as one of the greatest climbs of its era. In 1974 George Lowe and Chris Jones climbed the first route, a line that takes advantage of the most moderate ground on the face to gain a final steep pillar that leads to the top of the face. In 1985 David Cheesmond and Barry Blanchard climbed the proud north pillar of the same face. Both climbs were done in summer, and each took nearly a week. Neither has been repeated.

On April 4, 2004 Marko Prezelj, from Slovenia, and I skied up Wooley Creek, over Wooley Shoulder, down Habel Creek, and crossed a glacier to the base of the 4,500-foot north face. That day we bivvied at the base of the lowest rockband after fixing half a pitch. We carried food for five days and fuel for six. We had one synthetic sleeping bag, a 5'x8' tarp, and a shovel blade that fitted our ice tool shafts. Our rack was 13 nuts, 10 cams, 12 pitons, and 6 ice screws. Extra clothing consisted of a change of socks each and a synthetic belay (DAS) parka each. The leader would climb with a light pack and with leashless tools. The second would climb with a heavier pack, sometimes with the leader's pack hanging off his harness, and with leashed tools.

The initial rockband, though short, gave us a taste of what was to come. The first pitch offered steep and difficult drytooling in thin cracks, and necessitated some pulling on gear. The second pitch required a tension traverse from the belay and insecure mixed climbing on poorly adhered ice with hard-won rock gear for protection. A clear pattern soon developed for most of the 17 "hard" pitches: we didn't know if the pitch would go until we reached the end of the rack and/or the rope and built an anchor. This kept the adventure high, a feeling we both consider important to a successful outing—more important than whether we complete a route.

The end of the first full day on the face (April 5) saw us fixing a pitch halfway up the face at the point where our new line joined the 1974 Jones-Lowe route. We bivvied comfortably on the highest snowband that traverses the face.

On April 6 we ascended the ropes we had fixed the evening before and Marko led the first block of the day, four pitches of steep rock climbing. Much of it was freeclimbed by drytooling, but there were sections of aid as well, including what we presumed to be the "thin A3/A4" pitch described by George Lowe and Chris Jones. After that long lead, I started my block, finishing my third pitch of the day at a thin crack in a steep headwall 30 minutes after sunset. I fixed the ropes there and descended to Marko's belay. Being the size of one boot, it was the biggest stance we had seen since the morning. With some chopping we were able to enlarge the stance to approximately 12 inches by 20 inches, just big enough for three, sometimes four, butt-cheeks. We dug snow out of cracks and scooped it off of other small ledges, and hung in our harnesses to prepare food and water.

At this time I decided to

Steve House appreciating his modern tools one pitch before losing his plastic boot, day two. *Marko Prezelj*

change my damp socks. When replacing the outer shell of my left boot the loop on the back of the boot suddenly broke. We briefly saw the shell hovering in the light of our headlamps before it quietly disappeared down the face. After much cursing, and some discussion, Marko and I decided that it would be easier, quicker, and safer to continue to the top of the route and travel out by traversing the long, but non-technical, Columbia Icefields to the Athabasca Glacier and the Icefields Center.

It was an austere pair that finished their dinner of soup and dehydrated mashed potatoes and rigged their tarp overhead before squeezing onto the ledge. Our feet were on a backpack, and we pulled the sleeping bag over us and spent an uncomfortable night. Our repose was cut short at 5 a.m. when winds near the summit started to cause spindrift to dump on our ineffectively-rigged tarp and get into our sleeping bag. At approximately this point George Lowe and Chris Jones had "six pitons, some worthless nuts, and three ice screws" (*AAJ 1975*).

Finishing up the headwall at the top of the exit gully, day three. *Steve House*

Unable to use the stove in the spindrift-shower, Marko and I started without food or water and ascended the fixed pitch. Marko then lead one traversing pitch towards the exit ice gully at the top of the face, which I followed with one normal boot-crampon combination and one inner boot lined with plastic bags and wrapped with athletic tape to protect it from abrasion. From the end of that pitch we made a very traversing rappel, during which one of the rope sheaths was badly damaged. From that stance a short, 20-foot lower brought Marko into the exit ice gully, which to our consternation, was completely devoid of ice. Marko led a long and difficult mixed pitch up patchy ice and steep crack systems on the right side of the vertical gully, which brought us to within half a ropelength of the end of the true difficulties.

One short steep bit of ice climbing put us on the summit ice slopes, which we climbed in ten 60-meter pitches to the North Twin-Twin Towers col. From here we were able to ascend toward the summit of North Twin and reach a suitable bivouac at 7 p.m. below the summit cornice. Being quite dehydrated from a long day without water, we cooked until 1 a.m., and then fell asleep for seven hours.

At 10 a.m. on the 8th, we continued over the summit of North Twin and onto the Columbia Icefields where we used a GPS to navigate our way in a complete whiteout to the Athabasca Glacier. After nine nearly continuous hours of walking, we reached the Icefields parkway. It took us well over an hour to thumb a ride 10 kilometers north to our waiting van. (We later calculated that with perfect navigation it would have been a 14-mile traverse.)

I never had any problems with my foot getting cold, and we returned to the highway with 1.5 gas canisters and no food. We carried off all of our gear and ropes. Our skis, poles, and skins remained in the Habel Creek drainage, but were retrieved by a pair of young climbers a week later, whom we paid for their efforts.

At the summit bivy, House prepares his inner boot for the long walk over the Columbia Icefields. *Marko Prezelj*

Marko and I found the ambiance on the face to be excellent, and its remoteness kept the sense of adventure high. Marko compared it to climbing in the Himalaya for its feeling of isolation. Our attitude was not evolutionary. We carried minimal, simple equipment in pursuit of adventure on this greatest of Canadian north walls. We expected to climb until we failed, and as occasionally happens, we didn't fail. Our attitude was old school, the quest for adventure, which is exactly what we found.

SUMMARY OF STATISTICS

AREA: Canadian Rockies

ASCENT: Second ascent of the Lowe-Jones route (5.10 A3) on the north face of North Twin, with a new variation (5.9, A2) to the first half. Steve House and Marko Prezelj. April 5-7, 2004.

*Prezelj is pronounced "PREY-zell."

Feature articles on North Twin routes can be found in American Alpine Journals *with the following dates: Henry Abrons 1966, George Lowe 1975, David Cheesmond 1986, and Barry Blanchard's tribute to the Jones-Lowe Route in 2002. Abrons, who made the first ascent of the northwest ridge, wrote "So dark, sheer, and gloomy is the North Face of North Twin, like a bad dream, that I shall say very little about it." But he did make one prediction: the "awesome face … must become one of the great face problems for the next generation."*

A MOUNTAIN UNVEILED

A revealing analysis of Cerro Torre's tallest tale.

ROLANDO GARIBOTTI

Cesare Maestri standing before a two-meter model of Cerro Torre crafted by Elio Orlandi.
The occasion is a meeting in Male, Italy, in 1999 to commemorate the fortieth anniversary
of Maestri's claim to the first ascent of Cerro Torre. Maestri was unable to identify his route
line on the model and had to be helped by Orlandi and Maurizio Giarolli.
Ken Wilson/Baton Wicks Archive

If someone told you he had just run a 10-minute mile you would shrug your shoulders and say "so what." If someone said he had just run a three-minute mile you would be amazed and skeptical, and a reasonable response would be to ask for evidence. Mountaineering reports sometimes fall into the latter category, and if evidence is not forthcoming one is left with the difficult decision of how to assess these claims.

It is not for journalists to doubt the word of climbers, but what they can and should do is to obtain convincing accounts of climbs before according them proper credit. It is essential that magazine and journal editors are not credulous, for we all rely on the accuracy of such records.

One of the best-known cases in modern times is Cesare Maestri's claim to have completed, in a mere seven days the first ascent of Cerro Torre, in 1959. This supposed ascent was carried out with Austrian Toni Egger, who, according to Maestri's account, fell to his death during the descent, taking with him their only camera. While this supposed climb was initially taken at face value, climbers gradually started to take a closer look. Maestri's claim clearly surpassed all the highest achievements of its day in terms of difficulty, speed, and style. The great French alpinist Lionel Terray called it "the most important alpinistic endeavor of all time," a description still accurate today, considering that Maestri's claimed line is still unrepeated despite numerous attempts by some of the world's finest alpinists.

The jagged Cerro Torre is located in the Chalten Massif in southern Patagonia, in a group of dramatic peaks that include the well-known Cerro Fitz Roy. Cerro Torre is one of the most startling mountains in the world and would rank among the world's hardest if it wasn't for Maestri's very own "Compressor Route" on its south-east ridge. Maestri came close to climbing this line in 1970 when, using a gas-operated air compressor, he placed some 400 bolts to reach a point about 35 meters below the summit, which he considered a valid ascent.

Starting in the late 1960s, serious doubts arose regarding the supposed 1959 ascent. Such doubts first originated in Italy from the likes of Carlo Mauri, a well-respected alpinist from Lecco who had attempted the Torre's west face in 1958. Later, it was the British who picked up the inquiry, particularly Ken Wilson, editor of the renowned Mountain magazine. Later still, this subject was to become a staple of countless magazine articles. Maestri had numerous opportunities to present a plausible scenario, in conferences, interviews, and magazine articles, yet, he has repeatedly failed to make a convincing case.

Today the controversy remains unresolved. As 2004 commemorates the thirtieth anniversary of the first undisputed ascent of Cerro Torre (completed by a large Ragni di Lecco team led by Casimiro Ferrari via the west face), it seems appropriate to bring closure to this topic. This fine ascent remains eclipsed by the 1959 claims and the 1970 "bolt-aided" near miss.

Raised in northern Patagonia, I have had the opportunity to climb in the Chalten Massif countless times, making ascents of many of the area's towers, including the first complete ascent of the north face of Fitz Roy in 1996, and the first alpine-style ascent of Fitz Roy's southwest face in 1999. I became intrigued with the Egger-Maestri episode after meeting many of those involved in the early history of the area, including Folco Doro Altan, Walter Bonatti, Cesarino Fava, Casimiro Ferrari, John Bragg, and Jim Donini, among many others. Realizing that there were serious doubts concerning Maestri's claims, and that there were a number of key issues not previously addressed, I decided to investigate the matter in hopes of shedding more light on the issue.

Earlier attempts to validate Maestri's claims failed to take account of all the available material: one of the major hurdles has apparently been the variety of languages in which the important information was available. My knowledge of the languages concerned was invaluable researching

The east flank of the Cerro Torre group, showing: (1) Compressor route, (2) Devil's Directisima, Fistravec-Jeglic-Karo-Knez-Kozjek-Podgornik, 1986, (3) Calza-Giovanazzi-Gobbi-Salvaterra, 2001, (4) Bragg-Donini-Wilson, 1976 route, (5) Giarolli-Orlandi, 1998, (6) Salvaterra and partners, (7) Bonapace and partners, (8) Central Ice Gully, Bonapace-Dunser-Ponholzer, 1994, (9) Burke-Proctor, 1981 line, (10) Ponholzer-Steiger, 1998 line. (a) lower dihedral; (b) Egger-Fava-Maestri gear cache and likely highest point attained, (c) triangular snowfield, (d) middle buttress, (e) English box portaledge, (f) east dihedral, (g) Col of Conquest, (h) north ridge, (i) north face, (j) east face, (k) southeast ridge, (l) Alimonta-Claus-Maestri, 1971 highpoint. *Rolando Garibotti (2)*

this article. My analysis is based primarily on the various accounts written by Cesare Maestri and Cesarino Fava, many of which I translated personally from the original Italian. Fava's accounts are vital considering his claim to have climbed with Egger and Maestri to the Col of Conquest (the col between Torre Egger and Cerro Torre) during the claimed first ascent. Because no trace of the trio's passage has ever been found more than 300 meters up the wall, and since the first-hand accounts of Maestri's purported ascent above that point are vague and contradictory, Fava's descriptions are worthy of close inspection.

THE LOWER DIHEDRAL

In late January 1959, Egger, Fava, and Maestri began climbing the 1,200-meter-high east face, beginning with a 300-meter dihedral (the "lower dihedral"). Fava describes this feature: "The 300-meter lower dihedral took several days of exhausting work; three days in which Cesare danced chillingly among bolts and aiders."[1.1] Maestri states: "This dihedral presents difficulties of up to the fifth and sixth grade, including long sections of difficult aid climbing, some of which required bolts. We fixed ropes all the way to its end, where we made a gear deposit with all the equipment we had left."[2.1] He later describes the fixed ropes as 12-mm hemp ropes.

In his book *Arrampicare e il mio mestiere*[3] Maestri describes at length the four days it took them to climb and fix ropes on the lower dihedral. In this account, Maestri repeatedly comments on the difficulty of the climbing and the amount of physical effort required. On January 12 he notes: "Today was very tiring... only managed to climb 30 meters."[3.1] On the next day: "Every meter up here takes a lot of effort, the climbing is very hard, the wall is steep and blank. I manage, slowly, one meter at a time."[3.2] He goes on to say, "I am so very tired."[3.3] After a day in which they were not able to climb due to bad weather, Maestri describes January 15, "I am exhausted and it's barely the start of the day."[3.4] Later that same day he describes reaching a small ledge below a triangular snowfield above the end of the dihedral: "Below me are 300 meters of difficult climbing, another obstacle that we have surpassed, but at this point I am completely exhausted.... I have continuous cramps in my arms and my hands are totally trashed...."[3.5] After these few days of activity Maestri became sick and had to rest for several days before being able to descend from the snow cave they had dug near the base of the face—their so-called third camp—to their second camp, located at the foot of the formation known as El Mocho.

This initial 300-meter dihedral presents difficulties far less severe than the upper portion

The east flank of the Cerro Torre group, showing approximately Maestri and Egger's purported line of ascent (1) and descent (2), as described by Maestri. Also shown: (a) gear cache and end of fixed ropes—no trace of passage has been found above this point, (b) first bivouac, Col of Conquest, (c) second bivouac—2,720m according to Maestri, (d) third and fourth bivouacs-2,980m according to Maestri, (e) fifth bivouac—2,550m according to Maestri, (f) sixth bivouac and site of Egger's death according to Maestri. Please see the photo on the following page for Maestri's detailed route lines on the north face.

The north face of Cerro Torre, as seen from the top of Torre Egger, showing: (1) Burke-Proctor, 1981 line, (2) Ponholzer-Steiger, 1998 approximate line, (3) Chiapa-Conti-Ferrari-Negri, 1974 route—(P) marks the site where the photo on page 146 was taken, (4) Maestri and Egger's reported line of ascent as marked by Maestri in a photograph in *L'Europeo 704*, April 1959, page 34, showing ascent and descent bivouac sites (x), (5) Maestri and Egger's reported line of ascent as marked by Maestri in a photograph in *La Montagne*, April 1960, page 210, showing bivouac sites (o)—note how much the lines and bivouac sites differ. *Jay Smith*

of their claimed line, and considering the effort that Maestri describes in surmounting the lower dihedral, one cannot help but wonder how, in a matter of a two weeks they managed to acquire the additional fitness and skill necessary to complete the visionary ascent they later claimed.

TO THE COL OF CONQUEST

The following 10 days brought continuous storms, and therefore Egger, Fava, and Maestri, together with their support team—four young Argentinean university students (three of Italian origin), Augusto and Gianni Dalbagni, Juan Pedro Spickerman, and Angel Vincitorio—descended to base camp and even lower to rest.

Eventually the weather improved, and on January 28 they began their final attempt. Maestri writes: "…in silence Fava, Egger, and I tie in at the base of the east face."[2.2] Fava, who was along to help carry equipment, describes ascending the fixed ropes they had left in place ten days earlier: "Pulling with our arms, we go up the fixed ropes of the lower dihedral using a prusik knot for safety."[1.2] Maestri describes a somewhat more complicated technique: "We go up to the base of the lower dihedral all together, and, using the fixed ropes, we surmount it. I go up first and belay Cesarino, who belays Toni, while I go up the next fixed line before repeating the whole process again."[3.6] These two descriptions give a good picture of the equipment and tedious techniques the three men had at their disposal in 1959—the 12mm hemp ropes, the tiring and slow prusik techniques, and the belays while prusiking—and thus indicate a time-consuming process.

Maestri relates that upon reaching the triangular snowfield at the top of the lower dihedral, "We cross it, making a diagonal traverse to a series of cracks that lead from the edge of the snowfield to the base of the big, overhanging east dihedral... It is about 150 meters from the snowfield to here, with difficulties in the fourth and fifth grade [about US 5.6]; pitons used 15-20."[2.3] The above description, even though vague, clearly implies that the trio supposedly climbed on rock above the triangular snowfield, and not the obvious central ice gully. The parties that have since climbed through this section, including Bragg/Donini/Wilson, Wyvill/Campbell-Kelly, Proctor/Burke, Bonapace /Ponholzer and Salvaterra have all found that the terrain in this middle section is far more difficult than what Maestri describes, involving either difficult aid or fairly difficult free-climbing (5.9 to 5.10).

From the base of the overhanging east dihedral to the Col of Conquest, Maestri recounts climbing "fourth, fifth, and one section of the sixth grade [US 5.9]."[2.4] In another account he says of this section: "Now the wall becomes a bit harder, and every now and then there are sections of difficulties of the sixth grade."[3.7] Both quotes, when compared to his description in the previous paragraph, clearly imply that Maestri found the terrain between the base of the east dihedral and the col harder than the section below. Again, this directly contradicts the findings of those who have since climbed to the Col of Conquest via the same route. The technical difficulties are much more pronounced in the section directly above the triangular snowfield, while the so called "traverse" from the base of the overhanging east dihedral to the col, which Maestri describes as difficult, is in fact very easy. John Bragg, Jim Donini, and Jay Wilson climbed Maestri's claimed line as far as the Col of Conquest during their 1976 first ascent of Torre Egger. Donini later commented, "You peek around the corner and there is a ramp system going into the col about 120 meters long, and that's where Maestri claimed that it was very difficult doing that traverse, and from below it looks like a blank wall, when in fact you turn the corner and there is a ramp that is easy, it is not hard at all... from below you can't see the ramp."[4]

An aerial view of the Cerro Torre group from the northwest, showing from left to right Cerro Standhardt, Torre Egger, and Cerro Torre, as well as: (1) Burke-Proctor, 1981 line, (2) Ponholzer-Steiger, 1998 approximate line, (3) Bonapace-Dunser-Ponholzer, 1993, (4) Giarolli-Orlandi-Ravizza, 1994 line, (5) Chiapa-Conti-Ferrari-Negri, 1974 route. Also: (a) Col of Hope, (b) Col of Conquest, (c) north ridge (rising directly above the Col of Conquest; in his writings Maestri refers to it as "northwest" ridge), (d) north face, (e) northwest face, (f) west face, (g) the Helmet, (h) Punta Shanti, (i) Punta Herron, (j) Lago Viedma, (k) Cerro Solo. *Pat Morrow*

Egger, Fava, and Maestri claim to have climbed at a blistering speed up the 700 meters to the col, with Maestri describing that they arrived "around three in the afternoon...."[5.1] This would have been 11 hours[2.1] after they began from the foot of the face. Taking into account the techniques and equipment used in 1959, it would be unprecedented if they had managed to move so swiftly. Contemporary ascents on Fitz Roy and the Paine Towers suggest that such fast times with 1950s gear were virtually impossible.

In spite of the scale of the task at hand and the early hour, Egger and Maestri supposedly decided to spend the night at the col, while Fava, having done his share taking a load to this point, returned to the ground. Considering that Fava had to carry an extra rope—a 200-meter rope according to their descriptions—plus additional gear for him to descend safely, one wonders what else could he have carried to make his arduous climb to the col worthwhile? The 200-meter rope alone would have weighed at least 16 kilograms.

Fava recounts how Egger encouraged him to descend immediately, which he supposedly did. After being lowered across the "big traverse," which, as described earlier, is in fact a slanting ramp that slashes across the base of the north face, Fava recovered one of their 200-meter perlon ropes, which had supposedly been left fixed, and started descending on his own, "using Dülfer technique, separating the ropes by putting the ice axe between them."[1.3] After his incredibly long and very fast day climbing to the Col of Conquest, Fava, though using a rudimentary and slow rappel system, managed to make a very speedy descent. He writes: "I arrived at the glacier at dark, as the highest point of Fitz Roy was still glowing with the last rays of sun,"[1.4] a fact confirmed by Maestri, who writes, "In the late evening, when the sun illuminated only the top of Fitz Roy, Cesarino arrived at the glacier."[3.8]

The claimed speeds of both the team's ascent to the col and Fava's solo descent are indeed puzzling. Fava claimed to have climbed and descended 700 meters of difficult terrain in a mere 16 hours. This is would have been an unlikely feat in 1959, but the matter becomes muddier. In 1999 Fava completely revised his account in his book *Patagonia: Terra di sogni infrati.*[6] In it Fava writes, "Night surprised me at the upper edge of the triangular snowfield. Still clipped to the ropes, I dug into the snow to make myself a small snow cave...."[6.1] He later describes how he spent the night and eventually regained the fixed ropes and got down to their lower camp the following morning.[6.2,7] He also mentions that he rappelled using what appears to be an unusual and potentially dangerous (due to rope burning) double prusik technique,[6.3] using one as a brake and one for safety, as opposed to his earlier Dülfer rappel description.[1.3] In neither account does Fava give a precise description of his descent from the col or how he completed the descent so quickly.

While Egger and Maestri continued upward, Fava supposedly spent the following six days at the base of the mountain awaiting his companions' return. His description of these few days is important and is addressed later.

THE ICE SHEET

Above the Col of Conquest, Maestri claims to have been able to ascend courtesy of a sheet of ice that covered the north ridge in its entirety. Maestri: "… we attack a crust of snow and ice of variable thickness, from 20 centimetres to one meter, which was carried by the wind and pressed against the blank slabs of the north ridge. For 300 meters we go up climbing on air."[8.1] Clearly this description is too vague to be evaluated seriously, and yet it is a good example of the lack of detail given by Maestri regarding the upper portion of their claimed climb (whereas the initial 300 meters are described in great detail). Often times, during, and immediately after severe storms,

Cerro Torre is coated with a thin veil of frost, which to the unfamiliar eye might look like potentially climbable ice. However, this veil is only a layer of frozen humidity, with no solid bond to the rock, which would provide no purchase for a climber, and which promptly falls off. Nobody has ever found the ice conditions Maestri described and there are no comparable climbs where wind blown frost encrusted on an exposed and near vertical blank granite ridge has proved climbable. Maestri later made puzzling comments regarding the ice on his supposed route. When referring to Carlo Mauri's west face attempt in 1970, and comparing it to his supposed1959 ascent he said, "I watched parts of their film on television—a solid wall of ice. But on our side, we never encountered a wall of ice."[9]

Near the location Bragg and Burke describe as the possible site of Toni Egger's fatal accident. *Jim Donini*

Both Toni Egger and Cesare Maestri were accomplished climbers. Egger, a guide, was one of the best climbers of his time, with many fine ascents in the Dolomites, as well as the western Alps, Turkey, and Peru. Some of his finest ascents include the northwest face of Piz Badile, countless ascents in the Dolomites (including a 95-minute solo ascent of Spigolo Giallo on Cima Piccola), and the heralded first ascent of Nevado Jirishanca in the Peruvian Andes. Maestri had done countless fine solo ascents in the Dolomites, including the first solo of the Solleder route on Civetta's northeast face and the first solo of the Solda-Conforto Route on the south face of Marmolada. In contrast with Egger, Maestri had climbed little outside his home turf, the Dolomites. One of the rare exceptions was in 1955, when he completed a solo winter ascent of the southwest ridge of the Matterhorn. In spite of their superb credentials, the difficulties they faced on Cerro Torre are in an entirely different league, far surpassing those found on these earlier ascents.

Above the col, Egger and Maestri supposedly carried heavy packs while they "climbed on air."[8.1] Maestri writes: "We take a 200-meter rope, which we use doubled, 10 etriers, 30 pitons, 100 bolts, 30 ice-screws, wooden wedges, 30 meters of cord, food for three or four days, and all the bivouacking equipment. The packs are very heavy, weighing some 25 kilograms [55 pounds]."[3.9] Considering the weight of equipment at the time, could they have carried all this up such a difficult climb?

Maestri reports that they placed 30 bolts and used 15 ice-screws during that second day on the tower.[2.5] Regarding the bolts, he comments "to make a two and a half centimeter hole more than 500 hammer blows are necessary"[8.2] and it takes "approximately 35 to 40 minutes"[3.10] for each.

Phil Burke leading difficult mixed climbing in the upper portion of the north face. For the location where this photo was taken see the photo on page 142 (P marks the spot). *Tom Proctor*

This is not surprising considering the hard granite and the equipment of the time. Thirty bolts at 35 minutes each is more than 17 hours, an extraordinary amount of time considering the speed with which they claimed to have climbed the upper part of the mountain. Also, the straight-pick toothless ice axes, and thick pointed crampons from that time were completely inadequate to swiftly dance up near vertical ice, to say nothing of providing the neccesary security for bolting maneuvers.

Regarding their supposed line above the col, Maestri writes: "we have two options: to cut via ramps and gullies the whole west face [the face right of the col, probably of northwest orientation], to enter a chimney...or to benefit from the unusual snow conditions that cover a 300-meter section of the north face.... We choose this second option, since the north face is better protected from the wind."[2.6] He also states: "We climbed the face, not the ridge leading to the col itself. It is not as steep as you might expect. Our line was about 100 meters to the left of the ridge."[10.1] Regarding the terrain they found that day, he goes on: "The angle of the climbing was about the same as that of the gullies between the ice towers on the southeast ridge....about 45-50 degrees, I suppose. The same sort of thing, anyway, and the same general conditions."[10] These two statements confirm that Maestri's descriptions are implausible. The lower portion of the north face is nearly vertical, not 50-degree terrain that remotely resembles the ice towers on the southeast ridge. Jim Donini describes it as a "typical granite big-wall, absent of horizontal ledges or traverse lines."[11] Further questions arise from the fact that two parties who have climbed the first and only crack system left of the ridge found no evidence of Maestri's passage. More on this later.

On their second day above the Col of Conquest, Maestri reports climbing "toward the west flank, since the north side is too steep and extremely difficult."[2.7] He says they covered 250 meters, using 20 pitons, and found the terrain at an "angle between 50 to 60 degrees."[2.8] Once again, this description differs substantially with the terrain encountered later by other climbers (seen from a distance, the angle of that flank of the mountain is quite uniform, nearly 80 degrees).

On January 31, presumably their fourth day on the wall, Egger and Maestri, bivouacking 150 meters below the top, supposedly climbed over the summit ice mushrooms without great difficulty, reached the summit, and started their descent. That Maestri does not give a precise description of how they surpassed the notoriously difficult summit mushrooms, which hang prominently over the north and northwest faces, is quite telling. Englishman Phil Burke describes his and Tom Proctor's experience during a near miss on the north face a mere 50 meters to the left of where Maestri is supposed to have passed: "The ice was just overhanging mush, impossible to climb. I flayed with the now useless tools, stuck my arms in, edged up, but there was no purchase or traction."[4]

The Descent

Maestri says that at the summit the weather started deteriorating: "We felt safe only with the ice axes planted deep in the snow so as not to be blown off by the wind."[2.9] The first few rappels from the summit were apparently all from snow mushrooms and ice screws, with the exception of the last two of the day, which "we made using bolts, having at that point dropped below the limit of the ice…"[2.10] After supposedly spending the night in the same spot as the previous night, they continued down. "The first of February we continue descending, the warm wind melting the snow that falls noisily… There is not a single possibility of placing normal pitons. For every rappel we are forced to place two bolts under the continuous spindrift."[2.11]

Maestri continues: "We decided to descend diagonally across the north face instead of going directly to the col so as to arrive to the lower end of the traverse since, after Cesarino recovered the rope we had left fixed there, the traverse would have been a major obstacle for us."[12.1] Again, in this case, Maestri appears to imply that the traverse from the base of the east dihedral to the col was difficult, when in fact all other teams have found it straightforward. A diagonal descent across the mostly blank and very steep north face would clearly prove much more troublesome than a few rappels down a ramp, especially since they would not be

Looking down from the upper portion of Torre Egger during its first ascent in 1974. To the right is the snow of the Col of Conquest. The blank face above the snow is the lower portion of Cerro Torre's north face where Maestri and Egger claim to have climbed. The ramps that slash across the base of this face are the easy ramps leading to the Col of Conquest, which Maestri described as being quite difficult. *Jim Donini*

Daniele Chiappa and a friend on the summit of Cerro Torre, 1974. Chiappa, Mario Conti, Casimiro Ferrari, and Pino Negri were the first to reach the summit. *Baton Wicks Archive.*

able to re-use the many bolts they claim to have placed along the line of ascent.

It supposedly took them two full days to descend to the vicinity of their fixed ropes that reached the end of the lower dihedral. "Around 7 p.m. on February 2, barely 100 meters from the fixed ropes, we decided to spend the night on the right edge of the triangular snowfield. I drilled some bolts and we started digging a hole in order to spend the night."[2.12] Maestri claims to have placed three bolts at this location (these have never been found despite numerous parties climbing through this area), and describes being too tired to continue.[3.11] Egger was apparently unsure about this bivouac and decided to have a look below. Maestri was supposedly lowering him when Egger got hit by an avalanche that apparently cut his rope and swept him down the abyss, taking with him their only camera and much of the gear. Considering that it was their third day descending, and that they were supposedly tantalizingly close to the fixed lines, Egger's eagerness to continue seems quite understandable.

After collecting himself from the loss of his partner, Maestri claims to have spent the night at that location and, "At dawn on February 3 I exit from my hole… I start descending with the piece of rope that I have left."[2.13] He continues: "Hours go by until I get to the fixed ropes, along which I descend. The wall is hell; just a few meters above the glacier my feet slip and I don't manage to hold myself with my hands and therefore I fall…. The spirit of survival takes me across the tormented glacier to a point some 300 meters away from Camp 3, where Cesarino had stayed alone for six days waiting, and therefore it is he who found me a few hours later…."[2.14]

SUBSEQUENT ATTEMPTS AND OBSERVATIONS

Maestri describes the hardware used as follows: "All in all we placed 120 pitons, 65 ice-screws, 70 bolts, and 20 wooden wedges. At the start we took two 200 meter ropes, 10 etriers, 50 pitons, 100 bolts, 30 ice-screws…."[2.15] Since much of this equipment would have been left in place as rappel anchors, it is surprising that nothing has ever been found above the end of the lower dihedral, 300 meters above the ground. In the last 30 years at least 10 different parties have climbed past that point, seven of which reached the Col of Conquest.

During their ascent of Torre Egger, Bragg, Donini, and Wilson were the first to follow Maestri's footsteps to the Col of Conquest. They found copious amounts of gear in the lower dihedral, but *nothing* above. Also particularly suspicious was a large deposit of obviously unused gear—including ropes, two packs, many pitons, and wooden wedges—which they found on a small ledge at the top of the lower dihedral, 40 feet below the triangular snowfield. This gear could not have been taken further up the climb and dumped on the descent, because Maestri claims that Egger fell and took what was left of the summit gear with him. Maestri explained that two days before the final attempt they had made the decision to climb alpine style above the gear cache, therefore using less equipment than they had originally intended. However, Egger, Fava and Maestri had reached this point only once before the summit push, so it would have been unlikely that the three men would have been able to carry all the equipment found at this location plus all the equipment that was described as used on the final climb. Donini also points out that the last pitch leading up to Maestri's gear cache was fixed in its entirety, with the rope running through aid placements spaced very close together, with clove hitches on every other piton. Why would Maestri leave and not clean that pitch?

Bragg and Donini started off believing Maestri's claim but lost faith during their climb, when their own observations were inconsistent with Maestri's story. Bragg commented that they were particularly surprised to not find any gear on the traverse to the col, where Egger, Fava, and Maestri claimed to have fixed a rope: "There seemed to be only one natural traverse line into the col, and as the climbing was mostly easy in this section, it seems unlikely that they would have gone a different way. Yet we found nothing."[13] It is also troubling that the four parties that managed to climb a significant amount of terrain on the north and northwest faces above the col found no trace of the 60 or so bolts Maestri claims to have placed there, nor did they see any evidence of passage on Maestri's claimed descent line in the center of the north face.

In 1978 Ben Campbell-Kelly and Brian Wyvill climbed the initial 450 meters of Maestri's line, including the buttress up and right of the triangular snowfield, then moved left to attempt the impressive east dihedral, at the base of which they placed a box-style portaledge, which they left fixed.[14] In 1981, using the same portaledge, Englishmen Phil Burke and Tom Proctor, among the finest English climbers of the era, pushed the line further to the top of the east dihedral. From that point they made a 25-meter traverse to the edge of the north face, followed by a 65-meter horizontal traverse to the only major groove system in the heart of the face. Before retreating, they climbed 100 meters

Casimiro Ferrari approaching the summit mushroom above the west face during the first ascent of Cerro Torre, 1974. *Daniele Chiappa/Baton Wicks Archive*

more up the rightmost of two obvious grooves. Burke, a highly competent climber, said that the second-to-last pitch was the hardest of his life and required hooking the drooped-pick axes into the ice at the back of a crack. The last pitch, which was aborted, stopped at a blank wall beneath the snow of the first snow shoulder, a mere 30 meters below the summit ridge.[15] Burke: "The grade would be modern ED 3/4, with high standard rock pitches and particularly difficult ice pitches from 70° to overhanging, as well as dry tooling on one pitch, where I fell jumping from a sky-hook for a good hold! The average angle of the wall is more than 70°."[11] Proctor reported that the north face and ridge were much like El Capitan, very steep and without many climbable features. Their descriptions clearly establish how steep and featureless the terrain is, contradicting Maestri's description of 45-50 degree terrain, and demonstrate how unlikely it would be for such a wall to be covered by climbable, wind-blown frost as Maestri claimed.

In 1999 Austrians Toni Ponholzer and Franz Steiger climbed an obvious crack system on the north face, just to the left of the north ridge, to about 200 meters below the summit.[16] On the lower 300 meters of the north face itself, their line coincides almost exactly with the line Maestri claims to have climbed on the first day above the Col of Conquest,[10.1] where he claims to have placed 30 bolts in a single day. The Austrians enjoyed dry conditions, which allowed them a close look at the face and ridge. They saw no traces of passage. (Two Italians, Maurizio Giarolli and Elio Orlandi, had climbed 150 meters up this line in 1998 and similarly found no evidence of passage.)[17] Ponholzer, who by all accounts is an extremely well-versed mountaineer and rock climber, has made six attempts to climb above the Col of Conquest. Only on his last attempt, totally familiar with the terrain, was he able to match Egger, Fava, and Maestri's supposed speed: reaching the col in one day.

Between the English (Burke-Proctor) and Austrian (Ponholzer-Steiger) attempts, most of the north face has been explored. Considering that Maestri's route line[8.3] and descriptions clearly delineate two separate lines for the ascent and descent, on which Maestri claims to have left copious quantities of equipment, it is hard to explain why no gear has been spotted.

The northwest face, which lies on the opposite side of the north ridge, has also seen a few visitors. Italians Maurizio Giarolli, Elio Orlandi, and Odoardo Ravizza climbed to the north ridge itself from the west, reaching it at a point 300 meters below the summit.[18] Austrians Bonapace, Dunser, and Ponholzer crossed the Col of Conquest and climbed up the west side to 100 meters below the Italian's highpoint.[19] Neither party found any trace of passage, even though Orlandi went as far as rappelling 50 meters straight down the north ridge from their highpoint and made several pendulums in hopes of finding something (Maestri claims that he and Egger moved to the northwest face on their second day of climbing above the col).

In 1998, some 500 meters from the ground, right next to the "English box portaledge," Giarolli and Orlandi found one ice piton that they claimed was from Maestri's team. In an article by Mark Synnot in the May 1999 issue of Climbing magazine, this claim was used as new evidence to support Maestri's case.[20] As it turns out, the piton has been identified by Phil Burke as one of his. Near the same location, Giarolli and Orlandi claimed to have found a handful of hemp rope they believe to be Maestri's. But once again this is most likely attributable to the English teams. Proctor points out that on one occasion a 200-meter rope with a knot at the end jammed straight down from their box site and that he was forced to rappel all the way down the jammed rope and jumar back up. He did not rappel down their route, but went down the edge of the central gully to the south; he saw no sign of any equipment. Even though there was some rockfall down the gully, Proctor believes that this would have been the obvious line of ascent for Maestri rather than the middle buttress.

Fava's Camp

According to Cesarino Fava's diary, published in 1959,[1] after climbing to the Col of Conquest Fava returned to the snow cave (Camp 3) at the foot of the mountain on the evening of January 28. He claims to have spent the following six days waiting for his companions. It is difficult to understand why after such a long ascent to the Col of Conquest and the ensuing harrowing solo descent he did not descend to Camp 2, at the base of El Mocho, where the support team waited for him. Although one could argue that Fava might have been unwilling to descend the glacier on his own due to the hazardous nature of solo glacier travel, some curious facts arise from the original accounts. The young Argentinean support team report having visited the snow cave (Camp 3) the day after Fava's return, January 29, and found it empty.[21.1] That same day Fava, in his own account, describes descending the glacier to the slabs below, within striking distance of Camp 2. "On the twenty-ninth I went outside when the sun was already high...I returned to the snow cave when the shade of the Torre invaded the slabs of El Mocho, where I had descended to hang out in the sun."[1.5] Apparently the dangers of solo glacier travel did not much concern Fava, and somehow it appears that the two parties passed each other without meeting when traveling to and from the snow cave. Since the glacier provides only one obvious and safe route, this would have been impossible. Also, considering that the slabs of El Mocho that Fava describes descending to on January 29 are a mere half-hour away from Camp 2, one wonders why Fava would have decided against continuing down, especially when, according to Maestri's account in *Arrampicare e il mio mestiere,* Fava was clearly eager to have some company.[3.12] In his 1999 book, *Patagonia Terra di sogni infranti*, Fava tells a very different story: he describes having been at the base of the east face when Dalbagni, Spickermann, and Vincitorio came up.[6.4] However, since the snow cave was located a mere 400 horizontal meters from the face it seems unlikely that they would not have seen each other or established contact.

On February 3 Fava claims that, having lost all hope, he decided to descend to Camp 2. As he was departing from the snow cave, he supposedly looked toward the face one last time and noticed a curious black object that turned out to be a very tired Maestri. That same day they claim to have descended to Camp 2. The following day Fava, together with Dalbagni and Spickermann returned to Camp 3 in an attempt to find Egger, but terrible weather conditions soon forced them to give up the search.[6.5]

Fava's contradictions and lack of clarity cast substantial doubt on the reliability of his accounts. In the past, climbers accepted his recounting of the portion of the climb in which he was directly involved. One could easily argue that by claiming the first ascent of such a great prize, Maestri had substantial incentive to fabricate this ascent; yet, Fava appears to have had little to gain. However, when one takes into account the deep rivalry and competition within the Italian community in Buenos Aires at the time, between Patagonian veteran Folco Doro Altan and a group of émigrés from the Trento province, including Tito Lucchini and Fava himself, it becomes apparent that the weight of failure or success was as heavy for Fava as it was for Maestri. This rivalry had led two different expeditions to vie for the same peak in 1958, with Altan's team, including Walter Bonatti and Carlo Mauri, attacking it from the west, and Fava and Lucchini's team, including Maestri and other fine Trento climb-ers, from the east.

Further curious facts arise from Gianni Dalbagni's diary. Dalbagni, as mentioned earlier, was one of the four students who helped ferry loads throughout Maestri's expedition. His diary was published as a 16-article series, starting in March 1959 in an Italian language newspaper

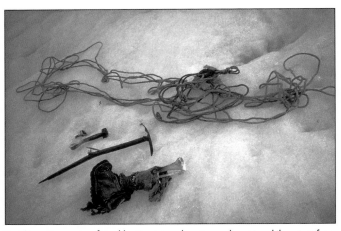

Toni Egger's remains, found by Donini and partners almost two kilometers from the base of the wall. *Jim Donini*

circulating in Buenos Aires.[21] Regarding the weather conditions, Dalbagni provides the following information. He describes the night of January 27 as one of very heavy rain, and only points out weather improvement in the early hours of January 29. Remember that Egger, Fava, and Maestri are supposed to have started their high-speed climb to the Col of Conquest in the early hours of the twenty-eighth. Of their ascent to the snow cave (Camp 3) on January 29, Dalbagni says that in spite of the blue skies the wind was extremely strong: "Even with our feet deep in the snow and the ice axes planted up to their head, the wind kept pushing us back… In the steep crest the walking got very exciting due to the strong gusts of wind…."[21.2] This day, according to Maestri, he and Egger climbed above the Col of Conquest, on the exposed north ridge. One can only guess how strong the winds must have been up high considering the conditions at the base of the protected east face.

On January 30, Dalbagni describes perfect weather, but the next morning brings some clouds, and by mid-day rain engulfs him and his companions while strolling on the glacier, forcing them to a quick return to camp. On this day Maestri claims to have reached the summit. Of the first two days of February, Dalbagni writes: "Clouds with unremitting wind, snow, and rain."[21.3] February 3: "It snowed all night; the strong wind even brought a lot of snow inside. Outside it's a white chaos."[21.4] Chalten Massif weather conditions are always worse up high, with much stronger winds and more precipitation. For those who have had the chance to climb in this area, it becomes apparent that the weather information provided by Dalbagni hardly describes the type of extended good weather that a brilliant, very fast, and extremely difficult alpine ascent such as the one described by Maestri would require to be carried out.

EARLY DOUBTS

Doubts about Maestri's account arose immediately upon his return to Buenos Aires when an article in a local magazine directly implied that Maestri might be responsible for Egger's death.[22] This led to a request by the Italian Consulate in Buenos Aires for the members of the expedition to give depositions about the events, but the matter was soon forgotten. (I tried to locate these depositions in Buenos Aires but found that they were shipped many years ago to Italy's national archive in Rome.)

It was not until 1970 that public statements casting doubt on Maestri's ascent were published in Italy. Renowned alpinist Carlo Mauri, returning from a failed attempt on Cerro Torre, commented via telegram to the press "... we return, safe and sound from the impossible Cerro Torre,"[23.1] implying that the mountain had never been climbed. Not long afterward, Franco Rho, a sports journalist well connected to climbing circles, described Mauri's failed attempt in one of Italy's major newspapers: "...he was not able to reach the summit of Cerro Torre, of that terrible Cerro Torre where no man has ever set foot."[24.1] Around that same time the English media, particularly Ken Wilson, editor of *Mountain* magazine, picked up the matter. Wilson's suspicions were aroused after Pete Crew, Martin Boysen, Mick Burke, Jose Luis Fonrouge, and Dougal Haston failed to climb the southeast ridge in 1968. Haston had climbed the Eiger Direct in winter; Crew and Boysen has made the first winter ascent of the Phillip/Flamm route on the Civetta north face, and Fonrouge, had done the second ascent of FitzRoy, via the Supercanaleta. This was an extremely strong team noted for fast climbing, yet they made slow and laborious progress, exactly the same as all other teams on the mountain except for Maestri and Egger. When they returned, Crew told Wilson that the whole team doubted Maestri's claim in light of the sheer scale, difficulty, and weather of the Torre, as well as the vagueness of Maestri's descriptions. In 1976 what Bragg, Donini, and Wilson found, and did not find, added more fuel to the fire.

The lack of conclusive information and the many contradictions pointed out in this article are strong evidence against Maestri's claims. It is quite obvious that Maestri's descriptions do not match the terrain he claims to have climbed, terrain that still today, almost 50 years later and in spite of significant advances in equipment and technique, continues to repel all attempts. Maestri, as well as Fava, has had countless occasions to provide plausible evidence and to answer satisfactorily the numerous questions put forth by his critics, but has consistently failed to do so. It is indeed strange that Maestri would be so unwilling to provide a detailed and thorough description of what would be the finest climb ever. One might conclude that his unwillingness to do so constitutes evasion.

Curiously, on several occasions Maestri has dismissed the difficulty of his supposed climb. For example: "... I wish to state that, from the technical point of view, it was one of the easiest climbs of my life. It was certainly the most dangerous, and the only deadly one, but technically it was just a race, a race over a snow sheet."[25] Another example: "For Toni Egger, Cerro Torre was nothing—a Sunday stroll... You see, the serious difficulties—the grade 6 stuff—are in the lower part, which Fava had already helped us equip with fixed ropes."[9] Such comments, including the implication that the lower dihedral might be the crux of his claimed line, contradict reality.

CONCLUSIONS

What might be the reason why two people have apparently conspired to construct such a story? A likely explanation, and this is mere speculation, might have been the need they felt to make Egger's death somewhat more worthy, less painful, telling a story that spoke of glory and triumph, and not solely of tragedy. Fava himself gives a hint when he explains, "But why do we torment ourselves? Toni disappeared after having climbed in perfect alpine style the most difficult mountain in the world. A masterpiece. The great French alpinist Lionel Terray called it 'the most important alpinistic endeavor of all time.' Before it disappears behind a plateau I see in the distance the most beautiful and luminous crypt in the world, the one that protects the unforgettable Toni Egger. It is not only important how one lives; it is also important how one dies."[6.6]

Fava's commitment and devotion to Egger was never questioned. In early 1961 he returned to the area hoping to recover Egger's body but was foiled by heavy snowfall. During that same trip Fava placed a commemorative plaque honoring the Austrian near the base of the east face.[26] Eggers's body was not discovered until 1975, when Bragg, Donini, and Mick Coffey came upon it a couple of kilometers from the base of Cerro Torre. It is unclear if the glacier could have moved Egger's body that far in only 16 years, if indeed he fell from the wall as Maestri describes. In early 2003 more of Egger's remains were found not far from the 1975 location. His camera has never been found.

To speculate what might have happened to Egger is not this article's intent. However, the area of the triangular snowfield is particularly dangerous, being exposed to falling ice, as well as to avalanches that sweep the gully at the top of the lower dihedral, just above Maestri's gear cache. It was in this gully in 1976 that John Bragg found a prominent block sticking out of the ice, with a double 3/8" perlon rope wrapped around it. The rope struck him as remarkably similar to that which they had found on Egger's remains a year earlier. A chill ran down his spine when he noticed that the double end of the rope was broken and frayed exactly as Egger's had been, and for a brief instant he had a vision that this was where Egger had died, leading out toward the snowfield. A week or two later, while rappelling, Bragg kicked off a monstrous avalanche from the snowfield which swept the very gully where he had found the frayed rope. He describes that gully as "a prime spot to be taken by an avalanche, the double rope catching around the block and then breaking.... Who knows?"[13] Both Donini and Burke had similar feelings regarding Egger's death. Burke writes: "Around the cache site the route is very prone to avalanches coming off the ice field, which channels all falling ice off the east face down the large corner system of the route. We initially thought that Egger was at this point when struck, hence all the gear being abandoned with complete pitches roped with carabiners on every peg. I very nearly got taken out here and just managed to shelter under an overhang."[11] As Burke implies, an accident at this location would be the best explanation for Maestri's team leaving the pitch leading to the cache completely fixed.

Frustrated over the doubts being voiced about his claims, Maestri returned to Cerro Torre in 1970.[24.2] As mentioned earlier, he attacked the southeast ridge with a 200-pound air compressor, which he used to place some 400 bolts, reaching a point about 35 meters below the summit, from where, still on vertical rock, he retreated. He alleged that the snow mushroom above was not part of the mountain and that it would "blow off one of these days." The amount of equipment and the style he used during this attempt helped spark further doubts regarding his 1959 claims. So striking was the contrast between these two so-called "ascents" that they appeared contradictory.

Taking all of the factors into account, Maestri and Fava's descriptions of what took place in 1959 are completely unreliable. All a reasonable person could conclude would be that that in 1959, Maestri et al. attempted to climb the east face and reached a point 300 meters up the face in the vicinity of the triangular snowfield. Accounts of further progress are so imprecise and contradicted by other facts that they should be disregarded.

The evidence convinces me that Italians Daniele Chiappa, Mario Conti, Casimiro Ferrari, and Pino Negri were the first to stand on Cerro Torre's summit when, on January 13, 1974, they completed their ascent of the west face. History has yet to give this ascent it's rightful place.

REFERENCES:

The list below is an abbreviated version of the complete list of citations and bibliography. The complete list, with the original Italian that was translated for this article, can be found at www.AmericanAlpineClub.org (click on *American Alpine Journal*).

1. Cesarino Fava, "Dal Diario di Cesarino Fava," *Bollettino Società Alpinisti Tridentini* (March-April 1959): pp. 22-31.
2. Cesare Maestri, "Il Cerro Torre," *Club Alpino Italiano Rivista Mensile* vol. LXXX (July-Aug. 1961): pp. 205-211.
3. Cesare Maestri, *Arrampicare e il mio mestiere*, (Milano, Garzati, 1961): pp.109-171.
4. Alan Kearney, *Mountaineering in Patagonia* (Seattle, Cloudcap, 1993.)
5. Cesare Maestri, *Il Ragno delle Dolomiti*, (Milano, Rizzoli, 1981.)
6. Cesarino Fava, *Patagonia, Terra di sogni infratti*, (Torino: Centro Documentazione Alpina, 1999.)
7. Fabrizio Torchio, "Cosi arrivorono sul Torre," *L'Adige* [Trento, Italy] (24 April, 1999.)
8. Cesare Maestri, "E Venne la morte Bianca," *L'Europeo 704* (12 April, 1959): pp. 30-36.
9. Guido Carretto, "Cerro Torre Enigma: Maestri Speaks," *Mountain 9* (May 1970): p. 32.
10. Ken Wilson et al. "Cesare Maestri," *Mountain 23* (Sept. 1972): pp. 30-37.
11. Personal comunication.
12. Cesare Maestri, "La Conquista del Cerro Torre," *Bollettino Società Alpinisti Tridentini* (March-April 1959): pp. 1-9.
13. John Bragg, letter to Ken Wilson (2 Oct., 1976)
14. *American Alpine Journal* 1979 p.256; and *Mountain 61* p.13.
15. Phil Burke, "Cerro Torre: East Face," *Mountain 79* (May-June 1981): pp. 40-43; and *AAJ 1982* p.193-194.
16. *AAJ 1999*, p.333; and *High Mountain Sports 203* p.81-82.
17. *Alp 172* p.108.
18. *AAJ 1995* p.212-213; and *Alp 126* p.28-29.
19. Tommy Bonapace, "Cara de Hielo," *Gipfelsturmer* [Insbruck, Austria] (1996): p.21.
20. Mark Synott, "The Maestri Enigma," *Climbing 185* (May 1999): pp. 72-81, 130-134.
21. Gianni Dalbagni, "La dura conquista del Cerro Torre," *Corriere degli Italiani* [Buenos Aires] (March-April 1959). Sixteen articles starting on March 23, 1959.
22. Juan Roghi, "La Tragica Noche sobre los Andes," *El Hogar 2570* [Buenos Aires] (6 March, 1959): pp. 77-81.
23. Franco Rho, "Carlo Mauri non ha chiuso con il Cerro Torre," *Rasegna Alpina 15* (March-April 1959): pp. 84-91.
24. Cesare Maestri, *2000 metri della nostra vita*, (Milano, Garzati, 1972).
25. Male Conference [Trento, Italy] (1999) transcript record .
26. "Tentativo di Cesarino Fava per il ricupero di Toni Egger," *Bollettino Società Alpinisti Tridentini* (Jan.-Feb. 1961): p. 15.

This article has been adapted from Tom Dauer's upcoming book Cerro Torre: Mythos Patagonien. *(AS-Verlag, Zürich 2004).*

A NOTE ON THE AUTHOR:

Rolando Garibotti has visited the Fitz Roy and Cerro Torre massif over a dozen times, the first at age 15 when he climbed Aguja Guillaumet. His finest ascents in that area include the first complete ascent of Tehuelche on the north face of Fitz Roy in 1996 and the second ascent of the Slovak Route on Fitz Roy's southwest face in 1999, both alpine style. Born in Italy, raised in Argentina, and currently living in the U.S., he considers himself a Bariloche national, as this is the place where he first developed his passion for the mountains and where, one day, he hopes to enjoy his old age. For the last five years he has been working on a guidebook to the Chalten Massif, which should be published soon.

CLIMBS AND EXPEDITIONS
2004

Accounts from the various climbs and expeditions of the world are listed geographically from north to south and from west to east within the noted countries. We begin our coverage with the Contiguous United States and move to Alaska in order for the climbs in Alaska's Wrangell–St. Elias Mountains to segue into the St. Elias climbs in Canada.

We encourage all climbers to submit accounts of notable activity, especially long new routes (generally defined as U.S. commitment Grade IV—full-day climbs—or longer). Please submit reports as early as possible (see Submissions Guidelines at www.AmericanAlpineClub.org).

For conversions of meters to feet, multiply by 3.28; for feet to meters, multiply by 0.30.

Unless otherwise noted, all reports are from the 2003 calendar year.

NORTH AMERICA
CONTIGUOUS UNITED STATES

Washington

Washington, trends and new routes. The summer of 2003 unfolded as the driest in a century, with rainfall 70-85% below normal. Seattle temperatures topped 70 degrees for a record 61 consecutive days. The unusual number of hot, dry days resulted in closed campgrounds, limited wilderness access, and fire bans. Pesky fires like the Farewell Creek in the Pasayten Wilderness, which was spotted June 29, obscured views throughout the Cascades, burned until autumn rains, and exhausted federal funds. Alpine glaciers and snow routes took on new character, as new climbing options appeared in the receding wake. A project by Lowell Skoog documented change by retracing, 50 years to the date, the photography of Tom Miller and the Mountaineers' crossing of the Ptarmigan Traverse (www.alpenglow.org/climbing/ptarmigan-1953/index.html). What characteristically would be easy glacier and snow travel in late summer turned to ankle-bending kilometers of talus and scree and mind-numbimg on/off crampon cycles. Washington's weather did, however, promote a number of luxurious and comfortable high alpine traverses. To further support the record of regional climbing, local enthusiasts established the Northwest Mountaineering Journal site (www.nwmj.org/). The goal is to collect regional accounts of mountaineering that does not meet the *AAJ* criterion of Grade IV. In addition to individual reports below, the following summarizes other significant new alpine routes.

On the northeast side of Vasiliki Ridge (a mountain with a broad summit from which many pinnacles rise), Jordan Peters and Mike Layton established the Carlo Rossi Memorial Tower route (III 5.10dX), up a tower that had likely been climbed before. The route, climbed on September 13, ascends the tower's east ridge for many pitches, traverses to the south face of the summit tower, and continues to the summit. The crux was a 5.10dX offwidth on which the rock was "total garbage." In general, however, the rock is good. Other pitches included a 5.8 open book with a fun roof, and a summit pitch that required "walking the plank."

In April, also on the northeast side of Vasilki Ridge, Mark Bunker and Colin Haley climbed what is likely a new route on Ares Tower that is parallel to, and just right of, the route Never Enough. Their route (IV AI3 M4) followed gullies and chimneys on generally good rock.

Paisiano Pinnacle received a new route (III 5.10c) in mid-July from Scott Harpell and partner. The route starts at the West Ridge notch, climbs roofs and cracks up and across to the dihedral route, Rampage, then toward the skyline, following more cracks, an offwidth, and a final chimney.

Jay Brazier and Eric Sweet climbed a new line on the western flank of Mt. Shuksan on November 8, between the Upper Curtis Glacier and the Sulphide Glacier. The route (Satan's Sidewalk, 280m, III 5.7X, WI3+) is the obvious late-season ice flow 200m left of Hell's Highway. Access to the ice was gained by climbing corners and ramps to the left for 60m. The second pitch traversed right, onto the ice. The remaining three pitches followed the ice to the Sulphide Glacier.

In July 1999 Mike Preiss soloed a new route (III 5.8) on the south face of Mt. Garfield's West Peak onsight, without bolts or pins, self-belaying the harder pitches, with one bivy. The March 2004 *Rock and Ice* reported a variation (Infinite Bliss, 23 pitches, V 5.10b, by Steve Martin and Leland Windham) which is a fully bolted sport route that climbs the upper face straight-on. The middle third of the original solo and the variation are approximately the same line. On the original solo, a traverse in from the trees to a large shelf bypassed the four- to five-pitch lower third of the bolted variation. On the upper third Mike climbed a chimney/corner on the left and finished with four or five pitches on a rock rib (5.8), exiting the face 40-50' left of the highest point.

On February 6-7 Sean Courage, Tim Matsui, and Andreas Schmidt made what they believe to be the first winter ascent of Mt. Buckner. They'd planned to traverse Sahale Peak and climb Buckner's North Face, but due to wind and "general lethargy" ascended the Southwest Face. Schmidt traversed to the slightly lower East Summit, as they couldn't recall which summit was higher.

On Pyramid Peak's northeast face, a new route (and the first on the face) was climbed on February 9 by Robert Rogoz, Coley Gentzel, and Chris Koziarz. The route (IV+ M4) climbed 400' up the gully on the far left side of the face before cutting to the right, up a groove, and onto the northeast face proper. From here they climbed seven pitches of steep névé, thin ice, and difficult mixed climbing to the summit. While leading the crux pitch, Rogoz jammed the shafts of his ice tools into a vertical crack. The climbers descended by the standard southeast slopes and Colonial Glacier. The route name, It Ain't Over MFers (a Polish rap song by Liroy), was decided upon after wandering around in the dark returning to the car, then getting in a car wreck at 2 a.m. It is recommended that teams bring a set of nuts, a set of cams, several pitons, a few short screws, and protection for frozen turf.

GORDY SKOOG, *AAC, and* COLIN HALEY, *AAC*

Southern Picket Range, Complete Enchainment. In July this long-standing east-to-west challenge was completed by Mark Bunker, Colin Haley, and Wayne Wallace. All 14 major summits in the southern Pickets were climbed during the four-day traverse, several by new routes. The peaks along the Complete Southern Pickets Traverse (VI 5.10+) are as follows: July 25: Little McMillan Spire, southeast face, III 5.8; East McMillan Spire, east ridge, II 5.6; West McMillan Spire, east ridge/face, III 5.8. July 26: Inspiration Peak, east ridge, III 5.9; Pyramid Peak, east ridge/face, II 5.8; Mt. Degenhart, east ridge, class 4; Mt. Terror, east ridge, II 5.6; The Rake, east ridge, IV 5.9. July 27: East Twin Needle, southeast ridge/face, II 5.10a; West Twin Needle, east ridge, class 3; Himmelhorn, east ridge/north face, II 5.10+; Ottohorn, east ridge, class 4; Frenzlespitz, southeast ridge/face, II 5.6. July 28: Chopping Block, northeast face, II 5.6. A total of about 50 technical pitches in all. Three routes were first ascents: The Rake, East Twin Needle, and Himmelhorn. For more information, see Wallace's article earlier in this Journal.

The Chopping Block, first winter ascent. On February 14, 2004, I hiked in via Goodell Creek and The Barrier to climb the Southeast Face route. The next day, from below the east face, I climbed a steep, north-facing gully to gain the southeast ridge, which consisted mostly of steep, wind packed snow and had two short but tricky mixed sections. I descended by the southeast ridge as well, rappelling over the mixed sections from pitons and a shrub, and downclimbing the rest. After returning to camp I immediately packed up and hiked out, because the week-old snow crust was being rapidly covered by fresh, unstable snow.

COLIN HALEY, *AAC*

Inspiration Peak, first winter ascent. On February 7 Forrest Murphy and I left the Goodell Creek trailhead early and, using snowshoes, made it to a camp midway up the Terror Glacier that afternoon. The unusually low snowpack helped make the approach reasonable. On the 8th we snowshoed the rest of the way up the Terror Glacier to the base of Inspiration's south face, at its far left side. We climbed the south-facing gully, which was mostly steep snow, to the col between Inspiration Peak and the Pyramid. Halfway up this gully, we were pleased to find that a flow of water-ice came down the right side of a chockstone that otherwise would be the crux of the route. From the Inspiration-Pyramid col we climbed the West Ridge in three 60m pitches. The rock was covered in rime ice which was, in places, thick enough that we could gingerly swing our ice tools. We downclimbed our last pitch and made three single-rope rappels, off of pitons and a chockstone, back to the Pyramid-Inspiration col. As the sun was now shining on our ascent gully, we hurriedly downclimbed most of it, but made one rappel over the chockstone and one directly below it. We returned to camp on the Terror Glacier, packed up, began the long hike out, and reached the car at 10 p.m.

COLIN HALEY, *AAC*

Graybeard, north face routes. In November 2002, I climbed two separate routes on the north face of Graybeard, both of which I believe to be new. The first began from the prominent field of névé at the base of the 1984 Skoog-Skoog Route. From the right side of the névé I climbed a short 5th-class chimney to gain the rib immediately right of their couloir and followed that rib to the west ridge. The climbing was mostly low-5th- and 4th-class rock, with sections of steep snow. The second route was completed several days later and followed a large left-facing ramp/dihedral system that leads to a prominent gully/funnel on the upper third of the face. I found enjoyable but not overly steep water ice in the corner system, broken by steep bits of rock which I circumvented wherever possible. I back-roped a few times to pitons, which remain on the face. I enjoyed firm snow in the upper funnel, which led to a spectacular notch in the ridge. Both routes continued to the summit and descended via the broken west ridge to Easy Pass, and each was completed as a day-trip. I had excellent fall conditions, with wet October snow cemented onto the face by a cold spell that lasted for three weeks in late November and early December. Others expecting to repeat these routes should endeavor to find similar conditions, as the climbing would be loose and dangerous with less-cemented snow and boring with more snow (as in the spring).

STEVE HOUSE, *AAC*

Easy-Heather Traverse, repeat with variations. In July 2001 I traversed the ridgeline of peaks from Easy Pass to Heather Pass along the north boundary of the south block of North Cascades National Park. I began at 6:06 a.m. from the Easy Pass trailhead and followed the trail to Easy Pass. I left the trail and climbed the first peak, Graybeard, and continued along the crest, covering 15 miles, with 11,000' of elevation gain and 10,000' of elevation loss, before I returned to the North Cascades Highway at the Heather Pass trailhead at 6:34 p.m. I went to the highest point of every summit, including Graybeard, Fisher Peak, Little Horn, all of the Ragged Ridge summits, Black Peak, and Corteo Peak.

I know that part of my traverse covered new terrain, but I don't know which parts. Beckey only mentions the summits (obviously), but there are big parts of this ridgeline that were technical but not near summits, so probably had not been traveled. That said, there were lots of little "summits" along the ridge that I went to because I figured no one had been there, and it was part of the game I'd set for myself. The conditions were very dry. I wore sticky-rubber running shoes and carried a camel-back. I could only get water at one location, just before Fisher Peak, about one-third of the way across. The climbing was up to about 5.7, the downclimbing and traversing up to about 5.6, and there was lots and lots of 4th/easy 5th, which is why it was worthwhile.

STEVE HOUSE, *AAC*

Mount Logan, Northwest Ridge. So ends my fascination this year with remote Mt. Logan. My first solo foray led to the fastest ascent to date: just over 24 hours car-to-car. That was a long day in July. On October 1 I found my own little version of the Hummingbird Ridge, the previously unclimbed, endless Northwest Ridge (V 5.8X). The topo map doesn't lie: the ridge is over a mile long and has almost 3,000' of vertical. Just getting there took more than I bargained for. After leaving the trail at Junction Camp, I bushwhacked through to the second lake, and then was lucky to find the "Wrinkle In Time" to reach the fantastic Logan Creek Valley. The Wrinkle, which I followed on a deer path from the second lake, is a bizarre triangle-shaped terrain feature that is separated from the west side of the Logan Creek Valley. It forms two valleys, one of which actually flows up the Logan Creek Valley. It was the only way I could see to get into the otherwise impenetrable valley. You may find it on a close-up topo, but neither the lakes nor The Wrinkle show up on the Green Trails map. Good bivy among bear scat. The climb itself is endless, exposed, and committing, involving much fourth class and five rappels to clear its abundant gendarmes. It gets harder as it goes, too. There are two reasons this route wasn't done before: it's almost unreachable, and the climbing is in big-fear territory. Not that it's all that loose, but the ambiance is intimidating, and if you blow the route-finding, the going is desperate and scary.

WAYNE WALLACE, *AAC*

Kurt Buchwald and Peter Avolio cruising on the Northeast Buttress of Bonanza Peak. *Martin Volken*

Bonanza Peak, three-summit traverse. On August 21 and 22 Kurt Buchwald, Peter Avolio, and I completed the first ridge traverse (V 5.7/5.8) of all three summits of Bonanza Peak. The route involves an approach via the Mary Green Glacier, climbing the Northeast Buttress to the main summit, a link-up to the west summit and from there a link-up to the southwest summit. Getting off the mountain meant descending from there to the Isella Glacier, traversing the glacier to the base of the Holden Ridge, crossing the ridge, and descending the Mary Green Glacier to Holden Lake. The approach was made to climber's right of the Mary Green Glacier, which provided easy access to the base of the Northeast Buttress at 8,350' (three hours from Holden Lake). The ridge got steep and narrow right away. The rock was mostly solid but lichen-covered. At several spots we climbed on or around the crest, in the 5.7 range, with wild exposure. It took a little less than four hours on the ridge to the main summit, and the Northeast Buttress alone is worth the trip. From the main summit we descended northwest on a steep and scary talus-covered ridge for 100', turned north, and downclimbed to a notch via exposed 4th and easy 5th class. Continuing, we stayed on or slightly north of the ridge until we got to the base of a smaller summit 150' horizontally from the main summit. This wild section was one of the many highlights of the traverse. On the second half of the main-to-west-summit traverse the exposure was the same, but the climbing turned into a class 4 "walk on the wild side." From the west summit we continued toward the southwest summit on mediocre but easy rock to where the ridge narrowed, and the rock quality tested our nerves. Avoiding the ridge on the north side at times, we eventually got to a greenish tower that had a fresh-looking breakout zone on its north side. We crossed to the south side, where the terrain mellowed, and bivied next to a snow patch just below the crest and above the Isella Glacier. From the bivy site we descended the next morning, in blustery conditions, toward a notch at around 9,000'. This notch forms the top of a 1,000-foot couloir, which is used for the Isella Glacier route. From the notch we continued on easy ridges and ledges, until the steepening south face forced us onto the ridge. We followed the ridge until an obvious talus-filled gully on the north side let us make quick progress. The terrain stayed easy and guided us around to the south side. Toward the end we traversed under a steep wall, until easy terrain let us proceed to the summit. From the southwest summit we descended easy, but somewhat dangerous, ledges down to the upper snowfields of the Isella Glacier. From here we traversed high on the Isella Glacier toward the Southeast (a.k.a. Holden) Ridge and a chimney that leads up to the saddle on that ridge. The chimney went at about 5.7 (near its start) on solid rock with loose surface stones. We belayed a full pitch that got us to easy fourth class terrain, which led to the col. A long rappel then brought us to the safety of the Mary Green Glacier, from which we reached our ascent route. The route is a full Cascadian adventure in a spectacular setting. You get to climb on an exposed ridge at over 9,000' for many hours, which is rare in the Cascades. Total time from Lake Holden to Lake Holden was about 19 hours.

MARTIN VOLKEN

Mt. Formidable. The complete East Ridge follows the crest from the Spider–Formidable Col to the summit. *Martin Volken*

Mt. Formidable, complete East Ridge. On July 30 Kurt Buchwald and I completed the ridgecrest traverse (IV 5.7) from the Spider-Formidable Col to the summit of Mt. Formidable. From the Spider-Formidable col at 7,350', we moved northwest and around a rotten tower on the left into the first notch, to get onto better rock. We then climbed generally near the crest to a flat, easy ridge. Next we climbed a blocky ridge on good rock, generally staying a bit north of the crest to the top of a first distinct tower. Then a rappel (or downclimb) was made into the next notch on the north side of the ridge, reaching a spot at the base of a two-pitch headwall, which leads toward the distinct summit that we called the "Two County Summit" (Chelan and Skagit). Climbing the two-pitch headwall (5.6 or 5.7) slightly north of the ridge, we found good rock and awesome ambiance. An easy but exposed blocky ridge brought us to the Two County Summit. Climbing over small towers, we gained horizontal, walkable terrain with stunning exposure and continued down easily to the next notch (first ideal bailout spot to the south). We continued up a steep, narrow tower with exposure and good rock. We next encountered a series of lofty gendarmes that involved steep rappels, which made for slower going and harder bailouts. Eventually we gained the notch that leads to a distinct summit just east of the Formidable Glacier (another north or south bailout option). From the Formidable Glacier col we stayed on the crest, crossing over the subsummit (not very good rock) to the summit proper, which didn't present any new challenges. This last section takes a little longer than the southern ledges described in the Beckey guide, but the scenery is wild and the rock good. We descended the summit ridge a short way and then a distinct couloir heading south. The route can be split into three sections: section one goes from the Spider-Formidable col to the Two County Summit. Section two goes from that summit to the Formidable Glacier. Section three goes from the Formidable Glacier to the summit. The second section is certainly the most complex and time-consuming, even though the hardest climbing occurs on the way to the Two County Summit. The ridge is about 2km long, involves a lot of exposed 4th- and easy 5th-class climbing, and offers pitches of 5.6 to 5.7 in the center section. We spent 11 hours moving from the Col to the summit of Formidable and approximately 13 hours from camp to camp. It resembles the Torment-Forbidden traverse in many ways. The route features more complicated ups and downs than the T-F traverse, but it is more reasonable to bail in two or three places.

MARTIN VOLKEN

The 1,100-foot Witch Doctor Wall of Exfoliation Dome, showing Voodoo Wall on the left, and Solaris on the right. *Dave Burdick*

Witch Doctor Wall, Voodoo Wall and Solaris. The summer saw two aid climbs put up on Exfoliation Dome's 1,100' Witch Doctor Wall in the Darrington area. The Voodoo Wall (IV 5.10 A2), established by David Burdick and Michael Swanicke, starts on stepped ledges 400 feet uphill from the original 1969 route. The climb then follows a series of steep left-facing flakes and corners for seven pitches to the ridge crest. A moderate amount of nailing is required, though most of the route consists of clean aid and free climbing.

David Whitelaw, Chris Greyell, and Mark Hanna established Solaris (IV 5.10b A2+), a slightly longer and more sustained climb featuring a long and elegant offwidth, as well as many sections of thin nailing. Solaris is located 200 feet to the right of the Voodoo Wall. Both routes are equipped with bolted chain belays and are featured in the new guidebook *Rattle & Slim: Darrington Selected Rock Climbs.*

DAVID BURDICK

Little Big Chief Mountain, Falcon Route. Jeff Hansell and I made this new route (IV 5.9) on September 10, 2001. Little Big Chief Mountain is located in the seldom-visited Summit Chief Valley in the North Central Cascades. The Summit Chief Valley is a tributary of the Middle Fork of the Snoqualmie River Valley. The route is never really hard, but is remote and demands a variety of alpine skills. From the end of the Middle Fork Valley Road, hike up the valley for about three hours. At a small steel bridge, leave the trail and hike cross-country in a southerly direction to the entrance of the Summit Chief Valley. The objective should be visible on the east side of the valley. Hike up into the Summit Chief Valley until you reach the flat gravel wash at about 4,650'. There are great low-impact camp spots.

From camp ascend a talus field for 900 feet to the base of the route at a prominent left-trending gully. Follow this for 50 feet; move right to a dead tree. Go up and right to another dead tree and continue to easier terrain. Ascend sloping heather benches to the prominent right-trending ramp and follow it to the beginning of difficulties, just left of the prominent chimney. The first pitch features an undercling to the right (5.8). On the second pitch, climb a groove for 60 feet, then move left onto a rib and into another groove. On pitch four climb a steep headwall (5.9) to yet another groove. Follow this groove on pitches five and six (5.7/5.8) to easy terrain and a big ledge, which is at the elevation of the top of the prow to your left. Pitch seven trends slightly right to a ridge near the summit crest. On pitch eight keep traversing right on exposed rock to the crest (5.7). Class 4 climbing on the narrow ridge leads to the 7,225' summit.

Descend the ridge to the south for several hundred feet, then turn left and gain a pocket glacier. Go down the pocket glacier and trend left over glacier-polished slabs. Keep trending left and reach the ridge crest at 5,400'. One to two rappels then take you back into the Summit Chief Valley. Continue trending left, follow goat ledges, then descend through steep forest to camp.

MARTIN VOLKEN

Blockhouse, East Face Route. On June 14 Ron Cotman and I completed an aesthetic, complicated route on the Blockhouse's east face, in Leavenworth's Cashmere Crags group, accessed by the Hook Creek drainage in the Icicle Canyon. Our original ascent took three days and seven belays, due to hand-drilling and technical aid sections, but a competent party should be able to complete the ascent in a day or two and only five pitches. A few sections were originally aided due to the need for cleaning cracks for gear placements, but could probably be repeated free by a competent party.

Approach toward the gully between the Blockhouse and the Crocodile Fang. The route starts just a few feet up from a large tree, with a short traverse onto a ledge (5.9) and a move up into a black corner (C1) that ends at a ledge. Pitch two climbs to another ledge and past a large flake to a bolt (A1 or 5.10). Climb above the bolt to the base of a hand crack. Pass the belay bolt and climb the crack to an exposed traverse left on a large ledge. Pitch three climbs the crack past a small roof (C1) and continues leftward past the roof to a crack (A2+). Climb the crack trending leftward to a tree snag (A2+). The fourth pitch climbs up past a large loose block into a slot chimney (5.9) and face climbs up and right to the base of a corner (5.10). The fifth pitch climbs the corner (5.10) to the base of a headwall. Climb the headwall (A1) and a short free section at the top. Grade III 5.10 A2+. Bring a large rack, to 4", that includes knifeblades, Bugaboos, angles, and Lost Arrows and bring two ropes for rappels. Descend the route via tricky rappels, at the tree snag continuing to a station 150 feet below.

TONY BENTLEY

Dragontail Peak, first winter ascent of Serpentine Ridge. Ade Miller (Alpine Club, U.K.) and I climbed Dragontail Peak (8,840') by the popular summer line The Serpentine Ridge on March 13, 2004. The route starts with a single pitch ice smear (AI3) to a snowfield traverse and two mixed pitches to the ledge below the 5.8 twin cracks, approximately following the summer line. From this point we climbed the rock of the summer route. Several pitches of 5.7 and 5.8 climbing with some aid moves (A0) led to a moderately angled iced up crack, which proved to be the crux of the route. The climbing above this point eased, and several areas of unpleasant loose rock in the summer were covered by snow making the upper section of the route very enjoyable. The final short rock pitch to the summit was easily skirted to the left via a short snow gully (4th class in summer). We summited just before dark after twelve and a half hours on the route and descended back to our bivy site via Asgard Pass.

ALASDAIR TURNER

Mt. Snoqualmie, North Face, first free ascent and speed ascent of New York Gully. Thanks to a weak snow year and cold temperatures in January and February, N.Y.G. received more ascents over a few weeks than the handful it's seen since its first ascent by Jim Ruche and Bob Cotter in February 1991. This 1,300-foot alpine line was climbed originally at grade IV 5.8 A2 WI4, with most teams bypassing the final aid pitch via an unconsolidated snow ramp to the right or a snow-covered 5.7 face to the left. On February 13 Andreas Schmidt and I, both from Seattle, left the car at 7:50 a.m., with hopes for an under-eight-hour car-to-car ascent and a free climb of the aid finish. Prior teams experienced sloppy post-holing on the approach and downclimb, making for a long day. We lucked out with a hard snowpack and gained the 1,100-foot flank of the Phantom Slide in 35 minutes, stashed our packs, and dropped over and down the northwest ridge for 500 feet to the base of the gully. We simul-climbed the first 700 feet of easy 5th class over snow-and-ice-covered rock to the base of a long chimney/corner. For two pitches, excellent climbing up frozen moss, and blocks connected by thin, insipient ice smears allowed us to move fast with good protection. On the final pitch Andreas quickly worked the crux, starting with a perfect 15-foot crack that pinched down to a bottomed corner, exposing just enough ice for delicate movement. Dry-tooling and clipping fixed pins for pro, he finished the pitch in no time, feeling the moves to be around M5+/6-. After Andreas brought me up for our standard cheesy high-five, we glissaded in 10 minutes down just-firm-enough snow to our packs—only to discover that one of my tools had popped out of my pack. Just great. Andreas snickered, knowing how I despise hiking, especially when it's brought on by my own gaucherie. He quickly made it back to my SUV to punch the clock at 12:22 p.m., while I scorned myself for having to climb back up 500 feet to retrieve my tool. Small price, I guess, for such a great outing in Washington's illusive winter alpine conditions.

ROGER STRONG, *Seattle, Washington*

California

YOSEMITE VALLEY

Yosemite Valley, various activity. The big news in the Valley this year, once again, was the freeing of big wall routes, specifically on El Capitan. While this activity has become more popular, the usual suspects remain at the forefront. Yuji Hirayama continued his quest to be the first person to onsight one of the big free climbs. He's onsighted 5.13 on Washington Column and Sentinel Rock, but never a complete route on El Cap. Hirayama tried to onsight the Salathé in 1998, but took three falls. This year he attempted El Niño (30 pitches, 5.13c or 5.14a, two falls, fifth free ascent, five days) and Golden Gate (41 pitches, 5.13b, three falls, third free ascent, two days). While he fell just short of the onsights, he did complete the free ascents of both routes. A route that eluded Hirayama's free attempts was Lurking Fear, whose crux slab pitches have baffled all but Tommy Caldwell and Beth Rodden. Hirayama had to be satisfied with the speed record on Lurking Fear. Climbing with Nick Fowler, he led the entire route, and they topped out in 3h04m. Hirayama used short-fixing techniques, as on most aid speed climbs, but he'd free climb mid-5.12 cracks with 60 feet of slack, while Nick jugged. He didn't self-belay, save for the short-fixed rope. Hirayama brought no piece larger than for hand-size cracks and led the notorious 100-foot fist crack without one piece of gear.

The Huber brothers were once again pushing the boundaries, with a visionary effort to free the Zodiac—the first radically steep route on El Cap to go free. It didn't fall easily, though, as the Hubers worked on it all spring without success. Like Yuji, they consoled themselves with the speed record (2h31m20s—the fastest ascent of any grade VI on El Cap), continuing the trend of cutting-edge free climbing to annihilate previous marks that primarily used aid techniques. They pushed the boundaries further than Hirayama and Fowler by constant use of short-fixing. When the second arrived at the short-fixed anchor, the leader would immediately short-fix the rope again, no matter where he was, frequently using a single piece of protection as the short anchor, thus combining 5.13 climbing with radically dangerous aid techniques.

The Hubers returned in October to complete a continuous free ascent, utilizing a number of variations, including a start that doesn't really join the route until the sixth pitch. This leads one to wonder what it means to free a route and where the true free crux of the Zodiac lies (hint: it's within the first six pitches). Their route should be known as the Free Zodiac, like the free variations to the Nose and the Salathé.

Tommy Caldwell, still interested in freeing big walls, had two impressive ticks. Climbing with his wife Beth Rodden, he freed every pitch on the West Buttress of El Cap, though not in a single push. Matt Wilder had previously freed all but one pitch and had, according to Caldwell, already freed the hardest pitch, at 5.13c. Rodden was stopped just short of a free ascent by one of those pesky offwidths, this one 5.12c. Caldwell, climbing with Topher Donahue, also nabbed the second (or third, if we count Alex and Thomas separately) free ascent of the Zodiac shortly after the Hubers.

Jim Herson finally consummated his multiyear love affair, some would say obsession, with the Salathé Wall. After numerous attempts with various partners, Herson became the fifth person to free-climb the route. While he did have to break the headwall into three pitches, ala Piana-Skinner, he became the only person to lead the crux 5.13c 19th pitch in a single go.

All other free ascents either broke up this pitch or avoided it via the Bermuda Dunes' offwidths.

Half Dome saw more free attention this year, and the original 5.11d rating for the ZigZags is apparently a sandbag. First, Micah Dash and David Bloom made possibly the first all-free (entire team) one-day ascent. Dash rated the last ZigZag pitch at 5.12b/c or "Boulder Canyon 5.13b." Dash and Bloom climbed the Higbee Hedral (5.12a) to bypass the bolt ladder and pendulum of the Robbins Traverse.

El Niño, the Huber's free variation to the North American Wall, drew attention besides Hirayama's ascent, and saw a change in the rating. A broken hold on an upper pitch turned that pitch into the crux, and Iker Pou first free climbed it at 5.14a while sending the rest of the route free. Steve Schneider and Brian Cork, with support from Schneider's wife Heather Baer, also freed the route, using a new four-pitch 5.13a variation to avoid the upper troublesome pitch.

Nick Martino continued his impressive speed climbing. With Renan Ozturk he joined the elite group of people to link the Nose and the Northwest Face of Half Dome in less than 24 hours. Ammon McNeely and Ben Vander Klooster broke the speed record on Wet Denim Daydream on the west face of the Leaning Tower. They did the A4 route in 5h6m40s, onsight, and car-to-car in eight hours.

New routes this year included Nick Fowler's Hard Farm Labor (IV 5.12?), an eight-pitch route left of The Rostrum. The original line hasn't gone free, but James Adamson freed a 5.11c variation to the sixth pitch. Adamson called the route "a real gift."

Eric Kohl was once again solo, once again on the Falls Wall (in autumn, when Yosemite Falls is dry), and, once again rated a route PDK (Pretty Damn Klaus). Does this guy need to learn a new tune? The most memorable pitch of the new route, called Witching Hour, involved 27 consecutive heads.

Higher Cathedral Rock saw lots of new route action. Rob Miller put up Gemini on the beautiful shield feature to the left of the Northeast Buttress. Jon Blair, Mark Garbarini, and Bryan "Coiler" Kay put up The Wild Apes' Route (V 5.9 A3+), which starts left of Mary's Tears and angles up right to the striking Banana Chute, just left of the Crucifix. It finishes out the Gravity Ceiling, which was partially free-climbed by Cedar Wright at 5.13a. The entire route has not gone free. On the north face of Higher Cathedral Rock, Kay teamed with Josh Thompson and Jamie Mundo to create The High Life (V 5.9 A3), an 11-pitch route.

On Washington Column, between the Great Slab Route and the Bad Wall, Kay and Thompson put up Tora Bora (V 5.9 A3+).

Finally in the new route arena, Ammon McNeely, with his brother Gabriel and his son Austin, linked Shortest Straw to Surgeon General to the Zodiac, including two new pitches. They named the route Jose Memorial Variation in honor of Jose Pereyra and Joe Crowe, who both perished in climbing accidents. Austin, at 13 years of age, becomes the youngest person involved in a first ascent on El Capitan.

Previously unreported is route activity in the Ribbon Falls area by Sean Jones and friends in recent years. The two outstanding routes are Gates of Delirium (19 pitches, V 5.12c) and Sky People linked to Persephone Butterfly (17 pitches, V 5.11d). Delirium is no harder than 5.11d after the crux entry pitch, and only two pitches are harder than 5.11b. The route is reportedly high-quality crack climbing, and fixed anchors up to the top of the tenth pitch allow for rappelling the route or continuing to the summit.

BILL WRIGHT, *AAC, Satan's Minions Scrambling Club*

Ribbon Falls area, new routes. Nearly a decade after the passing of my father, I was searching for the ideal place to put a route up in his honor, and so my journey to Ribbon Falls began. On Father's Day 2000 I hiked to the top, camped, and started in on the headwall, a 300-foot steep, golden wall littered with unclimbed cracks. A strip of forest separates the headwall from the 1,700-foot wall below. From this trip and many others we ended up with 17 pitches, ranging from 5.10a to 5.12a. The routes include Harold (5.11b), White Eagle Woman (5.10a), The Dreaming Tree (5.12a), Zeus (5.10c), Paiute Pride (5.10b), Universal Garden (5.11d), and Persephone Butterfly (5.11d). Partners included Tucker Tech, Blair Dixson, Boone Jones, Lonnie Kauk, and Brian Ketron. This wall became dedicated to an array of people, past and present.

In spring 2001 I went to the bottom of the amphitheatre with Phil Kettner and established Sky People, a 14-pitch Grade V 5.11d. The route went onsight and has only one protection bolt. Pro includes doubles to 2" and one each to 4". The climbing on Sky People is comparable to Sentinel, similar to the Chouinard-Herbert. It takes you to the forested ledge, giving you a choice of the exits listed above. Combining Sky People with any of the upper routes, you get 17 pitches in about 2,000 feet.

I then turned my focus to the right side of the amphitheatre. Jake Jones and I aided the 1,000-foot corner up the right side of the

Sean Jones repeating his new route, Gates of Delirium. *Shawn Reader*

golden fin to inspect the potential for a new free route. After 1,000 feet it became apparent that the route would go, as it there joins Keel Haul, East Portal Route, and Solar Power Arête routes. Knowing that these routes go at 5.9, we descended, headed home, and waited for the weather to cooperate.

We returned on November 18, 2002, and in 10 hours redpointed our new route, The Gates of Delirium (V 5.12c). It is 19 pitches long, with pro including wires and double cams to 2", one each to 4-1/2". The route has fixed anchors for the first 10 pitches, to allow for retreat if you don't summit. These 10 pitches are similar to The Rostrum or Astroman. The second half of the route kicks back in angle and becomes more of a scenic adventure, for a total length of about 2,200 feet.

The technical crux comes on pitch one, a 5.12 houdini funk corner into a 5.11d finger crack. Lots of 5.10 jamming and stemming fill the middle of the route. Pitch eight may prove to be the real crux for some, a burly 5.10c offwidth. Pitch nine offers a steep chimney into 5.11b finger-and-stemming section and an incredible belay atop the fin. The 5.11d 10th pitch is wild and steep, and projects you out over the route below. This steep pitch is capped by a bombay chimney and another 5.11 crux of flared fingers and stemming. With the harder climbing behind you, 1,200 feet of 5.9 and under takes you to the summit.

The views and exposure on these routes are amazing. In three years and many trips back I've seen no one, only ravens and a million rainbows. Oh the rainbows…maybe I have seen someone after all.

SEAN JONES

El Capitan, West Buttress, first free ascent; Free Zodiac, second free ascent. I get more obsessed with Yosemite every year. No matter how many times I see El Cap, my palms sweat and my heartbeat quickens. I spend hours examining its cracks, contours, and faces. Someday my energy will focus elsewhere, but for now I thrive on El Cap.

In spring 2003 my wife Beth Rodden and I decided to try to free climb the West Buttress. Steve Schneider had attempted it as a free climb many years ago, and Matt Wilder had been working on it the previous spring. It is an obvious weakness and therefore a candidate for a free climb. In early May Beth and I headed up for a one-day recon. The climbing went smoothly until early afternoon. As I led out the 200-foot traverse of pitch 11, clouds came out of nowhere. Within 10 minutes we were in a downpour, and for several hours were pounded by sleet and rain. Just before hypothermia set in we managed to traverse to nearby Lurking Fear and rappel to the ground. We ended the day exhausted and humbled, wondering if we should ever go up on the big stone again.

As adventure climbers know, the pain soon faded, and within a few days we were starting up again. We projected the climb for six weeks. Beth redpointed the crux pitches, but it became clear that at this speed we would not be able to finish the climb within our allotted time. She traded her chalk bag for jumars and supported me to the top.

I later learned that Matt Wilder had done more than just attempt the route; he had nearly completed the first free ascent. He had established some improbable free variations and equipped and cleaned the route for free climbing. In short, he put a hell of a lot of work into it and deserves more credit for the first free ascent than I do. When I learned about Matt's efforts I felt horrible. New free routes on El Cap are like gold, and I felt like I had stolen it from him. I contacted him, explained, and told him that I was sorry. He said that there were no hard feelings and he was glad we had a good time on the climb.

I had aid climbed Zodiac with my dad in early October. We passed the Huber brothers, who were working on the first free ascent. The free climbing in the middle of the route looked like some of the wildest climbing I had ever seen. I made plans to return over Thanksgiving with my friend Topher Donahue. With good weather I was able to free-climb the route over six days. Topher free-climbed all but three pitches. On both of my 2003 El Cap free-climbs, I climbed with partners who hoped to free-climb the routes. In both cases they abandoned their free-climbing goals to ensure that I was successful. I can't believe how lucky I am to have such great friends.

TOMMY CALDWELL, *AAC*

El Capitan, Zodiac, warp speed and free variation. After an exploratory ascent in spring 2002 with Valley local Ammon McNeely, I knew that the Zodiac could be climbed free. In spring 2003 my brother Thomas and I started working to free-climb it. We succeeded in doing all the moves free on a variation, but failed to do a continuous redpoint ascent. We planned to return in the fall to complete the redpoint, but did not leave before setting the speed record. After ascents in 4h07m and 3h08m, we climbed the Zodiac in 2h31m20s. This time was made possible by rigorous short fixing-tactics.

The continuous redpoint ascent finally happened at the beginning of October. In our quest for cooler conditions, however, we made one serious miscalculation: Zodiac gets no afternoon shade in the fall. We could only climb the friction-intensive crux pitches in early morning or late evening, when the sun was below the rim. This resulted in serious ledge time, the consumption of several books, and 68 hours needed for the redpoint—though the time spent actually climbing was no more than 18 hours.

Typical of El Cap routes, several sections of the original aid line did not go free. Our free variation begins 60m right of Zodiac, in the gray rock, and links various corners and ramps to meet Zodiac after four pitches. Another variation avoids the long bolt ladder on Zodiac's fifth pitch. This variation rejoins the original just before the short bolt ladder of the sixth pitch. The free crux lies in the heart of the Gray Circle, an El Cap landmark and the route's most conspicuous feature. The third Circle pitch involves a holdless 5.13+ stemming corner. Next comes the route's crux, the 5.13d Nipple pitch, so named for the arching fingertip pin-scar undercling that runs out the overhanging main wall and culminates at a point, the Nipple, where the crack widens abruptly to four inches, ending the difficulties. After that the doors are open, and the free line, more or less, follows the original line to the top.

ALEXANDER HUBER, *Germany*

SIERRA NEVADA

Ruby Wall Cirque, Boom Town and Billy from the Hills. In June 2000 Jason Lakey and I completed a new route in the Ruby Wall Cirque in Little Lakes Valley above Rock Creek Lake. We climbed the main formation right of the descent gully used for Pteradon. [The third tower, with the second tower hosting the route Pteradon and the first being the main Ruby Wall—Ed.] Our route, Boom Town (IV 5.10b), was done ground-up, onsight, with no bolts drilled. The pitches are new except the first, where we found a drilled anchor at the ledge where the pitch ends. We were told by Mike Strassman that whoever did the first pitch went no farther. We returned during the summer of 2001 and did a route to the left of Boom Town. This route, Billy from the Hills (IV 5.10b C1), was also done ground-up, onsight, with a few moves of C1 at the end of the first pitch. We swung leads on both of the nine-pitch routes, using a 70m rope for both ascents. Two ropes are required for the descent for an overhanging 60m rappel to exit the gully. Rumor has it that Boom Town was the first route to have summited the formation.

DAVID LANE, *AAC*

Mt. Mills, Northwest Ridge. Jackie Carroll and I climbed this spectacular ridge in an unintended two-day push from Rock Creek Lake. From Mills Lake we crested the North Ridge of Mt. Mills, only to find that our dog had followed us over 4th class ground. Sending her back to camp, we crossed the ridge and descended via one rappel into the Fourth Recess. We crossed Fourth Recess and began Mills's northwest ridge where the divide between the Fourth and Third Recesses meet the ridge. (One could add to the adventure by starting the ridge between this point and Third Recess Peak, undoubtedly a Grade V, or climb one of the Grade IV's on Third Recess Peak to access the ridge.) Airy class 5 climbing led over several gendarmes and knife-edge arêtes for many pitches, including an exposed 5.8 overhanging mantle. Beyond several large towers, a gap in the ridge required a short rappel. We thought the ridge would become easier, but no. Exposed climbing on the north side of the ridge (and a tunnel inside the ridge) past snow-covered ledges and ice-filled cracks found us below the summit plateau at nightfall. Without sleeping bags, food, or water, we shivered the night away in below-freezing temperatures, summiting at 8 a.m. the next day. We descended the chute to the north of the standard 3rd class route, which we found horribly loose and sandy for a standard route, necessitating belays and short-roping. The dog greeted us at the base after spending an epic night on the north ridge, and we arrived in camp at sunset the following day. We rated the route IV 5.8. Total number of pitches was around 20.

MIKE STRASSMAN, *AAC*

Birch Mountain, north ridge, attempt and tragedy. I had scoped out a line on this long ridge and questioned Sierra veteran Doug Robinson as to whether it had been ascended. He became secretive, and, probing further, I discovered that he also intended to make the first ascent that spring. We decided to do it together, but I live in the eastern Sierra and he doesn't, so I went without him. On the first attempt we didn't even leave the car, as a spring snowstorm had the ridge looking like K2. The second attempt, with Cindy Springer, showed what a long winter it had been. One look at the slog up the 2,000 feet of talus from base camp turned that trip into a reconnaissance. On the third attempt, in mid-July, I was in better shape and had enlisted the rope-gun talents of mountain guide Seth Dilles. A last-minute addition to the party was Keith Kramer, a long-time big-wall partner of Seth's from Yosemite. I feared that three on a rope might make the ridge a difficult undertaking to achieve in one day, but Seth felt that Keith was strong enough and experienced enough to move quickly. A recent fire had made the approach up Birch Creek relatively easy, but the 2,000-foot talus slog was another matter. Keith began exhibiting classic signs of altitude sickness, and we urged him to rest and drink water. After he vomited several times we suggested that descent was the best medicine and offered to lead him back to a meadow at 10,000'. He assured us he could make it down, and his footing seemed strong and balanced as he walked down the talus. This was the last time we saw Keith Kramer.

We started to fix the first pitch, an overhanging crack, and Seth took a stout fall, and he too vomited. The altitude didn't seem to be affecting any of us benevolently. We bivied at the base and woke up before sunrise to attack the ridge. The first 10 pitches were high Sierra granite at a moderate grade. We saw smoke in the meadow below and could hear Keith yelling words of encouragement, so we figured he was all right. After ascending the first tower in 13 pitches, we realized that we were only a third of the way up the ridge and would not make the summit by nightfall. We retreated via two shaky rappels, tricky downclimbing, and traversing two ridges to the west. Out of food and water, we found a waterfall, then were dumped on by an afternoon storm, just as we found a comfortable cave. We arrived at the base of the ridge at sunset and quickly made our way down the talus to the meadow, where a stick in the ground assured us that Keith had been there and was surely on his way down. But upon arriving at the car at 2 a.m., it was obvious that Keith had not made it out. We searched the lower reaches of the canyon until dawn, and then called Search and Rescue. Keith was found the following day tangled in the willows of the creek. The coroner ruled the cause of death as exposure. Keith Kramer was a jovial man who was well-known in the Mammoth Lakes community for his crazy antics and light heart. He will be sorely missed. Seth Dilles, Doug Robinson, and I intend to climb the ridge in spring 2004, name it for Keith Kramer (K2), and spread his ashes from the summit.

MIKE STRASSMAN, *AAC*

East Fuller Butte, Walking with Walt. After three false starts over 18 months, two due to 110°+ summer temperatures and one due to a "10% chance of light, scattered showers" that turned into a blizzard in September 2002, Sigrid and Lynnea Anderson, Kenny Rose, and I finally completed this route (V 5.10d C2) in mid-October 2003. This route features 11 pitches of enjoyable, clean rock in the wilderness setting of the upper San Joaquin River and has fine views of the upper San Joaquin River Gorge and the Sierra high country. It also features a one-hour downhill approach, a mostly level one-hour return, and a year-round spring at the base of the climb. Although the free-climbing is rated 5.10d, and

East Fuller Butte. The route follows the left skyline and the bottom 400 feet are hidden by the trees. *Jerry Anderson*

much of the route either does or will go free, there is no mandatory free-climbing over 5.5. We used three Lost Arrows on each of the first two pitches, but after a few ascents the route should go entirely clean, and all but pitch eight are C1. The route was named for the late Walt Shipley.

The climb begins several hundred feet downhill and to the left of the Fred Beckey Southeast Face Route (IV 5.8 A2), done in 1972. It starts just right of a small left-facing corner and follows a perfect, straight-in, right-arching crack leading to a large left-facing corner system. From there the route follows the only possible line. There is a poor bivy ledge for three or four people at the end of the fourth pitch, but excellent por-

Let's see, where does the route go? Perfect Sierra granite on East Fuller Butte. *Jerry Anderson*

taledge bivies at the end of pitches five and seven. Please check with the Sierra National Forest North Fork office for possible Peregrine Falcon closures lasting through midsummer. For topo and additional information, e-mail campfour_org@hotmail.com.

JERRY ANDERSON, *AAC*

The Obelisk, Far Out and other new routes. Lucho Rivera and I enjoyed several summer adventures in the rock-climbing wonderland that is the Sierra Nevada. First was a new route on the steep face of the East Ridge of Mt. Russell. The route offered six pitches of continuous, devious 5.10. Clouds moved in throughout the day, and we topped out 10 minutes before a downpour. Psyched by our route on Mt. Russell and our repeats of classics on The Incredible Hulk, we wanted to explore other rock formations of the Sierra. We somewhat arbitrarily settled on The Obelisk, a free-standing dome overlooking Kings Canyon. Without a topographic map or accurate directions, we were off-route from the get-go and tacked five miles onto the 12-mile approach. What we thought would be a one-day approach took two days. When we finally arrived we were disappointed to see that most of the obvious lines on The Obelisk had been done, but, after consulting the guidebook, we realized the steepest face had not been climbed. The giant roof 200 feet from the summit looked like it would require aid, but I have had enough experience to know that you never know if something is free-climbable until you're there, so the next day Lucho and I went for it. We carried a hammer and a few pins in case the upper bit required aid. Each pitch had a meant-to-be feel to it, with smooth and golden footholds and edges appearing where and when they were needed. After five classic crack and dihedral pitches, we were at the base of the roof. I cleared rocks from the stance and called for the hammer and pins so that I could get protection

was mostly 5.4 with occasional 5.8 moves. Threatening clouds, our diminishing supply of bolts, and routefinding challenges kept the adventure level high. We rapped the route, finishing with not much light left. This route could become popular.

Brian Smoot

Zion, new routes and speed ascents. I was fortunate in 2003 to have good partners and lots of climbing time in Zion N.P. My season started on February 15. My partner Ammon McNeely and I arrived in the park Saturday morning after working late on a rigging job Friday night. Saturday afternoon we hiked to the base of the Streaked Wall and climbed two or three "approach" pitches, arriving at the luxurious Rubicon Ledge well after dark. The next morning we woke and made the first one-day ascent of Latitudes (VI 5.9 A4+), in 18 hours and 40 minutes. Paul Gagner, of the first-ascent party, was helpful with approach and descent information. I feel this speed ascent is as noteworthy as any other big wall alpine ascent that I know of. The size and technical difficulty of this wall brought us one step closer to achieving fast ascents on the hardest routes in the big mountains of the world.

Ball and Chain's crux. *Andrew McGarry*

Two weeks later Ammon and I attempted to climb five Zion walls in a day. Our achievement was cut short by fatigue, darkness, and cold, but we were successful on three walls that day, all in record time. We first climbed Prodigal Sun (V 5.8 C2) in 2:36. (Thank you to Ron Olevsky for the first ascent. I believe first ascensionists are not appreciated enough for their efforts.) From the summit of Angel's Landing we ran to the top of Moonlight Buttress (V 5.10 C1), rappelled, and climbed Moonlight in 1:57. I apologize to the party that was high on Moonlight filming a video for obcenities I uttered. I point out to the public that the trade routes in Zion see a lot of traffic, and rock and anchors must often be shared. Expect traffic jams on trade routes—you won't be disappointed if you don't find them. Ammon and I finished with an ascent of Lunar Ecstacy (V 5.9 C2+) in 4:09. We were out of gas after rapping Moonlight again, in the dark, and opted for burritos at the local Bit and Spur.

I worked on the FFA of the seven-pitch Ball and Chain on Angel's Landing during September weekends. This work finally came to fruition October 1. The route was free-climbed except for having to stand on the belay from the fifth anchor. There were three 5.12+ pitches in a row, with each pitch requiring mastery of a different technique. I added three bolts to the route but none to the existing aid path.

On October 12 Ammon and I climbed Spaceshot in 1:36:54. This left us time to get to town and attend our friends Dean and Jill's wedding. In 37:14 during the next two days Ammon, Kurt Arend, and I did a new hard route on the right side of Angel's Landing. This route was named South of Heaven (VI 5.8 A4+), and has six pitches: A4, A3+, 5.8 A2, A3, A4+, and 5.5. Hole count: five for belays, four for protection, one Threader.

In December I came back to the park with Kurt and did a new route up the center of Red Arch Mountain. This route, eyeballed by many over the years, is now a reality. It is named Red Awakening (VI 5.7 A4+) and starts left of center up a bushy, dirty section to a small, open pad, continuing up the face via cracks and thin seams under the impressive red arch. The massive roof, climbed with knifeblades, is not to be missed. The steep next pitch did not offer the features we hoped for and accounted for a lot of holes. Six belay holes and 43 lead holes were drilled in the eight pitches (5.7, A1, 5.6 A1, A3, A4+, A3+, A4, and 5.6 A4). For topos and in-depth stories about these ascents, visit Ammon's site www.rocknrun.net or Zion Rock and Mountain Guides in Springdale.

BRIAN MCCRAY

Colorado

Rocky Mountain National Park, rapid ascents and enchainments. On the Diamond of Long's Peak in early July, Tommy Caldwell and Topher Donahue climbed five routes, totaling 30 guidebook pitches, in 23 hours car-to-car (probably the most routes climbed on the Diamond in a day), in the process doubling the number of Diamond routes Caldwell has climbed. The pair rappelled from Table Ledge to Broadway, where they had food and water, after each route. The five routes were Yellow Wall (5.11a), Pervertical Sanctuary (5.10d), D7 (5.11c), Curving Vine (5.11a/b), and Casual Route (5.10a). Donahue reports, "We climbed on twin ropes and did minimal simul-climbing. We never climbed faster than seemed fun, and although we wanted to see how many routes we could do, we weren't really gunning for a goal or anything. With true speed-climbing tactics it would be possible to squeeze in another one or do our link-up a lot faster."

Also in July Jonny Copp and Kelly Cordes completed what's likely the first enchainment of the three biggest technical rock faces in the park. They climbed the east face of Long's Peak (14,255') via the Crack of Delight (5.7) to the Casual Route (5.10a), with the Forrest Finish (5.9), then the northwest face of Chief's Head (13,579') via Path of Elders (5.9) to Birds of Fire (5.10d), and finally the Central Ramp (5.8) route on the east face of Mt. Alice (13,310'). They tagged each summit, covered about 20 horizontal miles and climbed 28 guidebook pitches (but simul-climbed throughout). Total time from the Long's trailhead to the Wild Basin trailhead was roughly 22 hours, 45 minutes.

In March 2004 Copp and Josh Wharton made the fastest winter ascent of the Diamond, via the most logical winter route, D7. Traveling incredibly light for winter on the Diamond (a single rope, for example), they reached Broadway via the North Chimney, climbed D7 with short-fixing techniques in one block lead, and finished with upper Kiener's route, continuing to the summit and descending the North Face. They returned to the Long's trailhead 14 hours and 17 minutes after leaving—an impressive time even for a summer round-trip.

Compiled from conversations with the climbers

BLACK CANYON OF THE GUNNISON

Cheap Hooker. The Black Canyon hosts some of the country's most adventurous rock climbs and is notorious for epics, runout climbing, difficult route finding, and chossy rock. This past year saw Topher Donahue and I up a few new routes. The Hooker Buttress saw its first ascent in May 1975, by Michael Covington and Billy Westbay, with another route added in 1984, by Katie Cassidy and Earl Wiggins. These routes, The Hooker (IV 5.10+R) and Cheap Shot (V 5.10X), which from the overlooks on both South and North Chasm Views look really impressive, have had only a handful of ascents. The guidebook characterizes these routes as poorly protected, with long runouts, and "hard, consistent, and serious."

Topher and I, lured by these descriptions, hatched a plan to do a new route on the Hooker Buttress. It would take us three tries to complete. We started by rappelling 800 feet off the rim, in between The Hooker and Cheap Shot, to try to see how good the climbing could be. After reaching a ledge under a roof, we set off on our recon. The roof looked large, intimidating, run out, and questionable. Topher climbed a corner out to the lip of the roof at 5.11+ and made a stellar hand-and-face traverse for a 160-foot pitch. The trail rope hung 20 feet out. Two pitches later we ran into the crux 5.12- crack as it started to rain. Topher freed this pitch, having placed two pins in a seam below a thin, technical face, and I finished up in a long, unprotected corner. The top section of the route proved to be on hard granite with incredible exposure and great free-climbing. We returned to try it from the bottom, but only made it up four pitches before we ran out of time and hiked out.

Seven months later we hiked back into the canyon with two gallons of water and clothing for a bivy. The first pitch is a 70m 5.9 corner. On the second pitch traverse on solid crispy edges up a slab, past a bolt, to a technical 5.11 face and a belay below a pegmatite band. Pitch three starts up a corner into a peg band and traverses left for over 100 feet, with only two bolts and a few RPs in peg crystals for pro. It's runout, but you're climbing at the top edge of the pegmatite on solid black 5.9 edges.

Head up a corner on bullet-hard face holds to a cam placement and run out another peg band to a belay. Climbing past a roof and up a corner leads into the third peg band. There is one bolt on this 70-foot-plus 5.9 section, which leads to the main corner of the upper wall. Topher then climbed a stellar 5.10+ corner pitch on the best rock I've seen in the canyon. Battleship-gray, laser-cut sheer granite with bomber gear and excellent face climbing leads to the belay we had rapped to the previous year, and we continued to the top.

This route (V 5.12- [5.9X]) is exceptionally good and well worth the effort. We drilled six bolts, on lead, and left the three pins in place. This 10-pitch route is about 1,700-feet long, not including the 400-foot scrambling approach, and was completed in a day, all free and with no falls, on May 27.

JARED OGDEN

Woke Up Punk. Zack Smith and I climbed a new 10-pitch route in the Black Canyon in the fall. Our route is located in the SOB Gully, in the area between Debutante's Ball and Casual Route. The first three pitches were climbed by Scott Hollander and me in the spring. Woke Up Punk (5.12- PG/R) connects features up the middle of this strip of rock. No bolts were placed, but a pin was fixed on pitch three and at the belay on pitch four. The climbing was on good rock with unique features. The bouldery crux appeared on pitch four. Good second day route for a strong party. Topo can be found at the North Rim ranger station.

JOSH GROSS, *Moab, UT*

Wishmaker, first free ascent. In September Topher Donahue and I masde the first free ascent onsight of Wishmaker (IV 5.11+R [5.10X]), a route just to the right of Lost Cities, in the Hairdo Gully on the north side of the canyon. Pike Howard made the first ascent but aided a few sections and suggested we try to free it. Wishmaker shares its first pitch with Lost Cities, then branches off right into a series of thin cracks and slabby faces. The second pitch follows a diagonal crack to a ledge. The third pitch follows a barn-door crack off a ledge (hard to protect—tiny cams and RPs) to a scary mantle, followed by unprotectable 5.10 climbing. Falling on this pitch is not an option. I suggest that the next party add a bolt. The crux fourth pitch climbs a sustained finger crack leading to a traverse and is a bit runout. The fifth pitch climbs a funky roof slot to a great crack that finishes below a roof on a ledge. Pitch six climbs steep hands-and-fingers to a big ledge. Pitch seven climbs out a roof to a hands crack, traverses a face, and finishes up a corner. We hiked out from here, but you could climb the last four pitches of Lost Cities to the rim. We removed a lot of loose rock, so the route is safer for future parties.

JARED OGDEN

Hallucinogen Wall, free attempt. In September and October I tried to free climb this route twice. On the first attempt, with Mike Shepard, we rapped to pitch 14 and climbed out from the top of pitch 14, all free at 5.12. Pitch 14 is a bolt ladder and will never go free. On the second attempt Topher Donahue and I climbed all free up to pitch five, at 5.11-. From here I led free past three bolts and finished through the pendulum to Fantasy Island using some aid. Topher followed to the pendulum point, lowered to a series of face holds leading left from my free high point, and on top rope climbed across this face to Fantasy Island at 5.12c/d. He then led pitch seven free, at 5.12a. Pitch eight is protected by RPs and rusty fixed heads, so I freed between them, with Topher following free at 5.11+. The next five pitches are A3 heading, hooking, and bolt ladders and will never be free climbed. We found free passage up to pitch nine in a day and rapped. At least future parties know that much of the route can be free-climbed. We didn't add any bolts or change the route in any way.

JARED OGDEN

Charm School Boutique and Dylan Wall free. In spring 2003 Allan Porter and I completed a new line on North Chasm View Wall, beginning on the Journey Home route and finishing on the Cruise, climbing the smooth shield between those two major crack lines. From the large belay ledge at the top of the first pitch of Journey Home, we traversed 60 feet left (reversing a traverse on the Dylan Wall and Highway 61 routes) to a belay stance, putting us at the start of an unclimbed crack system.

The first pitch above the traverse—an overhanging dihedral leading to technical seams and corners, with very thin gear—was 5.12, took several trips to redpoint, and ends at a small belay ledge where we placed the route's only bolt. From the ledge we aided a thin, vertical corner (50 feet of A2+, with a few pins left fixed, the only aid), hand-traversed left, then finished over bulges to another belay. A short corner ended in the biggest blank section on the route, passed via a very long, old-school 5.10+ pitch with runouts and pegmatite. Allan led the last independent pitch late in the day, through a weird-smelling cave and out across a band of roofs to hit the upper Cruise at bolts on the ninth guidebook pitch, 300 feet below the top of the wall.

The name Charm School Boutique comes from a funky women's shop in Glenwood Springs, where you could find all sorts of bizarre and startling things, kind of like our route.

I first saw the line a year or so earlier with Jason Keith, during an ascent of the Dylan Wall. We climbed that route almost all free (the first "near-free" ascent probably was done by Robert Warren in the mid-1990s), and then explored the lower part of the line that would become Charm School. Later, Tracy Martin and I freed the remaining aid on the Dylan Wall (about 10 feet) at 5.12-, traversing off into the gully once we joined the Journey Home. (The first ascent of the Dylan Wall, we learned from Colorado Springs climbers, included the first ascent of all but the first pitch of the popular Journey Home, which is now started much higher in the approach gully.)

Charm School Boutique is a logical direct finish for the Dylan Wall, avoiding the traverse to the Journey Home crack system. On the last of a half dozen forays, involving lots of approaching and retreating in the gully, Allan and I climbed the last of the missing pieces of this line, but the full link-up and 50 feet of aid remains. Done free, the A2+ will probably be hard 5.12, and exciting but passably safe without bolts.

JEFF ACHEY

Wyoming

GRAND TETON NATIONAL PARK

Ice conditions. The most-classic ice routes of Grand Teton National Park melted out for the second year in a row. The Black Ice Couloir on the Grand Teton became unclimbable in the midsummer (2003), and the ice in the Northwest Couloir of Middle Teton was mostly gone as well. Even the usually reliable Enclosure Couloir on the Grand showed gaps near the top. Rangers blamed ongoing drought and eight consecutive weeks of 90-degree heat in the Jackson area for the meltdown.

DOUGALD MACDONALD, *AAC, adapted from www.climbing.com*

Grand Traverse, first winter ascent. On January 24, 2004, after more than three weeks of unseasonably dry and warm weather, two parties set out to complete a long-standing project in the Tetons: the Grand Traverse in winter. Perennial winter activists Renny Jackson and Hans Johnstone set out around 3 a.m., and Stephen Koch and I followed around 3:30. Both parties skied to near Glacier Gulch and climbed couloirs and ramps up the South-southwest shoulder of Teewinot to start the traverse. Renny and Hans set a blistering pace over mostly firm, crusty snow, topping out on Teewinot around 10 a.m. Stephen and I didn't catch up with them until just past the West Prong of Teewinot. The steep, narrow ridge between there and the East Prong of Mt. Owen is some of the trickier terrain on the traverse and was the site of a near miss the previous year when Renny stepped off of a collapsing cornice just in time. The four of us moved together and shared ropes during rappels off the south ridge of Owen into Gunsight Notch and out onto the Grandstand. Hans broke trail into the dark to the top of the Grandstand, where the four of us bivvied just below the North Ridge. One of Renny's boot liners was soaked, and his foot badly needed warming. The next day he had to climb the five technical pitches (up to

5.6) up a variation of the Italian Cracks in bitterly cold conditions with numb toes. He and Hans stopped at the Lower Saddle and availed themselves of a tent and stove from the Climbing Rangers' rescue cache to dry Renny's liner. Stephen and I, with an eye on threatening clouds, pushed on up the Northwest Couloir of Middle Teton, to bivy between the Middle and South Teton. That night a minor storm moved in, with moderate winds and light snow.

The next day Stephen and I hesitantly continued through poor visibility and periods of heavy snow with gusty winds. Hans and Renny spent that day and a second night on the Lower Saddle before completing the Traverse on day four in better weather. Stephen and I bypassed two features, an unnamed hump between Ice Cream Cone and Gilkey's Tower and one of the twin summits on Gilkey's Tower, which Renny and Hans apparently climbed. Stephen and I had carried snowshoes in case my wife, Carina Ostberg, wasn't able to dig up an extra pair for me and stash them in Garnet Canyon. Turns out we needn't have, as the delivery came through, and there were skis waiting at the Platforms in Garnet Canyon. Hans and Renny had cached skis in the Meadows in Garnet Canyon, so neither party had to suffer an ignoble and tedious slog back to the car after a truly satisfying winter foray.

MARK NEWCOMB, *AAC*

Grand Teton, The Golden Pillar and other new Teton free climbs. On July 11 Hans Johnstone and I opened a classic, flashable, hard crack line (V 5.12-) on the golden pillar of overhanging rock west of the normal North Face route on the Grand Teton. The purity of the line, combined with the quality rock and hard climbing, should make this route a Teton classic. Armed for alpine free climbing, Hans and I spiked up the glacier, jumped the 'schrund, chimneyed the remnant snow block, and sprinted under the barrage of stonefall out onto the Grandstand. We 3rd classed to the base of the Golden Pillar and readied ourselves for sustained jamming. After a short 5.7 pitch, we cranked the steep, gold finger-and-hand crack (48m, 5.11b) that still had chalk on it from our 2002 attempt. The crack continues at 5.10b. A step left brings you to the crux: an overhanging corner and fist crack through a roof. Unload the big cams and pump and scum to the lip (45m, 5.12a). The roof pitch deposits you on the first ledge. We followed the normal route to the third ledge. Forty meters east of the Pendulum Pitch we climbed the Rugged Prima Donna Pitch in a shallow left-facing corner. Use your pitons here as you boulder, stem, and lieback to a nice ledge (31m, 5.11aR/X). The last pitch is a classic problem, with bouldering on small crimps into perfect fingerlocks followed by steep stemming and jamming (5.12a). From here it's a wee scramble of 150m to the summit.

On Cathedral Rock in Death Canyon, Evan Howe, Doug Workman, and I established The Fountainhead (IV 5.12a) in September. This 200m route climbs the steep, clean left side of the wall right of Lots Slot. Much ground-up work created a worthy seven-pitch free climb. Also of note is the maturity of Rock Springs Buttress, south of the ski area. It's accessed by aerial tram and is 170m tall, at an altitude of over 9,000'. Rock Springs Buttress could be one of the best new summer crags in the country. Important new routes here include Raspberry Arete (5.12a), Sole Super Power (5.13b), and Zion Storm Trooper (5.12d). A free topo can be found at the Teton Rock Gym in Jackson.

GREG COLLINS

SOUTH FORK OF SHOSHONE RIVER

Needle Mountain, north face. To climb the north face of Needle Mountain (12,106') has long been a goal of mine. After three unsuccessful attempts I finally made it to the top on September 27-28—7,000 feet from the floor of the South Fork's valley near Cody, 3,000-4,000 feet of which were vertical rock and ice.

My previous attempts were in the winter and spring; knowing how difficult access is, I decided to try in the fall. After the first good snow we decided this was our window of opportunity. We had three days of good weather to get up and back down. It was nearly 3,000 feet of bushwhacking before we got to put our harnesses on. The route goes up the east side of the north face, following a chimney system. Most of the route was 3rd classed, climbing runnels of ice and steep rock at a moderate grade.

My partner, Dave Elphingstone of Colorado, and I moved light and fast, packing no sleeping bags or tent, only climbing gear and water. All we packed to eat were Power Bars and GU. We began at 6 a.m. on September 27 and were on top of the peak by 6 p.m.

We were out of water by the time we reached the top, and an alpinist's nightmare became our reality. The stove would not fire up; my bad luck on this mountain was continuing. We worked down the ridgeline for five hours, carrying snow in our helmets and packs, before we found wood for a fire. We rested for a few hours while melting snow and rehydrating. Without sleeping bags or a tent, we had to keep the fire going. We made our way back to the base by the next noon. We were on the move for 30 hours with a few hours' rest. We traveled about 23 miles with over 13,000 feet of elevation gain and loss. The route has a high level of commitment, being so remote. [Further information on this and other routes in the Cody area can be found at: www.coldfear.com.—Ed.]

AARON MULKEY

Idaho

Old Hyndman Peak, Bear/Chicken Variation. Brian Wood and I set out in early October 2000 to explore the northeast face of Old Hyndman Peak in the Pioneer Range for possible early season ice climbs. We bivied at the base of the north ridge and the following morning ascended the ice couloir climbed as part of the 1975 Northeast Face route. We found the couloir in good condition and climbed nearly 1,000 feet of alpine ice up to 65°, with occasional short sections of verglas-covered slabs and an interesting chimney pitch of about M4. At the second major left bend in the couloir, where the 1975 route exits onto fourth-class terrain, Brain and I continued up and left via an icy corner and ramp for one full pitch of sustained mixed climbing, to reach a broad ledge. From this ledge we followed the path of least resistance: ice runnels and steep friable rock, up to 5.9, for five pitches. Protection was difficult to obtain on several of the pitches, and the rock is of poor quality. The rock quality improved for the last two pitches of steep corner-and-crack climbing on the left margin of the northeast face. We descended the East Ridge in the dark and traversed the cirque to the east, ascending two other peaks before finding a reasonable descent back into Wildhorse Canyon. Our route was 2,500 feet long, 5.9 mixed, and took 23 hours round trip from the moraine below the northeast face.

DEAN LORDS

Peak 11, 308', White Line Couloir. In May, Travis Michaelis, Abe Dickerson, and I made the first complete ascent of the 1,200-foot White Line Couloir, on Peak 11,308' (2.3 miles southwest of Borah Peak, in the Lost River Range). I previously climbed just the couloir in 1996 but due to avalanche conditions I descended without reaching the summit. The southwest face of 11,308' is a complex series of towers and couloirs. The White Line ascends the leftmost couloir on this face. The route starts in a chimney on the left edge of the couloir, thus avoiding a large chockstone, before entering the couloir proper. Once in the couloir, 50° snow with short sections of 60° water ice wind upward for 700'. At this point the couloir cuts left, and a steep chimney in the left wall is climbed for a ropelength. This pitch is the crux (M5 WI4+). Continue up the narrow couloir for two more pitches of enjoyable mixed climbing until the top of the ridge is reached. Pass underneath the chockstone and descend 100 feet into the west face bowl. About 800 feet of snow climbing on the extreme right edge of the bowl reaches the summit. We then descended one of the many south couloirs. Travis and Abe confirmed both the difficulty and aesthetics of the route, calling it a sure classic. Ten hours round trip from Whiskey Springs.

DEAN LORDS

Borah Peak, Psycho Therapy. On September 18, following the first major snow of the year, Brian Wood and I established Psycho Therapy (1,200', 5.9+ M6 AI4) on the north face of Borah Peak. This route follows the obvious couloir and black shaft of rock on the far right side of the face. The route starts with two pitches of alpine ice and a few mixed sections, before entering the shaft (a.k.a. Shock Treatment). The shaft is sustained for three pitches and involves steep climbing on icy runnels, snow-covered rock, and two large chockstones. After the second chockstone the angle eases and one and a half pitches of ice and rock in a wild setting finish in a steep notch on the northwest ridge. Brian and I spent 22 hours round trip from the mouth of Rock Creek. With more ice in the shaft, this route could be less difficult.

DEAN LORDS

Borah Peak, where Psycho Therapy follows the obvious shaft. *Dean Lords*

Bell Mountain, Hell's Bells. Brian Wood and I took advantage of a cold spell in early June, 2002, to establish Hell's Bells (1,100 feet) on the northwest face of Bell Mountain in the Lemhi Range. The northwest face is cut by two large gully systems. Hell's Bells ascends the left-hand gully for three pitches of thin ice and easy mixed climbing. The second pitch was the crux, consisting of a thin WI3+ flow, followed by several tricky M4 moves to regain the narrow gully. The third pitch reached a large bowl in the center of the face. From the bowl we climbed up and right for a pitch to reach a buttress. The buttress involved two fun and exposed rock pitches (easy fifth class on solid rock) to reach the north ridge. From the north ridge a few hundred feet of exposed scrambling led to the summit and an easy descent down the southwest gully. Thirteen hours round trip from Basinger Canyon.

DEAN LORDS

Montana

Mt. Brown, Mile of Smiles. The gullies on the lower northwest face of Mt. Brown (8,365'), in Glacier National Park, have become popular early-season climbs. They offer endless WI 2-4 climbing 15 minutes from the road. Many climbers announce they're headed to the summit 5,200 feet above, only to run out of time or energy before they run out of ice. Include me among those suitors, at least until November 2, when everything fell into place. My route took me up the west (right) gully to the prominent falls, through a hidden cleft where the gully forks at 6,200', up the west side of the face above, and out the summit ridge. The 2,500 feet of climbing below the fork consisted of a frozen creek bed and short steps, followed by a 75-foot WI 3+ curtain and nearly 1,000 feet of WI 3 gullies and steps. At the fork, I climbed left up a series of beautiful, narrow pillars to a deep chimney with rotten-looking ice. Lower-angle terrain to the right seemed to offer better ice, but mixed moves on snow-covered rock led onto a series of sloping ledges and steps frosted with thin, brittle ice. The climbing was delicate and committing. My mom would have nightmares, if she knew. The ice eventually improved, and after 200 feet I exited over a short pillar of good ice at 6,900'. The next 1,200 feet consisted of third class climbing up snow, rock, and intermittent WI 2-3 ice on the west side of the face. I exited the face just west of the false summit, at 8,200'. From the false summit, I traversed out the summit ridge and back, which proved the slowest part of the climb. The ridge involved over a quarter mile of 4th- and easy 5th-class climbing on snow-covered rock. Strong winds and single-digit temperatures kept me from lingering at the summit. I regained the false summit eight hours after I started climbing, then trotted down to the fire lookout and the trail. I reached my car (thankfully shuttled by friends) two hours later, just at dark. The climb was one of the most enjoyable days I've ever spent in the mountains. Mile of Smiles, 5,200 feet, IV 5.2 WI3+.

BLASE REARDON

Alaska

KIGLUAIK MOUNTAINS

Seward Peninsula, various ascents. In April I climbed the east face of Mt. Osborne (4,714') with Phillip Hofstetter. The climb was 2,500' of moderate 45° snow, ice, and cliff bands. Osborne is the monarch of the Kigluaik Range, 35 miles north of Nome, along the spine of the Seward Peninsula. It is unclear whether the Kigluaik (called the "Sawtooths" by locals) should be classified as large hills or smallish mountains; either way, they offer tors abounding with a hodgepodge of marble, basalt, schist, and granite. We approached via snow-machine up the Grand Central Valley. The summit ridge of Osborne is studded with a fence-like procession of tors (granite formations, typically no more than a pitch high, poking out of an eroded ridge); the highest, heavily rimed in winter, is surmounted via a short pitch of 5.6. During various summer attempts in 2002 and 2003, I climbed, solo, all three summits of Tigaraha (3,500'+). Tigaraha is capped with prominent granite tors, between the Sinuk and Windy drainages, almost Arrigetchian in proportion (though no Shot Tower, it's prominent and notable in quality). I climbed the north tower from an obvious notch in one long rope length of 5.8 A1. The south tower is a class 4 scramble. The main tower has a classic five-pitch friction arête (I found a lone rappel sling low on the route). The notch can be accessed from Windy via 2,000' of burly class 4 scrambling, or from the Sinuk via a loose ice gully. Tigaraha is likely mismarked on the USGS map, which locates it on the wrong side of the Sinuk drainage. I climbed the mountain the map says is Tigaraha, a lumpen choss pile with a scary class 4/5 summit block. I believe that all my climbs were first ascents, with the possible exception of the main tower of Tigaraha (I'm not sure if the party who left the sling continued).

IAN MCRAE

ALASKA RANGE

Geographical note: While the well-known peaks in Denali National Park are often called "the Alaska Range," these peaks form just one part of the immense Alaska Range, which contains many significant subranges, including the Hayes and Delta ranges, and the Revelation, Kichatna, and Tordrillo mountains.

HAYES RANGE

Various new routes. Between March 29 and April 7, 2002, Rich Chappell, Jose Rueter, Mike Sterling, and I made first ascents in the Hayes Range. Jim Cummings of Delta flew us to the west fork of the Gillam Glacier, beneath the west face of Mt. Hess. We were lucky to be able to land, given low snow accumulation and recent high winds. Temperatures ranged from –20 to +15° F during the trip.

In two days we had our ski camp put in at 6,500' on the east fork of the Gillam and had completed a reconnaissance up to the 8,600' col southeast of the south peak of Mt. Giddings. Cramponing was excellent, but avalanche blocks off the west face of Mt. Geist crossed our ascent tracks.

On April 1 we made what is likely the third ascent of Mt. Giddings (10,180') via a new route up the south buttress. It took six hours to ascend, four to descend, being predominantly 3rd class snow, with a few sections of rotten-rock ridge that we 4th classed. On a pulverized rock band at 9,200' we discovered water ice and whiffs of sulphur—geothermal activity? We remained roped on the summit, due to large crevasses. The views to the Tanana River, Donnelly Dome, and Mt. Hayes (13,832') were magnificent, due to the peak's central location and the perfect weather.

After repositioning camp farther up the glacier, at 7,360', we headed back up to the col just west of Peak 9,610' and climbed three pitches of 45° blue ice to its top. We descended from this summit heading northeast on the rocky ridge to Mt. Skarland (10,315'), but fear of frostbite turned us around despite fantastic views of the entire west basin of Mt. Hayes. Our retreat back over Peak 9,610', south to the col, and then west through the icefall went flawlessly.

Again we moved camp, down to 5,600', and on April 5 completed the first ascent of the north peak (10,065') of Giddings. We gained its west ridge at 9,200' by climbing a depression on the main southwest face. The upper ridge was 45°, protected with screws and pickets. The route took seven hours up, four down. Access to the base of the climb was by ski up the fine pocket tributary glacier beneath Peak 8,320' and northeast from the Gillam Glacier's east fork, upon which we had camped. We flew out on April 7 in continuing perfect weather. Such a blessing, on the heights, with the most agreeable of bergkameraden!

PHILIP S. MARSHALL, *Three Corner Round Pack Outfit*

The west face of Balchen is lit by the sun. *Jeff apple Benowitz*

Mt. Balchen, west face. In early March Michael Williams and I landed on the west side of the dry Gillam Glacier on a snow-covered gravel bar. We hiked and skied 15 miles up to the base of the west buttress of Mt. Balchen (11,140'). Above our base camp at 7,000' we were confronted with a large rotten granite wall that blocked access to the mountain's upper reaches. On a clear, cold day of 25 below (F) we bypassed the 1,500' rock headwall via a low-angle snow couloir that was topped with fun mixed climbing. Further progress was impeded by a series of large rock gendarmes. We traversed underneath the gendarmes via snow and occasional low 5th class rock moves. The final obstacle to the easier ice and snow above was a dead-vertical pitch of rotten rock and thin ice with sparse pro. Above, 60° water ice, an 80° rime snow dome, and a broken summit ridge (from the 2002 earthquake) led to the top. Rappel anchors were difficult to come by on the descent. The 4,000' climb took us 12 hours and was the third ascent of the peak and first winter ascent.

JEFF APPLE BENOWITZ

The southwest ridge of Mt. Balchen divides sun from shadow in the center of the peak on the left.
Jeff apple Benowitz

DELTA RANGE

Peak 7,600' and Mt. Kimball. On August 12 I laid eyes on Bethan Gilmartin for the first time. August 13 found us driving to the Richardson Highway Monument and starting to hike east toward Mt. Kimball (10,200'). Due to inclement weather and poor map reading we ended up climbing the wrong peak, Peak 7,600', which is on the south side of the right fork of the Gakona Glacier (the fork at the head of the west fork of the Chistonchina River); we climbed its northeast spur. From the summit we saw Mt. Kimball 20 miles away. After further hiking we set up base camp at 4,000 feet on the Chistochina Glacier. We made the second ascent of Kimball's southeast ridge and the first one-day ascent of the mountain. Along the way we found a long pitch of rock with much 5.9. We summited a 200' gendarme via vertical ice and overhanging rime, but the next gendarme looked a tad taller. We climbed in a ground blizzard, and the view from the "top" was thus compromised. After our 6,000-foot day we tried to raft out on the Chistochina River. Bears, mud, and a raft that wouldn't hold air found us eating 20-year-old Kit-Kats we found in an abandoned mine shack. To say the least, we got our money's worth from our internet "date." When I got back to town, I compared my photos to slides taken by the ridge's first ascensionists and talked to one of them about their ascent. I think the route and the summit were drastically affected by the 2002 earthquake. The most damage to roads and structures from the quake happened in the area of Kimball.

JEFF APPLE BENOWITZ

DENALI NATIONAL PARK

Denali National Park and Preserve, summary. The 2003 mountaineering season was eclipsed by the tragic crash of a McKinley Air Service flight in late May. En route to base camp, all four on board died when the plane crashed at South Hunter Pass. We lost good friends, including Keli Mahoney, a wonderful pilot who had flown many missions for the NPS over the years, and Bruce Andrews, a gifted guide with Alaska Mountaineering School.

The season saw several high-altitude rescues and several incidents that generated concern over the factors going into climbers' decisions when calling for a rescue. In response, those who are rescued (aerial evacuation or ground rescue) while climbing in Denali National Park and Preserve may be obligated to pay for air or ground ambulance costs. [Editor's note: AAC membership includes limited rescue insurance.] If a climber is rescued, his or her permit will be voided.

A point worth noting is that during 2002 five climber falls at Denali Pass required rescue (or recovery, in the case of the one fatality). During 2003 NPS rangers placed pickets along the length of the traverse to Denali Pass. This was done for the protection of rangers performing rescues but also benefited climbers that chose to utilize them. As a result, in 2003 there were no major incidents here and at least one instance, witnessed by a ranger, where the pickets helped to arrest the fall of a climber who was using the pickets as part of a running belay.

The number of climbers on Denali was down slightly from previous years, with 1,179 climbers (including 125 women) attempting Denali, 58% of whom reached the summit. The West Buttress continues to be by far the most popular route (952 climbers). Two climbers did, however, summit via a rare repeat of the Milan Krissak Memorial route on the south face. Guided expeditions accounted for 30% of climbers on Denali. Climbers came from 45 nations (including Costa Rica, Lebanon, Saudi Arabia, Sri Lanka, and Zimbabwe), the most common being United States (685), United Kingdom (87), Canada (52), France (41), and Spain (34). June 12 was a record-setting summit day, with 115 climbers reaching the top. The second busiest day was June 22, with 42 summits.

Of 34 climbers attempting Foraker, only 2 (6%) reached the top. There were no winter summits on Denali or Foraker this year, and Foraker activity coincided with the most popular period for Denali, May and June.

As training for an alpine speed-climbing competition in Central Asia, Chad Kellogg made a speedy ascent of the West Buttress. At 02:15hrs on June 17, Kellogg left base camp, climbed the West Buttress in 14 hours and 22 minutes, and was back in base camp at 23:55. Kellogg had climbed to the summit twice the previous week (once via the Upper West Rib) in order to acclimatize.

Elsewhere in the park new routes were climbed, notably on the east face of The Citadel in the Kichatna Spires and on the Father and Sons Wall. Mt. Hunter was descended on skis. Clean Mountain Cans (CMCs) were used successfully again at the17,200' high camp on the West Buttress, which made a huge difference in keeping the camp free of human-waste impact.

We were again privileged to operate under the medical direction Drs. Jen Dow and Peter Hackett, with many capable medical volunteers who made a difference for a lot of climbers. A crew from National Geographic "Ultimate Explorer" filmed the South District ranger operations, spending three months filming on Denali and throughout Talkeetna. The two-hour film aired on MSNBC in early November. For our cooperation in making the film, the Park will receive digital footage for an informational film to be used at the Park's main visitor center.

We are proud of two postseason awards. The partnership between Denali's mountaineering rangers and the mountaineering Volunteers-In-Parks (VIPs) was honored in Washington, D.C. at the annual "Take Pride in America" awards ceremony. Secretary of the Interior Gale Norton presented the award to Dahr Jamail, representing the Denali volunteers, and mountaineering ranger Meg Perdue. "These winners represent the epitome of good citizenship," said Secretary Norton. The National Outdoor Leadership School (NOLS) honored Roger Robinson, Denali Mountaineering Ranger, for his dedication to wilderness education and innovative land management. Roger was presented the distinguished Stewardship Award at the 14th annual NOLS awards ceremony on October 11, in Lander, Wyoming. Congratulations! More information can be found at: www.nps.gov/dena/home/mountaineering/index.htm.

DENALI NATIONAL PARK/TALKEETNA RANGER STATION

Mt. McKinley from Seattle. Erden Eruç bicycled from Seattle to Talkeetna, then walked, with friends, 67 miles into the Southeast Fork Kahiltna Glacier base camp, and climbed the West Buttress to the summit with two others. Due to time constraints (Eruç's wedding), he flew out to Talkeetna before pedaling home—a roundtrip distance of 5,546 miles. He plans to return to complete the Kahiltna-Talkeetna portion on foot, as part of his human-powered Six Summits Project. This will take Erden to the highest summits on five other continents à la Göran Kropp. For more on the tribute to Göran, and Erden's non-profit for education and inspiration, see: www.around-n-over.org.

Mt. McKinley's northwest face, Father and Sons Wall, The Great White Fright. Having barely survived the crux of any Alaskan trip, we dragged ourselves from the acrid atmosphere of the Fairview and flew to Kahiltna base camp. Exchanging hangover for altitude, we caught our first glimpse of the Father and Sons Wall while acclimatizing. After 10 days of bad weather, with plenty more forecast, we were looking for a short sharp hit.

With a predicted weather window of 24 hours or so, it would have to be light, fast, and sexy. Packing two duvets, a bivi sac, a stove, six tortillas, and 20 chocolate bars, we set off from 11,000' on the West Buttress. Five hours later we had descended and crossed to the base of the 6,500' Father and Sons Wall. Ours was to be a great-looking line of unclimbed ice runnels linking three rock bands, but first we had to dash a few hundred feet up the enclosed gully that splits the vast walls of the Father and Sons to the left and the Washburn to the right. For those few minutes we would be at the mercy of the "Howitzer." This huge serac wall, teetering 6,000 feet above, had been silent; indeed there seemed little evidence of recent shelling. I was in front and looked up as I heard a distant rumble.

"Oh my God!" An almighty plume had already gathered, as chunks of serac ricocheted down the gully. Subsidiary plumes and missiles were firing out of the vast white chaos as it gathered speed and volume. We were in Hollywood, part of an impressive and quite realistic special-effects and stunt sequence. It was like that bit in the movie, K2.

I ran to the side with adrenalin-fueled speed, but there was nowhere to run, kid, nowhere to hide. I thrashed at the rock wall looking for a crack and hammered my axe in as far as possible. A quick glance down and Paul had run to the side and was scaling a vertical ice smear protected by a small rock rib, but he was in the narrows.

A glance up and "Oh boy, it's a biggun." The avalanche filled the gully, the surging mass reaching maybe a hundred meters up the flanks. I braced; this was it.

It seemed to take forever to arrive; I suppose 6,000

The Father and Sons Wall on the northwest face of Mt. McKinley, showing: (1) The Great White Fright, 2003 (2) First Born (Helmuth-House, 1995), (3) Extraterrestrial Brothers (Cool-Parnell, 2001). For perspective on the wall's location, see Brad Washburn's photo in *AAJ* 1997, p. 46. *Paul Ramsden*

feet is a long way to come down. A rush of wind hit us before the real onslaught. And then a myriad of internal vortices, velocities, and vacuums pulled us and sucked the air from our lungs as we were pummeled and sandblasted. But no big hits. It lasted an age, and even once it had passed, a fine tail of powder whipped around us for some time.

Looking down, I saw a crusted snowman starting to make his way up the slope toward me. There was never any doubt about continuing, as neither of us fancied descending the gully and crossing the debris in the basin below. The quickest way out was up. Besides, we had barely swung an ice tool yet.

The remaining 6,000 feet went in a blur of squeaky ice runnels, tricky mixed pitches, the odd slush-puppy icefall, and finally a calf-wrenching treadmill of blue ice.

With only a couple of brief rests, we reached the top of the face not a moment too soon. Terribly aware of our exhausted state, we were not keen on being caught by weather, which was quickly deteriorating. Sleep deprivation and fatigue had been haunting us, and it was becoming increasingly difficult to shrug off the hallucinations, head spins, and general apathy. So the last thing we needed was ferocious heat and knee-deep breakable crust, but there you go.

Eventually we reached the West Buttress, and after a straightforward descent back to our tent, we finished our journey after about 50 hours of almost continuous climbing and 62 without sleep. We graded the route alpine ED, for whatever that's worth. [Editor's note: None of the Father and Sons Wall routes have continued to the summit of Mt. McKinley.]

GUY WILLETT, *U.K. and The Fairview*

Beauty is a rare...

patience for purity   **Thunder Ridge**

The lower west buttress of Mt. McKinley. Beauty and Thunder have been shown for reference; numerous other routes have been climbed on this face. *Brendan Cusick*

Mt. McKinley, West Buttress, Patience for Purity. On June 12 and 13 Robert Adams and I climbed a new 3,500' route (Patience for Purity, Alaska Grade IV, 5.9 AI85°) on the western end of the west buttress of Denali. After an eight-day storm, which required much patience, we descended intending to climb a new line on the northwest face of the Buttress (a.k.a. Washburn Wall), but we were thwarted by new snow. We turned to the unclimbed mixed ridge and face rising directly out of the Squirrel Hill area. The route ascends to the left of the Thunder Ridge route and to the right of the 1984 Uppers Peters Glacier Couloir. Initially, at 10 a.m., we went up a low-angle snow ramp from 12,700' to 13,100'. Then we ascended ice as steep as 80° and chimneys before ascending a snow ramp to 85° mixed terrain, where we met the ridge crest proper. The following seven pitches were rock up to 5.9, mixed with low-angle, snow-covered rock. From here we followed a 60° ice gully for one pitch before finding a comfortable two-hour brew site at 7:30 p.m. at 14,600'. We were able to simul-climb the following 1,000' before being forced off a direct line to the top of the buttress by very deep snow. From here we traversed left to the 1984 route, where we encountered ice and mixed ground for two and a half pitches before exiting into the upper snow basin on the top of the buttress at 1:30 a.m. We battled fierce winds and cold temperatures for the following six hours to the top of the fixed lines, where we descended to the 14K camp, arriving at 10 a.m. on the 13th. The purity of the route was maintained by climbing single push over a 26-hour period (15 hours on the route itself).

BRENDAN CUSICK, *AAC*

Kahiltna Dome, Choo-Choo Express. On April 23 Erick Lawson and David Mullins climbed a route, which they called Choo-Choo Express, directly up the east face of Kahiltna Dome. They left their camp at ca 9,000' on the Kahiltna Glacier, descended about 400' to avoid crevasses, then made a steep, rising traverse to about 10,000'. From there they continued straight up the east face until joining the broad Northeast Ridge (1951) at ca 12,000', where Lawson fell into a crevasse. The pair descended this ridge, without continuing to the summit, until reaching a col from where they rappelled straight down over cornices, chopping bollards and thus leaving no gear. The route has constant 40-60° snow and ice, some 75° snow, and three pitches of vertical ice (up to about 100' each) over seracs.

From TALKEETNA RANGER STATION *files and personal communication with* LAWSON

Mt. McKinley, Isis Face, second ascent. The few seconds seemed like eternity. There was no answer, only the glacier echoing our calls. I had this sour feeling that a tragedy might happen. After all these days of fighting together, it felt unfair.

The plane was swimming in snow at the West Fork base camp. We lost nearly one week with the first airdrop at the Mountain House, but this we preferred to eating more burgers in Talkeetna while waiting for flyable weather and landable snow.

We were motivated to climb, and for a warm-up the Colton-Leach route on the Rooster Comb seemed in shape. The next day, May 20, we found ourselves on an elegant 900m line of mostly good ice. We moved fast in two parties, Deux (Manu Guy) with Foué (François Savary), and Manu Pellisier with me. The last four wicked pitches took us more time than the rest, probably because we followed a thin line too far to the right. After some body-weight ice screws, we solved one dilemma by putting a left foot on a strong man's helmet (starring Manu and Manu—do not try this at home!). After 15 hours of climbing, we started the Abalakov threads game and reached base camp around 5 a.m. The 24-hour push prepared us for a mountain of pancakes and roasted pig with garlic.

On May 24 we were ready again and pulled our sledges to Isis Face. We'd prepared the packs for five to six days, and the beasts weren't light. The most detailed information we had of the line was a small photo with the bivouac indicated. We had been dreaming of this face for a year, and I could hardly believe that we were in the footsteps of the "maitre" (master) as we called Jack Tackle, surrounded by a perfect landscape. The first day we gained more than 900m of altitude, cruising in the couloirs of ice flutes and sugar-snow mushrooms. Nearly all day we moved together. These uniquely Alaskan features led to a perfect bivy under a sunny sky.

The next day started happily, and the sun was still smiling when we reached the first rock pillar. But after an easy pitch, bad weather greeted us. Friends and wires froze as Manu led the mixed pitches. We followed as fast as possible, not just to gain time but also to rewarm shivering bodies. The wind got really strong, and, 600m higher, we became aware that there was no way back.

The third day was a day with wind but without view. The second rock pillar's surprise was the eternal spindrift, and about eight challenging mixed pitches. In the middle were the eyes of Isis, two snowfields we had been examining since we arrived. The sunny holiday became a survival scene. In the twilight we climbed the last snowfield, which had the steepest bad snow we had seen on the route. Occasionally we found a spot of ice for protection, but the deadmen placements only meant less weight on our harnesses. Isis found us on top of the South Buttress at 5 a.m. on the 26th, but in poor shape, and she kept us in her stormy arms for 30 hours more. While we dug out tents and melted snow, our thoughts focused more around home than this great climb. Our bodies were burned out, with some frozen fingers and toes. At home we had planned to try for the summit of Denali, but at the moment we knew it wasn't realistic.

The descent on the South Buttress was a blank spot in our minds, as well in the rangers' library. We left our snow hole around 2 p.m. on the 28th under a hot sun. The endless ridge, jumps above ugly bergschrunds, and the deep snow exhausted us. Long rappels and hide and seek in the labyrinth of seracs. We believed this risky game was finished when, around midnight, we reached the West Fork Ruth Glacier, only 10 km of "walking" from base camp. Suddenly Deux disappeared into a crevasse.

The uncertain moments without his voice woke us up. Finally, from 20 meters below the glacier, his voice cut the silence. We were happier than at the end of the climb.

Epilogue: "Too much is as bad as nothing at all." Neither Deux's injured shoulder, nor our agreement with the pilot to prepare his landing strip was reason enough for him to pick up us at base camp. After two round trips to the Mountain House ferrying equipment, we were angry with this part of the world. Fortunately, a canoe trip on a nearby lake to catch rainbow trout and a real dinner made us forget the evils.

Thanks to Jack Tackle for this great line and to Millet, Simond, GMHM, and Sandstone for support.

ILDI PELLISSIER, *France*

Going Monk on Peak 13,790' (Mt. Andrews). *Jonathan Copp*

Peak 13,790' (Mt. Andrews), Going Monk. On May 30 Jonny Copp and I climbed a new route on Peak 13,790' (as marked on the Mt. McKinley A-3 quad map), located on the south side of the East Fork Kahiltna Glacier; this is the last peak at the southeast terminus of Denali's South Buttress. Although the peak had been climbed before (from the south and east), we proposed—unofficially, but with widespread support from the local climbing community and the peak's prior ascensionists that we were able to contact—that the peak be known as Mt. Andrews, after our friend Bruce Andrews, a guide and Alaskan regular who died in the airplane crash on May 28 (see Denali National Park and Preserve, summary, above).

Going Monk begins on a north-facing snow-and-ice field at the peak's west end, continues through a rock band via an ice ribbon, and then ascends the crest of the west ridge on ice and through mixed rock towers. The route gains 4,300' vertical and was climbed in a 24-hour round trip from the base (15 hours base-summit). Aside from the two crux pitches (AI6 and M6), which we pitched out, we found moderate terrain (with a few short, tricky spots) that we simul-climbed throughout.

Upon gaining the low-angled summit ridge, we were hit by a storm and punched through numerous crevasses en route to the summit. We descended by rappel. While skiing from the base in a whiteout, I fell into a crevasse, but we returned safely.

KELLY CORDES, *AAC*

Mt. Hunter, first ski descent. This was my first trip to Alaska. I was invited to attempt a ski descent of Mt. Hunter during May with Lorne Glick, John "Weedy" Whedon, and Andrew McLean. Our intended route was a variation of the West Ridge from the south, via the Ramen Couloir, which reaches the West Ridge route at 11,000'. The Ramen Couloir was climbed in the early 90s.

After three days of waiting for weather, Lorne, Weedy, Andrew, and I received a beautiful day for our flight onto the Kahiltna Glacier. We established a comfortable base camp and punched a route up through the icefall to our advanced camp. We stashed tent, stove, ice tools, coffee, and rum, and took a look at our intended route, before descending to base camp for the evening.

I awoke to the sound of snow hitting the tent. By morning there were 8 inches of fresh snow, and it was still snowing. The storm was on us for four days and produced 16 inches of new snow. We were packing gear for the trip through the icefall to our upper camp when we heard and felt a distinctive "thwack!" Tons of ice calved off the upper plateau of Hunter and raked down the 5,000-vertical-foot wall, gathering speed and snow. With a powder cloud thousands of feet high it barreled across the mile-wide valley and blasted the opposing wall. Clearly we needed to wait for conditions to stabilize.

Two frigid days later we worked through the maze of ice towers to advanced base camp. Our gear stash had been spared by the avalanche. We decided to head up the next day, after one more cold day for snow stabilization and caloric power loading. The next night, May 14 at 9:00, after eating and relaxing, we began the ascent.

We breached the Ramen Couloir and reached the west ridge at 11,000'. The sun set an hour before, and the reality of an Alaskan night without bivi gear set in. It was cold, so cold that stopping for more than a few minutes became uncomfortable. We were skinning now, as the angle had relaxed considerably. Nearing Mt. Hunter's 13,000'-plateau lip, we were forced to trade skis for crampons for a few hundred feet. We gained the plateau as surrounding peaks began to bathe in creamy pink predawn alpenglow.

We hit the summit ridge at about 14,200' and received our first sunshine for the day. On top we were rewarded with remarkable views of Denali and Foraker. All other peaks were insignificant in comparison. Soon reality set in. It was time to ski this sucker. I have never been more exhausted trying to ski. The snow on the summit ridge was wind-scoured hell, the kind that loosens your dental work. Soon we found ourselves at the saddle where we exited the west face. A 1,000', 45° face, garnished with a massive cornice, leads down to the 13,000' plateau. We skied down to the plateau without wasting time. At the lip of the plateau we took a break to brew up and power down food.

Starting again, we were faced with the most heinous part of the ski descent. Right off the lip, with 5,000' of exposure, sat 30' of blue ice. We skied carefully. Together again we gazed down the next 2,000' of the northwest side of the west ridge: dessert time, with boot-top to knee-deep recrystallized powder with surface hoar. The snow was so good it felt like we were cheating, but with every pristine-powder turn we were forced closer to the 3,000' south-facing, glop-plastered icy moment of truth.

One at a time we worked down the convex, increasingly steep headwall that caps the final couloir. The exposure was dizzying. Like fingernails on a chalkboard we scratched our way down to safety. Finally we skied out onto the flats. We congratulated each other and started cele-brating when, seconds after we exited the couloir, a raging wet slide blasted over

Descending the west face of Thunder Mountain. *Lorne Glick*

cliffs and dumped into our line, erasing the lower 1,200' of our tracks. We said, "Let's get the hell out of here." Feeling very lucky, we scooted on to advanced base camp and finished our fifth of rum. No one stopped smiling as we kicked back in the sun and let what we pulled off set in. It took 16 hours from our 8,000' ABC to the 14,575' summit and back.

ARMOND DUBUQUE

Mt. Hunter, South Ridge, third ascent. In mid-June Forrest Murphy and I climbed Mt. Hunter's South Ridge. It was likely the third ascent. We opted for the "direct start variation," made by the 1986 second ascent. Here we found high-quality mixed climbing to M5-, with long stretches of moderate mixed ice terrain. After a psychologically demanding journey across the Happy Cowboy Pinnacles and up the Changabang Arête, we visited the South Summit and descended the West Ridge, reaching Kahiltna base camp five days after leaving our camp on the Tokositna Glacier.

Previous traverses of Hunter to Kahiltna base camp via the South Ridge or the adjoining Southeast Spur took a minimum of 12 days and 13 days, respectively. The difference in our case was stable weather. (A major buttress located between these routes was climbed in 2001 [*AAJ* 2002, pp. 230-231]; this team descended the Southwest Ridge route, reaching the Thunder Glac-ier after 10 days on the mountain). The technical difficulties of the South Ridge were not extreme, but we found the route to be committing, consistently challenging, and requiring almost every alpine skill imaginable. This somewhat forgotten route has some of the finest rock in the Alaska Range, and offers a grand course in all aspects of Alaskan alpine climbing.

MARK WESTMAN

Thunder Mountain, ski descent of west face. This 2,000' face is prominent on the flight to Kahiltna Base. On April 25 Andrew McLean and I gained the upper glacier by traversing in from the west above a steep narrow icefall. After skinning across the bergshrund we cramponed up and into a couloir on the left side of the face. It ended on a knife-edged corniced ridge. On belay, I looked over into the Thunder Glacier cirque and at the 150 yards of tiptoeing to get to the West Summit Plateau. We skied. Snow conditions and position were fantastic. A K2 Cessna flew by, wagging his wings. In retrospect, to gain the plateau we should have veered up and right at two-thirds height, maybe avoiding the fall line of the humungous cornice.

LORNE GLICK

Peak 12,380' (Kahiltna Queen*), South Face Couloir and Distant Lights. It's maddening how many things can go wrong in this game of ours. The weather is a tough opponent, and gets the upper hand at some point. Snow is forever fickle. Personal fitness never seems right. Someone forgets crucial gear. Someone gets some sort of bug. At least one logistic element—transport, permits, or people—proves impossible. Something, usually important, breaks.

Sitting beside Paul Roderick as he skimmed the Cessna over the icefall that guards the upper section of the Tokositna Glacier and headed back to Talkeetna, Malcolm Bass and I couldn't believe how different this trip had been. The whole thing had gone right. Two new classic lines on the south face of Kahiltna Queen, climbed in a style which for us was new and fun, in a spell of perfect weather, superb cracks, only 13 days since leaving the U.K. We couldn't think of anything that had gone wrong.

Malcolm and Paul Figg had seen the south face of The Queen in 2001, when they were grinding their way up the east ridge of Hunter. Their photos were encouraging, showing an 1,100m face of soaring granite buttresses split by at least two compelling couloir lines. The face had only been climbed once, in May 1977, when Alan Kearney, Mal Ulrich, and Chuck Sink climbed the broad gully on the far left side of the face to a junction with the southwest ridge and continued to the summit. The couloir lines looked eminently doable, though both had invisible sections that added to the intrigue.

Malcolm and I sat outside the tent staring at the face in late April. To get a better look into the couloirs' obscured recesses, we'd skied down the glacier toward Mt. Huntington and back up toward the stunted southeast side of the Mini-Moonflower. We were sure the right-hand line would go and planned for a 24-hour climb, taking a skinny rack, twin 7.5mm ropes, duvets, a gas canister and lightweight burner, a kettle, 15 GU's each, 2 liters of carbo drink each, cheese and nuts, a bothy bag, chocolate espresso beans, and caffeine tablets.

We'd never set off to climb something like this light and fast, but during the 15-minute ski to the base, the advantages quickly became obvious. With Pertex shells over thermals and light mountain marathon sacks we made good time up the 300m snow apron, before skirting sideways into the couloir proper. There was a moment of doubt as the debris funneling down the couloir increased, and we questioned our decision to start climbing at 9:15 a.m. However, up was the safest option, and the climbing got better. Combining moving together and long pitches, mostly on moderate snow surrounded by fantastic rock architecture, we reached the narrower upper section of the couloir and steep mixed steps of classic Scottish 4. From there we broke right onto the mixed upper face, weaving around blocky steps and encountering the spice of bullet-hard ice. The broad summit ridge was heaven, as we'd been on the go for 18

The south face of peak 12,380' (aka Kahiltna Queen and Humble Peak). Left: Distant Lights (Bass-Yearsley, 2003). Right: South Face Couloir (Bass-Yearsley, 2003). Not visible on the left is the 1977 Kearney-Sink-Ulrich route, which ascends a broad couloir to the southwest ridge, then continues up the ridge (left skyline) to the summit. *Malcolm Bass*

Simon Yearsley in the lower section of Distant Lights. *Malcolm Bass*

hours. A surprisingly easy stroll/stagger led us past an Alaskan-special ridgecrest crevasse to the summit. Scuttling down to where we'd crested the ridge, we tried to sleep in the bothy bag. After four hours of kind of sleeping, kind of resting, we gave up and started to abseil. On the way up, just round the corner from the crux step, we hadn't noticed a commodious ledge under a protective wall, with a perfect gear crack and perfect bowl shape. We saw it now, and spent three hours sleeping, brewing, and drinking. The rest of the descent was easier, though time-consuming, and downclimbing and abseils got us back to the tent at 1:30 a.m.

We spent the next four days eating and sleeping, with a light storm and a change to colder, northerly winds. This right-hand couloir, South Face Couloir, had been superb. The left-hand couloir was to be even better.

Planning to leave at a more sensible 5:00 p.m., we got bored and headed off at midday. The couloir was narrower, with more pitches of superb ice, again set amid wild architecture. A steep pitch reminiscent of Mad Hatter's Gully led to a 15m vertical step. Placing two screws, Malcolm dispatched this obvious crux, and I would have followed in the same style if it weren't for a pulled tool leaving me with a deep cut above my eye and blood pouring. But this was the trip where everything was going right, so the cut wasn't allowed to be deep, and the blood had to clot quickly, which it did.

From a broad triangular amphitheater we followed the narrowing left branch, and steep mixed chimneys led to the only loose section, a shattered col ("Crockery Col"), followed by half a pitch of badly stacked washing-up. With darkness gathering, the ground changed as we left the gully below. We spent the night weaving slowly through what from below we'd named "The Great White"—600m of complex rocky spurs, blocky steps, and exposed hanging snowfields. Breaking onto the ridge, this time in brilliant dawn, was breathtaking, and we grinned and gazed. We also were wasted and forsook the short trudge to the summit this time,

Simon Yearsley on Distant Lights. *Malcolm Bass*

heading down South Face Couloir to the perfect ledge and another brew-and-sleep fest.

The descent was even slower than last time, with cruddy snow meaning more abseils to swallow our diminishing rack. Exhaustion and auditory hallucinations threatened to spoil things. Flat ground arrived at the right time, and we collapsed into the tent after 40 hours on the go, feasting on anything not sweet, after sucking GUs for so long, cranking up the CD player, grinning inanely.

Then things got even better. A fortuitous radio call saw Paul's Cessna back within a few hours. Hastily thrown-together gear stuffed in the plane, we were off to beers, Greg's 40th birthday party in Talkeetna's sublime birch woods, and more grinning.

SIMON YEARSLEY, *The Alpine Club (U.K.)*

Geographical note: Though Peak 12,380' is frequently called Kahiltna Queen, presumably due to its prominence at the head of the Southeast Fork Kahiltna Glacier, it is also known as Humble Peak, which is the name given by Kearney-Sink-Ulrich after their 1977 ascent.

Peak 11,520', north face to summit ridge. A new route was climbed by Marty Beare and me on May 14 and 15 on the northern aspect of Peak 11,520'. The route ascends an obvious couloir that extends from the valley floor (8,500' on the west fork of the Tokositna Glacier) to the summit cornice (11,500'), finishing just east of the summit. Most of the route consists of 50-60° ice, with three steeper ramps giving short sections of 75-85° climbing. The steepest, most sustained ice is found at the foot of the couloir. The route gives approximately 20 pitches of climbing. Estimated grade: Alaskan 3+, AI 4/4+. Location: 151 deg.01`E, 62 deg.57.5`N. Descent was via the couloir, using V-threads and rock gear during a snowstorm. Beware spindrift avalanches!

PAT DEAVOLL, *New Zealand*

RUTH GORGE

The northeast face of Mt. Dickey. Byrch and McNeill climbed the obvious drip of ice on the right starting up from the rock buttress.
Karen McNeill

Mt. Dickey, northeast face ice. Flying into the Ruth Gorge, I caught sight of an obvious drip of ice on the northeast face of Mt. Dickey. On May 20 Christine Byrch and I left our camp below the Don Sheldon Mountain House in the Ruth Amphitheater. We skied down to Mt. Dickey and stashed our skis south of a rock rib that separates Barril from the northern end of Dickey's east face.

Initially we postholed up 1,500' of snow that led to the base of the ice. The drip had formed between serac bands on the upper face. From looking at maps we knew that the route wasn't threatened from above. The ice was in perfect shape, and we climbed 240m of WI4+ ice. From the top of the ice, Christine and I ascended 300m of snow, interspersed with a little ice, followed by more snow. This took us to the ridge proper.

After brewing up we headed toward the summit, which lay more than 1.5km away. Initially we kept to the ridge, but part way along had to descend to lower slopes, as the cornices were huge. The going became slower, until we finally decided to descend Pittock Pass back to our camp.

Our skis were still at the base of Mt. Barrill. Walking around to retrieve them was out of the question, so on May 22 we climbed over Mt. Barrill and descended the Japanese Couloir, which landed us close to the skis. On our return to camp we discovered that Adam Rosenthal and Jack Jeffries had climbed the route on Dickey the day after us.

On May 25 Christine and I skied around Mt. Dickey, making a side trip to the summit. From the top we realized that we were probably 300m from the summit when we turned back after our earlier climb. Having communicated with several Alaskan veterans, I believe the route on Mt. Dickey to be a first ascent.

KAREN MCNEILL, *Canada*

Skiing in for the Eye Tooth. (1) The Dream in the Spirit of Mugs (Bonapace-Haas-Orgler, 1994). (2) The Talkeetna Standard (Hollenbaugh-House, 2003). *Jeff Hollenbaugh*

Eye Tooth, The Talkeetna Standard; Mt. Dickey, Roberts-Rowell-Ward route, second ascent. Steve House and I were flown to the Mountain House on September 17. Dry conditions made this the only landing site available. That afternoon we skied down the Ruth Glacier to assess conditions and take advantage of the high pressure that was providing clear, calm, and cold conditions (-10°F at night, 25°F daytime temperatures). Our hopes of finding ephemeral melt-freeze ice lines were quickly dashed, as we were hard-pressed to find blue ice on anything, a mere dusting of snow on north faces, and dry south faces. Desperate to get on something while the high pressure lasted, we chose a line Steve had looked at on the Eye Tooth.

On September 18 we left camp on the Ruth Glacier around 8:30 a.m. A two-hour approach brought us to the base of a snow cone on the west side of the Eye Tooth (just right of the start to the Orgler route, Dream in the Spirit of Mugs). The cone provided access to a snow slope leading to névé runnels and short sections of ice up to 70°, with most of the snow in the 60° range. We soloed and made good time to a point below a notch in the ridge between the Eye Tooth and the Sugar Tooth. The rock leading to the notch

Jeff Hollenbaugh on the south ridge of the Eye Tooth. The headwall was climbed via the right-most obvious crack above. *Steve House*

The east face of Mt. Dickey, showing the 1974 Roberts-Rowell-Ward route repeated by Hollenbaugh and House in 2003. *Jeff Hollenbaugh*

was steep and deteriorated, and we traversed a snow ledge left (north) to the base of a mixed pitch where we roped up. This 5.7 pitch led to a water ice pitch (V), which put us on easy snow by which we gained the south ridge of the Eye Tooth, having climbed 1,800 feet. Four pitches up the south ridge (up to 5.8) brought us to the base of a headwall and a ledge where we excavated a bivy platform a little after 6:00 p.m. The next morning the headwall was negotiated, and the route continued to offer fun on excellent granite (up to 5.9, interspersed with ridge-climbing). We shared the final several pitches of the Orgler route to the summit. Returning to the bivy ledge at 5:00 p.m., we spent another night, as the weather was perfect, and we could not think of a better perch from which to take in the Aurora Borealis. The next morning we rappelled the ridge for two raps to a plumb-line descent, climber's-left of our ascent route, to gain the lower snow slopes. We packed up camp on the Ruth and skied to our well-stocked camp at the Mountain House. The route gained 3,300 vertical feet, and we belayed 15 pitches, up to WI5 and 5.9.

The high pressure held, and while we could have flown out immediately and been satisfied with the Eye Tooth, we knew that you can't turn your back on such weather in the Alaska Range. While skiing back up the Ruth, we looked at other lines. In the back our minds was the east face of Mt. Dickey—5,000 vertical feet, one of the biggest walls anywhere—with six routes and no repeats. On the Eye Tooth we proved we could climb rock in double boots—important knowledge, as Dickey is primarily rock, and we had not brought rock shoes. Steve said, "I think it's time to step it up a notch." We chose the 1974 Roberts-Rowell-Ward line, as it seemed the most feasible, given the conditions and equipment constraints.

We packed three days' food and fuel and moved advanced camp down the Ruth to near the toe of the southeast buttress of Mt. Dickey, the general line that the route followed. The next morning, September 23, we started up, climbing three blocks using 75m ropes, for a total of 14 pitches up to 5.9 A1. By and large, the rock was good, outside of two rotten pitches just below the bivy, where we stopped at 10:30 p.m. Unable to find a sufficient ledge, we occupied a perch the size of the top of a clothes drier, where we could sit side-by-side in our single sleeping bag and lean against the wall.

Day two found the weather holding, and the morning sun got us out of the bag at 7 a.m. The second day proved to be both the technical crux and the route-finding crux (unless you consider the white-out descent). Five pitches brought us to an area of extremely poor rock and few feasible-looking options. After spending several hours looking for alternatives, we followed what seemed the only line of weakness out of the rotten-rock area. Just as it seemed our route was unlikely at best, we encountered pitons from the first ascent, driven directly into the rock, as David Roberts had explained to Jon Waterman in a letter we had seen a copy of. On the next pitch we encountered the only bolt placed on the 1974 ascent. While not overly joyous about a 29-year-old 1/4" bolt, I was thrilled to know we were on a route that was climbable. We pendulumed right, into the only obvious system, and I led into the night, mostly on aid, as snow began falling at 10:20 p.m. Three pitches and a short leader-fall later, I arrived at a snow arête that could be chopped down to form a platform; it was 2:15 a.m. The ledge was too small for cooking, the snow blowing too hard, and us too tired. We rigged a small tarp over us and tried to sleep.

On the third morning Steve led a 5.9 mixed pitch to a good ledge, where we were able to brew up. The three or four inches of new snow made climbing difficult and slow. Five more pitches (up to 5.9 A0) in constant snow brought us to the exit ledge, which we simul-climbed for 500' to the top of the face proper. Climbing moderate snow for another 650', we arrived at the summit plateau in a whiteout at 4:30 p.m. The altimeter told us we were within 100' of the summit, but had we been standing on it, we would not have known, the visibility was so poor.

The heavily crevassed descent was arduous in zero-visibility, though the compass bearings Steve had plotted proved invaluable. As we navigated major crevasses and a serac band, at times he was obscured 100' away. As darkness fell, just below 747 Pass, Steve fell in a large crevasse; the tight rope between us kept the event minor. Around midnight we found our tent, crawled in, brewed, and repaired ourselves with sleep.

It should be mentioned that while the first-ascent team fixed five pitches (ca 900') and had a cache on the summit plateau, their climbing this route in only three days in 1974 was an amazing achievement. Twenty-nine years after, we did little to improve on the style or time of the first ascent.

The climbing was never easy (much 5.7-5.9 in double boots and, on occasion, crampons), and we belayed the entire face in pitches. The vertical relief is almost exactly 5,000', and we climbed 31 pitches, up to 5.9 A2. Given the length of the route, the poor rock is minimal. Where it is poor, it is extremely so, but nothing worse than one would encounter in other great alpine ranges.

This was Steve's second trip to Alaska at the end of September, and he is now "three for two," having climbed a new route on the Moose's Tooth on his first September trip, in 2000. Alaskans we talked to said there is usually a high-pressure spell sometime in September; we were lucky enough to hit it. Historically September is one of the greater precipitation months. A year ago Colby Coombs was trapped on the Eldridge Glacier in 6' feet of unpackable snow during the same dates as our trip this year. Just as teams have been able to start the Alaska season earlier in March and April and come away with great results, there is perhaps a good opportunity for late-season routes as well.

JEFF "POUCHE" HOLLENBAUGH

London Bridge, Miss Keli, and various activity. We (Iwan Wolf, Urs Stöcker, Markus Stofer, Bruno Hasler) took advantage of the first sunny day to fly into the Ruth Gorge with Talkeetna Air Taxi, on May 7. We set up our base camp at the base of Mt. Dickey's southeast ridge. During the next couple of days accumulating snow created severe avalanche danger, which forced us to abandon our original plan to climb Mt. Johnson's east ridge. The impressive red pillar of Mt. Dickey's

London Bridge 7380 ft

Miss Keli

On The Frozen Roads of Our Incertitude, 2003

The Trailer Park

The London Bridge formation's two new routes and the start of The Trailer Park (Cordes-DeCapio, 2000) for reference. *Seb Constant*

south face caught our attention instead, but after two days on the wall, we turned around because of technical difficulties and bad rock. On a second attempt, we made our way up in teams of two and climbed nine pitches, totaling 480m. The difficulties did not surpass 5.9 A3 M4 50°. The quality of the rock became worse and worse, until we felt like we were digging in deep sand. A No. 5 angle, hammered into crackless rock, could be retrieved with one finger. Belaying was impossible. As the rock did not seem to be improving, we turned around again, and finally combated Mt. Dickey on skis by the west-southwest ridge. Via Pittcock Col and Mountain Hut we then cruised down to BC.

As Iwan, Urs, and I approached our next project, the nearly 1,000m-high west face of London Bridge, Markus headed back to Talkeetna. Urs mastered the first pitch through tricky, unstable ice structures. Parts of these ice structures broke when I was following. The route became more friendly as we made our way up, only to confront us again with a challenging exit at the end. We succeeded in doing an attractive first ascent with the rating 5.9 WI4 M6+. The scenic route allows efficient climbing in good conditions. Descending over the Coffee Glacier and Coffee Glacier Col, we did not encounter exceptional difficulties. Back in BC experienced glacier pilot Keli Mahoney offered us two six-packs of cold beer. However, on May 28 Keli died in a plane crash. In her honor we named our route "Miss Keli."

Next we set up camp on the West Fork Ruth Glacier. On May 24, shortly after midnight, we left to climb Mt. Huntington's French Ridge in an uncompromisingly light alpine style— without technical equipment, sleeping bags, or a tent. The climbing on the French Ridge turned out to be very challenging, with the snow being badly bound. Possibilities for belaying were scarce. The ridge was full of dangerous cornices, and I experienced a breathtaking fall. After 24 hours of non-stop climbing, we had to bring our adventure to an end only 50m below the summit because objective dangers were too high. Nevertheless, we succeeded in a speed ascent of [most of] the French Ridge, compared to the five days normally necessary for this route. We descended the West Face Couloir to the Tokositna Glacier and then flew to the West Fork Ruth Glacier. It was snowing so heavily that we had to use a compass and GPS to find base camp.

BRUNO HASLER, *Switzerland*

London Bridge, On the Frozen Roads of Our Incertitudes, and various repeats. P.J. from Doug Geeting Aviation dropped Jerome Mercader and I on the Ruth Glacier, below Mt. Barrill, on May 1. The following day we climbed the Ham and Eggs Gully (15h round trip from our base camp) to warm up. But then clouds came from the south, bringing bad weather. Our tent, like a small ship, sank slowly into the fresh snow (8' in 10 days).

When fine weather returned, the peaks were daubed with a white that slid with the first rays of sun. With all that fresh snow we had doubts, and when the time for action returned, we still had doubts. We wanted to attempt the west face of London Bridge (7,380'/2,250m), which is on the east side of the lower Ruth Gorge, across from Mt. Bradley and just north of London Tower. Our alarm clock didn't wake us. It was half-snowing but the sun appeared, so we headed down the glacier. On May 16 we started up a 1,300' approach snow couloir with steepness up to 45°. Where the couloir turns right, we climbed a narrow gully straight up (350' high, 60°snow and ice) in the middle of the face to the base of a headwall. Here Jerome lost a glove. We traversed a thin icefall on the left, climbed a thin but well-protected WI5 pitch, and reached the crux: an uncertain pitch (WI 5+) with a final M6 section poorly protected with knifeblades and short ice screws. I hung my backpack on a Friend, and, while gathering the two bags, Jerome dropped his, with our food and some water. Above was a nice pitch (WI4) and a 90' traverse to the left to join another gully, which is the wall's exit key. Two pitches in the gully (WI3; 70° max) brought us to the final snow slope (490', 50-55°), which we followed to the left to gain a corniced col and the summit ridge (M5 on the left side of the cornice). From the col we climbed the rocky ridge (5.8) and a short snow ridge to the rocky summit.

We downclimbed and rappelled the short east face to the Coffee Glacier, then walked south along its right side (don't try to cut across the northeast slopes of London Tower), up to the pass below Hut Tower, and down the other side to the Ruth—a long journey through deep snow. Our passage On the Frozen Roads of Our Incertitudes (3,110', V WI5 M6, 9:30 on route) left us two old vegetables in our small tent 20+ hours after leaving it, under the sunrise on McKinley.

On May 19 we made the second ascent of The Trailer Park (Cordes-DeCapio, 2000), with two variations, on the west face of London Tower (7,500'/2,286m). It was 3,200', VI M6+ WI6, and took us 14 hours for the climb and 22 hours round-trip from base camp. It's a long and sustained route that keeps giving, a cocktail of snow and ice with hard dry sections. We respected the spirit of the first ascent by removing all our gear. It's still a wild and challenging mixed route. The logical descent is by the east side and then the same way back as for the London Bridge. It's a long way back, but more aesthetic.

SEB CONSTANT, *France*

Mt. Bradley, East Ridge, attempt. Jay Rowe and I went into the Ruth Gorge during the last week in June 2002. We first repeated the Orgler route on the west face of Hüttenturm, a fantastic moderate 12-pitch climb done in T-shirts under blue skies. The next day we jumped onto the East Ridge of Mt. Bradley, also first ascended by Orgler. The climbing was as he described and very fun. We belayed every pitch, and got about 4,000 feet up the 4,600-foot route. Here we encountered a 50° snow couloir that was actively sloughing. We watched it for a half hour and decided that too much was coming down for us to continue. As we rested, a huge wet snow avalanche engulfed the gully from wall to wall, confirming our decision to go down. Countless rappels in mist and rain got us to the bottom. We were on the move for 60 hours. Future climbers should note that the couloir, which must be crossed or ascended, can be a significant hazard in wet conditions.

PETER HAEUSSLER, *Chugiak, Alaska*

KICHATNA SPIRES

Kichatna Spire, North Ridge variation. On June 6 Eddie Phay, Jed Brown, and I had Paul Roderick fly us onto the Shadows Glacier, racked-up and ready to go. Nineteen hours after landing, we were on top of Kichatna Spire. Our route followed the original North Ridge/Hidden Couloir route to a notch. From the notch we shared only a few pitches with the first-ascent line. We exited the notch via 600 feet of direct aid (A1) and iced-up 5.9 off-width climbing. Then we had to do a 60m rap off of a rock spike down into an ice slot. From here the climb was mostly iced-up chimneys (WI4). Having three ice axes and a wall hammer between three climbers complicated our movements. It took nine hours to rappel (the wind stuck our rope good) and downclimb the route. It was the first true alpine ascent of the peak and first one-day ascent to boot. I liken the climbing effort to the regular route on Half Dome, but a tad bit more remote and sans topo. With beta the route could be done quite fast. A recent mag article claimed Kichatna Spire to be the hardest summit in North America to reach. Our ascent begs that question. After our ascent weather kept us tent-bound except for one day, when we attempted a line on the east face of 6,790'. We were turned back by direct aid on extremely rotten rock. We were in the range for 16 days.

JEFF APPLE BENOWITZ

Modern wall climbers enjoying their portable beds on Last Cry of the Butterfly.
David Kaszlikowski/StudioWspin.com.pl

The Citadel, Last Cry of the Butterfly. Marcin Tomaszewski, David Kaszlikowski, and I, supported by the Polish Climbing Association (PZA), arrived in the Kichatnas on April 18, in perfect weather. We landed on the sunny Shadows Glacier, looked around at the surrounding walls, and despite our plan to attempt the unclimbed south face of Kichatna Spire, we headed for The Citadel.

The wall was pointed out to us by the pilot, Paul Roderick, who thought that the wall probably hosted at least one route. This wall is a beauty, slightly smaller than Kichatna Spire, but with a spectacular yellow 2,500' granite prow rising directly from the glacier. Without delay we started our climb and soon discovered traces of a line just right of the prow. Therefore, we committed to the prow proper, and headed for the flawless overhanging granite. For most of the way we were able to find thin to medium-size cracks, with tricky sections of moderate aid (up to A4). We established two hanging portaledge camps on the prow, and set up a third one on what we had thought to be the top of The Citadel. We were running out of supplies, it being the third week of our climb, when we were surprised to learn that the summit was still nowhere in sight.

After a few more days and 12 more pitches (mostly free climbing, alpine ridges, and steep ice/snow cols), we reached the summit. We shared our last tea, pondering the most beautiful mountains we have ever seen. On the way down, the weather began deteriorating, with heavy clouds covering the mountains and high winds. We thought we could hear voices above, from the direction of the summit. We thought we must have been hallucinating, until one of us saw a small figure on the snow-swept face. Another party was heading to the top of The Citadel. [Editor's note: This was the Supa Dupa Couloir team, see report below.] We reached the portaledges and hid before the real storm hit. We

The Citadel, showing: (1) Approximate line of East Buttress route (Black-Embick-Graber-Long, 1976); (2) Last Cry of the Butterfly (Belczynski-Kaszilowski-Tomaszewski, 2003); (3) Supa Dupa Couloir (McAleese-Sanders-Turner, 2003). Off The Wall Madness (McAleese-Turner, 2002) traverses in as per (1) but begins the wall betwen (1) and (2), joining (1) about halfway up the wall and following it to the top of the buttress (no summit). *Twid Turner*

waited 40 hours, finished our supplies, and began rappelling to base camp in a continuing storm. Statistics: Last Cry of The Butterfly, east face of The Citadel, 3,700' climbing (VI 5.10+ A4 80° ice). Route climbed (with fixing and rappels included): April 19-May 5.

CHRIS BELCZYNSKI, *Torun Climbing Club, Poland*

The Citadel, Supa Dupa Couloir. While climbing Off the Wall Madness in 2002, Twid Turner and I were amazed by a couloir running vertically, straight to the summit. In 2003 we were back for more, accompanied by Ollie Sanders. The Shadows Glacier was to be our home, and we put base camp in a great position directly beneath The Citadel. Our line was unmistakable from the glacier: a striking 1,000m thin white line that dug deep into the east face; for most of the way we were able to touch both walls, and at the top we had a clear view down the route to the tent. A trip on day 1 over the col beneath Gurney Peak and around to the other side gave us an idea of conditions and a chance to come up with a plan for tackling the Supa Dupa Couloir.

Our early season arrival meant dark nights and cold temperatures—perfect for ice, not so hot for the early starts. But so to it: we set off

Stu McAleese squeezes up the Citadel's Supa Dupa Couloir. *Twid Turner*

early and were soon soloing the initial snow and ice slopes in the red morning light. The gully took shape 200m up: time to tie on and use the huge rack. We knew we had our work cut out, with endless ice disappearing to blue sky. At least it was going to be fun. Unsure of the weather and with no idea what was in store, we decided to fix ropes and come back the next day if the weather held. Luck was on our side, and we soon regained our high point, with food and equipment for three days in heavy rucksacks and a haul bag. Pitch after pitch fueled our addiction, leaving us wanting more, curious as to what was ahead, and, more importantly, would it go? Two key sections proved crucial in linking the line. Leering above me I saw the first. We'd had our suspicions down on the glacier as to whether there was any ice here. With the couloir here narrowed to the width of my hips, but with ice in the back, vertical for 60m, I could barely hang in there. Christened the "No Hips Pitch," it didn't go without a fight. Tired and ready for a break, we found ourselves at an easier section of snow, three meters wide and at the average angle of Green Gully on Ben Nevis. Two hours of hacking ice and an avalanche later, we were dug in for the night. Constant spindrift pattering on our bivy bags ensured that we woke restless and feeling weak. However, ahead lay our wake-up call: more steep ice. The climbing on the second day was far more sustained, often 90° ice, with little shelter for the poor belayers apart from the haul bag, except when we found an ice cave behind pillars in the upper couloir. With 22 pitches of out-there ice behind us, we stood on the summit of The Citadel at 8 p.m. on May 3. Though tempted by exhaustion to bivy again, we descended through the night because the weather was changing. It was one of the best decisions we made. We arrived early in the morning to falling snow that was to last for 24 hours and leave a meter on the ground at base camp. Many thanks to the MEF, the BMC, and the Sports Council for Wales, who supported the expedition. An alpinist's dream, the Supa Dupa Couloir (ED4 WI6).

STU MCALEESE, *Wales*

TORDRILLO MOUNTAINS

Mt. Gerdine, Northwest Ridge and various activity. On April 4 Johnny Soderstrom, Zach Shlosar, and I flew in with Paul Roderick of Talkeetna Air Taxi. Flying into this fairly unexplored area was quite an experience, being surrounded by untouched granite towers, pillars of ice, and 3,000' couloirs. Having received Mountaineering Fellowship Grants from the AAC, Johnny and I recruited Zach for the unclimbed northwest ridge of Mt. Gerdine (11,258'). We were landed on the main flow of the Hayes Glacier at 4,700', six miles down the east fork from the base of the route. We put in a camp at the base of the Hayes Volcano, at 6,000'. With the base of Mt. Gerdine being guarded by an icefall, we were forced to climb the Hayes Volcano to Point 8,300', which made for a great ski or snowboard trip down. Not finding a route around, we were forced to traverse the Hayes Volcano, descend a gully on the backside, and travel across a slope exposed to ice fall, weaving through cracks to intersect the northwest ridge at 7,300'. We found the lower ridge scoured by the wind, leaving it beautiful hard blue ice. The ridge was straightforward; we belayed a few steps of ice and simul-climbed the rest, with the angle varying between 40° and 75°. At 9,600' we came to a balcony dividing the upper and lower ridges, which made a good camp. The temperature fell to about −15°F as darkness came. After cooking for a few hours outside, I crawled into the tent to warm up and found that a big toe was frozen. With my foot in Zach's armpit, the three of us dozed off in our cozy Bibler. The next morning, April 7, we awoke to blue skies and a throbbing toe. Thinking that I could wait a couple of hours to go down, Johnny and Zach headed for the summit, as I stayed in camp. They found the upper ridge to be fun, straightforward climbing on névé, with the angle varying between 40° and 70°. After negotiating a few bergschrunds they reached the summit, with a view encompassing Denali and the Alaska Range, the Kichatnas, Revelations, Neacolas, Cook Inlet, the Chugach, and the Talkeetna mountains. After rapping off a bollard from the summit, they hurried back to camp, and we packed and descended. With a few variations we descended the line of ascent, using seven V-threads, one picket, and much downclimbing. Back at the runway we spent three days trying to contact a plane for an early pickup. Johnny and Zach took advantage of the nice weather and skied a couple of couloirs to the east of camp. On the front of Peak 6,330' there are seven rock towers with couloirs between most of them. We named this formation the Seven Dwarves after they skied the two south couloirs. On April 11 Paul circled over and flew us home to Talkeetna. Happy with our shortened trip to this new area, we left with a first ascent of Mt. Gerdine's Northwest Ridge (4,000', AK grade 3, AI3), first descents of the Hayes Volcano and the two southern couloirs of the Seven Dwarves, and a purple toe.

JARED VILHAUER

Mt. Gerdine, looking east from north ridge of Peak 10,030'. Routes: (2) Hayes Point (9,600'), southwest ridge; (3) Mt.Gerdine (11,258'), southwest ridge; (6) Peak 10,300', south ridge. *Guenter Zimmerman*

Hayes Glacier, various ascents. From April 30 to May 15 Uwe Nootbaar, Thomas Speck, and I made four first ascents on unclimbed peaks or points and climbed Mt. Gerdine (11,258', fifth ascent) by a partly new route. The peaks are shown on the USGS Tyonek C-7 map. On April 30 we flew into the upper Hayes Glacier, at 6,000', where we established our base camp. On May 1 we skied up a small glacier northwest of Peak 9,670' (1.6 mi west of Mt. Gerdine) to a bergschrund at 7,500' and climbed the northwest face of Peak 9,670' by an 1,800' snow couloir

(40-50°). We climbed to the left of a huge rock tower located in the middle of the face, to reach the north ridge of Peak 9,670' at 9,300', near another rock tower. On May 2 we skied southeast up the Hayes Glacier and climbed a snow slope (1,000', 40°) to an 8,500' plateau at the top of the north branch of the Triumvirate Glacier. Turning northeast we followed a snow ridge to a point at about 9,600' (1.7 miles south of Mt. Gerdine, on the C-7 map between the letters B of the adjacent words Borough). Since it stands at the end of the Hayes Glacier, and is not a true peak but part of a ridge (the high point of which is Peak 10,510'), we named it Hayes Point.

The north ridge of Peak 10,030' (Surprise Peak), looking southwest from the glacier northwest of Peak 9,670'. *Guenter Zimmerman*

On May 3 we climbed Mt. Gerdine (11,258') via the southwest ridge. We started from base camp on skis, traveling southeast, and after a mile gained a snow plateau at 7,455'. We climbed a 40-45° snow slope to a little peak at 8,600' and followed a short horizontal snow-and-rock ridge to a saddle. We then climbed 30-40° snow slopes to the right of a rock ridge to 9,300', below a big serac.

The south couloir of Peak 9,620' (Argentiere Peak). *Guenter Zimmerman*

Above the serac (a short 70° passage) we crossed a snow plateau, climbed the southwest ridge of Peak 10,270', and finally a 50° ridge to the summit of Mt. Gerdine.

The following days the weather was bad, but on May 7 we climbed the north ridge of Peak 10,030', 3.7 miles southwest of Mt. Gerdine, up several 45° slopes and in a foot of new snow. We named it Surprise Peak, because of a surprising crevasse near the summit.

The weather was again bad for a few days. On May 11 we climbed the 1,600', 45° south couloir of Peak 9,620', which is 2.1 miles west of Mt. Gerdine and 1.0 mile north of Peak 9,670', We named Peak 9,620' Argentiere Peak for its similarity to the Aiguille Argentiere near Chamonix, France. After another period of bad weather, on May 14 we passed Hayes Point south on skis and climbed a snow point (ca 10,300', 1.4 mi south of Mt. Gerdine) via its short, easy south ridge. In perfect weather we flew out to Talkeetna on May 15.

DR. GUENTER ZIMMERMANN, *Deutscher Alpenverein (German Alpine Club)*

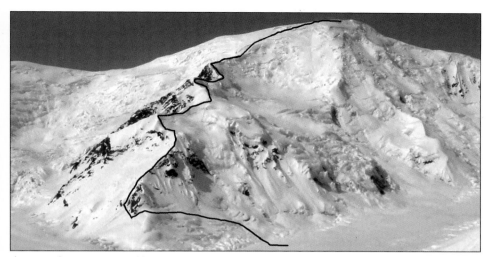

The East Ridge route on Nagishlamina in the Tordrillos. *Rod Hancock*

Nagishlamina, East Ridge. In May Brad Gessner, Doug Munoz, Stuart Parks, and I, all of Anchorage, completed a new route on, and made the second ascent of, 11,068' Nagishlamina, one of five peaks over 11,000' in the Tordrillo Range. Our line climbed the east ridge of Nagishlamina, which divides the east and southeast forks of the Capps Glacier. We rated the climb Alaska Grade II+, for sustained cornice and knife-edge ridge climbing, ice to 70°, and extreme remoteness. The climb took four days, including two storm days. The flight from Talkeetna took one hour, and our pilot was able to land at approximately 5,200' on the east fork of the Capps Glacier, adjacent to the east ridge. From base camp we traversed south onto the east ridge a few hundred feet above the ridge's heavily crevassed toe. We passed to the south side of the east ridge and gained the ridge proper a few hundred feet above. The rounded snow-dome summit was reached in good weather on day four, after which the ridge was descended to base camp.

The Tordrillos are located 80 miles west of Anchorage and are clearly visible from the city. Nagishlamina sits between its more famous neighbors Mt. Spur and Mt. Torbert and was first climbed from the southwest in 1989. Despite the area's proximity to Anchorage and the skyline views these peaks afford, the Tordrillos are rarely visited, offer difficult logistics, and big price tags. Although Anchorage is closer, Talkeetna seems to be the best flight base, due to the numerous skilled glacier pilots. Plan on spending $600-$1,000 per person to get in and out.

ROD HANCOCK

CHUGACH MOUNTAINS

Winter traverse of the range; Mt. Marcus Baker, South Ridge–Knik variation. During the summer of 2003 we started talking about a winter traverse of the Chugach Range, from Prince William Sound to the road system. If we encountered favorable conditions, an ascent of Mt. Marcus Baker would be attempted. We laid plans for a winter trip and reconvened in Talkeetna on January 21, 2004.

At noon on January 25 we beached in a small rocky cove about one-half mile from the face of the Harvard Glacier, on the western side of the fjord. After moving our gear above the high-tide mark, we started bushwhacking and found ourselves on the glacier in only three hours. On day two we continued beyond our previous day's cache and moved camp all the way to 1,700' on the direct south ridge. Negotiating the lower glacier in the winter proved easier than expected, since many of the slots were filled with water and frozen. High pressure remained, and the first five days saw some of the coldest temperatures of the trip, dropping to –20°F. We established camp three at 4,400' on the 28th, and the climbing began. Over the next two days we negotiated a beautiful ridge, never terribly exposed, and made camp four at 5,900'.

Spectacular ridge climbing connected this camp and the next, at 6,500', which we moved into on February 4, as it snowed. This was a decision point. The most direct line to the top of Marcus Baker continued up the south ridge over point 8,565' (which we dubbed "The Tooth") and then over a large snow dome at 10,300', en route to the 13,176' summit. Unfortunately, with the new snow we felt that the hazards were too high to continue ridge climbing. We left the ridge and decided to explore the upper Radcliffe Glacier and see if we could negotiate the icefalls and connect with the Knik Glacier.

We salvaged a half a day on the 6th, when the sun came out around 11 a.m., and wallowed down and out onto the Radcliffe. With the weather so unstable, we made a cache only two miles from camp five in hopes of reusing our trail, and were able to move and build camp six in a storm. As we sat out the 8th we studied the maps until our eyes hurt. Only 1.8 miles of broken glacier to go to the smoothness of the Knik and a known route up and down. One more day of good weather, and we would know if our route would go. We confirmed the route on the 9th, and we returned to camp in high spirits, knowing we could get to the Knik.

Following a storm day, more trail-breaking saw us on the Knik Glacier on February 10. For the first time we were able to call our families, and we requested a resupply so that we could wait for a summit bid. (A note about communication: We had a cell phone that did not connect to the local service, and the only call we could place was to an operator at Copper Valley Wireless. These operators were superhelpful in passing along messages. We believe a marine VHF would have worked well.) On the 12th we headed up with all remaining food. At 10,200' we built a bomber snow cave in a giant moat that became home for the next 60 hours. The 15th was worth the wait, calm and clear, one of the most spectacular days in the hills either of us has had. We fully enjoyed our climb to the summit and on the way down saw the grub arrive. The route from the water to the Knik at 8,400' was probably new, though the rest has been done many times. Also, we assume that the range has been crossed in winter before, but we never researched it.

On the 16th we descended from high camp all the way to the alder trees. The evening of the 17th found us near the toe of the Knik, sharing a campfire with moose. Mission accomplished mid-afternoon of the 18th at the Hunter Creek Bridge on the Knik River road.

JOHNNY SODERSTROM AND JOE REICHERT

Mt. Marcus Baker, attempt via Pi Ridge. In a Whittier, Alaska, warehouse of dry-docked boats we studied maps and photos of College Fjord. Rain drummed on the metal roof, and our breath spilled out in plumes of fog. Mik Shain and I were planning a trip that would fuse maritime adventure with climbing exploration and involve several climates. In an 18-day effort we hoped to pioneer a route from the sea to the summit of the highest point in the Chugach, Mt. Marcus

Baker (13,176'). I had just completed a 600-mile solo kayaking trip down the Copper River and through Prince William Sound from Glennallen to Seward. Mik had just finished a stint on Denali as a mountaineering ranger.

We chose a ridge that bounded the Smith Glacier to the east. We hoped the ridge would lead to the Knik Glacier at 9,000'. From the Knik, the summit seemed an easy eight miles. On July 20, with ice axes and packs strapped to our kayaks, we began the 60-mile paddle to the ridge. We feasted on salmon we caught during our days on the ocean.

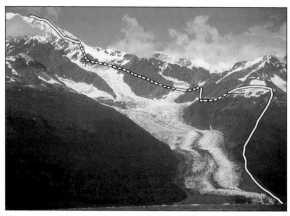

The route on Marcus Baker's Pi Ridge. *Jeff Pflueger*

Where the Smith Glacier calves into College Fjord, we hefted 10 days' of supplies onto our backs and began climbing in the rain. Our route became a wondrous journey so bountiful with challenges, matched by creative solutions, that we could only digest it one savory moment at a time.

From the sea to 3,000' we thrashed through alder thickets, dodging devil's club, cow parsnip, and bears. Occasional easy 5th-class rock provided faster climbing. One

Mik Shain looking down at the fjord from Marcus Baker's Pi Ridge. *Jeff Pflueger*

failed chest-beating contest with an aggressive bear sent us in a panicked run, ice axes waving above us. Unending rain and poor visibility pinned us at our 4,000' camp for four days. To avoid a series of gendarmes, we continued in the rain along the margin of the Smith Glacier and up a 5.6 gully to the crest of the ridge. The gully is just southeast of an icefall spilling from the Baltimore Glacier.

We camped at 4,400' at the Baltimore. We continued along the Baltimore's margin to a spur that rose west to regain the ridge. Slushy point releases avalanched all around in cascades of mud, rock, and snow. Our position on the snowy crest was safe, though twice I nearly buried Mik as he belayed me. At 7,300' we were again on the ridge. We camped.

The climbing above was spectacular: a knife-edge ridge followed by a crevassed maze and steep snow. We reveled in our tenuous position. An azure sky, brilliant snow, and an unending glacial landscape punctuated by black spires of Chugach rock contained us in a boundless wilderness vessel. Our path seemed the only passage from the sea. At 8,700', an easy climb along a cornice and up a mound appeared to be all that separated us from the Knik Glacier. We were out of food, fuel, and time, and another storm had arrived from the Aleutians. We had pioneered a route from the sea to where we stood, but we would not reach the top of Marcus Baker this time. Two days later we were back at sea level. During the climb we had read aloud The Life of Pi—a parable about the nature of reality, a survival story of a boy, Pi Patel, on an improbable ocean voyage. Our climb and the story became the same the night we returned to the sea and finished the last pages, igniting a discussion about perception, reality, their relation, and our creative roles in both. Our route was Pi Ridge: AK Grade 3, 6 miles, 8,700' gain.

JEFF PFLUEGER

ALASKA WRANGELL MOUNTAINS

Peaks 10,478', 9,900', and 10,088'. From May 8 to 17, James Dietzmann, Paul Templeton, and I did three possible first ascents of 10,000' peaks in the Wrangells. We had bad weather for most of the trip and were lucky to get any climbs in at all between storms. I had hoped to climb some of the bigger peaks, but it wasn't to be on this trip.

Kelly Bay of Wrangell Mountain Air dropped us off at roughly 7,700' on an eastern fork of the Russell Glacier north of Mt. Churchill near the volcanic cone of Mt. Sulzer, which Bob Jacobs climbed in 1980 from the White River. It is a nice area with some big icefalls to negotiate. I had hoped to get great pictures looking to the south, but that wasn't to be either.

We climbed Peak 10,478' on May 9 via an easy glacier and ramp from the west, finishing on the south ridge for the last few hundred feet. It was very windy and the weather was changing. We could see only clouds above 11,000 feet. On the 11th we climbed Peak 10,091' to its eastern summit of 9,900'+ via a steep, south-facing gully that tops out at 9,700 feet or so between the two summits. On May 12 we skied southwest from camp using a glacier system and icefall to reach a 9,600' saddle between Peak 10,088' and, to the south, Peak 10,400'+. We then ascended the south ridge of Peak 10,088' to the summit. It was not technical, mainly a narrow ridge walk to a pointy summit. We barely made it back to camp when the next storm blew in. We had hoped to climb Peaks 10,400'+ and 10,600'+ on the 12th, but the weather shorted our day. On the other days we also couldn't climb because of storms. Our pickup on the 16th was delayed by weather until the 17th. These were probably first ascents, but I don't make that statement as fact, just probability.

DANNY KOST, *AAC*

ALASKA SAINT ELIAS MOUNTAINS

WRANGELL-SAINT ELIAS NATIONAL PARK

Mt. Gunnar Naslund, Uncle Gunny's Weight-Loss Program; Mt. Huxley, first ascent. On April 22 Carlos Buhler and I were flown onto a spur of the Barnard Glacier below the unclimbed 3,000' east face of Mt. Gunnar Naslund (Peak 12,659', located 10-15 miles southeast of Mt. Bona and 20 miles west of Mt. Bear). Weather was perfect for our eight days in the range. We acclimated on the 23rd by doing the first ascent of the ca 11,600' peak above base camp to the east of Gunnar

Uncle Gunny's Weight-Loss Program leads directly to the summit of Mt. Gunnar Naslund; the line on the right is the descent. *Carlos Buhler*

Naslund. We ascended the west face to the south ridge and named it (unofficially) Mt. Huxley, for the environmental-studies college we both graduated from.

On April 26 we started at midnight. We planned to go light, making a continuous push without the encumbrance of overnight gear. Our one nod to safety was a stove with enough fuel to brew three quarts of water. We soloed the first 1,000', roping up at the constriction in the central couloir draining the upper face. We swapped leads, racing against the coming sun to reach the mixed band that guards the upper half of the face. I drew the mixed band, which got my attention with a sloping mantle covered in grainy snow to exit. Carlos drew steep rotten snow that required both of us to summon a little extra. Shattered rock bands provided adequate belay anchors, but belays took more time to set up than climbing between them. We had promised ourselves we would belay on the upper face, and we did, even after we realized we were going to spend a night near the top of the face. After 22 hours on the go we set to chopping a ledge out of rotten, then compact, ice. We were 300 feet below the summit. Two hours of effort kept us warm until midnight, when we sat down for a cold bivy. We had only day packs and climbing clothes—no pads, bags, bivy sacks, or tent. In only a few minutes shivering commenced. We beat circulation back into our limbs and half-heartedly chopped at the ledge to produce more body heat. Most of the night was passed by trying to be comfortable shivering. I heard Carlos asleep snoring many times, only to jolt awake a few minutes later. Meanwhile a great northern lights show was going on. I was too wasted to fully appreciate it, but I did watch it to pass time. At 4:00 a.m. Carlos climbed down below our ice-screw belay and ran in place to warm up. He ran for 30 minutes and fell asleep on his return to the ledge. His sleep only lasted a few minutes, as he was awakened again by shivering. After sunrise we soaked up an hour of warmth before we got going. We topped the face and had a nervous traverse over the summit ridge and a monster

Good Neighbor Peak and Mt. Vancouver viewed from Pt. 2,930m on Latus Pass Arm. *Roger Wallis*

cornice that stuck out 100' over the face.

Our descent down the east ridge was involved, with multiple rappels off of buried snow-filled stuff sacks. We downclimbed moderate-to-steep sections for hours, finally arriving at a gully which led back to the glacier 2,000' below. We committed to the gully and began "burning" the rack as each rap station ate gear. When we finally arrived on the glacier below, each of us had downclimbed 400' sections to string together scarce rap stations. We were out of pitons, slings, and a good portion of the wired nuts. We hadn't found any ice that would enable an ice rappel. We staggered into base camp after 42 hours of effort. Carlos swore that he was done with light-and-fast modern style. I'm still not sure what I learned, as I am soon headed back to Alaska for more.

GLENN DUNMIRE, *AAC*

Good Neighbor Peak, southeast ridge and clarification; Mt. Vancouver, St. Elias Range, Alaska and Canada. Paul Barry and I climbed a new route on the southeast face of Good Neighbor Peak (15,700') during May 18-21. We also completed the two-mile traverse to the higher summit of Mt. Vancouver (15,787') before descending our route. Ours was the fifth ascent of Good Neighbor Peak and the sixth of Mt. Vancouver. Only the 1967 Centennial expedition had reported climbing both peaks. Our southeast ridge route on Good Neighbor (Alaska Grade 3) is bounded on the left by the 1967 Centennial (south-southeast) Rib and the 1979 East Buttress route on the right. All three routes are visible in the Bradford Washburn photograph highlighting the adjacent South Spur (*AAJ 1994*, p. 88). Further research identified a similar Washburn photograph from the 1992 *Canadian Alpine Journal* (p. 13) that incorrectly labeled our then-unclimbed route as the Centennial Rib, confirmed by articles in the 1968 *AAJ* and *Expedition Yukon*, published in

1972. The traverse between Good Neighbor Peak and Mt. Vancouver is best seen in a Washburn photograph in the 1978 *AAJ* (p. 544).

Paul Claus of Ultima Thule Outfitters landed us one mile south of our ridge at 7,800' on the Valerie Glacier (Alaska) on May 17. The next morning, Paul and I cached our skis in the bergshrund at 9,300' and started climbing east-facing snow slopes to gain our ridge. Four pitches of 50° snow led to the knife-edge crest that we followed for two pitches to the base of a prominent red rock pyramid at 10,000'. This start avoided difficult rock lower down, where the ridge spine meets the glacier. We belayed three rotten class 5 pitches, then scrambled to the top of a small snow dome, at 10,650' atop the rock pyramid, where we camped after 11 hours of climbing. The next morning we descended steeply for 100' to a col. Above, four pitches of 45° snow led to a two-pitch knife-edge ice ridge, all of which we protected with running belays using pickets and ice screws. At 11,100' our rocky ridge blended into the glaciated upper southeast face. Technical terrain transitioned to post-holing through knee-to- thigh-deep snow until monstrous crevasses forced a 1/2-mile traverse west toward the Centennial Route. We wallowed an ascending trough up and left, intersecting the Centennial Route at 13,700', placing our second and final camp at 14,300' just below the crest of the east buttress after 10 hours of climbing. Paul and I left camp at 8 a.m. the following morning and made a descending traverse into the prominent 14,100' col on the east buttress proper. We simul-climbed the final exposed 1,500' to Good Neighbor Peak, bypassing most technical difficulties on the north, reaching the summit at noon and crossing into Canada. The two-mile ridge to Mt. Vancouver was interrupted by three intermediate summits, the last of which proved the most difficult, with its exposed knife-edge ridge. At 5:30 p.m. Paul and I stood atop Canada's Mt. Vancouver, becoming its first visitors in 26 years. Six hours of careful downclimbing found us back at high camp, completing our 15-hour day. Our fourth and final day was spent descending to base camp, rappelling most of the ridge below 11,100'. Paul Claus returned for us on May 27 to shuttle us 50 miles north to Canada's King Peak (16,995'), where we made our third unsuccessful attempt in three years.

DAVE HART, *AAC*

Mount Vancouver (15,787') and Good Neighbor Peak (15,700') complete climbing history. All climbs are described in the following year's AAJ.

   1949: Mt. Vancouver (first ascent), via northwest ridge
   1967: Good Neighbor and Vancouver, (first ascent of Good Neighbor), via south-south
      east rib
   1968: Good Neighbor, via west-south ridge
   1975: Vancouver, via north buttress
   1975: Vancouver, via northeast ridge
   1977: Vancouver, via west face
   1979: Good Neighbor (to 15,000'), via east buttress
   1993: Good Neighbor, via south spur
   1994: Good Neighbor, via south spur
   2003: Good Neighbor and Vancouver, via southeast ridge

DAVE HART, *AAC*

Mt. Foresta from the Hubbard Glacier base camp showing East Ridge route. *Paul Knott*

Mt. Foresta, East Ridge to north peak and altitude note. On May 3, Erik Monasterio and I landed at 4,040' on the Hubbard Glacier, courtesy of Paul Swanstrom from Haines. Conditions were unusual, with crevasse lines extending into the glacier and a melt-freeze crust on the surface. We elected to tackle Mt. Foresta, aiming for the unclimbed north peak. This pointed summit is marked on the 1:250,000 map as the highest at 11,960' (3,645m). It is quite separate from the south peak (11,040', 3,365m), climbed by Fred Beckey's party in 1979 and reportedly higher. There have been no further reported ascents of the mountain.

We climbed the East Ridge, which we joined at 6,400' (1,951m) via a shallow snow rib in a northeast-facing cwm. The snow in the cwm was wind-deposited and less stable than we wished. On the ridge itself large detached cornices over a sharp granite crest made for insecure climbing. We felt progressively more committed as we overcame numerous hidden obstacles, including steep rock steps and poorly bridged gaps in the cornice. After we had been six hours on the ridge, the going finally eased, and we made good progress on hard névé to a camp at 8,620' (2,635m). Similar conditions above led us, surprisingly quickly, to the summit on May 8. The GPS and altimeter read 10,960' (3,341m), exactly 1,000' below the map height. Visually, the south peak was a little higher, consistent with the 80' difference between its map height and our measured height.

In warmer conditions our descent was even more unnerving, with an unrelenting choice between the hanging cornice and the spiky granite edge. We camped near the top of the snow rib hoping for a freeze, but the weather deteriorated overnight. The snow in the cwm felt wet and poorly bonded. We descended without incident, but had to rely entirely on GPS waypoints to navigate back to base camp in what were rapidly becoming full storm conditions. A meter of snow fell on the glacier during the next 48 hours. After this we attempted to penetrate the icefall leading to the east rib of Mt. Vancouver, but found it essentially impassable. Its condition had worsened radically since my 1999 attempt to approach the same route.

PAUL KNOTT, *Alpine Club, New Zealand*

Canada

ST. ELIAS RANGE

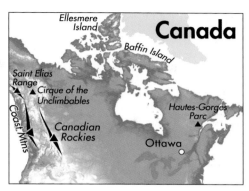

Various ascents and attempts. In May 2002 Tim Connelly and I guided an American Alpine Institute group in the St. Elias Range. Paul Claus of Ultima Thule flew us to an unnamed glacier cirque south of the Goat Creek Glacier and north of the Bagley Icefield. With near-perfect weather for nine days, we ascended five peaks, all possible first ascents. We began by climbing Peak 8,861' via the east ridge, and a neighboring peak just to the east. We found ice and snow up to 50° on both climbs. Peaks 7,900' and 8,435' turned out to be interesting climbs up west ridges, with short ice steps and some 4th-class mixed terrain. Tim led the highlight climb of the area, the northeast face of Peak 8,412', with three pitches of ice up to 60°, ending at the intersection of three distinct ridges. My team repeated this ascent the next day. The climbing potential in the St. Elias is still vast, and entails an expedition to a truly remote wilderness.

In June 2002 Dan Shutteroff and I guided a different AAI group into the St. Elias Range. This time Paul Claus flew us into onto a section of glacier at the confluence of the Baldwin and Frasier glaciers. We made the second ascent of the west face of Point 10,142' and attempted its still unclimbed north face, finding six pitches of unconsolidated snow and ice up to 80°. A ridge, which looked to be mixed snow and ice and low-5th-class rock, continued for another 1,000 feet or so. We made the second ascent of Peak 9,450' by a new route up the pyramid-shaped east face, finding snow slopes up to 55° and a spectacular summit. Climbing the north ridge of Peak 9,970' (a new route and, I believe, the second ascent of the peak), we found 40-50° snow-and-ice slopes, with a 15' vertical section of ice. We also climbed Point 8,184' and a peak just to the northeast of it, beyond a prominent col, where we found 40° degree snow slopes and brilliant views of Mt. Vancouver and Mt. St. Elias. Both these peaks were climbed via south and southwest slopes.

JAY HACK, *Mugatu Alpine Club*

KLUANE NATIONAL PARK RESERVE

Kluane National Park Reserve, mountaineering summary and statistics. During 2003 in Kluane National Park Reserve, 140 persons participated in 42 mountaineering expeditions. This accounted for 2,279 person-days in the Icefields of Kluane. This is somewhat higher use than in the previous year.

The weather this year was, as usual, unpredictable. Early in the climbing season a huge high-pressure system made for excellent traveling, and climbers fortunate enough to be in the St. Elias Ranges had successful trips. Unfortunately, during the main climbing period the weather was stormy and snow conditions poor, thus accounting for the low success rate on the major peaks, particularly Mt. Logan. On the King Trench route, only two out of 18 expeditions made the summit. With low snow last winter and an advancing icefall high on the route, difficult routefinding conditions existed. Many open crevasses have made this route more difficult over the past few years.

As usual most expeditions went to Mt. Logan. Twenty-nine attempted Logan—eight via the King Trench route, nine the East Ridge, one the Catenary, and one the Southeast Face. Only six expeditions reached one of the main summits. One success was a traverse of the mountain from the East Ridge to the King Trench.

Other mountains that saw climbing expeditions included King Peak (2), Queen Mary (3), Vancouver (2), Foresta (1), Kennedy (2), Hubbard (1), Walsh (1), Wood (1), and Steel/Lucania (1). In addition a research team was on Mt. Logan, and there were four ski-touring expeditions, including one that circumskied the Mt. Logan massif. The St. Elias Ranges offer excellent ski touring, and it was good to see more people taking advantage of this activity.

There were no major search and rescue operations. A few climbing teams self-evacuated or looked after injured or sick members of their team—thus the advantage of building self-reliance into one's climbing plans.

Anyone interested in mountaineering or ski-touring in Kluane National Park Reserve should contact Mountaineering Warden, Kluane National Park Reserve, Box 5495, Haines Jct, Yukon, Y0B 1L0; call 867-634-7279; fax 867-634-7277; or email kluane_info@pc.gc.ca. Ask for a "mountaineer's package." Alternatively, visit the parks website at www.parkscanada.gc.ca/kluane. Application forms and assumption-of-risk forms can be downloaded from this site.

RICK STALEY, *Mountaineering Warden, Kluane National Park Reserve*

Good Neighbor Peak, southeast ridge and clarification, and traverse to Mt. Vancouver. See the Alaska section of Climbs & Expeditions for this report.

Latus Pass Arm, various ascents and attempts. There are four main tributaries on the south side of Kaskawulsh Glacier: South Arm, Stairway, Cascade, and, farthest from Slims River, the Latus Pass Arm. In July we made a short visit to the Latus Pass Arm, to evaluate its potential as a site for an Alpine Club of Canada Centennial Camp in 2006.

As ski-touring terrain, the Latus Pass Arm is well-known because it provides an excellent route from the upper Hubbard/upper Kaska-wulsh iceshed, via the Latus Pass, to the upper Lowell Glacier and the country lying beyond to the south and east. However, as a mountaineering area it has received little

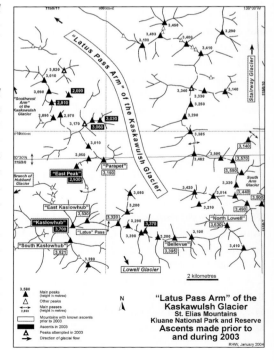

"Latus Pass Arm" of the
Kaskawulsh Glacier
St. Elias Mountains
Kluane National Park and Reserve
Ascents made prior to
and during 2003

Peaks near Latus Pass Arm. Roger Wallis

attention, probably because of the poor rock quality and the lack of major peaks, with Kaslowhub (3,700m) being the highest. The area was first explored by Bradford Washburn's 1935 Lowell Glacier Expedition. The first ascents appeared to have been made in 1961 by a large Seattle Mountaineers party. Since then a number of peaks have been climbed.

Our plan in 2003 was to place a base camp at 2,600m and explore the side glaciers and mountains at the head (southern end) of the Latus Pass Arm Glacier. However, due to unfavorable weather and poor flying/landing conditions, Andy Williams had to drop us off at 2,350m, eight kilometers north of our intended base. During our stay it snowed or rained, with fog and/or whiteout on seven of the nine climbing days. We only had freezing temperatures on three nights, and the frozen surface was gone by noon.

We completed the following climbs: Point 3,030m: first ascent, via southwest ridge; Simon Carr, Bill McKenzie. Point 3,060m: first ascent via north cirque and west ridge; Roger Wallis, Ted Rosen, Bill McKenzie, Simon Carr, Mark McDermott. Point 2,690m: first ascent, via west slope; Mark McDermott, Simon Carr. Point 2,810m: first ascent, via south ridge; Paul Geddes. Point 3,370m: first ascent, via southeast ridge from east col; Paul Geddes, Willa Harasym, Ted Rosen, Roger Wallis. Mt. Kaslowhub (3,700m): 4th ascent(?), via north-northeast ramp, and ski descent (4,000'); Paul Geddes, Willa Harasym, Ted Rosen. East Peak (2,930m): 2nd ascent, via south ridge; Roger Wallis.

Climbs attempted but not completed: Point 3,050m: via south col and south ridge; Paul Geddes, Willa Harasym, Ted Rosen. Point 3,170m: via north cirque and east ridge; Roger Wallis, Ted Rosen, Bill McKenzie, Simon Carr, Mark McDermott. Point 3,340m: via southwst cirque and south ridge; Bill McKenzie, Simon Carr, Mark McDermott. Point 3,020m: via east ridge; Bill McKenzie and Simon Carr.

The Latus Pass area has a number of moderately challenging peaks in the height range 2,900-3,700m, many of which remain unclimbed. There are attractive snow-and-ice routes, but the rock quality is appalling, and some of the snow-and-ice routes are threatened by seracs, crevasse systems, and cornices. Really cold nights with hard frozen snow are required to make climbing safe and enjoyable. Hence early June might be the best time for climbing.

ROGER WALLIS, *Toronto Section, Alpine Club of Canada*

BAFFIN ISLAND

Mt. Asgard, east face of South Tower. In July I soloed a new route on the 2,000' east face of the South Tower of Mount Asgard on Baffin Island. My route (VI 5.10 A2) consisted of mostly free climbing with an equal mixture of well-protected crack and runout face. I ascended the route in 16 long pitches and descended via 14 long rappels. The climb required 24 hours of climbing from the glacier to the true summit. No bolts were placed and no cracks were "cleaned." The summit was reached July 27.

JIM BEYER, *adapted from* Alpinist *Magazine*

Wide open spaces and waves of sastrugi on the Baffin Icefield Traverse. *Greg Horne*

Icefield traverse and Peak 1,850m, southwest ridge. From April 14 to May 5 Louise Jarry, Vicki Sahanatien, Doug Stern, Vivian Wasiuta, and I made a ski traverse of an unnamed icefield on the Cumberland Peninsula from Iqalugajut Fiord to Kaniqturusiq Fiord (south fork of Padle Fiord), all east of Kingnait Pass. This was the first complete traverse of the icefield from its southern edge to its northern limit, and we made the first ascent of the highest peak in this icefield. The ground logistics consisted of a snowmobile drop-off from Pangnirtung and a pickup from Qikiqtaruaq.

This icefield had been previously visited by Mike O'Reilly et al. in 1974 (*CAJ 1975*, p. 99). They climbed 10 peaks. George Van Cochran et al. briefly spent some time there in 1977 (*CAJ 1978*, p. 36), and there is a vague report in the 1977 *CAJ* (p. 90) of a spring traverse by four skiers "from Padle Fiord to Kingnait Fiord over the glaciers and icecaps south of the Padle–Kingnait trough." No other details of this trip were reported.

From Iqalugajut Fiord we skied up a valley with a series of lakes to pass #1 (350m), with a small lake on its east side. We crossed the Kuugajuaq River valley, skied up a side drainage, crossed pass #2, and camped near the southern end of the icefield. We made a steep, cramponed pull of our sleds onto the edge of the icefield, traversed a gentle plateau, crossed pass #3, a

Vivian Wasiuta enjoying a sled-free day on the Baffin Icefield Traverse. *Greg Horne*

microwatershed crest, descended into a glacial basin, and climbed toward pass #4.

On April 20 we easily skied up to glaciated pass #4 (1,143m) and down the north side. We descended onto a valley glacier draining towards Nallussiaq Fiord and ascended it briefly, before crampon-hauling to pass #5 (1,130m), which is between Peak 1,520m and its 1,160m south shoulder. We skied around the east side of a 1,407m nunatak and coasted into a glacial basin. From a low point of 690m we headed north toward glacial pass #6 (1,143m). The north side of the pass appeared steep enough that we set up a three-rope lower of our sleds.

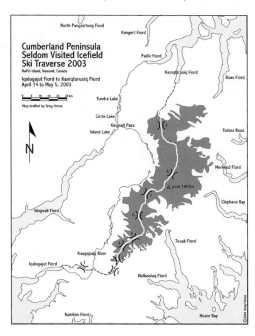

Another basin was crossed to glacial Pass #7 (1,295m). The descent ended in a jumble of moraines. We now reached one of the major valley glaciers flowing from the core of the icefield toward Touak Fiord. The "Walking Weasel Glacier," so named for the uncharacteristic tracks observed, was crossed to a camp positioned for the next day's climb. On April 25 we short-roped up the rocky-spur southwest ridge of the highest peak (1,850m) (Zone 20W, 477775E 7336700N, NAD 27) of this unnamed icefield. The summit was a classic alpine snow arête.

A 10km move of camp to the north,

just north of glacial pass #8 (1,275m), placed us in a great position to make numerous ascents as side trips. The next morning we woke to the sound of snow falling on our tents. For the following eight days we slowly advanced north in a whiteout, as 40cm of fresh, wet snow fell during the storm. The foul weather continued long enough that any thoughts of peakbagging vaporized, and reaching the ocean took priority. As we reached our last pass, glacier Pass #9, north-northeast of Peak 5,930', the clouds lifted long enough to see the ground horizon and pick a reasonable descent line.

The snout of the retreating glacier was a debris-piled, hummocky obstacle course in flat light, making for tiring, slow traveling. This valley and the south end of Kaniqturusiq Fiord are sheltered from significant winds. Through the night of May 6-7 we returned to Qikiqtarjuaq by snowmobile in about seven hours.

GREG HORNE, *Alpine Club of Canada*

VAMPIRE SPIRES

The Phoenix in the Vampire Spires, showing Freebird on the right (Childers-Shull-Young, 1998) and Wallflowers on the left (Caton-Patterson, 2003). X marks Caton and Patterson's highpoint. *Jasmin Caton*

Phoenix, Wallflowers to near summit. On June 30 a tiny Hughes 500 helicopter dropped Amelia Patterson and me at the base of a stunning 2,500' granite face known as the Phoenix. It is the largest feature in the Vampire Spires group of the Ragged Range in Canada's Northwest Territories, 15 miles north of the famed Cirque of the Unclimbables. Thanks to our adventurous spirits and the generous support of the Alpine Club of Canada, we hoped to complete the first female ascent of the Phoenix, either by establishing a new route or completing a second ascent of one of the several previously climbed routes on the granite face.

After fixing and hauling three pitches, we committed ourselves to our route and spent five nights on the face. We climbed 13 long pitches, mainly aiding the dirt-and-vegetation-choked coarse cracks characteristic of the region. There were no nights, due to the midnight sun, but we were frequently forced to take cover in our cramped portaledge by daily rain showers and our fatigue. Less than 200' from the summit an ice-filled chimney halted our progress. With nowhere to place pro and no ice gear, we retreated.

Our route, which we named Wallflowers (VI 5.8 C2+) to commemorate the colorful flora destroyed by our efforts, linked the unfinished After School Special with the upper four pitches of Freebird (Childers-Shull-Young, 1998) in 13 pitches, one of which was previously unclimbed. We placed no protection bolts, five belay bolts, and used only clean aid. The route could go free with enormous amounts of cleaning and a willingness to climb sharp offwidths.

Thanks to The Alpine Club of Canada's Jen Higgins Memorial Fund, other sponsors, and many fellow dirtbags who lent us gear.

JASMIN CATON, *Canada*

Fortress, You Enjoy Myself. On a rainy July 20 Pat Goodman and I, with financial support from a Balance Bar Grant, were helicoptered into the Vampire Spires, getting dropped off 30m from what would be our home for the next 24 days. We immediately set up camp, where we were imprisoned for the next 36 hours by rain. This set the tone for our stay.

The weather finally broke, and we were able to scope the route we intended to climb: Cornerstone (V 5.10 A2), climbed by Matt Childers and Cogie Reed in 1998. Theirs was the first ascent of the 1,500' wall called the Fortress. While scoping the line, we noticed anchors leading up the headwall via an impressive crack system. Two pitches led to a chimney, which topped out at a ledge on the third pitch of the Cornerstone. We decided to climb these pitches, so that we could further investigate the route. Although we were unable to find literary documentation, we had heard rumors about a German team floating the Nahani River, hiking in, and climbing. Climbing these two wet, loose pitches, we found anchors every 25 meters, with 1/4" Petzl self-drive bolts and aluminum hangers, as well as bolts at hard free moves, for a total of over 27 bolts. Whoever established these pitches used exceptionally light hardware, set anchors up for single rappels, and was obviously very conscious of weight, thus reinforcing the belief that it was a team that had floated the river and hiked in. We then climbed the chimney and, upon reaching the ledge, got our first look at what would be the crux of the route: a clean left-facing dihedral that eventually thinned to tips and continued through a roof-like chimney feature. However, the weather deteriorated, forcing us to retreat.

After several rainy days the skies cleared and we attempted the route via the original start of the Cornerstone. We reached the same ledge as on our previous attempt and again retreated due to weather. We made several attempts, invariably being defeated by storms, never making it more than five pitches up the wall.

Eventually the rain turned to snow, and we tried a new route on the neighboring Vampire Spire, waiting for the weather to come around. Being an aid invalid, I belayed Pat for two days on an aid route, which, at about the midway point, shallowed out into a water-groove bashy-flare. We would have none of this, considering we were on a free-climbing trip. Defeated again.

Finally, at 11 o'clock on a mid-August day (we had lost track of time), on a surge of coffee-induced manic motivation, everything from chalk to ropes to bones still damp from a six-inch snowstorm two days prior, we set off on an ill-prepared attempt, forgetting headlamps, tape, gloves, extra food, and water. Neither of us expected the rock to be dry, nor did we believe that we would make it up more than a couple of pitches. Nevertheless we found ourselves at our high point, with blue skies and virgin rock overhead. We diverged from the Cornerstone and continued for another six pitches until it was too dark and we were too exhausted to climb further. We huddled on a two-foot ledge in a rotten, wet gully, unsure of our location in relation to the summit, shivering for what might have been five hours. When we started climbing again, we reached the summit in just two pitches.

Pat and I made what we believe to be the second ascent of the Fortress, as well as the first free ascent. We climbed the first four pitches of the Cornerstone (only the first pitch had been freed) and eight more pitches, of which none appeared to have been climbed, to create You Enjoy Myself (V 5.12). We placed one bolt at the fourth belay. To be honest, I admit that after our second or third attempt we left two fixed lines, but we removed them on the following attempt, dissatisfied with the idea of not climbing in proper alpine fashion. On our final go we climbed the route in a single push, freeing every pitch from bottom to top.

HANK JONES

CIRQUE OF THE UNCLIMBABLES

Unnamed spire, attempt. Bryan Palminiter and I attempted a new line on an unnamed spire to the right of the Lotus Flower Tower in August. Since our return, we have learned that the high point of our attempt came within 50 feet of intersecting a Belgian line on the same formation, which was mislabeled "Tathagata Tower" in the 1979 AAJ (p. 205). The spire appears to be the right (northwest) buttress of the Lotus Flower Tower, but has a distinct summit (best seen when mist blows between it and the main tower). It can be recognized from below by right-slanting black rock at the base and a large square-cut roof with a left-facing corner on the lower head-wall. There is a smaller, slender triangular spire (with no recorded climbing history) between the Lotus Flower Tower and the one we attempted.

We started left of the black slabs and climbed three 60m easy 5th class approach pitches. The first followed blocky crack systems to below a 10-foot step. After passing this 5.9 step, the route trends up left to the base of the main wall. The main wall starts above and is quite vertical, with rock similar to that on the Lotus Flower Tower. We chose a large straight-in crack near the right edge. We followed the crack and nearby flakes and face features for two 100-foot pitches of 5.9/10-. We explored a little higher on more difficult ground before time forced us to turn around. We were attempting to reach the right arête of the spire, where we would have (unknowingly) joined the 1977 Belgian line. Several excellent lines are visible to the left of our line, and we were surprised there was no record of them being climbed. While in the Cirque we also climbed the regular route on the Lotus Flower Tower and climbed Unicorn Peak.

KEVIN JONES

East Huey Spire, Don't Panic It's Organic. Scott Hollander and I climbed a new route on East Huey this summer. Our trip was fortunate to have great weather, but it still rained most afternoons. After our two and a half days of travel from the states we were happy to have arrived in Fairy Meadows. If you can afford it, I recommended renting a chopper to Fairy Meadows. Unfortunately, we hiked up from the lake. Scott and I established Don't Panic It's Organic (IV 5.10+ C1) over two days. Our route name commemorates the extensive cleaning of vegetation required of us. DPIO is located left of Riders on the Storm, in the prominent, right-facing corner system. Above this corner, it meanders up right to the top of the buttress. Rap stations were rigged with mostly nuts, though one anchor required two bolts. Scott and I believe that the bottom of Riders on the Storm and the top of our route would make a great free climb.

JOSH GROSS, *Moab, Utah*

East Huey Spire, Riders on the Storm. In July, after five days of travel from Colorado, Evan Stevens and I unloaded our gear from the plane at Glacier Lake and trekked through three miles of hell. After losing the "trail," we took six hours of bushwhacking through alder thickets and scrambling up loose talus to reach Fairy Meadows.

The following afternoon Evan and I did some reconnaissance. Since it was still relatively early season, snow capped the peaks' summits and melted onto their faces. Flattop Peak was loaded with several feet of snow, spilling snowmelt onto the face we'd intended to climb. East Huey Spire caught our eye, with a dry line up splitter granite cracks. We climbed the first two pitches (which had been climbed previously) and scoped the rest of the route through binoculars. It looked promising and had never been climbed to the summit.

The next day dawned clear and we attempted the Lotus Flower Tower, but were thunderstormed off at pitch 13. We spent the rest of the trip working on our new route on East Huey Spire. We found evidence of a 1997 attempt by Paul Friberg and Kurt Blair on the first five pitches, which they rated 5.10 A2. We freed these pitches at 5.11c; the quality was Yosemitesque, with little cleaning required on pitches one through four. Pitches five to seven involved difficult climbing up a beautiful splitter. Pitch six was the crux, at 5.12b (or C2). Neither Evan nor I could free it without falling. Pitch seven traversed out of the splitter (5.11b) into a nearby corner, where the free climbing eased to 5.10. We followed the corner for several pitches and freed all of these pitches (previously aid climbed and named "Don't Panic It's Organic"). There was one dangerously loose and wet pitch that went free at 5.10bR. The final pitch (5.11+) was an unclimbed line that went up a steep three-inch crack and onto a sparse arête directly to the summit.

We topped out on our fourth day of working the route, using two fixed ropes to bypass the initial pitches and save strength to free the upper pitches on the summit push. All other attempts to free the face were made from the ground up, freeing every pitch as we went. After six days of climbing and gardening with nut tools and wire brushes, there were two pitches that we didn't free. Pitch six would go at 5.12b/c. Our route, Riders on the Storm, should become an ultraclassic and is guaranteed to be repeated by the masses. There is a good chance it will be freed by a stronger team in the near future.

JOHANN ABERGER

COAST MOUNTAINS

Coast Mountains, remote areas summary. It was a reasonable summer in the remote sections of the Coast Mountains, but not as many "big" routes were done as in 2002. The most productive group were 10 people from the ACC Vancouver Section who enjoyed mostly hot sunny weather on the Upper Tellot Glacier in the Waddington Range in late July and early August. Many established routes were climbed, with the biggest undertaking being the 1,500m TD South Ridge of Serra Two. This got both a complete ascent from Sunny Knob, by Ade Miller and Rob Nugent, and a variation of its 500m upper portion, reached by a traverse across the southeast faces of Serras One and Two, by Janez Ales and Graham Rowbotham. Ales and Rowbotham also made three attempts to climb the Grand Cappuccino, none of which were successful.

Several new routes and variations were completed:
Stiletto Needle, variation direct start to Abrons–Milliken (2 pitches, 5.10); Ales, Rowbotham.
The Blade, left variation start to the East Buttress (2 pitches, 5.9); Miller, Nugent.
Tellot Spire #1, southeast face: Triple Crescent (4 pitches, D+ 5.11- A1); Ales, Luca Bellin, Rowbotham.
Dragonback East Peak, South Spur (3 pitches, AD+ 5.8); Toby Froschauer, Jeff Hunt, Jesse Mason.
Serra Two, east ridge, O Sole Mio (7 pitches, D+ 5.10+); Bellin, Serl.
Serra One, north face, Armonia (4 pitches, D+ WI3+ M4/5); Bellin, Serl.
In September Soren Svinth and Kasper Berkowitz climbed about 120m of mixed ground linking the start of the Northeast Face of Stiletto Peak to the upper part of the Chilton-Must, producing Academic Exercise. Climbing was mostly on 60° snow and ice with rock protection, with short 75° sections and one short vertical step.
Chris Barner and Paul Rydeen, of the Vancouver Island-based Heathens climbing club, had a prolific summer, roaming several sections of the Coast Mountains. In the Reliance Glacier area they repeated the 1,000m Southeast Ridge of Reliance, then climbed the following routes, likely new:
The 200m Northeast Rib on the Swan's Tail (south of Silver Swan Peak, earlier called "Lyn Peak").
The Southeast Face (200m, 50°) and Northeast Ridge (300m, 5.6/5.7) of Furrowed Peak, immediately southeast of Determination Mountain.
The Northeast Ridge of Oriana (3-4 pitches, 5.7).

They then joined their friends Alana Theroret and Darren Wilman at the Plummer Hut in the Waddington Range, where they climbed the 100m Southwest Face to the upper West Ridge of Athos Spire. They also managed two pitches of 5.9 climbing on the south face of Harvard Spire before abandoning the attempt, finding the rock much poorer than a certain recently published guidebook indicates. They finished their summer with a few days on Royal Glacier in the southern Niut Range. Here they did the possible first ascent of the NTS 8,530'/TRIM 2,602m peak at the head of Royal Glacier and climbed the Northeast Face (250m, ice) of Royal Peak.

Fred Beckey lured Ray Borbon, Dave Parker, Matt Perkins, and Bill Pilling onto the

Monarch Icefield in August. The latter four climbed the fine Northeast Buttress of Princess Mountain (350m, AD/AD+), descending the original 1953 Atkinson-Broda-Dudra-Rode Northwest Ridge and finding it surprisingly long and complicated—perhaps no surprise after all, considering the strength of the earlier party. They also did the nontechnical probable first ascent of a 9,100' peak ("Turtlehead") between Princess and Page, via its south rib.

Perhaps the outstanding ascent of the season was the solo of the 700m slanting couloir on the north face of Blackhorn in the northern Niut Range, in late September, by Colin Haley. He flew in with Dan Aylward and Don Serl, but a warm night (+4ºC at 4 a.m.) and occasional clattering stones convinced the latter two to wander up onto the north ridge. Undeterred, Colin sped up the 50°–60° route in 2-1/2 hours, encountering strenuously brittle ice but almost no rockfall. The walkout took the afternoon of the climbing day and the morning of the next, but was not as bushy and tangled as feared and, at times, verged on enjoyable.

DON SERL, Alpine Club of Canada, AAC

Southwest British Columbia (southern Coast Mountains and Canadian Cascades) summary. For a variety of reasons 2003 was not as busy as 2002. Some of the activists were elsewhere, otherwise occupied, or injured. Fires burning throughout the backcountry from July through September also curtailed activity. Nonetheless, it was a fairly productive year.

First, however, a few routes completed in 2002 but not mentioned in last year's summary should be noted for the sake of completeness, especially as they are fairly significant. In Cathedral Park, just north of the American border on the eastern side of the Cascades, Mike Crapo and Jordan Struthers established Goats Go To Heaven, Sheep Go To Hell (10 pitches, TD- IV 5.11a V2) on the rock pillar between the south face of Mt. Grimface and the 1994 Beckey-Condon-Must route on Macabre Tower. The route is reportedly sustained at 5.10; the V2 refers to an unprotected boulder problem forming one of the cruxes. Meanwhile, at the other end of southwestern B.C., on the impressively deep fjord of Princess Louisa Inlet northwest of Powell River, Peter Rowat and John Brodie established PLI Trail (17 pitches, ED1/2 V 5.10+) on the lower part of the immense Princess Louisa Wall. They had begun attempts on this 1,400m wall back in 1986. The route, as presently defined, reaches a prominent pinnacle about halfway up the wall. It is felt by the first-ascent party to offer a completed route in its own right. The remaining 700m appears to require aid and is an ongoing project. The PLI Wall was noted as a potential "biggest wall in Canada" as early as 1971 by the climbers of the day, but PLI Trail appears to be the first actual route on the wall. A nearby peak sports an even more impressive, Trango Tower-like feature: a 1,000m slab leading to the base of a 1,200m overhanging headwall. Sadly, the rock quality on this feature is said to be poor.

In the Squamish area, 2003 saw numerous significant ascents, new routes, and crowds. Perhaps the hardest new long route was Yukon Gold (III 5.12+A0) on the Zodiac Wall, by Matt Maddaloni and Mateo Antonelli. However, the route that is likely to see the most traffic emerged once again from under the jumars, gardening implements, and wire brush of local guide Kris Wild. The Millenium Falcon (IV 5.11a/b) is a completely new 14-pitch line in the Western Dihedrals area, running from base to summit, and offers a great alternative to the classic Grand Wall for parties competent at the grade.

In the Powell River area, 2003 was fairly quiet on the new routes front. Thanks to the new guidebook, there was a marked increase in the number of visitors, but the main activists were relatively inactive, and no major new lines went up.

Spring saw little new route activity in the alpine terrain, partly due to unsettled conditions. The deaths of Guy Edwards and John Millar on Devil's Thumb probably influenced many climbers to take it easy as well. At the memorial, Sean Easton and Jeremy Frimer met, decided to climb, and within a few days flew into Tantalus. Frimer writes, "For me it was about making light of a tough situation—like John and Guy would have—by making a new friend and then celebrating lives lived by living my life." The obvious northwest couloir was a line many had been eying; it gave a long 50° snow climb with four steeper mixed pitches at the top (D+ IV M-unrated). The pair descended via the north ridge, bivvied in a gentle pass between Tantalus and Pelion, then continued to Sigurd Creek and out to the Squamish Valley on foot.

When the dry spell began in mid-June, alpine activity began in earnest. In the mountains near Squamish, Craig McGee and Jim Martinello climbed a direct line on the south face of Mt. Ashlu. Smooth Hooky (D II/III 5.11) features several 60-70m rope-stretching pitches on immaculate rock and is named for the tactics Martinello employed to skip work for the ascent.

On Mt. Habrich, a popular granite horn close to Squamish, McGee with Brad White climbed a new line on the south face. This six pitch, D+ III 5.11+ A0 line takes rock between Gambit Grooves and Drug Stabbin' Time, climbing straight up from the lower pitches of the Diachronous Variation to Drug Stabbin', and is the hardest route on the peak.

Farther north, several new routes were climbed in the mountains north of Pemberton. Jeremy Frimer, John Crowley, and Geoff Hill climbed a six-pitch line on the southeast pillar of Mt. Aragorn. Flareathon (D III 5.10b) follows mostly wide, rounded cracks. Jordan Peters and Steven Harng explored a nearby valley and found several small granite towers, which they dubbed the Incisors. Incisor Edge climbs the north ridge of the western tower at about D- III 5.8. South of Mt. Sloan, Peters became obsessed with a granite spire mentioned in the local guidebook as possibly unclimbed. After several trips foiled by bad weather and partner epics, he summited to discover a cairn. The first ascent was made in the 1940s. However, the South Ridge route he established on Peak 8,380', now dubbed Mt. Land after pioneering local climber Gerben Land, was apparently a new route (PD+ 5.6).

East of Vancouver, the Fraser Valley also saw lots of activity. A couple of large, established, but unrepeated routes saw exploratory pushes but remained unrepeated. On the new route front, the South Nesakwatch Spire saw several parties, intrigued by last year's burst of development. Nebulous descriptions of existing lines resulted in many variations in the 5.10- to 5.11- range. Detailed topos will appear in the next editions of the appropriate guidebooks. Across the valley on the subpeaks of Slesse, Ken Laing and Michael Spagnut climbed a six-pitch route on the east face of Labour Day Summit (III, D, 5.10-). On the southeast (third) summit of Slesse, the Flight 810 Buttress marked as "incomplete" on the photo topo in *AAJ 2003*, p. 258, was completed by Drew Brayshaw and Fern Webb. A 12-pitch route goes at 5.8 via a start from the gully to the south, or a 17-pitch route (5.9) via a direct start from the buttress toe; either variation is worth an alpine D+ and a Grade IV.

In the Chehalis area, Steven Harng and Reinhard Fabische pushed into the relatively unexplored southwest corner of the group and found large granite slabs on Skwellepil Creek. They climbed one route on a face below Stonerabbit Peak. Featuring blank stemming corners, Stoned Rabbits is six pitches long and rated 10d/11aR. An alpine grade was not given, due to the more craglike nature of this subalpine face.

The Anderson River group of granite domes and spires was off-limits for much of the summer due to forest fires and locked forestry gates. However, before access control tightened down, Shaun Neufeld, Drew Brayshaw, and Dwayne Barg managed to sneak in and establish The Proof Is in the Pudding (D III 5.10c) on the south face of Ibex Peak. This route is amazingly clean and solid for an alpine climb and is highly recommended.

The late fall and winter of 2003-2004 saw several protracted spells of cold weather and produced the best ice for several years. Details will be published in the long-awaited second edition of West Coast Ice, which should be out in time for the 2004-2005 winter season.

DREW BRAYSHAW, *Canada, AAC*

Greyskull Valley. The Greyskull Valley Expedition included Laura Schmonsees, Trevor Deighton, Andy Rich, and myself. The expedition spent 23 days in June in the Coast Range on the border of British Columbia and Alaska. On June 8 we flew in from Skagway, Alaska, via helicopter to the unexplored valley and established a base camp on a rocky outcrop surrounded by unnamed glaciers and granite peaks. The valley is located about seven miles southwest of Mt. Foster.

The overall weather was extremely unsettled—only three days were without precipitation. We free-climbed and aided 1,000 feet up the north-northeast face of the main tower (Castle Greyskull), before being driven back by storms, lack of continuous crack systems, and friable rock.

On June 28 Andy and I attempted a long alpine route on the same tower, to the east of the aid route. Warm temperatures and slush stopped us after several hard (WI5) pitches. That same evening

2003 attempts on Castle Greyskull. Alas, the vertical white line is just a spindrift avalanche. *David Anderson*

Laura and Trevor made a 4th class ascent of a peak ("Sweetness") to the northeast of base camp. Rock climbing in the valley was limited by poor rock quality and bad weather, but alpine routes earlier in the year might have better results.

DAVE ANDERSON, *AAC*

Princess Mountain, Northeast Buttress. Fred Beckey planned our gathering, and we flew into the Monarch Icefield in early August. Matt Perkins, David Parker, Bill Pilling, Fred, and I set up a camp below the west face of Monarch Mountain. The following morning we set off, without Fred, to explore a possible direct east-to-west route toward Princess Mountain. Matt had seen a photo of a buttress that appeared unclimbed and worth investigating. Fred was nursing a rib injury from a trip the week before. He elected to rest until he was feeling more fit to climb. As always, though, we were rewarded with his unique humor.

The next day the rest of us crossed the pass that Dudra and Broda had traveled in the early 1950s en route to climbing Monarch, then headed west again to an easy-looking mountain with an elevation of approximately 9,100'. There was a pass on its south rib, and we ascended the rib by walking. There was no sign of human travel on the mountain, so David and I made a cairn on top. We called this mountain The Turtlehead. There was a mountain to the south we called

Approaching the Northeast Buttress route on Princess Mountain.
Ray Borbon

Flat Top Mountain—over 9,000', with horrible-looking rock and a large, north-facing, low-angle glacier. Flat Top looked nice but would not be an objective for this trip.

The next day we crossed the Dudra-Broda pass again to The Turtlehead and explored west, toward Princess Mountain. We did not know what to expect but encountered only snow slopes, with some crevasses but no icefalls. This shortcut eliminated much time that might have been used traveling north to the main body of the Monarch Icefield.

We camped below the eastern side of Princess Mountain, and the following morning headed onto its northeast buttress, through crevasses and a rotten-snow 'schrund. The four of us climbed mixed terrain, steep snow, ice, and good rock to the summit of Princess. I estimate the difficulty at about 5.5, steep snow and ice, with a little mixed climbing.

On our descent, possibly due to the year's low snowfall, we encountered very different conditions from what Dudra described 50 years before. From the main summit we had to downclimb a pitch of 4th class rock and then traverse and climb to the west snow summit. We descended the Dudra–Broda ascent route on the north arête, then continued south and east to reach camp after sundown. This proved to be a good idea, as opposed to descending snow and ice faces directly, since parts of those descents would have left us above huge crevasses impassable without a parachute or glider. We retraced our route back to Monarch Mountain the next morning.

RAY BORBON, *Kaskade Trad Klan*

Mt. Blackhorn, Northwest Couloir. On September 27 I made what I believe was the first ascent of Blackhorn Mountain's Northwest Couloir. Mike King flew Don Serl, Dan Aylward, and me from Bluff Lake to the base of the couloir on the evening before, and we quickly fell asleep on the scree. When we woke at 4 a.m. it felt unsettlingly warm, and we debated whether the couloir would be safe. Don and Dan decided that it wasn't worth the risk, but I decided to head up with a minimum of equipment so I could move fast. I was able to stay on névé for the initial snow cone and the first 100m of the couloir, but after that the climb was on hard, brittle ice. The angle was about 50°, and earlier in the summer the climb would probably have been fairly easy, but in the late-season conditions I found it challenging. From the top of the couloir I reached the summit via 100m of 3rd and 4th class rock. I descended the North Ridge route for a long ways, mostly on its east side (3rd class), before dropping west, back into the scree basin below the northwest face.

We hiked out to Bluff Lake in one and a half days via Whitesaddle Creek. It was an enjoyable climb in a wonderful setting, and it should be noted that Don, in what I understand to be his usual pleasant and easy-going way, was not annoyed that I "stole" his project. I wouldn't have known of Blackhorn Mountain if Don hadn't invited me along.

COLIN HALEY, *Seattle, WA*

NORTHERN SELKIRK MOUNTAINS

ADAMANT GROUP

Geographical note: The Adamant Group, sometimes mistakenly called the Adamant Range or Mountains, is a subgroup of the Northern Selkirks. Thanks to David P. Jones, author of the Selkirks North and Selkirks South guidebooks, for the clarification and assistance with Selkirk information.

Colossal, Flight of the Prototype; Pole Dance Tower, first ascent. In August Vera Schulte Pelkum and I were honored to go climbing with guides from the CMH Adamant Lodge in the granitic Adamant Range, north of the more famous Bugaboos. We used a helicopter to access the remote range and, with the Canadian guide Erich Unterberger, were able to do the first ascent of Pole Dance Tower at 5.9+ in four pitches. It is the northernmost tower on the unclimbed northwest ridge of Colossal. We climbed the west ridge of the tower, starting from a notch where the granite meets underlying sedimentary choss. We named the formation in honor of the Canadians' ability to throw a raging party just about anywhere. The longer face to the south promises long and excellent climbs.

North of Unicorn Peak sits Colossal, a peak with a sheer south face that was unclimbed at the time of our visit. After two efforts Erich, Vera, and I managed a free route on superb rock to the top of the 400m face, entailing two pitches of 5.12 and several exciting 5.11 sections. The route starts in the center of the face and angles right into clean corners before veering back left to top out just to the south of the summit. We named it Flight of the Prototype, after a 10m whipper Vera took on our first attempt.

TOPHER DONAHUE

The Horn, West Buttress. On July 31 and August 1, during a spell of perfect weather, Rodger DeBeyer and I climbed a 22-pitch route on the West Buttress (V 5.10+ A1) of The Horn. [The Horn and Unicorn Peak, especially as seen from the southwest, are commonly confused. The Horn is a subsummit, slightly south and west of Unicorn Peak—Ed.]. From a camp below Ironman

The Horn's West Buttress. The ascent route closely follows the left skyline. *Rodger DeBeyer*

Buttress we descended the Austerity Glacier to Unicorn Meadows and the base of the buttress. Rodger and I climbed about 10 pitches of beautiful cracks and featured slabs on black rock to the huge halfway ledge, where we bivouacked. The next morning we made our way through shattered gray rock to break out onto the ridge proper, where we enjoyed a couple of spicy au cheval pitches. Several more pitches of fine crack climbing deposited us on the summit. A couple of raps and gulps of water in a tarn, and we climbed up and over the col to the Austerity Glacier camp.

This was my third effort on the route in two years. The week before the successful ascent, Conor Reynolds and I pushed the route to the halfway ledge, where we ran out of time and water. We placed two bolts to get to the ledge—one placed on lead to protect a blank section, and another to bypass a grunty overhang (A1).

TIM MCALLISTER, *Canada*

PURCELL MOUNTAINS

BUGABOOS

South Howser Tower, Catalonian Route, first free ascent. There we were, back in the Bugaboos, in August, on another blue-sky day. Beginning in the dark, we were excited. Not sure what we were up against or where the Catalonian Route (VI 5.10 A2) went, we knew we were in for an adventure. Having found the start the previous day, Dave Edgar headed up the polished slab with headlamp bobbing. A few moderate pitches to cut the chill, and we hung a left as the wall steepened. A clean corner with a perfect finger crack dissolved into tiered overlaps. Aid or free?

Some wandering about provided the answer. Up we went and quickly found the Catalonian's bivy with a fixed pin, so we were on route after all. Again it was Dave's turn to take on the evil (we were leading in blocks, with the second jugging), so into the wet chimney he went, loose flakes and all. He styled it with class, and our pace kept up. Overhanging moves, a shift change, and a couple of thin pitches put us in an open area headed for the summit ridge. A storm that had been beckoning finally hit, and we picked up the pace. Off route with no pro, I downclimbed and settled on the correct option. By passing a small roof on the right, we had gotten all the aid sections to go onsight at 5.11. Cruising past, Dave took the lead, and we simul-climbed to join the Beckey-Chouinard, reach the top, and descend. A quick dash down the rappels, blowing snow, a stuck rope that came free at the last second, and we were on the glacier, 17 hours or so roundtrip from the base. The storm dissipated. We romped down the packed trail and glissaded below the col, making

Dave Edgar at it again on the Catalonian Route, South Howser Tower. *Chris Geisler*

quick time back to camp for dinner and laughs. We remembered what climbing was all about that day—lots of fun with a close friend, some uncertainty, and the persistence to figure out the answers.

CHRIS GEISLER, *wandering in Canada*

South Howser Tower, Soul Cinders; East Pigeon Feather Peak, Ride the Snafflehound; other activity. During an amazing high pressure system from August 25 to September 4, Renan Ozturk and I climbed two new routes in the Bugaboos. Camped below South Howser, we were the only people in the range, as, unbeknown to us, B.C. Parks were closed due to forest fires.

We started by establishing a six-pitch free line in the Pigeon Feathers. Ride the Snafflehound (III 5.10a) ascends the previously unclimbed northwest rib (Snaffle Puss Pillar) of East Pigeon Feather Peak. The route follows corners and splitters on the left side of the pillar for three pitches, before it gains the ridgeline arête and rides the snafflehound for three more pitches to the summit.

Renan Ozturk cornered and loving it on Soul Cinders. *Nick Martino*

South Howser Spire and the Minaret: (1) Beckey-Chouinard (20-22 pitches, TD+ IV 5.10; first ascent: Beckey-Chouinard, 1961; first free ascent: Accomazzo-Sorenson, 1975; first free solo: Ken Trout, 1977; first winter ascent: Hein-Flavelle, 1981). (1v.) Lost in the Towers Variation (TD+ IV 5.11; FA: Kamara-Walseth, 1980; FFA: Trump and partner, 1999). (2) Catalonian Route (20p. ED1 V 5.11; FA: Burgada-Cabau-Masana-Wenciesko, 1983; FFA: Edgar-Geisler, 2004). (3) Soul Cinders (18p. with 70m rope, ED1 V 5.11 C2; FA: Martino-Ozturk, 2004). (4) Bad Hair Day (18-24p., ED1 V 5.12-; FA: Scully-Wirtz, 2002). (5) Italian Pillar (14-20p., ED1 V 5.10+ A4; FA: DeFrancesco-Stedile, 1987). (6) Retinal Circus (12-18p., ED1 V 5.11 A2; FA: Martin-Smith, 2002). (7) Doubting the Millennium (12-18p., ED1 V 5.10 A3; FA: Schultz-Sell, 1999). (8) Southwest Pillar (12-18p., ED1 V 5.10+ A3; FA: Jones-Rogan, 1972). The reason for the variance in number of pitches is because some people only climb to the top of the Minaret and others to the top of the South Howser Tower. *Photo, route lines, and info courtesy of Marc Piché, co-author of the new* The Bugaboos Guide: Rock and Alpine Climbs in the Bugaboo Spires and Vowells.

In a failed attempt to free the Southwest Pillar of The Minaret (A3), we freed the first six pitches, up to 5.12a. No bolts were placed, but we placed and removed one piton on the first pitch.

Our second new route was an independent line on South Howser between the Catalonian Route and The Minaret. Soul Cinders (V 5.11 C2) entails 20 pitches of chimneys and corners in perfect rock. It was done in 14 hours camp-to-camp, with no hammer or bolt kit.

Before leaving we climbed North Howser via All Along the Watchtower (VI 5.12). French-freeing and short-fixing, we climbed it in daylight from the base to the summit ridge. In the morning we gained the true summit and left a dreadlock of hair, in the absence of pencil or paper. Out of food, we were forced to leave the Bugaboos' towering walls basking in sunshine.

NICK MARTINO

Wide Awake Tower, Wild Fire. Being a Canadian Rockies climber bred on shattered limestone and blocky quartzite, I spent the spring and summer road-tripping, determined to learn how to climb cracks. After a couple of months of Indian Creek hand jams and Squamish finger locks, Matt Maddaloni and I hooked up for a week of Bugaboo granite. With 17 trips to this magical playground under my belt, I have had the opportunity to scope some stunning unclimbed gems. As a recent father, I figured that traveling halfway around the world to alpine climb didn't make sense when we have stuff as good as Pakistan or Patagonia right in our backyard. This was Matt's first excursion to the Bugs, and he figured he shouldn't do a new route until he had climbed a classic. So, for his first Bugaboo experience, within an hour of arriving at base camp below the west face of the Howsers, he ran off and soloed the Beckey-Chouinard Route (V 5.10) on South Howser Tower, in less than four hours roundtrip .

With that out of the way, we could focus on the unclimbed northwest face of Wide Awake Tower in the Pigeon Feather group. This 1,200' Rostrum-like pillar of splintered granite had been looked at, talked about, but not attempted, due to its remoteness and apparent difficulty. In 1997 Brian Webster and I had attempted the golden southwest face but were thwarted after only two pitches by weather. In 1999 Californians Todd Offenbacher and Nils Davis completed this same line, naming it Wide Awake. However, the intimidating northwest face remained unchallenged.

Over six days Matt and I aided, cleaned, scrubbed, and fixed ropes, then freed the pitches on lead, until we were close enough to blast for the top. This "aid-point" style produced a high-quality 11-pitch free route, with six pitches of overhanging 5.11 crack climbing. Highlights include Matt's send of two 5.11+ pitches: Pitch 1, power underclinging protected by a mix of bolts and fixed pitons; and pitch 3, an overhanging, enduro, thin-hands-to-fist crack. We named the route Wild Fire (V 5.11d) because of numerous out-of-control forest fires that blazed in the valleys below.

SEAN ISAAC, *Canada*

Wild Fire, the first route on the northwest face of Wide Awake Tower. *Sean Isaac*

CANADIAN ROCKIES

Canadian Rockies, summary. Ironically, the first significant ascent of the summer of 2003 was an alpine ice climb. These are, after all, the Canadian Rockies, where summer is but a brief interlude in the long, long winter. In late June the young Canmore team of Ben Firth, Greg Thaczuk, and Eamonn Walsh made the second ascent of Rights of Passage (1,000m, IV) on the northwest face of Mt. Kitchener in the Columbia Icefields. Local hardman Eric Dumerac and visiting French all-rounder Philippe Pellet had established the route in the fall of 2002. It received considerable attention after the overhanging glacial ice crux was graded an unprecedented WI8. (Given the nature of the climbing medium, an Alpine Ice rather than a Water Ice grade might be more appropriate, and might help better place the route in the

Sean Isaac jamming pitch two (5.11-) of Wild Fire. *Chris Atkinson*

context of earlier climbs.) The second ascent did little to resolve the grading controversy. Firth, who linked the two overhanging sections into one pitch, found the climbing strenuous but psychologically undemanding. This is unlike most hard ice climbing, where technical difficulty and danger usually go hand in hand.

In July the big limestone cliffs of the Bow Valley east of Canmore saw some notable repeats. Rich Akitt and Raphael Slawinski made the second ascent and the FFA of Quantum Leap (295m, 5.11d) on the south face of Mt. Yamnuska. Steve DeMaio and Jeff Marshall had established the route in 1990 as the third in a trilogy of ground-breaking routes on the cliff, the other two being modestly named Astro Yam and Above and Beyond (the names should be seen in the context of the then-fierce rivalry between traditional and sport climbers). Quantum Leap was named after a 12m factor-two fall Marshall sustained on the fourth pitch on an early attempt. Later in July Rolando Garibotti and Slawinski made the second ascent of Le Jour Le Plus Long (515m, 5.11a) on the northeast face of Windtower. This remarkable route had been put up in June 2000 by visiting Quebecois climbers Francois Roy and Remy Bernier. In a bold move, they headed up on a major first ascent carrying only clean gear—not a big deal on granite, but almost unheard of on Rockies limestone. As a result, there is not a single piece of fixed gear until the last pitch, where it joins the classic Homer-Wood route (570m, 5.10a). This adventurous state of affairs is a stark contrast to the belay and protection retrobolts proliferating on many of the Bow Valley's classic long routes in the names of convenience and safety.

That being said, the compact nature of Rockies limestone means that bolts often open up some of the best rock. The canyons of the Ghost Valley, a front-range area north of the Bow Valley best known for its ice climbs, are lined with endless walls of impeccable limestone (some enthusiastic locals have referred to the place as a limestone Yosemite). Braving the summer heat, long-time new-route activist Andy Genereux and visiting Colorado climber Chris Kalous bolted two seven-pitch routes that are likely the hardest multipitch sport routes in the Canadian Rockies. Premonition and Cowboy Poetry both feature multiple back-to-back 5.12 pitches, and share the crux 5.12c last pitch. Kalous redpointed every pitch on both climbs, and hopes to return this summer to redpoint the routes in a single push for proper free ascents.

In the alpine arena, a group of Jasper locals continued to explore the backcountry of the northern Rockies. Mt. Overlord is an unofficially named peak one kilometer north of Mt. Bridgland, northwest of Jasper. In July Carl Diehl and Dana Ruddy climbed Overlord's Northeast Ridge (900m, IV 5.7). They likened this feature to the East Ridge of Oubliette, the classic line of the Tonquin Valley. Also in July Ruddy teamed up with reclusive hardman Dave Marra and Sean VanAsten to climb the East Buttress (900m, V 5.10+) of Overlord. In the words of the first ascensionists, "poor quality rock in the lower half of the route is followed by immaculate quartzite of the upper part ... excellent gear, excellent climbing, on excellent rock—a classic in waiting." In September Marra, Ruddy, and Chris Delworth made the long, challenging approach to Dragon Peak. This quartzite peak with a spectacular east face is visible up the Athabasca River from Sunwapta Falls, along the Icefields Parkway. The trio started up the middle of three obvious arêtes in establishing the East Face (850m, V 5.8). Near the top, they avoided the blank-looking headwall by a leftward traverse to another arête, which led to the southeast ridge.

Also in September Slawinski and Peter Smolik made what was likely only the third ascent of the Northeast Ridge (V 5.10a) of Mt. Alberta. The lack of traffic may have had something to do with the guidebook reference to several "spooky pitches" reputedly featuring 5.10 climbing on loose rock, with no protection or belays. Slawinski and Smolik soloed or simul-climbed most of the climb, belaying only five 60m pitches on the steep headwall. They never did find the "spooky pitches"; instead they found consistently interesting and safe climbing leading to one of the Rockies' most spectacular summits. This beautiful route deserves to be climbed more frequently, being incomparably more enjoyable than the rubble of the normal (Japanese) route.

After a dry summer marred by massive forest fires, it might be expected that the ice season would be merely average. But a wet fall made for exceptional early season ice. The northeast face of Mt. Rundle is home to such legendary climbs as The Terminator and Sea of Vapours. It is also easily visible from the Trans-Canada Highway between Canmore and Banff, making these ice climbs the most watched in the range. As a result, when never-before-seen ice forms on Rundle, competition is fierce. Barry Blanchard and Phillippe Pellet were first to attempt a thin smear that appeared out of nowhere some 300m left of Shampoo Planet. However, they climbed only the initial two-thirds of the route, so the first ascent of The Oracle (450m, WI4+X M4) fell to Steve Holeczi, Rob Owens, and Brian Webster in early November. They found the route "very engaging and cerebral with very long runouts" on very thin ice.

Although The Terminator did, in fact, marginally touch down, Guy Lacelle and Owens ploughed up to it through the heavy snows of December not to climb the pillar, but to attempt a proper free ascent of T2. T2 is the mixed start to the usually unformed first pitch of The Terminator. Serge Angelucci and Jeff Everett made the visionary first ascent of this variation back in 1993. Although they did not use aid to gain the ice, they did employ yo-yo tactics. Moreover, they never linked the mixed start with the upper ice in a continuous push. As Lacelle and Owens traversed below the route, the fragile pillar suddenly collapsed, raking the slope between them. Regrouping, they succeeded in making a redpoint ascent of the mixed start (which now sported far less ice than in 1993), with strenuous M7 climbing using traditional gear. Running out of daylight, they retreated after the first pitch. In February Akitt and Slawinski likely made the first integral ascent of T2, climbing directly from the valley bottom up the rarely formed approach ice, on-sighting the mixed start, and continuing up the remaining two long pitches of steep ice. In March the T2 Integrale received several additional ascents by Europeans attending the Canmore Ice Festival.

Farther north, the Weeping Wall, given its proximity to the road, might have been thought climbed out. But last fall a beautiful line formed on the Upper Weeping Wall 100m left of the massive Weeping Pillar. In December Delworth and Marra snagged the first ascent of Master of Puppets (160m WI6). Two rope lengths of moderate ice lead to the most striking feature of the route, a slender freestanding pillar. From the top of the pillar another pitch of steep ice leads to the top of the wall. This exceptional line saw numerous ascents before the crux pillar fell off during an early February heat wave. Lacelle said it was among the ten best ice routes he has done—high praise indeed!

Blurring the line between waterfall and alpine climbing, in February Marra and American Tom Schnugg climbed For Fathers (1,000m, WI6) in the bowl to the right of Slipstream on Snow Dome. This bowl is a serious place, threatened by seracs from three sides. They attempted to finish up the serac, but after a narrow escape when a chunk of it collapsed, retreated down the route. (See a following report.)

On a lighter note Will Gadd and Slawinski brought the ice season to a close with an intriguing, if contrived, link-up of classics of three genres. On a beautiful day in late March, starting shortly after midnight they climbed the Regular North Face (III M3) of Mt. Athabasca. Returning to the car seven hours later, they drove to Polar Circus (700m, WI5), which they round-tripped in just over four hours. They then made the three-hour drive to Yamnuska, where they climbed Direttissima (325m, 5.8) in two and a half hours base-to-summit, topping out just as it was getting dark. Their day included experiences ranging from frostbite on the summit of Athabasca to sweltering sun on the Yamnuska approach.

The past year in the Rockies was most remarkable for a revival in winter alpine climbing. The New England duo of Ben Gilmore and Kevin Mahoney kicked things off in December with a strong attempt on The Wild Thing (VI 5.9 A3 WI5) on the northeast face of Mt. Chephren. Rather than take the original start up the left-hand gully, they attempted the direct start up the gully directly below the upper difficulties. They reported excellent climbing with several WI5 pitches. They bivvied below the A3 chimney, then the following day attempted to free the crux aid section. They freed all but the slabby tension traverse at hard M6 or M7 ("hard to say, since everything feels harder when you're getting pounded by spindrift"—Mahoney). They climbed one further pitch in what was now a full-on storm before retreating owing to concern about avalanche hazard on the descent.

In February Firth and Slawinski made the long-awaited first winter ascent of the Greenwood-Locke route (V 5.9) on the north face of Mt. Temple. This route had seen several strong attempts, notably in 1988 by Trevor Jones, Sean Dougherty, and Chas Yonge. After four days on the face, Jones, Dougherty, and Yonge made it to within two pitches of easier ground before being forced down by a storm. Firth and Slawinski climbed the route with one bivouac on the face and one on the descent. In March Slawinski was back on Temple's north face with Valeri Babanov, the well-known Russian climber and recent addition to the Rockies scene. Over two days they made the second ascent and first winter ascent of the obscure Robinson-Orvig route (V 5.9 A2), a.k.a. the Sphinx Face, freeing the aid at the catch-all new-wave Rockies grade of M6. Bad weather on the second day prevented them from continuing to the summit, and they rappelled and downclimbed the route. (A full report on these climbs follows.) Two weeks later and just outside of regulation winter, Scott Semple and Walsh made the first one-day ascent of the Sphinx Face. Leaving the car at 3:45 a.m., they reached the East Ridge at 6:30 p.m. Like Babanov and Slawinski, they also descended the route. Far from being the "supreme test of climbing cool," as it is described in the guidebook, the Sphinx Face offers a reasonably quick and enjoyable way up the north face of Mt. Temple in winter, and deserves to be climbed more frequently.

The biggest news of the season came in early April, when Steve House and Marko Prezelj made the third ascent of the north face of North Twin, outside of regulation winter but in what were winter conditions. In a dramatic demonstration of the evolution of winter climbing, they dry-tooled most of the route, with the leader climbing leashless for ease and convenience. [See a feature article earlier in this Journal.—Ed.]

RAPHAEL SLAWINSKI, *Canada, AAC*

North Twin, north face, House-Prezelj. In early April 2004 American Steve House and Slovenian Marko Prezelj made the third ascent (Lowe-Jones, 1974; Blanchard-Cheesmond, 1985) of the daunting 4,500' north face of North Twin, one of the great prizes of North American alpinism. Their route takes an independent start before joining the Lowe-Jones in the upper half and finishing via that route. As the ascent was essentially a continuation of the 2003-04 winter climbing season, we are covering it in this year's Journal. See House's feature article earlier in this Journal for details.

Mt. Kitchener, Rights of Passage, second ascent. The welcoming heat of late June had us on the Icefields Parkway to attempt Eric Dumerac's route, Rights of Passage. Eamonn Walsh, Greg Thaczuk, and I left in early afternoon and made our way to the base of the route. By making a short bivy at the base and leaving at midnight, we could climb the lower section of the route with good névé, as it is mainly a steep couloir with short rock steps.

As expected the lower section went quickly, with Greg and Eamonn slogging me into the ground. They reached the base of the steep serac headwall and waited patiently as I lumbered to catch up, wheezing like a geriatric smoker. The serac headwall was quite formidable, 100m high, 110° overhanging. Curiously, there was a single rope hanging anchored at about half height, severed close to the base [stuck rope from the first ascent—Ed.]. "Maybe Eric is not the only one who's been up here?" we wondered.

Eamonn blazed up the first pitch, soloing and dragging a line, while Greg purged weight and I panted my way into my harness, trying to salvage time. At the base of the crux pitches we rock-paper-scissored for the first difficult lead. I won. Thus motivated, I used the experience of my only two ice leads of the past winter to grovel, muckle, and sketch my way up the flat, steep, plating ice. Two hours later I was at a comfortable ledge, with a full arm pump and screaming barfies that Satan would be proud of inflicting. "Yep, ice climbing. Still as great as I remembered it," I said to myself. I looked around; to my surprise I had linked both crux pitches into one. "Thank God. I can't bear climbing another piece of ice. Eamonn's going to be pissed, though." The boys followed, harassing me every swing, and Eamonn set off on the final lead, a most excellent ice chimney that went between the left-hand edge of the serac and Kitchener's rock face. We rapped the route, elated, and were back at the car after 24 hours of being out, having survived WI8 and a few eventful river crossings. The ice was difficult but not psychologically stimulating. It begs the question of whether difficult leads come from the physical end of things or the mental stimulation of a thin death lead. I would argue the latter.

BEN FIRTH, *Canada*

Ben Firth leading the crux (WI8?, AI8?) of Rights of Passage. *Greg Thazcuk*

Approaching the serac headwall on Rights of Passage, Mt. Kitchener. *Ben Firth*

Snow Dome, For Fathers to serac base. This route is an obvious line, 600m to climber's right of Slipstream (approach as for that route). Ski in, park da sticks, grab your picks, strap your balls on, and move like the Devil himself is chasing you, scramble and climb the serac-flavored ice tongue via center-left (450m, up to grade 3 ice), no rest for the wicked, head over to the base of the line via the upper cirque (watch, some of the crevasses are too big to name), dance and climb like no one's watchin' up many pitches of tiered WI2-4, then 90m of WI5 to an ice cave

Snow Dome, with Slipstream the prominent ice line on the left and For Fathers the marked line on the right. *Tom Schnugg*

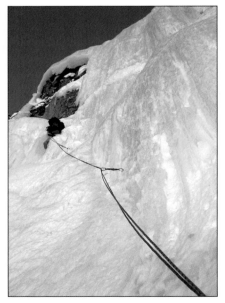

David Marra where the ice is still good on For Fathers. *Tom Schnugg*

on the right, exhale, then in again—WI6 for the next full pitch, belay on climber's right ice rib, look up at a way out, like taxes and mother-in-laws, and attempt it … why? 'cause topping out is faster than having to swallow your tongue and rapping, sooooo … we moved up on the right side, put in two screws, and lightly climbed into a slight gully feature for 18 feet, got on the delicate serac ice without swinging, just light hooking, tried to chip a hook then … I could smell death … the scream of an ancient animal, I awoke the dead … tried to make myself small and made a stupid face … nothing happened for enough time to think I was okay... then …… Boom! … 10' wide x 5' thick x 30' high crashed all around me, above me, and one wedge the size of a microwave divided me between my tools and my head, hitting my waist, causing my first-ever ice ride in 14 years of ice climbing. There was so much ice falling with me, that's all Tom Schnugg could see. My 13cm screw with no Screamer held, I'd landed on my side after the biggest football team north of the border had their way with me. Tom lowered me, barely making it to the belay. After a quick check, and in shock, I tried two other possible ways, no apples. The last time I tried to top out: more serac screams and shifting iceness. Fuck it, the route ends here, half a rope of unclimbable, multifaceted, very symmetrical, matrix-like wedges and shapes stops any man or woman from standing on top. We rapped the route and got back to Jasper by 10:30 that night.

DAVID MARRA, *Canada*

Mt. Temple north face, winter ascents of Greenwood-Locke and Robinson-Orvig a.k.a. Sphynx Face. "It is impossible to say how first the idea entered my brain; but, once conceived, it haunted me day and night." – Edgar Allan Poe, *The Tell-Tale Heart.*

I must have already been thinking of a winter attempt on the Greenwood-Locke on the north face of Temple when, after climbing the route in the summer of 1999, I drew up a topo complete with potential bivi spots. I knew the history of winter attempts on the route: storms, retreats, stubborn returns. The mountains we climb are only partly inanimate rock and ice; they are also made of the fact and legend of climbers' struggles. My own first winter attempt (if it could be called that) came in 2001. Eric Dumerac and I made the mistake of camping below the route, so we were already cold and uncomfortable come morning. Muttering about the face being too snowy and out of condition, we skied back to the parking lot. Attempt number two, in 2003, bogged down in the parking lot, when Ben Firth and I noted that 30cm of snow had fallen overnight.

This past winter we took the thing seriously indeed. We spent several days on Yamnuska climbing steep 5.8 corners with big boots, gloves, and tools, learning what works. Ben and I were veterans of the young discipline of M-climbing, its dead-points, figure-fours, and heel hooks. We liked to believe that this seemingly contrived activity was relevant beyond the Gulag and the Cineplex. The Greenwood-Locke in winter, a snowed-up alpine rock climb, would give us a chance to walk the talk.

The alarm went off at 3 a.m. We wolfed down breakfast driving from Canmore to Lake Louise, and soon were skiing through starry darkness. By the time we broke out of the trees below the face it was daylight. Stashing our skis, we headed up. Snow conditions were mostly good, though in a few places we wallowed up disconcertingly steep slopes. In early afternoon we bumped up against the steep rock of the upper face. We banged in a belay, geared up, and, after a swig of water, started up. The initial groove had a vein of ice, but that soon ran out. After that it was hooking small limestone edges, then front-pointing up them, cleaning snow from cracks for cams or blasting through it with pins. The leader climbed with a light pack, while the second jumared with a heavier one. Free-climbing mattered to us, and jugging represented a definite compromise, but there was no denying it was faster.

By the end of the afternoon we had climbed five ropelengths. Rather than continue and frig around in the dark, we fixed a rope and rappelled to a ledge one pitch lower. By chopping into the crest of a snow rib, we fashioned a platform that would take most of our bivi tent. It is amazing the difference that being zipped up inside even an imperfectly pitched tent makes. Once we had brewed up, sleep came easily. The morning was well advanced by the time we had jugged our fixed line and sorted ourselves out for the next lead. Chopping through the cornice topping a groove to a small, windy stance, we congratulated ourselves for deciding to stop early the night before. Pitch followed pitch, none desperate but all challenging: a knife-edge of snow traversed a cheval, a steep snow-choked groove, a clean headwall with front-points biting into tiny dimples. We were moving fast, wasting no time, and enjoying ourselves.

Dry-tooling over a bulge at the top of the last hard pitch, we were ecstatic. The few moderate traversing pitches that remained were a mere formality, and soon we were on top, if that is what a scree slope a few hundred meters below the actual summit could be called. The Ten Peaks and the Goodsirs stuck out of a sea of valley cloud. We lingered in the yellow rays of the setting sun, but then it was time to go. Eschewing the summit, we traversed the windswept west slopes and ran down the tourist route. Reaching Sentinel Pass ahead of Ben, I watched stars appear in the cloudless sky. The next morning we retrieved our skis and by early afternoon were back at the car.

During the drive back we were already making plans to attempt the obscure Robinson-Orvig, a.k.a. the Sphinx Face, of Temple. A few days before the appointed date, however, Ben emailed saying that he was unable to go. Weather and snow conditions were good, and I tried to think of who else might be interested. The guidebook, with its talk of "atrocious rock" was not going to make it easy to find someone. Then I thought of Valeri Babanov, who had just moved to Calgary. We had met the previous weekend at the Canmore Ice Festival, but I had long known of him by reputation. I picked up the phone. "North face of Temple ... probably no more than one night out...." Never having even seen the face, Valeri flipped through the guidebook. Yes, it looked nice; yes, he was interested.

I picked him up at 4 a.m. During the drive we sorted out translations of such terms as "secure" and "on belay" and by 10 a.m. were stashing our skis. It was surprisingly cold; within a few minutes of stopping I was wearing everything I had, but still shivering. There was nothing for it but to start climbing. A short quartzite band yielded quickly, and soon we were slogging up the snowfields that make up the bulk of the route. Hour after hour went by, the steep buttress of the Greenwood-Jones on our right flowed down past us, yet the crumbling yellow bastions guarding the top of the Sphinx Face did not seem to be getting closer.

It was late afternoon by the time we were anchored at the base of the crux chimney. Valeri, unfazed by his first climb in the Rockies, racked up for the lead. As he fought up the chimney, a week of late nights preparing lectures and grading papers caught up with me, and I struggled to stay awake. I woke up following the pitch; rock and protection were better then anticipated, but the steep climbing demanded attention. From the belay I looked up at the exit, blocked by overhanging chockstones. It was late, and the narrow confines of the chimney were not a comfortable place to spend the night. I grabbed the rack, stepped over Valeri, and, crampons scratching on the smooth limestone, squirmed upwards. A few meters up I hooked what looked to be blocks frozen in place. But as I weighted them they yielded; slamming onto my other tool, I watched helplessly as they crashed down the chimney.

Valeri was doubled over in pain, but after a minute or two he straightened up and indicated I could continue. A few meters higher I sent down another block. Miraculously, again we narrowly avoided disaster. Dry-tooling over the chockstones proved easier than anticipated, and soon I was cruising up the low-angle but loose gully above. By the time I found a solid belay in the shattered tile it was almost dark. Valeri came up on Tiblocs, manhandling the pack I had left halfway up the chimney. Scratching a small platform out of frozen scree, we settled down to Ichiban and tea. The night was relatively warm, and from our small perch we could look down on the lights of Lake Louise twinkling below.

Top: Mt. Temple, showing the Sphinx Face on the left and the Greenwood-Locke on the right. *Ben Firth*
Bottom: During the second day of a winter ascent of the Greenwood-Locke, Ben Firth jumars on the final crux headwall. The leader climbed with a light pack and the second jugged with a heavy one.

A blast of snow woke me up. From inside my warm sleeping bag I looked out on a changed world. Clouds enshrouded most of the neighboring peaks, and wind drove powder snow across the face. Foregoing breakfast, we packed up and kicked steps across the ledge to the base of the exit gully. One long pitch later we were sitting astride the crest of the east ridge. The plume blowing off the upper ridge convinced us to give the summit a miss. We rappelled down the south side and found ourselves in a different world: no wind, no visibility, bottomless snow. Looking for the descent couloir would be dangerous, which left but one option.

We had not pulled the ropes, so we yarded up them as we wallowed back to the ridge. A long rappel landed us on the traverse ledge where we had spent the night. We retraced our steps to the top of the crux chimney and set anchors, keeping a wary eye out for dislodged rocks. Cramponing down the slopes below amid streams of spindrift, we kept the rope on in case the first person set off a slab. But luck was with us, and we reached the bottom without incident. We laughed when we got to our skis: pummeled by the windblast of a serac avalanche, they stuck out of the snow at odd angles. Cutting across the fresh debris, we headed toward the valley. Though Temple reared up cold and white, collapsed snow bridges over the creek told of coming spring.

RAPHAEL SLAWINKSI, *Canada, AAC*

Mt. Stephen, Great Western. Great Western lies on the north face of Mt. Stephen (3,199m) in Yoho National Park, by the town of Field. The line follows a series of mixed gullies, ice runnels, and hanging ice pillars. The ice pillars do not always form but are essential to a quality experience. The route starts, basically, at the road, with a half-hour approach. While the majority of terrain is quite moderate, there are several distinct cruxes and over 1,900m of relief.

Start by climbing Extra Lite (245m, WI4). Above, Great Western follows lower-angle terrain up and left, aiming for a deep gash that presents several pitches of high-quality mixed climbing, including one short pitch (crux, M7 offwidth) past a massive chockstone. Above this gash the terrain eases off and opens up.

Continue to a cliffband that houses the first pillar (60m, WI5R). Above, several moderate mixed pitches are followed to the second pillar (50m, WI5). This pillar leads to several high-quality moderate mixed pitches until the terrain opens up and kicks back. Up to this point it may be possible to escape to the right and follow easy, albeit avalanche-prone, slopes to the west ridge. Follow open snow gullies up and left to gain the North Ridge. Climb an endless amount of terrain, combining sections of the ridge with more exposed snow/mixed gullies west of the ridge. Retreat at this point would be very involved. The final pitch climbs a short gully to the east of the ridge. The first ascensionists bivvied in a snow cave one pitch below the summit. Descent is down the South Ridge for 100m and then down a steep—and avalanche-prone—gully to the west. Once the angle eases, pick your way through the alpine terrain heading south-west, avoiding exposure to potentially dangerous slopes. Once below treeline, follow the drainage to Field. The "Fossil Bed" trail may be gained eventually on the ridge north of the drainage. Descent takes three to five hours, depending on conditions. Take a full rack including pitons and 8 ice screws. The first ascent, by Scott Semple and me on April 8 and 9 took 32.5 hours car-to-car, including a seven-hour bivy near the summit.

ROB OWENS, *Canada*

Mt. Inflexible, East Face Funfun. David Marra invited me on a secret mission on December 7, 2002. All I knew was that it was in Kananaskis Country and was unclimbed. We parked 2km up Mt. Fortress Road, 100 feet before the first "End of Avalanche Zone" sign. The approach was in great shape, as there was not much snow. We stayed right in open terrain, traversing right at the headwall into a snow bowl. I didn't see the route, which was on the east face, until I was below the initial pitch at first light. This was Grade 3 thin ice, 50m, and did not require roping-up. Another 15 minutes or so of snow climbing brought us to the "Ice Pitch." Dave did a grand lead on rotten, detached, hollow and unprotectable WI4+R (60m). We then simul-climbed 180 meters of low-angle ice with some easy mixed sections. A long section of snow climbing followed. Gear was obsolete. Fortunately the next crux pitch, at 5.9 and thin WI4 (60 meters), presented itself with adequate gear. More snow climbing, which we running-belayed, brought us to a 60-meter 5.6 mixed section, again, presenting great gear. This was followed by 20 meters of WI4 5.8, a 5-meter 5.9 roof, more snow, 15 meters of 5.7 mixed, and 45m of snow to the ridge. The descent was a walk off, southeast into a col, skier's left into another bowl and east down a valley. We followed a game trail along a creek for three and a half hours to Smith-Dorrien Road (car shuttle)—200 meters prior to Smith-Dorrien, we crossed a service road for a water system.

This 1,000-meter route must be climbed early season with excellent snow conditions (and/or little snow), and climbers should be able to climb mixed terrain with runout gear. All anchors are on rock. Required rack: 7 short screws, 1-2 long screws, 6-7 pins (3-4 blades), 4-5 cams up to 1 inch, a handfull of nuts.

JIA CONDON, *Canada*

QUEBEC

Cran des Érables, Hot Salami and winter potential. At the end of December, Frédéric Maltais and I climbed a new route and probably made the first winter ascent of Cran des Érables, a cliff in the Hautes-Gorges Park, Quebec. To reach the cliff, we traveled by night with mountain bikes on a closed road. After about 27km and a couple of falls on the icy road, we went by foot and bivvied near the cliff base. We planned to try a winter ascent of an existing rock route, but in the morning we discovered that the wall was mostly covered by ice, so we changed our plans and headed for an aesthetic, arching ice strip. We named the route Hot Salami (210m, M5+ WI5). The route offered excellent climbing on moderate to steep ice and on good granite with poor protection in some sections. Depending on ice condition, this unfrequented wall probably has other great winter routes to be discovered.

SACHA FRIEDLIN, *Quebec*

Greenland

THE FAR NORTH

Jensenland, explorations of most northerly land. This was the seventh in a series of joint European and American expeditions to explore the peninsulas, mountains, and islands at the extreme North of Greenland. Our exploration of the world's most northerly mountain chain and adjacent islands began in 1995 with a preliminary survey expedition and was followed by a comprehensive field expedition in 1996. We were searching for Oodaap Island, discovered by Uva Petersen in 1978, and thought to be the world's most northerly point of land. In the course of our 1996 searches we reached a seamount at 83 40 34N. It was several hundred meters north of Oodaap. Our third examination of this feature revealed it emerging as an island 1.5m above sea level, approximately 20m long. In 1997 it was recognized by a Danish Polar Centre team as the world's most northerly known point of land.

In 1998 we surveyed the region again from the air and found at least two rock features further out, near the edge of the continental shelf. In 2003 we returned with Hauge Andersson, director of the Danish Polar Centre, to resurvey the area. From Bliss Bugt camp we set up an advance camp on July 5 along the Jensenland coast near Kaffeklubben Island. On July 6, six members of the expedition crossed an extensive lead onto the sea ice and reached Kaffeklubben. From Kaffeklubben we proceeded northwest along the directional axis of Kaffeklubben to 83 41 05N, 30 45 33W. At this site we found an ice ridge up to 7m high extending for many hundred meters. It appeared to be overriding a seamount–island ridge beneath it. This ridge was one of our islands. We surveyed the entire area, collecting rock specimens and photographing. We were the first humans to reach the site. We celebrated with lunch. From here we set out on a heading north over a false island at 83 42 20N, 30 42 79W toward the edge of the continental shelf and then east to the intersection of the line that connected Kaffeklubben with the 1996 island and Oodaap.

Circumventing an ice ridge at 83 42 05N, 30 38 50W, we beheld a stunning sight. It was a rock feature over 4m high and over 20m long. It seemed to be an island. It was certainly a specimen of land of some variety. So near the continental shelf edge, we thought it must, at last, be the world's most northerly point of land, the Ultima Thule, with no other possibilities beyond. Peter Skafte noted a pattern of vegetation (lichens) that suggested a long history in its current disposition and formation. He also noted that our 1998 photographs confirmed both this feature and 83 41 in their current general positions. The ice associated with the feature seemed to be superficial. We treated it as an island and built a cairn on the summit. It was our little mountain. We had now explored what we believe to be all possible island sites at the edge of the world. After 18 hours on the sea, we returned to advance camp with some euphoria.

Not that we had achieved this day the final word on the identity and status of the world's most northerly land. We had not. But we had, this day, completed the first field survey of all apparent possibilities. We are all very fond of 83 42. But if its cosmetic good looks have deceived us into too much optimism about its rock/ice content, then 83 41 would again become important. If 83

41 completely disappears, the 1996 island resumes its 1997 status. If that disappears again, as it sometimes wants to do, then Oodaap and Kaffeklubben remain. These expeditions from 1995 to 2003 were the first to explore the sum of all these places. Whatever the outcome, that is my and my colleagues final satisfaction.

The 1996 expedition had explored the H.H. Bennedict Range, the middle section of the world's most

Ultima Thule? One of the possible most northerly points of land on Earth, a sea mount off the northern coast of Greenland, in 2003. *Dennis Schmitt*

northerly mountain chain, and climbed Stjernebannertinde, above the Borup Icefield and the 30km Moore Glacier. Very prominent from the north coast, it is that range's highest peak. Equally prominent at the far eastern edge of the peninsula is the highest peak of the Daly Bjerge, surrounded by the confluence of the Bertelsen and Moore Glaciers. But for our single ascent along the western margin in 1996, the Daly Bjerge were unexplored until July 2000 when we made an approach march up the Bertelsen Glacier toward the base of this highest peak. This march was stopped by severe winter storms. In 2003 four climbers set out across the Moore Glacier in a fearful race against storms that never quite emerged. All previous expeditions on the Moore Glacier were our own and we, at last, reached the icecap at its source. From here some glacial terraces and the south ridge led to the summit icecap of the Daly Bjerge's highest peak. We reached the summit (4,780') at midnight on July 12. This climb concludes my 20 years of expeditions exploring the mountains, peninsulas, islands, and ice shelves of the extreme high Arctic. The early expeditions in Baffin, Ellesmere, and Axel Heiberg Islands were to find their conclusion in North Greenland. These were the realms left unexplored from the times of Peary, Rasmussen and Koch. The expeditions I led were not alone in this, but they were an important part of it. Eigel Knut, Hauge Andersson, and John Peacock were there before. Hauge Andersson will also be there after.

One controversy that arose in the course of these expeditions concerned the world's most northerly mountain. My colleagues and I made the first ascent of that mountain, above the northeastern mouth of Sands Fjord, in 1998, exploring the entire mountain and following the northwest ridge all the way to the edge of Sands Fjord. In 1999 we made the second ascent. In two years of climbing on the mountain we left no measurable points unreached, though we left cairns only on the main summit and the landmark "three teeth." A 2001 expedition claimed the second ascent of the mountain along with some first ascents along its ridges, apparently not grasping our exhaustive history on the mountain. Eighteen species of birds were identified in the course of these expeditions as well as a number of mammal species including polar bear, wolf, harp seal, ring seal, musk oxen, fox, hare, and weasel. Members from 2003 include Marilyn Geninatti, Ans Hoefnagel, Patricia Thouvenin, Peter Skafte, Mara Bolen, Andy Rash, Alan Schick, and Rich Jali. Frank Landsberger was the assisting leader.

DENNIS SCHMITT

Jensenland, historical timeline of the search for the northernmost point of land on Earth. Based on the results from the 1996 American Top Of The World Expedition (co-leaders Ken Zerbst and myself [editor's note: this is the expedition mentioned by Dennis Schmitt in the previous report]) and the 2001 Return To The Top Of The World Expedition (co-leaders Theresa Baker, Ken Zerbst, and myself) as well as collaborative research with Hauge Andersson of the Danish Polar Centre and Willy Weng and Tony Higgins of the Department of Geological Mapping (GEUS) in Copenhagen, Denmark, a definitive timeline can be established regarding the search for the northernmost point of land on Earth.

From the early 1900s when American explorer Robert Peary visited what is now known as Cape Morris Jesup on the northernmost tip of Greenland, the Cape and Kaffeklubben Island—which lies approximately 35 km to the east—have been at the center of debate as to which lies farther north. In 1978, the Danish Geodetic Institute initiated a surveying expedition to finally determine which feature was the northernmost point of land on Earth.

JULY 28, 1978: Uffe Petersen, member of the Danish Geodetic Institute, discovered Oodaaq Island north of Kaffeklubben Island at 83 degrees 40'32.5" N – 30 degrees 40' 10.1" (by trigonometric survey).

1979: Two visits of Oodaaq Island occurred. These visits were the last confirmed sightings of Oodaaq Island at its coordinate positions.

JULY 7, 1996: The 1996 American Top Of The World (ATOW) Expedition discovers a potential new island during their aerial recon of the region at 83 degrees 42' 11.0" N – 30 degrees 33' 14.0" (G.P.S. coordinates/military filter applied).

JULY 10, 1996: The 1996 ATOW Expedition, while conducting an on-ice search for Oodaaq Island discovers a new island at 83 degrees 40' 34.8" N – 30 degrees 38' 38.6" W. A second potential island was reached on the return to Kaffeklubben Island, approximately half way between Kaffeklubben Island and the island at 83 degrees 42' 11.0" N.

1997: Based on photographs from 1996 ATOW Expedition that appeared in the May, 1997 issue of *LIFE Magazine*, Rene Forsberg and the Danish KMS reaches by helicopter yet another new island at 83 degrees 40' 15.1" N – 30 degrees 30' 34.5" W (G.P.S. coordinates).

JULY 1998: The EuroAmerican Expedition spots an island during an aerial recon that lies approximately 3.75 km. north of Kaffeklubben Island (no G.P.S. coordinates were taken of this sighting).

MAY/JUNE, 2001: Collaborative research by Andersson, Higgins, Weng, and the 2001 Return To The Top Of The World (RTOW) Expedition verifies that the 1978 Oodaaq Island, the 1996 ATOW Island, and the 1997 KMS Island are three separate, unique islands with the 1996 ATOW Island being the farthest north of the three.

JULY 13, 2001: Hauge Andersson of the Danish Polar Center accompanies the 2001 RTOW Expedition on a joint aerial reconnaissance that finds no evidence of the 1978 Oodaaq Island. A potential new island was noted at 83 degrees 41' 06" N – 30 degrees 45' 36" W during the recon.

JULY 6, 2003: The 2003 EuroAmerican Expedition visits probably the same island identified from the July 7, 1996 aerial recon and the 1998 aerial recon. This island, located at the 83 degrees 42' 05" N – 30 degrees 38' 49"W (G.P.S. coordinates/no military filter), is the fourth "new" island north of the pronounced Kaffeklubben Island since the original discovery of Oodaaq Island in 1978.

Members of the 1996 ATOW Expedition were Ken Zerbst, Theresa Baker, Steve Gardiner, Jim

Schaefer, Galen Rowell, Joe Sears, Bob Palais, Peter Skafte, Dennis Schmitt, and John Jancik. Members of the 2001 RTOW Expedition were Zerbst, Baker, Gardiner, Schaefer, Sears, Jancik, Vernon Tejas, Jim McCrain, and David Baker.

Clarification: The 1996 ATOW Expedition made the first ever exploration into the easternmost mountain range in North Peary Land. This set of mountains and glaciers, called the Daly Range, were visited starting on July 20, 1996 during which two first ascents in the western half of the range were made.

The 2001 RTOW Expedition mapped 14 peaks and recorded their G.P.S. summit locations, neighboring saddles, and all respective altitudes. A 1998 expedition had claimed the northernmost mountain on Earth (*AAJ 1999*) without conducting an exploration of Cape Christian IV, where four peaks of similar latitude to summits located on the east side of Sands Fjord are located. My teammates and I undertook an exhaustive documented field program to definitely determine the northernmost mountain on Earth. Our results are published in the *AAJ* 2002 and the book Under The Midnight Sun, as well as submitted to the Department of Geological Mapping (GEUS) in Copenhagen, Denmark.

JOHN JANCIK

Editor's note: The above timeline was slightly abbreviated for economy of space. Neither of the Jensenland reports was independently verified by the AAJ. *If you have questions about these explorations, please contact the participants. Some information on the islands as of 2001 can be found at the Danish Polar Centre website, www.dpc.dk.*

East Greenland

Staunings Alps, Dansketinde, first ascents of south and southwest ridges. On July 15, Hamish Irvine, Colwyn Jones (Medical Officer), Jonathan Preston, and myself (leader), forming the Scottish Mountaineering Club East Greenland Expedition, were flown by helicopter from Mesters Vig to a landing at Col Major (2,100m) near Dansketinde (2,930m), the highest peak in the Staunings Alps.

The major aim of the expedition was the first ascent of the stunning, unclimbed south ridge of Dansketinde, with the first ascent of the southwest ridge a secondary objective. The only other major ridge on this spectacular peak is the northwest ridge, which was first climbed by Preston and Reid in 1996. The weather throughout the expedition was mixed, with the team experiencing alternately clear, calm days, which were perfect for climbing, clear but extremely windy days, and days of total white-out that were often accompanied by wind and considerable spindrift.

On July 16 the whole team first acclimatized by climbing Dansketinde via the Original Route. Jones and Preston had climbed this route in 1996 and found last year's ascent to be a little more difficult, due to crevasses that had not been present previously. However, the round trip was accomplished in nine hours and marker wands left during the descent to aid future navigation in poor conditions. On the 19th all four climbed a lower and more or less independent section of the south ridge (PD) to a snow col at the start of the main ridge. From here an easy descent was made.

On the 22nd all four climbers made an attempt on the main part of the south ridge, leaving base camp at 3 a.m. and starting the first rock pitch at 4.30. Around 11 p.m., having been climbing for some 18 hours at grades of up to British VS, this attempt petered out about two-thirds of the

Dansketinde aerial photo. Route info: Northwest Ridge (TD, Preston-Reid, 1996), Southwest Ridge (Irvine-Jones-Preston-Reid, 2003), South Ridge (Irvine-Preston-Reid, 2003), Southeast Face (D, Morrison-Pettifer to summit ridge, Hulme-Ritchie to summit, both 1994), Original Route in hidden couloir (D/D+, Diehl-Haller, 1954). *Colin Read*

way up the ridge, below a steep and verglassed wall. The weather was very cold and windy, and the team was now exhausted. An escape was effected over the next six hours by making 15 abseils down the face below.

On the 29th and leaving camp at 8:20 p.m., the whole party climbed the southwest ridge, following a route some 50m below the crest on the west flank. This gave a great natural line with numerous pitches of Scottish grade IV and V ice and mixed climbing. We reached the western summit at 6 p.m. A snow arête joins this to the main summit, from where the team descended the Original Route to base camp, arriving at 1:45 a.m. The overall grade was felt to be TD+.

On August 2, Irvine, Preston and I left basecamp at 4:15 p.m. to make a second attempt on the 900m south ridge. Conditions were perfect and we made rapid progress to the previous high point. The intimidating wall was now free of verglas and turned out to be merely Severe in grade. We overcame the final headwall via an unusual through-route up a chimney (Scottish V) and reached the summit at 5 p.m. The descent was particularly unpleasant with waist-deep, sugary snow in places and not until 10:30 p.m. did we reach base camp—a round trip of 30 hours. With pitches of VS and Scottish V, and the major difficulties high on the route, we graded it TD+. The team was flown out by helicopter at 10:30 a.m. the next morning and arrived back in the U.K. two days later.

The following notes may be useful to future expeditions. (a) Traveling from London (and probably elsewhere in the UK), ammunition now needs to be carried in a purpose-made, lockable, padded, metal container: an MSR saucepan will not do. (b) The Bell 222 helicopter currently based at Constable Point/Mesters Vig can only carry ca 500kg to 2,000m. On the journey out it managed ca 600kg, however, as the pilot said, it was downhill all the way. (c) A1-Jet fuel was obtained at Mesters Vig. Despite this being kerosene-like in appearance, the one MSR XGK fitted with a gasoline jet worked much better, though the performance of another MSR XGK improved noticeably after a thorough clean. (d) No glass jars or tins were taken. All rubbish (including the marker wands) was burned prior to leaving base camp and the entire residue removed by helicopter. (e) A descent from Col Major southwest to the Gully Gletscher appears impassible due to crevasses.

STEPHEN REID, *Scottish Mountaineering Club, U.K..*

Jonathan Preston high on the South Ridge of Dansketinde. *Stephen Reid*

Knud Rasmussen and Liverpool Land, various ascents. In July 2002 Tim Mosedale and companions spent two weeks in Liverpool Land, then flew south to Knud Rasmussen Land. During their exploration of both areas they climbed a total of 15 peaks, of which 10 were first ascents. Difficulties ranged from easy snow plods at F to more interesting day excursions at Alpine AD. The weather in 2002 was unusually bad for this part of Greenland, limiting the amount of climbing achieved. From mid-July to mid-August 2003 Mosedale returned to the Central Knud Rasmussen with five other companions but the outcome of this trip is not known.

LINDSAY GRIFFIN, *High Mountain INFO*

Knud Rasmussen Land, first ascents. From July 22 to August 16 a five-man British team of Bob Dawson, John and Mark Doplock, Jon Lancaster, and Steve Long visited Knud Rasmussen Land, one of the least frequented regions of East Greenland, situated ca 40km from Gunnbjorns Fjeld (Watkins Mountains). They were landed in the eastern sector of the range on the glacier at 69 08N, 28 15W, where they set up camp at ca 1,700m. This area had not previously been visited by mountaineers and for the next 20 days they moved camp twice, climbing a total of 20 peaks, all of them first ascents with difficulties up to Scottish III. They soon discovered that the rock was extremely rotten and friable, so proceeded to concentrate on snow and ice routes toward the eastern end of the glacier. Particularly fine were two enjoyable ridge traverses and the highest summit was 2,620m, with a height gain of ca 600m from the glacier. The weather was generally settled with temperatures down to -10°C and gave good climbing conditions from midnight to midday.

LINDSAY GRIFFIN, *High Mountain INFO*

Knud Rasmussen Land, first ascents. A team of young British climbers (average age 25) completed 16 ascents of previously unclimbed peaks in the West Knud Rasmussen Land, ca 40km northeast of the Watkins Mountains. From June 13 to July 22 Richard Fallows, Chris Jones, Tim

Rogers, and I climbed peaks up to 3,085m in altitude and with difficulties up to PD+. We also completed ca 150km of ski touring.

JIM SMITH, *U.K.*

Rignys Bjerg, numerous first ascents. The eight-member British team of Bob Appleyard, Guy Beaumont, Martin Bohl, Rob Coles, Sean and Sue Dolan, Mike Palmer, and Phillip Smithson chose a previously visited glacier system in the Western Rignys Bjerg Mountains and spent July exploring and climbing in the region. The vast majority of previously climbed peaks lay to the northeast of their landing site, so the team planned to concentrate on the more southerly areas to the east and west of the main glacier system, with particular interest in the high unclimbed peaks of Pt. 2,680m, some distance to the northwest, and both Pts 2,380m and 2,390m (previously referred to as Rignys Bjerg) somewhat nearer to the southeast.

They enjoyed mainly excellent weather during their three week stay in July and were able to complete a climbing bonanza. They ascended a total of 34 peaks up to 2,797m in height, 22 of which were first ascents. The horizontal-strata rock that characterizes this range is poor and mountain ascents are typified by moderate snow and ice routes, or ridge traverses. The expedition was also able to carry out basic geographical and geological survey work in this unmapped area.

LINDSAY GRIFFIN, *High Mountain INFO*

Lemon Mountains, first ascents and new routes. The increasingly popular Lemon Mountains were visited by a 10-member Scottish expedition comprising Alison Callum, Iain Hall, Andy Lole, Brian Moretta, Phil Reynolds, John Sanders, Andy Saxby, Claire and Graham Stein, and Jago Trasler. The team planned to climb new peaks and routes around the Hedgehog Glacier but due to poor conditions was forced to land 35km from its intended site and spend two days hauling gear on pulks (four days on return due to the 1,000m of height gain) to an eventual base camp on the Hedgehog. Despite poor snow conditions due to very warm weather, creating avalanche conditions that failed to drop below a level 4 throughout the trip, nine new routes, some on previously unvisited peaks, were climbed in the area between the Courtauld and Lucy Glaciers. These included: the Acolyte to 2,100m (N68 38, W31 35) at PD/Scottish III (Hall-Sanders, June 16-17); the east ridge of the Mitre to 2,010m (Saxby-Trasler, June 23-24, eight pitches of rock climbing to British 4b); the Cornet (1,191m, Callum-Hall-Moretta-Reynolds, ca June 24); south east ridge of the Bishop to 2,200m (Lole-G. Stein, June 23-24, 14 pitches of rock to British 5b with one point of aid); the Reverend to 2,235m at PD (Hall-Moretta-Sanders-Reynolds, June 30-July 1); two new peaks of 2,087m (N68 40, W31 33) and 1,951m (N68 40, W31 32) by Hall, Moretta, and Reynolds around July 2; the south ridge of the Altar (Lole-G. Stein, 300m of moving together and two pitches of British 4a); first ascent of the Matron (N68 32, W31 44) to 1,461 (Moretta-Reynolds, mixed climbing at PD). Expedition members also made nine additional attempts at other routes but were unsuccessful. There then followed a last minute, all-out push to reach their rendezvous point with the aircraft at the pre-arranged time. Despite just making it, sod's law meant that the aircraft's arrival was suitably delayed by bad weather.

LINDSAY GRIFFIN, *High Mountain INFO*

Southern Kangerdlugssuaq, Kronprins Frederiks Berge, first ascents. From July 23 to August 15 eight British climbers (Pete Brooks, Bill Church, Brian Davison, Clive Dandridge, Pete Nelson, Mick Pettipher, Graham Robinson, and Dave Wilkinson) visited the mountains on the south side of the Kangerdlugssuaq Fjord. The team was flown in by a ski-equipped Twin Otter to a base camp at 1,700m at the head of both the Nordre Parallel and Sondre Parallel glaciers (N68 30). The expedition essentially planned to complete exploration of this region of the Kronsprins Frederiks Berge. The sector to the northwest and closer to the icecap was visited in 1990 by Stan Wooley's British expedition, which made extensive ski trips throughout the region climbing many of the highest peaks. One of the members, Phil Bartlett, led a subsequent trip in 1998 to the peaks around Redekammen (2,555m) to the west. Members of that expedition made the first ascent of Redekammen and numerous other neighboring summits, leaving the southern sector of peaks, closest to the coast, untouched.

During three weeks in this southern area in 2003, our expedition made a number of trips from a central base camp using skis and pulks, temporarily camping at 10 different locations. The weather was generally very good for the first two weeks but became unsettled in the last week (coinciding with the heat wave across Europe). Nevertheless, expedition members managed to make a total of 35 first ascents on peaks that were almost-certainly previously unclimbed. Most of these do not have spot heights on the map (Danish Geographical Survey) and many more errors were found on the map to this area than on the equivalent sheet to Redekammen.

Peaks climbed lay in an arc around base camp from south through north to east, with the furthest north being the group containing Crystal Peak (2,480m), Middle Peak (2,310m), Curving Peak (2,490m) and unnamed 2,310m (all climbed by Brooks and Pettipher, accompanied by Dandridge on the first only). The highest peak climbed (ca 2,600m), and also probably one of the steepest, was The Castle, which lay directly southwest of base camp and was climbed on August 8 by Church, Davison, and Wilkinson. Due east of base camp, Dome Peak (the north peak of Pt. 2,100m) gave some technical rock climbing on the southeast ridge and was climbed solo by Davison on August 13. There is scope for numerous more first ascents of new peaks and more adventurous routes on the already climbed summits.

BRIAN DAVISON, *U.K.*

Thor's Land, Queen Lilliana, first ascent. John Burcham, myself and brother Andy, together with Shinichi Sakamoto again visited the fjords near Thor's Land north of Tassilaq in East Greenland. The 200-mile boat journey from Tassilaq needed two boats, the second carrying only gear. By the second day we were seeing large plates of sea ice, which displayed dozens of black and white spotted seals basking in the afternoon sun. As is the Inuit way, we hunted seal for that night's dinner.

To give the two captains some rest, we stopped at the ruins of an abandoned hunting village, where boiled seal meat made a tasty supper. Our Inuit hosts offered us a delicacy, raw seal liver. I tried not to be rude, but the moment I got the raw, slimy, black flesh into my mouth, I almost gagged. It reminded me of the braised ox penis I tried a few years ago on an expedition to China. I now know at least two kinds of food in this world I do not like.

The next morning we explored five mysterious fjords with granite towers and walls on both sides jutting straight up 4,000–5,000'. We were overwhelmed by their sheer majesty. According to my maps, some were more than a mile high. Miraculously, golden, sandy beaches called to us for an Arctic sun-bathe. I never thought beaches, so beautiful that they reminded me of California, would be found near the Arctic. As we rounded a sharp corner at the end of the last fjord that we planned to explore, a set of perfect twin towers appeared in the distance. We unloaded, set up base camp, and made arrangements to be picked up three weeks later. In a nearby river, we caught fresh Arctic char and salmon for dinner. I enjoyed some of the best meals in my life at this base camp. Next morning

Mike and Andy Libecki in harmony in front of the sister towers, with their route line on Mt. Queen Lilliana drawn in. *John Burcham*

John, Sakamoto, and I started to organize gear, while my brother caught more salmon and made us breakfast, then accompanied our packing on the banjo.

One thing that was very different about our granite monster from the rest of the walls we scoped in the fjords, was the approach. Our chosen wall was at least six miles inland, while the others were only a few hundred yards from the ocean. Moving our gear from base camp to the wall proved to be a major crux (but not the crux by any means). Armies of hideous gnats sui-cide-attacked with full force and provided easily my worst memory of any expedition. For the next week, taking only one rest day, we established an advanced camp ca 3,000' above the fjord, a total distance covered by each person of around 40 miles. Andy took one last trip down to base camp, returning with his banjo and more salmon, then we spent two days closely assessing the tower before deciding on an obvious ridge into a steep ar_te. Splitter cracks waited for our hands and fingers to take advantage of the entire way.

With less than two weeks until our planned departure, we focused intently on the climb. A 300', fourth-class approach from our advanced camp led to 600' of casual and quite fun 5.6/5.7 climbing. From there we gained 1,500' on a casual ridge that offered a convenient second high camp in a small wind-protected alcove. After a storm forced three days rest, we climbed on and the crux of the route became evident: loose rock, and lots of it. We fixed three pitches that afternoon.

It was the second loosest route I had ever been on, and I was quite worried. The next day we gained another three pitches, barely avoiding chopping our ropes or limbs with the loose rock. Another storm lasted 30 hours and despite dampened spirits, we committed to a non-stop push as soon as the storm finished. Climbing the insanely loose rock, we moved slowly to be as safe as possible, gaining another 2,000'. We all agreed that if anyone on lead stated it was too dangerous to continue, we would retreat without question. Once above most of the loose stuff, we cruised through some wonderful free climbing to reach the summit ridge. An easy 800' walk took us to the top. Since I always try to honor the year's theme, I pulled out my Chinese Year of the Ram mask and danced on the summit. Not for the first time, my partners questioned my mental state.

Just a few minutes shy of exactly 24 hours from the time we started that morning, we had made it up to the summit and back down to our high camp. We slept and relaxed the entire next day before descending to our camp, where fresh salmon and fine-tuned banjo rhythms brought our journey to a close. Our expedition lasted from August 2–September 2, and we named our new route Way of the Banjo (4,500' IV 5.10b). I'd like to call the tower Mt. Queen Lilliana after my new daughter.

MIKE LIBECKI, *AAC*

Schweizerland, Tupilak region, new routes. In July the five-woman team of Justine Curgenven, Di Gilbert, Rosie Golden, Catrin Thomas, and I skied into the 16th September Glacier in Schweizerland to climb alpine routes. Delayed by freight problems and bad weather on route to Tupilak, the team had only nine days at base camp before having to ski out. Luckily they had nine days of perfect weather and managed to climb eight routes in all, six of which they believe to be new.

Three of the team (Curgenven, Golden, and me) started with an attempt on a new route up the south face of Tupilak (2,264m), but found that due to the unusually hot summer that Greenland was experiencing along with the rest of Europe, the approach up the extremely seracked glacier below the face was too dangerous. Instead, we opted to climb the very long south ridge of the west peak of Tupilak. We found the rock on the ridge to be incredibly varied, ranging from sections of perfect granite, giving some delightful climbing at around British 5b, to some of loosest rock ever. We finally stopped, after 17 hours climbing, on the Grey Tower below the West Peak, giving the route an overall grade of TD-. The ascent, and descent by the same route, was completed in a round trip of 28 hours from the tent and was felt to be reminiscent of the South Pillar of the Barre des Ecrins (French Alps).

At the same time Gilbert and Thomas were investigating the potential of the previously climbed Pt. 1,720 m (east of base camp next to the Beacon and called Schartenspitze by the 2000 Austrian team), ascending the west arête, a simple, but delightful snow crest at PD.

After a rest day we made a reconnaissance of the northeast face of Pt. 1,760m, one-and-a-half hours south of base camp. Curgenven, Golden, and I climbed the 800m northeast face by a direct line up the center. This route comprised excellent granite flakes and cracks, with 11 pitches up to British 5a. The first 300m of the route was on easy mixed ground, above which lay 500m of excellent rock. We descended the route via the ice couloir climbed by the Austrian pair of Julian Neumayer and Jorg Susnik in 2000, who made the probable first ascent of the adjacent Sonnblick (ca 1,800m). The route took an overall time of 17 hours. We named this peak The Coven, and our route Hubble, Bubble, Toil and Trouble, after all the delays

The Coven is the far left peak. *Sue Savege*

Unfinished Symphony on the south face of Pt. 1,720m (Schartenspitze). *Sue Savege*

with freight and bad weather.

Meanwhile, Gilbert and Thomas spent 24 hours on the 1973 Swiss Route up the 1,100m south (central) pillar of Rodebjerg (2,140m). This previously climbed route is graded D+ (pitches of Severe) and whilst the pair agreed that it is a stunning line, the rock was found to be disappointingly loose. However, they did note the potential for much steeper, 1,000m lines (which might be difficult to protect with natural gear) on the east face of the peak.

After a brief rest Gilbert and Thomas climbed a six-pitch rock route on the south face of Pt. 1,720m (Schartenspitze). This proved an excellent route on sound granite and was named Unfinished Symphony. The overall grade was British HVS and the pair descended the same line, leaving some gear in place.

The full team then had a mass onslaught on the northeast face of The Coven, with Gilbert, Thomas, and I climbing the 800m northeast arête, descending via the Austrian ice couloir, where we left a great deal of abseil tat in place. We graded the route TD- and for this part of the world it was a short day out at just 14+ hours. Meanwhile, Curgenven and Golden climbed a variant start just left of the northeast arête but finished up the same line as Gilbert, Thomas, and myself.

With bad weather creeping in, the team left camp early and skied west to exit the mountains over the Slangen Pass and down via the Tasilak Mountain Hut to the Tasilak Fjord; three long days in all.

We noted the potential for excellent, long, and steep rock routes on the east face Rodebjerg, the south face of The Coven, and a seemingly unexplored peak to the northwest of the Slangen Pass

SUE SAVEGE, *U.K.*

South Greenland

CAPE FAREWELL REGION

South Greenland, Ice Cap first ascents. Scottish mountaineers, Douglas Campbell and Malcolm Thorburn, had visited the ice cap northeast of Narssarssuaq in 1997 and 1999. In order to save the additional costs and hassle of bringing pulks into the region for subsequent expeditions, the pair has stashed them securely on the edge of the ice cap at the end of each trip. In the summer of 2003 the pair was again flown to this site by helicopter and after checking that the equipment was in full working order after four years in the elements, they set out on a 150km journey. They had an initial ambitious plan to reach four previously unvisited areas, with potential for up to 15 first ascents of previously unclimbed peaks up to 2,820m. However, last year the generally good weather that they had experienced on previous trips was missing and they were faced with difficult skiing conditions, rendering distances of no more than three to five km to be traveled each day. At one stage they were forced to sit out bad weather in their tent for six days. This meant that they were unable to reach their intended objectives, but they still managed to make ascents of five peaks on their committing journey, three of these being previously unclimbed. Peaks in this region are generally of the non-technical nunatak variety but well over 2,000m in altitude.

LINDSAY GRIFFIN, *High Mountain INFO*

Sermersoq Island, southwest face of The Needle. In 2002 French climbers, Pierre Mayet, Marrhieu Noury and Marie Ponson climbed a new route on the Needle (which they referred to as the Sermersoq Dibona, after its resemblance to the famous granite aiguille in the Ecrins Massif). The southwest face, which is clearly visible from the town of Nanortalik, gave the French 500m of climbing and is now the hardest route on the island. Dibonaland has 13 pitches up to F6a+ and A1 but the team stopped 15m short of the summit due to adverse weather and very high wind. On June 19 they climbed the first 11 pitches of superb knobbly granite but were forced to descend. They returned on the 21st and completed their 350m-high route. The Needle is a striking, course-grained granite, 1,200+m summit in the central range of the island and was climbed during the first expedition to Sermersoq. In 1957 British mountaineers, G Francis and D Fletcher, climbed the north face; a six-pitch climb at V with one aid point. This route has been repeated twice; in 1993 and 2003.

Prior to this, in six hours on June 17, the three French also climbed a six-pitch (250m) route, christened Buffet Froid (5+/6a with a beautiful diedre), on the southwest face of a nearby, pyramidal, slabby summit, leaving a cairn at the top.

LINDSAY GRIFFIN, *High Mountain INFO*

Sermersoq Island, new routes and repeat ascents. In August 2003 a six-member British party comprising: Kate Boobyer, Derek and Sarah Fuller, Derek's parents Brian and Sue Fuller, and Henry Lickorish, climbed a total of 23 peaks on Sermersoq, the island immediately north of Nanortalik in South Greenland. Nine of these peaks were previously virgin and a number of new routes were added to formerly climbed mountains.

Considering its ease of access, Sermersoq has a surprisingly limited mountaineering history, most parties having continued further east from Nanortalik to attempt bigger things. The island's climbing potential was first explored in 1957 by a small British party, which among other peaks climbed The Needle, the most prominent Aiguille seen from Nanortalik. In 1971 Phil Gribbon, a frequent visitor to Greenland, led an expedition from St. Andrews University, Scotland. The main objective was exploratory mountaineering in the Tasermiut Fjord, but while waiting (for three weeks) for the ship carrying the equipment to arrive in Nanortalik, the team climbed many of the easier peaks in the southern part of the island. However, they did not touch the main group of granite spires to the north.

A two-man British team climbed five moderate peaks in this northern group during 1977 and one of the team, Mike Banks, returned again 16 years later in 1993. This was the first serious attempt to climb peaks in the north, and 12 summits were successfully ascended by Banks's mature four-man team. Seven of these peaks were first ascents. However, one notable failure took place on Svatakkerne (Danish for Saw Tooth), at 1,276m the highest peak on Sermersoq and situated in the northwest. The unfinished route was completed two years later by Paul Marshall and Jeremy Lee (east-southeast ridge, then south face to west ridge at TD, VI+). No other climbing teams appear to have visited the island until 2002, when the French climbed a hard new route on The Needle (recorded elsewhere in this Journal).

The 2003 party's new route achievements include: Geneva Peak (ca 900m), fourth and fifth ascents via north ridge (V) and southeast face (VI+); Savtakkerene North Peak (ca 1,100m), first ascent via north ridge (IV+); Fullersoq (1,010m), first ascent via the north ridge (easy); Mount Doom (1,080m), first ascent via south ridge; Misty Mountain (1,120m), first ascent via the south ridge (III); Otley Peak (980m), first ascent via the east ridge (III); Sapangarssuaq (1,050m), first ascent via southeast ridge (III+); Akuliatitsoq (960m), first ascent via the east ridge; Boulder Peak (ca 900m), first ascent via the west ridge; Neyland Peak (ca 1,100m), first ascent via the south ridge; Kent Peak (ca 1,000m), second ascent via the north ridge. There were also many repeats of existing routes including the Original Route (north face) on the Needle (V with one aid point; fourth ascent of the peak) and the Original 1995 Route on Savtakkerne, where a probable variant was made to the final pitch at the same standard (VI/VI+). There were also several failed attempts due to poor weather, notably on the north ridge of 1,060m Half Dome, which is probably the finest remaining unclimbed peak on the island.

SUE FULLER, *U.K.*

Nalumasortoq, south-southwest face of Left Pillar, new route. At the end of June a four-member team from Spanish TV arrived in Greenland. We flew to Narssarssuaq and then Iñaki San Vicente and I paddled sea kayaks for eight days to the Tasermiut Fjord, landing below the towers of Ulamertorssuaq and Nalumasortoq. From July 9–16, San Vicente, Ferran Latorre and myself climbed a new route on the left hand pillar of Nalumasortoq, just left of Life is Beautiful. The route is a classic line following an obvious series of cracks and corners on the black part of the wall. Black unfortunately means lichen and we spent much time cleaning the route. In fact, we debated over naming our line, Black Roses. Over three days from the 9th–11th we fixed to the eighth pitch. Then on the 15th we climbed two more pitches and returned to bivouac at the top of the seventh pitch, where there is a good ledge. The first nine pitches are between F6a and 6c/7a. On the next three pitches we used some aid but climbed the remaining two free. The last pitch was perhaps the most dirty; completely covered in thick black lichen. On the 16th we climbed to the top and returned to the bivouac, rappelling to the ground on the following day. The route has 14 pitches and was filmed for the television documentary series Al Filo de lo Imposible.

JOSE CARLOS TAMAYO, *Spain*

Nalumasortoq, first free ascent of the left pillar. Timmy O'Neill and I wandered off to the remote fjords of Greenland for big-wall freeclimbing. Arriving in the fishing village of Nanortalik, we checked into the hostel of Neils, our charter guide into the fjord. In the hostel we met three Danish climbers on their return from the Tasermiut Fjord. These climbers were excited about having put up a new route on Nalumasortoq. They told us their route might go free; they also thought the British Route could go free, just 30' left of their new route.

After a few beers and lots of discussion I dug out some topos collected from the *AAJ.* The Danes looked through them and before we knew it they had all left the room. Timmy and I looked at each other and asked, "Was it something I said?" Later they returned to the hut with a topo that I had given them. The topo was from a yet-to-be-published article from the *AAJ 2003* that I had received from a friend showing that the Danes's 'new' route had in fact been climbed the previous summer by Chris Chitty, Ari Menitove, and Steve Su using no bolts or fixed protection. The Danes, by contrast, had placed many bolts on the same line. Upon this revelation Timmy and I decided that our objective would be to free the British Route (Anderson-Dring-Dring-Tattersall), first climbed in 1995 at E4 A2 without bolts or pitons for either protection or direct aid (but some bolts used on main belays).

The boat dropped us at base camp for some good fishing and mussel gathering as the rain kept us off the walls. The other sport in camp was hiding from the black flies and mosquitoes capable of carrying a grown man away. We continued

during this time to set up high camp three miles up the river valley. Our camp was surrounded by incredible wild flowers and a small arctic fox often visited us. Ten days of bad weather ensued, and it was with low morale that we finally attempted to free the British Route. Our high point was 10 pitches off the deck on wet and dirty rock. We on-sighted all pitches to the high point, but the 11th pitch stymied our progress and we retreated.

Our second attempt, after a few days of rest, took us to the summit of the massif with one hang on the 17th pitch, which I eventually redpointed and rated 5.12+.

On our final attempt, freeclimbing from the ground up, we summited in 16 continuous hours. We climbed in blocks, with the leader climbing every pitch clean while placing protection, and the second jumaring. The lead climber, after fixing a line, hauled a small pack with provisions for the day. The route contained 18 pitches in total, no pitch easier than 5.10 and the hardest being 12+. No bolts were placed, no fixed gear, and the entire route went clean

Tim O'Neill on the first free ascent of the left pillar of Nalumasortoq. *Nathan Martin*

(placing no bolts or pins and with no hangs). We summited in ample time to enjoy the sunset, and while rappelling the route we encountered the aurora borealis dancing across the sky.

We later attempted a new route on the Central Pillar. In total we climbed 10 pitches on it. I then encountered a very difficult face-climbing traverse in which I placed two bolts by hand.

This and the time of day turned us back to camp. When we tried to return to the Central Pillar the weather changed for the worst and the remainder of our trip was spent in a tent, leaving me with aspirations of returning during the next season.

NATHAN MARTIN

Nalumasortoq (2,045m), new route on south-southwest face of Central Pillar and first free ascent on any of the pillars. Ulamertorssuaq, Moby Dick attempt. On June 26, 2001 Petr Balcar, Pavel Jonák, Václav ·atava and Martin Vrkoslav from the Czech Republic left Copenhagen airport for Narssarssuaq, Greenland. Three days later we reached the Tasermiut fjord and met the French expedition, who provided some information about prior weather and access to our wall.

At home we had planned to climb a new route in the center of the pillar left of Cheese Finger at three o'clock, basing our ideas on a far from perfect photograph. Reality was somewhat different. However, a look through the binoculars revealed a line that seemed climbable with the exception of several vague sections.

We had only one two-man portaledge, so our tactics involved one pair climbing for two days, fixing rope on the route, while the other pair rested ready to take over for the next stint. After 10 days we reached the summit ridge, having climbed 17 pitches of vertical and overhanging granite with difficulties up to VIII+ and A2/3. We placed three bolts on the first, second, and fifth, plus double-bolt belays on every belay. Our objective was then to try to climb as much of the route as possible free. Four days were spent trying to redpoint the previously aided pitches. By the end of that period we had managed to free all the pitches except the first (due to bad weather). Four days later the weather turned better again and Vaclav and Pavel managed to climb this pitch free as well.

Turkish Garland Figs (IX) gives ca 700 m of cracks (some of which are thin) and corners in mostly vertical and overhanging granite of excellent quality save for the first pitch. Five pitches are straight IX- or above and the crux is a thin crack on pitch 13. All pitches have been climbed free in pink point or on-sight. Some bolts were added in a few pitches for the sake of our and subsequent free ascents. The ideal place for the portaledge is on pitch 9. Those repeating the route will need to take 2x60m of rope, nuts, cams, and microcams. There is no need to carry either pitons or large cams.

Our second objective was to repeat Moby Dick (31 pitches, IX+) on Ulamertorssuaq. Due to poor weather we not able to start the route until four days prior to our planned departure from the fjord, and as Martin had to leave early due to work commitments, we climbed as a threesome. We reached the Black Man Ledge in a long day and on the following day climbed and fixed six pitches. The weather got worse on the third day and we were forced to retreat from the 28th pitch (the crux is the compact wall on the 29th pitch). The grade was IX/IX+ and all pitches of VIII and below were climbed on-sight. Although we did not climb the whole route, we were able to make a good grade comparison with our own route.

Our team included people with knowledge of Alpine climbing and crack climbing on the Czech sandstone but little experience on big walls. This had been evident at the beginning when we made slower progress. However, in a few days there were no problems. The weather was also on our side during most of our time on Nalumasortoq and we enjoyed two weeks of Greenland summer without a drop of rain.

We would like to thank the French team, who left us a few ropes that were handy for the

The ca 600m pillars on the south-southwest face of Nalumasortoq (2,045m), Tasermiut Fjord, South Greenland. (1) Jumpin' Zack Flash (eight pitches, 5.10 A2, Chitty-Menitova-Su, 2002). (2) Spanish Route (14 pitches, 6c/7a and some aid, Latorre-San Vicente-Tamayo, 2003). (3) Life is Beautiful (5.9 A2+, Suzuki-Yamaeka, 2000). (4) Sekitori (5.10 A4, Kanehara-Suitsu, 1997). (5) Mussel Power (E4 6a A3+, Gore-Karo-Penning, 1996). (6) Original British Route (E4 A2, Anderson-Dring-Dring-Tattersall, 1995; second ascent and first one-day ascent of the pillars in 2002; FFA in 2003 at 5.12+). (7) Ekstra Lagret (5.11a A1, Chitty-Menitova-Su, 2002; repeated in 2003). (8) Umwelten (E5 A1, Thomas-Turner, 1996). (9) Turkish Garland Figs (17 pitches, IX, Balcar-Jonák-Satava/Vrkoslav, 2001). (10). Vertical Dream (7a A2, Castella-Dalphin-Lehner-Truffer-Zambetti, 1998; climbs the first six pitches of Cheese Finger almost free before breaking out left). (11) One Way Ticket (20 pitches, 6b A4, Ahmedkhanov-Dorfman-Lastochkin-Lifanov-Rozov-Seregin, 2003). (12) Cheese Finger at Three O'Clock (6b A3+, Berthet-Brambati-Dalphin-Flugi-Vitali, 1996). (13) Conspiracy Planet (VII A3+, Fluder-Golab-Piecuch-Tomaszewski, 2000). (14) Non C'e Due Senza Tre (6c A3, Arpin-Manica-Vando, 2000; climbed almost free at 5.11c with several rest points and moves of easy aid in 2002 during the second ascent; FFA in 2003 at 5.11+). (15) South Face (TD, 5+, Chapoutot-Domenech-Gorgeon-Guillot-Perrotet, 1975). (16) South East Ridge–Austrian Route (Aberman and friends from Lienz, 1974). *Nathan Martin*

ascent and Rene Nielsen from the Nanortalik Tourist Centre, who took care of us after our return. In addition thanks to our sponsors: Czech Mountaineering Association, LANEX (ropes), Adr –Design (haul bag), PETZL, VauDe, Hudy Sport, Schwarzkopf Sport, and others….

VACLAV ·ATAVA, *Czech Mountaineering Association.*

Nalumasortoq (2,045m), south-southwest face of Central Pillar, new route, One Way Ticket. In July the first Russian team to climb in Greenland visited the Tasermiut Fjord with two main goals: the first ascent of a new big wall route on Nalumatorsoq and to make what would probably be the first BASE jump on the island. The leader of the Russian Extreme Project was Valeri Rozov, climber, BASE jumper and three times World champion sky diver. Other team members were Tim Ahmedkhanov, Lev Dorfman (cameraman), Alexander Lastochkin, Dmitry Lifanov (cameraman), and Arkady Seregin.

The plan was to establish a new route on the Central Pillar, with Rozov making BASE jumps both from the wall and from the summit. In 2002 he jumped from the top of Great Sail Peak in the Stewart Valley on Baffin Island's east coast after completing a new route, Rubicon, on the ca 1,100m northwest face. On the south-southwest face of the Central Pillar there was

Valeri Rozov making a quick descent from his new route on Nalumasortoq. *Russian Extreme Project*

no obvious independent start. The team had hoped to climb a directissima and initially spent a couple of days on the first pitch of a possible line to the right of the Swiss-Italian route, Cheese Finger at Three O'Clock (Berthet-Brambati-Dalphin-Flugi-Vitali, 1996: 6b A3+). They soon decided against this because of the difficulties (A3+) and flaky, loose rock. Instead they climbed the first seven pitches of Cheese Finger before breaking out left.

Starting on July 10 the Russians fixed these (the team had 300m of static) and three additional pitches above, before establishing the first portaledge camp. The first three pitches were V and the eighth was 6b and A2. The remainder was continuous A2.

On the 17th Rozov decided to jump from the double portaledge at the top of Pitch 10. However, getting this organized involved quite a lot of man power and with all six members grouped in one place, the two-man portaledge became overloaded, creaked and groaned, and eventually broke. Rozov needed a very stable platform for take off to make sure he could launch well clear of the wall, so half an hour was spent reconstructing the double ledge (using ice screws) into a single one. Rozov jumped successfully.

After a day's rest at base camp the four members of the climbing team, Ahmedkhanov, Lastochkin, Rozov, and Seregin, spent five nights at the portaledge camp fixing pitches 11 to 19. The first of these pitches was A4, the next three A2, then came a pitch of A3 to by-pass a wet chimney. Pitches 16-18 were A2 and the 19th, 6a A2. During this period there were two days of storm when it was impossible to climb. The rain was heavy, soaking everything including their video cameras and tapes. However, the polar summer days presented the opportunity to work in two shifts, each pair climbing for around 10 hours apiece.

On July 23 the four left the portaledge and reached the summit at 2 p.m., the last and 20th pitch to the summit being grade V free climbing. They then had to wait five hours on top for the weather to improve sufficiently for their Icarus, Rozov, to fly. It was cold, windy and appeared as if they were going to have to descend to the portaledges and come back up for a second try next day. However, at 7.30 p.m. the clouds disappeared from the valley for 10 minutes. This was enough to allow Rozov, equipped with a winged suit, to take off. Descending to a ledge just 10m below the summit, Rozov jumped and enjoyed 35 seconds of free flight before he opened his parachute. For him it was a One Way Ticket and this is what the Russians decided to call their 975m route (climbing length from the snowfield). The remaining three descended to the portaledges and spent the whole of the next day stripping the route and bringing the gear down to base camp.

One Way Ticket: 20 pitches, A4 6b, one Petzel and one removable Russian bolt used at each belay, several bolts used while climbing, and some of the pitches involved bat hooking. Interestingly, Lastochkin and Rozov used the traditional Russian hook-leg ladders in preference to aiders, their main disadvantage being the inconvenience of changing from aid to free and back again.

VALERI ROZOV AND ARKADY SEREGIN, *Russia.*

Editor's note: at the time of writing it is not clear how this route differs from Vertical Dream (Castella-Dalphin-Lehner-Truffer-Zambetti, 1998: 7a and A2), the line Christian Dalphin came back to climb two years after his ascent of Cheese Finger. Vertical Dream climbs the first six pitches of Cheese Finger almost free (6c and 7a with half a pitch of A2), then, where Cheese Finger moves right into a big corner system, Vertical Dream breaks out left and climbs a crack system (A2 and 6a, although the climbers felt it might go free at 7b/7c) left of the pillar crest. This has not been recorded in many international publications but was mentioned in AAJ 1999. If the two routes are independent, which seems likely, then One Way Ticket follows a parallel crack system between the two Dalphin routes.

Nalumasortoq, south southwest face of Right Pillar, first all free ascent of Non C'e Due Senza Tre, and first ascent of a new route on Half Dome. For 30 days Micah Dash and I lived out of a cave located several miles from the Tasermiut Fjord in southern Greenland. Our simple home provided shelter, not only from the rain but from the hordes of mosquitoes and biting flies, which rarely entered the cool damp interior. Over this time we made five attempts to free the striking crack system of Non C'e Due Senza Tre, which splits the Right Pillar of Nalumasortoq. Our last attempt placed us a rope length from the summit after swinging leads up 2,500' of immaculate granite.

I have never been able to stay focused on long term climbing projects, preferring the excitement of going into the unknown. This is by far the longest that I had spent on one route. My motivation for another attempt had gone, there were too many virgin lines on the walls surrounding us. I told Micah that it was time for a change of pace. Micah has an obsessive personality and was fixated with completing the route, but he kindly agreed to switch focus to a dome directly opposite the Right Pillar. We determined, from Timmy O'Neill's and Nathan Martin's *AAJ*, that this had been named Half Dome by a Swiss party. The Swiss made the first ascent; free, incorporating fixed ropes and a drill. [Editor's note: Castella, Lehner, Truffer, and Zambetti climbed the route Les Temps sont Dur—15 pitches all

Half Dome, showing the Dash-Friday route, as viewed from half way up Nalumasortoq. The wall on the right is the backside of Ulamertorssuaq. *Thad Friday* free at 6c—to the left of the vertical north face in 1998. It's possible the name Half Dome was first coined by a British party, who had the north face as one of their objectives the same year.]

The dome reminded me of Fairview Dome in Tuolumne Meadows, except it dwarfs its California cousin. Standing at the base racking up, we greatly underestimated the dome's size: this lead us to leave everything except our small free rack and water bottles. From the belays on Nalumasortoq we had seen a crack that started halfway up the wall and continued to the summit. The rock below the crack looked highly featured but there seemed to be only inter- mittent opportunities for protection. As we started up doubts arose about the possibilities of safely reaching the crack. The difficulty of the climbing was not a problem for us, but the lack of gear was. There was enough to lure us higher, but there were many serious sections where we had to climb 20-30' above gear at 5.10 standard. After swinging leads up seven meandering pitches, we finally reached what we thought from the ground would be a hand crack. It turned out to be a flaring chimney with a finger crack in the back. After several pitches of 10-, the angle started to decrease, but we still were still some way from the top. In an effort to summit before darkness, we decided to simul-climb the remaining 500'. After a few moments of anxious relaxation on the summit, we rappelled into the darkness without headlamps, off the backside into the unknown. The 1,600' route currently remains unnamed but the grade is 5.10X

During the climb, as I was belaying Micah, my gaze would drift over to the Right Pillar of Nalumasortoq and the amazing line we had come so close to sending. This little break from our project had provided me with the inspiration I needed to head back up for our sixth attempt on the Right Pillar. Three days after climbing the dome, we completed the first all free ascent of the Right Pillar via Non C'e Due Senza Tre (2,700', 5.11+). It turned out to be the best route Micah or I have ever climbed. A lead article on this climb is found earlier in this Journal.

THAD FRIDAY

Historical note: In August 2002 Chris Chitty, Ari Menitove, and Steve Su came close to making the first free ascent of the French-Italian route, Non C'e Due Senza Tre (Jérôme Arpin, Mario Manica, Francesco Vaudo, and except for the final day, Giancarlo Ruffino, June 2000; 850m 19 pitches, VI 6c A3). They were forced to rest on gear for a few moves near the top and climb a variation top pitch. However, the A3 pitch was free climbed at 5.11a with bad gear and the overall rating of the climb was felt to be 5.11c.

Agdlerussakasit (1,750m), east face, new route on east face; The Butler (900m) and Mark (900m), first ascents. Overlooking Torssukatak Sound the seaward face of Agdlerussakasit, which is pos- sibly one of the largest sea cliffs in the world, leads to several subsidiary summits. One of these, referred to as the Thumbnail, was first climbed in August 2000 by Ben Bransby, Matt Dickinson, Ian Parnell, and Gareth Parry, to give a ca 1,350m route (vertical height) at E6 6b.

Last July the Irish-Australian pair of James Mehigan and Richard Sonnerdale started more or less at the same point as the 2000 British Route and in one day slanted up the walls left of the Thumbnail to the half-way terrace, where they were able to escape to the left and down a snow couloir to the fjord. They later returned to complete the upper half of the face, slanting back right to hit the ridge just above the summit of the Thumbnail. No fixed ropes were used on The Cruise Line (July 23 and 28, 1,350m and 20 pitches), which was naturally protected throughout and graded E3 5c.

Our expedition also made first ascents of other peaks. Dewi Durban and I climbed The Butler (900m) via the south face. The 200m route, climbed on July 25 and named The Cripple and the Tortoise, was E2 5c and A1. This followed an attempt to climb the west face on July 15, where the line was aborted after 120m of E2 5c. We also climbed another 900m summit, which we named Mark. This is a formation further up from the Baroness on the right. Mehigan and Sonnerdale climbed the west face of this on July 16 via the 450m Called into

Pamiagdluk Island from Torssukatak Sound. "Mark" is the wall half-hidden on the left. The tusk at left is the Baroness (FA Creamer-Anderson, 2001). The Baron is the high summit in the middle (still unclimbed). The Butler is hidden between the Baron and Baroness. *Jon Roberts*

Question (E2 5b). On the 31st Mehigan returned with me and we almost climbed another route on the left side of the west face, retreating due to lack of protection on the compact slabs leading to the crest of the north ridge. Other routes up to ca 300m and E2 5c were climbed on crags near to base camp.

One of the main objectives of our expedition was to raise money for UNICEF's Southern Africa appeal (target around £1,000), hoping that by doing so we can increase awareness of the situation in that area.

JON ROBERTS, *U.K.*

Agdlerussakasit east face, Maujit Qoqarsassia (1,560 m) first ascent and new route. The members of our expedition were Jesus Bosque (cameraman), Cecilia Buil (Spain), Gorka Ferro (kayaker), and Roberta Nunez (Brazil). From Nanortalik we paddled in single kayaks to base camp opposite the Thumbnail in Torssukatak Sound. This 80km journey took three days and part of it took place on the open sea. On August 1 we all crossed the fjord in our kayaks and reached the foot of the wall. From there Bosque, Nunez, and I climbed up 50m from the water's edge and reached a big ledge, above which rose a huge chimney-dihedral system. We slept the night here, while Ferro returned to base camp.

Our idea was to climb the slabs on the right of this chimney system to reach the halfway terrace, and even at this point we could see that

"Mark," showing (1) Arms Trader (Mehigan-Roberts) and (2) Called into Question (Mehigan-Sonnerdale). *Jon Roberts*

Agdlerussakasit east face (top): (1) Hidrofilia (2003), (2) The Cruise Line (2003), British Route (2000). Lower photos are from the first ascent of Hidrofilia. *Jesus Bosque (3)*

the portaledge and much of the food and equipment we were carrying was unnecessary. While Nunez and I would climb, Bosque would jumar behind, filming our ascent. We climbed for three days, spending two more nights on the wall and in the end having to climb part of the chimney. This was generally damp and sometimes running with water. Several sections were rotten and run out. On August 4 we reached the midway terrace and decided to escape by following it left to the snow couloir and descending to the water's edge.

After this the weather was bad and it wasn't until the 9th that Bosque, Nunez and myself managed to return to the terrace. Arriving at 5 p.m., we set up our bivouac for the night and rested for the next day's exertions. At 5 the following morning Nunez and I started up the wall above, left of the depression that would normally carry a waterfall. Bosque remained on the terrace. We took little gear and in contrast to the lower section, managed to climb 800m completely free. The rock and weather were perfect. All around the view was dominated by water and as we climbed higher we could see more and more potential for big wall climbing in this region.

Our route lay well left of the 2000 British first ascent and ended on a much higher summit, which we named Maujit Qoqarsassia (1,560m). We reached the top at 6 p.m. and called our two friends by radio. We saw no sign of any previous ascent and as we had to rappel from the very top, we believe this summit to be previously unvisited.

We set off down, thinking that we would be back at the terrace in a few hours. However, our rope jammed twice and we spent much time going up and down to retrieve it. In the end it was dusk as we started the final rappels. After a total of 15 rappels we arrived on the terrace at midnight. We rested here for two hours, then it started to rain, so we packed up and retreated across the terrace and down the couloir. By the time we were starting across the fjord in our kayaks, it was night once more. Not only was it raining but the wind was also beginning to rise. Forty-four hours after leaving the terrace for our final ascent, we arrived back at our tents wet and tired but happy. The weather remained bad for the next three days.

Nunez and I christened our all-female ascent, Hidrofilia. It gave 1,620m of climbing over effectively six days and had 31 pitches up to 6c+/7a and A2+. No fixed ropes or bolts were used and very little gear was left on the route.

CECILIA BUIL, *Spain*

Pamiagdluk Island, The Baroness, second ascent of Venus Envy; Prins Christian Sund, Igdlorssuit Havn, repeat ascents and new routes. Sarah Whitehouse and I again visited the Cape Farewell region of South Greenland. We first landed at Pamiagdluk Island, where we made the second ascent of Venus Envy, a 15-pitch route on the Baroness put up in 2001 by Airlie Anderson and Lucy Creamer at E4/5 6a. We fixed ropes and made several variations. At the pinnacle that forms the third pitch above the lower snow terrace, we climbed the left rather than the right side. Although the grade is the same (E4 6a), this allowed the pitch to be climbed with a standard rack. (The right side, followed on the original ascent is an off-width that requires a #6 Friend.) However, the next pitch (also E4 6a) is still a bold off-width requiring a #6 Friend. Near the top of the route we also climbed a ramp system left of the original finish, which gave two hard pitches of E3/4 (one of which was particularly bold at 5c, the other more technical at good 6a), followed by VS climbing. We named it the Blue Jeans variant. We also repeated the first three pitches of The Fur Trappers (ca 650m, 17 pitches, E4 6a and A1, Niall Grimes and Ian Hey, 2001) on the same formation. The Baroness is a splendid piece of rock with much scope for hard climbing on the yet untouched left side of the wall and no obvious easy way off the far side. However, it faces northwest and does not receive the sun until after 2 p.m.

We were then transported to Prins Christian Sund, where we overlapped four days with another British party climbing above Igdlorssuit Havn (see elsewhere). Here, we repeated Cryptic Crossword, an 11-pitch route on the right side of the left wing of Igdlorssuit Havn Tower's main face. This route has now been climbed a lot and is arguably the most popular climb in South Greenland. We were able to make the ascent entirely without aid, free climbing the tension traverse/lower at E3 5c, the same as the original route grade given by first ascensionists Matt Heason and Adam Jackson in 2001, and confirmed by several subsequent ascents by other members of their party the same year. We also did a one-day ascent of Wonderful Purple Head (25 pitches, E2 5c), another route climbed on the Tower in 2001 by Dean Grindell and Mark Harris, who linked the start of Wonderful World (800m, E4 6a C1) with Action Man's Purple Head (23 pitches, E2 5b). However, this is a big face and the line we followed may not be entirely that of the first ascensionists. In any case we felt the grade to be E3 5c possibly even E4 6a. Finally, we climbed a new route right of Homebrew Hangover on the much shorter sea cliffs above base camp, we graded Zip Drive E3 5c. We experienced brilliant weather throughout our stay and plan to return again this year.

TONY WHITEHOUSE, *U.K.*

Prins Christian Sund, Igdlorssuit Havn Tower, new routes and first free ascents on the west face. An eight-man team comprising some of the best rock climbers in Britain visited the western end of Prins Christian Sund in the Cape Farewell region of South Greenland. Two of the team, Miles Gibson and Steve McClure, completed a new 23-pitch route on the west face of Igdlorssuit Havn Tower (1,160m), an excellent 900m line that the pair graded E7 6c and named Twenty-one.

The route takes the most obvious feature on the face, an impressive, left-facing, central corner system, which was climbed ground-up, using nothing but natural gear and approximately 450m of fixed rope. Unfortunately, closer inspection revealed the 400m corner to be guarded by around 250m of compact slabby rock and the pair had two attempts to find a line through the slabs. On the second they discovered a series of cracks leading left through unprotected slabs and arêtes to gain the base of the corner in 13 pitches. Rope was fixed to this point, above which the climbers progressed in capsule style using a portaledge. A wet roof high on the route proved particularly troublesome, with McClure reporting it to feel like F8b under the conditions. This was pitch 21, climbed after four attempts. Above, much easier ground led to the top.

The 800m-high seaward face of the granite tower was first climbed by a five-man Croatian-Slovenian team in 1996 via a line further right. They named their 24-pitch route Ujarak (6c A3), after the boat that eventually picked them up at the end of a long 12-day wait, when their prearranged lift failed to materialize. This line was free climbed by four other members of the British team: Nick Boden, Tom Briggs, Adrian Jebb, and Rob Mirfon. The ninth pitch, rated A3, was first aided and then top-roped at E7 6b, whereas the A1 bolt ladder above eventually succumbed at E7c+. Ropes were fixed to the top of pitch 12, after which the remaining ground was climbed on-sight over one-and-a-half days with an intervening bivouac. Natural protection and existing in-situ gear were used throughout. On the 1996 ascent 12 pitches had involved the use of aid but the route now goes completely free at E7 6c.

In 2001 Max Dutson and Dave Lucas, from Matt Heason's British expedition to the same area, added Wonderful World to the face, giving 23 pitches to E4 6a and C1/C2. Heason's brother, Ben, was also part of last summer's team and repeated the line with Simon Moore. The pair free climbed the entire route on-sight over two days, notably the excellent corner of pitch 15 at E6 6b. At the top, a new four-pitch variant, dubbed The Turning Point, was created with one pitch of E5 and another of E6. Much of this was climbed at night with the top reached at 2 a.m.

Several shorter routes on the cliffs nearer to base camp were also climbed at grades up to E7 and Heason also soloed Cryptic Crossword (E3 5c), but Twenty-one and the free version of Ujarak are, almost certainly, the hardest major free rock climbs in Greenland to date. (Editor's note: E7 6c translates to approximately 5.13+.)

LINDSAY GRIFFIN, *High Mountain INFO*

Mexico

CHIHUAHUA

El Pilar, La Crux de Navidad. This route climbs the long diagonal crack on the east face of El Pilar. El Pilar is an isolated tower of solid volcanic rock (rhyolite?). Look for the beautiful dihedral halfway up. Start behind trees on boulders at the northeast corner of the tower. The route required no cleaning and was climbed onsight in December 2003 by Alex and Nathalie Catlin. There is a lot of loose rock on ledges. (There was natural rockfall while we where there.) Our rack consisted of small wires, including double micro wires, and double cams to three inches.

Pitch one follows a steep, wide crack to a belay where the angle kicks back. On pitch two stay left of the crack. Belay on the last good stance. Pitch three continues up the crack to the dihedral, past horizontals and another crack, to a good ledge. On pitch four traverse left to the only large pine tree. On pitch five climb the three-tiered face above the pine tree. Finish by scrambling up through trees. Descend by rapping Cindy Tolle's route on the south face (20m, 40m, 25m). (Tolle's route is 5.8, 5.9, 5.9+, 5.8. Run one and two together. The third pitch is excellent. Standard rack.)

ALEX CATLIN

PARQUE NACIONAL CASCADA DE BASASEACHIC

Summary of climbing on El Gigante. This year saw at least two repeats of Logical Progression and the establishment of two new long routes (described in the reports that follow this one). Neither ascent of Logical Progression was clean, so the route remains without a free ascent and grade confirmation. Both parties called the route "very hard" and both complained of lichen.

The two new routes were established by the same core group, but in different styles. The first, Man On Fire, was climbed ground-up, with all the bolts drilled free, on lead. This purist tactic was possible because of the route's 5.10d grade and the climbers' willingness to climb through very loose rock. The route required extensive subsequent cleaning to make it safe. The second and fourth pitches still need another pass, which they will hopefully get in March 2004 (caution until then!).

After this post-ascent cleaning and careful readings of Jeff Achey's, Kurt Albert's, and Royal Robbins' statements (*AAJ 2003*), we decided to clean the second route from the top, and climb it ground-up. All did not go as planned. The first rap bolts went in to make possible the descent of the 18th pitch traverse. Then we had the good fortune to run into Carlos Garcia. Of the people who objected to rap-bolting El Gigante, his opinion counted the most with us, as he has been the most active local first ascensionist. Hauling the drill back up to drill off hooks was a huge hassle, and we felt that the end result would be the same if we just put in the bolts on the way down. Carlos gave us the okay, and so pitches 15, 16, and 17 were bolted in this style. We do, however, agree with Achey that rap-bolted and sport-bolted are not synonymous. I doubt many climbers will find the route overprotected. Below the 15th pitch we could follow crack lines down to the 7th pitch of Man On Fire.

Two additional words on the style debate: As for freedom, I am with Robbins. There will be more rap-drilling in Candameña Canyon; I hope that those who do it have the dedication to clean their routes well. Nathalie Catlin and I, however, having tried rap-bolting, are going back to ground-up ascents. Finally, I was saddened by Rodulfo Araujo's suggestion that some of Candameña's first ascensionists come to Mexico "to do what they don't dare do in their home country." From what I have seen, this has not been the case, and I hope it never will be. Many of us come to Mexico because of our love for the country and its people. I hope the trust and respect we have been building in many climbing areas continues to grow.

ALEX CATLIN

El Gigante, Man On Fire. This 21-pitch route (5.10d/A0 or 5.12a) was established by Alex and Nathalie Catlin, Cindy Tolle, and Bobby Longoria, Katie Bluementhal, and Tony Scott, in September 2003 (FFA later in September, by Alex and Nathalie Catlin). The bolts, except for two, were drilled on lead and entirely free (no hooks or other aid). On pitch six's safe variation, however, two bolts were drilled on aid. Superpurists can take their chances with the loose blocks. We drilled approximately 70 lead bolts and 60 anchor bolts. All anchor material, except for tree rappels, is metal, not slings. The route was established in two phases. We worked from the ground for five days, fixing seven pitches, and then spent three days climbing to the summit and another day descending and cleaning. Although the rock quality was good overall, the 2nd, 4th, 11th, and 12th pitches contained significant loose rock. The 4th required gardening as well.

Nathalie and I returned in November. We cleaned pitches 9 to18 on rappel, making them safe if not perfect. With Matt Greco we climbed a prettier variation to the 19th pitch. Nathalie and I also added a new finish (pitches 20 and 21). These were all climbed in the original style.

Suggested Access: Drive to the plateau above El Gigante. (If you need guides or porters, ask for Lalo at Las Estrellas in Basaseachi; he will hook you up.) Walk down the gully that runs northeast along the north side of the cliff to the river, good bivy caves, and the trail up to the northwest shoulder of El Gigante. There you will find a large camping spot (Rancho Santiago). The route climbs the buttress immediately above camp. Walk up the ridge from Rancho Santiago for three minutes to the base of the route; there look for bolts.

Climb past three bolts to a dihedral. On pitch two pass between two palms. On pitch four traverse right from a bushy corner past bolts. On pitch six, climb a seam and follow bolts right. (The original line continued up the seam to a palm, but involved dangerous blocks.) To the right of pitch eight is a bolted bivy ledge. Pitch nine leads past bolts to an overhanging crack, the top of a pillar, and another bivy possibility. Pitch 12 zigs out left past an arête, then zags back right to the arête. On pitch 14 climb left to a gully and ascend it, before angling left to the top of a garden/ledge with a bivy site. A fixed rope may help you find your way. From the left end of the ledge begin climbing again at a small corner with oak trees. Climb a crack until palms force you to the arête. Climb past rappel anchors up to a nice ledge. Pitch 16 climbs a perfect crack to a cool cave. Pitch 17 climbs the arête to the left to a garden. On pitch 18 climb the right wall and finish by angling farther right. Pitch 19 follows a way cool thin crack, pitches 20 and 21 an arête that leads to the summit.

Descent: Rap anchors enable you to descend east from the summit to the saddle between the two summits. If you left a second rope and/or haul bag at the top of the 19th pitch, you can walk down west from here to retrieve it. You can then follow a good trail east along a ridge to your car (one hour). Alternately, three tree rappels (20m, 25m, 50m) get you down to the pitch 15 rappel-anchors, then a 40m rap to the bivy. Descend the fixed line to the top of the pitch 13. A 40m traversing rappel gets you to the top of pitch 11. Rappels of 40m or less then get you to the ground.

Rack: Standard wires, double cams one-half to three inches, the three smallest tri-cams, slings, ten draws, and double ropes. I did not bring a larger piece, making the 16th pitch 5.9R, but I did wedge a few chockstones.

ALEX CATLIN

El Gigante, Los Sueños del Gigante. This 22-pitch route (5.11d/A0 or 5.12d) was established in mixed style, by Alex and Nathalie Catlin and Matt Greco, in December 2003. The route was cleaned on rappel over three weeks (and could use more). Many pitches required no bolts. Others are fully bolted, some bolts being drilled free, on lead, others on rappel. We believe the route justifies the style and hope that others who climb it will agree. A double set of cams and one dozen draws are needed. The approach is the same as for Man on Fire, and the first six pitches of the two routes coincide.

Pitch seven starts as Man on Fire's does but continues right past the anchors to the bivy bolts. Pitch eight follows a diagonal corner to a crack and the top of a pillar. Pitch nine takes a thin crack right around an arête to a hand crack. Pitch 10 passes a small roof. On pitch 11 climb an overhanging crack and traverse right from a bolt. Above, retreat would be complicated. Pitch 12 is another steep splitter crack. On pitch 13 follow a corner to a long ledge. Pitch 14 begins with a hard move to a thin crack that turns into a seam; eventually move right to a good bivy ledge. On pitch 15 we left fixed a short piece of cheater rope at the otherwise 5.12d crux. The next two pitches, in contrast to the crack pitches below, involve bolted pockets, and pitch 18 involves a traverse right to a bivy cave. On pitch 19 take the crack out the roof of the cave, then traverse right. Pitch 20 is more pocket climbing, with 2,000 feet of exposure. From a flat spot left of the belay (where you can leave your haul bag and spare rope, to be picked up on descent) finish the route with two pitches up the arête above. Descent: Scramble east from the summit to a saddle, and after retrieving your gear, follow the trail east to your car.

ALEX CATLIN

El Gigante, Bernat Pudent. Last summer we flew from Catalonia to Mexico. We had seen pictures of the impressive west face of El Gigante and our goal was to open a new route. Although June seemed too late to climb this sunny wall, we decided to try it. We fixed the first six pitches in three days, before we left base camp. The temperature was about 40-43°C from 12:00 to 18:00, and we hadn't enough bottles to pull up enough water, so we decided to climb in minimalist style, hauling less than 40kg of water and food, one portaledge, and the climbing gear. Planning to stay one week or less on the face, we had to open three or four pitches a day, so there wasn't time to manage heavy haulbags. As it turned out we needed seven days to reach the top. We placed 20 8mm bolts and 17 rivets for belays, hand-drilled, and three rivets in pitches, two of them to avoid loose rocks hanging over a belay. We didn't drill any holes for hooks. The route begins to the right of Faded Glory, near a small group of trees, and follows a crack system to a half-moon-shaped roof, easily seen from the bottom, situated in the middle of the cliff. From this roof the route goes to the right, following a small ledge with sharp, spiky plants; you have to jump from plant to plant. After this the wall is less steep, and there is less aid climbing. The route has 26 pitches and a difficulty of 5.11c, with precarious protection and A3+. We named it Bernat Pudent (1,160m, ED+ 6c+[5.11c] A3+), Catalan for the Nezara prasina—thousands of these small, stinky insects filled the cracks.

As practical information we think that June is too late to climb El Gigante. During the last three days there were soft rains. If you want to climb on good rock, El Gigante isn't the place. If you need the help of local people to reach base camp or return from the top, we suggest contacting Don Santiago in Huajumar or Don Rafael in Las Estrellas. They are excellent people who are very helpful and not only interested in money.

DAVID FONT I VENTURA *and* JORDI SERVOSA I ROCA, *Catalonia*

NUEVO LEÓN

PARQUE NACIONAL CUMBRES DE MONTERREY

Trad at the Potrero Chico. The bolt Mecca of northeastern Mexico was profaned by a series of long trad routes this year. The rock's poor quality made these very bold adventures. Dane Bass and Sue from the Gunks started things off with The Scariest Ride in the Park (30 pitches, 5.9X), which starts at the overlook in Virgin Canyon. They finished this 3,000' ridge on their second attempt, taking two days. Paco Medina and Alejandro Garcés climbed the ridge above Stairway to Nowhere, calling it Robin Hood. We lack details of this ascent, but it is 5.10X, over 3,000' long, and uses the rappel descent of Time Wave Zero (a 22-pitch route by Jimmy Carse and partner). Finally, Alex and Nathalie Catlin climbed Devotion, which starts 30 feet right of Pride (14 pitches, 5.11d), in a style known as Potrero trad. The rules are to climb ground-up, on lead, with a drill but no hooks. The result is a fully bolted route and lots of excitement for the first ascensionists.

ALEX CATLIN

La Huasteca, Abuelo Fuego. Tatewari is a stunning 550-meter limestone wall in the Canon de Escaleras, near Monterrey. After the 2001 sport-climb first ascent by Carlos Garcia and Francisco Trad, in June 2002 a group of locals (Francisco Medina, Paul Vera, and I, Jimmy Carse) ascended a new route in traditional style. The route follows a prominent crack system, with an incredible rock-pillar bridge, formed by the pillar having toppled against the main wall on the fourth pitch. There are several bivy ledges. Four bolts were placed on lead, as well as anchors, using a hand drill. The main sources of pro were angles, Lost Arrows, stoppers, and a few tied-off bushes and palm trees. There was one aid pitch: lots of hook moves, with one bolt and a sketchy pin. There were several loose freeclimbing leads as well, with poor protection and no falls. Who knows if the pro would have held? We slept one night on natural ledges on pitch five, accompanied by Rafa Cornelius and Adrian "Orejo" who jugged behind us with food and beer. They bailed early the next morning, due to constant rockfall caused by us climbing above. This route went at 5.10X A3+, was led in 12 pitches of 40-60 meters, and was lots of fun.

JIMMY CARSE, *Team Tzolkin*

Peru

CORDILLERA BLANCA

Nevado Pucahirca Norte I, The Power of Perspective. In August 1979 Jack Miller organized the first commercial trek from the village of Huilca, on the western slopes of the northern Cordillera Blanca, up the Quebrada Alpamayo and over the main divide separating the remote eastern Cordillera Blanca from the more inhabited western drainages. I was fortunate to be among Jack's trekking guides on that circumnavigation of Alpamayo and the Pucahircas. During our forays to find the best route, we drove, coaxed, shoved, and dragged our unwilling burros over appalling passes. I'll never forget the drizzly day we came over the final pass of the main divide and dropped into the Sajuna Lake valley. The Pucahirca peaks (in Quechua, "puca" means "red" and "hirca" means "mountain") looming in the clouds were among the most impressive I'd seen—soaring walls split by huge faces and couloirs leading to jagged summit ridges.

Twenty-four years later images of those isolated red walls propelled Thaddeus Josephson (Bozeman, Montana), Crista Lee Mitchell (Halifax, Nova Scotia), and me to explore from Sajuna Lake for routes up those faces. In mid-June 2003 the three of us hired burros, arrieros, and Huaraz-cook Alejandro Sainz to make the three and one-half day journey from Huilca to Laguna Sajuna. However, my health was poor, so we descended to Pomabamba village. A horrible 22-hour bus journey returned us to Huaraz, where my goal was to regain my health and strength. In mid-July, with my health improved, Thaddeus and I returned to Laguna Sajuna for

Nevado Pucahirca Norte I, showing the only route on the face, The Power of Perspective. *Carlos Buhler*

a second look at the Pucahircas. Our journey to the lake was made more efficient by hiring a private vehicle to drive us to Pomabamba and a 4-wheel-drive van to follow a rough track to the shores of Sajuna, where we had set up camp a month earlier.

We originally thought to make the complicated approach to the base of these faces by negotiating the dangerous icefall of the lower Pucahirca Glacier. However, we spotted a 200m gully of rotten rock leading to a high notch in the ridge that comes down from Pucahirca

Thaddeus Josephson negotiating steep ice on Nevado Pucahirca Norte I. *Carlos Buhler*

Norte II's west face and encloses the Pucahirca Glacier. From the notch we saw it was possible to descend easily to the glacier on the opposite side and access Pucahirca Norte's 1,000m west faces without setting foot in the icefall. (Due to the north-south crest of the Pucahirca Norte peaks, these "eastern" peaks of the Cordillera have flanks on Lake Sajuna that actually face west.)

The next day we climbed the gully, traversed the upper Pucahirca Glacier to the base of the west face of Pucahirca Norte I, and climbed four ice pitches to the top of a small, safe, glacial-ice buttress at the base of the face. We spent our first bivy here, which was our last night in a tent. One hundred meters above us, blocking our route, sat an alarming, overhanging serac about 60m high but passable on the right. This was the first of three scary ice cliffs we had to deal with.

Thaddeus writes: "The next morning we climbed through unconsolidated snow and poor ice threatened by the huge seracs looming above. This was a very unsettling activity for me, as this was my first "real" alpine route and first exposure to such uncontrollable objective dangers. When I reached the top of the next pitch I found Carlos sitting in a hole he had dug for himself; apparently this was the belay! Snow holes and serac falls? I began questioning the madness of these alpine endeavors."

We bivouacked in a crevasse on the face and continued climbing up gullies, past the second set of ice cliffs on our left. Thaddeus writes: "The next day we encountered some fine ice pitches with solid belays, allowing us to move quickly in more secure conditions. Over the next two days we climbed through everything from wind twisted ice bulges to fragile mixed ground."

We chopped out two additional bivouacs on the face before gaining Puca's summit ridge. The crux was passing the large, ice-covered cliff at the top of the face. In an afternoon and the following day, we negotiated this obstacle on its right side. Two slow, technical leads on mixed rock and ice gave us access to the upper slopes. On the afternoon of day five, we were about 40 vertical meters under the summit when driving wind and snow prevented progress. We knew we were close, but could not go on.

Thaddeus describes our situation: "With a dwindling food and fuel supply our concerns mounted when we were pinned in a whiteout for 18 hours, just below the summit. As we melted snow the following morning, the increasing light revealed that the storm had passed, and we were able to continue. We reached the summit of Pucahirca Norte I (6,047m) at 8:25 a.m. on July 27, mentally and physically exhausted, but proud of our accomplishment."

At first we believed we could descend the opposite side of Pucahirca, and therefore we wasted four hours exploring this possibility. But 200m down we found the glacier crumbling into a complex icefall and decided to drag ourselves back up to the summit slopes for plan B, descending our route. For the remainder of that day and all of the next we rappelled, using many Abalakov threads and buried stuff sacks filled with snow as anchors. On July 28 we reached BC to find our cook Mauro waiting patiently with a fabulous meal. We spent the next two days fishing in Lake Sajuna with hooks and line we'd bought in Huaraz and worms the locals dug up. When our vehicle and driver didn't arrive, we made the arduous 40km hike to Pomabamba and soaked in the hot springs to relieve leg cramps. Thaddeus named the route The Power of Perspective (1,000m, TD+), in response to this game of alpine climbing.

CARLOS BUHLER, *AAC*

Nevado Alpamayo, tragedies. Alpamayo (5,947m), once selected as the world's most beautiful mountain, sees many ascents, but, in the last years, also many accidents. On July 21, 2003 an avalanche swept away a group 150m short of the summit ridge. Eight mountaineers (four Germans, two Israelis, an Argentine, and a Dutch) were killed, and others injured. The accident occurred on the Franco-Vasque Canal ["canal" is ice fluting] route on the southwest face. In June a Japanese climber died from high altitude illness, and in July 2002 three of eight members of a European team died in an avalanche.

MARCELO SCANU, *Argentina*

Nevado Quitaraju, south face, clarification. The Bullock-Powell Route (*AAJ* 2002, p. 295-6) begins to the right of the Slovenian Route, but after continuing near that line for several pitches, diverges left to attain the arête very close to the summit.

ANTONIO GÓMEZ BOHÓRQUEZ, *Spain*

La Esfinge, Welcome to the Slabs of Koricancha. On June 18, Slovaks Dusan Beranek, Rado Staruch, and I reached the top of La Esfinge (5,325m), having climbed a new route, Welcome to the Slabs of Koricancha (650m, 13 pitches, V 5.13b), via the largest slabs on the east face. We spent 10 days on this amazing granite tower in the Parón Valley and named the route in honor of the Incan sun temple in Cuzco. The route starts at 4,650m at the base of the east face, next to Ganxets Glacé (VI 5.9 A2, Ortuño-Salvadó, 1996). Ganxets Glacé leads to a ledge in the middle of the wall and continues to the right through an impressive chimney. Welcome To the Slabs connects with Ganxets Glacé at the ledge, via a direct line, and continues left and up through the slabs between two distinct black water streaks to the route Here Comes the Sun (VI 5.11 A3, Bigger-Regan, 2000).

We first climbed the route using aid at 7b+ (5.12c) A1, but with an all-free line in our minds. We placed 29 bolts at belays and 68 on the pitches, using a power drill and delicate hooking. We fixed the route to the ledge in the middle of the wall and set up portaledges. From there we climbed three difficult slab pitches between the black water streaks and four easier pitches directly to the top of The Sphinx. On June 23 Dusan, belayed by me, succeeded in free-climbing the route in one day in redpoint style. On June 25 and 26 Rado Staruch and I also climbed the route free, with Rado onsighting the crux sixth pitch (5.13b).

VLADO LINEK, SLOVAKIA, *adapted from Alpinist #5*

La Esfinge, southeast face, The Furious Gods. On January 1, 2003 Jeff Beaulieu and Vincent Légaré, of Quebec, Canada, reached the summit of La Esfinge (The Sphinx) by a new route. The Furious Gods (La Colera de los Dioses) (800m, VII 5.10 A4) took 17 days to climb. They placed no bolts on the pitches but 19 at belays. In the topo they left in the Casa de Guías they wrote, "Lots of rockfall. Bring lots of heads and small pitons. Don't forget a full double set of hooks." They also wrote, "1st route on the South Face," but their route is technically on the southeast face. Also, it is the second route on that face (in contrast to the extremely popular east face), with the existing route (ca 800m, UIAA-VI+ A4) established in August 1988 by Antonio Gómez Bohórquez and Iñaki San Vicente.

Compiled with information from the CASA DE GUÍAS *and* ANTONIO GÓMEZ BOHÓRQUEZ, *Spain*

The southeast face of La Esfinge: (1) The Furious Gods (Beaulieu-Légaré, 2003), (2) Bohórquez–San Vicente (1988). Route lines and photo: *Antonio Gómez Bohórquez, author of Cordillera Blanca, Escaladas (ISBN 84-607-7937-8)*

La Esfinge, El Diente de la Esfinge. In March 2003 Boud Docter (Holland), Geoff Hall (Australia), and Dave Lucas (U.K.) established a five-pitch alternative start to Cruz del Sur. The variation starts to the right with a first-pitch 7a crux. It then slants up to join the parent route. The first three pitches of Cruz del Sur were also climbed onsight and found surprisingly reasonable. However, due to constantly unsettled weather, no routes were completed.

LINDSAY GRIFFIN, *High Mountain INFO*

Chacraraju Este, En el Alto, el Viento sera Nuestra Recompensa, to summit ridge. Aymeric Clouet and I took two days to reach a camp under the face between the moraine and the glacier. This year the right moraine from Laguna 69 was the only safe access to routes on Chacraraju East

(6,001m). The direct approach was threatened by big seracs. We pushed ahead to the bottom of the face to make a track through the new snow for the next morning. We were too excited and a bit anxious to get much sleep. We woke on August 15 at 12:30 a.m., left camp with a light rucksack with only climbing gear, water, food, and a jacket at 1 a.m., and began climbing the first ice-flute gully in the center of the south face around 3 a.m. In spindrift we quickly climbed steep snow slopes cut by a short icy wall. The sun lit the top cornices and the blowing snow when we reached the rock bastion. A cornice fell just behind us and ploughed the gully below—ouch! Afraid, lucky, and frozen by the wind, Aymeric led the first pitch, forced by thin, vertical ice to find protection in rock.

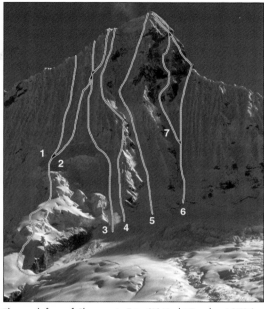

The south face of Chacraraju Este: (1) Kochi-Tanaka, 1972 (no summit); (2) Arnow-Fowler-Mooz, 1988 (no summit); (3) Richey-Brewer, 1978; (4) Escolar-García-Silverio, 1984 (no summit); (5) Jaeger, 1978; (6) Kondo-Yoshino-Hayashi-Hashimoto-Manabe-Ishii, 1976; (7) Clouet-Jourdain, 2003. Route info from: Antonio Gómez Bohórquez. Photo courtesy: Brad Johnson, Classic Climbs in the Cordillera Blanca, www.peaksandplaces.com

Above was an impressive wall, steep and overhanging, with huge stalactites. Only one line seemed possible. We crossed a few ice flutes on the right to reach it. Two incredible mixed-climbing pitches then drove us to a big, crazy ice spider! It was a climbing dream—ice-axe jamming, rock, firm snow...a few sparks...free...just pleasure. But as time was a consideration, I chose the more stable icicle on the right: one of the spider's legs. A good choice: overhanging, but less overhanging than other options. At the belay Aymeric could hear my softer placements resonate. Night was falling, and Aymeric dropped his water bottle. In two pitches of steep ice flutes we reached enormous snow mushrooms, the arête, and an even stronger, icier wind. We followed the Japanese route (Kondo-Yoshino, 1976) up the southeast ridge, with two old bolts so high on a slab that I had to jump to clip one. Since 1976 the snow level has decreased. In the cold we climbed one more pitch, hard mixed climbing that required me to take off my gloves. Frozen, we had no choice but to descend. The summit was 100m above, and the snow arête looked easier, but the wind was too much for our hands and feet. Then began a long descent, thirsty and bitter cold. During the day the wind never abated, and there was no sun on this southern hemisphere south face. We first abseiled on Japanese pitons and bolts, then on Abalakov threads, snow anchors, and two pitons. At 5 a.m. we arrived at camp, overly tired after 28 continuous hours but filled by our adventure and hot soup, even without the summit. En lo Alto, el Viento sera Nuestra Recompensa ("up high, the wind is your reward") (700m, ED+ VI WI5+ M6) We climbed with the memory of three good friends: Arnaud Drouet, Marshal Musemeci, and François Dupety.

DIDIER JOURDAIN, *France*

Editor's note: In 2002 Clouet and Drouet retreated high off this line. Jourdain climbed on Chacraraju twice that season, once to the summit ridge of Oeste (the west peak, 6,112m), with partners, via the difficult 1977 Bouchard-Meunier route in 28 hours round trip from Laguna 69. He also climbed, solo, on Este's Jaeger Route (incorrectly reported as being on Oeste in AAJ 2003, p. 298; also incorrect was the report of him reaching the summit) to 5m below the summit ridge, retreating below immense cornices with horrific snow (he reports needing over three hours to climb his final 100m) and in a storm. Drouet, Musemeci, and Dupety were killed by a serac avalanche in the Mt. Blanc massif in July 2003, just before this trip. All five are or were members of the French national team of young alpinists. See the feature article on Jourdain and Clouet's ascent of Jirishanca in this Journal.

Huandoy Este, showing Adam's Variation. The route continues on the ridge to the summit. *Adam Kovacs*

Huandoy Norte and Este, Alexandra and Adam's Variation. I arrived in Peru with the idea of climbing all four Huandoy summits. I came alone and decided to climb alone. I approached each Huandoy from the east (except when attempting the southwest face of the west peak), which is easily accessed with a collectivo (bus) going up to the Pisco base camp in the Llanganuco Valley. This is also the least expensive way of reaching the Huandoys. From there I could reach the edge of the glacier and the bivouac sites for my climbs.

The northeast side of Huandoy Sur (6,160m) was my first climb. On the approach I had a cup of tea and fried salmon in the Pisco Hut, which friends were taking care of. In case of a storm I wouldn't have to wait under a wet rock for days. Anyway, the east side was a natural choice, and I climbed it early, as it receives the first rays of the sun. The face consists of mostly snow-and-ice climbing, with a short mixed section to cross the rock band in the lower part. The band is tricky but doesn't require much more than carefulness. The main icefield is 50-60°. The upper runnels are confusing because they divide several times and are much steeper than the rest of the face. The runnel that I climbed, which led directly to the top, has three difficult steps, of which the last is the most difficult. The first two are 75°, but the last has a short section of 95°, which

I avoided by climbing to the side on a fragile snow flute—less steep but more delicate. The runnel exits 10-15m from the summit. The descent involved some moderate climbing down the 200-300m high north face, which is mostly 50° with a short section of 65°. The main difficulty was descending ser-acs to easier mixed ground below the saddle between the north and south peaks. It demanded vertical downclimbing, but could have been easily overcome by a single rappel. The northeast face (Astier Route, MD/MDsup) was a marvelous

Huandoy Norte: Alexandra and the descent (left). *Adam Kovacs*

climb; the last runnels had the most waterfall-like feeling you can ask for on a 6,000m peak.

Next was the southeast face of Huandoy Este (5,900m), which I climbed in early July. The day I arrived I made a trail up the glacier. In daylight it wasn't difficult to reach the face, and there was no real crevasse danger. I started at 2 a.m. and reached the base in 1-1/2 hours. This face is relatively short but sustained in steepness, with mixed climbing, around M4, and a difficult section of fragile honeycomb ice to reach the ridge to the left of the summit. [The route starts just left of the American Route, soloed by Alex Lowe in 1984—Ed.] Otherwise marvelous ice climbing, 55-75°. The descent was the main difficulty. I climbed to the summit and down a runnel on the right side of the buttress separating Huandoy Este and Norte. Old slings were in place, but I had no rope, and climbing down the first 150m was very difficult. The runnel was also exposed to large, free-hanging icicles that would have cleaned the runnel had they come down. It was a serious mixed route, and after much research, I concluded it was a new route (Adam's Variation, 550m, MD).

I finally climbed Huandoy Norte (6,395m). I bivvied to the left of the snow gully of the French Route. At 12:30 a.m. I departed, crossed the bergschrund, passed the French gully, and traversed onto the east face. I climbed straight up on 55° snow until I reached an ice gully; the adjacent face mostly consists of loose rock. This 70° gully led to a little snowfield under a band of icicles. I traversed left under the icicles, on less-steep rock and ice, until I reached an ice flute that took me to the upper ice runnels (80°, then 60-65°). The exit to the upper snow plateau was the hardest part of the climb, consisting of steep, fragile ice, just like the exit on the south-east face of Huandoy Este. From the exit I needed another half hour to reach the summit. The snow was soft and deep, and I had to circle large crevasses: the scariest part of the climb. I believe what I climbed to be a new route (Alexandra, 1,000-1,100m, MD+ 55-75° (80° max)). [This route is right of the 1976 Polish route—Ed.] Without a full moon I could not have found my way up the face. I descended the southeast slopes to the saddle and continued down the east face on its leftmost side. This is the so-called easy, normal route but it isn't easy, with ice to 60° and danger when the sun hits. I had to wait several hours under a rock overhang for the continual whistling of ice and stones to stop.

ADAM KOVACS, *Sweden*

Huandoy Sur, 11-second descent. In 1997 Frenchmen Jérôme Blanc-Gras and Yannick Graziani made the second ascent of the French Route (800m, 5+ A2+[New Wave], Desmaison-Faivre-Ottmann-Salomon, 1976) on the overhanging, shaded south face of Huandoy Sur (6,160m)—one of the most daunting rock walls in the Cordillera Blanca. Last July, apparently dissatisfied with their 1997 style of descent, Blanc-Gras returned with his brother Christophe and Lionel Deborde, neither of whom had been to such altitude. The trio climbed the Southwest Ridge in poor conditions on July 15, taking 16 hours to the summit and requiring a forced bivy. In the morning they found an appealing perch at around 5,800m, above the steepest part of the south face, and jumped off, enjoying an 11-second fall and the first known BASE jump in the Blanca.

From LINDSAY GRIFFIN *and personal communication with* JÉRÔME BLANC-GRAS

Chopicalqui, significant repeats. The Spanish climber Jordi Corominas made a rare repeat and possibly the first solo of what is thought to be the 1979 Japanese Route (Kamuro-Uejima) on the south face of Chopicalqui (6,395m). The steep face has a serac barrier low on it, a snow-and-ice slope in the middle, and a rib at the top, leading to the Southeast Ridge below where it meets the Southwest Ridge (1,200m, TD). Corominas descended the normal route on the Southwest Ridge, itself a serious undertaking.

Slovenian Tadej Zorman made a probable second ascent of Strah in Sceca (Fear and Happiness) on the west face, more than 20 years after its first ascent. This route was climbed in June 1982 by the legendary Slovenians Marjan Freser and Franci Knez, and takes a slanting line up the center of the face to reach the Northwest Ridge between the north and main summits. The climb, which originally took two days, is about 1,000m high, TD (50-60°), and is threatened by serac formations that characterize this central part of the face.

LINDSAY GRIFFIN, *High Mountain INFO*

Nevado Ulta, Personal Jesus. In August, Jim Earl and I established a new route up the 1,000-meter north face of Nevado Ulta. The route begins on the left side of the northwest bowl (sometimes called the north bowl), starting farther left than the Berube-Frimer 2002 attempt, but otherwise approximately following that line. This "direct start" (headlamp-induced route-finding error) avoids an obvious couloir in favor of 200 meters of fifth-class rock, but joins the 2002 attempt where it begins to angle back to the right, as shown in the photo on p. 302 of the 2003 *AAJ.* Jim and I continued to the obvious north ridge and finished along the right edge of the northeast face (farther right than the original 1961 route). The new route included difficulties up to M7, and we climbed it in a 22-hour push to the summit. The descent was complicated by Jim's suffering from HAPE. We think this is the first new route to the summit of Nevado Ulta since 1985.

KELLY CORDES, *AAC*

Nevado Ulta, west-northwest face. Previously unreported and scarcely known is an August 1985 ascent of an ice-and-mixed line, thought to be on the far left side of the west-northwest face (called the northwest face in the photo on p. 275 of the 2001 *AAJ*; also shown as the shaded face on the right in the photo on p. 302 of the 2003 *AAJ*). Chris Hassig and Jonathan Stevens climbed a long couloir with technically difficult mixed ground, continuing to the summit. They climbed the route in a long day, made a forced bivouac, and descended the next day. While rappelling Hassig fell to his death and took the ropes with him, but Stevens survived.

Based on information from ANTONIO GÓMEZ BOHÓRQUEZ, JEFF HOLLENBAUGH,*and* JONATHAN STEVENS

Nevado Copa, South Ridge. From June 13-16, an expedition led by Valerio Bertoglio, with UIAGM guides Fabrizio Manoni, Enrico Rosso, Miguel Martinez, and me headed toward Camp Lejiacocha at the base Nevado Copa (6,188m) to attempt the first ascent of the peak's 1,500m-long south ridge. [Note: The upper sections of the ridge, accessed from the southeast face, had been climbed, but an integral ascent of the ridge had not been made—Ed.] We took provisions for two days, but it turned out to be a four-day ascent, and after two days provisions began to run out. We had to ration food, water, headlamp batteries, and fuel. The cold was intense, stiffening our muscles and increasing our fatigue each day.

During the second bivy, at 5,700m, an impressive avalanche plummeted from the crest all the way to Laguna Paccharuri. It was a horrible thing. The dust of the avalanche reached 5,400m, almost touching our recently prepared bivy. We were afraid of dying, but we succeeded in briefly filming the avalanche. The following day we intended to reach the summit, but encountered various difficulties involving both rock and ice. On the last day we had neither food nor water. It was a day of fasting, and we could not push ourselves without the greatest determination. We thought that after the walls of rock and ice, everything would be much easier, but it was not so. A thick fog hindered the ascent, adding to the difficulty of reaching the summit. Miguel and I led the last part of the route, climbing an 80° wall in a direct line for 40-50m.

We arrived at the summit of Copa at 16:00. Then fatigue and uncertainty became our main concerns. "We have finished the climb—where is base camp?" After we had descended for an hour, classmates from Don Bosco School [A school founded to train young Peruvian alpinists to be local guides—Ed.] came to help us, bringing water. It was an unforgettable encounter, a profound moment of friendship between us all. We cried, from the emotion of reaching such a hard summit, then finding a team of friends awaiting us, ready to help and alleviate the fatigue accumulated over the previous days. We arrived at the base camp around 21:00, where more friends awaited us with a good meal. Although tired and without strength, we decided to continue down. Already it was 22:00, but the support of friends helped.

CÉSAR ROSALES, *Peru (translated by Molly Loomis)*

Tocllaraju, MGLA to Northwest Ridge. On July1 Mitja Glescic, and I climbed a new route on the west face of Tocllaraju (6,032m). The route begins in the middle of the rocky section on the left side of the wall and then angles slightly to the right. The first pitch is the most difficult, about 90° with bad ice and rock (mixed). Most of the climbing was 60-70° snow and ice in the middle of the couloir, which goes slightly to the right below the seracs. The route arrives on the Northwest Ridge at about 5,900m, and we descended from there by the normal route. Our route, MGLA, is about 400 meters high. (TD+ 90°(max)/60-70°(avg)). In deep snow, it took three hours from camp to reach the face, then four hours for the climbing.

ARCON JERNEJ, *Slovenia*

Editor's note: Although no record exists of this exact line having been previously climbed, it should be noted that the route follows no distinct or defining feature, particularly above the first pitch through the rock band. This broad face, like many Peruvian snow-and-ice faces, offers countless possibilities. Multitudes of variations are known to have been climbed to the popular West Face Direct (Calcagno-Carara-Lafranconi-Zappelli, 1980; just right of MGLA) and to the Northwest Ridge route, although documenting them all is impossible.

Churup, correcting the correction. On p. 306 of the 2003 AAJ *is a correction to a report in the* 2002 AAJ *(p. 302) about a new route on Churup. The correction reads, "The route completed in 1972…is to the right (not the left) of the Malinche route." Actually, this "correction" restates the erroneous description of the 2002 report. The 1972 route (Fear route) on Churup is to the left (not the right) of the Malinche route.*

CORDILLERA CHAUPIJANCA

Shicra, west face and southeast ridge. On July 5 Evelio Echevarría, Consuelo Amorós (my wife), and I left the mining town Pachapaqui, and reached the foot of the snowy peak local muleteers call Shicra (5,195-5,198m, per altimeter). This is the peak the 1972 Italian Expedition wanted to name "Nevado Cuidad de Macerata" (ca 5,000m). On July 9 Evelio ascended the eastern summit of an unnamed rocky peak (ca 4,900m) situated beyond a pass to the right of the peak the Italian expedition proposed calling "Margaroliraju" (5,205m). This same day Consuelo and I ascended Shicra via the right side of the west glacier to gain the corniced southeast ridge, which we climbed to the summit. We believe this is a new route and the second ascent of the peak. The Italians ascended the peak via the western glacier. The Peruvian geographic authorities did not recognize the Italian names, and the names do not appear on Peru's National Geographic Institute's maps.

ANTONIO GÓMEZ BOHÓRQUEZ, *Spain (Translated by Molly Loomis)*

CORDILLERA HUAYHUASH

Nomenclature in the Huayhuash. Since the Cordillera Huayhuash was first surveyed in 1927 by the American Geographic Society expedition, confusion over peak names and heights have surfaced. In cases where confusion over peak names exist the *AAJ* has turned to the ascension record to determine what has prevailed over the years and by which name the peak has generally become known. Transliteration of Quechua to German and English has also added to the confusion. For example, in the case of the prominent peak located midway between Yerupaja and Jirishanca, we have chosen to use the name of Yerupaja Chico (instead of El Toro), as it first appeared on the 1939 Kinzl/Schneider map, and we retain the name of El Toro for Yerupaja Chico's South Summit, since that name also has a long history of use. Peak heights are more complicated. Until the appearance of new topographic maps at the scales of 1:100,000 and 1:25,000, the 1939 map was the authority on the subject. Jan Kielkowski's guidebooks, published in the early 1990s, introduced peaks heights that are slightly lower; they are based on IGN maps. Jill Neate, in Mountaineering in the Andes, has generally used the heights published on the 1939 map. The 2002 Alpine Mapping Guild map of the range attempted to resolve this issue by using IGN heights when available and those from other sources when not.

MARTIN GAMACHE, *Alpine Mapping Guild, AAC*

Jirishanca summary. The impressive southeast aspect of Jirishanca (6,094m [sometimes given as 6,126m]) was a focal point of Huayhuash activity in 2003. In June, Brits Nick Bullock and Al Powell, returning after a near disaster in 2002 when they were avalanched off the start, climbed in alpine style a bold, difficult line (Fear and Loathing) up the central ice depression, branching right to join the East Buttress route (1957 Egger-Jungmair) after 17 pitches. They continued for approximately eight more pitches up the technical and corniced summit ridge of the 1957 route, retreating a couple of ropelengths below the summit.

In September young French alpinists Aymeric Clouet and Didier Jourdain established a difficult new route up the steep 900m, east-facing rock wall. The route—Tambo, Churros y Amigos—parallels much of the 1973 Japanese route, just right of the central ice face. At the start Clouet and Jourdain used 300 meters of fixed ropes, which they removed, but they carried no bolts. A red sling in a linule (rock hole) 15m up the first pitch marks the start of the route, but belays are not equipped (only rappel anchors). Above the rock wall their route joins the 1957 route and continues to the summit, likely the first time Jirishanca's summit has been reached from its formidable eastern side since the 1973, 49-day Japanese siege (some sources say 45 days). The French route shares approximately 4m of the Japanese route, on which old fixed ropes remain. Both the British and French climbs are covered in a feature article earlier in this Journal, as is the history of climbing on this face.

In July a team of three Italians climbed a route on the right side of the east-facing rock wall (see report below). Although the French climbers mentioned above report seeing 10mm belay bolts beside good cracks on the Italian line, and the Italian route was certainly a stylistic contrast to the above two routes, rumors of the Italians placing 150 or more bolts are greatly exaggerated.

Accomplished Austrian alpinists Alex Fidi and Julian Neumayer, who were in the area around the time of Bullock and Powell and who had plans for the same face, were killed in an avalanche below nearby Jirishanca Chico. Although the specifics will never be known, it appears that they were headed for an acclimatization climb on Jirishanca Chico's unclimbed southwest face when a large avalanche released. Bullock, Powell, Mark Richey (president of the American Alpine Club), and members of the Yungay rescue group USAM (Unidad de Salvamento de Alta Montana—www.huaraz.org/usam) conducted an initial search, recovering the climbers' packs and a helmet. USAM, a well-trained volunteer organization, continued the search in the ensuing days and proved instrumental in recovering the bodies.

Jirishanca, Suerte to East Buttress. During July 11-21 Italians Stefano DeLuca, Alessandro Piccini, and Paolo Stoppini (with Valerio Poggiani at base camp) established a line on the right side of the east-face rock wall, beginning just right of a yellow overhang to the right of the Japanese 1973 route. The first four pitches are similar to a previous Slovenian attempt. After several days of fixing and three days of rest, the Italians bivvied on the final ascent at 5,500m and continued up the following day. The route climbs 10 or 11 pitches of rock to reach a ramp that angles right and continues on mixed rock, snow, and ice, before finishing around 5,700m, just above where the 1957 East Buttress route (which begins from the other side) reaches the ridge crest. The route is 18 pitches total.

Fixed ropes (which they removed) and a power drill were used. In the initial five or six rock pitches, they placed bolts at the belays and three to four per pitch "where they were necessary." Higher, in the icy portions, they placed few. A few more than 40 bolts were placed on the route.

Difficulties are 6c+/A2 (hooks and rivets) and V/5+ ice. They named the route Suerte ("luck"), since that is what their arriero told them every time they left camp.

Compiled from correspondence and conversation with PAOLO STOPPINI, *Italy*

Limitless Madness. *Matej Mejovsek*

Yerupaja, Limitless Madness to summit ridge. My latest adventure began at the end of June. We were three Slovenians—Matevz Kramer, Tadej Zorman, and me—whose goal was to climb a new route in the Cordillera Huayhuash. I had climbed the Southwest Face of Sarapo (6,127m) and the West Face of Trapecio (5,644m), and I knew from my experiences that Huayhuash mountains are serious. There are no normal routes, and the glaciers are active and dangerous.

Our first few weeks in the Andes were spent acclimatizing on peaks around Huaraz, but we then felt it was time for something more serious. We chose Yerupaja (6,617m), the highest and mightiest mountain in the Huayhuash. On this mountain there are no good or bad ascents, only inventive ones. We chose to try a new, daring route on the northeast face. After two tiring days of driving over bumpy roads and donkey transport of supplies, we reached our base camp at the tip of Laguna Carhuacocha, with perfect views of Yerupaja and neighboring Jirishanca. Compared to many commercial trekking camps, ours was modest and environmentally friendly. We established friendly relations with the family Abalos, who stubbornly live there year-round, at 4,200m. We respect their immense will!

During the next few days we carried climbing gear and food up to our 4,700m ABC. One look at the beginning of the route told us it would be hard. The northeast face saw its last ascent 26 years ago, in 1977 (Dovzan, Manfreda). Italians climbed the east ridge in 1982. Because of global warming, information from these earlier teams is no longer of use, as the glacier and face have changed so much in the last 20 years. We could not determine what exactly they climbed.

We decided on an alpine-style ascent, going up and down in one push. After a few rest days we began climbing left of a hanging glacier, and found within a few pitches how serious the ascent would be. There were 300m of mixed climbing (5c WI5), and having gear and food for four days made it even more challenging. The lower part of the route was threatened by cracking seracs above, and now and then a few tons of snow and ice fell near us. We began to realize the definition of craziness, and why this face had been unclimbed for over 20 years.

Yerupaja, left to right: Limitless Madness (2003), Habeler-Messner (1969), Dix-Jones (1968). Others: Dovzan-Manfreda (1977), right of the above routes on the NE face; Hayashi-Kondo-Yoshino (1976), right skyline; Majerl-Wurm (1969), promiinent sun-shade rib on left, continuing up the left skyline; Badone-Penasa-Vialardi (1982), left skyline. *Jeremy Frimer*

The middle section of the face tested our limits with steep seracs and solid WI6. After 14 hours of hard climbing we finally finished with that craziness. We set up a tent at 5,500m on a huge snow plateau. As we cooked, we discussed the tactics for the next day. The night was calm. We continued up the middle section of the face, through the largest gully, which was closed by a rock band on the left side. Our morning warm-up consisted of rock and overhanging seracs, followed by a pitch of WI6 and rock climbing of 5b. This route was not what we had anticipated—we began thinking we could do it freestyle, with no technical climbing. Above, our route's difficulties resembled those of the upper part of the Jackson route on Les Droites above Chamonix. Around 9 a.m. the face became alive with huge rocks flying by. We felt totally exposed, as everything from above was funneled into our gully. The serious technical climbing kept us from moving as fast as we needed to go. However, analyzing the alternatives, we decided to continue. We wanted to escape from this shit right away! We climbed close to the rock, on the left side of the gully. This section paralleled the route Dix and Jones established in 1966, 200m to the right.

At last the vertical face began to kick back, but by then we were tiring and feeling the effect of altitude. We pushed through this section toward a huge serac that blocked the ideal line to the top of the face. Our lack of energy made us move slowly up a long snow face. When we were just below the serac, the weather changed, and the face soon was covered by fog and snowfall. The air became even colder—at least as low as −20° Celsius. We passed rocks to our left and headed to the ridge. Again the climbing became harder, and we used lots of time on the mixed steep part that led us to the east ridge. The falling snow was more serious, and little avalanches began coming down the face. By now we were simply exhausted.

We continued over the ridge toward the summit, but as we reached 6,550m the storm became intense. We waited a while, then decided to descend our route. The night was long, but knowing there was no alternative, we gathered every bit of energy and will we had left. The ascent to 6,550m took 26 hours. We were tired and longed to be back on solid ground, but had to descend by carefully constructing solid rappels. We made about 30 rappels with 60m double ropes.

Early in the morning we reached the tent on the snow plateau. We spent a few hours there before continuing our descent, and late in the evening arrived in base camp. We named the route Limitless Madness (1,900m, VI 5c WI6). It was pure madness: hard climbing, falling rocks and seracs, hot sun, and bitterly cold nights. We had wanted an adventure, and we got it!

MATEJ MEJOVSEK, *Slovenia*

Editor's note: Given its proximity and relation to existing lines, this ascent provokes an interesting question, which is well presented by Lindsay Griffin, editor of the Mountain INFO section of the U.K. magazine High Mountain Sports. Lindsay writes, "On paper their line is barely a variation to that climbed in 1969 by Habeler and Messner, but the Slovenians feel justified that the route is indeed new, as the ground they climbed bore no relation to that followed by previous ascensionists. They note that both 1968 and '69 lines would now be totally lethal, and in christening their route Limitless Madness, have opened an ethical debate on what constitutes a new route in alpine ranges of the world suffering severe transformation due to climatic change. The Peruvian Andes has suffered more than most in this respect and publications reporting ascents in the future will need to reach a consensus on what constitutes a new line."

Puscanturpa Norte: (1) Northwest Ridge (Bianchi-Boselli-Buizza-Caneva-Da Polenza-Milani-Mora-Pozzoli, 1975). (2) Northwest Pillar (Manera-Sant'Unione, 1988). (3) Pasta Religion (Baudry-Daudet-Lombard, 2000). (4) northwest face variation (previously unreported: 600m, ED2 F6b+ A4, Balzan-Bones-Conforto-Zanetti, 2002). (5) Macanacota (Avrisani-Faure-Pouraz, 2000). (6) North Face (Antonietti-Bianchi-Mondinelli-Mora, 1984). *Route info and photo courtesy of Jeremy Frimer,* Cordillera Huayhuash: Select Treks and Climbs

Puscanturpa Norte, various activity. July saw multiple teams camped below Puscanturpa Norte (5,652m), hoping to complete routes on the columned rock buttress of the northwest face. British climbers Mark Pretty, Nic Sellars, and Sam Whittaker first attempted Pasta Religion (F7a+, Baudry-Daudet-Lombard, 2000) on the northwest face, ground-up, hoping for an onsight ascent. This might have been achieved were it not for a fall on the crux seventh pitch due to a broken hold. This pitch was then yo-yoed, while all others were climbed onsight. The climbing was often bold, routefinding could sometimes be tricky, and the difficulties were found to be high, with British 6b climbing on the third pitch, and the seventh and eighth graded E6 6b and E6 6a, respectively. After five days the team terminated their ascent at the top of the 12th pitch. After the first pitch (E3 6a) they note 10 consecutive pitches of E4 and above, or F6c+ to 7a+, making for a very sustained route. Above, looser terrain led to the summit ridge and a huge and hideous cornice. They then turned their attention to their proposed new line, but found it to be largely crackless. Their ethics forbade drilled protection, so with time running out the three left the area.

The summit ridge also stopped a three-man Basque team from Pamplona, consisting of Iñaki Araiz, Iker Garcia, and Iñaki Garreta, who made the second ascent of the other French route put up in 2000, Macanacota (F7b A2, Avrisani-Faure-Pouraz), a climb that meets Pasta Religion at the top of its 12th pitch. The Basque team, climbing in capsule style, fixed the initial 250m and then climbed the route with two nights on the wall. Although the rock is very good, they did not find perfect cracks, just discontinuous lines and many pockets. Nevertheless, the terrain was well suited to natural gear. The three completed 14 pitches to reach the top of the First Tower, then climbed a little over one-third of the steep and difficult snow/mixed arête that leads to the top of the Second Tower (and toward the summit), before retreating. They note that the left edge of the Second Tower would be considerably easier but is impossible to reach from the top of

The west face of Yanashinga. *Richard Hidalgo*

the First Tower. The Basques found the quality of climbing good, the route always sunny, and report one bolt at each belay. They also believe that the hard rock up to the top of the First Tower could be climbed without a bivouac, if parties were to leave ice gear behind and travel light.

To the left a third party, Peruvians Diego Fernandez and Guillermo Mejía, made an attempt on the 1984 Italian Route (Antonietti-Bianchi-Mondinelli-Mora), climbing more than halfway up the face on July 29, at 5.10a. However, they were forced down by bad weather.

LINDSAY GRIFFIN, *High Mountain INFO*

CORDILLERA CENTRAL

Correction, note on naming. On p. 294 of the 2002 AAJ there was a report about climbing in the "Cordillera Huarochirí." "Cordillera" refers to a range or chain of mountains. While the nomenclature of Peruvian places is complex, it has been made clear to us, through several sources, that Huarochirí is more accurately a large massif within the Cordillera Central (a commonly referenced range, but not named on most Peruvian maps), rather than its own cordillera.

Yanashinga, West Face. One could consider Yanashinga (5,250m) the most technical and dizzying mountain of the Tíclio group. It is located 135km east of Lima and has only two routes and not a single repeat. The central highway reaches 4,818m, and through here runs the highest railroad in the world. The West Face (350m, MD 5.10a) had been attempted before but without success. I had tried it, too, once arriving just 50m from the summit. Guillermo Mejía and I began the route once together, and together we wanted to complete it.

We camped at the foot of the glacier that comes off Nevado Santa Rosa. We began the climb early on December 19, via an ice ramp to the first belay station. The first three pitches involved rock, with moves up to 5.9. On the fourth pitch Guillermo found himself stopped on vertical rock, struggling to place protection. He had climbed an easy dihedral, but the exit was more difficult, and he hadn't placed a piece since the belay. Desperately he began cleaning in order to place something. The rock was bad, with big flakes one on top of another, and one of these flakes launched and fell close to me, breaking on the backpack and causing almost everything inside to fall out. The last two pitches were on horrible rock, without many options for protection, and loose rock fragments covered in snow and ice. On the summit, Guillermo could not properly anchor, so he belayed from inside a depression. We arrived on top around 6 p.m. We descended the east face, which left us a roundabout detour around the mountain to arrive back at camp.

RICHARD HIDALGO, *Peru (translated by Molly Loomis)*

Yanashinga, Direct South Face. José Li Linway, Diego Fernández, and I left the village of San Mateo (3,300m), arriving at Tíclio in the middle of the night and at the foot of the wall around 3:00 a.m on July 20. Roped as a team of three, with the third jumaring, we climbed two pitches of easy mixed terrain, followed a trough leading toward the central wall for two more pitches, then one more pitch traversing a lower ledge. Already we were at the foot of the great rock wall. The sixth pitch was a rock wall that ended in a leaning chimney. I had climbed 15m when I dislodged a flake, possibly 20kg. I held it in position for a moment, but its weight was too much, and I let it fall. It cut the rope up which José would jumar. Apparently José delayed taking out the lower anchor, and that saved his life. We lost about 12m of rope, which limited us on the following pitches. The following pitches reached M7 in difficulty, but exited onto a mixed slope with a good belay station. From here up to the summit we followed a pair of WI4 pitches. The final three pitches had the worst rock we'd ever climbed, rock held in place only by snow that precariously secured them. One pitch was impossible to protect. It took a huge amount of work preparing those three belay stations, and still they were bad. We finished the route (550m, M7 WI4 A2X) and arrived at the rocky summit at 8:30 p.m. We descended the east face, with a bivouac imminent, a clear sky, but intense cold.

GUILLERMO MEJÍA, *Peru (translated by Molly Loomis)*

Nevado Huaguruncho, Tancash. Huaguruncho, meaning "the white tusk," is the 24th highest mountain in Peru (according to web pages that give the summit an altitude of 5,780m [See note below for explanation—Ed]). Located in the Central Andes region, it is best reached from Huachón, about three hours from Ninacaca (on the road from la Oroya to Cerro de Pasco, seven hours from Lima). The Huaguruncho Range is not big, with only about 10 peaks above 5,300m, of which Huaguruncho is the highest. Its isolation makes it visible throughout the region. The range being near the jungle, the weather is typically wet and cloudy most days of July and August.

We were told in Pasco that Huaguruncho was a virgin mountain. "No strangers reached the top," because, the locals said, there is a big golden cross on the very summit, shinning in the morning sun, put there by descendents of the Incas using a secret tunnel. None of us found the cross—nor did the British expedition in 1956, the Norwegian-American in 1970, or the Japanese in 1975—but 28 years after the last ascent, they said we were the first, apparently believing us though we hadn't a cross to show. Or did they believe us?

We acclimatized by walking, bouldering, and rock climbing in the wonderful weird rock formations of the Bosque de Rocas de Huayllay (4,150m) for about two weeks. In the last days of May we walked around the mountain looking for a fast way to ascend. The east face and south ridge seemed to be five-day climbs, at least. We moved base camp to the north face, making Camp 1 on the Matthews Glacier where we spent three nights at 5,000m. Once there, we did not like the west ridge, which took the 1956 team more than a week to climb, but we saw a line without seracs that leads to the upper section of the ridge, at about 5,400m. The wall was not overly steep, but did involve a short M5 pitch. The ridge was Peruvian: deep snow, double-corniced, slow going. In a mist, we realized that there was no further up to go. We looked in vain for the cross, but it was nevertheless the summit! We climbed alpine style, and so enjoyed the ambiance of Andean tradition. The golden cross is not a legend but a fact, as the people believe in it more than in gringos' accounts, so maybe you can still make the first ascent of Huaguruncho, one of Peru's beauties that is not in the Blanca or Huayhuash.

Tancash, direct way by the north face (but not a direttissima, which would be suicidal) to the west ridge, May 29, 2003: 700m, MD- ("very difficult minus"). Oriol Baró, Xavi Farré, and Albert Bargués from the Centre Excursionista, Alta Ribagorça, and Jordi Marmolejo of the C.E. Lleida. All from Catalonia (Southeast Pyrenees).

XAVI FARRÉ, *Pyrenees*

Guillermo Mejia on pitch 6 (A2) on the south face of Yanashinga. *Diego Fernandez*

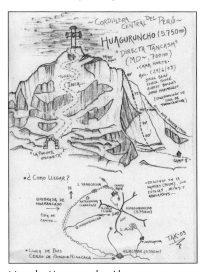

Nevado Huaguruncho (the more common spelling), revealing the secret Inca tunnel as well as Directa Tancash. Note: The British Route was actually 1956. *Jordi Marmolejo*

Note on elevation: The true altitude of Nevado Huaguruncho is unclear. Farré writes: "The official map from the Peruvian Geographical Institute, working on aerophotographical images, says 5,728m. Many webpages I've found say 5,784m. Our three altimeters became mad on the way up, same with our compass, and we didn't carry a GPS, so we cannot give data from the top. The drawing by Jordi Marmolejo says 5,750m—it's the height that Jordi remembered. I used 5,780m, based on various data I've seen. The true altitude is simply not known, but it's less than 6,000m, for sure."

CORDILLERA VILCABAMBA

Nevado Weqqe Suruchi, A Life Less Ordinary. The Panta Group lies in a sparsely populated area and consists of the most westerly cluster of glaciated peaks in the Vilcabamba. The principal summits are Panta itself (5,667m) and Camballa (5,551m). In 2002 Germans Christoph Nick and Frank Toma attempted the elegant, unclimbed, and unnamed peak at the end of the long ridge running south from Camballa (5,551m), but were foiled by poor snow and crevasse danger. In summer 2003 they returned to the Panta Valley for a second attempt. The peak is marked on the 1965 Swiss map as 5,349.1m. Again they were accompanied by their two arrieros and now-firm friends, brothers Alejandro and Hermenegildo Huaman Olarte from Yamana, without whose local knowledge the expedition would not have been successful. They were also joined by fellow German Metin Kavaz. Base camp was established in the Panta Valley, from where they climbed a small peak. The three Germans then carried loads through a steep couloir to rocky ledges under the glacier on the south flank of their main objective. On July 13 they set out from their high bivouac for a summit attempt. At 5,000m Kavaz and Toma had to retreat due to ill health, but Nick continued and in a bold effort crossed crevassed slopes and climbed a steep ice face to a glacier terrace below the summit. The last obstacle was surmounted via an easy ramp, and the summit ridge proved less dangerous than expected. At 11.30 a.m. he was on top, where he recorded an altimeter reading of 5,437m. The route, which was christened A Life Less Ordinary, was rated AD+, with short rock sections of UIAA II and III in the gully leading to the bivouac site. The peak had no local name, so the climbers took the liberty of christening it Nevado Weqqe Suruchi, which in Quechua means "tears of ice."

LINDSAY GRIFFIN, *High Mountain INFO*

Pumasillo Group, multiple ascents. Sean Easton and I spent 20 days in the Pumasillo group of the Cordillera Vilcabamba, in south-central Peru. It is quite hard to describe the mountains we climbed because the new government 1:100,000 topos have many errors, and the locals have several different names for the mountains. The following is a list of what we did, and the coordinates included are on or near the summit. Peaks one through eight are found on the Machu Picchu map.

> Peak 1: 5,108m (wrong on map) 18l 726321 8634376. Unnamed on map, locals call
>   it "Mandor," it lies on the Quelca-Mandor pass. We climbed the east face (10 pitches, 5.9).
> Peak 2: 5,050m (Cayco on map) 18l 726699 8534336. Incorrect summit altitude on
>   map, also called "Mandor," we climbed the north ridge (6 pitches, mixed 5.4).
> Peak 3: 4,935m 18l 727325 8533732. Unnamed on map, also called "Mandor,"
>   southernmost peak of group. We climbed the north ridge (3 pitches, 5.9).
> Peak 4: 5,210m 18l 732128 8532828. Unnamed on map, locals call it "Mayuyoc." We

approached from the south, dropped down and climbed the east face, 60° snow, 5.6. We found a tuna can on top, the only peak on which we saw evidence of previous ascents. [A 1959 Swiss expedition made the probable first ascent of this peak, calling it Nevado Paccha—Ed.]

Peak 5: 5,310m 18l 731959 8533616. A snow ridge just south of what the map incorrectly calls the south peak of Choquetecarpo. Hike up the steep snow of the south ridge.

Peak 6: 5,428 18l 731779 8534164. Choquetecarpo S peak on map. The locals call it "Panta" (although there is another Panta three valleys over). We climbed the east ridge, 50° snow. [The Panta Group lies further west—see above report—and should not be confused with the locals' name for this peak. The 1959 Swiss team who made the first ascent dubbed this peak "Pucapuca," and a New Zealand team in 1962 climbed this same east ridge route—Ed.]

Peak 7: 5,512m 18l 732621 8536496. Choquetecarpo on map. Called "Puca Puca" by the locals. We climbed the east ridge (1,100m, 5.8 M4 60°). [This peak was also first climbed by the 1959 Swiss expedition, and the east ridge had been climbed by a 1962 New Zealand team—Ed.]

Peak 8: 5,447m 18l740716 8530832. East peak of Sacsarayoc on map. Called "Sacsarayoc" by the locals. The rest of the massif is known as "Pumasillo." We climbed the north ridge up the 30m summit spire, 5.9.

On the trip I also climbed two other peaks, one with my brother Peter and one with another friend. Peter and I climbed a peak called Pitupaccha (5,090m), located above Incarajay, up the Quesqa valley from Wayabamba or Paucarcancha. We climbed the west ridge, easy 5th. Karen Perry and I climbed Jatunjasa (locally known as "Incachiriasca," 5,338m). We scrambled up the north face, with beautiful views of Salcantay.

CONNY AMELUNXEN, *Canada*

Historical note: The history of climbing in this region is obviously difficult to document, with multiple names and altitudes attributed to the various peaks. In the late 1950s and 1960s several expeditions explored the area, making many ascents. The 1962 New Zealand expedition made a sketch map of the entire massif that is commonly used by subsequent expeditions. Thanks to Lindsay Griffin for this history.

CORDILLERA VILCANOTA

Chumpe (Jatunriti) traverse, Colquecruz 1 attempt (Alcamarinayoc). Intrigued by the scarcity of information despite extensive research, Amy Bullard and I spent three weeks exploring and climbing in the northern Cordillera Vilcanota from April 21 to May 10. We saw no one during this time. We accessed the peaks from a base camp at Laguna Mullucocha after a long-day approach from Tinqui. On April 29 we climbed the west ridge of Nevado Chumpe (6,106m, also called Jatunriti) from a camp at 5,400m on the glacier on the northwest side of the peak. Descent was made to the north, down to the col between Chumpe and the Colquecruz massif. The climbing was straightforward and scenic on steep, consolidated snow, the round-trip traverse from camp taking under eight hours.

Colquecruz 1 (6,102m) is labeled Nevado Alcamarinayoc on Peru's Carta Nacional 1:100,000 Ocongate sheet. We approached its southwest face from the southeast, through a col

Chumpe, from the northwest. The route traversed the ridge over the summit. *Peter Carse*

The attempt on Colquecruz 1, a.k.a. Nevado Alcamarinayoc. *Peter Carse*

between it and Nevado Ichu Ananta. On May 4 we climbed the middle of the SW face to about 5,900m before turning back in a violent afternoon thunderstorm. Building ice-thread rappel anchors in the deep torrent of spindrift was memorable. The climbing was all on steep ice, with some hazard of falling ice and rock.

We don't know whether the routes are new. As far as we could gather from our research, Chumpe had been climbed from the north (ridge/face), northwest face, and the south. No traverses had been mentioned. Colquecruz 1 had been climbed in the early 1960s from the north side, and traversed west to east from a camp on the north side. We received useful information from Jorge Villena, the SAEC, and Luis Pineto, all in Cusco, as well as warm hospitality and arriero support from Hostal Tinqui.

PETER CARSE, *AAC*

CORDILLERA APOLOBAMBA

Ritipata, Palomani Grande, Palomani Tranca Central, and other ascents. John Biggar again visited the remote Peruvian Apolobamba, and as in 2002, the climbers traveled via Puno to the 4,700m mining village of Ananea. Base camp was again established by the shores of the beautiful Laguna Callumachaya, from where the whole team (Linda and John Biggar, Paul Cherry, Mark and Lizzy Hylton, Ken Pritchard, and Andy Rendel) first climbed the 300m Callumachaya Buttress to a spectacular high camp on the edge of the glacier at ca 5,000m. This route, which included two long ice pitches at Scottish II/III and some easy rock climbing, was certainly new, as 10 years ago the buttress was under the glacier. On August 6 all climbers made an ascent of Ritipata Oeste (ca 5,380m) by a west-to-east traverse. John Biggar, Cherry, Pritchard, and Rendel then climbed the easy Southwest Ridge of Ritipata (5,410m). This is a different Ritipata from the one marked on the Italian map drawn after the 1958 expedition, which was the first to visit this area. It is therefore felt that both peaks were previously unclimbed.

The team had hoped to tackle the unclimbed 500m-high east face of Callijon. However, this proved beyond the time and energy resources of the party. Instead they turned to the unclimbed south face of Palomani Grande (5,723m), a peak that rumor has it had first been climbed in the 1920s by a Captain in the Bolivian Army (and was certainly climbed by Italians in 1958). Leaving a camp in the Quebrada Palomani on the 11th, both Biggars, Cherry, Pritchard, and Rendel ascended the glacier to the southwest of the peak and reached a basin beneath the south face. From there a steep snow rib at PD led to the top. On the 12th John Biggar and Rendel set off from the same camp and later in the day reached the summit of Palomani Tranca Central (5,600m, AD). They traversed over a lower west summit (ca 5,450m), on which they found several little shrines. Was this evidence of an Inca ascent? Palomani Tranca Central was probably a first ascent, though the higher East Peak (5,638m) was first climbed in 1985 from the north by British climbers Jim Curran and Geoff Tier. Before departing, members of the expedition also made ascents of Asnococha (ca 5,250m), Huincho (5,204m) and Palomani Norte (5,629m) via established routes. The first was known ground, as it had been climbed by John Biggar in 2002, while the last had been unsuccessfully attempted in 2002, to within 50m of the top.

As during the 2002 visit, no other westerners were seen during the two-week expedition, and the weather was equally poor. However, this time snow conditions were considerably better, allowing objectives which had been written off as too dangerous in 2002 to be successfully tackled.

LINDSAY GRIFFIN, *High Mountain INFO*

Venezuela

Matawi Tepui (a.k.a. Kukenan Tepui), attempt and exploration. In the first week of February, climbers Federico Pizani, Luis Cisneros, Chris Gardner, and I, Maikey Lopera, and trekkers Dan Kopperud and Lindsey, as support crew, left from Caracas for southern Venezuela to attempt to climb and explore the west face of Matawi Tepui, located northeast of the Roraima Tepui. Our interest in climbing this tepui was that the west side was unexplored. I thought it would be a great opportunity to explore and climb this untouched face. Matawi Tepui (in local Pemon language, it means "The Place to Die") has been a mystery because of legends that surround its name.

After two days of traveling by bus, we were dropped off at the bridge on the Yuruani River. Our first leg of the approach was through savanna with the occasional jungle patch. We spent the first night at an abandoned Indian house, from which we "borrowed" a canoe to transport us across the Yuruani. We continued to a small tribe of Indians who screamed at us, trying to keep us from continuing our route. Two more days of walking put us at the edge of the jungle.

After four days of battling thick jungle, fighting off swarms of mosquitoes, and avoiding poisonous snakes, we reached the base of the wall. The next day, Luis and I carried loads to the base of our intended route, while Federico and Chris led the first three pitches. Chris had the honor of leading the first jungle pitches in wet weather. On the second day we committed to the wall, hauling gear and adding two more pitches, led mostly free by Federico. At the end of the fifth pitch the nice crack-and-corner system vanished into a sea of small and delicate features on the red sandstone. There we found a ledge where we set up camp. To our surprise the rock was bulletproof, making our drill bits and Petzl bolts worthless. Our only option was to drill 1/4" holes for rivets that we could use as anchors. Thankfully, we found a shallow crack in which we could back up anchors with Lost Arrows. Luis and I added two more pitches before we decided to bail due to the impossibility of safe anchors. Our last belay station consisted only of two 1/4" and one 5/8" rivets. The rock was so hard that in some instances drilling a 1/4" hole took 45 to 60 minutes. In addition, when we tried to set a rivet into a hole, it would deform rather than penetrate the depth of the hole, making the situation that much more dangerous. Becoming part of the legend was not part of our plan.

We rapped from the top of the seventh pitch and, in four raps, were on the ground. Some of the rap anchors consisted only of two rivets. Of the seven pitches, the first two were "jungle" climbing and were done in intense rain. Pitches three, four, and five consisted of crack climbing up to 5.12. We encountered much loose rock on these pitches. Pitch six was easy climbing from the ledge (5.6). The seventh pitch consisted of aid climbing on fragile features and rotten rock. From the base of the wall, two days of jungle traveling got us to Paraitepui, the nearest town.

MAIKEY LOPERA, VENEZUELA(*translated by* TRICIA KING)

Acopán Tepui. Pizza, Chocolate y Cerveza. In March, back in Venezuela again, we were preparing for another intense tepui (flat-topped mountain) experience. John Arran, nicknamed "La Máquina" by the Venezuelans, was particularly keen following last year's success on Cerro Autana. But this time there would be no José Pereyra to share the tepui experience—which he summed up last year as "a different kind of gnarly."

Accompanied by Venezuelan climber Alfredo Rangel, we were landed by our light aircraft on a patch of grassland near the Indian village of Yunek Ken in the Gran Sabana—a destination remote enough to escape the attention of even the Lonely Planet guide. Acopán's elegant, 300 million year-old bulging orange and gray walls gave the appearance of a fortress towering over the village. Our chosen line looked like an awesome proposition. It took two days, aided by the machete-wielding village chief, Leonardo, to break trail to the base.

Already a distant memory was the headache of planning an

Approaching Acopán Tepui's Pizza, Chocolate y Cerveza. *Anne Arran*

expedition deep into Venezuela in the aftermath of political unrest. Even the jungle approach, heavy loads, and irrepellable insects were no longer important. Bright red Gaijito de Piedera parrots welcomed us to the wall as we collected water at its base.

The fun began Tarzan-style, by us monkeying up 2"- thick vines for 35m. Four days of continuously surprising, bold face-climbing and steep cracks led to a 12m roof we hadn't seen from the ground. Alfredo had brought along a collection of lightweight Bolivian and Peruvian musical instruments which, along with his rap songs, had calmed many a stressful moment. Now a time of uncertainty: Could we overcome the monstrous roof? A reverse mantle and sloping hand-traverse, with legs dangling 400m above nothing, fortuitously led to more amenable ground.

After many close calls we made it to near the top, where the angle finally eased and I felt sure we'd cracked it. At one point John had to dyno for a bush on the lip of a roof, with no idea whether it would hold his weight.

Our 600m east-face route took six days and 21 pitches. We managed to free every pitch without falls. The route overhung by about 50m total with the hardest pitch cranking up to E6 6b (5.12bR), and the team avoided placing any pegs or bolts, even on belays. We spent a fun day scrambling around the summit's curious dike-like features and

Anne Arran on Pizza, Chocolate y Cerveza, Acopán Tepui. *John Arran*

wind-carved rock formations, before descending left of the climbing line, making full use of our 100m ropes. This expedition was supported by The British Mountaineering Council, UK Sport, Mount Everest Foundation, The North Face, Petzl, and Beal.

ANNE ARRAN, *U.K.*

Acopán Tepui, Unate Arête (a.k.a. Racquel Welsh Arête). Louise Thomas, Dave Turnball, Steve Mayers, and I traveled from St. Elena after meeting up with Alfredo Rangel, a local climber who had climbed at Acopán with John and Anne Arran. After flying in we took one days' march through the savanna and jungle to reach the base of the wall. The line was a huge 500m arête which had previously been tried by Italian climbers (70m climbed and bolted). Over 65 days we worked on the line and bivvied on top for a day. We fixed ropes and enjoyed base camp and party life. We aimed to have a holiday, not an epic. One could take portaledges, but with a big team we kept life simple. We did not place any pegs or bolts. It was a very pleasant rock climb, all pitches E2 to E5, all pitches free except the first, which had a few rest points because of a bees' nest. Solid, excellent sandstone, perfect for free climbing, took nuts and cams well. We climbed about 500m in about 20 pitches, including easy scrambling at the top. It's big and bulging and leads to the land that time forgot, hence the route's a.k.a. This is a class venue without a doubt. Acopán is 80 miles in circumference, with only three routes. We also repeated a route on the south tower—Jardineros de Grandes Paredes, 350m, about E3, first climbed by Italians with Venezuelan Ivan Calderon—a fantastic climb. The weather is hot but with a constant cool strong breeze.

MIKE "TWID" TURNER, *U.K.*

Guyana

Roraima, The Scorpion Wall. My dream of climbing a tepui began more than 10 years ago. An article in National Geographic captured my imagination, with its photos of huge virgin rock walls soaring above a remote, mysterious jungle. Tepuis, I learned, are the remnants of a sandstone plateau that once covered an area of roughly 200,000 square miles in the heart of the Amazon. Over millions of years erosion wore down this plateau and left about 100 table-topped rock formations sticking out of the jungle. The cliffs ringing them range from 1,000' to 3,000' high and extend in some places for miles. Tepuis represent some of the biggest, yet least explored, rock walls on the planet.

In 2001 I received a grant from the National Geographic Expeditions Council to lead a botanist and a biologist up a tepui wall to search for new species. While many people had studied the tops of tepuis, no one had investigated the walls themselves. We originally planned to do the trip in Venezuela, but found it impossible to get a permit from the government. We decided instead to climb and study a tepui

Bruce Means with a giant tarantula he found in camp. *Mark Synnott*

Kids playing outside Phillipai, the closest town to Roraima. *Jared Ogden*

called Roraima, which sits where Guyana, Venezuela, and Brazil meet. The president of Guyana personally invited us to approach and climb Roraima from the Guyanese side.

Our plan was to document the expedition for National Geographic Television, and at the last minute a host of people jumped on board: correspondent Mareya Mayor, scientists Bruce Means and Jesus Rivas, producer Peter Getzels, and his assistant Charlotte Mangin. Peter decided that this "A Team" would head down to Guyana first to pioneer a 50-mile trek across the jungle to the base of the wall. Then they would cut a heli pad so Jared Ogden, cameraman John Catto, and I could fly in.

Jared, John, and I arrived about a week after the A Team in 2003. We met the Guyana Defense Force and flew in with the country's only working helicopter to meet the others. After a two-day search above the jungle, we finally found them. It took nearly five days to cover the final mile of jungle to the wall. We often found ourselves climbing vertical walls covered in mud and poorly-rooted vegetation. The section of Roraima we wanted to climb is called the Prow, an overhanging 1,300-1,500' buttress on the north side. It had been climbed once, in 1971 by a British team made up of Mo Anthoine, Hamish MacInnes, Don Whillans, and Joe Brown.

We reached the base of the wall on March 29 under blue skies and immediately set to work. We chose a line a hundred yards or so to the left of the British Route. Our plan was to establish a free route. We fixed the first two pitches, to a hanging

Roraima Tepui, showing The Scorpion Wall. *Jared Ogden*

Mark Synnott leading the crux 5.11+ pitch through a roof about 800 feet above the jungle. *Jared Ogden*

garden, then brought Jesus Rivas up, so he could collect his scientific samples. The A Team then left, and Jared, John, and I committed to the wall. We spent the next four nights in portaledges. Every pitch was overhanging, and most of the climbing was in the 5.10-5.11 range, with two pitches of 5.11+. We placed six bolts, at belays. We climbed everything free until the very top of the wall, where we ran into more steep vegetation. In pouring rain we pulled on a few pieces of gear. The route was too overhanging to rappel, so we called for a helicopter pick-up when we reached the summit. The Scorpion Wall (9 pitches, VI 5.11+ A0) was one of my all-time best adventures.

MARK SYNNOTT, *AAC*

Bolivia

Ilusión, Ilusión Congelada. On June 14 we established a new route on Ilusión (5,330m) in the Condoriri Group of the Cordillera Real. The 400m route had WI6X, II-III (5.3) rock, and 40-70° snow, and required four hours to climb. The hardest and most serious part is the icefall in the middle of the west face, which is seen from the route to the glacier leading to Piramide Blanca. The approach is the same as for the Normal Route: head up the glacier that descends from Iluscionita and Ilusión to the left side of the col between the two mountains. About 100m before the col turn right and climb 60-70m of rock (UIAA II) to reach the base of the steep, thin icefall in the middle of the wall. Climb it (45m, 80-90°, one rock piton in the wall above the first ice mushroom) and reach the big shelf above the rock barrier (very thin ice—it collapsed after our ascent—start early in the morning!).

Climb straight up the snow, which steepens to 60°, to reach a 5m rock section (II-III), which leads to the snow shelf that crosses the face. Follow it to the snow slopes of the Direct

The frozen illusion, on Ilusión. *Branko Ivanek*

Route. Turn up left and climb the snow (150m, 70°) between the rock sections to reach the ridge. Follow it to the summit and descend the Normal or Direct Route.

BRANKO IVANEK *and* ANDREJ PECJAK, *Slovenia*

Ancohuma, Barrador Intimo; Pico del Norte, C'est la Vie, and other ascents. Climbing early in the year on the east face of Ancohuma (6,427m), Frenchmen Pierre Bogino and Simon Paris added a new ice/mixed line, which they named Barrador Intimo. The east face features three big pillars—the left one climbed by Arias and Mesili in 1970; the central one, which has 700m of rock at V+ and A1 followed by a 300m ice ridge, by Italians Zappelli et al. in 1978; and the right one (ca 750m, VI-) by Italians Agostino de Polenza et al. in 1979. How the new 800m French mixed route relates to these is unclear, but the pair report difficulties of V/5 and superb granite. From a camp below the face they climbed the route in 13 hours and descended the Normal Route, to regain their camp in an 18-hour round trip.

Bogino, this time with Alexis Loireau, also repeated the Via del Triangulo on the west face of Huayna Potosi (Hans Haztler-Alain Mesili, September 1971, ca. 750m, 55-60° mixed). Again, climbing so early in the season that they found delicate ice and mixed terrain at IV/5 (90°); they completed the route in 13 hours.

On the East Face of Pico del Norte (6,050m), the summit that marks the end of the long ridge running north from Illampu, Bogino and Paris added a route christened C'est la Vie. Again, the exact location of the climb on this broad and imposing face, which has plenty of scope in snowy conditions for many mixed lines, some potentially hard, is not clear. However, it is 600m high and IV/4 with some sections of 90° mixed and good rock. The weather was far from perfect, with thick mist leading to soggy snow, and the pair took 12 hours to complete their ascent. However, the fun had just started, as a difficult descent, most likely by the Normal Route, took longer, and the pair returned to their camp 25 hours after leaving.

LINDSAY GRIFFIN, *High Mountain INFO*

Argentina and Chile

NORTHERN ANDES, ARGENTINA

Citta di Rieti, first ascent. In January 2002 Italians Eliano Pessa and Arnaldo Milesmi, with Argentinean Patricio Cardù (Argentinean Federico Aguero Varela was the expedition's chief but did not summit), made a first ascent of a virgin mountain north of Cerro Bonete Chico (a volcano, part of the ridge connected to Bonete Chico) in Provincia de la Rioja. They had a difficult approach from Laguna Brava and from there they ascended the 6,200m peak, which they unofficially christened Citta di Rieti. They attempted Bonete Chico but were driven back by fierce winds at 6,550m.

MARCELO SCANU, *Buenos Aires, Argentina*

Cerro El Cóndor, possible first ascent and other ascents. In February and March some friends and I climbed Antofalla, a 6,409m (GPS 6,470m) volcano approximately 80km southeast of Llullaillaco. On the summit we found a 8m x 6m platform made by Incas, with a ring of stones and a long, thin volcanic block in the middle. Later we went to the Bonete-Pissis region. I climbed the "hills" on the east slopes of Bonete, between 6,100m and 6,330m high, hoping to find signs of Walter Penck, the German geographer who was once thought to be the first on Bonete, in 1913. However, I found nothing.

ALEXANDER VON GÖTZ, *Germany*

CENTRAL ANDES, CHILE

Elqui Valley and Los Corrales Valley, first ascents. In the upper Elqui Valley and on the Chilean-Argentinean border east of the town of Vicuña there seems to be a number of unclimbed mountains, all rising above very arid plains and valleys. The finest mountain in this district, the glaciated Nevado del Tapado (5,347m), was ascended in late September by Jorge Quinteros (Santiago), who was accompanying several foreign glaciologists. Earlier, in March, I made the first ascent of Peak 5,192m, which I christened Cerro Bachmann, after Walter Bachmann, the first mountaineer to explore and climb in the Elqui district (1953). The same day I descended to the Argentinean side and ascended Peak 5,163, which I named Cerro Olascoaga, after José M. Olascoaga, an Argentinean surveyor and mountaineer of the 1880s.

EVELIO ECHEVARRIA, *AAC*

Ojos del Salado, scientific determination of highest point. Ojos del Salado is, at 6,879m (IGMA), the highest mountain in Chile, third highest in the Andes, and the highest active volcano in the world. It's located on the Argentina-Chile frontier at 27°06'S / 68°32'W. Its main summit has twin rocky towers, 60m apart and separated by a 30m deep notch, technical on both sides. In February 1937 the Poles J. Wojsznis and J. Szczepanski made the first ascent of the mountain, reaching the eastern tower from Argentina. Nineteen years later, a mainly Chilean team achieved Ojo's third ascent and the first of the western tower, climbing from Chile. They claimed the first ascent of

Getting the equipment ready on top of the western summital tower. In front of it is the eastern one. *Darío Bracali*

the mountain, declaring that the western tower was 4m higher. Chile's Club Andinista denied that claim, accepting the Polish climb, but there has been much discussion about whether reaching the top of the eastern peak is really summiting Ojos. All kinds of opinions have been published, all based on visual perceptions based on simple local observations.

To end the controversy by scientific measurement, an expedition was organized to climb both towers simultaneously and make a topographic leveling between them. A team of eight mountaineers from all corners of Argentina gathered at the abandoned building at 4,500m at the Chilean foot of Ojos known as Murray. There, while acclimatizing, we were trained in the complex technique of topographical leveling by engineer Claudio Bravo, scientific director of the project. After a two-day climb by the normal Northern Route, Rolando Linzing and Dario Bracali reached the top of the western tower on November 11 at 11:30, carrying the 15kg of measuring equipment. A furious wind was blowing, making leveling the field level a hard job. Once that was accomplished, Dario took the graduated ruler to the eastern tower, through an easy technical pass beyond the notch. Rolando made two revised measurements and at 14:30 they started down. That night they reached Murray, where the following day the team analyzed the results.

In conclusion, the western tower is 54 +/-5 cm higher than the eastern one. As this difference is lower than one meter (the minimum that justifies considering a summit higher than another one) it can be stated that both towers of Ojos del Salado have the same altitude. So, the real summit is both of them.

CLAUDIO BRAVO *(CAT) and* DARIO BRACALI *(CAB & AAC), Argentina*

CENTRAL ANDES, ARGENTINA

Mercedario, La Conquista del Poniente. This mountain (6,770m), in Provincia de San Juan, is similar to Aconcagua in height, glaciers, and difficulties, but it hasn't had as many ascents. In 1999 a team of four from the city of San Juan went to the Valle del Colorado, the usual approach to all Mercedario's routes. They ascended to El Peine (The Comb), the ridge that unites Pico Polaco (ca 6,000m) with Mercedario. They reached 5,000m and then descended to

4,800m at the base of the west face. On their ascent of
Mercedario, they made two camps on the face, the
first at 5,700m and the second at 6,000m. The terrain
they ascended was mixed, with 60° ice and class 5
rock. They reached the summit on November 20,
1999, at 8 p.m. They pitched their tent at 6,600m at
nightfall and descended the next day.

MARCELO SCANU, *Buenos Aires, Argentina.*

Mercedario's 1999 route.

Nevado del Plomo, El Sendero del Léon and east ridge.
A remarkable ascent has been made on the 6,050m (also given as 6,070m) Nevado del Plomo
(a.k.a. El Plomo), a high peak in the Juncal Group, located east of Santiago on the Chilean-
Argentinean border and 5km south of the better-known Juncal (elevation often given as
6,110m), which have the most extensive glaciers in the Cordillera. The first recorded ascent was
in 1910, by German geologist and explorer Frederick Reichert. He reportedly climbed from the
Argentinean side, which is technically much harder than an approach from Chile, where the
west flank, above the Olivares Valley, is no more than a walk. Inca ruins remain just below the
summit. In Jill Neate's scholarly work, Mountaineering in the Andes, it is noted that the mountain
has an impressive southeast face, presumably unclimbed.

No more. In an 18-hour ascent on January 7 the resident German climber Jürgen Straub
made a solo ascent of a direct line on this huge face. He reached the foot of the ca 2,500m wall
with a Chilean partner early in the day, but before they had even come to grips with the ascent,
the Chilean's crampon broke, and the pair was forced down. After some discussion, Straub
decided to go it alone, while his friend made the probable first ascent of the much easier east
ridge. After a glacier approach and mixed climbing interrupted by snow/ice fields, Straub came
to the crux, a 350m rock pillar high on the wall. He climbed this, reporting difficulties up to
VII, after which the angle relented, and easier climbing led to the summit. The route, christened
El Sendero del Léon, was considered to be harder than the south face of Aconcagua.

LINDSAY GRIFFIN, *High Mountain INFO*

Erika and Yanina, first ascents; Gemelos Este, possible new route. Gemelos (The Twins) is a mountain
near Las Cuevas and the Aconcagua area, near the Chilean border in Argentina's Provincia de
Mendoza. A group directed by Glauco Muratti was active here in October 2002. There was much
snow, and the approach was a long one from Quebrada de Vargas, passing the Portezuelo Serrata
to the base of Gemelos. The group ascended two twin rock towers of ca 4,750-4,800m, both virgin,
christening them Erika and Yanina. The steepness was 50°. They also summited Gemelos Este
(5,180m) by a possible new route, the Glaciar del Vasco (Basque Glacier).

MARCELO SCANU, *Buenos Aires, Argentina*

Aconcagua, 2003-2004 season overview. This season Aconcagua beat its record for visitation.
The estimated number of people in Aconcagua Provincial Park was 7,000 (87% foreign, 13%

Argentineans) for the season (November 15, 2003 to March 15, 2004), 12% more than the previous season. The number of park rangers was increased to 36, and the Mendoza government may begin selling permits by internet. A lot of human waste was helicoptered out of the area, so it's much cleaner now. There is now internet access in Plaza de Mulas. The weather was not as good as in many parts of the Argentinean-Chilean Andes, with high winds and much snow in January. Some mountaineers were trapped in Confluencia by high temperatures and melting snow. Two Germans died on the Polish Glacier. Two Spanish balloonists were rescued in nearby mountains. On the other hand, a Spanish group summited with a two-year old female golden retriever named Rubia who wore a jacket, shoes, and sunglasses! [Canine gossip: There is controversy as to whether Rubia was the first canine to summit Aconcagua. A Chilean newspaper reported, some 10 year ago, an alleged ascent by a stray dog that tagged along with Germans and Austrians. We were unable to confirm with either the climbers or the pooch—Ed.] A winter ascent was made by Juan Benegas and Horacio Cunietti, who summited on August 27 by the Normal Route. They had strong winds and low temperatures (-40°C). A very important new route, with 2,500m vertical, was established by Slovenes Tomaz Humar and Ales Kozelj on the left part of the south face (left of the Slovene 1982 route).

MARCELO SCANU, *Buenos Aires, Argentina*

Aconcagua, Mobitel's Swallow–Johan's Route. Slovene mountaineers Tomaz Humar and Ales Kozelj climbed the south face of Aconcagua by a new route in the last days of December. The new route is dedicated to Humar's late partner Janez Jeglic, who suffered a fatal accident during their Nuptse expedition in 1997. This was the first time Humar climbed with a partner since the fatal ascent with Jeglic.

After failing on Nanga Parbat in the summer, Humar was regathering strength on less-challenging mountains, where he was joined by Ales Kozelj in October and November. Kozelj had been planning an expedition to Aconcagua with Matej Mosnik, but Mosnik had to drop out because of a knee injury. After two months of training together, Humar and Kozelj were the ones setting out for South America.

They left Ljubljana on November 26. Food and permits were acquired in Mendoza. They set up base camp at Plaza Francia, at an altitude of 4,200m. A fortnight of stormy weather followed. For acclimatization during this time they climbed Aconcagua's glacier and spent four days at 5,600m on a nearby mountain called Mirador.

The weather cleared on December 16. Humar and Kozelj moved up to ABC at 4,400m, and descended to the bottom of the glacier at 4,250m the following day. They started up the face on the afternoon of December 17. They encountered falling rocks in the entrance passage, some of which hit Humar's shoulders, but he escaped with just a few bruises. The entrance waterfall was followed by black ice (a mixture of ice, rocks, and water), then a 200m traverse to the right over frozen soil, and from there a 50m descent into a hollow among seracs. Since only frozen soil and receding ice could be found, instead of solid rock, this part of the route presented considerable danger. They continued across crevasses and seracs and ascended to 5,300m, where they dug a shelf by a waterfall and set up their first bivouac (B1).

On December 18 they continued by ascending the black ice next to the 500m-high Black Pyramid and reached a passage between seracs and rock. That proved to be one of the most dangerous parts of the route, due to falling rocks, ice, and water. Humar was hit by falling water.

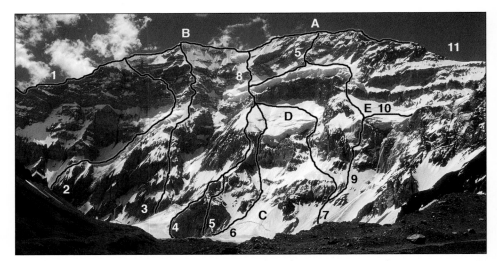

The notorious 2,400m choss pile also known as the south face of Aconcagua: (A) North Summit (6,962m), (B) South Summit (6,930m), (C) Lower Glacier, (D) Middle Glacier, (E) Pasic Glacier, (F) Upper Glacier. Routes (approximate lines): (1) Sun Line Route (ED1 5.10+ 90°, Romih-Sveticic, 1988), (2) Mobitel's Swallow–Johan's Route (VI+ A2 M5/6 90-100°, Humar-Kozelj, 2004), (3) Slovenian Route (ED1/2 5.9 A3 90°,Gantar-Podgornik-Podgornik-Rejc, 1982), (4) Slovenian Variation to the French Route (ED1 5.8, Discak-Crnilogar-Skamperle-Sveticic, 1982), (5) French Route (ED1 5.9, Bernardini-Dagory-Denis-Lasueur-Paragot-Poulet, 1954), (6) La Ruta de la Ruleta (ED1, Romih-Sveticic, 1988), (7) Central Route (D, Fonrouge-Schonberger, 1966), (8) Messner Variation to the French Route (ED1, Messner, 1974), (9) French Direct (ED1 5.7, ca. 1000m to join the Argentine Route, Chassagne-Dufour-Raveneau-Vallet, 1985), (10) Argentine Route (D, Aikes-Pellergrini, 1966), (11) Southeast Ridge (AD 5.9, Horak-Rocker-Sause, 1966). *Ken Sauls*

They reached crevasses 5,700m, dug a shelf in one of them, and set up B2.

On December 19 they continued their ascent, up the 150m high and, in places, slightly overhanging frozen waterfall. For the first time they hauled one of the rucksacks behind them. While the weather worsened, they crossed the waterfall in a blizzard and dug B3 at 6,100m. Because of the extreme cold, Kozelj suffered frostbite to his feet and hands.

On December 20 they proceeded into the "Small Bear" rock blockade, which was followed by a traverse some few hundred meters to the left. They climbed the "Traverse of Death" over a brittle rock pillar, crossing 300–400m to the bottom of the Swallow on 60-70° snow-covered ice . This crossing was itself risky, as they were climbing roped but unprotected. Once they reached the bottom of the Swallow they found blown snow stuck to the rock, forming a 15m-high pillar with no footing. They ascended to the top of the pillar and set up B4 at 6,300m, anchored by ice axes rammed into brittle rock.

On December 21 they began by descending to the bottom of the pillar, and then continued across the technically most demanding part of the face, forming the other part of the Swallow, which consists of a 100–120m overhanging rock barrier. They were forced to climb with bare hands due to the brittleness of the rock. Here they hauled their rucksacks again. The barrier was followed by perforated black ice and another 200m of mixed ground (rock, ice) to the peak of the face. They concluded their route at the face's summit and connected it to the Sun Line, set by Slavko Sveticic in 1988. They set up bivouac B5 at 6,750m.

On December 22, at 12:30 a.m., they set out toward the 6,930m south peak, the conclusion of 1982 Slovene Route, and reached it at 3:00 p.m. Two hours later they stood on the main summit, where they stayed for another hour. Humar and Kozelj agreed to name the route after both Humar's former partner and his sponsor of many years, calling attention to the route's shape at the same time: Mobitel's Swallow–Johan's Route (2,500m, VI+ (IV – V+) A2 M5–M6 90-100° (60°- 70°)). They descended by the normal route on the north side of the mountain to Plaza del Mulas at 4,300m, which they reached in only two and a half hours, at 8.30 p.m. On December 23 they travelled around the mountain on horseback and reached Plaza Francia at 6 p.m. The next day they cleaned up base camp and ABC. The expedition was made possible by Mobitel, Slovene national mobile telecommunications carrier and a loyal sponsor of Humar's endeavours.

From www.humar.com

The Avellano Towers: The Conquistador Ridge and the northeast prow attempt. *Dave Anderson*

CENTRAL PATAGONIA, CHILE

Avellano Tower, Conquistador Ridge. Dave Anderson, Steve Herlighy, and Jamie Selda (USA) and Nacho Grez (Chile) spent 27 days in the Avellano Valley, 80 miles south of the town of Coyhaique. Their main objective was a striking unclimbed granite wall, the Avellano Tower. The expedition was self-supported. Starting on March 13, 2004 the team began ferrying 1,000 lbs. of food and gear toward the Avellano Towers; they eventually hiked a total of 398 miles in and out of the mountains. Base camp was established near treeline at the base of the 4,000' Avellano Massif. The weather was unstable, even for Patagonia. The expedition experienced rain or snow at least part of every day they were in the mountains.

The climbers took advantage of the few hours of good weather they did receive. On March 20 the rain stopped for 14 hours. Climbing in two rope teams, the group ascended steep snow and rock to gain the north col of the Avellano Massif, then traversed across the west face.

On the south ridge the two teams combined and reached the summit of the Avellano Tower just after sunset. They spent the night rappelling and downclimbing, reaching base camp as the next storm moved into the valley. They named the route the Conquistador Ridge (IV 5.10 AI3).

After nine more days of rain and snow, the clouds lifted for 23 hours, allowing Anderson and Selda to attempt a direct line up the 2,500' northeast prow of the tower. The climbers navigated through a cracked-up hanging glacier to reach the base of the route. Unfortunately, the storms had encased the cracks with snow and ice, slowing their progress. After climbing 1,000' (5.10 A2), the pair was forced to retreat, as a new front blew in. The temperatures plummeted, and the rain turned to snow, forcing the climbers to pack up their base camp and hike out before the approaching winter made them permanent residents of the mountains.

The Avellano Valley offers a wide variety of objectives: snow walk-ups, low fifth-class ridge traverses, free-climbing on fine-grained granite, alpine snow and ice, and steep big walls. The mountains in this area are not subject to the extreme winds of other areas in Patagonia, but the valley does receive abundant precipitation

The expedition received generous support from the Mugs Stump Award, The National Outdoor Leadership School, and the Mazamas.

DAVE ANDERSON, *AAC*

SOUTHERN PATAGONIA, ARGENTINA

CHALTEN MASSIF

Season overview. The 2003-04 Patagonia season was one of marked contrasts, with much bad weather and heavy snowfall, but with one extended good weather period that lasted for an unprecedented nine days and sparked a flurry of activity (see individual reports below). During January the weather was uncharacteristically warm, creating dangerous conditions on the ice-capped Torre group, so most of the energy was focused on the drier Fitz Roy group. There were no ascents of Cerro Torre this season.

In early November the Supercanaleta route on Fitz Roy saw a couple of ascents, including one by a guided party. This was the first guided ascent of the route. Also on Fitz Roy, over a 10-day period in mid-November, Frenchmen Nicolas Fabbri, Jerome Huet, and Pierrick Keller climbed 700m of new terrain on the steep west-northwest pillar (immediately left of the Super-canaleta). They had hoped to climb the pillar all the way to the summit, but a tight schedule forced them to give up near where their line would join the French 1979 route. They used fixed ropes, which they left in place intending to return to complete their ascent. In all they climbed 22 pitches, with difficulties up to 6b and A2. In early February Italians Simone Pedeferri and Alberto Marazzi climbed a line parallel to and right of the Brenner-Moschioni route on the northeast pillar of Aguja Guillaumet. Their route includes six new pitches, with difficulties up to 6c/A0, before joining the Brenner-Moschioni, and is dubbed "Carlo." Strong winds forced them to turn around before reaching the summit. Also noteworthy was the first all-female ascent of Fitz Roy on February 6 by Slovenes Monika Kambic and Tina Di Batista, via the Franco-Argentine route. On that day 12 people climbed the mountain, nine via the Franco-Argentine route.

There were also a number of accidents. Sometime in January a German climber was killed by falling ice while attempting Cerro Standhardt. Toward the end of the early February good-weather period, temperatures above normal led to accidents, including one in which two Argentines fell 200 feet when their anchors pulled while descending from Fitz Roy's Franco-Argentine route. They suffered injuries that required the help of many climbers, as well as helicopter evacuation—a service usually not available since the closest helicopter is based 400 miles away. Another unfortunate event was a big fire caused by a careless smoker on the trail leading to Campo De Agostini; the fire burned many acres of native forest.

ROLANDO GARIBOTTI, *AAC, Club Andino Bariloche*

Punta Herron, Spigolo dei Bimbi, second ascent. On the evening of October 30 David Fasel, Ueli Steck, Ralph Weber, and I, all Swiss, set up base camp at the Campo De Agostini. It snowed like it was winter. The weather had apparently been nothing but snow and rain for the past three weeks. In the following three days we carried our climbing equipment to the Norwegian Camp, a bivy under the Medialuna Glacier, which was to be the starting point of our attempts. Due to bad weather the following few days were spent bouldering near base camp and near Chalten.

On November 9 the pressure rose and the weather improved, so we headed back up to the Norwegian camp. At 12:30 a.m. we set off to attempt the Cerro Standhardt–Punta Herron–Torre Egger traverse, but after hearing rumbling noises in the snow slope leading to Standhardt we judged the avalanche danger too high and postponed the project. We descended a bit and attempted the Titanic route on Torre Egger instead. By 6:00 p.m. we had climbed eight pitches, but, realizing that we were too late for an alpine-style attempt, we descended.

The weather was still great, so the next morning we discussed what to do next. We decided to attempt Punta Herron the following night. David was unsure, so he decided to go down. At midnight, November 12, it was time to get up again. We made good progress and with first light traversed the middle ramps of Cerro Standhardt, at the end of which we traversed west, then rappelled into the Colle dei Sogni between Standhardt and Herron. Out of this col, in 1991, Ermanno Salvaterra and partners climbed a line that they christened Spigolo dei Bimbi, ascending Punta Herron's north face. It was this line that we intended to follow. Although the cracks were full of ice, the next six pitches were a fantastic rock climb. Two uncomfortable pitches up the rime ice of the snow mushroom followed. At 5:30 p.m. we reached the beautiful summit of the Punta Herron. Ours was the second ascent of the Spigolo dei Bimbi route and the third ascent of Punta Herron. We planned to rappel one and a half pitches and then climb Torre Egger in just four pitches. But a talk with David at base camp over the radio gave us something to worry about. The pressure had fallen two millibars in two hours. The first signs of bad weather were noticeable on the inland ice. We were so near Torre Egger, but couldn't risk the long descent in a storm. If we had done the rappels, the climb over Egger would have been compulsory, because, due to objective dangers we were unwilling to descend the dihedral between Herron and Egger. Therefore, we did not continue. We rappelled back to the Colle dei Sogni and from there into unknown territory on the east face, between Herron and Standhardt. At 8:30 p.m., when our headlamp died, we decided to spend the night not far from the Norwegian Camp, which we reached the next morning by 10 a.m. In all we made 28 rappels. The storm was already of considerable strength, so we were glad we had decided to descend from Herron. We continued to Campo De Agostini, where David was waiting with a fantastic meal.

STEPHAN SIEGRIST, *Switzerland*

Cerro Rincon, correction on second ascent. Stephan Siegrist reported in the *AAJ 2001*, p. 293, that his team had made the second ascent of Cerro Rincon via a supposed new route. As it turns out, Siegrist, David Göttler, and Michi Wärthl had in fact repeated the first-ascent line climbed by Carlos Comesaña and Ismael Palma in 1971 (*AAJ 1972*, p.180). Also worth noting is that the side peak of Cerro Rincon that Siegrist and Wärthl then traversed to, climbed, and christened "Punta Amigos," thinking it unclimbed, had been climbed by Comesaña and Palma on their 1971 ascent. In short, Siegrist and partners retraced Comesaña and Palma's footsteps.

Aguja Guillaumet, new route. Marcin Szczotka and Mariusz Nowak established a new route on the west face of Aguja Guillaumet, to the left of the Padrijo route, just right of Comesaña-Fon-rouge. The route was climbed onsight on February 13, 2004, at UIAA VII (5.10d); 11 pitches, plus 3 on the summit ridge, 550-600m in length. They had good conditions (in general, west faces were in better condition), but when they were on the summit ridge, a big rockfall occurred to the left of their route, taking out their gear left at the bottom of the face, including boots, crampons, camera, and rucksack. Determined to get boots at least, they descended the debris during the night searching for the equipment. After a couple of hours, in poor light, they found remnants of their rucksack … and two pairs of boots. They felt like millionaires, since they would have had only climbing shoes for the two icefields, not to mention the five-hour trek to their tent at Rio Blanco. The camera is still at the bottom of the face.

JAKUB RADZIEJOWSKI, *Poland*

Aguja Mermoz, new variation. On February 7, 2004, Maciej Ciesielski and I added five new pitches, onsight at VII UIAA (5.10d) with one short tension traverse (new pitches: VII-, VII-/VII, VII-, VI+/A0 and V+), on the west face slabs between Ipermermoz and Cosas Patagonicas. These new pitches are nice but far from perfect: slabs with some rotten holds. We continued by freeing onsight the Ipermermoz route (Giordani-Levitti, 1996, originally VII+ A1), making a total of 14 pitches, plus 3 pitches on the summit ridge, 700m, 9 hours. Ours was the second ascent of Ipermermoz, and the first ascent of the route to the summit. (Giordani and Levitti stopped on the arête.)

JAKUB RADZIEJOWSKI, *Poland*

Fitz Roy, Linea de Eleganza (Elegant Line). True alpinism isn't solely the discovery of new walls, of new lines, of difficulties to overcome, but more than anything it involves the willingness to have open eyes and an open mind in order to reach the fringes of one's own imagination. Dreams often are never realized, but when I looked into Horacio's and Luca's joyful eyes, as they scrambled up the last easy slopes to Fitz Roy's summit, I understood that we had accomplished the dream of a lifetime, one that for them had even been impossible to fathom. Watching them, I saw them experiencing sensations and emotions far larger than the heart can contain, until the wind took my own thoughts away.

How time goes by! It had been 20 years since I had been up there, though for the last three years part of my brain had been occupied by Fitz Roy's northeast face. In 2001 Fabio Leoni, Rolando Larcher, and I had tricked ourselves into believing in the good will of fate, when we ventured 500 meters onto the steep flanks of the lower northeast face. However, after six

Aguja Guillaumet's west face: (1) Giordani Variation (Giordani, 1990); (2) Fonrouge-Comesaña (Fonrouge-Comesaña, 1965); (3) Polish route (Nowak-Szczotka, 2004); (4) Padrijo (Gatt-Gatt, 1993). Aguja Mermoz's west and northwest face: (5) Original Route (Cuiñas-Olaechea-Vieiro, 1974); (6) Ipermermoz (Giordani-Levitti, 1996); (7) Polish Variation (6c, Ciesielski-Radziejowski, 2004); (8) Cosas Patagonicas (Colombo-Canfaloniere-Corbetta-Galbiati-Maggioni-Spinelli-Tazzi, 1989); (9) Barriga Patagonica (Koren-Mali, 2000); (10) Northwest Ridge (Koren-Kouta, 2001). *Rolando Garibotti*

Cerro Fitz Roy's east face and north pillar: (1) Linea de Eleganza (Codo-Fava-Orlandi, 2004); (2) El Corazon (Ochsner-Pitelka, 1992); (3) Casarotto route (Casarotto, 1979) and Variation (Kearney-Knight, 1984). The major summits in the background: Aguja Poincenot (left), Cerro Torre and Torre Egger (right). *Elio Orlandi*

long, painful nights in our portaledge, hanging onto our hope, we endured the inevitable "fracaso" (failure) of our "Todo o Nada" (all or nothing) approach. We were chased away by avalanches in one of the most brutal storms that I can remember.

After the attempt with Fabio and Rolly, I returned to the northeast face twice before returning yet again in December 2003, convinced that such a strong call could not be a mistake. This time I was accompanied by the joyful enthusiasm of Fabio "Giac" Giacomelli's first time in Patagonia, and by Horacio Codò and Lucas Fava, both of whom had done minor ascents in the area. Horacio and Lucas live in Chalten, where Fitz Roy is their myth and an ever-present postcard in their daily lives.

Weather during the second half of December and most of January did not allow much progress, but in spite of the winter-like conditions, we surmounted the lower 600 meters, climbing cracks and dihedrals filled with ice, as well as difficult verglassed slabs. Because of the conditions, and mostly for safety, we fixed ropes up to a comfortable ledge half way: the "Gran Hotel Patagonicus." This ledge was a godsend, for it allowed us to equip the crucial slabs of the upper half of the route without returning to the ground.

In early January Giac's vacation time ended, and, heartbroken, he had to return to Italy. With Horacio and Luca we went back to the "cueva de hielo" (snow cave) in Paso Superior, where we waited patiently for a few more days. The wind rarely subsides, but I think that after we had waited so long, he understood our simplicity and took pity. Under a dreamy blue sky we walked incredulous toward the wall, tiptoeing as if not to disturb the stillness.

It is said that in every work of genius one finds again thoughts previously discarded. Climbing the elusive, never-ending slabs of the upper section, each day we felt discarded thoughts being reborn, transforming themselves into a beautiful and elegant line. At the end of every day we returned to the Gran Hotel Patagonicus, under the auspices of a moon that every day grew bigger.

Then, as in all stories with a happy ending, after six nights on the wall, including a very cold one near the summit, and seven days immersed in a dream, we woke suddenly, holding our breath as we watched Patagonia from above, from Fitz Roy's summit. Our only sorrow was a solitary falling stone that broke my hand the morning after we descended to our comfortable ledge, while we were retrieving ropes.

As I descended toward the glacier, I could not help but cringe upon seeing the dry rock, free of snow and ice after eight days of perfect weather. During our entire ascent we had found difficult conditions: snow on the lower wall, cracks filled with ice during our first four days on the upper portion, avalanches while the wall cleaned itself off. Looking at the clean granite, I wished I could redo our climb free, but my good luck had tricked me, sending me home with a bitter souvenir.

Linea di Eleganza (1,250m, VI 6c A3 90°/M7) follows an obvious line between El Corazon and Devils Dihedral. We reached the summit on February 7, 2004. We believe that in better conditions it would be possible to climb this route free.

ELIO ORLANDI, *Italy (translated by* ROLANDO GARIBOTTI)

Fitz Roy, Slovak Route, third ascent and first free ascent; Desmochada, El Facón. Patagonian weather seemed like it was never going to let up this season for any long spell. Does it ever? December brought more snow than all of most winters. In one night in late December the weather turned warm, rainy, and windy, and remained unseasonably warm until the end of January, making the Torre group a shooting range from falling ice and water. However, on January 31 the jet stream that battered the 50th parallel shifted well to the south and brought what turned out to be a monumental spell of high pressure. On February 5 Jvan "The Wad" Tresch (Switzerland), Ben "Super-Hijitus" Bransby (England), and I (Bean "Poroto" Bowers, from Bushlandia) headed up the Torre Glacier and established a bivy that was even with the Sitting Man Ridge below Fitz Roy's west face. We brought enough food and fuel for one day and two "meager" nights, wanting to go light and fast. Originally we had eyed a dihedral system on the left side of the face, but upon closer inspection it revealed little possibility of access and climbability, so we turned our attention to a free ascent of the Slovak route, and its third overall ascent. The route follows the 1,300m diagonal crack system that bisects the face from bottom left to upper right. We left our bivy at 6 a.m. and climbed the route at 5.10d in three long blocks, each leader freeing his pitches. The two followers climbed mostly but used jumars and one aider in awkward, hard, or icy spots, of which there were few. The crux was the moves from rock to rock on the summit ice slope, with the one ice axe and no crampons we brought to save weight and time. We arrived on the summit by 7 p.m. and descended the Franco-Argentine route on the east side of the mountain through the night. After a hearty cup of cocoa with Jonny Copp in Rio Blanco, we arrived in town for happy hour, a little over two days after leaving.

Fortunately the weather was bad for five days, during which we let our skin recuperate from the west face's rough granite, and slept. High pressure returned on February 12. We reloaded the packs with gear and food for a couple of days and headed back up the Torre glacier for rock climbing on Desmochada. Ice still wasn't refrozen into place sufficiently for us to venture into the waiting gun barrels of Egger and Stanhardt. We set our sights on a new line up Desmochada's southeast prow, to the right of El Condor (Bridwell-Dunmire-Smith, 1988), which was the route of this spire's only ascent. February 13 dawned with heavy, moist low clouds. We woke at 4 a.m. to our usual breakfast of coffee, oats, and a cigarette. We didn't hurry out of camp, due to the heavy haze above, but as Patagonia—the mountain-climbing Las Vegas—teaches: You can't win if you don't play. The worst that happens is that you "go for a hike." As we got in our morning hike with a hefty free-climbing rack, we began to break through the sea of low clouds and entered the realm of the giants, for a sunrise on the Torre group with the clouds below.

We began the route in the left center of the face, with a 5.9 chimney that led to three pitches of moderate-to-hard 5.10 splitters and a ledge at one-third height. A 60m class 4 traverse to the right put us right below the overhanging prow. A couple of hard crack pitches put us below the crux: 5.12a, shallow, rattly fingers in an overhanging dihedral. The next pitch sported 5.11+ thin hands through a dead-horizontal sickle roof, which was exited via a Harding Slot-like pod-chimney that ended in 5.11a fists. Above that a rope-stretcher 5.11c A0 offwidth to 5.11a hands got us into some easier 5.10 terrain that got us to the upper east face, where icy 5.10 slot climbing and an unprotected icy 5.10+ offwidth got us to the two final 5.10 pitches to the summit. We led a total of 16 pitches, arrived on top at sunset, hugged, and rappelled the less but still overhanging El Condor by headlamp. No sign remained of the first party [the El Condor party descended the backside, east and then north of the tower—Ed.]. We left mostly single "bombproof" stoppers for each rappel into space. We continued down the seemingly endless class 4 slabs to the Polish bivy, where we grabbed yet another beautiful sunrise before a well-deserved nap. We named the route El Facón (650m, V+ 5.12a A0), which means "the gaucho's

Aguja Desmochada's west and southwest face: (1) El Condor (Bridwell-Dunmire-Smith, 1988); (2) El Facón (Bowers-Bransby-Tresch, 2004). *Rolando Garibotti*

knife," for the cutter nature of the stone and the way our bodies felt the following day.

BEAN "POROTO" BOWERS, *PLT*

Historical note: In February 2000, Kevin Thaw and Alan Mullin free climbed most of the Slovak Route, retreating some 250m below the summit. The first ascensionists defined the route as ending on the summit, having twice retreated high on the route (once from a point similar to Thaw and Mullin's) before returning. For a report on the 2000 attempt, see 2000 AAJ, p. 282.

Aguja Rafael, Quilombo. When Zack Smith and I arrived at the Chalten Massif in Argentine Patagonia, the weather had been bad for over two months, with no sign of improvement. We established our high camp within a week, and amazingly the weather began to improve. We set out at the first sign of a break in the weather, even if it did not look perfect. Stratus and lots of high clouds loomed all day. We chose Aguja Rafael, a smaller objective, thinking that perhaps we could get up something. On January 30 we climbed a new route, via a beautiful, intimidating-looking crack line that cuts straight up the right side of the west face. The route turned out to be quite sustained, with four pitches of 5.11 and a few points of aid on two pitches; one of 5.10; and three of 5.9. After these eight pitches the route joins an existing line for four more pitches to the summit. The route consisted of a variety of climbing—crack, slab, face, a bit of aid—and we christened it "Quilombo," Argentine slang meaning "total mess." We chose this name because we got to the top in horrible-looking weather, and my hand got tweaked somewhere along the way, laying me up for the remainder of our trip.

HEIDI WIRTZ, *AAC*

Aguja Rafael, Artibelleza, first free ascent. Patagonia is always a crapshoot. Windy Patagonia ended up having a spell of great weather this season. Within 10 days of leaving Denver, John Dickey and I climbed on Aguja Rafael via the Anglo-American (1974) route to the top of the west buttress. We went down from there due to lack of clothing and questionable weather. Two days later Zack Smith and I climbed Chiaro Di Luna (750m, 6c) on Aguja Saint Exupery. Great route, definitely a Patagonia classic—awesome crack climbing. We couldn't believe the weather still held. Two days later John Dickey and I climbed again, on Aguja Rafael. We did the first free ascent of Artibelleza, all the way to the top (400m, 6c). Great climbing. We descended the same route. We ended up having about a week of stable weather this year.

JOSH GROSS, *Moab, UT*

Saint Exupery, Tical, and other ascents. This year's seven-week trip to Patagonia didn't start well. I flew out of London on New Year's Day while everyone else was ice skating in Fontainebleau. After four weeks of high winds, long hikes, tendonitis, knackered knees, and heavy rucksacks, Patagonia wasn't looking like the best idea. Jvan Tresch, Bean Bowers, and I were in the Torre Valley planning a traverse from Standhardt to Egger, but extremely warm conditions and our small necks forced us to move over to Polacos and try a bit of rock climbing.

Toward the end of January Bean needed a holiday from his holiday, and headed to Bariloche for a week's climbing. His departure triggered what turned out to be an eight-day spell of good weather. On 29 January Jvan and I headed up to Poincenot (3,002m) and soloed an unclimbed ramp below the Carrington-Rouse and above Southern Cross. We joined the Fonrouge-Rosasco route and climbed 200m farther, before the threat of bad weather forced us to retreat down the south face.

The 31st dawned fine, so we approached St. Exupery to try a new line close to the Crouch-Brooks attempt. The first five pitches were pleasant corner and chimney climbing, leading to the loose vein that crosses the mountain. Climbing through this vein proved the crux of the route: a scary and committing pitch, from which a fall could have resulted in serious injury. Luckily, the slab climbing just above was relatively amenable 5.11X. I spent most of last summer climbing on the excellent, esoteric, and friable crags of the Lleyn Peninsula in Wales, and am rather partial to kicking steps up sandy grooves and laybacking creaking flakes, so I thoroughly enjoyed myself (in retrospect).

We regained the golden granite, and more cracks, ramps, and flakes led us onto the south ridge and a junction with the Austrian Ridge route, approximately five pitches from the summit. We climbed the rather snowy upper section free. Jvan's anger increased with each unnecessary bolt and peg that we passed, until one bolt next to a perfect crack turned him into the Incredible Hulk, and he removed it with his bare hands. We reached the top in midafternoon and descended the northwest face.

February 2 saw us returning to the Poincenot line Jvan and I had attempted, this time aiming to reach the summit. By daybreak, though, our incompetent routefinding in the dark found us not only 500m below the start of the climbing, but also under the wrong mountain. Deciding that things were not meant to be, we headed up to the smaller, less-serious Aguja Rafael. An hour later, while we were climbing snow to the base, early morning sunlight lit the south face of Poincenot just above us, and we changed our minds yet again.

Aguja Saint Exupery's west and northwest face: (1) Tical (Bransby-Tresch, 2004); (2) Chiaro di Luna (Giordani-Manfrini-Valentini, 1987). *Rolando Garibotti*

Climbing with only 1.5 liters of water, a few power gels, and two belay jackets, we managed a free ascent of the Fonrouge route, at about 5.11. The crux pitch was a 45° ice slope, which Jvan crimped and smeared up in rock boots and chalk. We were back in Polakos after a 24-hour roundtrip.

We returned to Chalten the following day to celebrate and to restock food, feeling satisfied with our achievements and looking forward to plenty of rest in the bad weather which was sure to follow. Our recovery and hangovers were rudely interrupted early the next morning by Bean's return and the continuation of good weather.

BEN BRANSBY, *U.K.*

Aguja Saint Exupery, Austrian Ridge, first free ascent. Beginning on January 29, ten days after we arrived in Chalten, Jonny Copp and I were treated to nearly 16 days of continuous good weather, interrupted only occasionally by 10- to 15-hour periods of instability. At the start of the weather window we made a premature attempt on Fitz Roy's Franco-Argentine route, finding it encased in ice. Two days later, on February 2, the route was still locked in ice but we'd had enough of the arduous approach and decided to climb despite the conditions. Every pitch was a battle with ice-choked cracks and huge patches of rime. We reached the summit after 12 continuously difficult hours and arrived back at Rio Blanco base camp after 29 hours on the move.

Tired from Fitz Roy and sure that the benign clouds signaled an approaching storm, we wanted an objective that we might succeed on even if bad weather moved in. After deliberation in the Rio Blanco hut, we decided on a free-climbing attempt on St. Exupery's Austrian Ridge (5.10 A1): a soaring 700m skyline first climbed in 1987 (Barnthaler-Lidl). After an approach gully that proved to be the route's crux—a slushy vertical bergschrund followed by a mud groove that set a new standard for choss—we arrived at the base of the ridge proper. A sneaky traverse to the west avoided the route's initial wet A1 sections. Higher on the ridge we found relatively straightforward free climbing, interspersed with short sections up to 5.11a. We also found several bolts placed next to useable cracks. On the summit we celebrated our good fortune with our new friends Filip and WaWa, who had just made the first Polish ascent of St. Exupery via the well-traveled Italian Route. The Austrian Ridge is a beautiful free climb at a moderate grade and should become a popular alternative to the peak's normal routes.

JOSH WHARTON, *AAC*

Cerro Pereyra, first ascent; Aguja de L'S, The Thaw's not Houlding Wright. Heeding the barrage of ice blocks and rocks cascading down, Leo Houlding, Cedar Wright, and I abandoned our plans for the Maestri-Egger, and my compadres steered me toward the Compressor Route, Cerro Torre's southeast arête. Little else was safe.

The climbing usually begins with a steep snow slope and a pitch of mixed climbing, but warm conditions had collapsed the snow slope, requiring one to stay on rock: seven 60m pitches with a 5.9 move or two, but never sustained. The shoulder drew closer as did a cloud around the Torre's summit. Plan C came into effect: a small spire east of the shoulder—an unclimbed Patagonian summit! A single 5.10 pitch and a ridge traverse attained our fresh summit on February 26, "Cerro Pereyra," named in memory of a good friend who died while climbing in Mexico.

Finally, on March 9, right before we to leave, our vigil proved fruitful: A small high pressure system bumped south for long enough for us to poach a quick ascent. Cerro Torre remained

Engaged on Cerro Pereyra. *Kevin Thaw*

under rime cloaks, so a more rapidly achievable objective was chosen: the west face of Aguja de L' S. It's the shortest summit on the west-facing side of the valley, yet one of the longer climbs, as its technicalities begin at glacier level, rather than 3,000' up a loose gully. A truly enjoyable long moderate route (1,300m, 5.10). The first section is an arête of perfect rock formed by the left side of a larger buttress: We kept the ropes in the packs and free-soloed to the upper headwall. Some of the finest easy climbing ever! The highlight was a short 5.6 arête; climbed by laybacking the square-cut low-angle edge, with an admirable view of the glacier far below. The testy-looking upper headwall relinquished passage via a series of thin cracks just to the left of a long rust streak—never desperate, fun high-quality climbing with a 5.10 section or two per pitch, requiring 10 60m leads. Six on the headwall, then hike to the notch below the south summit, two more pitches ascend it, one across the ridge between summits, then the final pitch up the southwest arête of the north (main) summit. Rappel the north side of the north summit onto a plateau. One further rappel accesses St. Exupery's gully, and the rope-work is finalized. Satisfaction from a steep journey, absorbed in the expedition's dwindling hours! Fuel for the fire: not the main prize, but more moments for the memory bank, and Jose Luis Pereyra's impression on us all will reside with his name on a Southern Andean tower.

KEVIN THAW, *U.K.*

Cerro Solo, possible first traverse of the ridgeline. Earlier in the trip (see note above by Kevin Thaw), Cedar Wright soloed the ridgeline below Cerro Solo's true summit; this may have been the first traverse of the ridge. He writes, "I climbed ropeless, downclimbing from each of the nine or so 5th-class summits, encountering difficulties up to exposed 5.8. The rock was loose and required assorted equalization techniques."

HIELO CONTINENTAL

Patagonian Icecap, north to south unsupported traverse. Between late August and early October 2003 Swiss Thomas Ulrich and Norwegian Borge Ousland traversed, unsupported, the bulk of the Southern Patagonian Icecap. Ousland is well known for being the first man to accomplish an unsupported solo crossing from Siberia to Canada via the North Pole. Ulrich is a devoted Patagonian climber, responsible, among other things, for the first winter ascent of the west face of Cerro Torre. The pair started from the Chilean town of Caleta Tortel, paddling floating sleds for two days to the Jorge Montt glacier. After ferrying loads for a week and a half, they reached the icecap plateau, along which they headed south, using skis, pulling kayak/sleds, and at times benefiting from the use of kites. After crossing the notoriously difficult and dangerous Reichert Fault, they exited the icecap via the Tyndall Glacier, south and west of the Paine Massif, paddling down the Rio Serrano to reach the Ultima Esperanza fjord and Puerto Natales, having covered 460km in merely 54 days. Theirs is by far the most important unsupported traverse of Hielo Continental yet done. A detailed article describing this adventure will be published in the August 2004 National Geographic. A number of north-to-south traverses of the Patagonian Icecap have been done. In 1992 a Spanish-Argentine team entered via Glaciar Jorge Montt and exited via Valle Pingo to Lago Grey, but used a helicopter to surmount the Reichert Fault. Between November 1, 1998, and January 30, 1999, four Chileans, Pablo Besser, Rodrigo Fica, Mauricio Rojas, and Jose Montt, completed a traverse, entering via Glaciar Jorge Montt and exiting the network of glaciers south of Glaciar Balmaceda to the Seno Ultima Esperanza, 25km south of the Tyndall Glacier. The Chileans relied on a cache of food and equipment in the vicinity of the Reichert Fault, and did not paddle to and from the glaciers, relying instead on motorboats.

ROLANDO GARIBOTTI, *AAC, Club Andino Bariloche*

Cerro Murallon, The Lost World. Finally, after nearly three weeks of waiting and repeated shipments of gear and food, we stand before the Cerro Murallon with its wide north face. This immense face starts at the clearly defined northeast ridge and ends after nearly four km at the northwest pillar. Casimiro Ferrari had laid out a super climbing route there. Robert Jasper and Stefan Glowacz had already started setting up base camp. The cameraman Sebastian Tischler and I pulled the last haul-bags into camp with the pulka. In two days we dug a snow cave that had room for four people. However Stefan and I preferred the tent out front to the snow cave. Robert and Stefan made the first attempt onto the wall in order to examine it up close. They were gone a whole afternoon, and crossed the north wall from the Ferrari route to the back of the northwest pillar looking for a worthwhile route. When they returned to base camp the euphoria was dampened.

In the front part of the wall only Ferrari's pillar looked interesting. The middle part of the wall is overhung by seracs, which make a climbing route impossible. The northwest pillar looked like the only place one could risk an alpine style first ascent.

Early in the morning of December 3, Stefan, Robert, and I marched off. We followed the rock outcrops to the right past the pillar and then we could quickly climb on in easy terrain. At about 7 a.m. we already stood on the summit of the first pillar. The sun made Cerro Don Bosco radiant with its light. We took a rest and considered the way from there. Robert reconnoitered the best entrance onto the pillar.

Stefan Glowacz and Robert Jasper approaching the north side of Cerro Murallon. (1) Ferrari Route (VI 5.10 A2/3 80°, Aldè-Ferrari-Vitali, 1984), (2) The Lost World (1,000m, M8, Fengler-Glowacz-Jasper, 2003). Both routes closely follow the ridges as seen in this photo. *Klaus Fengler*

Blue sky, and not a cloud to be seen; it was our day. Robert got to work and lead for the first three rope lengths. Stefan cleaned the pitches and I jumared to the belays. The terrain became difficult. Robert was able to push his way up the cracks with his crampons on. After three lengths it was Stefan's turn, who preferred rock shoes. Stefan faltered during a traverse, where the protection was scant. To make matters worse he was moving into mixed terrain. Cursing and with great strain he got through this rope ropelength and was able to fix the next belay.

In good granite one can build super belays. Even the protection was easy to fix. The steep parts were behind us. Stefan and Robert alternately lead. As soon as the fissures were full of ice Robert continued climbing in a mixed style. About 5 p.m. we climbed out of the rock terrain. Over snow mushrooms and steep high expanses we reached the summit of Cerro Murallon. Our

Robert Jasper drytooling on The Lost World. *Klaus Fengler*

joy was immense. In the distance we could see the Lago Argentino and Fitz Roy. Robert planned the descent on a northeasterly direction over the glacier. In this direction we could get to the glacier that lay between Cerro Murallon and Cerro Don Bosco quite easily.

However already on the descent we encountered tremendous cloudbanks on the Chilean side. The wind picked up and soon we were more and more shrouded in icy fog. We had already descended one flank, however we could no longer find the way down. We waited and hoped the clouds would clear enough that we could find a safe way down. It became critical. Should we wait and look for a place to bivouac, or should we return to the summit and rappel via our ascent route? We decided to rappel. On the summit and to the north the visibility was still very good.

After a final rest and preparation we descended via our ascent route. Robert looked out for safe belays and then we rappelled in mammoth fashion into known territory. We needed the whole night for the rappel. Three times the rope got caught up in the rocks as we pulled them down. We needed to cut off a good 30 meters of rope, as we couldn't get the ropes free.

The new day had already arrived as we reached to our base camp exhausted after nearly 27 hours. In our new route "The Lost World" (1,000m, M8) we left behind a good rappel route. That same afternoon our cameraman Sebastian and I hiked out 14 hours from base camp to the "Rifugio Pascale" via the inland ice glacier. We slept there briefly and then hiked a further five hours back to the Estancia Christina. Sebastian reached his return trip on time and I had two days to wait until Stefan and Robert also returned safely.

KLAUS FENGLER, *Switzerland*

Editor's note: Fengler, Glowacz, and Jasper reached the west summit of Cerro Murallon, but did not reach its main summit. The main summit is the east summit, which is 60 meters higher and one kilometer east of the west summit, along a broad glaciated ridge. Murallon's main summit has had only two ascents to date (Ferrari and partners, 1984; Karo and partner, 2003). On some maps the west summit of Murallon is incorrectly marked as the highest point of the mountain.

SOUTHERN PATAGONIA, CHILE

TORRES DEL PAINE NATIONAL PARK

Cerro Almirante Nieto, various attempts; various other ascents. Grega Lacen and I, Slovenes, came to the park on December 1. The next day's weather was great, so we went up to try the beautiful, unclimbed northwest pillar of Almirante. It was harder than we expected. That day we did 350m of climbing up to 5.11-, on less-than-perfect rock. We then came to a blank section where we would need aid-climbing equipment or bolts. This gear was still in our bags, which had yet to be ferried to base camp, so we were forced to retreat. The weather then turned bad, with constant rain. On December 14 the weather showed a slight improvement, so we started from base camp at 6 a.m. and did the Bonington Route on the Central Tower in 24 hours round trip in bad conditions, cracks full of snow and ice. We climbed in big boots and mostly aided. We next tried the easier-looking southwest ridge of Cerro Almirante Nieto, which is unclimbed. I made nine attempts but was driven back by bad weather every time. After Grega left I tried with Nejc Bevk, also a Slovene. Our highest point was 120m below the top of the ridge. We did 11 long, free rock pitches (up to 5.10d) and around 300m of a snow-and-ice ramp (up to 60°). On our last attempt Nejc injured his hand from stonefall and was unable to climb for a week.

Later in January and in early February I went to the Chalten Massif, where I climbed Aguja De L'S via the Josh Aike Route (450m, 6a) with Slovenes Mojca Zerjav and Nastja Davidov, the Benitiers Route on El Mocho (500m, 6c A2) with Mojca, and the Franco-Argentine route on Fitz Roy with Israeli Jhonatan Ben Noshe. So that was my three-month trip to Patagonia: full of bad luck and not as I expected, but fine anyway.

TOMAZ JAKOFCIC, *Slovenia*

Central Tower of Paine, South African Route. A team of six Mountain Club of South Africa members—Alard Hüfner, Mark Seuring, Michael Mason, Dermot Brogan, Marianne Pretorius, and Voitec Modrzewski—spent December 2003 and January 2004 climbing the South African Route on the Central Tower of Paine. The east face of the Central Tower was first climbed in 1973/74 by a South African team of Paul Fatti, Mike Scott, Art McGarr, Mervyn Prior, Roger Fuggle, and Richard Smithers. At the time it was one of the largest rock faces ever climbed and a milestone in big-wall climbing. This route stayed unrepeated for 30 years. The route follows the obvious corner just right of the center of the tower, and is graded 5.10 A3. We free climbed the slabs of the first 400m and then aided most of the way to the shoulder, where we could free climb again.

Our first day on the rock was December 15, and we reached the summit ridge on January 13. During this period 15 days were spent actually climbing and the rest of the time was spent hauling gear and food or waiting for better weather.

We fixed lines most of the way, to about 250m below the summit of the 1.2km-high face. Ropes were cleaned on descent, but sections snagged on flakes, so we had to cut and leave them. It was fascinating to find sections of iced-up rope and old gear left by the pioneers 30 years ago. Mark, Marianne, Voitec, and I topped out on the summit ridge of the Central Tower. Dermot and Mike were unable to be with us, due to injuries and early flights home. Marianne was the first woman to climb the east face of the Central Tower. We reached the summit ridge at 19:00 in howling winds, gusting mist, and light snowfall. Due to these conditions and the long way back to the portaledges, we decided it was not safe to continue to the summit [only a few easy pitches remained to reach the summit—Ed.]. The joy of finally standing on the top of the South African Route was overwhelming. For 20 minutes we savored our excitement, as wind would clear the mist, revealing breathtaking views of beautiful scenery below.

ALARD HÜFNER, *The Mountain Club of South Africa*

South Tower of Paine, east face, Self Right to Suicide. In January and February 2004 Boguslaw Kowalski, Wojtek Wiwatowski, and I found ourselves in deserted Torres del Paine. Since we had heard much about bad weather in the area, we came ready for hard conditions. Either the reports are exaggerated, or we were lucky. With so much rock and nobody in sight, we had numerous options. We decided on the South Tower, since it has the highest summit and is the most remote of three towers. Besides, it hosted only three routes and a number of unfinished projects, compared to tens of routes on the other towers. At first we wanted to climb on the unclimbed south face, but it turns out to be several hundred feet shorter than the larger east face. Therefore, we shifted our interests to the east face and began our climb in the middle of the wall, intending to put a direct line to the top.

There was an old Swiss line (Piola-Sprungli, 1992) running through the middle of the wall until the upper portions, where it bears slightly to the right. We more or less, having no information on this route at the time, followed it for several pitches, though also climbing harder ground to the left and right of the Swiss line. Only higher up, where the wall became steeper and more compact, did we head through the most monolithic rock on the face, leaving the Swiss line to our right. We came across trashed gear and rappel stations in the middle of nowhere, obviously from past attempts on the east face direttissima.

After eight long days of a good fight we covered the crux four pitches leading us to the "Roof of Hope," the most prominent roof on the wall. It was the only hope for us, struggling through a featureless sea of granite, as it seemed that beginning at the roof we would find a continuous system leading to the summit.

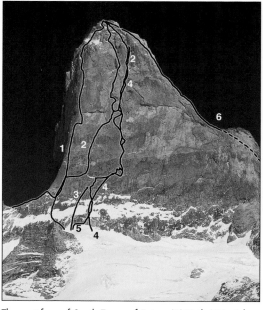

The east face of South Tower of Paine: (1) Hoth (27 pitches, 5.10+ A4 WI2/3, Amelunxen-Easton, 2000); (2) attempt (22 pitches to within 150m of summit, 5.10 A4, Davies-Gordon-Peer, 1985); (3) Slovenian attempt (1987); (4) En el Ojo del Huracán (18 pitches plus 250m easier terrain, 6b A4, Piola-Sprungli, 1992); (5) Self Right to Suicide (23 pitches, VI 5.10+ A4 55°, 2004); (6) North Ridge (27 pitches, VI- A1, Aiazzi-Aste-Casati-Nusdeo-Taldo, 1963). Route lines and information provided by Chris Belczynski. *Boguslaw Kowalski*

Once we placed our hands in the cracks above the roof and put the crampons into the hard ice of the final headwall, we were on top in no time. Drinking beer, of course!

We climbed in capsule style, with a week of fixing and 13 days on the wall. We reached the summit on February 12. We named our route Self Right to Suicide (VI 5.10 A4 55°). It gains 825m vertical, but the climbing distance, with traverses, pendulums, etc., is about 1,100m. We hand-drilled dozens of bat-hook holes to connect disappearing cracks and to hook around fragile features. A few bolts, besides the belay stations, were placed as well. Most of the route was an excellent expando adventure, and the entire trip was a first-class course in wall logistics. It took us two weeks to get our loads to the base, and a week down. The three weeks of climbing were challenging as well, with snow-swept slabs of the lower apron, waterfalls running through thin expandos in the middle wall, and freezing dihedrals on the upper headwall.

Incidentally, the South and Central Paine Towers are smaller than has been claimed. Their east faces at their highest are about 825m and 1,100m high, respectively. The unclimbed south face of the South Tower is therefore no more than 700m high. Although its base is lower than that of the east face, its steep portion ends much lower.

CHRIS BELCZYNSKI, *Torun Climbing Club, Poland*

Cuerno Oeste, Mas Ricas No Hay; Cuerno Chico, Hurly Burly. My partner Mark Davis and I arrived in Torres del Paine National Park in the first week of February 2003. Our initial objective was a new route on the west face of Torre Norte. We waited eight days at Campamento Japones, during which we twice tried to climb but were twice turned back by wind and snow. We then aborted the Towers and headed to the Bader Valley, also known as the Pingo Valley, which is reputed to have a better microclimate. Our luck changed, and our first day there was beautiful. We spied a nice-looking 1,200' line on the southeast face of Cuerno Oeste and began climbing at 10:30 a.m. on February 12. The route starts just to the right of an obvious 20' overhang (where we bivied) near the mouth of the valley, with 200' of class 4 and a 30' 5.6 dihedral. We traversed a ledge to the right, to a 5.7 corner. There we roped up and simul-climbed for 300 feet of 5.6-5.8, moving through crack systems and heading gradually

Chris Belczynski on Self Right To Suicide. *Boguslaw Kowalski*

left. At another ledge the climbing became more difficult, so we climbed the final 750-800' in pitches. This section begins with a 5.8 crack, traverses left through a 5.10 roof into a dihedral, and traverses left again, under a hanging flake into a chimney. After the chimney the climb moves out left through another roof to a crack that peters out. An A0 move was required to bridge a four-foot blank section to another crack, which leads to a ledge with rotten rock above. The route stops where the rotten rock begins. Mas Ricas No Hay (IV 5.10 A0).

A few days after climbing Cuerno Oeste we put up a 600' route on the east face of Cuerno Chico. We called the route Hurly Burly (5.9). Toward the end of February we tried a new line on Cuerno Oeste just to the right of Flight of the Condor. After 400' we hit a section of crumby rock, so we descended and traversed to Flight of the Condor. We climbed the first third of that route before a storm rolled in, and we descended in the rain. We had three climbing days during our month-long visit.

JOHN REYHER, *AAJ*

SOUTH OF PAINE

Mt. Burney, second ascent. Mt. Burney (1,768m) is a volcano that stands near the northwest corner of the Muñoz Gamero penninsula, which is about 2,000 square miles in area. Though it is a familiar landmark seen from ships passing through Smyth and Union channels between Punta Arenas and Puerto Natales, very little is known about this mountain, beside Eric Shipton's first ascent on March 10, 1973.

On March 6, 2003, after 2-1/2 days on the Pacific Ocean, the Pinguin dropped us off on a sandy beach in Puerto Muñoz Gamero. The expedition included 15 students and 4 NOLS instructors, including myself, carrying 600kg of food, 100kg of equipment, and 70 liters of fuel.

During 18 days of consistently bad weather, incessant rain and snow, we worked to get in position and be ready. On March 21, late in the morning, stable good weather suddenly arrived. After 8-1/2 hours of tricky glacier travel and a short section of steep ice, we reached the summit. The semicircular summit ridge was crowned by a number of spectacular ice pinnacles formed on an agglomerate of the tuff and lava blocks of which the crater rim of Mt. Burney is composed. The descent at night, after five hours of traveling, took place under a clear sky, with beautiful stars everywhere.

After the second ascent of this remote and historic mountain in the Magallanes region, we traveled east toward the sea and accomplished another goal, traversing the Muñoz Gamero peninsula west to east, finishing at Caleta Suarez. We covered 63km mostly of turba (Magallanes swamps) in 27 days, before being picked up by the Pinguin and her captain Conrado Alvarez.

Our group consisted of American students Zachary Blaylock, Drew Collins, Matt Citadin, Lucy Donaghy, Jen Gray, Lindsay Long, Tobias McDougal, Alex McLawhorn, Conner Mulvee, Evan Olson, Christopher Robin, Will Thames, Louis Urvois, and Tom Wilson, Chilean student Fiorenza Marinkovic, and instructors Ignacio Grez and Christian Steidle (Chile), Kat Rudert (Canada), and Chris Manges (U.S.).

CHRISTIAN STEIDLE, *Chile*

TIERRA DEL FUEGO, ARGENTINA

Isla de los Estados, inland traverse. This island was discovered in 1615 by Le Maire and afterward visited by many explorers, including James Cook. Many ships have wrecked on its difficult coasts. Because of difficult terrain and bad weather, no one had traversed the island. To commemorate the Argentine explorer Luis Piedrabuena, who was active on the island, a group of civilian and Argentine navy personnel crossed the island from west to east. The group consisted of civilian females Julieta Rimoldi and Verónica Schro and Argentine navy men Guillermo Tibaldi (chief), Antonio González, Gustavo Pérez, and Adrián Nuñez. They traversed many ridges and cols, many of them previously unvisited, although no summits were ascended. The expedition lasted for 22 days, the traverse ending on Februrary 16, 2004 in the lighthouse that inspired Jules Verne's novel, *The Lighthouse at the End of the World.*

MARCELO SCANU, *Buenos Aires, Argentina*

Antarctica

ELLSWORTH MOUNTAINS

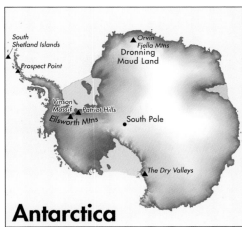

Sentinel Range, overview. The 2003-04 season saw a record number of people reach the summit of Vinson Massif (4,897m). A total of 75 people attempted the mountain and 74 were successful. This surpasses the previously most successful season, 2000-01, when 73 people summited out of 78 attempts.

Last season also saw the first Sherpa reach the summit. Lhakpa Rita summited twice while guiding clients, as did two other guides. At least 10 women reached the top, the most ever in one season, and one of them was one of two summiteers over 70 years old.

However, at one stage in late 2003, it looked like a Vinson season might not happen at all. Adventure Network International (ANI) had been the only operator of flights to inland Antarctica and had operated successfully every year since 1986. Around mid-year they decided to suspend operations this season for various reasons. Shortly after, the company, including the camp at Patriot Hills, was bought by a consortium that consisted mainly of ex-staff and owners. The new company—Antarctic Logistics & Expeditions (AL&E)—made their first flight in late November, and the experience and competence of their personnel resulted in a very successful and safe season.

The only new route last season was a variation on the long summit-day plod. Alain Hubert, of Belgium, guiding Christine Joris and Joao Garcia traversed east from the usual Camp 3 site on the col between Vinson and Shinn, then angled up to the eastern edge of the Vinson summit plateau. They followed this south over some minor ridge points before reaching the main summit pyramid from the east. This gave a very scenic outing, though slightly longer than the normal route.

Luis Fraga, Ramon Portilla, and Miguel Angel Vidal of Spain made an ascent of the right-hand side of the West Face Ice Stream, a moderate but sustained snow and ice route that is one of the faster ways to the summit of Vinson. The route had been climbed twice by Conrad Anker in 1999, the second time up to and over the summit. On his first ascent Anker skied the route from the top of the ice stream.

Three groups also reached the summit of Mt. Shinn (4,661m), the third-highest mountain in Antarctica.

DAMIEN GILDEA, *AAC, Australia*

Vinson Massif, West Face Ice Stream, repeat ascent. As reported above, on December 23 Luis Fraga, Miguel Angel Vidal, and I made a rare ascent of the 2,000-meter high West Face of Vinson (4,897m). We repeated the line first climbed in 1999 by Conrad Anker. Starting out at around 4:30 a.m., we unroped above the rimaye and progressed about 60 meters apart, worried

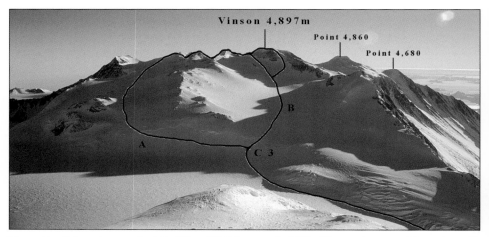

Vinson Massif from the summit of Mt. Shinn. (A) Hubert et. al., 2003; (B) normal route up Vinson from C3. *Damien Gildea*

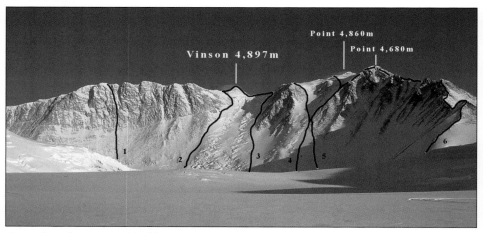

The west face of Mt. Vinson, with all known routes: (1) Linear Accelerator, Jay Smith, 1994; (2) Rudi's Runway, Rudi Lang, 1991; (3) Central Ice Stream–Right Side, Conrad Anker, 1999; (4) South Ice Stream, Jay & Jo Smith, 1993; (5) South Ice Stream to Point 4680, Alvarez-Juez, 1995; (6) West Ridge, Conrad Anker, 1999. Repeats: # 3 by Spanish, 2003; # 4 by Slovenians, 1997; # 5 partially repeated and skied by Anker and Anselme Baud, 1998; # 5 partially climbed in 1995 during unsuccessful attempt on Point 4860. *Route info and photo courtesy of Damien Gildea*

by wind slab in the middle section of the route. The first 800 meters were straightforward 45-50° but then it got steeper and the last 200 meters were on 55-60° hard bare ice. Fraga arrived at the top first, taking around eight-and-a-half hours, while I brought up the rear in 10 hours. The following day all three of us reached the summit and on Xmas Day descended the original 1991 Rudi Lang route on the far left side of the Central Ice Stream. The 2003 climb was my second ascent of the face. My first, and the most southerly of the five existing routes, followed an easier line up the right side of the South Ice Stream (though not to the summit), and was completed around the 18th January 1995 with the late Manolo Alvarez.

RAMON PORTILLA, *Spain*

An exploratory journey through the Ellsworth Mountains in 2002-03, and first ascent of Mt. Segers. On November 10, 2002 four Chilean mountaineers, Pablo Gutiérrez, Eugenio Guzmán, Ernesto Olivares, and I started a journey of over 400km through the almost unexplored east side of the Ellsworth Mountains, with the aim of finishing at Patriot Hills. We first flew by Twin Otter from Patriot Hills to the Newcomer Glacier, where on our first night the temperature dropped to –35°C. The next day we began pulling our four pulks, each one weighing 140kg. After four days we reached the first pass that would lead us into the heart of the Sentinel Range. We named it Light Pass and the crossing to the Embree Glacier proved easy.

Shoveling terraces was essential to descending the passes safely. *Rodrigo Jordan*

By contrast, sledging up the Embree proved steep and strenuous. We had to haul the pulks and on one day traveled less than 400 meters. Our first crux came toward the end, where we had to cross to the Ellen Glacier. On route we had hoped to attempt Mt. Todd, but after inspecting the pass we had to cross, and seeing

The first camp on Ellen Glacier provided this view of the highest mountains in Antarctica. *Eugenio Guzmán*

the difficulties involved we decided to concentrate all our efforts on reaching the Ellen Glacier.

It took a full 14 hours to rappel and lower sledges down the far side of Crocodile Pass, at one point negotiating a vertical ice step. Still hoping to bag a virgin summit we concentrated our efforts on one of the two remaining unclimbed 4,000m peaks of the Sentinel Range, Mt. Giovinetto. We left most of our supplies on the glacier and detoured for seven kilometers to camp at the base of the mountain. Unfortunately, once there we realized that the climb would take far longer than we anticipated, and we were not carrying enough food or fuel. Reluctantly we abandoned the idea.

Another difficult pass led to the Patton Glacier, and after 21 days we had our first official day-off to rest. We then continued along the glacier, at one point camping at the foot of 4,852m Mt. Tyree, and crossed a pass to the Crosswell Glacier. The traverse of the col was so straight-forward we name it Angel Pass.

On December 6 we completed 26 days of travel. We had consumed nearly half our food yet had only traveled 112km, a little more than one quarter of our intended trek. It seemed stupid to waste our meager resources on attempting a virgin peak, but our motivation to do so was still strong. We took two days out to try Mt. Segers and were rewarded with an outstanding view from the summit, which lies in the very heart of the Sentinels.

We then crossed the Dater Glacier to the Thomas Glacier, and to our dismay found the second crux of the journey: an immense crevasse field that took considerable time and effort to negotiate. We finally reached the Minnesota Glacier and crossed it to the Heritage Range.

On December 28, after climbing to a gap we called Non-steep Slope Pass, we could see the Union Glacier with its beautiful blue ice surface. By the 30th we had reached the last pass on our journey, Eureka Pass, already named by one of the members of the 1989-90 Trans Antarctic Expedition. From this pass we were delighted to see Patriot Hills, 60km distant. Our last camp was about 17km from the Patriot Hills Base and we covered the ground easily to arrive on January 2, 54 days and 403km after starting our journey.

RODRIGO JORDAN, *AAC*

DRONNING MAUD LAND

Fenris, Orvin Fjella Mountains, first ascent. In December 2003 Mike Libecki and I were landed at an altitude of ca 1,200m close to Ulvetanna in the Orvin Fjella mountains of Dronning Maud Land. Base camp was established at 71° 51,264 S, 08° 22,552 W. We first circumnavigated the Orvin Fjella range, on route repairing an unmanned weather station for Stanford University and NASA. By climbing a few moderate ridges, we discovered most of the rock to be highly decomposed.

After our ski tour we decided to attempt the unclimbed 600-meter west face of Fenris (2,680m). The first pitch proved the most difficult; over 70 meters of A4 on which no bolts were placed. Above, a crack system appeared to split the remainder of the wall, so we started up the face in capsule style on January 2, 2004. On the 15th we reached the knife-edge summit and began a series of 14 rappels back down the wall. Only bolted anchors were left behind. A full account of this climb by Mike Libecki appears earlier in this Journal.

JOSH HELLING, *AAC*

THE DRY VALLEYS

Mount Dido, first ascent of South Ridge. During a SAR training exercise in February 2002, Thai Verzone and I had the opportunity to make the first ascent of the South Ridge (IV 5.9) of Mt. Dido (1,976m) in the Olympus Range of Victoria Land's Dry Valleys. The first half of the route was straightforward and primarily low to mid 5th class climbing. The second half required careful route finding with two crux sections of 5.9. The ridge ended before the summit, and the final three pitches were on the exposed south face.

In total, we climbed 12 pitches in plastic boots on sandstone of varying quality. According to our best research, the tower had seen only one ascent previously, via the north ridge by a New Zealand party in the early 1980s. Before then, only a helicopter-born survey team had touched the summit. Descent involved rappelling and down-climbing our line of ascent.

The Dry Valleys have an immense amount of climbing potential, with rock climbs like ours and other climbs more alpine in nature. Access is tremendously challenging, and the commitment factor is extremely high. This is also an area of high scientific interest, so special care must be taken with the environment.

CHRIS SIMMONS, *AAC*

Historical note: the first recorded ascent was made by New Zealanders L. Main and R. Millington in November 1981. During the 1984-1985 summer, a four-member New Zealand team led by the late Rob Hall attempted the south ridge but was beaten by technical difficulties.

ANTARCTIC PENINSULA

Antarctic Peninsula brief summary. The Antarctic Peninsula was surprisingly quiet this year, with only two expeditions attempting mountain objectives. During November and December the Omega Foundation conducted its fifth Antarctic expedition in as many years, this time on Livingston Island in the South Shetland Islands. Later, in January, a group of Israeli and Palestinian adventurers sailed down the Peninsula to make a first ascent in the name of peace.

Livingston Island, South Shetland Islands, second ascent of Mt. Friesland and New Altitude. Livingston Island is around 60km long and much of it is gentle terrain. However, at the eastern end rises an impressive range of snowy peaks that I had first seen

Thai Versone leading one of the harder pitches on the final south face. *Chris Simmons*

The south ridge of Mt. Dido. The ridge is gained at its lowest point by a series of traversing ledges from the west, and follows the sunlit skyline for 12+ pitches. *Chris Simmons*

while visiting the area in 2001. Though mapped by the British Antarctic Survey in the 1950s, there was some ambiguity over the height, names and locations of some of the peaks. Myself and John Bath of Australia, with Rodrigo Fica and Osvaldo Usaj of Chile, sponsored by the Omega Foundation, aimed to climb several of the main peaks and ascertain their height (as Rodrigo and I had done on Mt. Shinn the previous year). In addition we wanted to match various peaks and features with names in existing Antarctic databases, such as the Composite Gazetteer of Antarctic Place Names compiled by the Scientific Committee on Antarctic Research (SCAR).

John Bath and Osvaldo Usaj approaching the summit of Mt. Bowles (822m) on Livingston Island. In the background, left to right: Falsa Aguja, Levski Peak, and Lyaskovets Peak. Mt. Friesland is out of picture to the right. *Damien Gildea*

The Omega team first flew to King George Island in a Dash-7 aircraft chartered by the Chilean airline DAP as part of their expansion of tourist activity in the area. We then transferred to a new DAP BO-105 helicopter and in three flights were transferred to a predetermined base camp site on Livingston. During the 26 days we spent on the island, only three days were really suitable for climbing. Two of those days were taken for flying in and out! The other good day was spent making the second known ascent of Mt. Bowles, a rounded peak north of the main range, which the Omega team measured at 822m. After the work on Bowles, we spent nearly two weeks unable to climb high due to combinations of wind, light snow, constant low cloud and fog, and two periods of severe blizzard conditions lasting several days. During this time some short ski journeys were made in the vicinity of the plateau and also to make a cache at the start of the ramp that led up to the east ridge of Mt. Friesland, the primary objective of the group, as it is the highest peak on the island.

Friesland was first climbed in December 1991 by two Spanish climbers from the nearby King Juan Carlos I base. Though Bulgarian scientific personnel had been active in this part of Livingston in the intervening period, they confirmed to us that they had not climbed any of the high peaks.

On December 19 John, Rodrigo, and I left camp in the evening to make a final attempt on Friesland. The long snowy ramp up to the ridge was much more crevassed than we had assumed and took time to negotiate in visibility that was usually around 20 meters or less. Upon reaching the ridge the weather deteriorated further, but we continued up until we came to a point where we could not see the way ahead due to low light levels (it was 2 a.m.) and a light snowfall. We then spent a cold and uncomfortable night bivouacked in a two-man tent with no sleeping bags, then continued to the top later that morning in slightly better weather. The ridge was severely crevassed and corniced, but otherwise held no difficulty. Fortunately, the weather held for around three hours while we were on the summit, enough time to run the GPS and eventually obtain a new height of 1,700m for Mt. Friesland. At various clearings in the weather, and on the spectacular helicopter flight out on December 22, we were able to confirm visually that Friesland is indeed the highest peak on the island. The Omega Foundation will use the new information from this expedition and other sources to produce a new map of Livingston Island later in 2004. More information can be found at www.theomegafoundation.org.

DAMIEN GILDEA, *AAC, Australia*

Unnamed Peak, First Ascent, Prospect Point, Antarctic Peninsula. A group of eight Palestinian and Israeli adventurers—the *Breaking The Ice* expedition—with another eight support crew, traveled well south down the Peninsula aboard the well-known yacht *Pelagic* and the new *Pelagic Australis.* Their aim was to make a first ascent of a virgin Antarctic mountain in the name of peace. The eight team members were Ziad Darwish, Doren Erel, Yarden Fanta, Olfat Haider, Suleiman al-Khateib, Heskel Nathaniel, Nasser Quass, and Avihu Shoshani. Most of the team had never climbed before, but were guided by Skip Novak (skipper of *Pelagic*), Doren Erel, and Denis Ducroz of France. Erel and Ducroz had both visited the Peninsula in January 1994 when, with Novak and sailing aboard *Pelagic,* they made the fourth ascent of the beautiful Mt. William on Anvers Island.

On January 16 all team members eventually summited a non-technical peak at the head of the glacier above Prospect Point. Their handheld GPS gave a height of 882m and a location of 66 01.08S 65 11.36W. On the summit, Nathaniel read a declaration that the team had prepared and called the peak *The Mountain of Israeli-Palestinian Friendship.* More information can be found at: www.breaking-the-ice.de.

DAMIEN GILDEA, *AAC, Australia*

SOUTH GEORGIA

Mount Paget, Alladyce Range, North East Spur. In November 2003 a Spanish team including José Carlos Tamayo made a rare ascent of Mt. Paget (2,935m), the highest peak on the island of South Georgia and the highest on British soil. They repeated the North East Spur, first climbed in 1980 by a five-member French expedition led by Philippe Cardis (traveling in the yacht Basile) during the second ascent of the mountain. The Spanish ascent of Paget was probably the fifth.

LINDSAY GRIFFIN, *High Mountain INFO*

Africa

MOROCCO

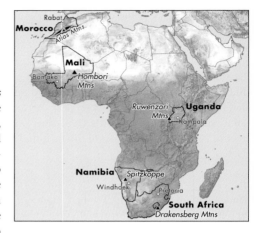

Atlas Mountains, Taghia Gorge, Les Rivieres Pourpres and Sul Filo della Notte. Visiting the remote Taghia Gorge in Morocco this October, Rolando Larcher, Maurizio Oviglia, and Michele Paissan established the stellar 12-pitch Sul Filo della Notte (V 5.13a; 5.12b obligatory) on the immaculate red limestone of the Tadrarate. Though climbers have been active here sporadically since 1974, the gorge's location in the Atlas Mountains, two hours from the nearest decent road and above a village with no electricity or telephone, had thus far kept development to a minimum. Nevertheless, this is an area to keep an eye on, with a handful of one-pitch routes up to 5.13c, Sul Filo della Notte, and the nearly 2000-foot 5.12b route Les Rivieres Pourpres put up in May 2003.

Adapted from www.rockandice.com

UGANDA

Approching Bujuku Lake, with the southern peaks of Mt. Stanley on the left and the northern peaks of Mt. Stanley on the right (Alexandra and Margherita). *Ralph Baldwin*

Rwenzori (Ruwenzori) Mountains, Mountains of the Moon, an historical overview and recent ascent of Mt. Stanley (Margherita Peak, 5,109m.). Rwenzori Mountains National Park is located on the border between Uganda and Zaire. It contains six major glaciated massifs of over 4,600m less than one degree from the equator (0°11'N, 29°47'E). Little climbing has occurred in this range over the past three decades due to the tyrannies of Amin and Obote, then the guerilla war on the mountain by rebel insurgents. The most recent closure was from 1994 to 2001.

Our group included Douglass Teschner, an American working in Kigali, Rwanda; John Skirving from Vashon, Washington, and myself from Wasilla, Alaska. We made an ascent of Margherita Peak, Africa's third highest peak, and a 60km approach and return over nine days, July 30–August 7. Although not as high as Mt. Kilimanjaro and Mt. Kenya, the Rwenzori comprise an alpine zone significantly larger and far less traveled than either. The first full season since reopening, 2002, saw only about 200 visitors, few of whom were climbers. Rwenzori Mountains National Park measures roughly 100km by 40km at the 1,500m level.

The wettest months are March to May and August to December. Rains can be very persistent and heavy on the trails with some monthly averages reported at 19 inches. We considered ourselves lucky to have had rain only on the last day. The thickly vegetated rock slopes of the approach and return as well as the deep mud of the high altitude bogs pose serious obstacles even in the supposedly dry season.

Ptolemy, the great Greek geographer, writing in ca A.D. 150 first suggested the source of the Nile River to be two large lakes whose waters were fed by snow melting on the "Mountains of the Moon." The European explorer, Henry Stanley called these mountains Rwenzori, after a local name meaning "hills of rain," when he "discovered" the range in 1888. The Rwenzori today are recognized as a vital water catchment, feeding the economically important lakes Edward and George, and constituting the highest and most permanent sources of the River Nile.

Intrepid explorer and climber, Prince Luigi di Savoia, the Duke of the Abruzzi, made the first comprehensive exploration and ascent of major peaks in 1906. H.W. Tilman and Eric Shipton visited the Rwenzori in January of 1932 and made the third ascent of Margherita Peak as well as several other major ascents. During the 1960s and 1970s, expatriates based out of Kampala and members of the Mountain Club of Uganda made many ascents and installed a hut system along the primary trails. These huts and their replacements are in use today. Rwenzori Mountains National Park was established in 1991 and recognized by the United Nations as a World Heritage Site in 1994.

Our climb began with the recognition that Teschner's job assignment in Rwanda provided an excellent base for a trip into the Rwenzori, an object of fascination for us for some time. Skirving and I traveled to Nairobi and then on to Kigali to meet Teschner. From Rwanda, we headed north by public bus, probably the most dangerous element of the entire expedition! The bus lurched around precipitous mountain roads at breakneck speeds with the driver leaning on the horn most of the time.

At Kasese, we made last minute purchases in the market, met representatives of Rwenzori Mountain Services (RMS), an NGO controlling access to the park, and booked into the Hotel Margherita for the night. In the morning, a taxi took us the final 20km to Nyakalengija at the end of a dirt road. Local Bakonjo people whose families have served as porters and trail guides for generations were lined up outside the park headquarters hoping to be hired as we arrived.

The Uganda Wildlife Authority administers the park and RMS is the sole concessionaire. Following the incidents at Bwindi National Park (1999) and Murchison Falls National Park (2001) in which rebel insurgents kidnapped and murdered visitors, trekking and peak ascents are tightly regulated. An armed ranger escort is mandatory as are guides and porters. RMS insists that all visitors be guided up all peaks. The guides proved useful in route-finding through the forest and on the glacier, but they need training in technical mountain skills. Our proposed trip required prepayment of US $600 cash per person including peak fees.

We reached the high hut, Elena (4,540m), on the fourth day after following the lower reaches of the Mubuku river and then the Bujuku river to its source. As we ascended, we passed through montane forest, thick bamboo stands, and dense thickets of tree-size heather. The giant grounsel and lobelia plants in the alpine zone reached 8 meters! Bujuku Lake (3,977m) at the head of the drainage is surrounded by three main massifs: Mt. Stanley to the west, Mt. Speke to the north, and Mt. Baker to the south.

The Stanley Plateau is about 1km by 0.5km and lies at 4,800m. We ascended Moebius (4,919m) to the final three-meter summit block, an easy third-class scramble and a good vantage point. The east face of Elena Peak (4,970m) looked to be a possibly interesting rock climb of about 200 meters at intermediate standard. However, the glaciers and snows are melting at an accelerated rate and rockfall can be a serious hazard in this area. Back at the hut, a clearing in the sky afforded a view of two large tower-like peaks guarding the entrance to the Coronation Glacier, Kitasamba (ca 4,863m) and Nyabubuya (ca 4,863m), deities to the local Bakonjo.

Our summit day started shortly after dawn in a snow squall that dropped six inches of snow on the Stanley Plateau. At the north end with the weather clearing, we dropped down a rocky gully at the foot of the east ridge of Alexandra Peak to connect with the Margherita Glacier. From a col, we climbed a short rock cliff to gain the east ridge of Margherita. The first 20 meters requires low-level fifth-class climbing over rock streaming with water, but RMS has installed a fixed rope to which one can clip. We were amazed to see our guides pull themselves up the rope hand-over-hand without clipping in.

Five and one-half hours from the hut, we topped out at the summit of Margherita Peak, highest point on the border between Uganda and Zaire. Depending on the weather conditions, route-finding can be difficult. However, we had a relatively easy time of it thanks to our mandatory guide, John Mudenge. In 1932, Tilman and Shipton camped on the Stanley Plateau for four days before the mists cleared sufficiently for them to climb Margherita.

The next morning before descending to Scott-Elliot Pass (4,370m) to complete our circuit back to Nyakalengija, we decided to make a short rock route. Teschner led four pitches (5.5) on cliff escarpments above the Elena hut. The rock was solid but slippery due to heavy moss cover in places. By observing photos and diagrams from Osmaston and Pasteur (1972), it is obvious that the glaciers have receded tremendously over the past 40 years exposing more rock, creating new route options, and making old ones longer. Osmaston is a good reference for established routes, but retreating glaciers have changed conditions, and glaciers may be gone in 20 years. Best new route options in the Rwenzori may involve longer mountaineering routes (300-900m), primarily on rock. If current park administration will permit easier access to the high peaks, there is great potential for new routes in this exotic range. The Mountain Club of Uganda, based out of Kampala, may have the most complete records of routes done to date.

The trek back to the trailhead took three and one-half days during which we passed the Kitandara Lakes, source of the Butawa River which flows westward down into Zaire. Scorched hillsides could be seen across the lakes where fire reportedly set by rebels had worked its way up the valley. The descent took us over Freshfield Pass (4,280m) and by Bujongolo, the large cave from which the Duke of Abruzzi launched his assault in 1906.

Our last night on the trail, we joined the porters and guides for supper and discussed the current political situation in Uganda. Rwenzori Mountains National Park is an exquisite African mountain wilderness with no infrastructure at this time other than a crude hut system. Major development is planned and increased visitation expected. Hopefully, the Bakonjo who have lived on this land for generations will be a part of the decision-making process. There is a very real need for training of local guides in mountain craft, and the organizing of guides and porters into entities that can ensure their well being.

Useful contacts: Rwenzori Mountaineering Services, P.O. Box 33, Kasese, Uganda; The Warden in Charge, Rwenzori Mountains National Park, P.O. Box 188, Kasese, Uganda; and U.S. Department of State (http://usembassy.state.gov). Useful references: Else, D. (1998) *Trekking in East Africa*, Lonely Planet Publications; Wielochowski, A. (1989) *Ruwenzori* (trail map); Osmaston, H. and D. Pasteur (1972) *Guide to the Ruwenzori* (out of print); and Tilman, H.W. (1938) *Snow On The Equator* (out of print).

RALPH BALDWIN, *AAC*

MALI

La Mano de Fatima, Kaga Tondo, Forsakala Bimbaso. Adventure and unexpected situations guided a group of Czech climbers during their trip to La Mano de Fatima. In spite of very high temperatures, four of them, Pavel Jonak, Vasek Satava, Petr Piechowicz, and Milan Benian repeated the route Harmattan Rodeo on the tower Kanga Pamari. The hardest pitch has a difficulty of 7c+/8a. Because of very high temperatures they repeated the route only in AF style. The first ascent was made by Paul Piana and Todd Skinner and rated 5.13a. The Czechs Tomas Zakora, Radek Tilnak, Ludek Slechta, and Tomas Bien climbed a new route on tower Kaga Tondo. They christened their route Forsakala Bimbaso (13 pitches, 7a AF).

JAN KREISINGER, *Czech Republic*

Hand of Fatima, first complete link-up (in a day). From mid November to mid December, I had the extreme pleasure of being part of a North Face –sponsored expedition during which we explored the surreal sub-Saharan dream-world of Mali as we ventured towards the legendary five fingers of the Hand of Fatima. We landed in the apocalypticaly industrialized capital city of Bamako and left as quickly as possible via three Land Cruisers. Along for the ride were videographer Kevin Kau, sound man Andrew, and the legendary still photographer Jimmy Chin,

Kevin Thaw on Kago Tondo, The Hand of Fatima. *Jimmy Chin*

The traverse of all the towers was from left to right (Suri Tondo is far right out of the photo). The first tower, Kaga Pamari was ascended from the notch up and down its right arête. Kaga Tondo by its left skyline, then down the face hidden from the camera. The others (Suri Tondo inclusive) were up and down their left skylines—3,500 feet of climbing. *Kevin Thaw*

with his assistant and rigger Evan Howe. Due to some last minute changes because of an injured partner, Kevin Thaw enthusiastically stood in and was to meet us in a week when we arrived at the Hand of Fatima.

Because there was no hurry to get to the Hand, we enjoyed a three-day detour into Dogon Country. The Dogons are amazing people who live in caves and mud-walled huts. The Dogon Country has the most impressive bouldering and cragging potential I have ever seen, on some of the highest quality quartzite boulders and walls on the planet. Above the Dogon habitations are walled-in caves from the Tellum Era. No one knows for sure how these people got to their caves hundreds of feet off the floor, but it is theorized that thousands of years ago there used to be thick jungle vegetation to climb. The Dogons are amazing wood carvers and craftsmen, and still practice their Animist (Voodoo) belief systems. Certainly the highlight of the trip was watching the people perform their mask dance, which includes some 20 men dressed in full regalia with beautifully constructed masks representing the different aspects of their culture. The mask representing their dwellings is nearly 20 feet tall, and some of the men dance on 10-foot stilts. Amazing.

We tore ourselves away from Dogon Country and headed further north to the Hand of Fatima. Along the way we saw the occasional Tuareg, a nomadic band of people who wear blue turbans, ride camels, and trade across the Sahara.

The largest face of the largest finger of the Hand of Fatima is 2,400 feet tall, and when Kevin Thaw arrived, we climbed the beautiful 5.10 regular route up the face as part of the film project. The Hand is home to thousands of birds of every shape and size, and Kevin and I theorized that the towers might actually be ancient petrified dung. After completing our film and photography obligations we were free to climb, and on a cool day for the Hand (about 90°F) we climbed and summited all five fingers via their shortest routes in about 11 hours, completing my vision of a desert push. On the final tower of the link-up hundreds of bats began to pour out of the crack we were climbing, and one of the 5.11 cruxes involved manteling a pile of bat dung with a bat carcass embedded in it. At one point a frantic bat slammed into my chest, nearly knocking me off my stance. While the climbing was amazing, by far the most enjoyable and memorable part of the journey was encountering all of the friendly, colorful people from a culture so vastly different from the Western with whom I live.

Statistics: This was the first time the five fingers of the Hand of Fatima have been climbed in one day. The link up involved about 30 pitches, or approximately 3,500 feet of technical climbing, plus much hateful hiking in the sticker-infested, chest-high, "Black Mamba Grass Fields." The technical crux came on the final tower of the link-up Suri Tondo, which went at 5.11d and involved hand jamming and finger locking in a crack soaked with bird and bat urine, but the bat-dung mantle—complete with half decomposed bat carcass—was DEFINITELY the most memorable 5.11 moment. The first route of the link up was a new route first ascended two days earlier by Jimmy Chin and Evan Howe. This was the most logical and least dung-infested way up the beautiful and slender Kaga Pamari, and yielded three 60m pitches up to 5.10dR, i.e., big runouts on solid 5.10 face.

CEDAR WRIGHT, *AAC*

Hand of Fatima, further notes to Wright's report. The Hand of Fatima towers close to the town of Hombori within a region mainly occupied by the Fulani tribe. Hombori's unique position shares tribal borders, so the regional market trades between many clans: Dogon, Hogon, Senufo and the still feared Tuareg from the barren Sahara only 70km north. Feared because in recent history they attempted a regional coup and occupied Hombori and the surrounding area, their insurgence finally suppressed by Mali's military.

Cedar Wright secured the Fulani Chief's permission to dwell and climb on their land. Kaga Tondo—the largest "finger"—was our first objective. In native Bambara it translates very simply as "Big Rock." Kaga Tondo's North Pillar is dubbed the world's longest sandstone route. The rock was of good quality, sometimes brittle and blocky, but never dangerously loose. Most importantly it proved a very, very fun outing. We neared the summit as residents enjoyed their feeding hour: cracks spilled all sizes of birds into the sky, including swifts, hawks, eagles, vultures, and a pair of massive storks with the proportions of a small Cessna. They created a wonderful and unique summit experience.

KEVIN THAW

NAMIBIA

Spitzkoppe, summary. This stunning granite outcrop in central Namibia has some of Southern Africa's finest climbing, with bouldering to 14-pitch trad and sport routes, and delicate face climbing to crazy cracks and chimneys. Spitzkoppe is located in the middle of the Namib Desert, one of the driest places on earth, and due to the hot temperatures it is recommended to climb only between April and September.

The summit of Spitzkoppe was first reached in 1946, and since then the number of routes

The southwest wall of Spitzkoppe, Namibia. The South African Grading system has been used for the following routes: (1) Active Side of Infinity (25 A0, Hüfner-Modrzewski-Seuring, 2002); (2) Beyond Suntan Lotion (24, Brogan-Modrzewski, 2002); (3) Nothing in Moderation (24) Broccardo-Hüfner-Seuring, 2001; (4) Watersports (20, Hüfner- Modrzewski-Pretorius, 2001); (5) Herero Arch (27 A0, Gargitter-Botte-Thaler-Trekwalder, 1999); (6) INXS (24, Cartwright-Smith- Seegers, 1991); (7) South West Wall (24, Haber- Holding-Ward, 1982); (8) Royal Flush (21, Edelstein-Mallory, 1983). *Alard Hüfner*

has slowly been increasing. In the late 1980s and early 1990s several big new routes were opened with the use of bolts, thus allowing the huge slabs of the southwest wall to be climbed.

The new millennium has seen a surge of big new routes being established on the South West Wall, both trad and sport. These are summarized on the accompanying photo, which uses the South African Grading System. Additional info: Spitzkoppe and Pontoks, *Namibia: A Climbers Guide*, by Eckhardt Haber (Blue Mountain Publishers, 2004); and www. alardsbigwallclimbing.com.

ALARD HÜFNER, *Mountain Club of South Africa*

SOUTH AFRICA

Drakensberg Mountains, Monk's Cowl (3,224m), Janschek-Mackenzie-Manson. The Drakensberg Mountains (Quathamba in Zulu, translated: "the barrier of spears") are not very frequented by climbers. Interest in this area has waned more and more as the attention of local climbers has moved in other directions. The escarpment stretches for 250km along the eastern boarder of Lesotho, with its adjacent freestanding spires. The entire length of the Drakensberg is wilderness and has been declared a World Heritage Site. The basalt escarpment is extremely beautiful and hosts a large variety of fauna and flora unique to this area. It is nearly free of development, and the only way to access these mountains is on foot. Various passes give natural passage to the Lesotho highlands, which on average are above 3,000m altitude.

Monk's Cowl is a very prominent freestanding spire that had caught my attention many years before. The 400-meter north wall is where Ian Manson and I focused our attention in the winter of 2000. At the base of the wall we looked for an appropriate place to start. There was no obvious line so we looked for a place that had enough features to climb on. Adjacent to where the route starts is a little overhang shelter. It was very convenient and we made much use of it later. The first four pitches climb a slab then lead into a faint dihedral system. Pitch 6 is the crux (5.12b), a memorable pitch to savor. It is a mixture of face,

The Monk's Cowl in the Drakensberg Mountains, showing its new route. *Peter Janschek*

crack, stemming a dihedral, and a very awkward mantle: sustained high quality climbing. From then on the difficulty eases to 5.10–5.11. In August 2000, Ian and I reached our highpoint at pitch 9. Running out of bolts and time, we had to postpone the completion of this route.

It was not until April 2003 that I could visit South Africa and this wonderful mountain range again. This time, however, Ian could not join me to continue working on this route. Luckily, my good friend Tom Mackenzie had time and enthusiasm.

We had stashed gear in the shelter at the base of the wall, long awaiting our return. It was mid April when we returned to the mountains. After fixing four of the pitches, we returned to the shelter. The weather had been very unstable, and that night we were given a spectacular thunderstorm display. Lightning bolts struck into the mountain directly above us. The typical summer weather pattern was still prevalent, with a daily thunderstorm. It was too dangerous to consider a bivi on the wall, which we logistically needed. At least we had all the gear at the base of the route and could try again at a later stage. With the changing seasons a turning point in the weather usually happens. When the adjacent plains cool and days become shorter with the approaching winter, thermal activity ceases and hence the thunderstorm clouds no longer form.

At the end of April we managed to get the timing right with the changing seasons. We climbed to our highpoint of three years ago and continued on for one more pitch. A typical alpine bivy, and the next day we reached the summit. The upper part of the wall is featured with bulging prows that we had to find our way through. Route finding was the difficult part, and having to drill on lead also slowed our progress. At 2 o'clock we were on the summit of this beautiful peak.

PETER JANSCHEK, *Austria*

Norway

Lofoten Islands, Vagakallen north face, Invasion in the Land of Vikings. The alarm clock sounds and our small troop prepares for the big day. The atmospheric pressure was high and we hoped that the beautiful March weather had returned. We departed at 4 a.m. and quickly swallowed the approach. We were light as all the gear was already at the bottom of the face. We realized that today would be the day to climb this face, or we would give it up, having only two days left before we had to depart.

On our first attempt, after finishing three easy pitches through a great slope of heavy snow and ice, we had arrived at the foot of the first difficulty of the face in bad weather. With the assistance of Julie and Pierre Normand we chopped a bivy site in the face. It began storming and although we had our sleeping bags and rucksacks, we ran out of gas. It was necessary to scout the route to see what was above. We wondered if the route would open up higher. It was 9 a.m. and the temperature already was 4°C!

The last pitch of Full Spin Drift, Vagakallen's north face. *Julie Gerber*

Leaving our gear under a large boulder, we descended to the hut to regroup.

Morale the next day wasn't at its highest. The sky was gray and the temperatures weren't much better than the day before. We covered the approach in 35 minutes and recovered the gear. We quickly ascended the first three lengths and attacked the first ice gully. I led the fine ice lines that zigzagged up the center of the face. The team followed quickly on the moderate terrain. Protection and belays were difficult because of the thin ice: 10-12cm on average. We continued three more pitches in deteriorating weather.

Two pitches from the top, the terrain became slightly more technical, to my pleasure! The first pitch started with dry tooling in a chimney, choked in places with snow, which led to a fine gully of mixed terrain. After a mixed departure and some shaky terrain, my search for a route led to a beautiful crossing where a snow slope opened the route to the top. I found a crack and placed two beautiful pitons there. The summit was ours! After the obligatory congratulations and enjoying the fine Norwegian alpine views, we started the descent. The night caught up with us on the descent and the sky revealed its stars, the lights of Svolvaer, and the fishing vessels at sea. By midnight everyone whirred into the hut with a great feeling of accomplishment.

Invasion in the Land of Vikings (north face) (650m, V French TD+ 4, Scottish 4+/5, M6), David Jonglez, Pierre Plaze, Perrine Marceron, Jean-Hugues Marchal, and Stéphane Mouret, March 11, 2004. Other expedition members: Julie Gerber, Cécile Chauvin, and Pierre Normand.

DAVID JONGLEZ, *French Alpine Club of Savoie*

Vagakallen's north face in winter: Invasion in the Land of Vikings. *David Jonglez*

Lofoton Islands, Vagakallen's Great Pillar. We always intended to visit Norway, inspired by the Troll Wall and pictures and reports from the Lofoton Islands, which lie 125 miles north of the Arctic Circle. Somehow Norway always slipped down the list until this summer. The Alps were suffering from a heat wave, so we decided to head north to Norway. We stood under the Troll Wall wanting to be impressed and inspired, but it was dark, wet, and oppressive.

From our camp at Kalle, Vagakallen's 940-meter Great Pillar dominated our view. With the potential difficulties of the 800-meter route combined with rapidly shortening days and mixed weather we decided to go with a portaledge and four to five days of food and water.

I was amazed as the route unfolded. The climbing just worked. Above the slabs the ground leaned back in to hideously steep grass and disintegrating rock before kicking back up to vertical. We made our first camp above grassy rubble on a rocky rib. The line

Louise Turner jugging on Vagakallen's Storm Pillar. Note that the Pillar can also be seen in the photo above. *Twid Turner*

Vagakallen's north face in shadow. *Twid Turner*

proved strong and the climbing generally excellent. We hoped to free the route and, so far, all had gone well. Twid was onsighting long pitches of E4 and E5, despite the impromptu snow showers. As we strained our necks upward, it was obvious the next pitch was similar to the crack in the headwall of El Cap's Shield. We thought: aid it now and free it later; it is only one pitch.

The third day we continued to push, aiming for a huge boulder where we planned to bivy. Above the aid pitch a tricky slab ended in a precarious traverse to a stunning jamming and layback crack. Two more pitches took us under the boulder, which formed a huge chimney we easily scrambled through to the top. It was dark by the time we hung the ledge and fired up the stove.

I was awakened by water seeping through my sleeve and into Twid's sleeping bag. It had begun to rain and water seeped down the ropes and our daisy chains. We pulled our bivy bags close around us to keep our bags dry. Through years of living in Scotland and Wales and as a frequent visitor to Patagonia, I can safely say that I am accustomed to rain but I had never experienced anything like those next 24 hours. Imagine sitting in a car wash for 24 hours, only that each hour it ups a notch on the water, power, and volume!

The next morning the rain eased and I set off up saturated ropes hoping and praying they would not jam, which of course, they did. Eleven hours later we stood at the base. Suddenly we were greeted by a group that merrily explained the predicament we were about to face. A tiny stream we had previously stepped over was now five feet wide and thigh deep. Twid looked over his shoulder. "This is not a problem," he declared as he waded straight in.

LOUISE THOMAS, *U.K.*

Russia

CENTRAL CAUCASUS

Ullu-Tau (4,207m), north face, new route. In June 2003 a team of Czech climbers Bohuslav Vlcek, Jan Skalik, and Ondra Vespalec climbed a new route on the 1,400-meter high north face of Ullu-Tau (4,207m). Ullu-Tau is at the end of Adyr-Su Valley in Central Kavkaz. The new route is on the right of the north face through a snow couloir and snow-ice threshold. They began climbing at 3 a.m. and were on top 14 hours later. They descended after a bivy the next day.

JAN KREISINGER, *Czech Republic*

SIBERIA

Czarsky Tron, southwest wall, new route. In February 2003 a team from Krasnoyarsk climbed a new route on the southwest face of Czarsky Tron (Czar's Throne, 2,500m) located in the Kodar Range, Eastern Siberia. The temperature on the arrival at base camp was –20°C. The extreme cold of last year (up to –50°C) came into mind. The team was flown by helicopter, which allowed them to save energy for the approach. They settled in an abandoned hut and dug a snow cave for nights near the base of the wall. It took 10 days to put in Camp I (after fixing six pitches) and Camp II (after fixing 11 pitches). The climbing was mostly hard aid. They proceeded up the 75° wall placing hooks, anchors, friends, and bolts. Free climbing seemed hardly possible because of poor rock. After establishing Camp II the team gathered in a portaledge for the summit push. It was getting warmer and the rising temperatures brought strong winds. They worked their way to the summit ridge with frozen fingers, the storm failing to calm down. After advancing 20 more meters, they finally reached the summit. The descent took a whole day and they arrived in base camp in darkness. This is possibly the hardest route on Czarsky Tron (1,000m, 6B). Members: Valery Balezin (leader), Alexander Kuharev, Alexey Sikilinda, Vladimir Arhipov, Egeny Dmitrienko, Anton Pugovkin, Sergey Cherezov, Uriy Glazyrin, Dmitry Tsyganov.

Y. GLAZIRIN, *www.Mountain.RU*

Agrada, east face, Mirror for the Hero. In August our team established a new route on the 2,340m Agrada, Barguzinsky Ridge, Ulzykha River Canyon. Mirror for the Hero (566m, 6B) ascends the center of the east face. The route opened in a corner with a wide complicated crack. Above the crack, a couloir opened up with lively rockfall. The couloir ended on a cornice compounded by a huge boulder we had to climb over. A steep grassy ledge offered some relief before gaining a wide couloir, which was climbed without a safe belay: a station on a single bolt. Another series of steep grassy ledges brought on a monolithic slab with blind cracks. Ice hooks were very useful to climb this section. We reached a smooth plate with a very poor relief where we used hooks to climb between cracks. Above the hook moves we gained an inclined rocky ledge where we began to fix almost vertical ropes. We accessed a corner with poor relief, but we were able to bolt it without any problems. After another corner we reached a system of cracks and grass. The hooks came out to help again. We found a nice ledge for a camp.

Further up, we freed a wide crack in wet and chilly weather. A very complicated couloir ended by a cornice and a complicated overhanging corner. A long internal corner revealed big lively edges as we made a belay station on an anchor bolt and settled into another camp. We fixed the main rope near two slanting cracks, using hooks to overcome them. We were climbing on a half rope on unpleasant lively slabs. Yet another steep grassy ledge opened up a long corner leading to the ridge straight under the top. From here, an easy ridge brought us to the summit. We spent a total of five days on the route, and placed 10 bolts. Members: O.P. Kolesov (leader), Sherstnev Igor, Lyalin Sergey, and Sherstnev Igor.

Recommendation to climbers: The specialty of this region is wet weather, especially in August, because of its proximity to Baikal. There is a lot of grass on the route, even on vertical rock. Hooks are necessary, and the rock is very tough, so I recommend bringing several drill bits, even for a Hilti.

O.P. KOLESOV, *Chairman of Federation of Mountaineering and Rock Climbing Republic of Bury-atiya, www.mountain.RU*

Afghanistan

Noshaq (7,492m), first ascent in 25 years. The Oxus Mission, organized by Mountain Wilderness International, had two main goals: to show that it was again possible and not risky to visit the mountains of the High Hindu Kush in northeast Afghanistan, and to help organize a training scheme for young Wakhan Valley inhabitants who wish to become professional mountain guides, trekking guides, high altitude porters, or who want to arrange modern outdoor activities. This second goal, a project submitted to the Afghan Government one year ago by Mountain Wilderness, could get adequate funding from Italy and Europe and would help improve the socio-economic status of young people in this remote mountain area. Mountain Wilderness is convinced that training courses and accompanying structural improvements (such as new guest-houses, storage facilities for mountain gear, courses for management and basic English) could also pave the way toward the local population accepting a project for a Wakhan National Park, which seems to be on the agenda of Dr. Nouristani, the Afghan Minister for the Environment and Territory.

The three main organizing staff of the Mission were: Carlo Alberto Pinelli (Italy, Head of Mission); Giorgio Mallucci (Italy, technical and logistic chief);

Noshaq, showing the line of ascent.
Carlo Alberto Pinelli

Maria Chiara Starace (Italy, base camp manager); Haj Safat Mir (Afghanistan, representing the Ministry for Tourism). The international climbing team: Fausto De Stefani (Italy), Lambert Colàs Toràn (Spain), Irena Mrak (Slovenia), Olivier Paulin (France), Marco Schenone (Italy-Switzerland), Jocelyne Audra (France), Christophe Faisy (physician–France), Sahid Akmal (Afghanistan). In addition we had an Italian film crew of Alessandro Ojetti, Giorgio Gregorio (Italy), and Gabriella Tiberti.

The 6,000m camp on Noshaq. The ridge in the middle distance above the tent belongs to the Aspe Safed Group, while the two snowy tops visible in the left distance are Ghul-Lasht Zom (6,665m on the right) and Ghul-Lasht Zom East (6,611m on the left). Both Ghul-Lasht summits lie on the border with Pakistan and have been climbed many times since their first ascents in 1965. Afghanistan's Central Hindu Kush can be seen in the distant haze on the right. *Giorgio Gregorio*

The team was due to leave Europe on June 25 but just two weeks prior we learned that the valley leading to the foot of Noshaq (7,492m—the highest mountain in Afghanistan) was probably blocked by two mine fields, placed some time ago by Commander Massoud's Mujaheddin to prevent Pakistani troops disguised as Talibani from crossing the border. In order to check this alarming news, the Mission had to postpone its departure by 15 days. De Stefani and Ojetti were sent ahead to reconnoiter the terrain.

On July 17 the whole team grouped at the village of Qaz-i-Deh on the banks of the Amu Darya (formerly the Oxus River in the times of Alexander the Great). With the help of the local Ismaelite religious chief and a very efficient officer from the new Afghan Army, assigned to the Mission by General Zulmai (Chief of Security in the Karzai Government), 136 porters were hired for the rather attractive salary of 10 US dollars a day. As the Army officer had personally directed the placement of the landmines about three years ago, he was able to find an alternative route, zigzagging up the steep left hand side of the valley (looking upstream), completely avoiding the mined area.

On July 19 the expedition reached the traditional site of Noshaq Base Camp (4,550m) to find not only traces of low stone walls, but—alas—also many piles of non-biodegradable garbage, abandoned by expeditions in the 1970s. During our stay at base camp, members cleared the whole area and nearby moraine, carrying back to Kabul over 200kg of old (and new) tins, jars, and gas bottles. Unfortunately, it was not possible to clean entirely the high altitude camps from debris left by over 30 expeditions.

We started our climb, without local high altitude porters, on July 21. Right from the beginning it was obvious that during the last quarter of a century the condition of the ice slopes had become more demanding and the lower section of the West Ridge, the normal route, had become a huge heap of rubble, which was impractical except for descent. Instead the team moved up the glacier on the north flank and then climbed a 1,000-meter snow ramp to gain the crest. The first high altitude camp was set up at 5,400m on a small, flat section formed by a big crevasse, which luckily was filled with snow. This is where the first group of De Stefani, Colàs, and Gregorio spent the night, planning to proceed the next day to choose a site for Camp 2. However, De Stefani's partners were not suitably acclimatized and it was not until the 25th that Camp 2 was established by De Stefani, Carrel, and Gregorio. During the night Gregorio became ill with AMS and Carrel volunteered to descend with him. Stefani carried on alone, overcoming the ca 400-meter rock barrier leading to the plateau below the West Summit. This was relatively rotten with steps of UIAA IV. Old fixed ropes were still visible. Stefani bivouacked on the plateau (he carried no tent) and experienced "one of the coldest nights of my long mountaineering career." Leaving at 3:30 a.m. he continued over the West and Central tops to reach the Main summit by noon. Amazingly, by 5 p.m. he had returned to Base Camp.

In the next days Carrel, Schenone, and Mrak also reached the summit. By the 10th everyone was back at Qaz-I-Deh.

CARLO ALBERTO PINELLI, *Mountain Wilderness International*

Historical note: Although records are not totally exact, this was approximately the 33rd ascent of Noshaq, a mountain that was first climbed in 1960 by a Japanese expedition via the South Ridge from the Qaz-i-Deh Glacier. The first ascent of the West Ridge, the line subsequently used as the Standard Route of ascent, took place in August 1963, when an Austrian expedition traversed all four main summits, in the process making first ascents of the West and East Tops. This was the route used by Andrzej Zawada's Polish expedition, which during February 1973 made the first winter ascent of any mountain above 7,000m. The last ascent before the Soviet invasion of the country took place in 1978.

Kyrgyzstan

TIEN SHAN

INYLCHEK REGION

Peak Gorky (6,050m), south face, Slovenia Direct. In July-August 2003 the region of famous peaks Pobeda and Khan-Tengri was visited by expedition from Slovenia. Its members were mostly young alpinists, climbing at such heights for the first time: Ales Cesen, Anze and Tine Marence, Darko Podgornik, and Peter Poljanec. The main goal of the expedition was the south face of Peak Gorky (6,050m), which had not been climbed before. The team arrived to Almaty, the former capitol of Kazakhstan by direct flight from Frankfurt, on July 21. On July 25, after transfer to Karkara camp near Kyrgyzstan border (to the east from Issyk-Kul Lake) and 40-minute helicopter flight, the expedition arrived to the base camp located on moraine at 4,100m between peaks Khan-Tengri and Pobeda. About 10 days were spent on acclimatization on nearby peaks (twice up to about 5,300m) and preparation of ABC in a snow cave at 4,750m in the lower part of south face of Peak Gorky. Meanwhile Peter Poljanec had to return home because of a twisted ankle.

Upon arrival to the base camp they noticed that the wall could be climbed following two logical lines: the direct line over the waterfall, which rises over rock level in the upper part of the wall, or over the snow and ice to the right side over the southeast fissure. This direct variant was taken as more beautiful and as a bigger challenge. Two unsuccessful tries followed. First one ended in the ABC camp, and the second one in the direct variant beneath the rock level, 300 meters under the top of the wall, because of the bad conditions (too thin, husk ice) and technical difficulties (they did not have enough equipment to get to the upper part of the wall).

The team did have success on the third try. They arrived to ABC cave in bad weather again, but in the evening a marvelous night with a full moon followed. Visibility was excellent. They started climbing at 11 p.m. Unattached the group progressed quickly and at the sunrise they were already 100 meters beneath the first snowdrift (at the height of 5,800 meters). Over it they discovered an interesting and difficult passage through a kind of snow-ice chimney. Wading in snow up to the waist on a slope followed. The exit over the last snowdrift and they were on the pre-peak Gorky, at around 6,000m. Because of approaching bad weather, they started to descend the south ridge (in the direction of the first-ascent in 1962), but that was hardly possible, with hollow snow up to the waist and snowdrift. Consequently they descended into the southern part of the wall after 200 meters. For some time the night descent took place in catastrophic weather conditions. It grew calmer in the lower part of the wall so they could descend directly into base camp. In the ideal conditions (shadow, good weather) the wall is really calm, but as soon as it starts snowing or the wall is touched by the sun, it comes alive. That is why they climbed the wall mostly at night. You can climb the wall at least over two more beautiful and logical lines: over the line of their first attempt (in better conditions) and the line of their descent.

Slovenija Direkt: climbed in two days (Aug. 11-12, 2003) on the south face of Peak Gorky, by Ales Cesen, Anze and Tine Marence, and Darko Podgornik (1,700m, V-VI, 5, 90°/50-65°). After successful climbing Peak Gorky (by the way named after Maxim Gorky, famous Soviet writer of early XX century) and short rest just enough time was left to try the to scale neighbor Khan-Tengri peak (7,010m) via normal route from South. This time the tour took three days. The first day they started from ABC at 4,200m and reached camp 3 (5,800m) near the West saddle between Khan-Tengri and Chapayev peak (6,371m). The second day they reached the summit (7,010m) and descended back to camp 3. The third day the team returned to the base camp and from there on flew with the helicopter the following day, back to the valley.

GREGOR SIFRER, *www.promontana.si, www.Mountain.RU*

KOKSHAAL-TOO

Borkolday Range, first ascents. The Borkoldoy range is a limestone massif situated north of the Dankova region of the West Kokshaal-Too. Apart from British expeditions in 1995 and 2002, which operated in the northeast and southwest corners of the group, the range is little-explored by mountaineers. In September 2003 an ISM expedition comprising Adrian Nelhams and myself (guides), Tony Allen, James Bruton, Jo da Silva, Steve Kempley, Nigel Kettle, Clive McCafferty, Neil Sutcliffe, and Jane Whitmore (expedition doctor), set up base camp at the head of the Kynar Valley. This long curving valley cuts deeply into the southeast part of the range, and on its south side is the massif dominated by Pik 5,060m, a giant rocky peak taking the form of a narrow crest running north to south.

First reconnaissance was made up the canyons either side of Pik 5,060m, and ABC established on the west side at 4,130m. From here Nelhams, Kettle, Allen & Sutcliffe traversed the fine mixed peak at the top of the canyon (Peak Mars, 4,905m, AD) while Bruton, da Silva, McCafferty, Whitmore, and I climbed the neighboring Peak Virgo (4,744m). Nelhams' team then attempted the fortress-like peak north of Peak Mars, but was stopped by a 50m barrier of steep compact rock near the summit. Bruton, da Silva, and I tried the huge north ridge of Pik 5,060m. We traversed its first summit (Mramorney Cupol [Marble Dome] 4,700m), but an hour beyond this they were stopped by a deep breech which would have been very difficult and time-consuming to cross. This peak remains a major and challenging objective.

The expedition then moved around to more accessible peaks on the north side of the range (two valleys west of the area explored by the 1995 British expedition) and enjoyed more success. Base camp was established in the Chon Tor valley, which divides higher up into two glaciated valleys. The team split and moved up to ABCs high on each glacier. From the east glacier Nelhams, Allen, Kempley, Kettle, and Sutcliffe climbed the southeast ridge of PE Peak (4,740m, PD), the west ridge of Peak Obsorny (4,914m, AD), and the south ridge of Gromovoy (Thunder) Peak (4,840m, PD+). They came close to success on the prominent triple-summited peak forming the east side of the valley, turning back due to avalanche danger. At the head of this glacier a superb snow peak characterized by soaring corniced ridges remains unclimbed.

From the western glacier Bruton, McCafferty, and I, with a second rope of da Silva, Whitmore, and Russian companion Sasha Miyusov, climbed the southwest ridge of Peak Tomos (4,869m, AD), the beautifully symmetrical snow peak that dominates the glacier. Another classic summit—Shutnik (Jester) 4,890m—was climbed by the north spur at PD+. Ascents were made of Scalnya Kiska (4,666m) and a fine rock pillar above ABC: Snezny Chelovek (Snowman) grade V. Finally, everyone with energy left joined Nelhams for the 4,542m peak above base camp, a stunning viewpoint in perfect weather.

PAT LITTLEJOHN, *U.K.*

Borkoldoj and Southern Kokshaal-Too, Pik 5,471 (Mt. Letavet), first ascent; Krylia Sovetov (Wings of the Soviets), second ascent. In the summer of 2003 our group—Mikhail Daineko, Dmitrii Konilov, Mikhail Ageev, Anna Perever-zeva, and myself as leader—visited the ranges of Borkoldoj and Western Kokshaal-Too on the border of Kyrgyzstan and China. Because of international disputes between the USSR and China for many years the region was practically closed and impossible to visit. Only beginning in the 1990s did groups of Russian, American, and European alpinists and tourists start to come to the area. We flew from Moscow to Bishkek. Then, we traveled by jeep along the mountain roads from the southern shore of Issyk-Kul' through several mountain passes to reach the river Naryn, to the border outpost Karasaj. From there we organized our cache into the valley of Uzengikush. Before us, until the Uzengikush valley, lay about 130 km of a difficult mountain road, which for several years had been left in neglect. Automobiles cover this stretch in 6-10 hours.

Visiting Borkoldoj, located to the north of Kokshaal-Too, we prepared to acclimate and to attempt to reach the highest point of the range: the unclimbed peak 5,171. Through several mountain passes (just lower than 5000m) we came out onto the largest glacier of the range Borkoldoj Dzhegolomaj and approached peak 5,171 from the southeast. Peak 5171 from the south-east abruptly ends with a rocky wall. The ascent of the mountain turned out to be more complicated than we had calculated drawing on available cartographic information, and could require three days. Since the fundamental part of the route was planned for Kokshaal-Too, we descended into the Uzengikush Valley to our cache.

We climbed along the Ajtali Glacier to the main range (Kokshaal-Too). Here an unclimbed peak 5,471 is located. Crossing the main ridge from a branch of the Rudnev glacier, located on the southern slopes, along a simple rocky-snowy south-eastern rib (500 meters vertical, steepness up to 40°, 2B) we climbed to the summit. We decided to call the peak Mt. Letavet in honor of the Russian geographer, alpinist, and scientist Avgust Letavet, who organized the first detailed expeditions in region before the Second World War.

In order to accomplish the second ascent of the peak Krylia Sovetov (Wings of the Soviets, 5,560m) (first ascent by E. Monaenkov in 1998; one of the highest points in the Kokshaal-Too range), we continued

View to Pik Letaveta (5,471m) from Nalivkin's glacier. The route follows the left skyline. *Danil Popov*

Krylia Sovetov (Wings of the Soviets) from the north. (1) Efimov and (2) Popov routes merge and follow the skyline ridge over the false summit to the pointy peak on the left. *Danil Popov*

through several mountain passes along the axial line of the main ridge to the glacier Sarychat Eastern. We began the ascent of Mount Wings of the Soviets along the western ridge across peak 5,120 and the false summit 5429. The route is rocky-icy-snowy (5A) and took 4 days. While crossing some of the key parts: circumvention of peak 5,120, ascent of the false summit (5,429) and the summit (5,560), 20 ropes were hung. During our overnight near the false summit a strong wind arose which destroyed the frame of one of the tents. We descended along the northern ridge onto the Pal'gov glacier, from where the approach route of the first-ascent team continued. After this we climbed to the upper reaches of the glacier Grigor'ev and continue by traversing peak Friendship (3A, 5,330 m., first ascent probably was done from the north in the 1960s, and in 1995 the traverse was first done by the group led by O. Chkhetiani), and descended (500 meters, steepness of 45-40°) onto the largest glacier of the Western Kokshaal-Too: the glacier Korzhenevsky. We concluded the expedition after 25 days at the border outpost Karakoz, where an auto collected us and took us to Issyk-Kul'.

Danil Popov, *Russia (translated by Henry Pickford)*

PAMIR-ALAI

KARAVSHIN

Peak October, October Victory. In the Ak-Su Valley three Czech climbers—M. Holecek, D. Stastny, and O. Vasek—established a new route on the northwest face of peak October (3,805m). They called the ascent October Victory, 8+/A4. The route was climbed capsule style in nine days. Furthermore, Czechs Martin Klonfar and Peter Wagenknecht repeated the route Traschinenko (6A/5.10/A2, 1982) on the northwest face of Pik Ak-Su in the Lailak region. The route consisted of 73 pitches, which they climbed in eight days, including the descent.

JAN KREISINGER, *Czech Republic*

Ak Su, north face, new route in winter. Before climbing Ak-Su (5,355m), we already had expedition experience on big walls in winter, which proved very useful. We decided to climb a new route because Balezin had seen the possibility of an interesting variation. The dream turned real. At the beginning of February, we settled at an excellent base tent 6km from the mountain, which became home for a month. On February 3 we started to climb fixing six ropes in two days. The weather was excellent, and on February 7 we started climbing to hang a portaledge. Then Ak-Su showed itself. The wind reached such force that when Evgeniy hauled the portaledge, it was not clear sometimes who was dragging whom: it "hung" ABOVE him.

That day Andrey climbed one pitch and looked like a snowball in glasses. As a result we hung the portaledge at pitch 13. A "white river" fell down the wall and visibility sometimes was no more than a meter. That evening all of us ran away to base camp. The bad weather continued a day longer, and after that we could see Ak-Su in all its magnificence, decorated with fresh snow. By this time we had already climbed 19 pitches and had come to the route's crux: five pitches of A3/A4, 70-80°, with lots of hooking. Reaching this site had taken five days, and now the weather became disgusting: daily snowfall, sometimes with a strong wind, stopped our progress. But our tactics and a good mood allowed us not to waste time during the bad weather; during the entire ascent there was only one day of forced rest. After that we decided to change two-man teams every day, giving ourselves rest after working on the route.

When only one pitch was left to the ledge under the "Nose" (also called "Snot") we decided that it was time to drag up all our gear (10 pitches higher). In the morning Malygin and Litvinov left to fix the ropes, and we hauled our belongings. That day the weather

The joys of winter on Ak Su's north face. *Anton Pugovkin*

tested our durability. The force of the snowfall that day was maximal, and we moved slowly. By 2 p.m. we had made five pitches, and it became clear that we could not reach the ledge before darkness; therefore I decided to hang the portaledge at the beginning of the crux. Finally we got inside after it had already been dark a long time. It was the decisive day of our ascent. That's when our firm confidence appeared: we would make the ascent in any way, sooner or later, because we could climb in such conditions.

Up to the "Nose" we had climbed a new route, but then we went out to Popov's route with an excellent relief. We could make only four pitches in two days. Above, there was a cascade of serious cornices and the overhang. After 5-6 pitches on the "roof," we found a bolt. It meant that Shabalin had descended the Nose somewhere around here. All this time the weather still was disgusting.

Every evening Zaharov encouraged us by radio: "Guys, you have to suffer a day—a change of moon phases will pass." And it was like this all 10 days. We must give due to modern Thinsulate insulation. Then there was our portaledge. Its roof had some patches because of falling stones, and a 1.5-meter hole along its external edge. By the end of the climb the platform looked pitiful: every possible patch and plug, from

The 5,000-foot north face of Ak Su, showing: (1) Kavunenko, 1984; (2) Pugovkin, 2004, (3) Popov, 1986; (4) Moshnikov, 1984; (5) Klenov, 1998; (6) Shabalin, 2002; (7) Shabalin, 1994; (8) Ruchkin, 1997. *Anton Pugovkin*

polyethylene packages and insulating pads, the tubes deformed by a wind. Going down we took only the tubes.

On February 23 the group successfully summited and the weather took pity on us: there wasn't any snowfall for two days, and we could enjoy fantastic views of wintered mountains from the top. It was too pleasant to see the sun, having lived for 10 days on the wall during bad weather. The next day the next snowfall let us know who was boss here. But it did not stop us any more. At 4 p.m. all of us already sat in a cave under a bergschrund, having descended the route.

Thus, for 20 days we managed to lay a new route on the north wall of this tremendous summit. In my opinion, it appeared the logical route in 34 pitches. There were no special technical difficulties on the route, though it is difficult to imagine how we would climb if we did not have anchor hooks and fifi hooks, which allowed to make reliable points on rocks in thin, bottoming cracks [Russian "fifi" hooks are something like giant skyhooks.—Ed]. And, without Evgeniy, who climbed the first 80% of the route as the leader, we would climb much longer. About the weather: in February there are plentiful snowfalls here, but the temperature during the ascent did not fall lower than –25°C. It was usually between –15° and –20°C.

Expedition members: Eugeny Dmitrienko, Dmitry Tsyganov, Sergey Cherezov, Andrey Litvinov, and Pavel Malygin. Reservists and assistants: Jury Glazyrin, V. Saveljev, and Viktor Tsygankov. Doctor: Alexander Kuharev. Trainers and heads: Zaharov Nikolay and Balezin Valery.

ANTON PUGOVKIN, *Russia (translated by Anna Piunova, www.Mountain.RU)*

Ak-Su North, Nose Direct. Due to terrorist activity, the government closed the Laylak Valley in the Pamir-Alai in 2000. Only in 2002 did they reopen the Laylak Ak-Su and the neighboring Karavshin Valley. In 1998, we had repeated the Popov Route on Ak-Su North, and I saw a system of cracks and corners crossing the huge overhangs that characterize the buttress high on the north face. It looked difficult, but possible. Best of all, it was only 50 meters left of our Nose Route (1994), on which we were forced to make holes for skyhooks and use bolts for protection through a 150m blank section. Now, we would try to climb a direct line without the holes!

We started on September 15 from Tashkent with a special permit from the Ministry of Foreign Affairs of Kyrgyzstan and a lot of papers from the Russian Mountaineering Federation. Because of the International Year of the Mountains, the government had been ordered to make the official procedures as easy as possible. However, two border crossings took a lot of time and made us very nervous. On September 20 we started climbing. We were alone in the valley: there were no alpinists, no tourists. Even the Kyrgyz herders had returned home from the summer camps in the upper part of the valley. We were very lucky to have Indian summer conditions. There were no waterfalls as there are in July, and no stone fall like in August; it was a little cold, but safe. In 16 days we opened a direct variation (1,500m, VI 5.9 A5) to the Nose Route, joining the latter route after eight new pitches. On October 5 we reached the top and rappelled down via the Cold Corner route. It was my tenth ascent of this wall, and the most difficult.

PAVEL SHABALIN, *Russia (adapted from Alpinist.com)*

Tajikistan

SOUTH-WESTERN PAMIR

Ishkashimsky and Shakhdarinsky ranges, 280km traverse with several ascents. In August-September our group from the sport club of the Moscow Aviation Institute led an autonomous expedition in the South-Western Pamir. This was the first significant expedition in this region after an 11-year period of civil war and an indefinite political situation in Tajikistan. Our group consisted of myself as leader, secondary leader Sergei Fetisov, Dmitrii Pribylov, Nadezhda Obukhova, Irina Bystrova, and Marina Nikonova participated in the first part of the tour. During 34 working days we covered a 280km linear route that encompassed the Ishkashimsky and Shakhdarinsky ranges. We crossed 15 passes, and ascended the highest points of each of these regions: Peak Mayakovsky 6,096 m, Peak Armed Forces 6,138 m, and Peak Karl Marx 6,723 m.

Two ascents were accomplished by classical routes: the ascent of Peak Mayakovsky from the south, by the route done by V. Budanov in 1947, 3A (icy-snowy); and that of Peak Karl Marx along its western ridge, by the route done by E. Beletsky in 1946, 4B (combined). The ascents of these mountains by Soviet alpinists after the Second World War began and formed the basis of the alpinism of this region. We did the third ascent of Peak of Armed Forces (Vooruzhen-nykh Sil) (6,138 m.) in the central part of the Shakhdarinsky range. This summit was climbed only once, in 1983, by a group led by Sollonikov along a wall route from the south 5B (rock). We led a new route along the north-western slope, 3A (ice-snow).

The linear thread of the route traversed almost the entire South-Western Pamir from the west to the east. The route was divided into two logically complete parts, between which we descended to the Pyandzh River, to the *kishlak* (Central Asian village) Shitkharv, where we'd left a cache of food and fuel before we started our tour. The South-Western Pamir is distinguished by its very severe conditions of acclimatization. The overwhelming majority of passes are higher than 5,000m, and the climate is very dry and hot, and likewise there are marked altitude changes between the passes and the bottoms of the valleys, which can drop to 2,500m.

At the start of our tour we completed first traverses of two of the lowest cols in the western spurs of the Ishkashimsky range, with heights of 4,650m and 4,850m, and only after this did we come out smoothly to an altitude level higher than 5,000m. On the tenth day of our tour we overcame the technically difficult mountain pass Surprise (3A, 5,300m), in the western ridge of Peak Mayakovsky.

Our base camp for the ascent of Peak Mayakovsky was set up on the mountain pass "50 Year Anniversary of LGU" [LGU = Leningrad State University] (5,270m). After the ascent we went down into the picturesque valley of the Daraidarshai River. This is one of the few places where in our age *ovrings* are still used—mountain paths made on steep rock faces, with birch pickets driven into fissures in the rock face, onto which are laid stakes, branches, earth, and stones. Such a path hangs above a 100-meter abyss.

The route to Mount Armed Forces led along the unbelievably beautiful valley of the Saryshitkharv River. Here there are many canyons, the walls of which at places reach half a kilo-meter in height, and many mineral springs. But in the lower part of the valley are located several islands of woods, quite rare for the South-Western Pamir. Our base camp was set up below Mount Armed Forces on the Saryshitkharv glacier, at 5,300m. We reached the summit on August 22.

Crossing two moderately difficult icy passes—Medyr 5,703, in the northern rib/edge of Peak Armed Forces; and Ratseka 5,850, between Peak Luknitsky and Peak Chibud—we came out at lake Zardiv. This place is the pearl of the Shakhdarinsky range, and in my opinion one of the most beautiful places in the Pamir. If you look from the northern edge of the lake, then it appears that the mighty walls of the summits are rising straight out of the lake. The change in elevation is about two kilometers. We approached the mountainous knot of Peak Karl Marx via four passes: Yamchun 5,340 (ancient caravan route from the valley of Shakhdara to Pyandzh), Dzhentiv 5,130, Tsakhinlovga 4,523, and Khodash 5,140m. In order to get to the plateau of Marx, in the upper reaches of the Nishgar glacier, we had to surmount two difficult passes in the southern spurs of the Shakhdarinsky range: Riga 5,620 and Oval'ny 5,740. From the plateau of Marx (5,550 m. base camp), we began our ascent of Peak Karl Marx, which we summated on September 3. The final mountain pass on our route was the Nishgar pass 3A 5,750—the descent from the plateau of Marx towards the north. We crossed over icefall of the Khatsak glacier, in the end we saw the two-kilometer walls of the peaks Karl Marx and Engels. The next day the poor weather caught up with us and the peaks were hidden in leaden-colored clouds.

PETR RYKALOV, *Russia (translated by Henry Pickford)*

Pakistan

Pakistan, 2003 overview. Approximately 54 expeditions took up permits for peaks over 6,500m. Mountains below this altitude are now exempt from royalty fees, though not from trekking and Sirdar fees for those situated in restricted areas. Despite this, 85 percent of the expeditions went to the Baltoro and 75 percent attempted 8,000m peaks. At the Ministry of Tourism the Secretary for Mountaineering appears motivated to improve services for climbers and in 2004 peak fees will remain 50 percent of the normal rate. Expeditions (to the Baltoro 8,000ers in particular) are now being allowed up to three permits.

2004 coincides with the Golden Jubilee of the first ascent of K2, and it is expected that the number of climbers and trekkers will substantially increase over 2002 and 2003 levels. However, there is still a serious terrorism threat in the North West Frontier. For the Baltoro there will be increased pollution problems, damage to the delicate environment, problems with porters, and of course increasing costs. Pakistan is now the cheapest country in which to climb an 8,000m peak, but the future of climbing there is limited if the concentration continues to center almost exclusively on the Baltoro and 8,000m peaks. To this end it is reported that the Ministry is considering the latest UIAA proposal (backed by some of the major local tour operators) to remove royalty fees to mountains below 7,000m in non-restricted areas. It is also promising to be more helpful to climbers by replying quickly to inquiries and remaining open for briefing six days a week.

LINDSAY GRIFFIN, *U.K.*

Pakistan, the implementation of more normal relationships with India. As India and Pakistan strive toward more normal relationships, the following measures have been agreed by both countries:

1. Opening of bus services between Delhi and Lahore.
2. Resumption of air flights from January 1, 2004.
3. Resumption of train services from two border points, Wagah and Kokhrapar, and the possibility of resuming shipping between Karachi and Bombay.
4. Resumption of diplomatic links at High Commission level and expansion of embassy staff.
5. Resumption of trade relations.
6. On Pakistan's initiative, guns have been silenced on the LOC in Kashmir and there is a cease fire in operation all along the Kashmir front up to the Siachen Glacier.
7. A delegation from the European Parliament (including Reinhold Messner) is visiting Pakistan to inspect the situation in Kashmir. Subsequently it will also visit the Indian occupied Kashmir. These efforts are encouraging for peace in this region.
8. On top of this the Indian Prime Minister decided to attend the SAARC conference

to be held in Islamabad in January 2004. The Indian PM has expressed his readiness to meet his Pakistani counterparts.

These measures have ended the political tension between the two countries and greatly improved the climate of peace in the region. Internally, the government has put a complete ban on religious extremist groups, closed their offices in Pakistan, and frozen their funds in Pakistani banks. Meanwhile, British Airways, in expectation of increased travel to Pakistan from the U.K. and Europe, resumed its London-Islamabad flights from December 1, 2003.

NAZIR SABIR, *Pakistan*

WEST HIMALAYA

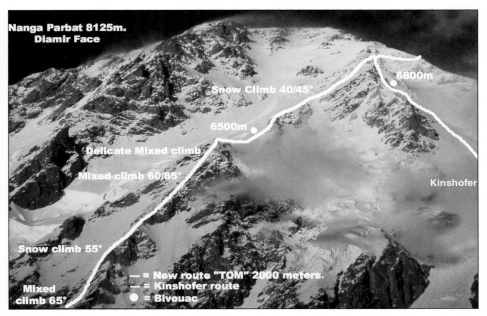

The Diamir Face of Nanga Parbat, showing the 2003 route "Tom" on the left, and the Kinshofer Route on the right. The summit, still a long way off, is not visible in this photo. *Jean Christophe Lafaille*

Nanga Parbat (8,126m), new route on Diamir Face. Of the five expeditions to Nanga Parbat, only two were successful and a total of 14 climbers reached the summit, bringing the total number of ascents of the mountain to 216 from 1953 up to its Golden Jubilee year. However, the Diamir Face of the peak proved the venue for the only new route on a very high mountain in Pakistan during 2003.

Jean Christophe Lafaille reached the 4,100m base camp below the face on June 5, a little later than other members of his team. Almost immediately he set off for the standard Kinshofer Route with Ed Viesturs, climbing up to Camp 2 at 6,100m, where they erected a tent. Bad weather drove them down, and the next time they regained the camp Lafaille was ill with suspected giardia and had to be escorted down by Viesturs. He recovered quickly on antibiotics and on

Simone Moro coming up the Tom Route on Nanga Parbat.
Jean Christophe Lafaille

June 16 was able to carry equipment to Camp 3 at ca 6,800m. However, before leaving for Pakistan, Lafaille had already made a photographic study of the broad buttress/spur to the left of the Kinshofer line and, disenchanted with the copious amount of fixed rope on the Standard Route, decided to investigate further. The Italian, Simone Moro, also had the same idea and the two paired for an alpine style ascent. The line lies parallel to, left of, but close to the 1978 Slovak Route (Belica/Just /Zatko/Zatko), which climbs the west face of Nanga Parbat North I. It finishes on easy ground at around 7,100m, with the continuation of the Kinshofer just to the right. The plan was to time their ascent so as to meet Viesturs at Camp 3 and continue with him to the summit.

At 11 p.m. the two left Camp 1 at 4,900m and an hour later were starting up the glacier. Once they were on the spur they unroped and climbed at their own pace up an ever steepening and narrowing couloir. The snow conditions were excellent. Around daybreak and close to the top of the first icefield, a route finding error cost them some time. Above, an icy couloir and snow covered slabs forced them to rope. The second ice field was climbed unroped and led to more mixed ground close to the top of the spur. Another delicate passage required the rope, after which they reached a horizontal arête at the top of the spur. The snow was now getting deeper and in worse condition as temperatures rose in the sun. At one stage the pair were optimistic about reaching the Kinshofer Route the same day but eventually decided to bivouac at ca 6,800m. This proved a wise decision as they were later hit by a sudden afternoon storm.

Next morning 45-50° slopes led up to the junction with the Kinshofer, from where they descended several hundred meters to join a waiting Viesturs at Camp 3. The new variation was in the bag but the summit still some distance off. On the 22nd all three set off for Camp 4 at 7,400m, already installed by the Kazakh members of the team who had summited earlier (Denis Urubko, the first to summit on the 17th, reportedly made the top in the amazingly fast time of three-and-a-half hours from camp). Moro, not happy with his acclimatization, decided to return before reaching camp. He went all the way back to base, hoping to make another attempt later. Unfortunately, when he did so he was thwarted by very strong winds.

That afternoon it snowed once more but the next day dawned cold and clear. By 11:45 a.m., after a grueling seven-hour climb through deep and unstable powder, both Lafaille and Viesturs were standing on the summit; 44-year-old Viesturs later remarking that it was one of the most physically challenging days of his career.

After a second night at Camp 4 both climbers descended to base camp on the 24th, and the following day Lafaille was already on his way out for a new adventure. The new line was named "Tom and Martina" after both Lafaille's and Moro's children.

This success, not long after Dhaulagiri, the summit of which he reached, alone, on May 20, was doubly impressive, as in January 37-year-old Lafaille had sustained a broken collar bone and a blow to the head, which resulted in partial amnesia, after taking a 20-meter fall from an ice pitch in Vail, Colorado. He was stopped from hitting the ground by the only ice screw placed below.

Lafaille went on to climb the main summit of Broad Peak with Viesturs on July 15, thereby completing a hat trick of 8,000m peaks in less than two months. However, his success on Broad Peak could well have ended tragically and is another interesting example of how even after nearly three months at high altitudes, an excellent acclimatization, and on the third 8,000m peak of the season, high altitude mountain sickness can still strike those making a rapid ascent. Lafaille arrived at base camp on July 11 and was on the summit just four days later. On the descent he contracted pulmonary edema and although he managed to get himself back to the top camp, from there he had to be assisted down the mountain by other climbers, who were fortunately in camp at the time

LINDSAY GRIFFIN, *U.K.*

Nanga Parbat (8,126m), Rupal Face, new route attempt. The Slovenian, Tomaz Humar, was hoping to make an audacious solo ascent of a new route on the huge Rupal Face. From the beginning of July he made several attempts to acclimatize on the 1970 South East Pillar (aka Messner Route) with other climbers on his team but each time poor weather and conditions prevented him gaining much height. In the third week of July he made a fourth attempt on the almost 5,000m-high route with Croatian, Stipe Bozic. They camped above 6,000m. From there Humar set out solo to climb to 7,000m and return. However, at around 6,500m he gave up in the warm temperatures and deep unstable snow that had characterized conditions throughout his stay. As there was simply no chance that the face would improve, the team went home.

LINDSAY GRIFFIN, *U.K.*

KARAKORAM

RAKAPOSHI RANGE

Malubiting Central (7,260m), second ascent. On July 25 two Spanish climbers, Raúl Magdaleno and Álvaro Novellón, made the second ascent of Malubiting Central. The Malubiting group is a complex of high and rarely visited summits on the watershed ridge west of Spantik and the only previous ascent of the Central Summit was on August 2 1975, when it was climbed by Japanese, Hedeke Atsumi, Kazuhiko Moro, Masahide Onodera, and Toshinori Takahashi. They made four camps and finished up the west face from the upper Barpu Plateau to the summit. The Spanish more or less followed the Japanese route (and the line taken by the 1997 Swiss expedition that made the second ascent of the neighboring—and higher—west top).

Last summer's four-man Spanish expedition, led by Óscar Casero Vidal, approached via the traditional route, placed Camp I at 5,380m and fixed 300 meters of rope on the ice face below the Polan La. This proved a little dangerous and avalanche prone, with slopes between

45-60°. Camp 2 was placed on the La at around 5,840m. They then tried to get through a rock wall above but found their choice of line too threatened by seracs. At this stage one member had run out of time and was forced to descend. He was accompanied by a second member leaving only Magdaleno and Novellón to make a further attempt. This time the pair tackled the wall more directly with 100 meters of difficult climbing. Then, after camping out twice more (Camp 3 under a serac at 6,100m and Camp 4 at 6,400m on a small plateau), they reached the summit at 1:30 p.m., three days after setting out from Camp 2.

LINDSAY GRIFFIN, *U.K.*

HISPAR MUZTAGH

Khunyang Chhish (7,852m), west ridge attempt and Pt. 6,100m. Locals say Khunyang Chhish means "the corner peak." In 1892 Martin Conway wrote about Khunyang Chhish and in 1908 Workman published a photo of it in the book *The Call of the Snowy Hispar.* A joint Pakistani-British expedition led by E.J.E. Mills in 1962 was the first to attempt Khunyang Chhish. In 1965 a Japanese team led by Shiroki tried the south ridge. In 1971 a Polish expedition made the first ascent of the south ridge (Andrzej Heinrich, Jan Stryczynski, Ryszard Szafirski, and Andrzej Zawada). In 1979 a Japanese team led by Echizenya made the first ascent of the North Peak (7,200m). In 1980 and 1981 British teams attempted the northwest spur to north ridge, reaching 6,900m. In 1988 a British team led by Andrew Wingfield made the second ascent via the northwest spur to the north ridge.

I have been interested in Khunyang Chhish for a long time. When I was at K2 Base camp as the leader of 1985 Japanese expedition, I met the late Andrzej Zawada, leader of the 1971 Polish Khunyang Chhish expedition and the first to summit. Since then, I dreamed of climbing Khunyang Chhish some day. In 1994, after I climbed Muztagh Ata, I visited Pakistan to research routes on Khunyang Chhish. In 1995, 1996, 1999, and 2002 I made subsequent visits to the area and made several attempts. In 2003 a group of climbers approached me about trying Khunyang Chhish yet a fourth time. After getting acclimatized on Rashphari Peak (5,058m), we left Hispar and stayed at Furoling Chhish the following day. With 78 porters we reached our base camp (4,200m) on May 30.

We began climbing on June 1 and checked the foot of the complicated west ridge. In the first week we climbed a total of 23 pitches of mixed ice, snow, and rock. We returned to base camp because of snowfall and strong wind. Days later, after the weather cleared, we reached a broad snow shoulder after resorting to aid climbing to pass a difficult rock section. More bad weather allowed only 11 pitches to be climbed over the next few days.

C1 was established on June 21 and over the next week we climbed 21 more pitches. Part of the team reached the end of the snow ridge. From here we checked the route ahead. The descent to a col seemed very risky because of avalanche, so on June 29 we descended once more to base camp. The route became very dangerous due to melting snow and ice, and there was much rockfall that damaged our ropes.

On June 30 we had a meeting to decide on a plan for the final push. The route to the 7,350m West Peak of Khunyang Chhish didn't appear to be too difficult for us but our supplies were running low. We decided to climb only the 6,100m snow peak on the ridge, which no one had climbed before. On July 3 Kazuya Hiraide (who has skied from the top of Cho Oyu),

Takeshi Yamakawa, and HAP Shaheen Baig reached the summit of the snow peak. On July 4 Tosio Sakairi, Masakatsu Tamura, Kazuo Tobita, and HAP Muhammad Hussain also reached the summit. On July 9 we left base camp in the rain.

KAZUO TOBITA, *Japanese Alpine Club*

Khunyang Chhish East (ca7,400m), southwest face attempt. The Polish Khunyang Chhish East Expedition comprised Janusz Golab, Stanislaw Piecuch, and myself, Grzegorz Skorek. On July 31 we started our first acclimatization climb on the 6,500m Ice Cake Peak (on the south ridge of Khunyang Chhish). We spent the night at 6,200m. Next day we climbed to 6,300m and descended to the base camp. The weather was very hot and even at 6,300m we only needed to wear polar T-shirts. The snow was very heavy and the climb was very hard work. On August 5 we made a second acclimatization climb and reached the summit of Ice Cake. We spent a night on the top. This time the climbing was easier and faster. We

The Polish attempt on the southwest face of Khunyang Chhish East. *Grzegorz Skorek*

decided that after a few days rest we will start climbing our main objective, Khunyang Chhish East via the 2,500m, beautiful and steep southwest wall.

Unfortunately, the day we decided to start up the face the weather changed for the worse and stayed bad to August 15. After 10 days of rain and snow the weather improved and we decided to make a "last chance attempt." We started late in the afternoon because of avalanche danger and high temperatures, which precluded climbing on lower, icy part of the wall during the day. We climbed from 5 p.m. (on the 15th) to 4 a.m. (on the 16th). We climbed over 1,000 meters up the ice field (70° maximum). In order to climb faster we did not belay. We cut out a snow ledge at 4 a.m. and made a 1-1/2 hour bivouac. At 5:30 a.m. we started climbing again. We had to force a steep mixed section. I led very hard pitch (M7) but it was on very thin ice and completely without proper protection. Consequently, it took me 2-1/2 hours. Next pitch was much easier but I climbed only 30 meters because of the snow. It was terrible. We were now at an attitude of ca 6,000m and we couldn't climb because of the sun. The snow was too heavy to make even three or four steps. We had to wait until 5 p.m. to resume climbing again at night. This time the terrain was harder and we had to belay. The climbing became slower. We made our next bivouac at 6,300m.

Next day we started climbing early in the morning and reached an altitude of 6,700m by the afternoon. However, it was still too warm. The snow was heavy and we were now very tired after two nights of climbing. At 6,700m we made our third bivouac. Next morning the weather changed for the worse once again and we decided to go down. It wasn't easy because we had only 25 hooks and 10 ice screws. We had to rappel from one-hook belays. Fortunately, we reached the bottom of the wall without any falls.

Next morning we reached base camp. Our decision to retreat was correct as by now it was beginning to snow heavily. Soon there was over half-a-meter of fresh snow and this was the first time during our expedition that it had snowed in base camp.

In our opinion the south west face of Khunyang Chhish East is as big and hard as, for example, the north face of Jannu in Nepal. It is really one of the Karakoram's great climbing challenges.

GRZEGORZ SKOREK, *Poland*

Pumari Chhish South (7,350m), attempt on south face. Two French climbers were among the first to visit the range last year, making a couple of very spirited attempts to climb the south face of the virgin Pumari Chhish South (7,350m). Yannick Graziani and Christian Trommsdorff moved up the Hispar Glacier at the beginning of May and in winter conditions inspected various side glaciers to the north. They eventually opted to established a base camp at 4,500m on the Yutmaru Glacier and from there attempt a unnamed 6,181m peak south west of Kanjut Sar (and a little to the north of the impressive and virgin 6,400m Hispar Sar). During the third week in May the pair reached 5,400m on the elegant west ridge but was prevented from continuing further by windslab.

They then moved camp to the Pumari Glacier and attempted a 600-meter couloir leading up to the unclimbed south ridge of Khunyang Chhish East. Although the weather was fine, after a bivouac at 5,900m the pair realized that to continue in alpine style was impractical with their insufficient level of acclimatization, so they descended.

They now returned to the Yutmaru Glacier and attempted a new route on the flanks of Kanjut Sar (7,760m). The pair climbed a short distance up the south face of 7,330m Yutmaru Sar and then broke out right to a southwest facing spur leading up to an unnamed summit of ca 6,200m near the start of the long west-northwest ridge of Kanjut Sar. Climbing to a bivouac on this spur at around 5,800m they were again defeated by dangerous snow conditions and while retreating set off a huge windslab avalanche.

Still not happy with their depth of acclimatization, they decided nevertheless to make an attempt on the south face of Pumari Chhish, following the line attempted twice previously, in 1999 and 2000, by the New Zealand–British couple, Julie Ann Clyma and Roger Payne. This pair had opted for a leftward slanting, snow-covered ramp line, leading up to the crest of the southwest ridge. On both attempts from the West Yutmaru Glacier, they were driven back by bad weather, the first from 6,200m approximately one third of the way up the ramp and the second from only 5,300m.

Graziani and Trommsdorff climbed for 14 hours on the first day to a bivouac on the arête bordering the ramp at 6,100m. Next day two hours took them to the top of the ramp, where they then had to embark on the crux of the climb, 700 meters of rock and mixed climbing to reach the summit ridge. Three difficult mixed pitches took them to a small snow patch, above which they needed to aid up an overhanging 25-meter-high dihedral. There followed some fine mixed pitches before they were forced to construct a very bad bivouac at 6,750m. The weather turned, spindrift swamped them all night, and the next day there was no option but to go down.

After a week at base camp the pair set off again on the June 14 and after three days had climbed past their high point via more excellent mixed terrain to reach an altitude of 6,900m, a point they estimated to be just two pitches below the ridge. To that point they had climbed ca 2,300m with 60° snow, 90° ice, mixed climbing at M6, rock to French 6a and a vertical 20-meter pitch of A2, all on excellent granite. Then it began to snow. On the way down, at around 6,500m, they witnessed the huge seracs, which threaten the lower section of the face, explode. The resulting avalanche wiped the approach clean, filling the valley below with an enormous cloud and even affecting base camp some four kilometers distant. The two promptly descended and went home.

LINDSAY GRIFFIN, *U.K.*

Peak 6,920m, first ascent. A four-man Russian team comprising Valeri Bagov, Ivan Dusharin, Viktor Kolesnichenko, and (Russian-American) Lev Yoffe, made the first ascent of the unnamed Pk 6,920m, which lies on or close to the watershed ridge between Pumari Chhish and Yutmaru Sar. The expedition approached up the Hispar Glacier and then turned north for a few hours up the Yutmaru Glacier to establish base camp on the east side. A huge ca1,500-meter tall icefall blocks access to the Upper Yutmaru at around 6,000m and this had to be gained by a rather dangerous route to a flanking ridge. Placing two camps (5,600m and 6,300m), the team reached a point where it was possible to gain the upper glacier safely, but with a descent of close on 600m. They had hoped to be able to reach the top section of the upper Yazghil Glacier to the north of the divide and from then try either the unclimbed South Summit of Pumari Chhish (7,350m) to their west or Yutmaru Sar (7,330m) to their east. The latter has only been climbed once. In July 1980 a small Japanese party followed a similar route to that tried by the Russians last summer, first reaching the Upper Yutmaru Glacier, then ascending this to the west ridge of Yutmaru Sar, after which they crossed the top section of the Upper Yazghil Glacier and finally finished up the north ridge.

Unfortunately, the Russians decided at this point the amount of time left available to them was not enough to succeed with either project. Instead, they continued up the sharp ridge to a nameless summit of 6,920m (determined by GPS readings) and then withdrew to base camp. An application has been made to the Ministry of Tourism to call this peak United Russia.

LINDSAY GRIFFIN, *U.K.*

PANMAH MUZTAGH

Latok V (6,190m), attempt. The Japanese climber Moromu Omiya returned for his third attempt on the unclimbed 6,190m summit of Latok V. Omiya, who made the first ascent of Latok IV in 1980, attempted this small peak in both 1999 and 2000 via the south face. Last summer with two other companions he again tried the mountain but on the summit day was forced to give up just 70 meters below the top when it simply became too late to continue safely. The peak lies at the end of the southeast ridge of Latok III.

LINDSAY GRIFFIN, *U.K.*

Great Trango (6,257m), northwest face attempt. Four mountaineers from the Ukraine, Alexander Lavrinenko, Vladimir Mogila, Vitali Yarichveski, and Alexey Zhilin planned to try a new route up the huge northwest face of Great Trango left of the existing lines. In 1999 three routes were established on the previously virgin, almost 2,000m-high northwest face and since that time the wall has remained unvisited.

The climbers from the Ukraine reached base camp on July 2 and were on the route a week later. Their chosen line climbed slabby ground to reach the center of the prominent pillar left of the snow patch at ca 5,000m, a little below half-height on the face. From the top of this pillar they would slant up left across compact slabs to reach the edge of the hanging glacier and then up the relatively short headwall to the summit. The team first fixed seven pitches, then waited out bad weather at base camp before starting up the wall in capsule style. From this point it took around 20 days to reach their high point. Unfortunately a surprising lack of features and very dirty cracks, even on the more slabby ground, meant that only one third of the route could be free climbed. The headwall was covered in ice and had to be aided in shade temperatures of around –5°C. However, the line proved very sheltered from objective danger and although each belay features one bolt anchor, only a further 12 were placed on route. Because the route took much longer than expected, the climbers were forced to abandon their attempt an estimated 2-1/2 pitches (approximately 100 vertical meters) below the summit when all their food and fuel had been used. The route was rappelled in 2-1/2 days of rain and base camp regained on August 4. The team had made nine portaledge camps and climbed 46 pitches before descending on August 2, rating the difficulties as VI 5.11 A4 and likening the climbing to that found in the Karavashin region of Kyrghyzstan, only on a much bigger scale.

LINDSAY GRIFFIN, *U.K.*

Trango Tower (6,251m), almost-free ascent of Eternal Flame. This spring, Toni met Kurt Albert, who told him about his route, Eternal Flame, on the south face of Trango Tower and the possibility of free climbing it. The result was that three months later Toni, Nicolas, and I were in the Big Wall Valley of Eden that is Trango. On July 23 we reached base camp on the Trango glacier at 4,000m. Some expeditions had nearly finished. The tower was exactly like we dreamed, and our motivation began to increase.

From July 24 to 28 we carried all our gear to the base of the route. We also started to experience altitude sickness, so we realized we must take time to acclimatize. After two days, one day to climb, one to haul all our gear (120kg), we established Camp 2 on the shoulder at 5,400m. The next two days we climbed 14 pitches of Eternal Flame. The route is almost entirely a hand or finger crack. The cracks were nearly free from ice and the temperature was quite agreeable. To describe the climb: take all your best granite climbing and put it on one route. It's incredible; perfect and clean. We fixed ropes (ca 500 meters) as far as two hard pitches, then had to wait for four days of poor weather to clear before we could climb again. The temperature was now very cold but by the afternoon of August 7 we reached the summit. It was the first time any of us has visited the Himalaya/Karakoram and we stayed for an hour, dreaming in front of the giant peaks; K2, Broad Peak, G1, and G4.

After a rest day we went back up the route in poor weather to look at the two famous crux pitches. On our previous summit day we had climbed these two pitches using aid and they seemed very thin and blind. We tried the moves and—oh!, what a surprise—it's possible to climb them free. Unfortunately, we had to wait as it snowed everyday and the wall turned white. On the 13th we tried to climb, once more jumaring back up 500 meters of rope. The weather was snowy and windy, and made it almost impossible to climb such difficult moves; the shoes don't adhere, and the hands….

August 14 had to be our last day on the wall. The porters would arrive the following day and we had to take down all our gear. Although the weather was very unstable, it was at least a bit warmer. High on the face the rock was dry. I tried the 16th pitch first and it went at 7c (5.12d). Then the snow started to fall so I spent my first attempt on the 15th pitch finding new holds that would be good enough to use in the prevailing weather. My motivation was at its maximum; it was now or never. My last try was a good one (7c/7c+, 5.13a) and the pitch was now free.

With the weather conditions as they were, we needed 17 days on the wall to make an almost free ascent of the route. There still remains one aid pitch on a blank wall to challenge future parties. But this was a wonderful climb and my congratulations to the first ascensionists. [Editor's note: the team did not free climb pitch 10, which has a 15-meter section of blank granite with a bolt ladder. It appears to be unclimbable without aid, though the Swiss believe it might be possible to bypass this section via a two-pitch variation to the right.]

Eternal Flame (1,000m, 7b+ and A2, Albert-Güllich-Stiegler-Sykora, 1989). An almost free ascent was made by Denis Burdet and Nicolas Zambetti, both of Switzerland, and Toni Arbones of Spain. Access to The Shoulder via the Slovenian Route [Note: this avoids the original start climbed by the Germans, which requires an approach up a dangerously stone-swept couloir above the Dunge Glacier] gave nine pitches to 7a+ (5.12a). Eternal Flame above the Shoulder gave 22 pitches, 7c/7c+ (5.13a) max with one bolt ladder. The climbing was sustained 7a (5.12a) to 7b (5.12c) on 16 pitches and the two crux free pitches (15 and 16) are above 6,000m. The total length was 31 pitches.

DENIS BURDET, *Switzerland*

Trango Tower (6,251m), alpine style ascent of Eternal Flame (though not to summit). In early July Eternal Flame also received a very spirited attempt to free climb it by the French couple, Antoine and Sandrine de Choudens. This pair wanted to climb the whole route alpine style and for that needed prior acclimatization. To achieve this they walked in via the Hushe Valley, crossed the Gondorkoro La (5,650m) and reached Concordia in five days from the road at Hushe. Two more days were needed to reach base

Eternal Flame on the Trango Tower looms above. *Denis Burdet*

camp at 4,000m on the Trango Glacier. On July 14, two days after arriving at base, they spent six hours reaching the foot of the tower via the standard approach couloir, then climbed and fixed two pitches (7a+) of the Slovenian Route. On the 15th they climbed 10 pitches to the Shoulder and set up camp, fixing the first three pitches of Eternal Flame (7a+) before retiring for the night. The pair started next day at 3:30 a.m. jumaring the ropes then carrying on up a series of excellent cracks. The route continued to be steep and sustained and by midday the clouds were rolling in. At this stage their arms were so tired that aiding the remaining pitches became the only option. They eventually reached the junction with the original 1976 British Route just 80 meters below the top, but by this time night was fast approaching and it had begun to snow. Turning their backs on the easy mixed ground above, they reluctantly decided to go down, reaching their tent on the Shoulder at 11 p.m.

Next day was sunny and, exhausted from their previous efforts, the pair descended to base camp. Apart from the bolt ladder on pitch 10, it is thought that Antoine free climbed the route as far as pitch 20, after which he aided to the top. Tragically, this very accomplished climber (see his feature article in *AAJ* 2003), with many first ascents around the world including Everest without oxygen, was killed in Tibet the following autumn.

From information provided by the late Antoine de Choudens, France

Point 4,400m above the Trango Glacier, first ascent (Sadu). A few days after their climb on Eternal Flame, Antoine and Sandrine de Choudens set off on July 20 for what they hoped would prove a pleasant rock climb on one of the small buttresses above the Trango Glacier. Ten minutes walk from base camp placed them at the bottom of a pointed tower. Starting up the left side of the southwest face, they climbed for 350 meters (seven pitches) to a small subsidiary summit at ca 4,400m. Unfortunately, the cracks were not particularly good and the granite rather gravely, leading to some serious runouts. They reached the small top toward the end of the afternoon and rappelled a couloir on the right side of the face. The first three pitches of the route, named Sadu, were 6b, 6a, and 6c respectively, after which the standard eased a little, rising again to 6b on the final pitch. A few days later they had walked out via the Baltoro to Skardu. According to the Swiss climbers mentioned above, Antoine de Choudens did not think this was a recommendable route.

From information provided by the late Antoine de Choudens, France

MASHERBRUM RANGE

Masherbrum attempt, Charakusa Valley exploration, Haji Brakk first ascent. With Slovenians, Marko Prezelj and Matic Jost, I arrived at base camp below Masherbrum (7,855m) on May 31, after experiencing a difficult approach due to winter snow. We put our camp on the Mandu Glacier at approximately 4,200m. Unfortunately, we eventually realized that to access Masherbrum's North Ridge we first had to get to the Yermanendu Glacier, even though our decision to site base camp on the Mandu was well-researched through discussions with the leader of a previous expedition to the mountain (R. Renzler, Austrian Expedition 1985). Due to different glacier conditions and an abundance of snow, we were to cross a small pass above base camp many times to get to and from the Yermanendu Glacier.

A view of the Charakusa region from Haji Brakk. The arrow points up the 5.11 Anker-Croft 1998 route on Spansar Peak, which follows the obvious sharp ridge until the down-arrow rappels. X marks known-climbed summits. The highest peak on the right is Chogolisa. Masherbrum is just left of this view (see House feature article in this Journal for that view). *Steve House*

A few days after we arrived, Marko and I climbed a small 5,000m peak near base camp. Here we triggered a 30-40cm slab that ran down a steep couloir for ca 600 meters. We had been expecting a summer snow pack, but it turns out we were dealing with something different. Our next acclimatization foray was to ca 5,880m to the northwest of Biachedi, where we slept for two nights. Matic and I didn't feel too well, but Marko continued upward, only to be forced back from 6,000m due to poor conditions. We descended to base camp in a blustery storm.

It was now time to inspect the north ridge. Above the col a snowy crest led to the start of the ridge itself. While breaking trail, I triggered another slide, which hit Prezelj below and swept him 80 meters down the slope. Fortunately, he was unscathed, but for the rest of the trip all snow climbing was belayed. Later the same day Prezelj triggered another slab, this time 30cm deep. He was able to run on top of it until it broke up and slid away below. The following day we arrived at a nasty avalanche-prone slope that we were simply not prepared to cross, and at that point any attempt on Masherbrum was abandoned until conditions improved. Sadly, during the next three weeks conditions failed to change.

The trek out proved to be mostly pleasant, as we took three extra days and explored the Charakusa and the Nangma Valleys, which promise fantastic climbing venues for future trips. When the Slovenians left, I made a solo expedition back to the Charakusa. This valley is home to K7 (one ascent, by Japanese in 1984) and K6 (7,246m), and the soon-to-be-famous rock towers of Fati Brakk, Farhoud Brakk, and Spanser Brakk. Spanser Brakk was the site of Croft and Anker's 56-pitch, 5.11a ridge climb about four years ago. [For a photo see House's feature article in this Journal.]

On July 31 I climbed a new route on an unnamed and unclimbed peak that I called Haji Brakk after my good friend and cook, Ghulam Rasool, who became Haji this past year. Haji is the title given to those Muslims who have made the pilgrimage to the Muslim holy sites in Mecca and Medina. My trekking permit required a cook/guide, and allowed me to climb any peaks up to 6,500m. Haji Brakk is approximately 5,985m according to my altimeter watch. I climbed a broad ice face leading to an ice-choked chimney system. I self-belayed a total of five pitches. The chimneys gave sustained climbing up to mixed 5.9. The pitches on the summit tower were 5.7 and 5.6 on beautiful alpine granite. The route (measured from bergschrund to summit) was 1,200m, and I ascended and descended the line in 19 hours.

I saw just one westerner the entire time (an American trekker). This valley is the most amazing alpine area I have ever seen. Those climbers who have been here tend to return (e.g. Conrad Anker, who did his first trip with Rowell and Croft, and then another with Robinson and Chin). The variety of objectives is unmatched. From rock towers to super-alpine objectives, there is something for everyone. Plus most of the peaks are under 6,500m, which means no permit fee and no liaison officer. As the valley is just a two-day walk from the end of the road, this is a very affordable Karakoram expedition. These climbs are further described in an article earlier in this Journal. I would like to thank the Mugs Stump Award for financial assistance on this trip.

Steve House, *AAC*

Baltoro Muztagh

Gasherbrum IV (7,980m), attempt at west face. Andrew Lindblade and Athol Whimp made two attempts on Gasherbrum IV. Their main aim was the second ascent of the celebrated 1985 Route on the 2,500m west face climbed by Voytek Kurtyka and Robert Schauer, a climb that many people acknowledge to be one of the greatest alpine style ascents ever made in the Greater Ranges. Lindblade and Whimp were plagued by the bad weather that affected everyone in the region. On their main attempt they had one clear day, during which they climbed the initial couloir, but then the weather broke and there was heavy snowfall. Life became a survival issue as they waited inside their small tent. At one point it cleared and they managed to get a little higher on the very loose mixed ground of the main face. However, they were constantly battered by snow, wind, and spindrift slides, and when they eventually ran out of food and gas, having reached a height of ca 6,800m, there was no option but to go down. Another attempt, this time on the northwest ridge (first ascended in June 1986 by Greg Child, Tom Hargis, and Tim Macartney-Snape), was again thwarted by bad weather at around half-height.

Lindsay Griffin, *U.K.*

India

Ladakh
East Karakoram
Lahaul & Spiti
Pakistan
Himachal Pradesh
Kumaun & Garwal
Delhi
Nepal
Sikkim

India

Overview of foreign expeditions. Around 35 expeditions from various countries visited the Indian Himalaya during 2003. This was perhaps the smallest number of visiting teams in the last few years. Many expeditions cancelled after the threat of the SARS epidemic in Asia and the war in Iraq. Out of these 35 or so, around 20 teams attempted routine ascents of standard peaks that are nowadays considered commercial expedition targets, such as Satopanth, west ridge of Shivling, Kun, Stok Kangri, and Dzo Jungo (the last two named were climbed by 11 expeditions). Satopanth (7,075m), the highest of the Gangotri peaks, received its first French ascent by Pierre Malherbe and Jean-Noël Urban, who climbed to the summit in nine hours from their 6,000m camp. Forty-four-year old Urban then made the first ski descent of the mountain, removing his skis only for one section of narrow icy ridge.

Jammu and Kashmir received only three expeditions, but the Gangotri area remained as popular as ever, with 15 teams attempting different peaks. The most popular objective was, surprisingly, Thalay Sagar, with five expeditions, but Bhagirathi III and Shivling were also attempted by three teams each. The success rate was rather poor, many teams being thwarted by the bad weather that characterized both pre and post monsoon seasons.

Bureaucratic restrictions near and around the Nanda Devi Sanctuary created problems for various climbing teams. When these teams with permission from Delhi reached their starting points, some of them had to travel back to Dehra Dun, which is now the new capital of Uttaranchal State, to seek fresh permission from the State (local) Government.

Uttaranchal proposes to levy additional peak fees, as is done in Sikkim, which may cause severe financial hardship to visiting expeditions. Expeditions to Jammu and Kashmir still find it difficult to climb mountains due to bureaucratic problems such as the requirement of local police officers and liaison officers to join the team. Overall, as far as the foreign expeditions to India were concerned, this was perhaps a low point of the last few decades.

HARISH KAPADIA, *Honorary Editor, The Himalayan Journal*

Overview of Indian Expeditions. Seventy five Indian expeditions were organized by various clubs and associations within the country. In addition there were three expeditions organized by the Indian Mountaineering Foundation, bringing the total to a healthy 78. However, out of these more than 50 teams went to routine peaks and attempted them by very frequented standard routes. These included Jogin III, Bhagirathi II, Kalanag, Hanuman Tibba, Kedar Dome, Manali, and Thelu. In addition there were three expeditions each to the increasingly popular peaks (for Indians) of Chhamser and Lungser Kangri, Satopanth, and Shri Kailash, all by their Normal Routes.

HARISH KAPADIA, *Honorary Editor, The Himalayan Journal*

KASHMIR

Shafat Valley, first ascent of Kova Peak and Gulmatonga Tower. The Curbatts (the Crows) are a close-knit group of alpinists from Menaggio on Lake Como, Italy. In 2002 they planned to attempt a big granite wall on an unclimbed 5,500m peak in a side valley off Zanskar's Shafat Valley, the latter leading to the Kun Glacier. However, a combination of events thwarted this attempt. First, the airline lost their baggage and they were delayed 10 days in India before it eventually arrived. Then, the Indian army and the public safety officials

Unclimbed walls near Kova Peak. *Maurizio Orsi*

wouldn't allow entry to the valley. The mountain could only be photographed from a distance and all plans for climbing it had to be postponed. With time now at a premium the group had to make do with a much smaller peak of ca 4,600m, which they christened the Gulmatonga Tower. On this, they put up Waiting for Militants, a 1,000m-high rock climb with technical difficulties of VII+ and an overall grade of ED1.

In the summer of 2003 eight of us left Italy for Delhi, where this time we were able to obtain permission for the expedition from the Indian Mountaineering Foundation. From there, we flew to Kashmir with our liaison officer. Srinagar, the capital of Kashmir, is a like a decadent Venice. It has paid the price of political and military tension. Despite its beauty, it has been deserted by tourists for years.

Two days' bus travel brought us to the entrance of the Shafat valley, where we continued on foot, accompanied by a caravan of horses. We reached a site for base camp at 4,050 meters. The Kun Glacier was only a little further on and the 6,930m Pinnacle Peak, first climbed by the Bullock-Workmans in 1906, hovered above our heads. The Indian military was a constant presence (at times a bit cumbersome) during our stay, even though there were no apparent signs of great danger.

From base camp we continued up a large but yet unnamed lateral valley (which we affectionately nicknamed Dream Valley), traversed by an impetuous mountain stream, and closed by a huge granite wall. Between these, 5,500m Kova Peak (Kova means Crow in Hindi) formed an elegant and perfect cone. We set up Camp 1 on the highest meadow below boulders at ca 4,500m and spent a couple of days ferrying climbing gear from base camp and then upward to the foot of the wall.

Once we found a possible line, we needed eight days climbing to reach the summit. The most logical route took the southeast ridge, which we called The Flight of the Crows, in honor not only of its first climbers, the Curbatts, but also the large black crows, which are the only real inhabitants of the wall.

The first two-thirds of the route were fixed. Halfway up the ridge at 5,100m, a large ledge nicknamed "the coffee pot" provided a comfortable bivouac. The weather proved very changeable, sometimes turning more than once during the day. Snow and wind would beat our faces and cover the fixed ropes with ice, making it necessary on occasions to scrape them clean in order to jumar.

The route was made up of a series of slabs, corners, and long cracks for a length of about 1,350m, and rose for a vertical height of almost 1,000m. There were a total of 29 pitches with a sustained level of difficulty from V+ to VII-. The rock was a magnificent compact granite and almost always easy to protect with nuts and cams. On the whole we used few pitons and not more than a couple of bolts for protection, although all of the belays were hand bolted. The summit was reached on August 18 by three team members, but more of us followed on subsequent days.

After the climb we used our remaining days to bring down gear, trying to leave as little trace as possible of our passage on the climb and at Camp 1. Those who still had energy to spend finished exploring the Dream Valley, reaching the pass at the head of the glacier.

MAURIZIO ORSI, *The Curbatts, Italy*

LADAKH

East Karakoram, Argan Kangri (6,789 m), first or second ascent? The Indian Mountaineering Foundation sponsored an all ladies expedition to Argan Kangri in the Arganglas range east of the Nubra Valley. It was led by IMF Vice-President Rita Gombu Marwah. The nine-member team, accompanied by four high-altitude Sherpas, successfully climbed the peak on July 20. Four ladies and four Sherpas reached the summit; Kavita Burathoki, Reena Kaushik, P. M. Tamang, and Shushma Thakur, with Sherpas Dawa, Pasang Dorjee, Samgyal, and Sangepuri. The team operated from July 1-31.

This peak was attempted by the Indo-British expedition, jointly led by Sir Chris Bonington and Harish Kapadia, in the summer of 2001. They failed to climb what they thought to be an unclimbed mountain and the highest in the range. After their expedition Josef Hala, a noted researcher of mountain history from Prague, Czech Republic, drew attention to a previous report about this area dating back to 1970. In that year a peak in this region was reported to have been climbed by the Indian Army. That peak is located at a similar latitude and longitude, has the same height and lies on the same glacier. The Indians called it Phunangma after the name of the glacier at its foot. However, currently it is not conclusively known whether both peaks are one and the same. Please refer to the following note printed in the *Himalayan Journal*.

From a letter by Mr Josef Hala in the Himalayan Journal Vol. 58, p 254: Argan Kangri climb 1970; *The Himalayan Club Newsletter No. 28*, June 1971 (Page 2), compiled by Soli S. Mehta. LADAKH: PHUNANGMA 22,272 ft. First Ascent. This peak in Ladakh was climbed on 4 August 1970 by Capt. F. C. Bahaduri, Nk. S. K. Thapa, Nk. S. Tashi, Hav. S. S. Bhandari and two Sherpas. Capt. N. K. Kalia, Nk. P. Stobdon and a porter again climbed the peak on 5 August 1970. Maj. R. C. Naidu led the expedition. There is also a mention in Ichiro Yoshizawa (670 pages) *Concise Alphabetical Register of World Mountains*, published in Tokyo, 1984. PHUNANGMA

6,788m (34° 35' N: 77° 50' E). (Argan Kangri is 6,789m, with similar co-ordinates as the above peak. It must be noted that there are several peaks in the area within these same co-ordinates but not of a similar height. HK).

HARISH KAPADIA, *Honorary Editor, The Himalayan Journal*

Saser Kangri I, northwest ridge attempt and Saser Kangri IV ascent. A nine-member team from the Indian Navy made a spirited attempt to repeat the long and difficult northwest ridge of Saser Kangri I (7,672m) in the East Karakoram. This elegant line, which features steep snow and rock climbing leading to a sharp corniced upper ridge, was first climbed by Indian members of the 1987 Indo-British expedition (leader Col DK Kullar), which also made first ascents of Saser Kangri V (6,640m) and Saser Kangri IV (aka Cloud Peak; 7,415m although sometimes quoted as 7,364m).

The Navy team was led by myself and included a number of highly competent Sherpa staff. We reached Panamik in the Nubra Valley on the 30th August and started the approach to base camp the following day. Access to the western side of the Saser Group is not straightforward and the expedition was forced to fix ropes on narrow, exposed tracks around rock buttresses. Base camp at 4,750m was occupied on the 4th September and by the 8th an advanced base had been established at 5,360m on the South Phukpoche Glacier. The team now moved into the combe beneath the west face of Saser Kangri I and the unclimbed Plateau Peak (7,310m) to its right, where despite very poor weather we finally established Camp 1 on the 12th at 5,880m. This camp was at almost exactly the same location as that used by the 1987 expedition.

The lower half of the ridge faces west and 13 ropes were fixed up the south flank (60° maximum) to the crest. The line was quickly extended to around 6,600m, two pitches below the rock band. Climbing through this rocky barrier proved very taxing in the prevailing high winds and spindrift, with only four pitches maximum completed a day. However, by the 20th September this section had been successfully overcome and Camp 2 established at 7,000m on the snowfield above. Unfortunately, the next section of the ridge, leading to the col between Saser I and IV, had always been hidden from below, so it wasn't until the 21st that I led a group that discovered a maze of crevasses and serac walls blocking our upward path. These formations do not appear to have been present in 1987. Nevertheless, we opened the route to a point beyond the col at ca 7,300m, above which the ridge proved to have steep flanks and be highly corniced to the north. At this stage it seemed unlikely that further progress could be made and we opted to try the much nearer Saser IV.

Climbing on Saser. *Satyabrata Dam*

On the 22nd Viking Bhanoo, Amit Pande, Rajkumar, and Sange Sherpa summitted Saser IV. They left camp at 5 a.m. and were on the top by 9 a.m. The same day the expedition learned by radio of the tragedy on Panch Chuli (reported elsewhere). Many of the dead were close friends of ours. Three of the Saser Kangri Sherpas lost relatives and were immediately sent home to Darjeeling. This sealed the fate of the expedition and abandoned any further attempts on Saser I.

The Saser Kangri route. *Satyabrata Dam*

In good weather at 5 a.m. on the 23rd, having left camp a little after midnight, Pema Sherpa and I reached the summit of Saser IV. During the coldest part of the night the thermometer showed a temperature of -38°C. While we descended to Camp 1 a third team set off for the top but soon had to retreat as the weather closed in. A ferocious storm raged that day and into the following morning, when the group made a very difficult descent, blinded by the blizzard. Fortunately, the mountain was evacuated safely and base camp reached on the 25th.

COMMANDER SATYABRATA DAM, *Indian Navy and Himalayan Club.*

Editor's note: this was the fifth ascent of Saser IV, but there appears to be something of a dilemma about the number of ascents of Saser I. Second and third ascents of the northwest ridge of Saser I were recorded in 1988 and 1990. The 1988 ascent by Heera Lohia's Indian team fixed 600m of rope from the col to the 7,620m west summit of Saser I and report reaching the main top on the August 24. In 1990, a joint Indo-Taiwanese expedition led by Hakum Singh reported reaching the summit on July 24. Summiters included the well-known Indian female mountaineers, Deepu Sharma and Santosh Yadev. However, Commander Dam is of the opinion that the northwest ridge has not been climbed to the true summit of Saser Kangri I since 1987.

After a number of attempts (the first taking place in 1956) Saser I was first climbed via the south ridge from the east (Shyok) side in 1973 by a team from the Indo-Tibet Border Police. Before that time it was the highest unclimbed peak in India and was the highest first ascent by an Indian team at that time. This route was repeated in 1979 by the Indian Army. In 1995, while attempting a more direct variation to the northwest ridge, another ITBP expedition lost 13 of its climbers in an avalanche when they were retreating in bad weather from the summit camp.

LAHUL

Unnamed peak on the Spaghetti Glacier, Miyar Valley, The Last Minute Journey. Making an alpine ascent in the Himalaya is often a dream for young climbers. It's the same as packing only two bags and heading to the big mountains for the most beautiful adventure. We were lucky to fulfill our

Attempts and eventual success on the stormy wall of Miyar. The Last Minute Journey reaches the 5,845m foresummit. *Dodo Kopold*

dreams. In the middle of August two young Slovak mountaineers, Ivan Stefansky (25) and myself (23), approached a virgin 6,000+m peak near the head of the Miyar Valley; a little-frequented area. In 1998, Italians, Gianluca Bellin and Diego Stefani, had designs on the 6,000+m peak but had to make do with an ascent of neighboring Thunder Peak instead. Shortly after another Italian team, comprising Antonella Cicogna, Fabrizio Defrancesco, and Mario Manica, also reached the foot of the peak but were prevented from climbing by bad weather. In 2002 a strong Slovak team also planned to attempt the ca 700m big wall that forms the west face of this peak but was not able to reach the mountain and climbed elsewhere in the valley. In all, the complicated approach up the aptly named Spaghetti Glacier, and unstable weather were reasons why this summit had not been climbed.

In 2003 it was the same again with the weather. The monsoon was a never-ending story. Every day, snow and rain stopped any activity. In the morning the entire face was covered with snow and ice, while by afternoon it had changed to streams of icy water. In spite of these terrible conditions, there was a team of four Italians trying to climb the smooth slabs in the left part of the wall.

We decided to attempt the overhanging corner on the right side of the face. We hoped that after climbing a 200m-long crack the wall would be not so steep and we would be able to continue to the top on more mixed terrain. Our time was running out and progress of both teams was slow. Wet, icy cracks, together with rock and icefall from the ledge in the upper part of the face, were scary. Every meter climbed in these hopeless conditions drained our energies and our will to continue.

Every day we returned to our advanced base, situated one hour from the wall. This camp, pitched on the glacier, was not really comfortable, particularly during the long wait for better weather. After six days of rain and snow we decided to make our final attempt. We had fixed the hardest part of the face and it was now, theoretically, an easy matter to reach the less steep, upper section of the wall. However, running water in the chimney and constant rain prevented any progress. We retreated.

That same day the Italians decided to go home and we decided to channel our remaining energies into a bold-looking ice and mixed line to the left of the Italian attempt. We knew that during the night everything would be frozen and if we were quick enough we could climb all the ice faster than it disappeared.

We started at 1 a.m. and climbed most of the route using headlamps. The angle reached 70° but the crux was a section of vertical ice above 5,500m. In five hours we climbed a narrow corner system and by noon we were on the top of a 5,845m summit (two altimeter readings). We christened it Mt. Mahindra and named our 900m route, The Last Minute Journey (ED1). This was the end of our never-ending wait.

DODO KOPOLD, *Slovakia*

Editor's note: The two Slovaks reached a foresummit of the main peak, the highest point of which is thought to be ca 6,000m.

Unnamed peak on the Spaghetti Glacier, Miyar Valley. Four Italians, Roberto Iannilli, Marco Marciano, Moritz Tirler, and Giovanni Rivolta, attempted a route toward the left side of the big rock wall that forms the west face of the impressive unnamed ca 6,000+m summit north of Thunder Peak. They were hampered by very poor weather and eventually gave up at ca 5,700m after climbing over 400m at 6c and A2.

LINDSAY GRIFFIN, *High Mountain INFO*

CB 44, a previously unnamed peak in Central Lahul, probable first ascent. Our organization, Kolkata Trekkers Youth (formerly Calcutta Trekkers Youth) of West Bengal, organizes expeditions in unexplored regions, or to virgin or relatively unknown peaks, or peaks that require technical climbing. For our 18th mountaineering expedition we decided to climb Akela Qilla (CB 46, 6,005m), Tombu (CB 48, 5791m), and Jori (CB 49A, 5,791m) in the Kulti Valley of Himachal Pradesh.

The first successful expedition in this region of the Chandra Bhaga peaks was organized

A camp en route to climbing CB44 (5,938m), the pointy peak behind. *Sandip Majumden*

in 1955 by the R.A.F under the leadership of Tony Smythe. This team climbed CB 46 (now at least four ascents to date) and CB 48 (now at least two ascents to date). However, CB 49A does not appear to have any recorded ascent. Nearby there are many beautiful peaks. From the north these are: Taragiri, Tila ka Lahar, Ashagiri.

On August 29 we established Camp I above a hanging icefall, which we had bypassed via ca 250m of steep rock on the left side of the moraine. On September 2 Sonamji served bed tea at 3:35 a.m. and we left for the summit two hours later. We traversed onto the northeast side. Ashagiri (6,161m, climbed by the 1955 expedition) was the nearest objective, then unnamed peak (CB 44, 5,938m), and Akela Qila (6,005m). At 10:30 a.m. we put on crampons and climbed a steep face of around 75° for ca 250m. After tough climbing we reached a rock ridge at 11 a.m. and considering the prevailing weather and the time, we decided to climb CB 44. Perhaps the weather would not allow us to climb Akela Qila, Tambo, or Jori. Rajib was out of breath and I decided to wait here with him. But Sonam, Sandip, and Tikkim went on to climb CB 44, reaching the summit at 11:35 a.m. (32°27'N, 77°24'E). There appears to be no previously recorded ascent of this peak and we have no other information regarding whether this summit has been reached before.

ASHIM KUMAR GHOSH CHOWDHURY, *Kolkata Trekkers Youth*

HIMACHAL PRADESH

SPITI

Losar Valley, Pt 6,000m, (first?) ascent and Dawa Kangri, second ascent. A 10-member team from Kolkatta led by Ujjal Ray climbed in Spiti's Losar valley. They first climbed an unnamed peak of 6,000m. The summit was reached on August 28 by Rajan Aich, Surojit Bhowmick, Subrata Mukherjee, Deb Das Nandi, Tushar K. Sarkar, and Satyajit Shroff. The following day Bhowmick, Nandi, Ray, and Shroff made the second/third ascent of 6,140m Dawa Kangri, a peak first climbed on August 5 and 7, 2000, by a large Japanese expedition under the overall leadership of Takako Kata, which reached the summit via two different routes: the north face and northeast ridge.

HARISH KAPADIA, *Honorary Editor, The Himalayan Journal*

GANGOTRI

Gangotri National Park. Recently the Gangotri region gained national park status. The park has already reported a number of successfully completed projects and an on-going program is planned. This program is displayed at the park entrance a few kilometers from the road head at Gangotri. Projects are listed below with a somewhat liberal translation from the Indian English (I struggled with a number of words).

Project Enterprise of Achievements

1. Installation of eco-friendly incinerator at Gangotri.
2. Placing 50 garbage bins between Gangotri and Bhojbas.
3. Issue of 400 LPG connections at Gangotri and beyond.
4. Issue of 15 tubular frame structures with protective covering to replace existing shelters

made of bhojpatra wood.
5. Issue of 16 prefabricated latrines at Gangnani, Gangotri, Chirbas, and Bhojbas.
6. Cleaning various base camps beyond Gaumukh; over three tons garbage brought back.
7. An awareness program; construction of obelisks at Uttarkashi, Sukhitop, and
   Bhairongati. Issue of leaflets and holding of seminars.
8. Establishing nurseries at Rawara, Maneri, and Bhojbas.
9. Plantation of "over roplings" at Malla, Lata , Raithal Barsu, and Sukhi Top.
10. Facelift of Gangnani sulphur springs.
Future Activities
* Provision of solar light at Bhojbas, Chirbas, and Devoad.
* Setting up a hydro-electricity plant of 150 to 250 kW at Gangotri.
* Provision of LPG connections to all hotels, ashrams, and guest houses at
  Gangotri and beyond.
* Provision of toilets between Gangotri and Gaumukh.
* Afforestation between Uttarkashi and Harsil.
* Periodic cleaning at all base camps.
* Collection of garbage from Gangotri to Gaumukh.
* Strengthening existing nurseries.
* Plantation of bhojpatra trees at Bhojbas.
* Footbridge at Bhojbas on river Bhagirathi to prevent crossing of Gangotri Glacier.

This appears very timely, given the increasing popularity of the area with Indian tourists and pilgrims, who visit the source of the Ganges at Gaumukh (the Cow's Mouth) at the snout of the Gangotri glacier. The number of lodges has increased dramatically and as a result there is a lot of pressure on the environment. Most of the environmental damage comes from domestic tourism, as there is less awareness of best practice. The perception at the Indian Mountaineering Foundation is that the majority of foreign expeditions promote best practice and leave base camps in good condition. Let's make sure this trend continues.

ANDY PERKINS, *U.K.*

Kedar Dome, east face attempt. Cameron Lawson, Mark Synnott, and I arrived in the Gangotri during September, finding that a lingering monsoon was greatly shortening any post-monsoon weather window. The objective was the huge rock wall forming the east face of Kedar Dome (6,831m). We established base camp at Sundovan, close to the end of the mountain's north ridge, where there is some excellent quartzite bouldering. The east face rises above the Ghanohim Glacier and is around 2,000m high. In 1989 it was climbed to the end of the rock difficulties at 6,200m (but did not continued up the remaining 600m of easy-angled snow ridge to the summit) by the Hungarians Atilla Ozsvath and Sazboles Szebdro, at VII- and A2. The vertical height of their route was 1,300m. In 1999 Polish climbers Jancek Fluder, Janusz Golab, and Stanislaw Piecuch climbed a new and more direct line to the right, joining the Hungarian Route at the Yellow Tower (below 6,100m), before bad weather forced them down. Mani Stone has difficulties of VIII WI4 A3+. Lawson, Synnott, and I planned to repeat the Polish route in Alpine style but to complete the line to the summit of Kedar Dome.

We first went up the normal north face route to ca 5,480m and bivouacked for a night in order to aid acclimatization. Dangerous snow conditions prohibited any higher progress and the

Looking good before the fall, with Kedar Dome behind.
Kevin Thaw

weather was at best unstable. With little improvement in sight, Lawson joined the Americans, Anker, Chabot, and Millar, who were attempting the Shark's Fin on Meru, at the end of September. From around this moment things began to get better, with afternoon storms becoming far less frequent. Shortly after, Synnott and I were able to start on our Alpine style attempt. The first day took us 500m up the face, where the ground was not very technical and it was possible to climb unroped over significant sections. The second day was necessarily quite short due to the return of bad weather and only four pitches were achieved (5.9 to 5.10-). The third day dawned murky and it started precipitating by 9 a.m. The rest of the day was spent inside the tent, trying to conserve food and fuel. When day four brought no change, we stashed most of the gear was stashed and descended.

It was another week before the weather again looked promising and the pressure began to rise steadily. We packed and ascended back up to advanced base, where, of course, on arrival we were hit by a violent storm. However, the next day was sunny and any build-up of cloud proved benign. We gained something of a morale boost by regaining our high point in a single day, leading in blocks with the second jumaring carrying a huge sac. The next day also seemed very promising, with even less cloud build-up, boosting morale further. The unstable weather pattern appeared to have broken at last.

Starting out that morning we were able to move together for a few rope lengths, after which we pitched two good steep rock pitches in a crack system. From there a lengthy traverse led into a couloir approximately half-way up the face. In the couloir, Synnott fixed the lead 10mm rope and continued on a 6mm haul line while I jumared. Suddenly, the belay, which was three Friends in what appeared to be perfect cracks, failed. The belay block then narrowly missed me as I tumbled down the gully before fortunately being brought to a halt by the large rucksack. Inspection of the lead rope showed it had been badly damaged by the block and without a replacement we had no alternative but to go down.

KEVIN THAW, *U.K.*

Thalay Sagar, north face attempt. A skilled team of seven Koreans, with considerable 8,000m experience, was led by Lee Sang Cho. They attempted to make the second ascent of the 1997 Australian-New Zealand Route up the Central Couloir. The climbers appear to have found difficulties with thin ice and felt the route to be quite dangerous, eventually retreating from ca 6,400m near the head of the couloir.

HARISH KAPADIA, *Honorary Editor, The Himalayan Journal*

Thalay Sagar, north face, new route, One Way Ticket. Stéphane Benoist and Patrice Glairon-Rappaz from France discovered a very thin line of goulottes and ice smears running up the face just left of the Central Couloir and climbed it over 10 days using a portaledge. The route featured sustained climbing between 6,000m and 6,500m, with a very thinly iced crux slab at ca 6,300m. Difficult mixed climbing through the shale band towards the top led to the last four pitches of the Australian-New Zealand Route, up which the pair gained the summit on October 30. During the ascent the climbers were confined to their portaledge for three nights in a storm, after which temperatures never rose above −15°C. Named One Way Ticket, the new route was thought to be least ED3 in standard with difficulties of WI6 M6 F5+. A lead article on this ascent appears earlier in this Journal.

Thalay Sagar (6,903m), north face, new route attempt. Ben Gilmore and I attempted a new line on the north face of Thalay Sagar. The line follows the major weakness to the west (right) of the central buttress that was climbed in 1998 by a Russian team led by Alexander Klenov. It had previously been tried by an American team and a New Zealand team (climbed later last year by a Bulgarian expedition, see below). On our attempt we made it to ca 6,000m before being turned around by a storm. Our expedition started April 20, when we met in New Delhi. We spent a day purchasing provisions and meeting with the Indian Mountaineering Federation. There, we met our Liaison Officer and took care of all official business within a couple of hours. We left Delhi and traveled to Uttarkashi, where we finished obtaining supplies and met with the Director of the Nehru Institute of Mountaineering for a handshake and confirmation of our itinerary. We then traveled to Gangotri in nine hours, experiencing minor vehicle troubles along the way. There, we met our 10 porters and organized loads. The trek to base camp took five days, two days longer than expected due to weather.

Once installed in our 4,700m base camp, we hunkered down for four days in a storm that hammered us with snow and constant winds of 40-60 m.p.h. Two tents were destroyed and one damaged. We sent out the LO with the cook and his helper to get new tents and replace damaged food. We stayed at base camp repairing gear and reorganizing our thrashed camp until four days later the LO, cook, and helper returned. Then on May 10 we moved up to ABC at 5,200m. The next two weeks were spent acclimatizing, scouting the route, and waiting out bad weather.

On May 26 we set out on our proposed line, carrying two small packs containing only belay parkas, insulated pants, a stove, and two days of food and fuel. We were attempting the route in single push style. We climbed the first 400m unroped on easy snow and ice, and then ca 400m of mixed terrain. We stayed independent of fixed lines from previous attempts, free climbed every pitch, and left only minimal rappel anchors on the mountain. After climbing for several hours in a building storm, we decided to retreat. During our descent we encountered nearly constant spindrift avalanches, which made finding anchors very difficult. Back at ABC there was a short break in the weather but soon more snow returned. We left for home on May 30.

We would like to thank the Lyman Spitzer Award for its support.

KEVIN MAHONEY, *AAC*

Thalay Sagar, north face, new route. A Bulgarian team tackled the unclimbed right side of the face, well right of the 1999 Russian Direct and in the same vicinity as the line attempted by Lindblade and Whimp in 1996. They climbed in capsule style and used three portaledge camps, the last at ca 6,450m. After spending six nights on the face and equipping the route with fixed rope to around 6,600m, Nicola Levakov and Hristo Hristov set off on October 11 for a light-weight push to the summit. By the end of the day the two had reached the shoulder on the west ridge and without bivouac gear spent a night in a snow cave. The weather was very cold with strong winds but they survived the night, and the next day made the summit. This is one of the best Bulgarian ascents in the Himalaya for some years, though Levakov suffered serious frostbite and had to be evacuated by air. A lead article on this ascent appears earlier in this Journal.

Thalay Sagar, northeast face, new route. Dutch climbers Mike van Berkel, Cas van de Gevel, and Melvin Redeker fixed ropes to the col below the northeast spur and then climbed a new route on the northeast face. Very steep ice smears and an overhanging band of granite climbed on aid led to the southeast ridge, up which the team reached the summit on September 23. The 800m face was thought to warrant ED1 with grade 5 ice and rock to UIAA V+ and A1. A lead article appears earlier in this Journal.

Meru Central Summit (6,450m), an attempt on the Shark's Fin. A four-member Korean team led by Park Sik-Young attempted the east face of Meru Shark's Fin. They established base camp at Tapovan on May 29, then subsequently two camps on the face, the highest at 5,900m. However-er, due to persistent bad weather they were not able to climb higher than 6,000m. Further details are not known.

HARISH KAPADIA, *Honorary Editor, The Himalayan Journal*

Meru Central Summit (6,450m), an attempt on the Shark's Fin. Conrad Anker, Doug Chabot, and I arrived in Delhi in late August on our way to attempt Meru's conspicuous Shark's Fin. Though this summit had been reached by the prolific Russian alpinist, Valeri Babanov, in a well publicized 2001 solo effort, the first ascent of a direct line up the east face was what the previous 20 or so expeditions (and ours) had had in mind. Most of those expeditions favored big wall tactics to try to overcome the final 500m of the namesake rock fin via its southeast face. Of the few that even made it onto the face, only a couple got their haul bags past the initial 550m ice slope. We thought the little attempted northeast face of the fin (often plastered white in photos) offered a far more attractive possibility of an alpine-style climb.

At 10 p.m. on September 13 we crossed the bergschrund at 5,150m and started up the exposed slope. At 2 a.m. on the 17th, after two days of ice and rock (with difficulties up to 5.10X) and one day of sitting out poor weather, we reached our high point at 6,000m. A respite of "easy" snow turned out to be completely unconsolidated and around one meter deep plastered over 60° blank granite slabs. Without any ice, conditions were absolutely impossible.

Incredulous that our luck had turned so unexpectedly, we started rapping. Sixteen hours later we were safely back in ABC. Though we'd climbed higher than anyone on the northeast face of the Shark's Fin, the route had lost its appeal. We all felt the innocent-looking white patch that turned us around was most likely always a dead end and probably things only got worse above. Conditions would have to be really exceptional for the face to be "in."

I wasn't surprised that people have suggested a comparison to the notoriously uncooperative north face of Devil's Thumb in Alaska. But it's only true in regards to the number of attempts, grant dollars doled out to would-be ascensionists, and conditions on the northern half of the fin. The 500m of rock on the southeast face of the fin is always "in," and as for the 800m of ice and mixed leading up to it, only high avalanche conditions have been a semi-regular problem.

Having covered most of the lower 800m in one day during our attempt and considering Conrad thought the southeast face of the fin looked really "fun," it would seem the most coveted line on The Shark's Fin could be climbed without turning it into a dog-and-pony show. British climbers made a couple notable attempts in 1993 and 1997. Others, less inspired, left behind the pointless bolts we passed. I suspect the right people have simply been there at the wrong time and by all accounts, including our own experience with the weather, that's most of the time.

BRUCE MILLER, *AAC*

The infamous Shark's Fin on Meru, and Conrad Anker near the highpoint. *Doug Chabot (2)*

Unnamed Peak (6,193m). A two-member Polish team comprising Robert Sieklucki and Marcin Wernik attempted this unnamed peak near to Nandanvan. They reached the base of the mountain on April 19 and, not surprisingly considering that they had arrived so early in the season, found large quantities of snow. The route proved hard going and the pair were forced to give up at 5,450m.

HARISH KAPADIA, *Honorary Editor, The Himalayan Journal*

Bhagirathi enchainment attempt. Americans Jonathan Copp and Dylan Taylor were attempting the ambitious project of an enchainment from Bhagirathi III (6,454m) to Bhagirathi II (6,512m) over the smaller unclimbed summit of Bhagirathi IV. They planned to first reach the summit of Bhagirathi III via the quasi-classic Scottish Route on the south west pillar. Their best attempt reached ca 5,800m just below the shale band. To this point they had climbed for two-and-a-half days carrying just a single-skin Goretex tent, one sleeping bag and minimal food and fuel to complete the traverse. A storm moved in and pinned them down for three days, after which they had no option but to retreat. Subsequent attempts failed to regain their high point.

The ca1,350m Scottish Route (Bob Barton and Alan Fyffe, October 1982) was also attempted by Spanish, Joan Belmonte, Jordi Bonet, Joan Jover and Frederic Puig. They made two attempts in Alpine Style but only reached half-height on the pillar.

LINDSAY GRIFFIN, *High Mountain INFO*

Bhagirathi III, west face, ascent of Spanish (Catalan) Route. Three Swiss, Simon Anthamatten, Urs Stocker and Reiner Treppte, made the third ascent to the summit of the ca 1,350m Spanish Route, Impossible Star (Juan Aldeguer, Sergio Martinez, Jose Moreno, and Juan Thomas; May 1984) on the west face of 6,454m Bhagirathi III. The Swiss initially thought the Spanish Route lay more to the left and therefore hoped to climb a new route on the pillar. However, they soon realized their "new" line was the 1984 route and decided to attempt this anyway, free climbing as much as possible.

The three fixed about 600m (the first two pillars) of the route and established a camp at the top of their ropes. Due to the prevailing weather, they were only able to free climb the first third of the route (at 6c), after which it turned extremely cold (-10° to -20°C), ice remained in the cracks and the team was forced to use aid (A3+). The climbers felt that in warm and dry conditions the second pillar would be relatively easy (around 6a) but the third pillar involved quite hard aid climbing and they were somewhat doubtful if it could ever be climbed completely free. Certainly, in their opinion, it would be at least 7c/8a. However, in this section there is a well-featured overhang, where the rock is quite loose, ca 10m to the left of the established line. Also, to the right of the line is a gully system, where avalanches, originating from the top of the wall, tend to fall. However, as this gully is overhanging, any avalanche would tend to pass well out from the wall, leaving climbers relatively sheltered from objective danger. The rock here is also poor but both these adjacent lines offer technically rather easier climbing. From their high camp the three Swiss climbed to the summit in four days. As the upper third of the wall is overhanging, there was no snow and therefore no water. This forced the team to spend the first couple of days fixing ropes above the portaledge, before climbing to the top with an open bivouac at 6,000m. Here the temperature was around -20°C and the wind gusted to 60km/hour.

In 1984 the Catalan team fixed some rope on the base of the pillar and then climbed the route in capsule style, making hammock bivouacs. Although they left a considerable amount of equipment on the route (ropes in the upper section, many pegs, rubbish on the ledges and an unnecessary bolt), the line was completed more or less using natural gear throughout. On the second overall and first alpine-style ascent, which took place later the same year, Americans Scott Flavelle and David Lane cleaned most of the route. Despite this, the Swiss found considerable amounts of old fixed rope (which they didn't use and some of which they cleaned) but took the liberty of carrying a battery-powered drill to place a single 8mm bolt anchor at the end of each 60m pitch to facilitate constructing a better line for their fixed ropes. They spent a total of 18 days (out of 40 at or above base camp) climbing the route and feel that their style was acceptable given the conditions, which had already sent most other teams in the Gangotri packing for home. For a topo illustration of the routes on Bhagirathi III, see *AAJ* 1999, page 97.

LINDSAY GRIFFIN, *High Mountain INFO*

CENTRAL GARHWAL

Kamet (7,756m), new route via the northwest ridge. An eight-member Indian Navy expedition, employing Sherpas and High Altitude Porters, climbed both Kamet and neighboring Abi Gamin in the pre-monsoon period. We reached the road head at Ghamsali on May 18, and on the 23rd established base camp at 4,650m beside the frozen Vasundara Tal. We followed the Normal Route for both Kamet and Abi Gamin all the way to Meade's Col (7,100m), which separates the two mountains. Camp 1 was established at 4,960m, Camp 2 at 5,360m, 3 at 6,050m, 4 at 6,650m and 5, which was first occupied on June 10, on the Col. The route thus far had some avalanche danger and the weather had not proved favorable. Camp 5 was cold and windy, with average daytime temperatures hovering around −15°C and winds gusting to 100 knots. To our south the massive northeast face of Kamet rose like a gigantic column of ice, snaking away beyond our vision into the azure. To our north, the south face of Abi Gamin looked a nice and easy proposition. However, on the col a severe blizzard continued unabated.

At 4 a.m. on the morning of the 11th visibility cleared and the wind dropped. Surg Lt Viking Bhanoo, LMA Rakesh Kumar, and Sherpa Sange Puri set out for the Normal Route up Abi Gamin (7,354m) and reached the summit around 7:30 a.m. After they returned to C4, I followed their tracks, alone, to the summit, reaching it around 12:30 p.m.

A little after midnight of June 12, Sherpas Ang Tashi and Purva left with me for Kamet. Purva had to descend soon due to mountain sickness. Ang Tashi and I traversed to the northwest ridge and summited after 14 hours of climbing, descending back to Camp 5 in the dark. This was the first ascent of the ridge. A day later, having started out at 3 a.m., Lt Cdr Abhishek Kankan, Sange Puri, Mchera Rajkumar, and Samgyal reached the summit at 11:30 a.m. via the Normal Route up the northeast ridge. Everyone was back in base camp on the 15th, returning over a glacier that had now completely altered its appearance since we first arrived.

COMMANDER SATYABRATA DAM, *Indian Navy and Himalayan Club.*

Pt 6,175m, AAJ 2003, p370-371, correction. In the account of the first ascent of this peak in 2002 by an Irish expedition, it appears that the summit, subsequently christened Draiocht Parvat, was reached on May 13 and not April as stated. Also, it is now believed the summit that Shipton reached in 1934 was 6,075m Shri Parvat.

EASTERN GARHWAL

Lampak I and II, ascents. A 10-member team from the Punjab Police, led by PM Das, climbed both Lampak peaks, which lie south of the Girthi Ganga in the Eastern Garhwal. The expedition established base camp at 4,700m in the Kala Kharak to the west of the mountains, and then a higher camp at 5,127m, from which both peaks could be attempted. Further camps were then on both Lampak I and II. On June 7 Lampak II (6,181m) was climbed by the leader and seven other members (Nari Dhami, Inder Kumar, Kulvinder Kumar, Mohan Lal, Anand Singh, Palvinder Singh, and Sangram Singh), whereas on the 13th the more southerly Lampak I (6,325m) was climbed by the leader and three other members (Nari Dhami, Inder Kumar, and Sangram Singh). The latter was a major technical ascent by an Indian team on a peak above 6,000m. PM Das has made a full study of peaks and their nomenclature in this region and recorded the results in Volume 60 of the Himalayan Journal.

HARISH KAPADIA, *Honorary Editor, The Himalayan Journal*

Editor's note: The Lampak Group rises between the Siruanch and Kalla Glaciers above the road head at Malari (northeast of Joshimath) and is very rarely visited. The history of ascents in this group is rather confused, as originally Lampak was the name awarded to the sharp northerly peak of 6,181m, while 6,325m was designated Lampak South. The higher peak was first attempted by the 1950 Scottish Expedition (Tom MacKinnon, Bill Murray, Douglas Scott, and Tom Weir), via the east ridge from the Siruanch Valley. It was reported as being first climbed in 1969 by an Indian expedition from the Mountain Lovers' Association, which after failing to reach the col between (the then) Lampak South and 6,504m Gorur Parbat, climbed the southwest ridge to the summit. One year previously the 6,181m peak had been climbed by a team from Calcutta under Nemai Bose. Both peaks were climbed again on September 20, 1978 by a 12-member team from the Indian Military. The third ascent of 6,181m occurred in September 2001 via the southeast ridge.

Kalanka, north face, attempt. Kalanka is 6,931 meters and is joined to Changabang bordering the massive Nanda Devi Sanctuary. There is only one confirmed line on the north side of Kalanka, climbed by a Czech team. We set up base camp on May 1, and throughout the next week we continued to carry loads and get our fitness back.

On May 12 John Varco and I finally got a good work day in on the mountain, ascending the first 2,000' up a snow slope. We left a cache of food and gear at 18,500' and headed back down in bad weather. May 17 was our first night on the big wall portion of the mountain. We dug out a great bivy. The next 800 feet was 80-degree mixed climbing on extremely loose rock. We fixed all of this to what we called "The Meat," a rock structure where the route turns into a 90°-overhanging wall.

The weather continued to suck. May 27 was our 10th day on the mountain, and although we were making headway we were completely out of food. So we headed down to advanced base camp. Our remaining food consisted of 6 freeze-dried dinners, 20 GU packets, 10 energy bars, 1 package of Kool Aid, and 2 cough drops.

We returned to the ledge exhausted but happy to at least be back on the mountain. Our health was deteriorating from being up so high so long. John had lost about 15 pounds and had a chest infection producing a lot of green phlegm. Finally after nine days we reached the top of the north buttress.

We were both totally worked and had been completely out of food for four days. After much deliberation and weighing every possibility we decided to forgo the summit. We put all the gear together in two huge loads and headed down.

Depender surprised me with an amazing birthday cake he had made the day before. He had written my name in white icing and we celebrated a fantastic climb and adventure consuming the delicious cake under the stars with a circle of snowcapped peaks surrounding us. I looked over at John and smiled; he gave me a big hug, and all was right in my little alpine world.

SUE NOTT

KUMAON

Panch Chuli II (6,904m), ascents and tragedies. In one of the worst avalanche tragedies in the history of Himalayan mountaineering nine members of an Indo-Tibet Border Police team to Panch Chuli II (the highest of the Panch Chuli Group at 6,904m) in the Kumaon region of the Indian Himalaya were killed while descending the mountain on September 20 after a successful summit attempt. While exact details are not known, the team appears to have climbed the southwest ridge, the route of the 1973 first ascent by 18 climbers from another ITBP expedition led by Mahindra Singh and repeated in 1992 by three Indian members of an Indo-British expedition jointly led by Chris Bonington and Harish Kapadia. The 1992 party found the approach through the icefall to the upper Balati Plateau below the ridge objectively dangerous.

The 2003 ITBP team was attempting the mountain before the end of the monsoon, reported to be comparatively heavy last year. The members reached the top early in the morning of the 20th and were involved in

The north side of Kalanka, with the Nott-Varco attempt shown. *John Varco*
John Varco, high on the route. *Sue Nott*

the accident at around 12:30 p.m. the same day. A series of helicopter searches eventually discovered the bodies, which were brought down to base camp. All the climbers involved were very experienced mountaineers and several had been to Everest. Among them Sunil Dutt Sharma had climbed Kangchenjunga by the northeast ridge (1991) and Everest (1993), while Sange Sherpa was one of only two people (the other being his brother Kusang) to have climbed Everest from all three sides: from the south via the South Col and southeast ridge; from the north via the North Col and north ridge; from the east via the Kangshung Face. Four of the victims are reported to have been Everest summiteers.

The ITBP has produced many accomplished climbers over the years and has been responsible for a great many significant first ascents in the Indian Himalaya, so it is truly unfortunate that the two worst avalanche incidents in India have involved its members. In 1995 an ITBP expedition to Saser Kangri lost 13 of its climbers in an avalanche when they were descending in bad weather from the summit camp.

Within a month of this accident the peak was climbed again by the Indian Army, this time from the eastern side (exact route unknown but the peak was climbed via the northeast ridge by an Indian Gorka Regiment in August 1991 and again the following month via the east face by members of the Kumaon and Naga Regiment). During the descent from the successful summit bid on October 4, a fixed rope snapped, leaving one member killed and four injured. All were from the Kumaon Regiment.

LINDSAY GRIFFIN and HARISH KAPADIA

SIKKIM

New icefall climbing. In 2004, Adam George, Philippe Wheelock, and I (all from Colorado), with assistance from Kelsang Phuntsok and Tashi Sherpa from Sikkim, Carlene Grant from Canada, and Andreas Prammer from Austria undertook what we believe to be the first waterfall ice climbing in Sikkim. Research by Philippe Wheelock confirmed no other attempts at climbing ice in Sikkim, and local residents also reported that no other ice climbers have been seen. With the assistance of local guide and outfitter Kelsang Phuntsok, owner of Wisdom Travels, Wheelock made an initial reconnaissance of northern Sikkim, where plentiful ice was discovered in the Lachen and Yumthang valleys. Ice conditions varied but was found to be best at elevations between ca 3,200m and 4,600m. Indian military presence along Sikkim's north border makes winter road access very convenient and possible. Wheelock climbed a 75m, WI3 icefall in the Lachen valley with local Tashi Sherpa and Canadian climber Carlene Grant, who was traveling in the area.

Upon the arrival of George and me, the team set out for Yumthang Valley, where the ice was found to be in better shape. We were joined for a short time by Prammer. We based ourselves in the village of Lachung and made day trips to the higher Yumthang valley, where ice and we found mixed routes of varying length and difficulty. We put up 10 routes here, ranging from 60-180m in height with difficulties WI3 to WI5, including one partial mixed line at M4-M5. The largest concentration of climbs was found ca 4,300m in an area named the Terma Wall. This contained the highest quality ice and has potential for 20 routes arranged in two tiers.

Scope for longer and more difficult routes exists in the Yunthang valley. Last winter was reported to be warmer than normal and could account for many of the routes being poorly formed. Many routes were spotted but not climbed due to either poor ice conditions or approaches longer than those of other climbs.

In late February, George, Wheelock, and I trekked into Sikkim's West District in search of ice. The west proved to be drier than the north, with only a few climbs spotted along the Yuksum to Gocha La trekking route. Due to poor ice conditions we didn't climb, but we could have fine one to two-pitch climbs earlier in the season. January could prove to be a better month for ice climbing in Sikkim. The remote locations, variety of climbing and cultural diversity of Sikkim make for a truly rewarding trip. There is great potential for further development of ice climbing in this area.

RICHARD DURNAN, *AAC*

Climbing the Glass Noodle, Sikkim. *Richard Durnan*

Ratong Valley, Tieng Kg, new route Merenge Bilinbolonka; and Phori, possible first ascent. Spanish Basque climbers Garo Azuke and I climbed in western Sikkim during October. Our intended objective was an ascent of the virgin east face of Kabru South (7,317m, a peak with only one claimed ascent, by an Indian Army expedition in 1994), which is reached from the Ratong Valley. However, first we needed to acclimatize and, we chose the ca 6,000m peak of Tieng Kg. This is an impressive peak, which we think looks like a shorter version of Ama Dablam. It was climbed in 1992 from the southeast by an Indian military expedition.

We chose the elegant 800m-high west face. After two days of difficult and delicate climbing over poor quality rock, snow, and ice, we reached the top of the face and a small subsidiary summit around 200-300m distant and ca 70m lower than the main summit. The intervening ground looked complex and as we were cold and exhausted, we decided to descend from this point, which our altimeter put at 5,960m. We reached the high point on October 3 and named the new route Merenge Bilinbolonka (750m, VI 5+ M6).

We next moved camp to the Ratong Glacier for an attempt on Kabru but discovered that conditions on the proposed route looked bad and the line featured a dangerous icefall. We therefore decided to abandon this idea and instead to make an ascent of nearby Phori Peak

The Terma Wall, Sikkim. *Richard Durnan*

(5,837m), a fine pyramid. We began our ascent via the south-southwest face at 1:30 a.m. on October 17. After mostly snow and mixed climbing with some aid, we reached the top at 11:30 a.m. There were no signs of any prior ascent of the granite block forming the summit, from which we had to rappel. We christened the 600m route Debekatua Debekatzea (V 4+ M6 A1). Five rappels, each of 70m, put us on the glacier east of the peak and we returned to camp at 6:30 p.m.

This summit is supposed to have been attempted by Indian climbers, one of whom died on the mountain. We found a broken rope 20m below a foresummit of the peak, but nothing in the summit area. We also found a piton about 30m above the glacier during our rappel descent, but surmise that it probably belonged to the military, which uses this glacier for training. Our sirdar and agent in Darjeeling both thought the peak previously unclimbed.

ALAIN ANDRES, *Spain*

ARUNACHAL PRADESH

The Bailey Trail, a rare trek in Arunachal Pradesh. During the month of October a team of three Indians comprising Huzefa Electricwala, Dr. Kamal Limdi, and I trekked in the rarely frequented valleys of Arunachal Pradesh, North East India. We first drove to the northwest corner of the state, visiting the Bum La on the Tibetan border and nearby Zimithang and Lumpho. Just north of Zimithang, where the Thag La Ridge forms the natural border with Tibet, the Dalai Lama crossed on his escape to India in 1959. It was also a dispute about the position of this ridge and the exact alignment of the McMahon Line that precipitated the 1962 Indo-China war, fought with disastrous results.

In the second half of the trip we undertook a 22-day trek going along the old Bailey Trail from the ancient village of Thembang, a little distance to the north of the Bomdi La road pass, to a point close to the Tibetan frontier. This was the trail pioneered (from the border south-wards) by British Army officers Lt. Col. F.M. Bailey (author of the classic No Passport to Tibet) and Capt. H.T. Morshead in 1913. H.W. Tilman followed part of this route in 1938 when he was looking for views of the big peaks, Kangto and Gorichen. One of his Sherpas died due to an attack of malaria, and Tilman suffered severely from the same disease.

The forest around the trail was magnificent, with rain forest continuing to high altitudes. The views of mountains, available only in the mornings, were beautiful. On several occasions we could see Kangto (7,042m), a huge mountain rising on the horizon. Kangto is the only peak above 7,000m in Arunachal Pradesh (according to the latest maps) and the highest in the Indian Eastern Himalaya. The Gorichen group was seen from different angles. We reached two points, Pt. 4,640m and Pt. 4,983m, near the Tse La above Pota.

The area now welcomes trekkers and visitors but it does not have many facilities. Trekking is best during the period mid-September to mid-November: Arunachal Pradesh has some of the highest rainfall in the Himalaya and outside this period it either rains, snows, or (in winter) is snow-bound and misty.

Permits and Rules for entry:

The entire area of Arunachal Pradesh remains within the Inner Line. This is a line desig-nated on the map beyond which visitors must obtain a special permit. At present, the rules are as follows:

1. Indians: any Indian national is granted seven days permission to visit the open area of Arunachal Pradesh. This permit can be extended for seven days at a time as desired. Naturally, for a long trek or an expedition, a special permit has to be obtained from Itanagar, the capital of Arunachal Pradesh. This is easily given on payment of a small fee.

2. Foreigners: a group comprising a minimum of four foreigners can visit Arunachal Pradesh for travel or trekking. The current fee is $50 for a period of 10 days, which can be renewed for another 10-day trek. Generally, it is expected that foreigners would go through a travel agent registered in Arunachal Pradesh. There are no restrictions on photography (except in military areas) but foreigners are only allowed to visit open areas.

HARISH KAPADIA, *Honorary Editor, The Himalayan Journal*

Nepal

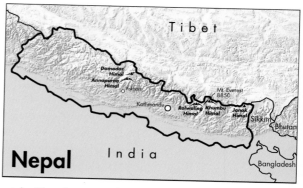

Pre-Monsoon 2003, overview. The spring marked the 50th anniversary of the first ascent of Everest and led to record numbers on the mountain. While there were well-over 100 expeditions to the permitted peaks in Nepal or on the Nepal/Tibet border (excluding Trekking Peaks), approximately half were to the world's highest mountain. Elsewhere, very few climbers attempted to break new ground, although a new and difficult variation finish was established to the Standard Route on Kangchenjunga and Japanese made the first ascent of a 7,000m border peak. One or two Trekking Peaks, recently opened by the Nepalese Government (e.g. Machermo), gained their first official ascents. In July there was more helpful news for tourists when the government abolished mandatory Environment Officers for trekkers visiting Upper Mustang, Humla, Upper Dolpo, and the Vyas region of Darchula. This, it is hoped, will encourage more trekking in these areas. In the same announcement the government granted free visas for all visitors from neighbouring countries such as Bangladesh, Bhutan, China, India, Sri Lanka, and Pakistan. It also granted Western tourists a free three-day transit visa and waived the visa fee for anyone re-entering the country within one year of a 15-day sojourn in Nepal.

Ministry of Tourism post monsoon statistics. The Ministry of Tourism reported that 76 expeditions comprising 490 members from 18 different countries were permitted to climb 36 peaks over 6,000m. The total amount raised in royalty fees was Rs 21,600,000, or a little over $300,000. The Government has now opened a total of 326 Expedition and Trekking peaks. Thirty three of these are designated Trekking Peaks and are administered by the Nepal Mountaineering Association. In the autumn the NMA issued permits to 2,292 members of 443 expeditions to climb on these lower altitude peaks.

Despite the Nepalese authorities' efforts to entice climbers to go to far-flung regions, half of the autumn's 123 expeditions went to just two mountains, only one of which was climbed inside Nepal. This one was Ama Dablam with 27 teams consisting of between one to 21 members each. Cho Oyu, which is on the border but, as is normal, was climbed from its Tibetan side only, had 36 teams, ranging in size from one to 24 members.

ELIZABETH HAWLEY AND BIKRUM PANDEY, *Nepal*

FAR WEST NEPAL

Raksha Urai, first ascent and tragedy. In the remote Api-Nampa-Saipal region of Far West Nepal, there is a small north-south range of mountains named Raksha Urai, which consists of several peaks (see note below). The highest of the group is Raksha Urai III, quoted as 6,593m, and has been attempted by several expeditions in the past.

In the autumn of 2003 a seven-member French team led by Arnaud Clère (together with Nepalis—Gurungs, not Sherpas) succeeded in putting the first people on top of any of the four peaks. Three of their members and one Nepali stood on the summit of Raksha III, which they said is about 6,600m high.

Because they had been delayed in reaching base camp by Maoist extortion (see elsewhere), the expedition's tight schedule left them only 10 days for climbing after their arrival at base camp. They set up base camp at 4,000m, east of the range near a stone hut designated on some trekking maps as Saipal village. While one party went exploring other mountains in the area, Clère, Catherine Coulaud, Gaël Farroux, and Keshab Raj Gurung attempted Raksha Urai.

They moved around to the northwest side, which none of the previous teams had attempted, to see whether they could climb from there up Raksha Urai II, which at 6,420m is the second-highest of the group. They quickly decided it was too technical for them, so they changed their objective to Raksha Urai III and returned to base camp.

They left base camp again on the 13th and bivouacked at 5,100m. The next day they moved up to a spot for their second bivouac below the col between Raksha Urai II and III. They bivouacked here at 5,800m and on the following day, the 15th, climbed to the 40-45° snow slope onto the col and then turned northward on Raksha Urai III's south ridge.

Most of the ridge itself was snow-covered with many small cornices and loose rock. On the final 200-300m there were several false tops before the true summit was reached. The four climbers had left their bivouac at 4:30 a.m., were on the top at 12:00, and soon began their descent.

By the time they had reached a point 500m from the col, Farroux and Gurung were in the lead and Clère and Coulaud could no longer see them. When the last two were at a place where they had a view of the whole ridge above and the mountainside below it, they spotted one body 400m down the flank of the ridge and two tracks in the snow. They were too tired to try going down the very steep slope where the body lay. They returned to their bivouac to sleep that night and were in base camp the next day.

ELIZABETH HAWLEY, NEPAL

Editor's note: The 1997 German expedition, the first to this range, defined the group as having six peaks, which they numbered from south to north as Raksha Urai I to VI. However, the 2001 Anglo-Canadian-New Zealand team, the fourth expedition to attempt any of the peaks in this range, are convinced the peak referred to by the Germans as Raksha Urai I is in fact Dhaulagiri/Dhaulasiri (not to be confused with the more well-known 8,000m peak), or certainly part of the Dhaulagiri Group, as it is not visible from the main valley and is separated from the other Raksha Urai peaks by a considerable distance. Also, Raksha Urai VI referred to by the Germans is, in the opinion of the British climbers, yet another separate mountain a little north and some way east of the main range. They therefore suggest the most logical nomenclature for the Raksha Urai Group to be four peaks (I to IV) from south to north, so the Germans' II now becomes I, etc. They also note that Raksha Urai III, the highest summit of the group and the one they attempted, is higher than the quoted 6,593m for Raksha Urai. They believe it to be more like 6,650m.

The 2003 French team received the first Vertical-Petzl award, which is a grant conferred on a group of non-professional climbers taking their first steps in the Greater Ranges. It is believed that Farroux and Keshab Raj Gurung fell toward the remote Salimor Valley to the west of the peak and were killed. The former, who was 30 and chief motivator of the expedition, was one of the most active climbers in the Grenoble section of the French Alpine Club, while the latter, just 23, was acting as Sirdar for the first time in his career and had just started a guide's course in Nepal.

KANJIROBA HIMAL

Norbu Kang, first official ascent. During the summer, Japanese led by Tamotsu Ohnishi made the first ascent of Norbu Kang, a recently opened 6,005m peak in the Upper Dolpo region of northwest Nepal. From a base camp pitched on June 20 at 4,805m, west of the mountain, they moved to a higher camp (5,250m) two days later, and on the 23rd climbed to the west col (5,490m), returning to high camp later that day. On the 25th they fixed 50m of rope on the north face, which they followed to the summit via snow/ice slopes broken by two crevasses. They were back in base camp the same day. The summiteers were Chhulsim Nuru Sherpa, Kanchha Dawa Sherpa, Ms. Tazuko Inoue, Koji Mizutani, Ohnishi, and Takehiko Yanigahara.

ELIZABETH HAWLEY, *Nepal*

DHAULAGIRI HIMAL

Dhaulagiri II, south face to east ridge, attempt. The seven-man Czech expedition led by Pavel Trefil chose the very rarely visited Dhaulagiri II (7,751m) as its objective for pre-monsoon 2003, hoping to repeat the 1978 Japanese Route (summit reached by Shorji Koiko and Yoshio Ogawa) from the Tsaurabong Glacier. This climbs a prominent snow/ice spur right of the south face to reach the east ridge at a small, pointed, snowy top on the long, lower, horizontal section of the crest. From here the elegant East Ridge is followed more steeply to the summit.

Our expedition took six days to reach Base Camp from Beni. There, we were faced with a difficult river crossing (the Japanese spent three days building a bridge during their expedition), followed by a large and equally taxing rock barrier to reach the glacier. We had only brought 200m of fixed rope plus a few rock pegs and ice screws but after one week were able to set foot on the glacier and establish a camp. During the next two weeks we attempted to climb the mountain but snow fell every afternoon and night, making conditions highly avalanche prone. By May 17 we had reached ca 6,700m on the crest of the east ridge but saw that the remaining 1,000m to the summit comprised 50° ice. We felt unable to progress any further without fixed ropes and decided to call off the expedition. It would appear that the post monsoon would generally be a better season for an attempt, as there would be less snow and avalanche danger. However, a ladder is advisable for the river crossing and in autumn there would be even more water.

PAVEL TREFIL, *Czech Republic*

The middle section of the Dhaulagiri Range seen from the north-east in winter. The highest summit visible is Dhaulagiri II (7,751m) with the large triangular north east snow/ice face. In front is Sita Chuchura (6,611m). The summits of Dhauligiri III (7,715m) and Dhauligiri V (7,618m) are visible on the ridge running back left from the summit of D II. *Jacques Belge*

Tashi Kang and Peak 6,195m, ascents. While acclimatizing for their attempt on the northeast ridge of Dhaulagiri, a group of primarily German climbers successfully reaced the top of two low 6,000m peaks in the Hidden Valley, north-northeast of Dhaulagiri I. Angela Beltrame from Switzerland, and Olaf Köhler, Frank Meutzner, Götz Wiegland, and Olaf Zill from Germany climbed a straightforward unnamed peak of 6,195m and Tashi Kang I (6,386m). They followed the rocky southwest ridge of Tashi Kang I to reach the upper section of the southeast ridge. The lower part of the route was steep and narrow, while the upper southeast ridge rose to an icy 60°. Overall, the climbers found the route to be technically quite difficult and reached the top on April 19. These ascents were partly for acclimatization, partly for pure adventure.

In the autumn Tashi Kang was climbed again by Francois Borghese, Frederic Dufau-Joel, and Paul Grobel, from Grobel's commercially-organized expedition to the popular 6,920m Tukuche (which was successful). The successful ascent took place on October 10 and a traverse was made of the mountain via the north ridge and a descent of the east face.

ELIZABETH HAWLEY, *Nepal*

Editor's note: There have been plenty of ascents in this region over the years, including a very successful German team in 1974 that climbed nine peaks, but the first official ascent of Tashi Kang I was not made until August 2002, when the summit was reached by four Japanese. It is not clear exactly which line they followed. Peak 6,195m lies immediately northwest of Tashi Kang and is separated from it by a high col. Both these peaks are relatively barren, with 6,195m having a rocky south face and small glacier close to the summit on the northern flank.

DAMODAR HIMAL

Putrung, attempt. One of the newly opened Mustang peaks, 6,466m Putrung in the southwestern Damodar Himal, was attempted by a seven-member Finnish expedition. Patrick Degerman's team tried the west-northwest ridge but was turned back at 6,050m on April 21.

ELIZABETH HAWLEY, *Nepal*

Saribung, a.k.a. Seliben (6,328m), first ascent. During October, Peter Ackroyd, Steve Furman, and I made the first ascent of this peak north of the Annapurnas. In 2002, while making the first ascent of 6,152m Gaugiri further north in the Damodar, Peter and I had viewed a handsome range of mountains to the south. To our knowledge this had been little explored, much less climbed. Upon our return to Kathmandu we consulted with Elizabeth Hawley, and then with the literature. It turned out that a few of the Damodar peaks had been climbed in the early 1980s by Japanese but until a couple of years ago the area had been closed to mountaineering. In the last few years, to try to increase tourism, Nepal has added over 150 peaks to the permitted list. Peter's and my ascent of Gaugiri was the first expedition to take advantage of the new regulations that made the organization needed to attempt peaks below 6,500m less bothersome.

As the three of us flew to Nepal, we planned to climb a peak named Birkuti, which had been given conflicting elevations between 6,300m and 6,900m. Upon meeting with Elizabeth Hawley in Kathmandu, we discovered that Birkuti had been climbed several times. A last minute scramble brought us a second peak permit, this one to Saribung. We were confident this had not been climbed. The peak was located much more in the center of the range and was therefore less accessible. It had been attempted twice previously by Japanese.

On October 2 we flew by white-knuckle charter from Kathmandu to Honge, an airstrip in the Manang Valley. From there we journeyed up the Phu Khola. Steve and I had explored the Phu Khola in 2000 and had made the first ascent of an unnamed 6,152m peak a couple of days northeast of the last village, Phu. We have named this peak Na Gore U South, after the deserted prehistoric ruins that stand near its foot. However, we had no idea of what the upper valley might present and were anxious to determine whether a pass into Tibet existed at the top.

A guide with horses was hired in the village of Phu and he led us to the upper part of the valley. We reached the edge of the Khamjungar Glacier in a couple of days. From this vantage point it was clear that there was no pass into Tibet, at least not where the map indicated it might be. Instead, there was a 600m wall of rock and ice. Our guide indicated that he had been into Tibet to trade salt but that the closest pass, a difficult one, existed far to the east.

As to what might lie up the Khamjungar Glacier, our guide had no information: the locals had no interest in a zone like this, which was devoid of grazing. The few peaks on the Khamjungar Glacier that had been climbed previously, had been reached from the north and west, never from the glacier itself. We were perhaps the first humans to set foot there, let alone traverse its ca13km length.

After several days of exploration of the glacier and its nasty moraine, and then finally sighting our objective, Saribung, which was only visible from a point above base camp, we established a high camp on the edge of the moraine at ca 5,730m. The day moving up to stay at this camp was punctuated with an early morning evacuation of a porter, who had contracted pulmonary edema. We sent five out of our 15 men down to the village of Phu with the porter. From there he was evacuated a couple of days later by helicopter and recovered completely.

On October 15 we negotiated the lower icefall and began encountering difficult snow conditions. We reached the north col and could see into the heart of the Damodar Range, which had only been explored by two or three Japanese teams over the last 20 years.

When the peak steepened to 70°-80° near its summit, we really wondered whether we would be able to get enough purchase in the miserable unconsolidated snow to gain elevation. We had to finish up a steep headwall at the top of the north ridge, which we had ascended to that point. The view from the top was incredible: monstrously twisted summits and glaciers all about us, the Annapurnas and Dhaulagiri to the south. To the north I could make out last year's peak, Gaugiri.

We headed out to Kathmandu by walking down the first part of the Annapurna Circuit trail to the road head at Besisahar. That journey was made more interesting when our hosts at one village rushed us into their house to hide us in darkness, having been notified that Maoist rebels, engaged in a bitter six-year civil war with the central government, had entered the village and "taken it over." They were said to be going house to house, extorting money. Because of American military aid to the Nepalese army, the anti-American sentiment had increased significantly. Our sirdar, who had suffered significant trouble from the Maoists in his own village, where they had extorted potatoes and money from him, was even more alarmed than our hosts. A modest amount of medicinal whiskey and cigar smoke by candlelight calmed our nerves. In the middle of the night, when it was not quite light enough to see, we took flight from the village, avoiding all conflict with the Maoists. We were soon down at the next village for breakfast, surrounded by Nepalese army troops.

A wild and remote area, the Damodar Himal offers untold exploration for those who are interested in such things. This was my fourth trip to the range in four years, and each one has produced at least one first ascent of a 6,000m peak.

JIM FRUSH, *AAC*

Editor's note: Tamotsu Ohnishi from Japan reached 6,000m on the north ridge in the summer of 2002 but was turned around by a sudden storm.

Gaugiri, second and third ascents by a new route. The 6,110m Gaugiri in upper Mustang, first ascended in 2002 via the southwest ridge by Peter Ackroyd and Jim Frush, as noted above, received second and third ascents in 2003. On September 8, Josep Aced, Adria Font, Francesc Zapater, all from Spain, and Sergi Benet from Andorra reached the summit via the north face to northeast ridge. Later, on the 21st of the month, Kenneth McConnell, Dendi Sherpa, and Ongdi Sherpa made the third ascent of the mountain via the northeast ridge.

ELIZABETH HAWLEY, *Nepal*

Amotsang reconnaissance and first ascents of Thansunjiti (6,084m) and Jomson (6,335m). One of the expeditions on newly opened mountains was unsuccessful in its bids to climb this previously unattempted summit. A French team under the leadership of Paulo Grobel first had to make some exploration of the area in order to determine the correct location of their peak, Amotsang (6,392m), which lies to the northwest of Pokharkan in the West Manang–Damodar Region. After this they then had to decide which line to take. In the end, they never set foot on the mountain.

While some members made first ascents of two nearby mountains, three French members and one of their Sherpas went looking for the best place to set up a base camp from where they could scale Amotsang. The expedition had originally expected to climb the west ridge but quickly realized this was not possible. Instead, the explorers went around its southern side and then northward to the east side. They concluded that the best approach would be from its east side. By now there was no time left for a serious attempt. "At least we know where the mountain is and where there is a route up it," Grobel remarked.

The two neighboring mountains climbed were: Thansunjiti (6,084m) on November 2 by Joycelyn Chavy, Hugues,de Varax, Yves Ebrayat, Frédéric Gaume, Grobel, Camille Jacquet, Neils Martin, Stephane Rouge, Ratna Man Lama, and Mingma Temba Sherpa via the north ridge; Jomson (6,335m) on November 4 by de Varax, Exbrayet, Gaume, Grobel, and Mingma Temba via the west ridge.

ELIZABETH HAWLEY, *Nepal*

ANNAPURNA HIMAL

Annapurna III (7,555m), first ascent of the southwest ridge. On November 6, Kenton Cool and Ian Parnell, both from the UK, and myself completed the first ascent of the ca 2,400m southwest ridge of Annapurna III. The route had been attempted in 1994 and 2000 by two strong Slovenian teams, numbering as large as 11 members. They had both employed the heavy-handed tactics of fixed rope and camps. The Anglo-American team acclimatized by climbing the lower one third of the route, loosely following an 18-pitch topo from the Slovenians. We encountered extremely loose rock and decaying in-situ ropes on the dangerous and challenging 600m buttress. We then bivouacked at ca 6,000m for two days and established a well-stocked camp for a forthcoming summit attempt. We then descended to base camp for a four-day rest.

On the successful summit attempt the team climbed alpine style, with two climbers leading all the lower rock buttress free at 5.10X without the use of any fixed rope (although both the rope and anchors were used for descent). After reaching the 6,000m camp, a further nine days were spent on the mountain.

The remaining climbing first involved 900m of committing snow and ice. This was followed by a 250m mixed rock band at 6,800m, which was climbed free at 5.8 and M5. Two days later the summit was reached via exposed knife-edge ridges of poor snow, resulting from extremely high winds. On reaching the top at 12:30 p.m. on November 6, we descended to a snow cave at 7,000m before continuing down for a further two-and-a-half days to base camp. [A lead story on this ascent appears earlier in this Journal.]

JOHN VARCO, *AAC*

PERI HIMAL

Gyajikang, unsuccessful attempt. An expedition from the Czech Republic led by Karel Plechac attempted this 7,038m peak to the northwest of Manaslu. The first and only recorded ascent of the mountain took place in October 1994 when a large Japanese-Nepalese expedition (joint climbing leaders Osamu Tanabe and Dinesh Chandra Pokhrel) put no less than 17 people on the summit. They fixed ca 1,500m of rope on the northwest spur, which joins the west ridge at 6,600m. The Czech climbers attempted to climb onto the northwest spur via the northeast flank but gave up on October 26 at 5,850m. This was the third attempt on this high peak south of the Himlung Group, the second taking place in the autumn of 2002, when a three-member Dutch-Belgian team reached 6,250m on the north face.

ELIZABETH HAWLEY, *Nepal*

Himlung, ascent. A Spanish expedition led by Inigo Loyola made the fourth ascent of Himlung (7,126m) in the Peri Himal. The previous three ascents have all been by the straightforward west ridge (Japanese in 1992; French in 2001 and French again in 2002). However, the Spanish report climbing the northwest face, arriving at the summit in two groups on April 18 and 20. The first party comprised Andoni Etxezarreta and Mitxel Insausti, while the second contained the leader with Ramon Iturrikastillo and Juan Jodar. A broad and relatively gently angled spur rises from the northwest to meet the west ridge close to the summit.

In the autumn seven separate permits were issued for this mountain and the west ridge was successfully climbed by six expeditions.

ELIZABETH HAWLEY, *Nepal*

LANGTANG HIMAL

Yansa Tsenji attempt. A British commercially-organized expedition led by David Pritt was unsuccessful in an attempt on the east ridge of this recently opened 6,643m peak on the north side of the Langtang Valley (northeast of Kyanjin Gompa). The team reached a high point of 6,120m on October 20. Although it is well-known that many if not most of the peaks above the Langtang have seen unauthorized ascents in the past, there is no officially-recorded ascent for this mountain, which is also known as Dragpoche Ri.

LINDSAY GRIFFIN, *High Mountain INFO*

JUGAL HIMAL

Triangle Peak, attempt on west (southwest) couloir. By October 1, 2001 all of our gear was at Pemthang Karpo Kharkha (4,675m), our campsite in the Langtang Valley. It used to be a classic stop for pirates on route to Xixabangma. Looking north from there, on the left wall of the Langtang Glacier, there is an arête descending between Karpo (6,875m) and Langtang Ri (7,205m). The route was more than evident: a couloir facing west, where ice appeared to run from bottom to top. There were no seracs but it still looked a pretty stiff climb, with ramps of blue ice, chutes, and columns. After making two acclimatization climbs to 5,800m we left on October 17 with big rucksacks and climbed from the 18th-20th. We progressed unroped at first up snow to 75°. The chute, sandwiched between two big rock walls, was two vertical pitches of poor snow ice, above which there were easier angled slopes of hard black ice. It was easy to see the drop between both front points of the same crampon. What surprised us was there was nowhere horizontal on which to bivouac. In the end we spent the night on the lower part of the second icefield. In addition, each of the two days we were on the face, mist enveloped us at midday. At 6,100m, in the middle of a monotonous 70° ice slope and with no real visibility, we decided to go down. Although we seemed to be around 150m below the col at the top of the couloir, the mist, wind, and almost constant stone and ice fall were both dangerous and miserable. If the mind is telling you it doesn't want to go on anymore, then there is no col that can serve as an excuse, even if it was almost within sight. We began a series of 100m rappels (we climbed on a 100m rope doubled and carried a spare of the same length and 8mm diameter in the rucksack) and bivouacked again in the same spot, reaching the bottom of the face on the following day.

The rockfall-prone west couloir leading to the west col of Triangle Peak. The Catalan attempt reached a point about 150m below the col. *Xavi Farré*

We achieved no summit, nor did we reach a ridge, so perhaps it is not relevant to give our climb a name. Our satisfaction was in climbing and returning in one piece. It was not a lengthy expedition but a major excursion. Furthermore, we can say to those who have already photographed this obvious line, "there is a way!" On the other hand, if we don't say anything, people will call the route the Spanish (or Catalan) 2001 attempt, whereas in fact we both come from the same state, in the Pyrenees, Rigagorca.

Ribagorca attempt: west (southwest) couloir to west col (6,240m) of 6,600m Triangle Peak (October 2001, 1300m, VII 5 M X). Triangle Peak is a summit on the wall between Pemthang Karpo Ri (aka Dome Blanc, 6,830m) and Pemthang Ri (6,842m) on the long wall that runs northwest from Lenpo Gang (Big White Peak) to Hagen's Col. There are many similar lines, all around 1,000-1,500m in height, leading to the ridge that forms the Nepal-Tibet border at ca 6,500m. Our line was chosen because it was only two hours across the Langtang Glacier and was not threatened by serac avalanche. However, it is important to emphasize that the stone fall was very serious.

XAVI FARRÉ, *Spain*

Historical note: Hagen's Col (mentioned above) was named for the Swiss mountain traveler Toni Hagen, who died in April 2003. Hagen worked as a geologist for the U.N. and from 1953 onward undertook the first geological survey of Nepal. He was the first foreigner to really trek the length and breadth of the country, making a total of 19 expeditions, visiting almost every valley and covering a distance of over 14,000km in around eight years. He took the first pictures of the south side of Xixabangma. Over the years many mountaineers gained great insight and inspiration from the books and photographs that he published.

LINDSAY GRIFFIN, *High Mountain INFO*

Gurkarpo Ri, another unsuccessful Korean attempt on this unclimbed peak. Koreans led by Kim Myung-Sin were back for another attempt on the unclimbed 6,891m Gurkarpo Ri, which is situated on the Tibetan border northwest of Lenpo Gang. It appears to be a very difficult peak that has thwarted at least three previous attempts: two by Koreans in the winters of 1993 and 2001, and an autumn 1999 attempt by Germans. Last year the Koreans were attempting the southeast face but got no further than 5,750m on September 25.

ELIZABETH HAWLEY, *Nepal*

MALAHANGUR HIMAL (KHUMBU)

Teng Kang Poche, first ascent of the northeast face to east ridge. During November 2003 Jules Cartwright and I made two attempts on the 1,600m northwest face of Teng Kang Poche (6,500m), the first of which also included Al Powell. An easy approach of one hour from the lodge at Thyongbo brought us to the start of the climb at 8 a.m. on the 14th. Finding good snow conditions, we climbed unroped up the initial snow cone and continued into a runnel/gully. The line chosen followed this gully system, which was 55-75° névé at Scottish II to IV. At one point a mixed corner had to be followed in order to bypass an overhang in the gully. This proved quite difficult and had short sections of Scottish V, 6 until we rejoined the original line. Slightly above this point, we cut a tent ledge for the first night (ca 4,800m).

The second day continued in the same vein, although we started to pitch the climbing, because despite being more or less the same grade, it was more sustained. At approximately 5 p.m. we cut a tent ledge for the second night. The pitch above proved the hardest so far at V, 6. That evening I fell ill, and was vomiting and delirious for 40 minutes. We decided to descend, and the next day, the 16th, rappelled from our high point at 5,400m and reached Thame by 3:30 p.m.

I recovered quickly but Powell's time had now run out and he was forced to leave. On our second attempt Cartwright and I made an 11-hour ascent to our previous high point. No food or gas was taken as a stash had been left there. However, the conditions were serious with very high winds and constant spindrift. In addition, a certain amount of stone and ice fall was encountered. Much of the ground we had previously climbed unroped now had to be pitched, as it was uncertain when the next lump of ice or rock would strike.

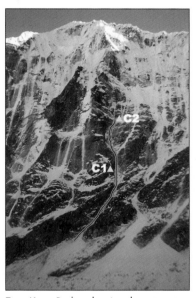

The night was a fraught affair. So was the following day sitting out the wind in hope of more favorable conditions. We spent a second night at our 5,400m camp but on the 24th we decided to abandon the attempt and escape in an early morning lull.

Well to the left of the prominent granite north pillar is a left-to-right ramp line, leading to the lowest point on the east ridge. I had stared at this line for two weeks and after our failure to climb a new route on the northwest face, decided it was time to have a look. I was

Teng Kang Poche, showing the attempt on the northwest face. *Nick Bullock*

now by myself as both Cartwright and Powell had returned to Britain. This line looked the most suitable for a solo attempt.

Starting at 1:30 a.m. on November 27, I climbed the lower slopes via a left-to-right path under the steep rock walls beneath the east ridge. Although the ground was not technical in the lower 600-800m, it was tiring due to deep unconsolidated snow and the laborious nature of traversing the undulating,

Teng Kang Poche's north face showing Nick Bullock's route of ascent (right) and descent (left). *Nick Bullock*

fluted ground. Below the lowest point of the east ridge I decided to continue right, aiming for runnels that appeared to lead directly to the summit. The shortest line to the ridge above me appeared to finish up mixed ground, which looked difficult in the half-light of dawn. After two previously unsuccessful attempts on the northwest face, I craved success and so opted for a more certain line. Or so I thought.

As daylight approached and I gained height, it became apparent I would have to cross a deep couloir. An active band of seracs on the east ridge towered above and gave me cause for concern. Deciding that crossing below the seracs was too risky, I climbed a rib of mixed ground until directly beneath them (100m, Scottish V, 5). The terrain prior to this had gradually increased in angle, being 60-80°, at a grade of Scottish IV/V, and quite tenuous due to the unconsolidated nature of the snow.

Moving left, I climbed steep, hard ice to reach the crest of the east ridge. I continued up this until ca 200m below the summit, where I bivouacked in a large crevasse as my hands and feet needed re-warming. It was 2:30 p.m. and I had taken 13 hours to reach this ca 6,350m point on the ridge.

The following morning I attempted to reach the summit but found the way above very crevassed and far too dangerous for a solo climber. I decided to go down and followed the ridge to its lowest point, where I made two 30m rappels on the northeast face and then down-climbed directly to reach my traverse line followed on the ascent. By 1:30 p.m. I had reached my starting point in the valley at 4,300m and later decided to name my route to the east ridge, Love and Hate (Alpine D+/TD-).

NICK BULLOCK, *U.K.*

Editor's note: the east ridge of Teng Kang Poche has probably been climbed on several occasions from the Lumding Valley to the south, and was certainly climbed in 1984.

Pharilapcha-Machermo Peak (6,017 m), first official ascent. The first authorized ascent of this recently permitted trekking peak in the Khumbu valley was made from the west in spring 2003. The team comprised Israfil Ashurly (Russia), Marcelo Rey Belo (Brazil), Juliana N. Bechara Belo (Brazil), Josko Bozic (Croatia), Stipe Bozic (Croatia), Valentine Grakovithch (Russia), Viktor Groselj (Slovenia), Vladimir Mesaric (Croatia), Vladimir Shataev (Russia), Rafael Vodisek (Slovenia), and a Sherpa team. Their route is said to follow the west ridge.

SEB CONSTANT, *France*

Pharilapcha-Machermo Peak (6,017 m), first ascent of north face (The Bonfire of the Vanities), and southwest side (The Bridge of Lost Desire). The north face of this peak, dominating Gokyo village, remained virgin. Climbing it had been a dream of mine for seven years, ever since the beauty of the lines running down that rocky, shady wall, like yogurt flowing over a dark surface, had impressed me during a trek in the Khumbu. Of course, I knew destiny would bring me there again, but when? Finally Jerome Mercader and I arrived in the autumn of 2003. Before our north face ascent we established The Bridge of Lost Desire on the southwest side during a reconnaissance of the peak. This showed us an easy descent for our north face attempt.

Because we are lazy boys we set up our base camp at a lodge in Machermo village, one day's walk from the foot of the face. Why do we require the services of a cook, sirdar, and staff on a mountain like this, when you can travel so light? We were just two friends ready for a long and sustained alpine-style adventure.

We climbed on the right side of the 1,000m north face via a system of gullies. We adopted a very light style, carrying rucksacks that weighed only eight kilos and held three days food, one canister of gas, a small stove, one small Thermarest, one sleeping bag, one bivouac tent constructed by myself (weighs only one kilo) and our climbing gear; five ice screws, a set of nuts, six pitons, and five cams. Due to the cold weather we had to climb in down suits.

In total we climbed 27 pitches, with two bivouacs on the face in the micro tent. Many pitches had very thin snow or ice covering the rock and were hard to protect due to the poor quality of the snow. The hardest thing was to put in rock protection. It was a challenging and amazing climb, and the style

The north face of Pharilapcha-Machermo, showing The Bonfire of the Vanities. *Seb Constant*

of our ascent required us to ponder on the prospect of retreat with our minimal rack. We summited on the third day, atop a thin snow ridge with a complete view of Everest and Cho-Oyu. And we finally had sun to warm our bodies.

We established The Bridge of Lost Desire (ca 350m, V M4 WI3), on November 18 in a 12-hour round trip from a 5,200m high camp. The route was 11 pitches to the summit ridge and

began at an obvious snow cone 600m to the right of the west col. First, there was a mixed wall (M4) above the rimaye, after which we followed a snow couloir for three pitches (50°). Above, was one M4 crux section to surmount a small step, after which two pitches in a snow couloir brought us to rocky terraces. From this point you can see the summit ridge, which we reached in three pitches (snow from 45-65°). Here you join the traditional route (I guess, because we saw a sling on a block). Two exposed pitches led to easy ground

The southwest face of Pharilapcha-Machermo, showing The Bridge of Lost Desires. *Seb Constant*

Jerome Mercader in action on the north face of Pharilapcha-Machermo.
Seb Constant

and the top. To descend we climbed down the couloir to the rocky terraces and then followed a loose, rocky ridge 20m to the right of the couloir. Before the last wall (above the rimaye) we crossed left to the couloir and made rappel.

Le Bucher des Vanités (The Bonfire Of The Vanities) (1,000m, VI M5 WI4), November 22-24. The route: three pitches (some M4) up the first wall to a long snow band that splits the lower part of the face. The first crux lies in the couloir system above (The Three Gullies; three pitches of snow and ice to 80/85°). We made a tight bivouac on a snow ledge at 5,670m. From here, a two-pitch traverse left enabled us to start the delicate M5 dance in the "Perdition Wall." A gully continued up right and gave five pitches to 65°, with the last crux on crumbly rock (M5) before joining the summit ridge. We made our second bivouac at 5,960m, just under the summit ridge. Next day, two pitches on the sharp ridge above led to easy ground and the summit. We down-climbed the southwest side of the peak by The Bridge of Lost Desires.

SEB CONSTANT, *France*

Hungchi, first ascent. A five-hour walk northward from Gokyo along the right bench of the Ngojumba Glacier brought us to a plateau commanding a good view of Everest, Cho Oyu, Gyachung Kang, and Hungchi (7,036m). We proceeded to base camp, which had an entire view of Hungchi and beyond. We passed a lovely grassland, studded with rocks we called "the Japanese Garden." Just out of advanced base camp the snow-covered slope gets gradually steeper and we began fixing ropes along the route to the foot of a long side ridge that leads directly to the main line of the southwest ridge. We reached the crest via 60° snow-covered slopes.

We followed the snow-covered ridge until we came to the base of a massive rock, where we pitched Camp 1. From there, we found a couloir on the rock face, fixed the main rope to the left of it, and continued up. Although it was technically a Grade III-IV section, the altitude made hammering a piton a difficult task. We ended up pitching Camp 2 right on the narrow ridge. After following the snow ridge for some time, we moved on to the eastern flank, traversing a 50-60° ice face.

With utmost care we followed the ridge, which was much narrower than expected and was a series of continual ups and downs. Finally we came to the foot of a snow wall on the right. This is where we had to retreat in 2001 because of soft snow.

Finally, at 12:10 a.m. on April 19 we stood on the summit. We anchored ourselves to a piton on the narrow summit, exchanged messages with base camp, and took pictures. Half-an-hour passed all too soon and mist began creeping in. We buried national flags of both countries under the snow, and left the summit. Expedition members were: Takashi Shiro (leader), Kanji

Shimizu, Tadashi Morita, and Katsuo Fukuhara. The Nepalese sirdar was Tul Bahadur Tamang, and the high altitude porters were Ram Kaji Tamang, Hitman Tamang, and Santaman Tamang. All these except Shiro reached the summit.

TAKASHI SHIRO, *Osaka Eiho Alpine Club*

Hungchi, which lies south of the Nup La on the eastern rim of the Ngojumba Glacier, which itself forms the Nepal-Tibet frontier, is sometimes referred to as Cha Khung or Gyuba Tshomotse, and Fungqi in Chinese. Some members of the 2003 Japanese expedition had taken part in the first official attempt on this mountain, which was made via the southwest ridge during the autumn of 2001. However, with permitted but unclimbed 7,000ers in Nepal at a premium, it will perhaps come as no surprise to find the Japanese were not the only party on the mountain. Summiting just five days later was a group of Koreans. Few details are known of their ascent but for the most part they followed in the footsteps of the Japanese. Their route only differed in the initial section, where it is believed they approached the crest of the southwest ridge via the southeast rather than the west flank. Kim Jeon-Am, Kim Seung-Koo, Kim Sung-Ho, Jeong Chan-Il, and Yoo Cheoi-Mok report reaching the summit on April 24.

LINDSAY GRIFFIN, *High Mountain INFO*

Cholatse (6,440m), north face attempt. Corean Alpine Club expedition leader, Kang Sung-woo, returned to the north face of Cholatse in 2003 after bad weather thwarted an attempt the previous year. In 2002 the intended line had been a new route up the right side of the face but after nearly five weeks with considerable rain, snow and associated avalanche danger, the team reached a high point of only 5,200m.

Kang's team in 2003, which included Hwang In-seon, Hwang Young-soon, Lee Young-joon, Kim Chae-ho and Yang Byeong-ok left Incheon on September 24 and reached base camp on October 5. The climbers spent just over a week establishing advanced base at 4,900m and then the following week fixing 13 roped pitches to 5,450m. Here, they established Camp 1 at a place dubbed The Turtle's Head, due to the distinguishing features of a prominent rib directly above.

Over the next four days alternating teams of two and three climbers worked their way up to 5,700m. The Turtle's Head

The Korean 2003 attempt on Cholatse's north face (left) and the French route of 1995. *Kang Sung-woo*

consisted of seven pitches varying from 75° to 110°. Lee Young-joon and Kim Chae-ho aided through the 100m crux section, then traversed, still on aid, 30m left to gain the mixed terrain of an adjoining gully. Looking up, the route to the summit appeared to lie directly up the small gully and all the difficult climbing appeared to be behind them. The previously named pair, together with Hwang Young-soon, then were forced to sit out poor weather at CI for five days, waiting for the next opportunity to climb.

When this opportunity arose, several days were spent cleaning snow-buried lines from base camp to Camp I. On October 28, Hwang Young-soon and Kim Chae-ho bivouacked at 5,600m in preparation for their summit bid. They cleared CI and after a rest climbed up to a second bivouac at 5,800m. On the 30th, a large icicle falling from above knocked Hwang Young-soon off balance at 6,000m; a piton popped and he took a 15m lead fall, damaging his leg. Hwang and Kim were forced to stop and bivouac for night. Hwang endured the pain of his seriously injured leg but began to suffer frostbite in the feet due to poor circulation. The two men were therefore forced to abort their summit bid.

Despite the motivation of the majority of remaining climbers to rest for a few more days and go for a second summit attempt, Kang, concerned about his team, wisely discouraged further attempts. Various members of the expedition had already sustained a broken shoulder, a fractured rib, severe frostbite, and a badly damaged ankle, and two of the team had been forced to leave early for further medical treatment. Although the summit was within reach, it was not the primary goal of Kang's agenda: for his climbers, climbing is breathing, breathing is living, and living is climbing another day.

PETER JENSEN-CHOI, *Corean Alpine Club and AAC*

Khangri Shar, attempt. Khangri Shar (6,811m) is one of many unclimbed peaks in the Nepal Himalaya opened for climbing by the Nepalese government in the fall of 2002. It is located west of Pumori in the Khumbu Himal in northeastern Nepal. The Changri Glacier flows into the Khumbu Glacier near Gorakshep, through the "Everest Highway." Khangri Shar soars dominantly between the heads of the East Changri Glacier and its side glacier on the Pumori side. We chose the side glacier as our route, naming it the "JAC Glacier."

The Khangri Glacier is often referred to as Changri Glacier on older maps. Locals call it "Changri"; therefore "Changri Shar" would be the most authentic name of the peak. (The col on the border was the same as that reached by the Americans in 1990 who unsuccessfully tried the northwest ridge of Pumori and referred to Khangri Shar as Chumo.)

Makoto Nebuka and Sherpa Anu made a reconnaissance in the winter of 2002, and identified three potential routes, only one of which was considered possible for our senior members— over 55 years old. This route leads to the summit via a col on the border and the east ridge. In pre-monsoon 2003 we crossed the Kongrama Pass (ca 5,300m) to acclimatize. We only had a expedition permit for a one-month period, so some of the members had to descend, as they had not recovered from altitude sickness.

Base camp was located on a plateau near a small glacial lake at the foot of Pumori. Four Sherpas went ahead and established the climbing route. We crossed the JAC Glacier tongue, then ascended a slope of the side moraine and began to climb a rock wall. Along the ridge we reached C1 on a glacier plateau at about 6,000m. We fixed 600m of rope from the foot of the wall to C1. We fixed 600m of rope from the foot of the wall to C1. Above, a superb rocky spur led directly up the southeast face to the summit would have been an exhilarating ascent for skilled climbers. We, however, continued toward the 6,497m col and the next morning began to climb, encountering crevasses about five meters in width, which forced us to give up the ascent. We returned to Namche Bazaar via the Everest Highway.

KANENORI EMOTO, *Japanese Alpine Club*

Mt. Everest Jubilee; an overview of events on Everest 50 years after its first ascent. Although some of the records discussed below actually took place on the Tibetan side of the mountain, it was felt appropriate to keep this overview of pre-monsoon Everest events on all flanks of the peak more or less complete.

It seemed the whole world's attention was focused on Mt. Everest this spring to mark the 50th anniversary of its first ascent. Not only climbing magazines but also periodicals of general interest devoted pages or even entire issues to it, and new books were published.

Nepalese organizations including the government sponsored a series of events and the King conferred honorary Nepalese citizenship on Hillary in recognition not only of his pioneer ascent with the late Tenzing Norgay Sherpa, but also for his tireless work over the following decades in bettering the lives of the people living in the Everest region with the construction of schools and hospitals and renovations of Buddhist monasteries. Hillary is the first foreigner ever to be made an honorary citizen.

On the 8,850m mountain were half the 137 expeditions attempting to climb any Nepalese Himalayan peak over ca 6,500m. The Everest teams numbered 35 on Nepal's side and 34 on the Tibetan slopes, and all but two of them attempted the standard routes via the South Col and southeast ridge from Nepal or by the North Col to the north face and north ridge. (By comparison, the largest previous numbers, in the millennium spring of 2000, were 27 on Nepal's side and 29 on the Tibetan side.)

Neither of the two expeditions to non-standard routes succeeded, but one demonstrated that it is still possible to find an unclimbed route on Everest and even perhaps a previously unattempted one. Ian Woodall, originally from Britain, and his wife Cathy O'Dowd, South African, both of whom had already summited Everest from its south and north sides, went with just one climbing Sherpa to try to forge a totally new route on the huge east face in Tibet. They had chosen one of three ribs between the so-called American buttress, near the south end of the vast face, and the east ridge in its middle.

But when the couple reached base camp, they found massive avalanching of hanging seracs in the area of the ribs and concluded that an attempt would require a fast, non-stop alpine-style effort, which they were not prepared to make. So they tackled the east ridge, a forbiddingly steep and difficult feature, which had defeated the two teams who tried it previously. They chose as their approach a snow ramp leading to the ridge from its southern side. However, O'Dowd and Ang Gyalzen Sherpa gave up at an altitude of just 5,800m on the ramp, 200m below the ridge. They had not brought gear to fix rope in deep snow, and after Woodall had become ill, only two climbers were still active.

In terms of numbers of climbers, expeditions ranged from just one independent individual on someone else's permit, to nearly 80 members and Sherpas from a joint Indo-Nepalese Army expedition to both Everest and its immediate neighbor, Lhotse. Climbers came from all over the world: Iceland, Estonia, Georgia, Andorra, Bhutan, Kuwait, South Africa, New Zealand, and

Ecuador, as well as from the usual countries such as the U.S., Britain, Spain, and Japan.

There might have been even more. A London newspaper reported that a British team had been forced to cancel their plans to go to the north side because by the time they wanted to reach Everest in early May—a rather late date—the Chinese government had already closed Tibet to all entrants in order to prevent the acute respiratory illness known as SARS from spreading into Tibet. A few Romanians also were refused entry to join a team already there. (The border was re-opened on July 1.) And when Hillary heard about plans by two New Zealand and two British skiers and skateboarders to race down the mountain from 7,000m to mark the anniversary of his ascent, he described the idea as "rather dangerous ... and not appropriate." They did not turn up.

Base camp at the Nepalese foot of the mountain was a sizable village of tents housing 441 climbers on the 35 Everest teams, plus their base camps staffs, members and Sherpas on other expeditions, 10 for Lhotse's west face and one for Nuptse's north side, bringing the total expedition personnel to at least 600. And then there were the staffs of a satellite communications tent, several small cafes, a medical clinic, a massage parlor for a brief time, some shops selling soap and t-shirts, plus numerous trekking groups. The total population at base camp perhaps occasionally reached the same figure as the entire population of the area's largest village, Namche Bazar, which is about 850.

One notable visitor was Reinhold Messner, who was appalled by the scene. He noted that tents stretched one kilometer from the bottom end to the top, and that the cafes were well patronized by the Sherpa "Icefall Doctors" who were trying to forget their dangerous daily task of repairing the Khumbu Icefall route, as seracs toppled over and crevasses widened.

Climbers on the Nepalese side complained this spring of having to wait a long time to go up or down the Hillary Step, where there were many others ahead of them in the queue: one leader reported that it had taken his summit party two-and-a-half hours on May 26 to climb the fairly short distance from the south summit to the top, whereas it would normally have taken them only one hour. An American, who frequently leads teams on the south side of Everest, believed that the competence of this spring's climbers was lower than before, and he cited the specific case of members belonging to a Japanese expedition as being "really, really slow."

The number of people who actually died on Everest this spring was remarkably low considering the large number on the mountain. Those who perished were just one Pole, Krysztof Liszewski, who fell to his death, perhaps blown off balance by the wind, one Nepalese summiter on the Indo-Nepalese army team, Bhim Bahadur Gurung, who was a victim of altitude sickness and fell into a crevasse in the Khumbu Icefall—the 20th person ever to die in the Icefall—and Karma Gyalzen Sherpa who succumbed to altitude sickness.

Some noted mountaineers, including Hillary and Messner, have publicly voiced strong views that the numbers of people given permits to climb Everest should be greatly restricted. This is for a variety of reasons: safety of others, pollution of the mountain with abandoned oxygen cylinders, broken tents, and other kinds of rubbish, the belief that climbers on Everest—or perhaps any mountain—should be limited to preserve the adventure of their accomplishment. Some urge that only climbers who have already had the experience of summiting at least one 8,000m peak be allowed to attempt Everest.

By no means was everybody successful this spring: one-third of the 69 teams did not make it to the top. A long period of very bad weather with fierce winds and considerable amounts of snowfall resulted in many tents being destroyed, supplies of food and gear being irretrievably buried, people losing top strength over the days and weeks on the mountain, and time running out. A number of these groups simply gave up and went home instead of waiting patiently for better weather.

Nevertheless a record number of mountaineers did succeed when weather finally permitted. From May 20 to 31 an astonishing 251 people, foreigners and Nepalese, men, women, and one 15-year-old child, stood on the summit of Everest. It had taken 25 years for the 251st person to reach the summit—October 1988.

On just one day in 2003, May 22, 103 summited. From the Nepalese side, there were 66 on the top that day, while 37 came up from Tibet. Before this season, the largest number on a single day was 89 on May 23, 2001 (47 from the south and 42 from the north), and during that month of May, 182 from both sides.

Notable among the men and women who succeeded were:

* The first Arab, Zaid Aasa Al-Refa'i, a Kuwaiti.

* The first black from any country, Sibusiso Vilane, of South Africa. He said he did his climb to show other black people that they can do it too. "It was very exciting to be the first black on the summit ... I am very proud." He added that he would like to climb another 8,000m mountain, and this one he would do for himself.

* The first one-armed person, an American, Gary Guller, who found his biggest problem was keeping his balance, especially when descending the Hillary Step, since he had no left arm or prothesis to help steady him. (A Sherpa who has no hands, Ungdi Tshering, got no higher than 7,300m but claims he is sure he will be able to get to the top if he can find sponsorship for another attempt.)

* The oldest summiter, 70, Yuichiro Miura, a Japanese who became famous in 1970 as the "man who skied down Everest" when he made a dramatic partial ski descent. In his climb to the top, he used a considerable amount of artificial oxygen: while sleeping in Camp II in the Western Cwm at 6,400m and throughout the rest of his ascent to the summit and descent to Camp II. Miura was five years older than the oldest person before him.

* The youngest, Mingkipa Sherpa, who said she was only 15 years and nine months old. The previous record-holder was a Nepalese Sherpa boy, Tashi Tshiri, who was just over 16 years old when he summited in May 2001.

* The first person to reach the top for the 13th time, Apa Sherpa, who is 42 years old. He made his first ascent in May 1990, summited every year after that except in 1996 and 2001, and went to the top twice in 1992. He says he may go to Everest again, since this is how he earns a living.

* The fastest ascent—in fact two of them in just four days—on the Nepalese side by Pemba Dorje Sherpa on May 21/22 and by Lhakpa Gelu on the 25th/26th. Both used bottled oxygen in the final stage of their climbs. Lhakpa Gelu climbed alone, while Pemba Dorje had a friend with him from the South Col. They were challenging the previous speed record for an ascent on the Nepalese side set by another Sherpa, Babu Chiri (Tshering), who reported he had summited on May 21, 2000, in just 16 hours, 56 minutes after he had left base camp the evening before. Pemba Dorje said it took him just 12 hours and 45 minutes to climb from bottom to top. Lhakpa Gelu said he himself spent only 10 hours and 56 minutes to do the entire ascent.

Pemba Dorje charged Lhakpa Gelu with lying about his times and continued to insist, in statements to both Nepal's tourism ministry and to the press, that he had made the fastest ascent. Lhakpa Gelu countered with his own statement to the ministry and added supporting documents. The government's liaison officer posted at base camp had recorded the time he set out at the start of his ascent; Apa Sherpa noted the time at which he himself reached the top, and

Lhakpa Gelu, Apa confirmed, had been there not much later. The ministry's verdict was not given immediately, but no one doubts Apa's evidence.

Lhakpa Gelu set up a brass Nepalese flag on an iron pole at the summit. As long as it stands, it can provide proof of success for anyone having a photo taken of himself standing next to it. The 1975 Chinese tripod provided proof for nearly a decade, and Lhakpa Gelu's flag was doing the same this spring.

* Another first, but on a much less serious note: the first person to play a guitar on the summit, Vernon Tejas from the U.S. He strummed his 1.4kg instrument very briefly.

ELIZABETH HAWLEY, *Nepal*

Everest, summer and autumn attempts with ski and snowboard. In stark contrast to the spring season, when 69 teams swarmed on the north and south sides of Everest, there was only one expedition on the entire mountain in the summer and just one other in the autumn, both of them American, and both with plans for ski and snowboard descents. Unfavorable snow conditions thwarted their attempts. The summer team consisting of Jimmy Chin and Stephen Koch were on the north side of the mountain and their activities are reported in the Tibet section of this Journal. In the autumn five Americans and six Sherpas, led by Wally Berg, nearly made history when they narrowly failed to make the first November ascent of Everest. Team members left the South Col on November 1 for their final summit attempt and by 8 a.m. had reached the South Summit. Here, they were "blasted by very abrupt strong winds" and forced to descend. Back at the Col they found all three tents had been torn apart.

ELIZABETH HAWLEY, *Nepal*

Nuptse East I, south face, pre-monsoon attempts. Immediately to the south of Everest is the jagged Nuptse, which has numerous summits with no easy access from its southern flanks. By coincidence, independent teams of highly-skilled European mountaineers, one led by Hans Kammerlander from Italy's South Tirol, and the other led by Valeri Babanov of Russia, came this spring to attempt the first ascent of the southeast pillar that leads directly to the 7,804m unclimbed peak known as Nuptse East I. This line is technically extremely demanding.

Kammerlander with Konard Auer, Alois Brugger, Wilfried Oberhofer, and a German camera crew arrived rather late, and seeing the Russians well-established on the pillar, opted for a line up the face to the left, more or less in the vicinity of the 2002 American-Canadian-Slovenian attempt. Ropes were fixed on the lower section and the team gained the upper section of the southwest-facing spur. They eventually established a high camp at 6,900m, before being driven down by very strong winds.

Babanov had made an unsuccessful solo attempt on the pillar in the autumn of 2002 and this time was accompanied by Vladimir Suviga. The Russian pair arrived in April and again established ropes on the pillar, this time surmounting the difficulties and reaching the top of the pillar at ca 6,400m, then continuing up snow slopes to establish a tent at ca 6,700m, before they, too, retreated in the high winds and stormy weather that also affected Kammerlander's team. When the weather cleared Babanov and Suviga left base camp late on May 4 and regained their high point. They then pushed on up to the final ca 400m mixed buttress. However, above 7,000m the weather turned poor with snow and strong winds. Ground down by the cold (estimated to be below –30°C) and insufficient acclimatization to this high altitude, the pair finally came to a halt on May 10 at ca 7,450m. Above, the mixed terrain looked hard and icy and the pair decided to retreat, hoping for another attempt later in the month. In the meantime the South Tyrol team had regained their high camp but once again been forced to retreat.

Subsequently, the weather did not allow either group to make another attempt and the Russians, who were the last to leave, finally abandoned their efforts because of too much snowfall, their exhaustion, and lack of time to get well-rested before resuming the climb.

ELIZABETH HAWLEY, *Nepal*

Nuptse East I (7,804m), first ascent. Last autumn's attempt on the southeast pillar of Nuptse East I was the third by Valeri Babanov of Russia. Babanov had made an unsuccessful solo attempt on this pillar in the autumn of 2002, and in the spring of 2003 returned with Vladimir Suviga as noted above. But he was not willing to give up, and now he knew the route well. This time, at last, Babanov, with Yuri Koshelenko, stood at the pointed summit of Nuptse East I in bright moonlight. They had made one attempt to make their way up the route on October 21 and 22 but only reached 6,900m, before very strong winds forced them to descend. The two Russians resumed climbing the 2,600m buttress on October 29 and in one continuous push, with three bivouacs, they gained the summit on November 3. A lead article on their climb is found earlier in this Journal, along with a chronology of attempts on the route.

Babanov was clearly very pleased to have achieved his goal at last. Not only had the two Russians made the first ascent of the southeast pillar and the first ascent of this 7,804m summit, but Babanov believes they had managed to reach the top of the highest unclimbed peak in the world.

Many of those who are knowledgeable about trends in mountaineering are admirers of Babanov. The equally well-known Slovenian climber, Tomaz Humar, who prefers faces to ridges himself, was quoted in a German Alpine Club magazine three years ago as commenting that, "the future of climbing belongs to the new Russian teams around Valeri Babanov. They practice classical alpinism with little equipment on technically extremely demanding routes.... To me, the future is the lightly-equipped conquest of technically demanding routes at great heights in alpine style." But the admiration is not shared unanimously. One American climber remarked in September, "Babanov uses bolts and I don't like that." Some climbers who made earlier pure alpine-style attempts on the southeast pillar have strongly complained about Babanov's use of fixed ropes.

ELIZABETH HAWLEY, *Nepal*

Nuptse, north face, The Crystal Snake. In terms of high-standard technical ascents at altitude the highlight of the season was the new route on the north face of Nuptse by Argentinean guides, Damian and Willie Benegas.

The brothers made their first sortie onto the face during early May and a second on the 15th of the month, when they climbed 10 hard pitches over good but brittle ice and wonderful orange granite. At 2 a.m. on the 16th the stove broke and the pair had no option other than to rappel, leaving most of their gear at the high point.

The third and final attempt began on the 18th. The first night they bivouacked at 6,500m, the second at 6,700m, and the third at 6,950m. At this point they exited from the steep triangular face onto the snowy crest of the north rib, having climbed ca 22 pitches up to 5.9 WI5 and M4 (for speed, pieces of gear were intermittently pulled on or hooked with ice tools). On the 21st they reached a small rock band on the rib at 7,100m and bivouacked for the fourth time.

The next day it snowed more or less continuously and the pair only managed a further 300m. The next day the weather began to improve and the summit was reached after midday. After rappelling the approximate line of the British Route they were back in the Western Cwm by 10 that night. The new route, 1,500m high and christened The Crystal Snake, involved 42 roped pitches and a considerable amount of unroped climbing during the last 800m on the crest of the rib. A lead article on this ascent appears earlier in this Journal.

Historical note: In October 1979 Georges Bettembourg, Brian Hall, Al Rouse, and Doug Scott climbed the snowy left flank of the north rib, joined its crest in the upper section, where they continued to the main summit to make the second ascent of Nuptse's 7,861m main summit. This route or variants to their original line have been repeated on three separate occasions to date, but by members of only two expeditions. In September 1996 Ralf Dujmovits and Axel Schlonvogt established a camp at 6,800m on the glacial shelf above the Western Cwm and directly below the start of the snow rib leading up the face to the crest of the rib. From this camp they climbed the intervening ca 1,000m to the summit in 12 hours. In May 1999 Andy Lapkiss, Jeff Rhoads, and Gyalzen Sherpa adopted the same tactic but started up the face right of the 1979 Route, crossed it, then followed a snow ramp left of and parallel to the crest of the spur to arrive directly at the summit. This was repeated the following day by Pete Athans climbing alone but from the same expedition.

LINDSAY GRIFFIN, *High Mountain INFO*

Lhotse south face, winter attempt. Two years had passed since the Tokai section of the Japanese Alpine Club tried the first winter ascent of Lhotse's giant south face. The attempt, which took place in December 2001, eventually failed at 7,600m due to a biting winter blizzard. A second expedition was organized in 2003, JAC's centenary. The idea was to train five top men in excellent physical condition and acclimatize by climbing an 8,000m peak immediately before the route, pushing for the summit as early as possible in winter.

On October 14, all five reached the top of Shishapangma Central and by November 14 base camp had been established at the foot of Lhotse's south face. However, we discovered that the bottom one-third was in worse condition than last time. On November 22 we set up Camp 1 on a rock rib at 5,900m. On November 28 Camp 2 was established at 7,100m and then on December 3 an interim C3 was placed at the site where the Slovenian team pitched their C4 many years ago.

Conditions were good, with rock fall less frequent than the last time. On December 5 we climbed past our high point of 2001 and on the 9th set up Camp 3 at 7,850m. How much we had dreamed about occupying a high camp, from which we could finally head for the summit! Everything, so far, had gone smoothly and according to plan. The summit would surely be in our hands.

But it was not to be. The crux of the entire face actually began above our top camp. We opted to follow the couloir to the right of the final crest and in order to reach it had to make a 200m descent rightward from Camp 3. By doing this we would avoid the seemingly difficult ridge up which Tomo Cesen climbed.

We found the couloir far from easy. From the beginning we struggled on the delicate traverse to reach it. The couloir itself comprised stiff pitches of climbing one after the other, and the two parties, led by Tanabe and Kitamura, worked away day after day, eventually reaching 8,250m.

The final attempt was made by Tanabe's party, which started out from base camp on December 18. That night at Camp 1 the weather forecast reported a probability of snowfall, which in turn implied a high risk of avalanches. Only 250m left. To this point there had been no serious injuries, although eight members out of a total of 20 had been hurt by stone-fall or suffered frostbite.

I concluded that there are only three possible ways in which this face can be climbed: an alpine-style ascent by a genius like Tomo Cesen, a sieged climb following the rock ridge throughout like that achieved by the former Soviet expedition, or a speedy ascent in pre-winter season.

OSAMU TANABE, *Japanese Alpine Club*

The south face of Lhotse, showing the route taken by the Japanese winter attempt, which reached a highpoint of 8,250m. *Chunichi Shimbun*

Kyashar (aka Peak 43, 6,770m), first official ascent. Climbing new routes in the Himalaya isn't what it used to be. Nowadays you just surf two browsers from the security of your own internet connection: one of these is a search engine and the other the incomparable Alpine Club Himalayan Index, which attempts to list every recorded attempt on every (Himalayan/Karakoram) peak above 6,000m. Our choice of first window was the list of 103 "New Peaks Opened to Expedition," produced two years ago by HM Government of Nepal. Lurking under the name Kyashar was the long-coveted Peak 43, familiar to any trekker on the Mera La. However, HMG Ministry of Tourism had muddied the waters by listing Pt. 6,770m in the upper Hongu as "Peak 43."

After flying to Lukla, Sam Broderick (US-Swiss), Andi Frank (Austrian), Kevin Riddell (Canadian), and I (UK) followed the standard Mera trek over the Zawtra La, up the Hinku Valley to Tangnag, and then on toward Mera La. Before this, we branched north to the Hinku Nup Glacier on the east side of Kyashar. By the time we reached Kangtega Base Camp on October 3 our hopes for the northeast face of Kyashar had been dampened by occasional views of steep snow flutes, mushrooms, and not inconsiderable sections of bare rock.

On Pt 6,261m, directly above us and across the glacier from Kangtega, Kevin and I took the southeast ridge, while Sam and Andi climbed up the southwest. Only Kevin and I reached the top, but all of us got a good, long look at the impressive east face of Kangtega (6,779m), the daunting northeast face of Kyashar, and the unstable north face of col 6,034m on the south side of the Kangtega Glacier, which we'd have to climb to get to the base of Kyashar.

Next, we set up a high camp at the base of the north face of col 6,034m to get a first-hand look at the snow conditions and for a more serious acclimatisation and reconnaissance exercise on the slopes on Kangtega. After a bad-weather break in base camp we all shared trail-breaking duties back to high camp and beyond, following the glacier below the impressive north buttress of the Kyashar ridge. Continuing through a zone of large crevasses brought us to shoulder at ca 6,400m with a view of Everest, Lhotse, Makalu, Ama Dablam, and, most importantly, the west side of Kyashar. A short hike across from high camp to the base of col 6,034m helped convince us that while the north side of Kyashar might be climbable, it is not protectable in post-monsoon snow conditions. We packed up and headed down to base camp.

Kevin had by now decided he was not happy with the prospect of technical climbing above 6,500m but Andi, Sam, and I had no problem in deciding to attempt the west ridge. Logistically, this would mean a single, alpine-style bid from Tangnag, leaving the clearing of base camp to our Sherpa staff.

Armed with leaden, five-day, full-alpine packs we descended to Tangnag (4,356m) and then ascended moraine west of the village to a bivouac. The next day involved climbing 800m of snow slope below the south face of Kyashar. This was completed before sunrise to avoid rockfall and we set up camp 50m below the 5,800m col separating the long northeast ridge of Kusum Kanguru from the west ridge of Kyashar.

Above the col lay a steep, 150m-high rock buttress. Andi and I took our two ropes to fix the first pitches. The rock quality was execrable and the climbing vertical for one 25m section, but morale-boosting protection was possible. We climbed a third pitch, less steep but equally loose, to find the end of the rock section, then descended for the night. The following morning, October 18, we jumared our ropes and started up the snow ridge at 8 a.m. The corniced ridge looked unpleasant, but turned out to be relatively straightforward: strong melting made the footing mostly firm on the south side, and where this dropped vertically, tracks could be made on the deep, soft north side. Above 6,400m, where the ridge becomes steep and rocky, we moved left into a couloir on the west face. One pitch of soft snow, three of perfect ice, and a lot of firm snow led to a long exit slope. In the lead, I arrived on the summit ridge just beside the highest point, and, after checking that it wasn't a cornice, belayed the team onto it at 4 p.m. The views of the Rolwaling, Solu-Khumbu, and Khumbakarna ranges were everything we could have asked for, while one glance down the northeast face confirmed that our final choice of route had not been a mistake.

After some compulsory food and drink we headed back into the west face and the lowering sun. Night fell in the couloir on the upper face, but the footprints on the ridge were clear to follow and the anchors in place in the rock band. At 1 a.m. on the 19th we were all safely back at high camp.

As the descent below the south face would require a 3 a.m. start, we enjoyed a semi-comatose 24-hour break. At the appointed hour we made two rappels and descended the snow slope to reach Tangnag in time for breakfast. Here we met Kevin, our porter crew, and a small army of other trekking groups, from whom we learned that every expedition in the valley after our own had been met near Tashing Ongma by some gentlemen with AK47s requesting a "donation" to the Maoist cause: Rs 1,000 per foreign trekker and Rs 500 per porter. While the porters returned to Lukla on time for Diwali, we completed our Hinku/Hongu/Khumbu experience by crossing via Mera to the relative solitude of the upper Hongu Valley. Snowstorm and avalanche danger on the Amphu Labsta brought us back to the crowded Khumbu, through which we descended to Dingboche, Namche and Lukla. The Kyashar team would like to thank the Akademischer Alpen-Club Zurich for the club's generous support of the expedition.

BRUCE NORMAND, *Switzerland*

MAHALANGUR HIMAL (BARUN)

Tutse attempt. A Danish expedition led by Claus Ostergaard made the first official attempt on Tutse (aka Peak 6, 6,758m) close to Makalu. The peak has only recently been opened by the Nepalese Government but is believed to have received at least one unauthorized ascent in the past by a party or parties with a permit for Makalu, acclimatizing on the smaller surrounding peaks. The team attempted the northeast ridge but failed at ca 5,000m. However, on October 23 Luise Hogedal Ortmann, Theje Ortmann, and the leader Ostergaard made an ascent of an unnamed 5,822m peak in the same area via its north ridge.

LINDSAY GRIFFIN, *High Mountain INFO*

KANGCHENJUNGA HIMAL

Jannu, north face attempt. The all-star team of Erhard Loretan, Frédéric Roux, Ueli Steck, and Stefan Siegrist attempted the north face of 7,710m Jannu but were defeated at around 7,100m by the storms and heavy snow fall that plagued the Kangchenjunga region during the season. The team began early, reaching base camp at the end of March. Although the lower pillar leading to the large ramp/snow basin at the foot of the face was quite snowy, conditions higher looked good. In fairly settled weather at the start of April the four had soon established ropes up to Camp 1 and climbed the basin to the foot of the face at around 6,200m. Later, Camp 2 was placed at this point.

After discovering some of Loretan's ropes from the previous year, the climbers reached the big serac on the face around April 20. However, the weather then became increasingly unsettled with large dumps of snow. Much time was spent at base camp, and it wasn't until the second week in May that they could resume the climb. By this stage the team had opted to climb the face by the easiest line. On the night of May 16 more bad weather moved in and a retreat became inevitable. With the monsoon rapidly approaching, the team decided to throw in the towel and remove all their equipment and ropes on the descent.

LINDSAY GRIFFIN, *High Mountain INFO*

Jannu, attempt on the direct north face. Big Walls–Russian Routes is the name loosely given to a series of expeditions that since 1996 have been trying to climb 10 major new routes on some of the most famous big walls around the World. Last autumn's expedition to attempt the coveted direct route up the north face of Jannu (7,710m) was led, as usual, by Alexander Odintsov and included Alexey Bolotov, Mikhial Davy, and Mikhail Pershin from Yerkaterinberg; Alexander Ruchkin, Ivan Samoilenko, and Nickolay Totmjanin (Everest without oxygen), who like the leader hail from St Petersberg; and Mikkail Mikhailov from Bishkek in Kyrgyzstan. After acclimatizing in the Tien Shan, the team arrived in Nepal in August, trekked to Jannu Base Camp, where they arrived on September 8, and then started work on the icefall. In this dangerous section to reach the glacier plateau at ca 5,600m below the wall, Mikhailov sustained fractured ribs, a hematoma in his lung and head injuries when he was hit by serac fall at 5,300m. He was evacuated to Kathmandu and then onward to a hospital in Bishkek.

Camp 2 was established at ca 6,000m and sometime toward the end of the month Odintsov suffered a cracked bone in his hand, forcing him down to the village of Ghunsa. Meanwhile, Samoilenko, the high-altitude cameraman, had returned to Kathmandu.

By October 4, and despite less than perfect weather or conditions, the remaining five climbers had pushed the route out to 7,000m on the face and dug a snow cave. They then managed to fix several more ropes up the quasi-vertical headwall above to ca 7,200m, higher than anyone before has reached on this part of the face. But it was not to be. Snowfall, which became heavy,

On May 26, 2004, the Russians completed their route on the north face of Jannu. There will be a feature on this climb in the *AAJ 2005*. *Lindsay Griffin*

drove them down to base camp. By October 12 there had been more than three days of constant snowfall, which was almost knee-deep above 5,000m and had completely buried the fixed ropes above. As winter descended on base camp, the threat of avalanche became too great to continue and the expedition was called off.

LINDSAY GRIFFIN, *High Mountain INFO*

Kangchenjunga, southwest face, partial new route/direct finish, La Luce del Nirvana. Of the five expeditions attempting 8,586m Kangchenjunga, two were successful with all summiteers reaching the top on the same day. Four of these teams were attempting the Standard Route up the southwest face, while the fifth, a multi-national expedition led by Ralf Djumovits, including experienced high-altitude climbers such as Veikka Gustafsson and Michi Wärthl, was trying the north face-north ridge via the 1979 British Route. However, they failed to get above their Camp III at 7,200m, having fixed ropes on the difficult mixed face leading up to the col on the north ridge. Heavy snowfall in the region thwarted most climbers and those who succeeded had simply positioned themselves for a summit attempt at the right time.

Summiting on May 20 from a high camp at 7,600m were Italians Christian Kuntner, Mario Merelli, and Silvio Mondinelli with the Spaniard Carlos Pauner, all from a five-person expedition led by the 8,000m collector, Kuntner, and Kobi Reichen from a Swiss expedition.

This five-person group reached Camp 2 at 7,000m on May 17 and Camp 3 (7,600m) on the 18th. They had a rest day on the 19th before leaving early on the 20th to continue their climb up the glaciated slopes above to the start of the Gangway at ca 7,950m. Here, instead of following the Normal Route up the Gangway and then out right across a series of ramps to reach the west ridge above a large tower, they broke out right on new ground and climbed directly up the mixed rocky face to the summit. This gave between 450-500m of quite difficult climbing, starting with a 150m gully from 45-65°, a 20m rock wall of UIAA IV+, and then a horizontal traverse to the right to gain a deep couloir that splits the middle of the face. This was climbed for 200m (45-50°), above which they were forced to climb a difficult rock buttress on the right to reach easier ground. The buttress had a system of corners at III-IV, with one little section, thought possibly to warrant V, at an altitude above 8,400m. Another 100-150m of relatively straightforward mixed ground led to the top, which understandably was not reached until quite late in the day, at approximately 4:30 p.m. This is reported to be Mondinelli's 10th 8,000m peak and Kuntner's 12th. The new finish has been christened La Luce del Nirvana.

During the descent and as night fell, they separated. The Italians and Swiss were quicker on this difficult ground and although for much of the time they could see Pauner's headlight above them, they had lost contact in poor weather by the time they had regained Camp 3 (7,600m) at 1 a.m. on the 21st. No ropes had been fixed on the upper section of the climb and Mondinelli, having spent the winter in the Karakoram attempting Broad Peak, must have been very well-acclimatized. The three left lights outside the tent during the night and also went out on several occasions to shout for Pauner but at 9 a.m. on the 21st, with no sight of the Spanish mountaineer, they continued their descent, reaching base camp at 7 p.m.

Fortunately, late on the 22nd the feeble light from a headlamp was seen on the lower part of the face and two Sherpas were immediately dispatched. They found Pauner alive and able to walk unaided but badly frostbitten in the fingers. He was escorted safely to base camp that night. Unable to regain the tents at Camp 3 on the night of the 20th-21st, he had been forced to bivouac in the open after reaching the base of the Gangway at around 8,000m. The following day he had descended slowly, reportedly taking a 100m fall at one point and eventually bivouacking for a second time between 7,400m-7,500m. Back in Spain he was later to loose two fingers and toes.

LINDSAY GRIFFIN, *High Mountain INFO*

Maoist activity, an overview of the post-monsoon season. Maoist rebels fighting against Nepal's constitutional monarchy have been earning quite a lot of money by extorting funds from groups of climbers and trekkers. Not all groups have met this problem, but many have. The rates vary from one area to another, but the standard rate seems to be $15–$20 per foreigner. Expeditions going anywhere in Nepal, except in the Khumbu north of the Lukla airfield, must budget for these "donations" to the Maoist cause.

The Khumbu region above Lukla is totally free of Maoists. Very probably one important reason for this is the tireless efforts of Sir Edmund Hillary over four decades to make a better life for the people there, through his construction of numerous schools and health facilities, and the Lukla airfield, which gives easy access to trekking and climbing groups. He has also showed continuing support for those schools, hospitals, and health posts. Khumbu residents make up a community that is close-knit, relatively prosperous, and well educated, so for them the Maoist championing of the underdog has no appeal.

However, elsewhere in the east, on the route to the Makalu area, this autumn's Danish expedition going to the recently-opened Tutse (Peak 6) found a banner across the trail at Sedua village reading, "Welcome to you, Makalu base camp. Entry tax for Maoist Party." Its fixed-price list was: Rs 5,000 (roughly $70) per tourist, Rs 1,000 per guide, Rs 500 per Sherpa cook, Rs 100 per kitchen boy, and Rs 50 per porter. Farther east, a French team going into the Kangchenjunga region for Gimmigela Chuli (The Twins), was also stopped and "taxed." But a Jannu expedition went so fast past Sedua that they escaped without having to pay the tax.

On the very popular trekking route north from Pokhara to the south side of the Anna-purna range, the office buildings of the Annapurna Conservation Area have been taken over by the rebels, forcing conservation staff to suspend their work. An Italian expedition to Annapurna III was charged Rs1,000 per foreigner but nothing for their Sherpas and other Nepalese staff. On the equally well frequented trail around the Annapurna massif, Maoists are seen in strength on the west side just south of the Kali Gandaki village of Marpha. They are collecting the same amount in the Marshyangdi Valley on the east side of the massif at Ngadi village, just north of the road-head town of Besisahar, where teams going to the north side of the Annapurna range leave their buses.

Much farther west, the French on their way to climb Raksha Urai had to stop at Chainpur village and wait for two days while two of their Nepalese staff went down a valley to meet the local Maoist leader. They were forced to pay the tariff demanded in his area. The team's trekking agent asked the team not to disclose how much they were forced to pay: trekking agents don't like discussions on this topic. The team members were told that if the climbers had been American, British, or Japanese, they would not have been allowed to continue on their way.

ELIZABETH HAWLEY, *Nepal*

Autumn fatalities. Ayumi Nozawai was one of seven climbers who died this autumn. He was part of a three-man Japanese expedition attempting the west ridge of 7,140m Nemjung. On October 2 the party had reached ca 6,000m, not quite at the start of the west ridge, when a snow avalanche suddenly swept down the mountainside. One member, Nobuteru Kawahara, was untouched, but the other two, who were above him, were caught by it. Kawahara succeeded in digging Hiroytaka Imamura out of the snow, and both searched for Nozawai. They found him not far away, buried almost up to his neck, and when they pulled him out, he was dead. They immediately abandoned the climb. Nozawai had, among others, climbed Api and Gasherbrum I, as well as making an attempt to 6,750m on the unclimbed north ridge of Kula Kangri in Tibet.

As noted elsewhere two climbers fell to their deaths on Raksha Urai. An experienced German professional expedition leader, Robert Rackl, also suffered a fatal fall: he was on Ama Dablam, and the probable cause was the breaking of a fixed rope. Avalanches swept to their deaths two South Koreans, Hwang Sun-Dug and Park Joo-Hoon, on Lhotse Shar. The leader of a Greek Cho Oyu team, Christos Barouchas, died of altitude sickness.

ELIZABETH HAWLEY, *Nepal*

China

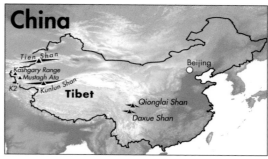

The effect of SARS in 2003. The outbreak of the SARS virus played havoc with many expeditions visiting China in the pre-monsoon season. On April 25 the Government of the Tibet Autonomous Region announced that it was closing its borders to both Chinese and Foreign tourists. Travel permits to enter Tibet were immediately withdrawn and two days later a similar pronouncement was made in Kathmandu and Zhangmu (the Tibet border post on the Friendship Highway connecting Kathmandu and Lhasa). Fortunately, most pre-monsoon mountaineering expeditions to popular destinations such as Everest, Cho Oyu, and Shishapangma (Xixabangma) had already entered the country, though other smaller trips with later departure dates were forced to cancel or postpone their plans to the autumn. At the end of May there were no confirmed cases of SARS in Tibet, though according to the Ministry of Health, the neighboring province of Sichuan had a total of 17.

Coming shortly after a spate of terrorist activities in Nepal, this dealt yet another body blow to the Nepalese tourist agencies, many of which derive considerable income from the organization of Tibetan tours. Fortunately, despite initial pessimistic predictions concerning the length of time the country would be closed, the Chinese Government officially re-opened Tibet to foreign visitors on July 1 and other regions were quick to follow.

XINJIANG

KUN LUN MOUNTAINS

Mustagh Ata, The Golden Eye, new route with ski descent. On July 18, "Sneaky" Pete Lardy, Chad McFadden, and Tom McMillan completed a route to the summit of Mustagh Ata (7,546m). The team then descended the route on skis and snowboard. The trio climbed from Camp 2, skipping Camp 3, in an 11-hour push. Pete Lardy set the record for the highest descent with a split snowboard. The route was named Golden Eye for a prominent region of yellow talus located near Camp 1.

The slopes of Mustagh Ata were made for ski mountaineering. In 1955 a joint Russian/Chinese team made the first ascent of the regular route. Ned Gillette, Jan Reynolds and Galen Rowell completed the second ascent and first ski descent in 1980. Since then, this route has become very popular, seeing about 75 ascents a year. In 2001, Dan Mazur, Walter Keller and Jon Otto made the first ascent of the east ridge, which involved technical ice climbing. *[Editor's note: ascents of Muztagh Ata by lines other than the original route have been reported since 1981, though the exact lines are unknown to us.]*

Located on the western slope, north of the Kartomak glacier, Golden Eye provides a moderate ascent, which was completed mostly on skis. It offers stellar turns down one of the highest descents in the world. Avalanche danger is minimal and crevasses are easily negotiated. The route was skied mostly unroped. This allowed for a rapid ascent of 14 days from our arrival at BC, most of the time in good weather. The lower part of the route shares the same approach as a French route on Mustagh South.

Mr. Guo Jin Wei, member of the 1985 U.S.–Chinese Ulugh Mustagh expedition, organized the trip. Total expedition cost was less than $3,000 per man Beijing to Beijing. This was approximately a 50% discount compared to list prices. Checked baggage allowances were a hardship (20 kg for economy air tickets). It costs about 50 Yuan/kg for excess baggage Beijing to Kashgar. We were surprised to find that Xinjiang has equal or even higher quality substitutes for most of the food that we brought from the U.S. We could have saved several hundred dollars by sending a shopping list to our agent in Urumchi.

Our Chinese agent from Xinjiang Mountaineering said that this was a first ascent. However, after some research I believe this route may have been first climbed in 1982. The evidence is not clear. But it makes no difference: it was a wonderful trip and a great life experience.

CHAD MCFADDEN, *AAC*

KASHGAR RANGE

The unclimbed Peak Gez (left) from the south. *Otto Chkhetiani*

Complete crossing of the southern section of the Chinese Pamir and first ascents of Pts 5,430m and 5,975m. Andrei Lebedev (leader), Otto Chkhetiani (assistant leader), Mikhail Babich (Saint Petersburg), Tatiana Belyaeva (Saint Petersburg), Yura Maksimovich, and Oleg Yanchevsky (both from Kiev) flew from Moscow to Kashgar via Urmchi. This was our third visit to the Kashgar Range.

We traveled south down the Karakoram Highway and turned east into the Tashkurgan Gorge. We found that a new road was currently under construction to Yarkand. After 20km we stopped in the Tadzhik village of Shindi (2,900m), where we bid farewell to our escorts and began following a path to the north.

For the first 20km of our journey we hired two donkeys to carry part of our load. In two

E.Kongur 7625

5975

The north ridge of the Pk 5,975 (Nikolaeva), and the great north face of East Kongur on the right. *Otto Chkhetiani*

days we crossed the straightforward Kok-Muinak Pass (4,515m) and descended to the Chikchiklyk Plateau, where there were many nomadic camps. It was through here that the legendary Syuan' Tszan traveled from India to China in the 6th century. From here we crossed the easy Yangi-Davan Pass (4,830m) to the picturesque Yangi-Kel lake. We continued to the upper reaches of the northern source of the lake and descended a stony path to Kengshibers, where we got a glimpse of the Koksel glacier flowing down from the eastern slopes of Muztagh Ata and Mount Tuyuk. We then crossed a 5,155m pass to reach the Southern Chat glacier, all the while having behind us a foreshortened view of the North and Main summits of Muztagh Ata, strangely reminiscent of Elbrus's twin peaks. Six pitches down an icy 45° slope led to the glacier and then the Teresaz-Su valley, heavily populated by Kirghiz.

It was three years since we had passed this way and we continued through a familiar canyon to the Chimgen glacier, which flows from the south east flanks of Kongur. In 2002 this isolated place was finally united with Yarkand via a motorable road across mountains to the east. From a moraine ridge on the Chimgen we were able to see Koksel (6,740m) and Kysylsel (6,605m), which we had crossed via an east to west traverse in 2000. An icy barrier blocked the way to the Gez-dar'ya gorge. We climbed upward, spending a night on a narrow arête, then traversing 60° ice slopes and carefully crossing a band of rotten cliffs to finally reach the crest. Here, we were able to ascend an unnamed summit of 5,430m, all the time to the sound of avalanches cascading down the eastern side of Kongur. To the north lay the unclimbed rock tower of Gez (5,696m), which is clearly visible from the Karakoram Highway. To reach this spot had involved 24 roped pitches.

From here a crumbly ridge ran south to Pt 5,975m. The traverse wasn't difficult (we roped for four pitches) but was exceeding tiring due to deep snow. On the morning of August 19 we reached the summit of Pt 5,975m, which we named Mt. Nikolaev in honor of the famous Russian high-altitude traveler and equipment manufacturer, who was lost in the vicinity of Pobeda (Tien Shan) during the winter of 1993. The grade of our route using the Russian system was 5A mixed climbing.

Descending 400 meters via a glacier flowing down from a col on the eastern side of Kongur, we climbed down a ridge line where, on a tricky band of cliffs, we found scraps of light-blue colored rope, apparently the remains of a Japanese attempt to climb Kongur via its east ridge in 1981. Twenty four roped pitches were required to complete the descent and we were not helped by inclement weather; snowfall and poor visibility. As the glacier appeared covered in avalanche debris from the slopes of Kongur, we took to the west ridge of Karatash, descending an ice slope in 12 pitches to reach the northern tributary of the Koksel Glacier.

Here, we found only green hills and spent the rest of our time exploring the western sources of the Koksel glacier, which had not been visited before by any European. The dominating summit in this region is Kongur Tybe and we continued past its heavily-gendarmed north ridge to begin our approach to the north ridge of Aklangam (6,995m). This peak was climbed from the south in 2002 by Andrei Lebedev and party. The northern route looked attractive, making Aklangam one of the most accessible peaks in this region. From an altitude of 5,400m we were once again able see the northern slopes of Kongur (7,719m). However, a snow storm that night pinned us down for 24 hours at ca 5,700m and after this cleared we were forced to descend in very dangerous avalanche conditions. On September 1, in the village of Gez, our 235km, 31-day unsupported journey ended and we had completed a crossing of the entire southern section of the Chinese Pamirs.

OTTO CHKHETIANI, *Russia*

DAXUE SHAN

Mt. Grosvenor, showing the two spring 2003 attempts (Cave-Fowler and McAdie-Nadin) and the Clyma-Payne route to the summit. *Roger Payne*

Mt. Grosvenor, first ascent. Our original plan had been to attempt Chomolhari, but we ran into problems when we discovered that a joint exercise was taking place between Chinese and Bhutanese military forces down in Yadong County. Not even Chinese were getting permits to travel to this area. Fortunately we had a good Plan B: to attempt the first ascent of Mt. Grosvenor (6,376m) in the Daxue Shan range of Sichuan. Mick Fowler had attempted it in the spring, so we had some beta on the approach. We traveled from Chengdu to Kanding, where we were able to sort out most of our provisions before moving to the village of Laoyunin and from there to the foot of the mountain.

The weather was appalling at the start and we had snow every day and most nights for our first 10 days. During this time we acclimatized and shifted gear to below the route. But miraculously, on November 2 the hoped-for good spell came through and we had sunshine and blue skies throughout our ascent. The temperatures were very cold though, and there was a ferocious wind. We made the ascent via the northwest face and west ridge, followed by a traverse down the east ridge to the Grosvenor-Jiazi col. The climbing on the north face was mostly Scottish grade 4-5 on very thin ice and névé with poor protection (no ice screws and very shattered rock on the side walls) and some grade 6 dry-tooling to fill in the blanks. The first day involved 15 pitches

Julie-Ann Clyma on the summit ridge of Mt. Grosvenor. *Roger Payne*

with the last three climbed in the dark. Above, we made a sitting bivouac at ca 5,900m on the crest of the ridge.

The first part of the ridge was really loose and both ropes got chopped, with the sheaths almost fully cut through (we repaired them with Elastoplasts). The remainder of the ridge gave fairly straightforward climbing on snow-covered slabs and occasional steeper steps. At the end of the second day we made a very windy camp on a snow shoulder at ca 6,100m, then the following day made it to the summit on easy (30-40°) but heavily-loaded snow slopes: scary! With such poor conditions on the north face we really didn't want to go back down that way, but it was a bit of a leap of faith to start the descent down the east ridge. We had only given it the most cursory of looks during our reconnaissance, but we knew that Americans had climbed Jiazi from the col between Grosvenor and Jiazi, so we figured if we could just get down to that point, there must be a way off.

As it happened, conditions on the south- and east-facing aspects were really good: loads of ice to make Abalakovs. We had another bivouac just below the summit at ca 6,200m, and then the next day made 12 rappels down the flank of the east ridge to a huge plateau. We traversed this and—yippee—found the col. At this point we thought we might make it off in one day, but the couloir below the col was nasty, so we spent the night at ca 5,700m in order to complete the rest of the descent in the morning cold.

There were more rappels and only just enough ice, so it was a real relief to pass the rimaye. Then, it was an extremely painful slog, which took us hours in knee- to thigh-deep

Roger Payne starting up the north face of Grosvenor. *Julie-Ann Clyma*

snow to get back round to the north side. We were forced to make another bivouac and on the final day had to suffer an excruciating climb back UP below the face to collect the gear we had left behind. We were so knackered and the snow was still so deep, that I wondered if we would make it. Anyway, we managed to drag our bodies up there, and made the descent to base camp, arriving at 8 p.m. Phew!

We found access to the Daxue Shan range to be excellent, with locals and officials in Kanding and the Sichuan and Chinese Mountaineering Associations extremely helpful and hospitable. There are other good lines to climb on both the northwest and north faces of Grosvenor. There are also five more virgin 6,000m peaks in the Daxue Shan, and only two ridges have been climbed on the very impressive Minya Konka (7,556m). Late October had heavy snowfall, but November brought clear cold conditions, making ascents on east and south aspects attractive. We were supported by the Alison Chadwick Memorial Fund, Nick Estcourt Award, Mount Everest Foundation, and British Mountaineering Council. A report with relevant logistical information is available by contacting roger.payne@uiaa.ch.

JULIE-ANN CLYMA *and* ROGER PAYNE, *U.K.*

Mt. Grosvenor, attempt on northwest face. In the spring of 2003 Grosvenor (6,367m) was still unclimbed. It has a spectacular northwest face, which we attempted as two separate pairs. Andy Cave and myself tried the central couloir directly below the summit, but were stopped on our third day by a very loose, slanting groove choked with powder snow. It was one of those difficult situations where we could have made more progress but there was no gear and the danger levels had risen to a point that we deemed unacceptable. So, despite the ground easing only 30 meters or so above us, we rappelled. A bolt or two would have solved the problem, but we regard such things as cheating.

Neil McAdie and Simon Nadin tried another line toward the right-hand side of the face. They managed five pitches before rappelling due to extremely heavy spindrift avalanches. I might add that it snowed or rained on every day we were in the region.

MICK FOWLER, *U.K.*

QIONGLAI RANGE

SIGUNIANG NATIONAL PARK

Tan Shan and Putala Shan, first ascents via difficult rock routes. My wife Tanja Grmovsek and I planned to visit the Qionglai Mountains in the spring of 2003 but due to the outbreak of the SARS virus just a few days before leaving for China we had to postpone to the autumn. In the

The 22-pitch Dalai Lama, on Putala Shan (5,428m). *Andrej Grmovsek*

end this time of year turned out perfect for rock climbing in the Siguniang region.

We always try to travel as simply as possible on our climbing expeditions. We were completely on our own, without a translator, in the land of Chinese characters. In the second half of September we arrived in Rilong, a small tourist town at the foot of the Siguniang Shan, an increasingly well-known region of the Qionglai Mountains. Our goal was to free climb some large granite walls in an area that is almost untouched by mountaineers. We didn't have much information about the mountains here, only inspiration from Tom Nakamura's article published in the *AAJ* 2003. However, we were also a bit scared due to the almost universal reports of bad weather and limited success by the few rock climbers who had previously visited these peaks. Because of this we opted to climb very light and fast.

We really had no idea where to find the big walls, so the first thing we did was to take a new tourist bus into the Shuangqiao Gou Valley. This valley is 35km long and had many interesting granite walls up to 1,000m high, almost all of which were unclimbed. We couldn't believe that all those walls were just waiting for climbers, so we quickly worked out a plan as to where, and how, we were going to climb in this paradise. Access to the valley was very simple. We just got off the bus, established base camp, and

The 11-pitch Don't Fly Away, on the Tan Shan Wall. *Andrej Grmovsek*

then hiked for four to seven hours up to the base of the walls. The weather in the Shuangqiao Gou was really strange. During the course of the day we could have all kinds of weather. But in general the weather was much better than we expected. It was very changeable but most days were without rain or snow.

We decided to first try a somewhat easier, lower wall for acclimatization. The approach was quite bad, involving very steep terrain and a lot of prickly vegetation. We tried to go as light as possible, but our sacs were still far from light. On September 25 in a one-day push we climbed Don't Fly

Andrej Grmovsek celebrating on the summit of Tan Shan. Tanja Grmovsek

Away (450m, 11 pitches, V, VIII/VIII+ obl.) on the south face of a nameless peak, which we later called Tan Shan. It is probably 4,943m high and was almost certainly unclimbed. For protection we used only Friends and found in general they were quite hard to place. This meant the climbing was sometimes really serious, especially on the hardest pitch, which had a 15-meter runout up a smooth slab. I took a fall on the crux and was held by just two cams of a small Friend placed in a flared crack under a small roof. The rock was very smooth and the climbing right at the limit. At one stage I thought we were going to have to retreat from half way up the wall. However, I managed the slab second try, but the protection was really quite scary.

After a few rest days we went for our second objective: the west face of Putala Shan (5,428m). The snow that had previously been lying on the face had now almost disappeared, so we left all our ice climbing equipment in the valley and took only climbing shoes, some clothes, a bivouac sack and a small bottle of water. The approach was again very steep with a lot of vegetation. We had hoped to climb the beautiful arête that forms the left side of the face, but after a closer look we decided for a more logical and faster line up the middle of the wall. We climbed as fast as possible and reached the north summit of this broad mountain in the evening. The lower part of the wall had been exposed to rock fall. The middle part was quite steep with nice climbing in crack systems and some off-widths. On the last 200m we found some snow on the ledges. Now the weather had become more changeable: very cloudy with some sun, and often misty and windy. We opted to make a freezing bivouac on the summit and rappel the wall the following day. We used only Friends and nuts for protection and belays, but left rappel anchors on our descent. The route is ca 1,300 meters long and the wall ca 800 meters high. We called the 22-pitch climb Dalai Lama (VI, VIII-), and we believe this also to be the first ascent of the peak. By the time we returned to the valley, the weather was changing. Next night 20cm of snow fell and we were really happy we were no longer on the wall. Because of this and the injuries I had sustained (I'd hurt my ribs), we decided to leave this beautiful area. But there are still many interesting walls to climb here and we shall probably return in the future. For more photographs of this trip see http://kitajska.odprava.net .

ANDREJ GRMOVSEK, *Slovenia*

Tibet

Chang Tang, unsupported crossing. Janne Corax and Nadine Saulnier from Sweden are claiming the first complete north to south crossing of the Chang Tang. The journey took 46 days, and although the pair hoped to climb several peaks en route (including Khanzangri), they were unable to do so, mainly due to strong winds and deep snow at low altitudes. The first western exploration of the high altitude desert region of the Chang Tang was probably made by fellow Swede, Sven Hedin, at the start of the 20th Century. A committing and unsupported south to north crossing was made in 1997 by Frank Kauper and Stefan Simmerer, and is recorded in the 1998 *AAJ*.

LINDSAY GRIFFIN, *HIGH Mountain INFO*

HIMALAYA

Shishapangma (Xixabangma), winter attempt via the southwest face. Before last year no one had attempted to climb 8,012m Shishapangma in winter, and until recently permission had never been granted. But if you wait hours for a bus in the end two come along. First to arrive were British climbers Andy Parkin and Victor Saunders. These two had gained permission to attempt the southwest face in 2001-2002, but in the end were unable to go. This winter they arrived in November, hoping to summit in early December. The pair decided to attempt the unrepeated Corredor Girona, a couloir on the right side of the face climbed more or less alpine style in September 1995 by Spaniards, Carles Figueras and Josep Permañé. Unfortunately, very fierce and bitterly cold winds prevented the British climbers from getting above an altitude of 6,500m, close to the bottom of the face.

LINDSAY GRIFFIN, *HIGH Mountain INFO*

Shishapangma (Xixabangma), attempt in winter and first winter ascent of the southwest face. Our aim was the southwest face and main peak (8,012m) of Xixabangma in winter. For our attempt we chose the Spanish Route toward the right side of the face. It has only been climbed once: in the summer of 1995 Carles Figueras and Josep Permaé climbed the face more or less in alpine style, but unfortunately were not able to reach the summit. They retreated from the final ridge at ca 7,900m. To our small team comprising Simone Moro (Italy), Piotr Morawski, Jan Szulc, and Darek Zaluski (the last three from Poland, with Zaluski also acting as cameraman), a completion of this route in winter seemed very attractive.

Our expedition started from Kathmandu on December 6. By the end of the month base camp had been established at 5,200m (two days walk from Nyalam), advanced base positioned one day higher at the foot of the glacier below the south face at 5,600m (there was no snow until this point), and camp 1 set up beneath a big serac below the face at 6,100m. On January 4, Morawski, Moro, and Zaluski reached 7,000m during their first attempt to establish camp 2. However, they found no place to put the tent and had already fixed almost 1,500m of rope

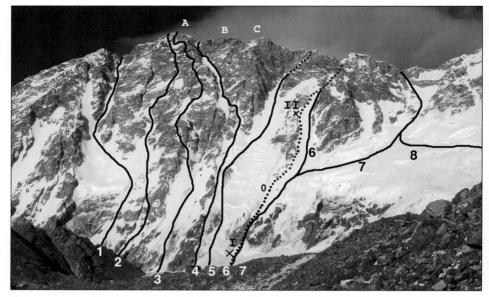

Shishapangma's southwest face, showing: (0) Winter expedition, Morawski-Moro, 2004, to the point C; (1) Kurtyka-Loretan-Troillet, 1990; (2) Korean route, Par Jun Hun–Kang Yeon Ryoung, 2002; (3) Slovenian route, Stremfelj, 1989; (4) British route, Baxter-Jones–Scott-McIntyre, 1982; (5) Polish route, Wielicki solo, 1993 (approximate line); (6) Spanish route, Figueras- Permaé, 1995; (7) British descent route, 1982; (8) Slovenian route (also descent) sometimes called "Normal route," Kozjek-Stremfelj, 1989. (A) Main Summit 8,027m (invisible, over the ridge); (B) terminous of the Spanish expedition (over the ridge); (C) winter-expedition 2004, 7,700m. (I) Camp I (6,100m); (II) Camp II (7,150m). Route info courtesy Piotr Morawski. *Darek Zaluski*

above camp I. On the 9th Morawski and Moro fixed another 200m and were finally able to establish camp 2 at 7,150m on a small platform. The preparations for a summit push began.

On January 17 Morawski and Moro set off from camp 2 around midnight. They wanted to fix another 400m of rope, but at 2 a.m., after fixing half that amount, they decided to come back to the tent and warm themselves up using a stove. It was below –50°C and the wind was really strong. The second attempt started at 6:00 a.m. They fixed the last 200 meters of rope, but did not reach the top of the face. Expecting the final ridge leading to the summit to be relatively easy, they set off up the last section of the couloir with a 60m Kevlar rope. Parts of the final section were very steep, and just before the top there was a rocky wall a few meters in height. At 11:30 a.m. Morawski stood on the ridge at 7,600m and a few minutes later was joined by Moro. It turned out that the way to the summit wasn't as easy as they had been told. The simplest solution, going straight down to the big plateau ca 100 meters below on the north flank of the mountain, was impossible. The rope was too short and the plateau was cut off from the face by a crevasse some six or seven meters wide. Instead they were forced to traverse the ridge to gain the plateau at 7,700m. However, this took time, and when they arrived it was already 3 p.m. It was too late to safely continue to the summit, which they felt was another three or four hours distant. The wind was getting stronger and an unplanned bivouac would have certainly resulted in severe frostbite. They did the only thing they could: descend.

Morawski went right down to camp 1 but Moro stayed at camp 2 with Zaluski, hoping to make another attempt the next day. However, the wind only blew stronger and the sky became overcast, so the pair broke camp and descended to base. All members were back in Kathmandu on the 22nd. The Spanish route to the top of the south face had been repeated, but the summit was not reached. However, this party proved that climbing Himalayan giants in winter by a very small team is indeed possible.

PIOTR MORAWSKI, *Poland*

Labchi Kang Group, first ascents. Duncan Chessell's Australian-Icelandic commercial expedition, which was successful on Cho Oyu, putting three out of its four members and two Sherpas on the summit over two days in mid May, first acclimatized on one of the neighbouring Labchi Kang summits. Also known as Labuche Kang and Choksiam, the main spine of the Labchi Kang Group lies northwest of the Rowaling and has three summits over 7,000m. The highest, Labchi Kang I (7,367m) was first climbed in October 1987 by a joint expedition from the Himalayan Association of Japan and the Tibet Mountaineering Association. Seven Japanese and eight Tibetans reached the top via the west ridge. Labchi Kang II (7,072m) was first climbed in April 1995 by all 10 members of a Swiss expedition. However, these high summits are surrounded by over a dozen unnamed peaks above 6,000m. Chessell had a permit to explore and climb in this area, so set off from Cho Oyu Base Camp with full mountaineering gear and 14 days food. The team first walked west up a valley that had no visible signs of previous human visit in the upper reaches. This valley led to a glacier and eventually a col at ca 6,400m, on which the climbers established a camp. They stayed there four nights and climbed two peaks on opposite sides of the col. One required eight pitches of moderate snow/ice climbing to reach the ca 6,800m summit. Both peaks were thought to be previously unclimbed. The team then returned to Base Camp.

This trip provided interesting and excellent acclimatization for Cho Oyu and as it took place on the lee (eastern) side of the Labchi Kang Group was much more enjoyable than struggling with the early season gales that plagued the northwest flank of Cho Oyu. While this deviation meant that the climbers arrived at Cho Oyu Advanced Base well after other expeditions, they were, together with another multi-national team, the first to summit (on May 11). They established only two camps on the mountain; the first at 6,400m and Camp 2 at 7,100m. On the 11th the summit was reached at 2:35 p.m. and Camp 2 regained by 6:30 that evening. The following day two more climbers from the same expedition, Anna Svavarsdotter and Tshering Bhote, also reached the top, with Svavarsdotter becoming the first Icelandic woman to climb any 8,000m peak. Tshering Bhote is an instructor with the Nepalese Mountaineering Association and was trained in Scotland. He recently came top of a six-week course at the Chamonix Guides School and hopes to eventually become a full IFMGA guide.

Acclimatizing on other peaks prior to an ascent of a high altitude mountain is more expensive and harder to organize, but is has been shown effective and there are many peaks in Tibet that can be added to an existing 8,000m permit for only a little more money, providing both share the same Base Camp. All team members on Chessell's expedition found this a much more enjoyable experience than ferrying loads on Cho Oyu.

LINDSAY GRIFFIN, *HIGH Mountain INFO*

Cho Oyu, Oiarzabal record. In the post monsoon of 2003 Cho Oyu was attempted by 36 teams, ranging in size from one to 24 members. The mountain can expect even more teams in the autumn of 2004 to mark the 50th anniversary of its first ascent on October 19, 1954, when it was climbed by two Austrians, Herbert Tichy—whose name is often used to identify what is now the normal route—and Sepp Joechler, plus Pasang Dawa Lama from India.

Among the 150 summiters on Cho Oyu was the veteran Spanish Basque, Juanito Oiarzabal, who set an impressive record by having been 20 times to the highest summit of 8,000m mountains, including all 14 of the world's 8,000m peaks. These include two ascents of Everest (in 1993 and 2001 by different routes). He had already summited Cho Oyu twice before (in 1985 and 2002) and he was again on the top, not just once but twice, 14 days apart. Already far into the fifth decade of his life, he says he has no plans to stop.

Oiarzabal's two Cho Oyu ascents this autumn put him ahead of the previous record holder, Ang Rita Sherpa, who, before his retirement from mountaineering, summited Everest ten times, Cho Oyu four times, Dhaulagiri I three times and Kangchenjunga once, giving him a total score of 18 summits over 8,000m at the end of 1996.

ELIZABETH HAWLEY, *Nepal*

Hungchi, attempt. The successful first ascent of Hungchi (7,036m) in April 2003 by Takashi Shiro's Japanese Osaka Eiho Alpine Club expedition is recorded elsewhere in the Journal. This team climbed from Nepal. However, it appears that an attempt on the mountain was also made from Tibet by Masakatsu Nakamura's five-member Japanese expedition from the Nagano Prefecture Mountaineering Federation. This team arrived at Everest Base Camp on October 21, and on the 24th established Camp 1 at 5,450m on the Central Rongbuk Glacier. The Japanese climbers then proceeded up the long Western Rongbuk, passing below the Pumori Glacier to the south and establishing intermediate camps at 5,600m, 5650m, Camp 2 at 5,700m, and Camp 3 (Advanced Base) at 5,800m. This took until the beginning of November, after which a reconnaissance was made of Hungchi's north face. Camp 4 was placed at 6,100m on the left side of the glacier bay below the face and then 650m of rope were fixed to the col on the northwest ridge. Finally, on November 10 Camp 5 was sited on the col at 6,600m.

A summit attempt was made the following day. The party first moved onto the south (Nepalese) flank of the north west ridge before returning to the crest and climbing it to a point about 200m below the summit. Here, they came across a steep wall of snow, which consumed a great deal of time and energy. Above, and in striking distance of the summit, the party found itself too late in the day to continue. They retreated from that point, made no further attempt and left base camp on the 13th.

TAMOTSU NAKAMURA, *Japan Alpine News*

Everest, overcrowding on the North Ridge. Climbers on the Tibetan side had similar complaints to those on the Nepal side. A Swiss expedition leader said that when he and his group on their way to the top reached 8,600m (28,200 feet), near the bottom of the Second Step, he could see 15 climbers ahead waiting to go up the ladder on the Step; clouds were rolling in and the wind was getting stronger, so he decided to retreat out of fear of a repetition of 1996. He noted that many of the climbers from other teams who did carry on to the top returned with frostbite or snow-blindness or even a broken leg, and he was very happy with his decision; his party descended safely and in good health.

Other climbers on the north side during their summit bids a few days before the Swiss were forced to climb up or down much more slowly than they were capable of doing because of inexperienced people blocking their way. Another problem created by the novices was falling discarded oxygen bottles, which had been carelessly dumped in soft snow; when the snow melted, the bottles fell, and a skilled American mountaineer had to leave for home after being hit on the back of his head by one of them.

ELIZABETH HAWLEY, *Nepal*

Everest, summer attempt to ski and snowboard the mountain. There was only one expedition to the mountain during the summer and they planned a ski/snowboard descent. The two climbing members were Jimmy Chin, the skier, and Stephen Koch, the snowboarder; they had with them two climbing Sherpas. They were on the north face with the intention of climbing to the summit via a direct line up the Japanese and Hornbein Couloirs, then descending the same route. But they went no higher than 7,000m, to a point near the top of the Japanese Couloir, in increasingly deep snow, which they report as not less than knee-high. On their first attempt in August the weather was warm, and wet snow stopped them at the start of the face. On the second attempt and having climbed through the night, they turned around at 8:30 a.m. on September 10. Their progress had become much too slow and the four climbers decided that under the prevailing conditions they would be very extended reaching their planned camp site at 7,800m. Unfortunately, conditions did not improve before their permit expired.

ELIZABETH HAWLEY, *Nepal*

NYANCHEN THANGLHA (NYAINQENTANGLHA) RANGE

Golden Dragon (6,653m). *Christian Haas*

Western Nyanchen Thanglha, Golden Dragon, White Pagoda, Yarlung Ri, previously unreported first ascents. In September 2000 Erich Gatt, Hansjoerg Pfaundler, and myself, Christian Haas, visited the Nyanchen Thanglha ca 80km north of Lhasa. Here, in an area which is still largely unexplored, we made several first ascents in alpine style. Base camp was established on September 15 in the Lan Puk Valley at 5,080m. On September 18 we slept for the first time at our 5,800m high camp. As we were using skis, the descent toward base camp next day proved quite fun, apart from minor tumbles due to wearing mountain boots on telemark skis.

During the descent Hansjoerg and I decided to try an easy-looking peak. After reaching a windy col via a steep rocky slope, we climbed the broad snowy southeast ridge. The last 100m was an extremely narrow snow arête, and at 2:30 p.m. we reached the summit of

The White Pagoda (Chorten Garpo in Tibetan, Ba ta Shan in Chinese). The ascent followed the right skyline, and the descent the left. *Christian Haas*

6,256m Yarlung Ri (N30°16,817; E090°28,494).

Three days later Erich woke us up at the high camp with his mouth-organ and then with Hansjoerg started out for the White Pagoda (Chorten Garpo in Tibetan; Ba ta Shan in Chinese). I remained behind with a headache. After climbing the steep and snowy south-southeast flank of the mountain they reached the northwest ridge and followed this, via some mixed terrain, to the 6,415m summit (N30°17,817; E090°29,738). In the meantime my headache had worsened, so I decided to go straight down to base camp.

Next day, September 23, I went back up to high camp to find that Erich and Hansjoerg had already left for Golden Dragon (Sir Duk in Tibetan; Jin Long in Chinese). It was already midday but I decided to start out for White Pagoda via the south ridge. Two steep, snow-covered ramps led up the south face to a small col on the south ridge. From here I followed the ridge—a sharp snow arête—to the summit, which I reached at around 4 p.m.

In the meantime Erich and Hansjoerg had succeeded in reaching the summit of the 6,653m Golden Dragon (N30°18,219; E090°28,826) via a route up the south face.

Next day it was my turn to climb Golden Dragon, repeating the same route followed by Erich and Hansjoerg. From the foot of the south face at 6,140m I climbed up snowy gullies and along ridges with short passages of crumbling rock. In the upper section the route followed a long steep snow slope we christened the White Sickle due to its shape. This never-ending slope continued right up to the crest of the summit ridge, west of the highest point. The angle was generally ca 50° with short passages of 60°. Several hundred meters along the highly corniced crest but moderately angled ridge led to the highest point, which I reached at around 1 p.m. I descended and that same day we walked back down to base camp with huge sacs to meet the shepherds who had come up to carry out our equipment next day. As far as we know there are no detailed maps for this area and we used only our eyes and a hand held GPS-device for documenting our travels.

CHRISTIAN HAAS, *Austria*

Beu-tse (6,270m), in Central Tibet. *John Town*

Beu-tse, first ascent. In September Derek Buckle, Martin Scott, Alasdair Scott, and I made the first ascent of Beu-tse (6,270m), which lies in Tolung Dechen County of Central Tibet, ca 16km south of the town of Yangpachen. The peak forms one of a small glaciated range of mountains running in a north-south direction and is the highest point of the extensive highland area bounded by the Yangpachen Valley to the north and west, the Yarlung Tsangpo to the south, and the Tolung valley to the east. The sharp pyramids of the two main summits are well seen from the Shigatse road near Yangpachen Monastery, as is the spectacular hanging glacier that falls between them to the west.

The only published photo is titled Da Kangri, and hence we were the British Da Kangri Expedition. However, the locals were adamant that our peak was in fact Beu-tse (Calf Peak) and that Da Kangri, also known as Da-tse (Horse Peak), lay elsewhere to the southwest. As is common in Tibet, their name applies to the group as a whole rather than any one peak. The range is close to the Western Nyanchen Tanglha, which stretches in a great arc along the opposite side of the Yangpachen Valley culminating to the south in Jomo Kangri (7,048m) and to the north in Nyanchen Tanglha itself (7,162m).

This is a well populated and accessible area, and Yangpachen can be reached from Lhasa in less than two hours by the main northern road. We arrived in Lhasa on September 9 and on the 11th drove to base camp at 4,645m in a high valley to the west of the mountain, close to the five houses of Nya. One choice of route was to climb steeply up the end of the long west ridge before following it to a high snow saddle and then turning south to reach the summit pyramid. In retrospect this would have been easiest, but instead we entered the hanging valley that ran along the northern side of the ridge, making our first camp by the entrance at 5,185m. We then climbed easily upward through moraines to the head of the valley, where we placed a second camp at 5,641m in the shelter of a steep rocky outcrop at the top of the initial snow slopes. A long snow slope then led steeply upward to the 6,000m saddle forming the end of the west ridge.

After a day spent acclimatizing, followed by two nights of snowfall, we eventually set off in pairs at 4:50 a.m. on September 21. The snow was in perfect condition, but the slope steepened rapidly from 45° to 60°-70° in the final stages. It was disorientating to haul up onto the flat expanses of a saddle, but the summit pyramid was not the push-over we expected, being steep, exposed, and heavily corniced. At 11:20 a.m. we reached the summit, though no-one went near the highest point of cornice, six or seven meters above our little snow ledges. It took until 7:30 p.m. to down-climb our route, which those who knew rated at D+/TD-.

JOHN TOWN, *U.K., Alpine Club*

NYAINQENTANGLA EAST RANGE

Chukporisum (6,359m), showing the route and 6,180m highpoint of the 2003 attempt. *Adam Thomas*

Niwu Valley, Chukporisum (6,359m), attempt. In September 2003 a team of four members traveled to the little-explored Nyainqentangla East range in Tibet. Situated 400km northeast of Lhasa, this range has seen little exploration or climbing to date and therefore promised a wealth of exploratory mountaineering. The team had permits to climb Nenang (6,870m), Chachaco (6,575m), and Jomo Taktse (6,582m). The team consisted of Phil Amos, Bryan Godfrey, and myself, all from Edinburgh, U.K., and Graham Rowbotham from Vancouver, Canada. Amos, Godfrey, and I arrived in Kathmandu, Nepal on September 14, with Rowbotham arriving the next day. This left just enough time to finalize visas before we flew to Lhasa on September 16.

We met up with the agent in Lhasa and did some last minute organization before leaving in three Land Cruisers on September 19. We experienced some very poor road conditions and were eventually stopped by landslides 40km short of Niwu, where we had planned to walk for three days to a base camp in the upper Niwu Valley. We waited for four days for enough horses to carry our equipment, and then walked for six days to get to base camp, which we established at 4,300m.

We spent four days exploring around base camp before realizing that due to problems of access and the available maps being inaccurate, none of the proposed peaks were feasible. We eventually decided to attempt a mountain previously unknown to us called Chukporisum (6,359m). On October 6 all four of us walked to an advanced base camp and spent the next 8 days on the attempt. Two days were spent ferrying loads, and then the mountain was attempted in pure alpine style from 5,140m. A summit attempt from a high camp at 6,040m ended at 6,180m in extreme cold and wind.

Entertainment on the Niwu Valley approach to Chukporisum.
Adam Thomas

Unfortunately, because of the time lost due to the landslides on the road while getting to the mountain, no time was left for any further attempts. We then sent our guide and cook out to Niwu and the roadhead with the gear while we proceeded to make a complete circumnavigation of the northern part of the range. This involved the first western crossing of a pass at 5,300m and another pass at 5,100m, in five days. We were back in Lhasa on October 26 before traveling back to Kathmandu overland in three days.

ADAM THOMAS, *U.K.*

KANGRI GARPO RANGE

Mt. Ruoni, attempt. The Kangri Garpo Range is located in the Zayul and Bomi Counties of Eastern Tibet. Since this region is close to the borders with both India and Myanmar, it has remained strictly off-limits to foreigners for many years. Even now the area remains shrouded in mystery. There are numerous 5,000-6,000m mountains surrounding unknown glaciers and only one of these peaks has ever been climbed. In 2001 three members of a New Zealand expedition led by John Nankervis climbed and skied down from the summit of a 5,650m snow dome above the Lhagu Glacier. The highest mountain in the range is called Ruoni (a.k.a. Bairiga, see below).

In 1882 a Pundit, Kishen Singh, approached the mountain from the south, and his route was repeated in 1933 by Kingdon-Ward and Kaulback, who named the peak Choembo. After that, neither mountaineering nor scientific expeditions visited the region until 1995, when Tamotsu Nakamura's party trekked in from the north. According to the former Soviet Union map, the height of Ruoni is recorded as 6,805m, while the 1:100,000 Chinese Peoples Liberation Army map gives it a height of 6,882m

After our expedition made the first ascent of Kula Kangri (7,554m) in 1986, I decided that Ruoni should be our next target and continued to negotiate with the Chinese Mountaineering

Mt. Ruoni, still unclimbed after a 2003 attempt. *Tomatsu Nakamura*

Association. Finally, in early 2002, special permission was granted by the CMA. It had indeed been a patient and tenacious effort lasting 16 years, and I was now over 70 years old.

In the fall of 2002 a three-member reconnaissance party was dispatched. They explored the Ata Glacier to a height of 4,800m and looked for a possible route to the summit. On October 2, 2003, the nine-member Kobe University East Tibet Mountaineering and Scientific Expedition arrived in Chengdu. I was chief leader, 72 years old, and the climbing leader was Prof. H. Kitaguchi. Nine days later we reached base camp at 4,150m on a lateral moraine of the North Ata Glacier.

On October 13, using 15 porters, we established an advanced base at 4,250m. At this point the Ata Glacier splits into two branches, one flowing north and the other south. Two days later Camp 1 was placed at 4,600m. From there, we decided to attempt the northeast ridge of Ruoni, which rises steeply to the summit from a col.

We climbed the ridge above Camp 1 and tried to traverse onto the upper part of the Ata Glacier in order to avoid an ice fall, but the ridge was too dangerous due to high avalanche risk. We therefore abandoned this route and on October 18, set up Camp 2 at 5,250m on a different line, which followed a smaller branch of the Ata Glacier. By the 23rd we had established a route to the col at ca 5,800m, only to find that directly above we would have to cross a sheer rock wall, overhung by a massive snow cornice. Although a search was made for alternate routes, poor visibility and 10 days of constant snowfall prevented us from making any further progress and we left base camp for Lhagu on November 2. In my opinion, the northeast ridge, while not easy, is definitely climbable if snow conditions and weather are good. The route favors a fast ascent by a small party.

KAZUMASA HIRAI, JAPAN *(translated by* TAMOTSU NAKAMURA, *Japan Alpine News)*

Kangri Garpo Range, exploration and naming of peaks. In spring 2001, the Fukuoka Section of the Japanese Alpine Club dispatched a reconnaissance survey team to the Kangri Garpo Range in Eastern Tibet. Many previously unknown peaks were named with respect to geographical characteristics and proper local names. In the spring of 2002, a second team visited the Mizui Valley, most probably the first foreigners ever to visit the area. They investigated peaks soaring higher than 6,000m.

In November 2003 a third expedition comprising Dr. Yukio Matsumoto (team leader), Takeshi Nakayama, Hideki Watanabe, Koji Sasaki, Miyoko Watanabe, Kazuki Tsuji, Tadaomi Fujino, and Nobuhiko Miyahara, set up base camps at both Lhagu and Mizui, from where they executed an extensive investigation of the region with the following three objectives: 1) to identify peaks on the principal mountain ridges of the Kangri Garpo Range; 2) to clarify the headwaters of the Lhagu Glacier Valley and surrounding peaks; 3) to identify the headwaters of the Mizui Glacier Valley.

The team succeeded in taking clear panoramic photographs of the peaks from four viewpoints on the road to the Dema La. The photo analysis revealed that there were 13 peaks higher than 6,000m. Of the 13 peaks, four had local names, but names for the other nine peaks could not be confirmed, as they cannot be seen from local villages due to geomorphologic barriers.

Hiyong (4,923m), which is located directly west of Lhagu Village, was successfully climbed by four members (T. Nakayama, H. Watanabe, K. Sasaki, and N. Miyahara). They established two camps on the route. During the ascent and while on the summit the four were able to precisely place on both the 1: 200,000 former Soviet Union map and the 1:250,000 Chinese map, Dojizangdoi (6,260m) and other peaks next to the deep headwaters of the Lhagu Glacier. Measurements were made using a Brunton compass and GPS-device.

A rugged and long ridge at an altitude of ca 6,000m divides the Mizui and Lhagu valleys. The former flows northward, while the latter drains to the southeast. The team tried to climb up to ca 4,500m in the Mizui Valley, in the process confirming the locations of Hamokongga (6,260m) and Gemsongu (6,450m).

All the peaks in the report except for the highest, Bairiga (Ruoni: 6,882m), were named by the present and previous survey expeditions from information provided by local people. A total of around 30 peaks were identified and named by the three expeditions. These names, which were translated into Tibetan, were approved by local villagers.

YUKIO MATSUMOTO, *Fukuoka Section, Japanese Alpine Club*
(*translated by* TAMOTSU NAKAMURA, *Japan Alpine News*)

OTHER MOUNTAIN ACTIVITIES

KHUMBU CLIMBING SCHOOL

The Sherpa people of Nepal visit the mountains for reasons quite different than the western climber. For the Sherpa of Nepal climbing is by and large a vocation. The level of risk these climbers accept while working is very high. Consequently, the Sherpas have the highest fatality rate of any nationality while on climbing expeditions. Despite being well known for their stamina and ability to carry heavy loads in the thin air of the Himalaya, they generally lack the years of training that western climbers have.

The goal of the Khumbu Climbing School (KCS), founded by the Alex Lowe Charitable Foundation, is to lower the injury and fatality rate among the Nepali climbers who work and climb in the Himalaya. This goal is to be achieved by improving the safety techniques of the Nepali climbers. The program is based on instruction, practice, application, and testing of technical climbing skills.

The inaugural school in winter 2004 provided instruction, practice, and testing of climbing skills. The instructors assessed the skill level of the participants and tailor the instruction. The western guides focused on presenting climbing as we were introduced to it: recreationally. The sense of enjoyment that one receives from climbing is as much of the message as the technical skills. The class took place in the village of Phortse, a one-day walk from Namche Bazaar in the Khumbu region. The course lasted seven days (February 15–20, 2004) and consisted of two classroom days and four days in the field. The course was planned in the winter to time it with the expedition off season. The instruction focused on ice climbing as the skills are similar to what is used on the high peaks. A series of ice flows on the northern flank of Khumbila Peak provided a practical schoolroom for instruction. At least a dozen climbs of varying degrees of difficulty exist within a several hour walk of Phortse.

Thirty-two students took part in the school this February. The class had eight novices with the balance having worked with climbing expeditions. The novices were split between attending as a way to gain employment in the trade and attending for recreational purposes. The experienced climbers have worked on expeditions to Everest, Cho Oyu, Manaslu, Makalu, Shishapangma, Ama Dablam, and as guides for the "trekking" peaks. The instructors came from the western U.S. All the instructors have been climbing and/or guiding for many years in an alpine setting: Conrad Anker, climber and private guide; Chris Booher, International Mountain Guides; Topher Donahue, photographer and guide; Steve Gipe M.D., climber and emergency medicine; Harry Kent, Kent Mountain Adventures; Adam Knoff, Mountain Link; Jon Krakauer, climber and writer.

The 2004 school produced a 40-minute video in Nepali focusing on the fundamentals of belaying and rope work. It was duplicated in Kathmandu into VHS and DVD formats and is being distributed free of charge to trekking agencies, tea houses, embassies, and the Nepal

Mountaineering Association. If you would like a copy of this film please contact info@ alexlowe.org.

The KCS is an ongoing enterprise. The hope is to have a school that is run and maintained by the people of Nepal. Our goal is to get the ball rolling and provide help in making the school a viable operation. Perhaps the best measure of the school's effectiveness was a comment from Palding, a student in this year's class: "I have always felt like a yak working for expeditions; now I am a climber."

CONRAD ANKER, *The Alex Lowe Charitable Foundation, AAC*

CLIMBER IMPACTS AND ACCESS IN PERU'S CORDILLERA BLANCA

The Cordillera Blanca is the world's highest tropical mountain range, with the greatest concentration of 6,000-meter peaks outside the Himalaya. It has attracted climbers and explorers from around the world since the early twentieth century. In 1975, most of the range was designated Huascarán National Park (HNP), and has since become part of a UNESCO Biosphere Reserve and a World Heritage Site. The area surrounding the park is also home to an estimated 230,000 residents, many of whom are descendants of the indigenous cultures that have inhabited the region since before the Incas. Much of the area now encompassed by the national park has long provided for local livelihoods, and many residents still depend on park land for various resources and as dry-season pasturage for livestock.

In recent decades, traditional ways of life in the Cordillera Blanca have been significantly affected by the region's burgeoning tourism infrastructure. HNP's spectacular and accessible mountain scenery draws high numbers of both domestic and international adventure tourists annually, yet climbing and trekking have remained largely unrestricted and free of the red tape and expense associated with permit systems in other countries. While tourism brings important economic opportunities for local residents, it has also created highly politicized conflicts over resource distribution and management as well as increased inter- and intra-community competition and environmental pressure.

I first became interested in tourism impacts in the Cordillera Blanca in early July of 1999 when I observed staggering numbers of trekkers and climbers in the Santa Cruz Valley and Alpamayo base camp (73 tents in the base camp and more than 100 people and 60 burros on the trail over a five-hour period). Later reports, including one by Cameron Burns in the AAJ 2001, also indicated that popular climbing routes and camping zones in the region were often overcrowded and increasingly trashed by heavy use.

As a Conservation Fellow in Environmental Studies at the University of Montana and with the sponsorship of the Doris Duke Charitable Foundation and an AAC Research Grant, I returned to the Cordillera Blanca during the summer of 2003 to begin a preliminary analysis of climbing and trekking impacts in HNP. Working as a research intern with The Mountain Institute's Andean Branch and under the auspices of HNP, I began collecting data on garbage and human waste accumulation, non-designated camps and trails, overcrowding, and the harvesting of fuelwood from native forests in a number of sites, including the popular Santa Cruz, Llanganuco, and Ishinca Valleys.

This research is, to my knowledge, the first attempt to gather ground-truthed data on visitor impacts in HNP, which is especially important at this time as park authorities are in the process of reviewing alternatives for new public-use regulations. Based on the language in the recent HNP Master Plan, there is concern among the climbing community that restrictions to access are likely to occur over the next three years throughout much of the park (see Jim Bartle's article in American Alpine News, Winter 2004, for details).

The proposed restrictions seem to be based on the premise that restricting recreational users to popular areas will both streamline park management and protect untrammeled ecosystems. Yet, while these changes would minimize the area managed for public use by HNP, my research indicated that cattle and other livestock had already degraded many of the park ecosystems to an extent that impacts from tourism were clearly secondary to those from agriculture-related grazing. This is not to say that impacts from tourism are inconsequential, but that they are occurring in environments with a long history of human and livestock use rather than in pristine ecosystems. I also found that the areas most degraded by tourism were, not surprisingly, those where use is already highly concentrated, and that, in general, less-visited areas (those frequented only by independent groups) showed few impacts from tourism. Undoubtedly, certain areas, particularly remaining Polylepis (Quenoa) cove forests, would benefit from restricted access, but in much of the park it seems that responsible adventure tourism will cause little additional impact. Whether these observations will help to inform future park planning and public-use regulations is impossible for me to say; but I am hopeful that they may, at least, illustrate the need for reliable field data.

Overall, the impacts from tourism in the popular valleys I studied were less severe than I expected from my observations in 1999 and from word-of-mouth accounts of previous conditions. Exceptions to this trend were the heavily used Pisco and Ishinca base camps where garbage and, especially, human waste accumulation was a significant problem by early August. The dearth of previously recorded data on both impacts and tourism levels made it impossible to make thorough comparisons to other years, but, according to numerous interviewees from the tourism sector, levels in both categories were significantly lower during the 2003 season than usual. As a result of these low levels, I am hesitant to draw too many conclusions regarding the severity of tourism impacts in HNP from my preliminary research, but I hope my observations will serve as a baseline record that can be used in conjunction with further monitoring efforts.

Two conclusions, however, are easily forthcoming: First, due to the lack of previous research on tourism impacts in HNP and because reliable data are essential for sound public-use planning, it is important to continue the monitoring I began in 2003 and to expand it to other parts of the park. Second, if we climbers are to maintain the freedom of use that has historically made the Cordillera Blanca so appealing, we must carefully minimize our impacts and work to show park managers and planners that we are a valuable and responsible constituency of Huascarán National Park.

ADAM FRENCH, *AAC*

MT. EVEREST ALPINE CONSERVATION AND RESTORATION PROJECT

On 30 May, 2003, the International Conservation Committee of the AAC announced that it will financially support a major new conservation initiative in Nepal's Sagarmatha National Park, home of Mt. Everest. "Community-Based Conservation and Restoration of the Mt. Everest Alpine Zone" will address the increasing impact of trekkers and climbers on the high altitude alpine landscapes. The project will be implemented in partnership with local Sherpa communities, local non-government organizations (NGOs), Nepal's Department of National Parks and Wildlife Conservation, and The Mountain Institute's (TMI) Nepal Program.

The project's primary concern is the continued over-harvesting of slow-growing shrubs and high altitude plants for tourist lodge fuel, a process I believe has accelerated since I first identified the problem during my dissertation research in 1984. Local people say that many of the hill slopes in the region have become "growing glacial moraines" during the past 20 years because of the increased erosion and instability that has resulted from these trends. The alpine ecosystems surrounding Mt. Everest, both in Nepal and Tibet, simply cannot endure this kind of pressure much longer.

The project was officially launched on May 28, 2003, the fiftieth anniversary of the first ascent of Mt. Everest, and has received a substantial amount of international publicity since then. It will be one of the first projects of its kind that combines community driven management and action with the results of extensive scientific research. AAC and TMI expect the program to set a precedent for similar projects in affected alpine regions throughout the mountain world, including the Andes and East African Highlands, within the near future.

The five-year project will be based on recommendations proposed by local Sherpa communities to protect and restore the heavily impacted alpine ecosystems of the upper Imja Khola watershed, gateway to the Everest base camp and popular trekking peaks. It will be implemented and directed by these communities in partnership with government agencies, NGOs, international NGOs, and the trekking and climbing communities. Activities will include strengthening community planning and implementation skills through training; the restoration of high impact areas; and increased education of both local people and tourists. Other activities planned include forming local Alpine User Groups; building porter shelters on trekking routes and stocking them with alternative fuels; constructing enclosures that protect the hillsides from overgrazing while promoting native plant re-establishment; and establishing restrictions on the harvesting of juniper shrubs.

During October-November 2003, TMI's Ang Rita Sherpa (Project Field Manager and son of Sir Edmund Hillary's head sirdar in 1953), Dumbar Thapa, and Vinod Aravind launched the project's Phase I activities by conducting a detailed survey of alpine lodges in the upper Imja Khola region. Project planning with Sherpa stakeholders, interested NGOs, and government partners was also initiated. At present, the Trekking Agents Association of Nepal (TAAN), Nepal Mountaineering Association (NMA), Sagarmatha Pollution Control Committee (SPCC), Sagarmatha National Park and Buffer Zone (SNPBZ), and local youth groups have all expressed interest in working with the project in the coming years.

As an indicator of the potential international interest for the project, Ang Rita Sherpa also walked out with $11,000 in donations from two trekkers met during the course of the fieldwork. We would like to extend a special thanks to Mr. Marcel Bach, Switzerland, and Dr. Sandra Cook, U.S.A., for their generous contributions to the Khumbu alpine project! Building on this promising beginning, TMI and AAC must continue to work hard to reach the project goal of $125,000 over the next five years, and AAC member contributions (as well as suggestions for other donors to approach) will be highly appreciated.

"This project will strengthen the capacities of local people to protect and restore their fragile landscape and will serve as a model for conservation in alpine zones throughout the world," said AAC International Conservation Chair Peter Ackroyd. "We are excited that this action, taken by the membership and leadership of the AAC, will encourage others to invest in protecting these mountain environments that so many people enjoy". For further information regarding the Khumbu alpine conservation and restoration project, please contact Dr. Alton Byers at abyers@mountain.org and Ang Rita Sherpa at angrita@mountain.org. For more information on The Mountain Institute, visit www.mountain.org.

DR. ALTON BYERS, *Director of Research and Education, The Mountain Institute*

UPDATE ON THE HIMALAYAN CATARACT PROJECT

The past year and a half has marked an exciting period of growth for the Himalayan Cataract Project and has furthered our mission of eliminating preventable and treatable blindness in mountainous Asia. We are making the transition from being an organization focused primarily on cataract surgery to one that is working to eliminate all types of preventable and treatable blindness. To this end, we have begun to focus our efforts on reaching the most remote and poorest people in the region, establishing self-sustaining cataract surgery facilities in the surrounding countries, and training ophthalmic sub-specialists in Nepal to become the teachers for the next generation of Himalayan ophthalmologists.

As always, education of medical personnel at all levels is playing a vital role in this development. At the paramedical level, we have established a training program for ophthalmic assistants. We are bringing intelligent young men and women from remote villages, who have completed the equivalent of our high school education, to Kathmandu for a three-year course. They return to their villages where we are establishing primary eye care centers. The ophthalmic assistants provide glasses and preventive care, treat infections and minor injuries, screen for diseases and surgical problems, and refer more serious problems to the nearest eye surgeon or arrange for a cataract team to come to their village. At the surgical level, we continue to train teams of doctors, nurses, and technicians from Bhutan, Tibet, India, and Pakistan to deliver modern cataract surgery. At the specialty level, we are supporting some of the best young ophthalmologists in Nepal to pursue fellowships in America or Australia.

Establishing a world-class eye care infrastructure remains central to our mission and is crucial in supporting the education of local providers. In 2003, we established four new primary eye care facilities in Nepal and performed over 9,000 surgeries in remote villages, including a cataract camp that was filmed by National Geographic Television in the kingdom of Mustang. In early 2004, we opened a permanent primary eye care facility in Kalimpong, West Bengal, the first of its kind in the region, and have plans to open a similar center in the Tibetan Amdo region of the Quinghai Province in China during the summer of 2004.

The core of our eye care infrastructure in the region is the Tilganga Eye Centre in Kathmandu. In 2003, we started a campaign to expand the Centre into a full tertiary care eye hospital. This expansion will allow us to accommodate the hundreds of patients who line up before dawn every morning seeking care and will also provide space to begin a full, American standard, three-year ophthalmology residency program in July 2004. The residency program will train the teachers for the next generation of ophthalmologists in mountainous Asia. For further information about the Himalayan Cataract Project, please visit our website, www.cureblindness.org.

GEOFFREY TABIN, *M.D. Co-Director, Himalayan Cataract Project, AAC*

Mountain Hut Competition

Europeans rely on mountain huts while climbing, whereas American climbers camp. The problem the American system is that dispersed tenting has a higher impact on fragile alpine areas than concentrated use around huts. With that in mind, some people are now wondering if the mountain hut culture should be imported to America. Replacing the old Glacier Lodge near the Palisade Group in the eastern Sierra Nevada, California, has provided the opportunity to invigorate this discussion. The old lodge burned down in 1998, and the plan is for it to be rebuilt using the winning design in 2003's The Mountain Hut Competition, conducted by the University of California at Berkeley College of Environmental Design.

As an avid user of European Alpine huts, I helped to sponsor this competition, though I was not a jurist. After nearly six years of groundwork, we were gratified to receive close to 500 individuals and teams who paid $35 apiece to enter the competition. The competition yielded a smorgasbord of interesting ideas for relating buildings to the surrounding landscape and for allowing people to interact with the environment more sustainably.

The central problems relating to structures on glaciers and other fragile montane ecosystems are energy, human waste disposal, solid waste disposal, and water sources and disposal. Also vital is how the building integrates into the landscape—even a beautiful structure should not call too much attention to itself. The old Glacier Lodge's misfortune provided the competition with a specific site to build on. The goal is for the Forest Service hut concessionaire to build this prototype hut. The Forest Service is interested in more huts in the 150 million non-Wilderness acres of National Forest land, hoping this might diminish the impact of individuals in the backcountry.

The winning entry came from Switzerland, earning the design team $15,000, while the four runners-up were American. Many worthy designs could not become finalists. One design dubbed "the whale" by the judges was a long, bulbous wooden structure that hovered above the landscape. It would fit perfectly into the arctic forests of Northern Finland, but it seemed out-of-place for the Sierra Nevada. Several structures would be constructed out of tent-like fabric. One finalist utilized PVC panels combined with zippers; it could be disassembled and moved from site to site. One proposal would have marched climbers up five stories of stairs to reach a hut on a pole—perhaps not ideal for sleepy 2 a.m. starts.

The tension between aesthetics and pragmatics—between a beautiful structure and what works technologically and is suitable for climbers—was apparent throughout the judging process. The winning design—by Hans Berrel, Maurice Berrel, and Charles Wulser—has two floors of four rooms each: a kitchen, a dining area, an equipment room, and a hutkeeper's apartment on the first floor; four dormitory rooms occupy the second floor, sleeping 16 people each. The rooms can be constructed at a lower elevation and flown by helicopter to the alpine site, where the pieces can be assembled. The entirety will be wrapped in roofing felt, into which stones from the site will be pressed to help blend the building into its landscape. The bunk platforms are built into the windows so that one is "sleeping with the stars," while hallways bring light into the building and provide a sense of space. The idea is to feel harmony with the outdoor experience, rather than confined to corridors and a warren of tiny rooms.

For more information about the competition, including photographs, please visit http://www/ced.berkeley.edu/competitions.

Jay Wiener, *AAC*

BOOK REVIEWS

EDITED BY DAVID STEVENSON

Everest: 50 Years on Top of the World, The Official History. GEORGE BAND. NEW YORK: BARNES & NOBLE, 2003. (IN ASSOCIATION WITH THE MOUNT EVEREST FOUNDATION, THE ROYAL GEOGRAPHICAL SOCIETY, AND THE ALPINE CLUB, LONDON.) 256 PAGES. HARDCOVER. $19.95.

Everest: Summit of Achievement. STEPHEN VENABLES, WITH JOANNA WRIGHT, JOHN KEAY, ED DOUGLAS, AND JUDY AND TASHI TENZING. NEW YORK: SIMON & SCHUSTER, 2003. (IN ASSOCIATION WITH THE ROYAL GEOGRAPHICAL SOCIETY, LONDON.) 252 PAGES. HARDCOVER. $50.00.

Chris Bonington's Everest. CHRIS BONINGTON. CAMDEN, MAINE/NEW YORK: RAGGED MOUNTAIN PRESS/MCGRAW-HILL, 2003. 256 PAGES. HARDCOVER. $29.95.

For mountaineers it was undoubtedly the crowning moment of the 20th century the day two climbers—an Asian roped to his New Zealand partner—first stood atop Earth's highest summit. Tensing Bhutia (later Tenzing Norgay Sherpa) was the 1953 British Mt. Everest's expedition's sirdar, while Edmund Percival Hillary—soon to be Sir Edmund Hillary—was a beekeeper. Both of these men's lives, and that of their expedition leader, Col. John Hunt (later Lord Hunt of Llanfairwaterdine) were forever altered by the worldwide media attention that rightfully glorified their achievement.

"Not many adventures ... ever achieve the status of allegory," wrote British author and Everest 1953 chronicler Jan Morris in Smithsonian in 2003, the 50-year Anniversary of Hillary and Tenzing's triumph. "... Perhaps only two such exploits have [in our time] been so charged with meaning that they have become in some sense transcendental. One was ... that giant step for all mankind, the arrival of Apollo 11 on the moon. The other was the first ascent of Mount Everest."

To commemorate the gala fiftieth anniversary of Everest's first ascent, London publishers released three new books in 2003. (Each also had an American imprint, given above.) While *Everest: 50 Years on Top of the World* and *Summit Of Achievement* are weighty, sumptuously designed coffee-table extravaganzas, *Chris Bonington's Everest* is more compact; yet all three virtually burst at the seams with skillfully reproduced photographs. And each book is not only a good read, but tells its portion of the Everest story in its own admirable way. However it is the quantity, high quality, and never-before-published status of many of the images in these three books that will make Everest aficionados salivate.

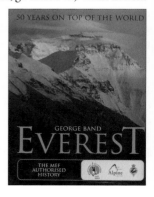

George Band, at the tender age of 23, was the youngest member of the successful 1953 British Everest expedition. After then making the first ascent of Kanchenjunga, the world's third tallest peak, two years later with Joe Brown, Band is eminently qualified to tell the story of Everest's conquest—and he does so with gusto. In *Everest: 50 Years on Top of the World, The Official History*, he tells the story of those golden days in intimate, fresh-scrubbed detail, in an unpretentious, engaging style that is informative, sometimes humorous, and rather like a fireside chat. As such Band's book stands apart from (and higher on the readability scale) than many Everest volumes. You become swept up in the drama and friendly English teamwork of the enterprise. You feel the tension of doggedly breaching the Khumbu Icefall and the unrelenting Lhotse Face as the excitement mounts to the historic quests of the two summit teams: first Bourdillon and Evans, then Tenzing and Hillary, pressing ever higher into altitudes and terrain unknown.

But is Band's book "The Official History" as the subtitle purports? Well, perhaps not. Although the mountain's discovery and early British attempts on Everest are all zestfully described (along with follow-up chapters on modern routes), *Everest: 50 Years on Top of the World, The Official History* is primarily an insider's view of the successful 1953 Everest ascent. But on that mark it scores high, and absolutely brims with amusing vignettes and never-before-seen photos (Hunt and Hillary sharing a pint at their 40th Everest reunion comes to mind, as does a candid snap of an older and wiser Noel Odell.) But look to Walt Unsworth's *Everest* for the definitive written history of the mountain, and to Peter Gillman's *Triumph & Tragedy, 80 Years on Everest* (1993) as the authoritative photographic and written chronicle of Earth's tallest peak.

Everest: Summit of Achievement, by volume and weight, is the most massive of the three books. Nothing less than a lavish feast of stunning imagery, the book is—and I say this unreservedly—a photographic masterpiece. Joanna Wright, Curator of Photography at the Royal Geographical Society Picture Library in London, assembled this magnificent visual opus from the society's 20,000-image collection, taken on nine Everest expeditions from 1921 to 1953. Clearly foremost in photographic criteria was that a picture had not been published. For jaded Everest admirers, this makes *Summit of Achievement* a true joy, even though the 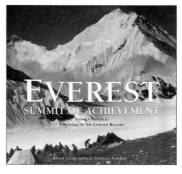 mountaineering action photos, while present, run almost secondary to the book's mission. The bulk of the image content shows us, in large format black and white, and hand-painted color, the culture of old Tibet. Through it we see the faces, daily life, and religious celebrations of the Tibetan people encountered during the first British forays to Everest in the 1920s and '30s; and the monasteries of Khampa Dzong, Shekar Dzong, and Rongbuk prior to their destruction during China's Cultural Revolution of the late 1960s.

To savor these photographs is to be transported back in time to the simpler days of the Dzatrul Rinpoche, the Head Lama of Rongbuk Monastery beneath Everest's north face, and the era of Tenzing Norgay's youth in the decades preceding China's military invasion and ruination of Tibet. Excellent, scholarly-penned chapters on the discovery and mapping of Everest by John Keay, and the religious traditions and sensibilities of the Tibetans residing near Everest by Ed Douglas add importance to the book. Likewise, a thoughtful contribution by Judy and Tashi Tenzing (Tenzing Norgay's grandson and two-time Everest summiter) on the multi-faceted contributions of Sherpa mountaineers to Everest's history. Himalayan climber Stephen Venables has the unenviable task—which he performs with his usual literary zeal, along with opinionated commentary from Reinhold Messner—of succinctly describing all the notable Everest expeditions from 1921 to 2003! All in all, this is an essential Everest book—to own, to read, to admire.

Of the three books, *Chris Bonington's Everest* hit the bookstore shelves first in 2003. Obviously this volume, a collected "best of" of Bonington's Everest writings and photographs, would sell a few extra copies during the Everest Anniversary Year, as Chris (now Sir Christian) is the most famous living British mountaineer. This even though the book has absolutely nothing to do with the anniversary of Everest's 1953 first ascent, since it chronicles Bonington's forays to the peak in 1972, 1975, 1982, and 1985. Book promotion aside, readers should not confuse his earlier autobiography, *The Everest Years: A Climber's Life* with *Chris Bonington's Everest.* The former covers Bonington's major Himalayan expeditions during a 15-year-period bracketed

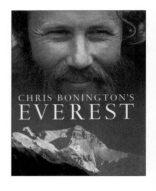

around (and including) his four Everest expeditions. *Chris Bonington's Everest* completes the Bonington oeuvre, being an excellent and highly enjoyable compendium of only his Everest experiences. Unpublished photographs (including numerous double page color spreads), diary entries, and postscriptal musings add depth, while a newly-minted introduction describes how he first heard Everest had been climbed. Lastly, an up-to-the-year-2003 conclusion yields a philosophical wrap-up of recent Everest trends: guided expeditions, offbeat firsts, and pointers to the few remaining potential new routes.

Chris Bonington has suffered as much as any mountaineer on Mt. Everest. From defeat and eventual triumph pioneering a new route up the massive southwest face; to the tragic and inexplicable disappearance of his partners Peter Boardman and Joe Tasker on the northeast ridge; to his own emotionally-charged ascent at age 50 via the South Col Route. In this year of the 50th Anniversary of Everest's first ascent, *Chris Bonington's Everest* is a valuable and beautiful testament to Chris's desire to push the boundaries of the possible while attaining the much sought-after summit of the world's highest mountain.

ED WEBSTER

Tenzing: Hero of Everest. ED DOUGLAS. WASHINGTON D.C.: NATIONAL GEOGRAPHIC PRESS, 2003. 304 PAGES. HARDCOVER, $25.00; PAPERBACK, $15.00.

I still buy plenty of climbing books, but I can rarely bring myself to read them. I review the picture captions and then unfairly decide to either get around to the book in my old age or to just let it collect dust forever. I'm glad that I chose to do more with Ed Douglas's new biography of Tenzing Norgay.

Like many an Everest enthusiast, I was pretty sure I already knew enough about the legends of the game … including the guys who were lucky enough to get on top first. Before I'd gotten very

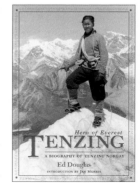

many pages into *Hero of Everest*, I discovered, once again, that I can't know enough about the pioneers of my life's game; that they were tougher and braver than I; and that luck had not-too-much-to-do with Tenzing Norgay's ultimately being in the right place at the right time. And I was pleased to find that Ed Douglas not only does read climbing books (lots of them), but obviously has gotten out in uncomfortable places enough over the years to understand them well.

In *Hero of Everest*, Douglas gives a fine overview of Tenzing's life and times. It turns out that in Tenzing's case, this is an absolutely essential combination … life and times. It is not enough to make do with an understanding of who the Sherpas are now, since the profession for which they have become famous was born in Tenzing's boyhood and, in essence, evolved with him. Nor can one get away with looking at a current map of the Himalaya in order to easily understand why a "Sherpa" like Tenzing was actually born in Tibet, but drew his identity from the Khumbu of Nepal, and then chose to live his life out as an Indian citizen in Darjeeling. And one simply cannot rely on a knowledge of what modern climbing is in order to grasp the enormity of Tenzing's achievement in teaching himself the game on his first expeditions with Eric Shipton, H.W. Tilman, and Frank Smythe. Douglas manages, while keeping the story moving along toward its natural climaxes, to put events and people into essential perspective.

I marveled that the author could build tension and anticipation in a story that most people on the planet think they already know the ending to. They make it to the top of the highest mountain in the world … and live. But there is tension, and it is due to Douglas's thorough examination of Tenzing Norgay's building obsession with Everest. By the time Tenzing does make the top, at age 39, he has outlived many of those he began work with. Douglas tells us just how few Sherpas came through the deadly learning curves of expedition climbing on Everest, Nanga Parbat, and K2 in the 1920's and 30's, leaving one thirsting for more knowledge of those sad epics. But more significantly, one comes to understand that the man who got "lucky" enough to be up there with Ed Hillary on May 29, 1953 had been the driving force behind three major Everest attempts in the space of a year. And this in a day when Everest attempts were long. As sirdar for the Swiss and then the British and as a full climbing member on these teams, Tenzing's duties were never-ending. He hadn't just been smiling and pleasant, he'd been relentlessly strong. In a time when European climbers were surprised to find such ambition among their hired help, they were even more surprised that Tenzing's drive could exceed their own.

Douglas keeps the suspense going after the Everest summit, but inevitably it is a sadder story and a more complex one. It is no great mystery when fame ruins the lives of even those born with every advantage. Tenzing's triumph, as a man who had none of the conventional advantages in life (he never learned to read), was that fame did not kill him. Where some might have taken easy shots at the "villains" who used Tenzing Norgay over the years, Douglas manages to explain how misunderstandings arose. He combined key interviews with careful readings of the recent works of others in order to come up with a remarkably balanced and even portrayal. True enough, after the Everest triumph one keeps reading in order to understand how such a seemingly happy, poised, gifted, and strong man could die lonely and troubled over status and money. But it isn't really some flaw in Tenzing's character that saddens here. More that even tigers of the snow must inevitably grow old. Ed Douglas objectively reveals a hero who was quite human, sensitive, and, in his way, grounded. Against all odds.

DAVE HAHN

Mountains of the Mind. ROBERT MACFARLANE. NEW YORK: PANTHEON BOOKS, 2003. 320 PAGES. HARDCOVER. $24.00

Imperial Ascent: Mountaineering, Masculinity, and Empire. PETER L. BAYERS. BOULDER: UNIVERSITY PRESS OF COLORADO, 2003. 174 PAGES. HARDCOVER. $29.95.

These two books have a common goal: to describe the cultural and historical factors that gave mountaineering form and meaning. But they go about it very differently. Let's start with Macfarlane's more familiar approach, a survey of the mostly literary influences that over three centuries transformed the European view of mountains from grotesque to enchanted, from the demonic to the sublime. As he writes on page 18, this "tremendous revolution in perception" caused "qualities for which mountains were once reviled—steepness, desolation, perilousness—to be numbered among their most prized aspects. So drastic was this revolution that to contemplate it now is to be reminded of a truth about landscape: that our responses to [it] are for the most part culturally devised … we do not see what is there, but largely what we think is there." And on page 165, about an early casualty on Mont Blanc, an American named Henry Bean: "He was sent to his death by ways of feeling set in motion many years before his birth. Because the ways we perceive and react to the forms of landscape are prompted, primed and reminded by those who have gone before, no death in the mountain is isolated from historical circumstance. Although we might like to believe that our experience at altitude is utterly individual, each of us is in fact heir to a complex and largely ¡ Predecessors who, in their turn, were influenced by the likes of de Saussure, Shelley, Wordsworth, Byron, Petrarch, Coleridge, Edmund Burke, Albert Smith, Ruskin, Bachelard, John Muir, and others whom Macfarlane discusses from the impressively wide reading one might expect from a fellow of Emmanuel College, Cambridge. To manifest the power of his antecedents, he interpolates recollection from his own experience in the hills of Scotland, the Alps, and the Tien Shan.

Macfarlane is a writer with more charm than intellectual rigor. His opening premise is not satisfactorily substantiated, in part because he cannot turn down a good digression. He writes with such brio that one hardly notices the transitions from topic to topic, the haphazard melding of the personal and the academic. Sometimes, however, the writing skills and the aliveness of his mind don't quite justify the diversions from theme—a discussion of children's literature, say, or a solipsistic rant about climbing fatalities, or an insert about Chinese scholars' rocks. But soon, like a clever magpie, Macfarlane proffers another seductive tidbit and the reader is entertained again. For example, during a hurried tour of the history of cartography he says the following with customary style and authority: "The Jungfrau and the Eiger were christened in the eleventh and twelfth centuries respectively, but it was during the 1800s that the micro-naming properly began. Niches, notches, shoulders, cols, ridges, glaciers, routes: all began to bear the names of climbers and explorers. Look at a large-scale map of the Alps now, and you will see the names jostling for space, radiating out of geological features like small black spokes."

In contrast, Bayers is an academic of an unamusing type. His sources are the likes of Foucault, Barthes, Terry Eagleton, Edward Said. From which anyone who has studied literature of the humanities in the last 20 years will know that we are in a country called "postmodernism." Appropriately therefore, this is a book about texts. Seven in fact: three about climbing Denali (Cook, Browne, and Stuck); and four about Everest (Younghusband, John Hunt, Tenzing Norgay, and Krakauer). These are all critiqued for the light they shed on the tropes of masculinity and imperialism. One needs a stomach for academic prose, but I found the going worth the effort, especially the dissection of Younghusband's chest-thumping *The Epic of Mount Everest* (1926) and the vestiges of the Empire in Hunt's *The Ascent of Everest* (1953). Of the former he says: "Through his portrayal of Mallory and Irvine's deaths, Younghusband's narrative capitalizes on the public sentiment towards the now idealized body of the dead male soldier [dead in the trenches of WWI]. Their warrior bodies lying high on the slopes of Everest represent the physical courage of their lived actions …" Of the latter, Bayers illuminates how: "Hunt is caught between his desires to legitimate Britain's imperial traditions while also trying to distance the expedition from the pejorative connotations of imperialism [and] in the end the narrative celebrates the masculine imperial ethos of the adventure tradition." The weakest chapter is the last. Krakauer's *Into Thin Air* is unconvincingly shoehorned into the argument by conflating imperialism with globalization and its Third World effects.

The message here is that there are more determinants of the climbing experience than you can shake a piton at. History, literature, culture, ideology, aesthetics—all bear on the motivation to climb. That's worth remembering in the light of the contemporary emphasis on the psychological. Remember the next time you tie onto a rope: there are ancient ghosts in the air.

JOHN THACKRAY

Where the Mountain Casts Its Shadow: The Dark Side of Extreme Adventure. MARIA COFFEY. NEW YORK: ST. MARTIN'S PRESS, 2003. 234 PAGES. HARDCOVER. $23.95.

You expect a lot from a book that garners awards at the Banff Mountain Book Festival. And *Where the Mountain Casts Its Shadow* delivers. The book tackles an unusual, historically under-examined subject in mountaineering literature: What is life like as a top high altitude mountaineer? What is the impact of that life on loved ones—partner, children, and parents—during the climber's life and after he (or she) is gone?

To get answers, Coffey interviewed many top climbers or their survivors—Conrad Anker, Chris Bonington, Anatoli Boukreev, Kitty Calhoun, John Harlin III, Lynn Hill, Alex Lowe, Joe Simpson, Ed Viesturs, and Jim Wickwire, to name but a few—and exhaustively researched the book with an impressive roster of noted sociologists, psychologists, and historians.

If Coffey's approach sounds clinical—about as exciting as watching a belay—rest assured, it's anything but. This book is a page-turner: Coffey's writing style is direct and ferociously honest, while her use of emotionally gripping anecdotes infuses an engaging, novelistic feel. Hollywood couldn't script stories more wrenching or ennobling than the death of Chris Kerrebrock in a

Denali crevasse while singing a boyhood song, or the poignant love story of New Mexican nurse practitioner Linda Wylie and Kazakhstan alpine superstar Anatoli Boukreev.

The seed for Coffey's book was planted in 1982, when Coffey's partner of two-and-a-half years, Joe Tasker, the great British mountaineer, disappeared with Pete Boardman on the unclimbed northeast ridge of Everest. Until that moment, Coffey felt she was drifting through life—30 years old, sedentary, immature, bored by her teaching job, passive, without passion or purpose. In Tasker, Coffey had found not only a boyfriend, but also, for the first time, status and direction.

When Tasker disappeared, Coffey wrote, his "death jolted me alive." In 1989 she published her first book, *Fragile Edge*, about dealing with Tasker's death. In the intervening years she completely overhauled her life: physically, in relocating from Britain to Canada; professionally, through crafting a calling as adventure guide and writer; and emotionally, by building a long marriage and discovering the zest and focus for which she admired Tasker. Coffey's impressive personal journey is reflected in the maturity and power of *Where the Mountain Casts Its Shadow*.

The book unfolds essentially into three sections. Initially, Coffey examines the many reasons why, despite appalling fatality rates, people do extreme climbing. These include addictive highs and hormonal rushes; cravings for extreme physical exertion and experiences; a sense of purpose; play and youthfulness; spiritual "flow"; artistic self expression; a direct connection with nature; and satisfaction from living on a heroic scale, exercising control in difficult situations, and experiencing "moments of perfection."

Coffey also lays out mountaineering's secondary rewards: exciting travel, wild parties, glamorous buzz, entree into a close-knit community, acceptance by an interesting group of friends, and for the top practitioners, even fame and prestige. (Bonington was knighted; Tasker and Scott met the Queen; blind Everest summiter Eric Weihenmayer visited the White House.)

The rewards, Coffey reveals, also extend to partners of mountaineers, who bask in "reflected glory," enjoying a dramatic, passionate, exciting, intense lifestyle, and gaining acceptance into the "protective circle" of the closely knit "climbing tribe," with its own rituals and active support network.

But in life there's always a price. In the book's second section Coffey shows us how climbers' partners pay for the climbing lifestyle, and what the cost is. For partners it means long separations, loneliness, the constant specter of widowhood (even today, the bereaved partners are invariably women), disrupted family routines, difficult "re-entry time" when the climber is home, as well as the emotional and physical absences when he is home but planning the next expedition. It also means dealing with the adulation heaped on the returning "hero," plus jealousy from the intense bonds her partner forms with climbing partners, and the awareness that he is emotionally centered outside the family.

And that list doesn't even take into account having to deal with endemic mountaineering personality traits such as restlessness, huge egos, single mindedness, self-importance, self-centeredness, and disdain for values like fidelity and truthfulness. Or what Coffey calls the "emotional toll of mopping up so much tragedy." For when an expedition death occurs, it's typically the partner at home who is stuck with the awful task of contacting and comforting the dead mountaineer's next of kin.

Yet it turns out that many women, like Jenny Lowe after Alex Lowe's death, opt to be "lifers" in the mountaineering community. After the death of a mountaineer partner, it is common for the woman to become romantically involved with another mountaineer.

The book's last section focuses on children and parents of mountaineers, who, unlike the climber or his partner, don't have a choice in the situation. The result is an invariably complex relationship.

For children this means mixed emotions and messages, such as dealing with a father gone for long stretches, including routine absences during birthdays and other important childhood milestones; feeling that Dad prefers the mountains to his family; and experiencing unusual childhood situations—for example, routine attendance at memorial services. The toll can be considerable and is often expressed in wild behavior, craving for ordinariness, anger at the mountaineering parent (often anger at the surviving parent), and later on, difficulty forming stable adult relationships.

"Ordinary" climbers will be fascinated by the voyeuristic peek into the world of top mountaineers this book offers. Coffey doesn't dish gossip gratuitously, but it emerges that the much-lionized Alex Lowe, for instance, was an emotionally distant son and father. Joe Tasker, Coffey reveals, not only cheated on her, but self-righteously and indignantly lied to her about it.

My biggest criticism of the book is a certain lack of perspective. It shows us how the death of a 35-year-old on Everest is particularly painful for the climber and particularly tragic for the loved ones. But what about 35-year-olds—or anyone, for that matter—who die in car crashes? After protracted battles with AIDS? Multiple sclerosis? Breast cancer? Are these deaths "less heroic"? Less painful? Less wrenching on family and friends?

That aside, *Where the Mountain Casts Its Shadow* is a gripping must-read. Despite the book's grim title, it manages to reveal some elements of sun, as well as the shadow, in the lives of the top mountaineers. And it helps the rest of us better understand and appreciate what their world is about.

SUSAN E. B. SCHWARTZ

The Naked Mountain. REINHOLD MESSNER. (TIM CARRUTHERS, TRANS-LATOR.) SEATTLE: THE MOUNTAINEERS BOOKS, 2003. 315 PAGES. HARDCOVER. $22.95.

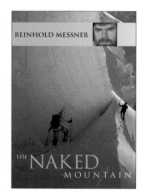

The Naked Mountain is Reinhold Messner's account of the 1970 expedition to climb Nanga Parbat's Rupal Face, led by Karl Her-rligkoffer. In it Messner recounts his and his brother Günther's success in gaining the summit, and the tragic events surrounding Günther's death on the descent.

Finally available in English and published in America last November, this is Messner's 40th book. Intense controversy sur-rounding Messner's account of Günther's death has swirled around this book since its German publication in 2002. Expedition members have accused him of sacrificing his brother in an attempt to traverse the mountain, and Messner has responded vig-orously—even with lawsuits. While I haven't read the contradictory accounts*, I did go back over the relevant sections in Messner's autobiography (*Reinhold Messner—Free Spirit*, 1991) and his *All 14 Eight Thousanders*, as well as a 2003 article by Greg Child in *Outside* that discusses the controversy. To say this is a somewhat incestuous and complicated tale is a huge under-statement, but not at all surprising.

Following a preamble and short introduction, the initial 100 or so pages set up the tale. These include background on Messner and Günther's boyhood and climbing partnership; the first attempt on Nanga Parbat in 1895, which claimed the life of English mountaineer A.F Mummery; the 1932 reconnaissance and 1934 expedition led by Willy Merkl, which took his life and those of nine others; and finally the 1953 expedition on which Hermann Buhl managed his heroic solo summit climb. It was Merkl's death that prompted his half-brother Herrligkoffer to vow to "continue the battle for Nanga Parbat" as Willi's legacy.

Much of the next section is told through excerpts from Reinhold's and Günther's diaries and letters home, interspersed with comments by other expedition members, including Herrligkoffer, which have been taken from their published accounts. Through these we get the timbre of the expedition, and a sense of the relations between the climbers, in particular the strained relationship between the young Messners and their leader. Reinhold uses this technique to advantage in portraying both the excitement and drudgery of expedition life. The closeness of his and Günther's relationship comes through clearly.

However, the real meat of the story is in the next hundred pages. An incorrect weather flare triggering Reinhold's decision to summit alone, Günther's last-minute impulse to follow him (against the expedition's plan), and the brothers' simul-climb to the summit set the stage for one of mountaineering's most poignant tragedies. Leaving the summit, Günther's altitude sickness and the brothers' lack of a rope make it impossible for them to reverse their ascent, forcing them to bivy at 8,000 meters in brutal temperatures. The following morning, in what must have been the ultimate frustration to the Messners, two of their party (Kuen and Scholz) pass within 200-300 feet of their position. Exhausted and apparently unable to make their condition understood to their teammates, Günther and Reinhold feel compelled to attempt a descent via the Diamir Face. On the descent the two become separated. Reinhold backtracks to try to find his brother, but finds only avalanche debris. Grief-stricken and delirious, he wanders the glacier calling out in agony.

The final chapters deal with Reinhold's epic journey back toward base camp, aided first by local villagers and then soldiers, finally meeting the retreating expedition team by chance. He relates the team's reactions and the events that followed. It is here, and in his discussion of his recovery, where his frustration and anger are most apparent. Excerpts from published statements by Herrligkoffer and other members of the team, alternating with Messner's italicized comments, present a fairly good summation of the controversy.

More than 30 years after these events took place, the reopened wound is an ugly thing. It challenges the reputation of one of the greatest figures in mountaineering history. As there were only two people who knew what happened on this climb, and one is dead, we can never be absolutely certain about the causes. For Reinhold Messner's most recent and most thorough explanation, read this book.

AL HOSPERS

Editor's note: Two books by 1970 Nanga Parbat team members were issued last year in response to the publication of The Naked Mountain. *They are Hans Saler's* Between Light and Shadow: The Messner Tragedy on Nanga Parbat *and Max Von Kienlin's* The Traverse: Günther Messner's Death on Nanga Parbat—Expedition Members Break Their Silence. *Court injunctions granted to Messner prohibit further editions of these books. Opportunities to read English translations will depend on the outcome of legal proceedings.*

The Beckoning Silence. JOE SIMPSON. SEATTLE:
THE MOUNTAINEERS BOOKS, 2003. 315 PAGES. PAPERBACK. $18.95.

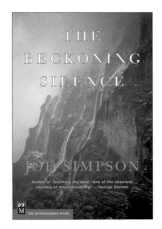

Of course Joe Simpson would have to cap off his climbing career
with an ascent of the notorious north face of the Eiger. As anyone
who's followed his adventures can tell you without even checking
his birth certificate, "Trouble" is Simpson's middle name. From
his teeth-clenching crawl off Siula Grande (captured in the
mountaineering classic *Touching the Void*); to his open air plunge
from the heights of Pachermo; to any one of a bushel of other
mishaps and disasters, Simpson has wallowed in a brand of high
altitude mayhem that would have turned lesser men into hand-
wringing Xanax-poppers.

It should therefore come as no surprise that as his latest
book opens our hero finds himself contemplating retirement.
The cumulative years of close calls and perished friends have left Simpson, on the threshold of
middle age and feeling it daily, wondering if there isn't a more appropriate way to be spending
his life. The thought crystallizes for him on Alea Jacta Est (Latin for "The Die is Cast"—some
climber-classicist's idea of a grim joke), a Grade V ice climb in the French Alps. In a classic Simpson
set piece, the author gives a heart-stopping description of his partner Ian Tattersal's decision to
risk both their lives attempting to dry-tool over a roof with Simpson belaying him, on no more
protection than two poorly placed knife blade pitons ready to pop.

Though Simpson survives this self-inflicted near miss, as well as another close shave in the
Andes, a slew of lethal accidents among his colleagues in the climbing community leads him to
consider hanging up his crampons. When Tattersal perishes in a freak paragliding accident and
Simpson's mother dies while the author is unreachable on a climbing holiday, he finds himself
ready to close the book on his thrill-seeking life.

Not, as it turns out, without a last hurrah: Simpson takes a jaunt on the American winter
testpiece Bridalvail Falls with his new partner, Ray Delaney, who's also contemplating retirement.
In the afterglow of this happy interlude, Delaney proposes the duo go out on the classic-to-end-
all-classics: the Eiger Nordwand. The last half of the book is devoted to Simpson's attempt on the
notorious vertical death trap. It includes an absorbing recitation of some of the more brutal
chapters in the mountain's history, and a chance encounter with legendary first ascender Anderl
Heckmair at an inn at the foot of the climb. Despite a platoon of ghosts and several operas-worth
of tragedy plaguing the mountain, it quickly becomes clear that the Eiger's reputation is more
ferocious than its current status. Thanks to advances in gear and a world-class mountain rescue
squad, when Simpson and Delaney begin their assault of the Nordwand no one has died on the
Eiger in a decade.

Naturally, with Simpson's infallibly bad timing that admirable record immediately goes
sour. The two friends find themselves sharing the route with a film crew, a second pair of
climbers, and a fast moving soloist. Though not unusual company on a coveted, easily accessible
route, events turn lethal when a sudden thunderstorm envelops the face in pounding hail,
lightning, and torrential rains. Simpson gets his nose rubbed in the famously awful Eiger weather,
but he and Delaney are fortunate to be only a pitch beneath the well-sheltered Swallow's Nest
belay as the storm hits, and they soon find themselves watching the bombardment from relative

safety. The storm initially verges on comic misadventure, but it soon becomes clear that others on the face have not fared so well. In an air of grim resignation, the pair beat a hasty retreat from unforgiving heights.

All this is thrillingly told in Simpson's justly celebrated prose style. The book becomes tedious only when he swaps his black leather role of existential philosopher for the tweedy jacket of the moralist. In this persona Simpson writes sanctimoniously about the controversial 1999 expedition to find the bodies of Mallory and Irvine on Everest, describing it as a desecration and freak show. His oddly inappropriate editorializing over Mallory's cairn is a jarring note in this mostly felicitous volume. Sermonizing over long dead corpses is entirely misplaced in book that includes "historical" photos of climbers dying or about to die on the Eiger Nordwand. As Simpson himself well knows, he has made a handsome living milking the public's appetite for pathos, providing detailed descriptions of the suffering and terror mountaineers visit upon themselves and, by extension, their loved ones.

Despite this unaccountable lapse, Simpson is otherwise a great armchair companion, broodingly articulate in repose, gallant and good-humored when the chips are down. He has spent his adult life in the state of engaged introspective that one longs for in the ideal adventure writer, and if *The Beckoning Silence* ranks a few grades lower than *Touching the Void*—and what doesn't?—it is still an adventure worth having, in company worth keeping. The reader is grateful for the strong hint at the volume's close that the mountains aren't finished with their famous prodigal son, despite all the talk of retirement.

RICHARD RYAN

Dougal Haston: The Philosophy of Risk. JEFF CONNOR. EDINBURGH: CANONGATE BOOKS, 2002. 225 PAGES. PAPERBACK. $15.00.

Jeff Connor is a seasoned journalist and author whose book on wild men of the Creag Dhu was well received. In researching this book Connor interviewed me, as he did others, on his visit to Leysin. Though our talk was brief, he left me with a sense that he would write an objective and balanced account of Haston's life.

When I was approached to review this book, curiosity prompted me to take a gander at what Amazon.com readers thought. I was both surprised and dismayed to find that readers who, like Connor himself, had never met Haston, had formed such strong and hostile opinions. For one reader Haston came across as an "egocentric hedonist notable only for his immense physical strength at altitude." For another he was "a nut case," and for yet another he was "not an admirable man" but "a wild drunk."

Though I found the book a "page-turner," by its end I was all too aware why the Amazon reviewers had formed such low opinions. In page after demeaning page, one is apprised of such trivia as how Haston scrounged smokes on the Mönch; or that he smoked the "Euro-chic Disque Bleus holding the cigarette with exaggerated care between thumb and first two fingers." Or how a Leysin guide informed him that "until you ski properly, you are not a complete mountaineer," a prospect apparently so horrifying (though he had already climbed the south faces of both Everest and Annapurna!) that he forthwith became an accomplished skier.

The reader's bent for vicarious hedonism is generously satisfied. We are informed of Haston's drunken binges, his insatiable womanizing, his appetite for gratuitous violence, his ruthless exploitation and/or ill treatment of friends. The "Clachaig incident" is exploited to cruel effect. And, the fact that he wore a "foulard" around his neck (as many of us did in those days), coupled with his pronounced interest in philosophy, is used to portray him as a pseudo-intellectual prima donna.

One must wonder how it came to pass that Connor, who had certainly done an amazing amount of legwork, and had interviewed many of those who had known and/or climbed with Haston, should write such an uncharitable and ofttimes prejudiced biography.

None of us who climbed and worked at ISM (International School of Mountaineering) with Dougal in those days would deny many of the faults Connor brings up. But did such behavior make him any worse a climber? Or even a worse person? Climbers have never claimed to be angelic. Certainly those of us who climbed in the sixties and seventies were far from being heavenly envoys. (To get a whiff of those times one may savor Alan and Adrian Burgess's *Book of Lies.*) Compared to many of the "lads" back then, Haston was quite temperate. Bev Clark, Davie Agnew, and Ellie Moriarty give honest, though all too limited, appraisals of Haston. They were truly his friends.

In any event, by book's end, having weathered the maligning of Haston's character; the unnecessary debunking of a wonderful person like Ian Clough; and trivia such as being told that the Dutch co-founder of the Vagabond Club was not heterosexual, the cognizant reader can only feel frustrated.

We are left with an unsatisfied appetite for more about Haston's mountaineering career, which spanned some of the most interesting years in our history. Though cut short by an avalanche, it was a career equal to those of most of the truly great climbers of the 20th century. And it was one that could never have been as colorfully eventful and as brilliantly successful if Haston had not been the generous, intuitive, intelligent, courageous—and somewhat flawed—person that he was.

Michel and Yvette Vaucher, who were on the ill-conceived 1971 International Everest Expedition, had nothing but praise for Haston when we met soon after their return. I recall their lauding his team spirit, endurance, and climbing abilities. In Connor's biography there are too few such words of praise. Quotes from Tut Braithwaite, Karl Golikow, and Doug Scott stand out in contrast.

It is regrettable that despite broad based and significant research Connor skims so deftly over Haston's many exciting British, Alpine, Andean, and Himalayan exploits. He touches on this or that climb, yet never in the depth they warrant.* Many of those living today who climbed with Haston surely could share an extensive collection of anecdotes. Why not quote more liberally from "The Bat and the Wicked" by Robin Smitt whom, in marked contrast to Haston, Connor seems to revere? Where is the story of his first Eiger ascent? Rusty Baillie, his partner on that climb, is still with us. There is very little on his amazing final bid for the summit on the 1966 Eiger Direct, one of the highlights in Alpine history. More anecdotes from Scott or Bonington would have been much appreciated.

In my opinion, the best part of this biography is not the slow-moving first section, where Haston is introduced more as a hooligan than an aspiring but wild young climber; nor the tabloid-ish middle. The book's finest moments are in the next to last chapter, "In High Places," which is the best written and most instructive. Despite the inevitable digs at Haston's persona (for example, the Whillans "rejection"), we are given a clearer perception of him. He comes across here as a man driven, assuredly, but also a man who carries his own weight, and a climbing partner you can depend on in a pinch.

I lived in Leysin with Dougal for 10 years. We climbed on the same crags, drank in the same pub, and guided at the same climbing school. The Dougal that I read about in this biography is not the Dougal that I knew. It is undeniable that he was somewhat taciturn, appeared enigmatic, and did not suffer fools. Thus, he was not easily approachable. But, I know of few people in my long climbing career whom I would rather have had by my side in a tough spot.

Despite Connor's many allusions to the contrary, I never knew Dougal to drive a car. The burden of memory that stemmed from an ill-fated night in Glencoe when his car struck and killed a pedestrian never left him. We touched on it only once. It was obviously a very painful subject. Hamish MacInnes once asked Haston why he did not drive. His answer was "Would you drive after what happened…?" MacInnes, who was closer to Haston than most, knew him to have in his inscrutable depths "strong and sensitive emotions." That is the Dougal I also am glad to have known.

T.E. Lawrence, Churchill, Shackleton, and Messner, to name only four outstanding figures, were not without character flaws. But it is what they accomplished despite (and at times because of) those shortcomings that makes them unforgettable. In Connor's book Haston is afforded no such credit.

Once as we walked under a blank, unclimbed face somewhere above Leysin, I said that the face would "go" with a few bolts for protection. Dougal felt that the face should be left alone until a climber came along who could climb it "clean." Likewise, readers would have been better served if the story of Haston's life had been left alone until someone came along who could write it clean.

LARRY WARE

Editor's note: For more on the climbing achievements of Dougal Haston, read In High Places *(1972), his autobiography. Also* Direttissima, *co-authored with Peter Gilman (1966);* The Eiger *(1974), a history of the Eigerwand by Haston; and* Changabang *(Bonington, 1975), which includes contributions by Haston. Readers may also gain insight into Haston by reading his* Calculated Risk: A Novel *(1979).*

Himalayan Vignettes: Garwhal and Sikkim Treks. KEKOO NAOROJI. BOMBAY, INDIA: THE HIMALAYAN CLUB, 2003. 236 PAGES. HARDCOVER. $60.00.

Himalayan Vignettes is a large format, coffee table photo-essay of expeditions to the Garwal and Sikkim by Indian trekker-photographer Kekoo Naoroji during the1950s. It is a work of love, primarily undertaken by his son, Rashid, and published with the support of friends and colleagues at the Himalayan Club in Bombay. Naoroji is a well-known member of the Club, and was instrumental in moving its headquarters from Calcutta to Bombay after Indian independence. He was an executive at Imperial Chemical Industries during the fifties and has a polymath's range of tastes and interests, including Western classical music, theater, mountaineering literature, and outdoor conservation. Naoroji's family is omnipresent in the introductory sections of the book and in the extracts from his expedition diary, which precede the photographs. Especially present and appreciated is his wife, Dosa, and her infinite patience and support of him in his quest to record visually some of the most remote areas of India. His diary entries always return to his family, and his greatest superlatives of the mountain terrain are put in the context of how he wishes his family were there to see it. It is Naoroji's humanity that truly adds poignancy to the text. No posturing here; just an appreciation for the early explorers of the Garwal and Sikkim, and of the supreme beauty of the Indian landscape. And sometimes, it must be admitted, a bit of venting about the discomforts, aggravations, and general headaches of treks to remote regions.

But as I said, this is primarily a picture book. When I received the review copy from the AAC Library, I opened the package and started leafing through it, as one does, to get an initial impression of the photographs. My first reaction was that some of them should not have been included because of his camera's technical limitations. (Naoroji primarily used a 35mm camera.) Several of the full-page images are quite grainy, and obviously benefit by being presented at reduced scale in the same frame as the blow-up. I assume the inclusion of these small insets means the publishers were well aware of the shortcomings of his photographic equipment. But, on subsequent perusals, remembering the message I once read in the liner notes of a vinyl record album, I softened my view. The record company advised that one should regard the recording problems (it was a "live" album) as one would "flaws in fine leather." This is precisely how to view the photographs of Kekoo Naoroji: what is lost in the clarity of certain images is more than repaid by his composition and artistry. Having said this, I should emphasize that the majority of photographs are well printed and in crisp focus.

Working mostly in black and white, Naoroji uses the medium to wonderful dramatic effect. I was not surprised that Naoroji's major interests in the arts were in drama and music; both are present in his images. His photographs of local people and of his porters in the pursuit of their everyday lives in the mountains not only make for a valuable ethnic document, but also great theater. For me, his starkly contrasting images of the high Himal conjure up musical themes of the great classical composers. One can almost hear Beethoven's symphonic works when looking at Naoroji's carefully composed photographs of Nanda Devi or Trisuli: the romantic, terrible beauty. As stated in the text, the photographs are reproduced using "the most modern of techniques," and we experience not only a fine aesthetic treat, but also have a visual yardstick with which to measure the environmental degradation that has taken place in the Indian Himalaya since the 1950s. It is sad to think that many of these remote areas have been largely deforested and have experienced major glacial shrinkage in the years since Naoroji's expeditions. This fact is aptly observed in the fine foreword written by British mountaineer Stephen Venables, who trekked the same areas 40 years after these photographs were taken.

Himalayan Vignettes will be appreciated by those longing for the pristine mountain world that existed in the not too distant past, when areas such as the Garwal and Sikkim were viewed as remote, strange, and dangerous. Armchair mountaineers will trace routes with their fingers, and those less ambitious will just enjoy the view. It is, simply, a fine addition to the library of any of those who love mountains.

JOHN OWEN

Range of Glaciers: The Exploration and Survey of the Northern Cascade Range. FRED BECKEY. PORTLAND AND SEATTLE: OREGON HISTORICAL SOCIETY AND UNIVERSITY OF WASHINGTON PRESS, 2003. 568 PAGES. $40.00.

Fred Beckey, world-renowned climber and historian, has written yet another definitive guide to the Cascade Mountains of the Northwestern United States. But this one is not a climbing guide.

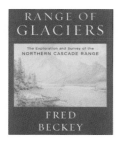

Range of Glaciers takes the reader on a journey through time and space that chronicles the economic, sociological, and recreational history of these mountains and the activities of the men who explored them. Beginning with the first settlers, Beckey leads us through the early surveys and mapping projects that exposed the challenges the Cascades posed to cross-range railroads and year-round travel. Accounts of the two Northwest Boundary Surveys paint a detailed picture of the politics endemic to surveying such an "unnatural boundary," as well as the problems of early mountain travel in the North Cascades. We next come to the building of the railroads across the passes, and the excitement of a minor mining boom. Later, attention is turned to the development and evolution of tourism, and mountaineering on the volcanoes.

The search for a mountain pass useable year-round is a particularly interesting story from a modern perspective. Today's highways, lazily crossing the Cascade passes, were once the scene of formidable railroad challenges. Beckey draws attention to the hardships of finding and building these passages, as well as how decisions made during the building of the railroads have had a permanent impact on our experience of the wilderness today. Tying past to present in this way makes the history particularly relevant to anyone who enjoys the wild spaces of the Cascades, and it is used effectively throughout the book.

Beckey also gives an interesting chronology of the early events and circumstances in the birth of Cascade mountaineering, including detailed narratives of early ascents in the range and the particular logistics needed to obtain them. Peppered throughout the history are specific (and often amusing) tactics used by the early mountaineers, such as the crevasse-crossing methods employed on the first ascent of Mt. Rainier. The logistical problems of gaining access to the mountains, and interactions with the Native American guides, are discussed in detail.

The writing in this book has a level of detail approaching that of a reference, which sometimes makes for dry reading. However, Beckey periodically relieves the monotony by including humorous anecdotes, such as Lt. Kautz's descriptions of the crumbling volcanic moraines along the Nisqually glacier of Mt Rainier as walls of "white granite"; and the whistling marmots he encountered as "mountain sheep." Also, each chapter ends with a fine selection of historical maps, drawings, and photographs, which give one a visual sense of what was known and how it felt to be there at the time.

Range of Glaciers is a meticulously researched and thoroughly detailed book that will appeal to anyone with a love for history or for the Cascade Mountains.

DAVID BURDICK

Frank Smythe: The Six Alpine/Himalayan Climbing Books (*Climbs and Ski Runs; The Kangchenjunga Adventure; Kamet Conquered; Camp Six; The Valley of Flowers; Mountaineering Holiday*). FRANK SMYTHE. SEATTLE: THE MOUNTAINEERS BOOKS; LONDON: BÂTON WICKS, 2000. 944 PAGES. HARDCOVER. $38.00

For anyone impassioned about bygone adventure in the distant ranges, The Mountaineers Books' Omnibus series may be the finest way to make contact. The photograph- and map-rich volumes include one by the Austrian Kurt Diemberger, two by the American John Muir, and fittingly, four by the prewar British climbers Eric Shipton, H.W. Tilman, and Frank Smythe. Many readers will agree that the early Brits, in their nailed boots and fedoras, largely shaped both the history and literature of modern mountaineering. England's postwar hardmen may have dispensed with step chopping and Sherpas on their own initiative, but they were hugely influenced by the rigid sportsmanship of their forebears. The world of contemporary climbing, with its stiff-upper-lip vernacular and alpine-style ethics, owes as large a debt to the early British pioneers as rock-and-roll pays to The Beatles.

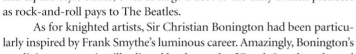

As for knighted artists, Sir Christian Bonington had been particularly inspired by Frank Smythe's luminous career. Amazingly, Bonington's prodigious output is still eclipsed by the work of Frank Smythe, who published 26 popular books in two decades. Smythe may have been only slightly less active on the crags, but he died at a young 49*.

As a wispy youth, Smythe had been inspired by Edward Whymper's successes. So Smythe, too, began with the requisite alpine apprenticeship, picking Mont Blanc's Route Major and Sentinelle Rouge plums. Early on, a reader can discern one of the many shimmers to Smythe's aesthetic armor: unlike most British alpinists of the day, he climbed without guides.

At high altitude, Smythe often slipped the leash and outdistanced even his partner Shipton. In 1931, Smythe made the first ascent of India's Kamet (25,447 feet), the highest peak yet climbed—until five years later, when Tilman bagged Nanda Devi, repeatedly called by the colonial-conscious Smythe the highest peak in the British empire. In the 1930s, Smythe kept up a dizzying agenda of climbing trips and his chronicles thereof: once to Kanchenjunga, twice to the Garwhal, three separate attempts on Everest, and a half dozen forays to the Alps.

The literal and figurative high point in these six books is Smythe's first attempt on Everest in 1933, *Camp Six*. (Early editions of it are still available for $20: proof positive that Smythe's books experienced numerous reprints.) This touchstone mountaineering tale has little of the disaster yet all of the durability of such later classics as *Annapurna*, *The Mountain of My Fear*, *Minus 148*, *Touching the Void*, and *Into Thin Air*—no doubt candidates for a future *Omnibus of Accident-Prone Expeditions*. The expedition's isolated fatality, sadly announced by Smythe: the mysterious crevasse disappearance of Policey, the Tibetan dog.

Caveat emptor: the politically correct modernist, while pining for a body count, might cringe at the imperialism of these British Grandfathers of Mountaineering. Readers will find unabashed whippings of thieving porters; the criticizing of uncovered sewage in monastery streets; vaunting about their telephone cable strung from basecamp up into high altitude; and, by story's end, the proudly announced telegram from the King of England, along with a wireless message ordering the Everest army back home.

"Nevertheless"—as they would say, poised over their basecamp teacups while debating the English plantations in Kenya—Smythe's pen builds suspense through the poky approach and camp buildup as he and Shipton climbed higher, looking for signs of Mallory. Even without the editor's subtle footnoting, even without the discovery of a naked body, Smythe's sleuthing was incredibly close to the mark.

As he climbed higher, cut off from all the approach-march colonialism, Smythe's description of the terrain and his lurking doubts ratchet up the narrative. The pacing of Camp 6 is clearly the work of a gifted writer; but then, even more unexpected, after Shipton turned back, Smythe's voice breaks through the time barrier. For a dozen stellar pages, Smythe becomes an ageless narrator, his observations oddly of a piece with those famed alpinists (but not so talented writers) who climbed a half century later. Other readers might also wonder if these latter-day authors were so inspired by Smythe that they couldn't help borrowing some of his prose.

As he boldly soloed into the Death Zone, he details an unseen companion—decades before these high-altitude doppelgangers became stock partners in mountaineering narratives. In two other passages, he lucidly describes overflying UFOs—spiking *Camp 6* book sales among the paranormal crowd. If not for unstable snow, forcing him back down, Smythe could have made history. During the descent to basecamp, he frostbit his feet badly enough to raise pus-filled blisters on his toes. He experimentally took his first whiff from an oxygen bottle and thought it unnecessary. Starved from high-altitude deprivations, his legs shrunken to sticks, he climbed back up without complaint, as if the mountain shrouded in white monsoon might actually give him another chance. Everest, he wrote, had beaten them.

Smythe used the whipping as empowerment. Like Shipton and Tilman, his lightweight expeditionary climbing and writing career surged. He let go of imperialism. In subsequent writings, he denounced bottled oxygen, pitons, and guides. One can't help but think, given the evolution of this visionary climbing purist, that if Smythe had been given the opportunity to grow old, he too would have cringed in 1953 as two oxygen-masked men, amid a plodding army of Brits, caused the anticlimactic subjugation of the world's highest mountain.

*On page 941, the editor successfully baited this reviewer [who grabbed a magnifying glass] to read the tiny, unasterisked footnote: "Smythe continued to climb during the war post-war years until his death in 1949 (to be summarized in a later volume)."

JONATHAN WATERMAN

Mountaineering: The Freedom of the Hills, 7TH EDITION. STEVEN M. COX, KRIS FULSAAS, EDITORS; CHAPTERS BY MEMBERS OF THE MOUNTAINEERS. SEATTLE: THE MOUNTAINEERS BOOKS, 2003. 575 PAGES. HARDCOVER, $37.95; PAPERBACK, $26.95.

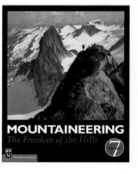

I took the Seattle Mountaineers' basic climbing course in 1970, at the age of 16. The course textbook was Freedom of the Hills, and I did my homework from a copy of its second edition, the one with the blue cover. Somewhere along the way I lost that copy. So when I was asked to review this new edition I was glad to find my wife's third edition (the green one) and compare them side by side. The older book takes me back to memories of knickers and Goldline, my first moves on rock, anßd a bunch of old guys in metal helmets tapping in pitons till you get that high ringing sound. The new edition reminds me that much has changed; that there is considerably more that must fit between the covers of any text that tries to be comprehensive, as *Freedom* always has. The most visible theme spanning the 30 years that separate these editions is The Mountaineers' fierce dedication to alpine mountaineering and to good information.

The particular strength of *Freedom* , now as in the earliest editions, is the sense that it is written for the well-rounded mountaineer—one who is faced with rock, snow, and ice, and who also has to venture into the wilderness in pursuit of his or her summits. Who may even get wet.

Obviously the book speaks to Pacific Northwest climbers. But it has worthwhile information for sport climbers and those from other regions as well. This is a real plus in a book that is intended to serve primarily as a teaching manual.

Open any climbing magazine and you can find an article reviewing 20 different kind of rock shoes, or the latest in sport climbing achievements, or the climbing in some exotic locale. Clearly, the technical aspects of our sport have become more involved over the years. It's this that accounts for the multiple editions of *Freedom* separating the one I used in 1970 from this most recent effort. Though I cannot speak for the editions in between the third and the seventh, the size and scope of this latest version is evidence that keeping up with developments is a formidable task. Fortunately it is a challenge The Mountaineers have met successfully. The new *Freedom* is replete with drawings, descriptions, and concise summations of the various aspects of our sport. Useful charts, graphs and tables detailing the most important points accompany many pages. On a technical basis there is nothing to find fault with in this exhaustive compendium—at least from the viewpoint of this semi-retired mountaineer. The explanations are superb, the drawings include relevant details and descriptions. I particularly like the clear depictions of various maneuvers in the rock climbing sections. For a book that has been written by committee, the various chapters are cohesive and read well. Its straightforward prose manages to instruct and enlighten a novice mountaineer, or provide information for those with more experience.

On the other hand, I notice a kind of homogenous quality about the new *Freedom*. By contrast, the third edition shows unmistakable signs of individual writing styles and the occasional polemic—like Harvey Manning's plea in the preface for wilderness activism, or the whimsical writing in the chapter on navigation. In the new edition's clearly depicted drawings, every character wears a helmet. Climbers are of both genders and are easy to follow throughout their complicated maneuvers. But they have no personality. Somehow, even when pictured on lead, they do not seem to sweat or break into a smile. What a contrast with the older edition's whimsical line drawings by Bob Cram! His climber smiles wryly, wipes his brow, and plunge-steps fiercely down the slope. He wears a Tyrolean hat and appears to be whistling. The older book is idiosyncratic. (It is also more convoluted and harder to read.) For me, despite impressive content and organization, the new book lacks the magic of the first few editions.

Both editions devote relatively few pages to the questions of access, stewardship of the land, the ethics of climbing and leadership, and what it means to have the "freedom of the hills." Yet in the older book the arguments seem more potent and less perfunctory then the seventh edition. Do we all agree nowadays? Have we all become zealous climbing automatons? Is there still magic and power out there in the mountains, amidst the technical wizardry and diagrams? I suppose it is hard for any instructional manual to speak of the magic and mystery of mountaineering. In 1975 they did it with a lot more pictures—great black and white shots of various Cascade Peaks. I look at them now: the long northeast buttress of Mt. Goode and the classic horn shape of Forbidden Peak. Though they speak to me today in different tones than they did to my 16-year-old self, they still beckon with immense charm. This new book doesn't reach me in the same way—but maybe I can try it out on my kids.

ALAN MILLAR

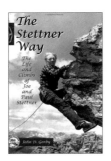

The Stettner Way: The Life and Climbs of Joe and Paul Stettner. JACK GORBY. GOLDEN: COLORADO MOUNTAIN CLUB PRESS, 2003. 210 PAGES. PAPERBACK. $14.95.

When I opened this book and began reading a description of the author's visit to Joe Stettner's home, only to run into paragraph after paragraph—then page after page—of quotes from Joe, I cringed. I'm no fan of long quotations; to me they usually signal a lack of storytelling ability.

But I was soon drawn in and within a couple of chapters (all extremely brief in this book), I was hooked. This remarkable tale of survival, escape, adventure, and mountaineering across two continents soon made me forget any of my beliefs about reporting styles. Indeed, it is exactly this style, and Jack Gorby's subtle presence—carefully nudging the story along—that makes this "as-told-to" account work so well.

The Stettner Way chronicles the lives of two of the most significant characters in American mountaineering from their humble beginnings in pre-World War I Germany to their fabulous though perhaps even humbler climbing careers overseas. Although the story might seem written for an audience of climbers, the plot is so intertwined with history, politics, travel, adventure, and romance that it's more like an epic—in fact, it's not hard to picture this book being made into a big Hollywood-style film.

After the death of their father at the hands of a street gang in 1919, the two teenaged brothers immersed themselves in mountains and mountaineering. Virtually untrained and with very little gear they accomplished an impressive string of ascents in the German Alps. By about 1925 it was apparent that Hitler, Goering, and Goebbels were on their way to power, and their mother urged Joe and Paul to leave Germany, which they did. Joe started a new life in Chicago; Paul first went to Sweden, then joined Joe in Chicago a year later.

This is where the story gets impressive. They lived most of their lives in Chicago, more than 1,000 miles from the nearest big mountains, and were decidedly working class. (Joe was a metal worker; Paul a photoengraver.) Yet with little money and little time off for holidays in the mountains, over the course of 20 years they were able to cobble together a string of nearly-annual trips and a handful of first ascents that made them legends. (The stories of driving motorcycles between Chicago and the mountains, on soft muddy roads, are epics in themselves.)

On their very first trip to Colorado in 1927 they made their historic first ascent of Stettners Ledges on the east face of Longs Peak, a climb that was the hardest in the state until well into the 1940s. In 1933, they did a new route up the huge northern side of Lone Eagle Peak. In 1936, Joe soloed Teeter-Totter Pillar, left of the Diamond, and in 1947 he led the first ascent of the east face of Monitor Peak in the San Juans, a climb worthy of respect even today. Interspersed with these ascents were dozens of climbs in the Tetons, Wind River Range, Glacier National Park, the Big Horn Mountains, and other ranges. And even after their glory days the two brothers continued to explore and climb whenever possible, often as leaders with the Chicago Mountaineering Club and the Iowa Mountaineers.

Gorby's research into and discussion of each of the Stettners' major routes is meticulous and artful. Since Joe and Paul never reported their ascents, leaving future climbers to claim them as new, controversy has clouded some of their achievements. But Gorby leaves readers with enough information to make up their own minds about the brothers' climbs.

There was much more to the brothers' lives than climbing, and Gorby gives us the whole picture. He completes the portrait with several very personal descriptions of visits to see Joe Stettner in his old age, both in Chicago and in Laramie, where he moved in his later years.

In all, Gorby has done the mountaineering community—especially us Coloradans—a tremendous service. He has gathered up all the relevant documentation and provided a clean, thorough account of the lives of two of America's greatest but least known climbing heroes. And he has told one heck of a story.

CAMERON M. BURNS

Mount McKinley's West Buttress: The First Ascent—Brad Washburn's Logbook, 1951. WILLISTON, VERMONT: TOP OF THE WORLD PRESS, 2003. 142 PAGES; 72 PHOTOS. PAPERBACK. **$23.00.** (There is also a hardbound limited edition, signed and numbered, and priced at $93.00—a dollar for every year of Washburn's age the year this book was published.)

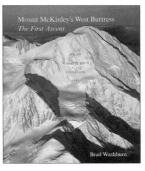

Few individuals have so powerful a bond with an individual mountain as does Bradford Washburn with Mt. McKinley. Washburn not only pioneered one of the most widely recognized and popular climbing routes in the history of mountaineering—the West Buttress—but he surveyed, photographed, mapped, researched, and wrote about this great peak. Of course, anyone who has even the slightest interest in McKinley knows that his aerial photography of this mountain is without peer and the 1:50,000 scale map he produced is one of the greatest of cartographic accomplishments.

While Brad Washburn has published numerous articles and contributed to an impressive array of books about McKinley, we finally have a book detailing the explorer-photographer-cartographer's McKinley triumphs and travails in his own words—and what a book it is.

This magnificent tome combines the best attributes of a coffee table book and a narrative. Publisher Greg Glade painstakingly transcribed Brad's field diary from cursive to Times Roman, and obviously was vigilant about straying as little as possible from the spirit of the original work, including underlined words, Brad's shorthand ("Fbks" for Fairbanks, "McK" for McKinley, etc.), and marginal notes. Glade edited virtually nothing—Washburn's diary didn't need any. The passages are elegant, fluid, his prose often memorable. Because it was a diary—something that Washburn probably never thought would be read by anyone other than himself—the writing is relaxed and utterly unpretentious. You forget you are reading a book and feel as if you are standing in Washburn's "Thermopac" insulated rubber boots, surveying the glacial landscape around the upper Kahiltna.

After just a few pages, it becomes clear that Brad Washburn is a renaissance explorer. His thoughts range from flying, to photography, to history, to surveying, to geology, and a variety of other interests. And he does more than just ponder these subjects: you learn how he forges new ground in them. Washburn clearly is no egomaniac. He often expresses concern for others on the mountain, and berates those who, in his eyes, act with disregard for others. It is wonderful to have such a lucid, autobiographical perspective of an explorer I have known primarily from the writings of others

In addition to the text, this book contains 79 duotone reproductions of Brad's stunning black and white images, four sketches, and two maps. As a matter of fact it took me a few days to begin actually reading the book, as I couldn't stop scanning Brad's tack-sharp, large format panchromatic images. Brad exposed thousands of 7 by 9-inch black and white images of Denali with his Fairchild K-9 aerial camera. This book contains the best of the best of these. Many of his 35-mm photos of day-to-day expeditioning are included also.

The production quality is high-end. The paper stock is bright and sturdy; the binding allows for easy, even perusing; and obviously, great care was taken during the pre-press and printing processes. (I couldn't find a speck of dust or any printing aberrations in the entire book.)

Mount McKinley's West Buttress: The First Ascent—Brad Washburn's Logbook, 1951 is a must-have title for any McKinleyophile—whether a seasoned guide, a prospective summiteer, or simply a dreamer.

ED DARACK

Yosemite: Half a Century of Dynamic Rock Climbing. ALEXANDER HUBER (AUTHOR) AND HEINZ ZAK (PHOTOGRAPHER). BIRMINGHAM, ALABAMA: MENASHA RIDGE PRESS, 2003. 176 PAGES. HARDCOVER. $45.00.

Heinz Zak's photos caught me first. He is quite simply the best climbing photographer out there. Part of his magic comes from a superhuman energy level, along with world-class climbing ability. He seems to have pictures of every possible facet of Yosemite, and they are all spectacular. But what makes Zak's photos so brilliant is the emotion that flows through from both sides of the camera. I got choked up looking at some of these photos.

Once I pulled myself together and actually started reading, I was even more impressed. The fact that this engaging and impeccably researched book was written by two Europeans is testimony to the Yosemite climbing scene's unique international spirit. They may live in Austria and Germany, but Heinz and Alex are virtual Yosemite locals. The essays—with contributions by such Yosemite notables as Allen Steck, Warren Harding, Royal Robbins, Mark Chapman, Jim Bridwell, Dean Potter, and Lynn Hill—cover every aspect of climbing life in the Valley. From bouldering to aid climbing to slacklining, to just plain living in Camp 4, nothing is left out. Even the activities of the Ahwahneechee natives in the Valley's "prehistory" are represented. Its comprehensive scope is one of the things that will earn this book a place among its classic predecessors.

Alex's greatest passion is free climbing on El Capitan, and this is where he sees the future of Yosemite climbing. The later essays and photos illustrate many of his free routes on the Big Stone. These feats represent lofty dreams for many who visit Yosemite, and Mark Chapman's final paragraph is an affecting reminder of the magic that the Valley holds for every climber.

History has progressed even in the short period since *Yosemite* was finished. Whether intentionally or not, Heinz Zak and Alex Huber have given themselves a lifelong task, and I look forward to future editions. But even if there are none, this book, like its namesake, is a place you'll visit again and again, always finding something new.

STEPH DAVIS

Ordeal by Piton: Writings from the Golden Age of Yosemite Climbing.
STEVE ROPER, EDITOR. PALO ALTO: STANFORD UNIVERSITY LIBRARY PRESS,
2003. 290 PAGES. PAPERBACK. $20.00.

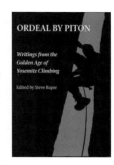

We are fortunate to have had Steve Roper to chronicle the evolution of
Yosemite climbing and its unique society. In his earlier *Camp 4*, which
contains his own reminiscences, and in this new anthology of others' writings, he has vividly captured the early climbing life of the Valley, preserving
and making accessible a special chapter in the history of our sport. Though
climbers who were there may need glasses to read them, revisiting these
stories will certainly evoke sharp memories of wonderfully misspent youths.

Many of the articles in *Ordeal by Piton* have appeared in *Summit, Ascent,* the *Sierra Club
Bulletin,* and the pages of this journal. But it is especially nice and useful to have the best of these
writings collected in one volume. (Gathering this material into book form evolved from a book
about the Stanford Alpine Club produced for a Stanford University Library exhibit four years
ago. Roper had written the introduction to the SAC exhibit book, which featured photographs
by Tom Frost, Henry Kendall, and Leigh Ortenburger and the writings of Stanford Alpine Club
members.)

Fifty-four articles are included, with contributions by David Brower, Royal Robbins, Layton
Kor, Chris Jones, Galen Rowell, Tom Higgins, Rob Wood, and others. Roper provides a short
introduction to each, supplying context and rationale for the selection. Among my favorites are
classics by Allen Steck, Sybille Hechtel, and Chuck Pratt.

Steck, who wrote the article "Ordeal by Piton" from which the book takes its title, here
recounts a moment from the first ascent of the Steck-Salathé on Sentinel Rock:

> *I remember watching, my lips tight and drawn, while a little bead of water seeped out and
> smoothly slid down the rock. It was barely enough to moisten my lips and wetten my
> mouth, yet is was a wonderful sensation.*

Chuck Pratt's "South Face of Mount Watkins," gets many climbers' votes for best-written
climbing story. This justly famous passage ends with a self-fulfilling prophecy:

> *As we unloaded packs at the parking lot, two young ladies approached us to ask if we were
> some of the Yosemite climbers. Yvon modestly pleaded guilty and pointed out our destination. They asked if it were true that Yosemite climbers chafe their hands on the granite to
> enable them to friction up vertical walls. We assured them that the preposterous myth was
> true. Then, with perfect timing, Harding yanked a bottle of wine and a six-pack out of
> the car, explaining that these were our rations for four days. We left the incredulous young
> ladies wondering about the sanity and good judgment of Yosemite climbers. And so the
> legend grows.*

I really enjoyed seeing Sibylle Hechtel's 1974 article in print with its proper title, "Walls
without Balls." It was simply called "Untitled" when it first appeared in the *AAJ.* (As Ad Carter
explained, while he loved Sibylle's title, the Board would not approve.) This article tells the story
of Sibylle's and Bev Johnson's first all-female ascent of El Cap. Hechtel writes:

> *This remains one of the most memorable and beautiful nights of my life. Despite any
> physical discomforts of my position, I was glad to be there. Serene in the knowledge that
> we were only three pitches below the top and would reach it early the next morning, I settled back to munch gorp and read Asimov. The rock swelled into a roof up to the right, a*

beautifully sculptured curve that I could just perceive in the beam of the headlamp. Cars twinkled by, 3,000 feet down, threading their way along the flowing moonlight below me where the river had been earlier that day. I leaned back to await my last sunrise here and, perchance to sleep.

Some, of course, will quibble with the selections, asking why this was left out or that included. But I am grateful to Roper for a job well done. Many of the book's photos are recognizable from his *Climber's Guide to Yosemite Valley*, published in 1964. It is nice to see them back in print. However, if I have any criticism of *Ordeal by Piton*, it is in the plain presentation. It would have been nice to have seen a book more along the lines of *Camp 4* with its lush black and white photographs.

Great writing and fond memories recreate a special time and place in Yosemite climbing history. It is not that the "Golden Age" was better than the years that followed. Who from that time is not awed by climbs of 5.14, or the climbing of El Cap three times in one day, or the Nose in … how fast was that? But, for us it was a special time, and it is a great pleasure to share our adventures and misspent youth with today's climbers through this new collection of old Yosemite tales.

ROBERT SCHNEIDER

Under A Sheltering Sky: Journeys To Mountain Heartlands. COLIN MONTEATH. CHRISTCHURCH, NEW ZEALAND: HEDGE-HOG HOUSE, 2003. 240 PAGES. HARDCOVER. $60.00.

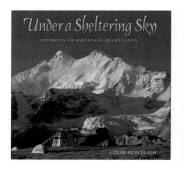

Under A Sheltering Sky is a large format photography book with unexpected visions of the enchanting beauty in mountain and polar worlds: a work replete with more pictures of faraway alpine places—Tibet, Bhutan, Mongolia, Greenland, Antarctica—than even Galen Rowell's most ambitious productions. The Altai, Mt. Kailas, Mt. Erebus, Shackleton Gap: these evocative names, and the book's 12 chapters, each chronicling a separate expedition, form a roadmap to the life well lived of New Zealand mountaineer Colin Monteath. Writes polar legend Sir Wally Herbert in his introduction: "Colin … is one of those rare individuals in our day and age—a romantic who is drawn to the wilder regions of the Earth, not by the call of instant fame to which so many of the modern 'explorers' all too eagerly respond, but by that far subtler insistence of spirit the more sensitive souls call wonder."

And so Colin takes us on his prolific journeys to some of the world's wildest and most remote quarters. His writing, colorful, insightful, humorous, and at times hypnotically evocative, complements his images; his descriptive passages are some of the best I have read. *Under A Sheltering Sky* weaves together the threads of Colin's personal experiences in these remotest regions with the fabric of historic tales—of Mallory, Younghusband, Nansen, Shackleton, and Kingdom-Ward, among others—who first explored them. Part adventure narrative, part historic travelogue, each chapter ends with a definitive bibliography of the books penned by these early explorers, complete with photographs of the books themselves from the author's extensive, well-read library.

Monteath's photographic eye has few, if any, contemporary rivals for capturing not only the decisive moment in images of people and animals, but the stunningly pure color of the alpine and polar landscapes. To hike in Shackleton's, Crean's, and Worsley's footsteps across South Georgia, from King Haakon Bay to the Stromness whaling station (to the very bathtub where they took their first baths in nearly two years!); to camp and climb the same route George Mallory and Guy Bullock took in Tibet's Kama and Kharta valleys as they tried to unravel the unknown approaches to Mt. Everest ... Ah, the stuff of legend, and the yearning for future adventures, lies within these pages! In a hopeful tone, Colin writes, "The more I travel, the more convinced I am that this is far from a shrinking planet with nothing left to discover ... For climbers with imagination and resolve, the scope for new routes knows no bounds."

I cannot recommend *Under A Sheltering Sky* highly enough—to young aspiring climbers and to older, more contemplative mountaineers alike. Go to Colin Monteath's website at hedge-hoghouse.com to obtain your copy of this exquisite book.

ED WEBSTER

Southeastern Rock, HARRISON SHULL. ASHEVILLE, NC: HARRISON SHULL, 2003. 144 PAGES, 250 PHOTOGRAPHS. HARDCOVER. $39.95.

Having accidentally tucked this book in the seat pocket of my van, I carried it around with me on a road trip for several months. Everywhere I went, anyone who had a chance to flip through its pages was instantly intrigued by the obvious climbing potential of the Southeastern states. As my friends looked at the photos they made comments like "Oh my god, where is that? Have you been there? Wow, this makes me want to go there."

I knew from personal experience that the South is host to world-class climbing, and to every genre of climbing one could want—from granite splitter cracks, to sandstone roofs, to Fontainbleau-esque bouldering. I had been, of course, to well-known areas such as the Red River Gorge, the Obed, the New River Gorge, and Tennessee Wall. I had even been to some of the lesser-known walls. But though I had spent six years of my life living there, Harrison Shull's *Southeastern Rock* made me realize that I hadn't even touched the climbing potential that was to be had. I was astounded by the quality of some of the obscure areas featured in its pages–places that I had never heard of, but which had been literally "out my back door."

The book covers 43 climbing areas spread across the 10 states that comprise the Southeast. Divided into chapters detailing every featured state, each includes an intro written by a seasoned local. The intros vary in style and form, but each includes a brief synopsis of the place, the climbing, and the people. After the intro, the reader gets snapshots, with page after page of brilliant photographs. There are moderate trad climbs, hard sport climbs, boulder problems, famous climbers, and unknown climbers. There are also blue skies, foliage thick with rhododendrons, fields covered with fall leaves, and local climbers' hangouts.

There is great diversity in the South, not only of style of rock, but of culture. One thing remains constant: southerners are very proud of their home states, and of the rock therein. There are a few areas Harrison included in his book that seem to be a stretch to call world class, or even high quality. But I'm sure there are proud locals who are right now taking offense to an outsider who has the audacity, without even having climbed at these areas, to claim that the climbing could be less than the best!

In his preface, Shull says that this book is not comprehensive, but merely a sampling of Southeast climbing, a drop in the bucket. He ought to know: he spent nearly 10 years traveling, living, photographing, and climbing throughout the region in order to make his dream of a climber's guide to the Southeast a reality.

Shull's ability not only to get southern climbers to acquiesce to the creation of this book, but also to contribute to and participate in it, has resulted in a valuable addition to America's rock climbing guidebooks. It's a boon for southerners and anybody else who would like to explore the routes and rocks of this vast but little-recognized climbing region.

KATIE BROWN

With a Camera in My Hands: William O. Field, Pioneer Glaciologist. WILLIAM O. FIELD, AS TOLD TO SUZANNE BROWN. ANCHORAGE: UNIVERSITY OF ALASKA PRESS, 2004. 350 BLACK AND WHITE PHOTOS, 46 MAPS, INCLUDING LINEWORK AND SHADED-RELIEF LANDFORMS. 208 PAGES. HARDCOVER, $59.95; PAPERBACK, $29.95.

This is the story of William Osgood Field, whose work in Alaska and Canada from the 1920s into the1950s did much to advance understanding of glacial phenomena and their relationship to global climate trends. Field has been called a founding "father of American glaciology," and this book, using diaries, tape recordings, and photographs, reveals the man behind the epithet. *With a Camera in My Hands* will reward anyone interested in the glacial systems of these regions, or in the career of the distinguished explorer, scientist, and AAC member.

The book's title turns out to be a key to one of Field's significant contributions. Keeping a camera on hand at all times, he made a practice of recording the condition of glaciers wherever he went. By returning at intervals to a site and occupying the exact location from which an earlier photo had been taken, he was able to update the photographic record, demonstrating patterns of movement, shape, and size from summer to summer, and eventually decade to decade. His collection of historic glacier photos by earlier explorers allowed him to extend the usefulness of the technique, in some cases providing a 100-year photographic record of glacial changes. Several of these time-lapse sequences are reproduced in the book.

Field's familiarity with glaciers and wilderness began at an early age. In the summer of 1920, when he was 16, he first visited the Canadian Rockies, returning again in 1921 and 1922. He climbed in the Alps in 1923, was elected to membership in the American Alpine Club in 1924, and was back in the Canadian Rockies that summer for a first ascent of South Twin. Alaska called him in 1925 and again in 1926, when he made the first of his many scientific trips. During his final year of college he served as president of the Harvard Mountaineering Club, and earned a degree in geology in 1926.

Field's initial glacial studies were in the Glacier Bay and Prince William Sound areas, and he made numerous visits to the Muir, Rendu, Grand Pacific, and Johns Hopkins glaciers in Glacier Bay, the Columbia Glacier in Prince William Sound, and also to the glaciers in College and Harriman Fiord. Though eventually his interests were to take him as far afield as Greenland, the Caucasus and Antarctica, his work among the coastal glaciers of Alaska was to be the dominant theme in his long and active career.

In 1940 he became a full-time research associate with the American Geographic Society in New York. Back in Alaska in the summer of 1941, Field led a survey of the glaciers in Glacier Bay. With him was Maynard Miller, then a Harvard geology student (and new AAC member). In 1946 the two initiated the idea of studying the health of Alaska glaciers, and in 1948 they founded the Juneau Icefield Research Project (JIRP), establishing several camps along the periphery of the icefield. Over the next decade more camps were established and scientific personnel added for glacial research and related meteorological, geological, and botanical studies. (Scanning *AAJ*s from the late forties and early fifties will reveal several articles penned by Miller and others about the project.) When JIRP evolved into a college-credit summer course, Field handed the reins to Miller and resumed his surveys of glaciers in other coastal areas of Alaska and British Columbia, and in the Canadian Rockies.

In 1957 Field participated in International Geophysical Year activities, becoming chairman of the Panel for Glaciology and also head of the new IGY World Data Center for Glaciology in North America, for which he organized its repository of glacier information. His last major project was authoring *Mountain Glaciers of the Northern Hemisphere*, in 1975.

There is a great deal more to tell about the man and his accomplishments. But it is much better done in his own words and photographs. We can be thankful that Suzanne Brown took it upon herself to produce an audio history of Bill Field's career, work with him on his extensive collection of photos and notes, and transform these valuable records into a living story. Likewise, that the University of Alaska Press has given it such an attractive tangible form. His scientific and historical activities are in good hands at the University of Alaska, Fairbanks, and at the Whyte Museum of the Canadian Rockies at Banff. William Osgood Field, American glaciologist and one of the AAC's great members, will not be forgotten.

DEE MOLENAAR

Spies in the Himalayas: Secret Missions and Perilous Climbs. M.S. KOHLI AND KENNETH CONBOY. LAWRENCE: UNIVERSITY OF KANSAS PRESS, 2003. 248 PAGES. HARDCOVER. $29.95.

It's hard to imagine climbers playing a role in the nuclear political drama of the Cold War, which one usually associates with secret agents in trench coats, top secret scientific facilities, and ultra-sophisticated military units. But they did. *Spies in the Himalayas* chronicles the several covert CIA-backed expeditions undertaken between 1965 and 1970, only bits of which have surfaced over the past four decades. These involved American and Indian climbers attempting to place a nuclear-powered listening device in the Indian Himalaya; their attempts to retrieve the device after it plummeted off Nanda Devi and into the headwaters of the Ganges River; and subsequent fall-back efforts to accomplish the objective.

The authors—Kohli, an Indian naval officer and top Indian climber assigned to run the various covert expeditions, and Conboy, a former U.S. think tank policy analyst—provide the historical and political context for these expeditions. The October 1964 detonation of the first Chinese atomic weapon caused the CIA to wonder whether the Chinese also possessed the rocket technology to launch atomic payloads. An intelligence-gathering project was proposed. India was a willing participant in this scheme because it had been involved in brief border skirmishes with the Chinese and there existed continual fear that the Red Army would invade India, as it had Tibet.

As the story begins, the goal is to plant a 125-pound plutonium-powered listening device on a Himalayan peak so that telemetry data from rocket tests can be obtained. The site must be sufficiently high and close to the Chinese border to "see" into the Chinese testing grounds, but isolated enough so that the device is neither obscured by adjacent peaks, nor likely to fall into Chinese hands. Initially 27,500-foot Kangchenjunga is the preferred peak, though eventually, for a host of factors, sights are lowered to 25,645-foot Nanda Devi.

American and Indian climbers are chosen for the expedition largely from the successful 1963 American and 1965 Indian Everest expeditions. The two teams unite in the U.S. during the summer of 1965 for a training exercise (ultimately making a failed 10-day attempt on Denali's South Face), then helicopter to a remote glacier in what is now Denali National Park to assemble the Rube Goldberg-like listening device. In mid-September they regroup in the Nanda Devi Sanctuary and begin their campaign for the summit in hopes of planting the listening device.

Political pressure to get the device to the summit and get it operational is intense. However, as climbers know, Mother Nature is immune to imposed deadlines. The expedition makes good headway establishing camps on the mountain, but by mid-October the post-monsoon climbing season is fast drawing to a close. Expedition members are poised to take the device from Camp Four to Camp Five when a storm sets in and Kohli makes the decision from base camp to abandon the climb. He orders the device and generator lashed to the mountain; they will come back the following spring to take it all the way to the summit.

Over the winter the CIA determines the listening device will work fine from a lesser altitude and a decision is made to retrieve the device and transport it to 22,510-foot Nanda Kot, a lower and less significant mountaineering objective. But when the return expedition arrives at Camp Four they receive a shock: *the listening device and nuclear-powered generator are nowhere to be found.* They have vanished from the mountain, presumably carried down the south face by an avalanche.

Several expeditions follow—some joint, some solely Indian—to find the missing Nanda Devi generator, to place a second listening device atop Nanda Kot, and then to establish a conventionally powered listening device atop an even smaller peak when conditions on Nanda Kot render the device useless for most of the year.

Spies in the Himalayas tries, but ultimately fails, to combine an intelligence history with mountaineering drama. Its dry prose adequately conveys the whos, whats, and wheres of the intelligence story, but we learn little about the climbers and their motivations to participate, or the climbing action taking place on these peaks. Dramatic falls and improbable saves come across as just another day on the mountain. Meanwhile, most of the climbers—but especially the Americans—appear as two-dimensional cutouts. In fact, we often are told more about the intelligence service desk jockeys than we do about the climbers.

Despite the plodding nature of the book, it does offer up a few mountaineering gems. We learn of Rob Schaller's solo ascent of Nanda Devi and the superhuman summit push by Gurcharan Bhangu and Sherpa Tashi from Camp Three, though neither is discussed with the detail or passion it deserves. Schaller's was the highest solo ascent then done by an American, while Bhangu and Tashi climbed the 4,500 feet from Camp Three to the summit and back in less time than all previous parties had done from Camp Five. In the hands of more capable authors, these mountaineering achievements would shine.

In the end, *Spies in the Himalayas* sidesteps the most significant questions about these expeditions: how and why a plutonium-powered generator found its way into the headwaters of the sacred Ganges River, which supports a half-billion Indians, there to remain. While it is easy in hindsight to second-guess decisions that were deemed necessary at the height of the Cold War, the environmental legacy of the nuclear arms race is hard to overlook. Former U.S. Defense Secretary Robert McNamara devoted a whole book to explaining how many of his Cold War decisions regarding Vietnam were wrong. It is unfortunate that Kohli spends little time reexamining his decision to leave the nuclear generator on the mountain without a proper installation, a decision that may affect his countrymen well into the future.

LLOYD ATHEARN

Himalayan Quest: Ed Viesturs on the 8,000 Meter Giants.
ED VIESTURS. WASHINGTON D.C.: NATIONAL GEOGRAPHIC PRESS, 2003. 159 PAGES. PAPERBACK. $20.00.

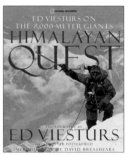

Himalayan Quest is a beautiful book that provides a spectacular series of photographs depicting Ed Viesturs' expeditions to 8,000-meter peaks. Those with an interest in the Himalayan giants will find the descriptions of his trips and personal adventures fascinating, and the photography certain to excite many armchair fantasies. Indeed, the photos alone are worth the price of the book.

It also gives us insight into Ed Viesturs, the man. Over the past dozen or so years Ed has quietly and methodically become America's most accomplished Himalayan climber. His climbing style is straightforward and safe, without much in the way of flare besides a purist's insistence on not using bottled oxygen. While he has attained all of his Himalayan summits without the use of supplemental oxygen, he has always made safety his primary concern. He has been involved in heroic rescues of other climbers at high altitude, yet he has wisely been able to avoid death-defying circumstances himself. Viesturs' other main focus is the simple joy of being in the mountains and sharing the experience with friends.

Ed's writing, like his climbing style, is straightforward and unadorned. You couldn't really call him a great storyteller. His approach to climbing denies him the nail-biting life-and-death dramas that are the stock-in-trade of some climbing authors. Together, these conditions guarantee text that will be neither riveting nor especially entertaining. However, those interested in what it is like to climb above 8,000 meters will no doubt overlook such shortcomings to read Viesturs' views on the subject.

The overall effect of reading this book is to gain insight into how Viesturs approaches the big peaks, and what this phenomenal Himalayan climber is like as a person. As a matter of fact, these insights would seem to suggest an ideal role model for future mountaineers. Viesturs has produced a very good book. We are fortunate that he has shared this much of his extraordinary world with us.

GEOFF TABIN

Good Morning Midnight: Life and Death in the Wild. CHIP BROWN. NEW YORK: RIVERHEAD BOOKS, 2003. 300 PAGES. HARDCOVER. $24.95.

A reviewer often struggles to separate his judgment of a book—the author's work—from his personal feelings about the subject's life. The book in the reader's hand may not be the same as the book in the writer's head. In the case of recent *AAJ* reviews of biographies, our readers are

a tough lot to please. Those who knew the great ones personally may not recognize the portrait the biographer has constructed, as in this year's review of *The Philosophy of Risk,* Jeff O'Connor's story of Dougal Haston's life. Other readers may not appreciate the man they construe from the biographer's language, as happened with last year's review of Robert Roper's *Fatal Mountaineer,* a biography of Willi Unsoeld.

In the case of Chip Brown's *Good Morning Midnight: Life and Death in the Wild,* the story of Guy Waterman's life and death, I like to think I am able to sort through these issues: I never met or corresponded with either Waterman or Brown. In the case of Brown's book, terrific. In the case of Guy Waterman, who am I to say? His is a profoundly sad story and when I finished the book I was deeply shaken. I related to it far less as a climber than as a father and a son.

What you probably know about Guy Waterman is this: that he orchestrated his own death by hypothermia on Mt. Lafayette in New Hampshire's White Mountains in mid winter of 2000. He hiked up to a spot near the summit and lay down in the snow to die—not far from a cairn he had made to honor his son Johnny, who disappeared climbing in the Alaska Range in 1981. Though there is much more to know about Guy Waterman's life, the reader of climbing literature is drawn to the story because of these two central events, Guy's suicide and Johnny's death in Alaska. The author is interested in answering the question, Why? And the space Brown devotes to Johnny's story—because it's dramatic, because it eerily prefigures Guy's death—suggests that he wishes to connect the two tragedies. But Brown is wary, perhaps overly so, of arriving at such a simple conclusion.

Even without the pair of dramatic deaths, Guy Waterman's life warrants a biography. Waterman married young, fathered three sons, played jazz piano, worked in Washington D.C. as a speechwriter, and drank too much. By all accounts he was miserable during these years and in a relatively short span of time quit his speechwriting work, stopped drinking, discovered hiking and climbing and made them central to his life, left his failing marriage, and set out to live deliberately. He remarried, and with Laura forged a new life off the grid, as self-sufficiently as possible, in a home of their own design and construction they called Barra. Together Guy and Laura wrote *Forest and Crag,* a history of the Northeast's mountains; *Wilderness Ethics;* and *Yankee Rock and Ice,* among other titles. Theirs was a highly disciplined, self-sustaining existence full of simple non-materialistic pleasures, including the respect and love of a wide circle of friends. They lived this way right up until Guy, abetted by Laura, took his own life at the age of 66. This is, of course, a gross simplification; Brown's work is to flesh this story out as best he can, in order to approach the *why* of it.

Guy's hiking and climbing life comes across as, if not downright odd, at least a lot different from most climbers I know. He climbed, for example, almost exclusively in his own home range. But it's not just the lack of interest in other mountains, it's how he chose to do his climbing: he acended all of the 48 peaks over 4,000 feet in the White Mountains, in winter, *and from all four points of the compass.* I know, of course, that many of us are single-minded and even obsessed with climbing, but the sort of obsession required for that endeavor seems perhaps more aligned with Guy's ingrained habit of recording and quantifying minutiae. We learn that in 10 years at Barra "he and Laura had canned 1,977 jars of fruits and vegetables ... hand-cut 68.7 cords of firewood ... been drenched by 322.16 inches of rain ... had picked 5,009 tomatoes." There are dozens of such examples, some more extreme, throughout the book.

Much is made of Guy's guilt and grieving over the loss of two sons and strained relationship with the third. Johnny Waterman is perhaps better known among mountaineers for his 145-day solo ascent of Mt. Hunter in 1978 than for his disappearance from the Ruth Glacier three years later. Johnny's story has been told before, and told well. Glenn Randall wrote about Johnny in *Breaking Point* (accurately described by Brown as "gripping and regrettably out of print"); Jonathan Waterman (not related to the New Hampshire Watermans), talks of him in In the *Shadow of Denali*; and Jon Krakauer refers to him in *Into the Wild*. Even without such able writers, Johnny's story would probably live on as myth. But Brown does a fine job of retelling here, and if we questioned Johnny's madness, this telling removes the doubt. If the loss of Johnny hit Guy hardest, it's no mystery—they were much alike. In a chapter on Johnny, from a paragraph about them both, Brown writes: "His mania for indiscriminate documentation bordered on madness as he tried to record the second-by-second flux of daily life." Though Brown is referring to the son, he's aptly describing the father as well.

Johnny's brother Bill's story is even more mysterious: a lost soul with drug problems, he too disappeared in Alaska, never to be heard from again. Johnny left tracks on the Ruth Glacier, Guy left a note, but Bill's disappearance was by far the most enigmatic; he left the fewest clues. It's clear that Guy grieved the loss of his sons. But it's not at all clear that he might have been able to save them from themselves, as indeed he could not do for himself.

Brown's biography is somewhat constrained by the apparent lack of participation of Guy's surviving son Jim and his first wife Emily. Though their marriage is described as horrific, we don't see much of it on the page. Guy's shortcomings as a parent, which seem to be at the center of his despair, are likewise more alluded to than shown.

If the book might seem overwrought with its chapter epigraphs from Byron, Dickinson, and Milton, to name only a few, and its repeated references to classical literature, these allusions are perfectly appropriate to a story of Waterman's life: passages from the classics were always in his thoughts. He had memorized the first eight books of *Paradise Lost*, and in his own writing reflected on his life in terms of classical references. It seems likely Waterman would have been pleased with these literary touches.

Certainly Brown got the climbing right (even if he meant *Goldline* and not "gold line," *Millar Mitts* and not "Miller Mitts"). I sensed the depth of his immersion in Guy's world when he observes that "the sixties were some of the last unself-conscious years of climbing." Debatable, perhaps, but in a very smart, provocative sense.

Browns' final verdict is sympathetic, even if throughout I felt he had been privately making judgments that he was unwilling to put on the page. He notes in one of many such moments, "Who in all decency could find fault in a man already finding so much fault with himself?", indicating perhaps more allegiance to his subjects than to his readers. Laura Waterman closed her own obituary for Guy with the lines: "For me it is right that the mystery of our essential individual selves remains unrevealed. Seek not to rend the veil." The biographer's job is, of course, quite the opposite, to rend the veil. Brown rends gently.

The story is tragic, in the classical sense that both the author and subject would seem to prefer. Reading it induces some sense of catharsis: surely I felt intense pity and fear. Beyond that I felt that Waterman's death was the world's loss, my own loss. Chip Brown may not reduce Waterman's life to a simple moral, or even any number of morals. Nonetheless I couldn't help thinking—and this is oversimplification—that although climbing might save us from any number of the world's ills, in the end it can't save us from ourselves.

DAVID STEVENSON

IN MEMORIAM

GUY EDWARDS 1972-2003

The northwest face of the Devil's Thumb, near Petersburg, Alaska, remains what is likely the most impressive unclimbed face in the Americas. It has been attempted by many times by people such as Alex Lowe, Jack Roberts, Dieter Klose, and Mike Bearzi. On April 13, 2003, Canadians Johnkim Millar (24) and Guy Edwards (30) started up the 6,500-foot face. They did not return.

Guy Edwards

A celebration of lives lived was held a recent Sunday at the top of one of Guy Edwards' favorite climbs, an 80-meter old growth Douglas fir in Lighthouse Park, Vancouver. Guy endlessly exuded exuberance, complete absorption, and a taste for the wacky. Running up the cables of the Lion's Gate Bridge or making first ascents of new buildings on the University of British Columbia campus were equal in intrigue to setting the standard on ice routes in the Rockies. His infectious enthusiasm and engagement made him famous.

Quietly famous. Guy avoided publicity. He greatly disliked putting together climbing résumés of technical ascents for grant applications, so I don't see that I should create one here. He is perhaps better known for his in-the-buck ascent of Pigeon Spire than for his speed records in Squamish.

Guy embraced a self-propelled, adventure-oriented climbing ethos that fit so well with the inaccessible Coast Mountains. Quite a few years ago he and I paddled from our homes in Vancouver and headed up Waddington without having gathered any route description—the summit that eluded us on that journey was just a detail of the voyage. Two years ago, he was the inspiration behind a classic journey for those who live on the Rainy Coast: heading up into the mountains north of his home in Vancouver and continuing by ski all the way to Skagway.

Switching seamlessly from buffoon to sage and back again, Guy inspired all those who knew him with enthusiasm. Yet almost unnoticed underneath was the drive that got him where he was and kept him on the edge. I wish that I had the opportunity to talk to him about the accidental symbolism of his death on the unclimbed north face of the jewel of the Coast Mountains, the Devil's Thumb.

VANCE CULBERT

ANDREW EMBICK, M.D. 1950-2003

Andrew Embick pioneered big walls, steep ice, and cold waters in Alaska and Canada from the mid-1970s through the nineties. He mentored and inspired a generation of Alaskan boaters and climbers. He was a father of two, brother of three, and friend to hundreds. He was a Rhodes scholar, Harvard educated doctor, author of two books, and an inventor of wild outdoor gear.

We Alaskans benefited immensely from his vision, creativity, hospitality, generosity, information, and humor. He was our Hemmingway, full of himself, hearty and arrogant, exuberant in his likes and dislikes, and he crafted classics in rock, ice, and river.

Embick's epic Grade VI walls included first ascents of the East Buttress of Middle Triple (listed in *50 Classic Climbs of North America*), the Northwest Buttress of Kitchatna Spire (with Jim Bridwell), the Citadel, and Mt. Jeffers, all in that nastiest of mountain ranges the "Kitchatna Spires" west of Denali. Embick climbed these Kitchatna Spire test pieces during the late 1970s when big walls and bad weather were still a novel combination. His first ascents on Serenity, Trinity, and Sunrise Spires are destined to become trade routes. His shorter works on Valdez ice during the early 1980s were equally classic: Wowie Zowie, Love's Way, Crystal Visions, Flying Cloud, and the first solo of Bridal Veil, each long, brittle, and steep. Altogether he made more than 50 first ascents in Valdez, culminating in *Blue Ice and Black Gold*, his ice climbing guidebook. Andrew also made more than 30 first kayak descents, culminating in his *Fast and Cold*, a whitewater guidebook to Alaska.

In 1984 he combined his passions by leading a kayak/climbing expedition sponsored by *National Geographic* to the Hunza region of Pakistan. That trip with Galen Rowell, Jack Tackle, Rob Lesser, Bob McDougall and others included a Grade VI first *ascent* of Lukpilla Brakk in the Biafo valley and a Grade VI first *descent* on the Braldu River. In 2002 Andy returned to Hunza for a medical sabbatical where he treated more than 1,500 Pakistani mountain people.

Embick was a complicated, conflicted man who drank fine scotch, cooked cordon bleu, and hunted big game. He joined the Sierra Club, the Alaskan, Harvard, and American Alpine Clubs as a life member of each. He was even the vice president of the AAC in 1985 and on its board of directors in 1986. Living in Valdez for more than two decades, he and his wife Kathy Todd practiced medicine and raised two daughters. During all this time, Embick opened his home to visiting climbers, boaters, and outdoor adventurers. And it wasn't just floor space he offered: it was the sauna, shop with tools, kitchen, and library.

Embick kept a mountaineering library likely unmatched by any north of Banff. The library included his meticulous journals, complete with topos of Kitchatna climbs, and was complemented by his encyclopedic scholarship of all things steep.

During the eighties and nineties his household formed the nexus of the Valdez Ice Climbing Festival. The Festival and Andy were also key ingredients in foreign exchanges with climbers from Japan and Russia in the mid-80s.

Andrew was quick to share not only his home, but his knowledge and talents. Whether medical advice or route beta, he would return a phone call or inquiry with an immediate answer. We often wondered where he found the time, as he was obviously managing many of his own projects simultaneously.

Embick popularized ice climbing (he was featured in *People*, *Sports Illustrated*, and *Smithsonian* as well as the climbing rags and journals) and cold water kayaking, both in print and through mentoring with young outdoorsmen and women. I count myself in that fortunate group, along with Mike Buck, Chris Roach, Steve Garvey, Evan Smith, and Kate Bull.

Andrew also established a biathalon range and network of Nordic ski trails in Valdez, a town with little flat space between mountain walls. Altercations with snowmachiners who were tearing up the trails alienated Embick from the community, a community he'd served for 20 years as physician, often gratis.

My wife and I dined at Anchorage's finest restaurant with Andy, recently back from his Pakistan sabbatical and 30 pounds lighter. He said he was repaying us for the $7 worth of headlamp bulbs we'd sent him so he could work in the light-less village of Shimshal.

Over a gourmet meal of pheasant, scallops, and rare beef, he told stories about Hunza patients lining up for treatment, how appreciative they were, how happy he'd been. He spoke of returning there to write a book about the fabled people of Hunza.

Less than a month after that dinner, we were shocked and dismayed when we learned Andy, like Hemmingway, took his own life.

Andrew's extraordinary brilliance left an indelible mark on the granite spires, blue ice, and pool-drops of Alaska. More importantly his generosity and exuberance left an indelible mark on the hearts of those who knew him.

ROMAN DIAL

WILLIAM J. MOSCONI 1951-2003

Bill Mosconi began his climbing career relatively late; he was nearly 30. He learned to ski in the Alps and tried sky diving. With characteristic pragmatism, Bill sought the best climbing mentor available to him, hiring Richard Goldstone as his instructor. Richard referred Bill to me in 1982 for ice climbing. We spent a December week in North Conway and decided to end with a day on Cannon Cliff. We roped up in an old stomped out plat-form and climbed up the tracks on the snow cone below the Black Dike. The entire slope gave way and we were swept down the talus field in an avalanche of a scale unlikely for New Hampshire. My descent was stopped by

Bill Mosconi in the Alps. *Courtesy The Explorers Club*

a scrubby birch tree about halfway down the slope—I was upside-down with broken ribs. After frantically extricating myself, still unable to breathe, I looked for Bill. About 30 yards above me, I saw a leg sticking out of the snow, near the edge of some small birches. I stupidly pulled on the rope still between us, trying to reach him as quickly as possible, thinking with horror that I had killed my client. As I approached, the leg kicked the air—to my great relief.

The conversation that followed was nearly as comical as the stories that followed. Gasping for breath—the wind was knocked out of me, with two cracked ribs—I said "Are you OK?"

"Of course," he said. "Are you?"

"Yes," I said, "But I'm sore. My side hurts."

He then looked at me with what I later learned was the "Mosconi Look," the baleful stare of ice blue eyes and an expression inscrutable behind his gigantic Austro-Hungarian Empire mustache.

"Bouch, we still have all the gear and after this, there won't be another avalanche. Right?"

I knew what he was about to say.

I said "Right."

"So, I came all this way, and I'm not coming back here to this podunk town, so let's fin-ish it." I had to explain that I hurt too much and besides, I was no longer in the mood for climbing.

Our next jaunt was Chamonix the following August. I was to meet Bill at Geneva airport. He would change into his climbing clothes in the car while we drove to Chamonix, and we would sleep at the base of a big route that night, the American Direct on the Dru. I didn't believe it possible for a New Yorker to go straight onto the Dru after a six-hour flight, and I changed the plan to the Cordier Route on the Pic du Roc—technically, a more difficult, and elegant route, but with less "engagement." We climbed it and descended to the Montenvers Hotel the next day. Bill could have climbed Dru straight off. I was wrong and he berated me for the rest of the trip after the big rains arrived.

It was awkward. I was his employee and I had failed him. But I knew that if he made the decisions, we would eventually have a bad accident. Bill had a most intimidating stare and he demanded rational explanations for decisions. My saying "I just don't have a good feeling about this route" was not acceptable. The intuitive decision making of climbing annoyed his own precise logic, but I couldn't let him bully me into a bad situation. But Bill could afford to climb anywhere and the fees I charged him were impressive and tempting. So I decided to quit being his guide. I told Bill that I would climb anywhere with him, any time, as a friend and not for money. The result was an extraordinary run of climbing that lasted several years and a friendship that developed into a lifelong relationship.

Unable to climb the Nose during a rainy spring, we climbed the East Buttress of El Capitan and the regular route up Higher Cathedral Spire. That summer, we went to the Dolomites.

Bill had a flair for drama. Hemingway mentioned the Hotel Della Poste in Cortina in one of his books, so we stayed there while we climbed. Our first season we climbed the Punta Fiamma, The Spigollo Giallo, the Comici Route of the Cima Grande, the Pilastro on the Tofana, the Micheluzzi-Buhl on the Ciavazzes. Our final objective was the North Face of the Civetta. The family who ran the Coldai Hut was intrigued with Bill, initially because of his striking Franz Josef mustache, then for his Italian surname, and finally for his coming from New York City dressed like a well-to-do mountain walker but aiming for the North Face of the Civetta. We settled on the Andrich-Fae, but rain cancelled our plans.

The second trip, we climbed the Steger on the Catinaccio, another route on the Tofana, but our main objective was still the Andrich Fae. When we walked back into the hut, the girls who ran the hut burst into laughter, saying "Mosconi, Andrich Fae!" with the thumbs up sign. Again it rained.

What occurred next was pure Bill.

"Bouch, I'm not staying here. Let's go to Venice." So we went to Venice where Bill booked us rooms at the Hotel Danielli, the luxury hotel preferred by discerning visitors to Venice for generations. Instead of festering in the rain in a drab hut, we visited the legendary Basilica of St. Mark, the Doge's Palace, and the Bridge of Sighs.

The next year, we again returned to the Dolomites for the Andrich Fae. It was to be our last climbing trip, but we didn't know it. We climbed the Fehrmann on the Campanile Basso as a warmup, then drove to the Civetta area. We attempted the West Face of the Torre Venezia. After climbing the easy but unprotected and mossy slabs, we climbed the traverse that begins the real climbing. That day, I didn't bring a helmet and was clunked by a stone kicked off above us. It knocked me out briefly, and took my desire to finish the route. My face covered with blood, we returned to the hut.

That was our last climb. A few weeks later I started flying paragliders and didn't climb for five years. During that time Bill stopped climbing also, and during that period his shoulders fell apart. When I resumed climbing again in 1993, Bill's shoulders could no longer take the stress. We made a half-hearted attempt to climb again in Chamonix in 1994, but we both knew our great climbing days together were behind us. In spite of that we stayed in close contact; we spoke several times a week, meeting once or twice a year in New York for American Alpine Club or Explorers Club functions. He was more than a friend; he was a great friend to me and I miss him terribly. [Editor's note: Bill Mosconi died suddenly in his sleep in New York City on July 29, leaving his wife Linda Ianeri and two young sons. An accountant and consultant by profession, Bill was the Treasurer of the Explorers Club.]

JOHN BOUCHARD, *AAC*

GEORGE R. SENNER 1924–2003

While in the Park Service at Mount Rainier National Park, I developed some of the closest friendships of my life, and many of us guides and park rangers met gals who later became our wives. It was there that my brother K and I also found our second brother, George Randolph Senner.

I first met George at the University of Washington in 1947, where as World War II veterans we were taking advantage of the G.I. Bill to further our education. George was among the vets of the 10th Mountain Division ("Mountain Troops") and, as he had also been serving as

George Senner.   *Dee Molenaar*

seasonal ranger at Mt. Rainier, we later became better acquainted through skiing, climbing, and participating in mountain search-and-rescue operations.

George had an interesting background. Born and raised on a Kansas farm, he and his folks moved to Tacoma where George went through public schools while noting Mt. Rainier on the southeastern horizon. With a friend he often biked to the mountain, peddling some 50 miles to Mowich Lake in the northwestern corner of the park, from where he began exploring the foothills peaks and snowfields.

While a senior in high school in 1942 George was called into the principal's office and confronted by man in an olive green uniform: Al Rose, chief ranger of Mount Rainier National Park. Apparently he had heard of George's cycling trips and was on a trip to town to seek out youths for summer work in the park, at a time when many college-age kids were being drafted into the army. He offered George a job as fire lookout at Anvil Rock during the summer of 1942. From then on George Senner was hooked on the mountain. During the summer evenings he often hiked the three miles to Paradise for a little night life before climbing back up to his post.

During World War II George served in the headquarters company of 85th Mountain Infantry Regiment of the famed 10th Mountain Division, and saw action in the Italian Campaign. Through the years he has maintained touch with his wartime buddies and made several return trips with his wife Glo to Italy to revisit scenes of those days of glory with the "Old 10th." George sent me a typed version of his war-time diary, and I found mention of several of his fellow mountain troopers, some who were or became members of the AAC: Glen Dawson, Bill Hackett, Bert Hirtle, Shorty Lange, and John Montagne.

It was at Paradise after the war that he met Gloria Olson, who worked as a waitress for the Park Company. After their marriage and upon his graduation from the UW with a major in geography, George took Glo to Europe, intending to stay only for the summer. But he found work in the Alps of Germany and Austria with the U.S. government. For awhile he managed the Schneefernerhaus atop the Zugspitze (Germany's highest peak), and later he was part of a team that evaluated and returned to Germans the property confiscated from them during the war. In their wide travels, much by bicycle, George and Glo became well acquainted with Europe and the

Alps, and this proved valuable to the trip K and I took with George through the Alps in 1973. The Senners' return to the U.S. was expedited with a Civil Service transfer from Europe to serving as a civilian advisor in the Army's Mountain and Cold Weather Training Command at Camp Hale. There he regained contact with some of his "Old 10th" buddies.

George had his career as sales rep for the Griffin Envelope Co./North Pacific Banknote Co. in Seattle, and made many friends in the local business community, even taking some up Mt. Rainier. Besides scrambling around together on Mt. Rainier—including taking Governor Dan Evans to the summit in 1965—and other Northwest volcanoes and peaks in the North Cascades and Olympics, George and I shared a rope in bringing Jim and Lou Whittaker down Mt. McKinley after their accident high on the mountain in 1960. Then in 1965 George arranged for me to join him in a climb of Mt. Kennedy in Yukon Territory, which culminated in our joining the party that took Senator Robert F. Kennedy to the summit.

Between pioneering new routes and serving in a number of rescue operations on Mt. Rainier and throughout the Cascades in the 1950s, George was a popular guide to the many friends, neophytes, and VIPs he took up The Mountain over many decades. He's been a member of the American Alpine Club since 1949 and was a charter member of the Seattle Mountain Rescue Unit in 1948, along with the 10th Mountain Division Association, the Pacific Northwest Ski Instructors Association, and the Ancient Skiers.

In our retirement years, as "Old Cronies Expeditions," George, my brother K and I, along with Elvin R. Bob ("Swede") Johnson and Kurt Beam, made a number of auto trips throughout the western U.S. and Canadian Rockies. These trips were enlivened with observations of the geologic settings and climbing history of the mountains, and I'll never forget the running descriptions by K—a real authority on the subject—of the geology of the Canyonlands of western Colorado and Utah. Meanwhile, during our cocktail hours in various motels along the route, George would relate the details of the many trips he shared with Glo in Europe and across the U.S.—his famous "Glo 'n' I" stories. For our later trips, George had acquired a camcorder and he prepared a great audiovisual record our trips to the Canadian Rockies and down the Oregon-California coast. Now that George, brother K, and Bob Johnson have passed on, these videos have provided Kurt and me with the clearest "contact" with our old cronies.

All of us who've known George will miss his cheery smile and personality—and sharing stories of mountains and mountaineers. Above all, we'll remember the great parties he and Glo hosted at their Seattle home, which kept many of us oldsters in touch with each other over the decades. Besides his wife Gloria, George is survived by daughters Kris, Gretchen, and Trudi and their families, all devoted mountain lovers and skiers.

DEE MOLENAAR, *AAC*

NECROLOGY

Bruce Andrews	David Gunstone	Landon G. Rockwell
George Van Brunt Cochran	Richard Hechtel	Ryan Sayers
John R. Durrance, M.D.	James Kurtz	George R. Senner
Guy Edwards	Ilse Letinger	Ira Spring
Andrew Embick, M.D.	William J. Mosconi	Mark Wagoner
Linnea Erickson	David Pengelly	Richard W. Wahlstrom
Don J. Forest	Polly Prescott	Rodman Wilson, M.D.
Roy M. Gorin	Jane C. Reid	Peter H. Wood

CLUB ACTIVITIES

EDITED BY FREDERICK O. JOHNSON

AAC, CASCADE SECTION. In 2003 the Cascade Section helped organize and sponsor two events in conjunction with a local web-based climbing group, cascadeclimbers.com. We also took part in a three-day mountaineering event hosted by REI in late February, which included talks and demos by such luminaries as Peter Croft and Mark Twight, giving the AAC some good exposure. In April we provided sponsorship in the form of prizes to the Sawtooth Film and Climbing Festival at Evergreen State College.

The first event, in June, was a slideshow and talk by Scott Backes. Scott drove from the flatlands of Minnesota to share his philosophy, experience, and advice from 27 years of cutting edge climbing. This was not just a slideshow. Scott used each of the five expeditions including, Mt. Kitchener in the Rockies in 1980, Fitzroy 1983, Denali 1985, Mt. Hunter 1984, and the single-push ascent of Denali in 2000 via the Czech Direct to show how these climbs changed his life and opened his mind to what is possible. He showed us how important it is to have mentors and teachers in the mountains. He made us think about why we climb and why it has become so attractive to more and more people to be able to escape the stressful, technological life of today. In the climb of the Czech Direct he taught us what can be achieved when you hone your body, mind, and skills, and have climbing partners with whom you have a deep connection and trust. In the questions and answers we learned tips and techniques for climbing light and fast using nutrition and equipment that was not available to the pioneers of this style of climbing. Altogether this was an excellent presentation and one to be recommended to other sections.

The second event was outdoors (a different approach!) in Leavenworth, as reported by Mike Beck of cascadeclimbers.com: "The rain may have gotten the climbers wet, but it didn't dampen their spirits. Nearly a hundred participants braved the weather to convene October 10-12 outside Leavenworth, Washington, to climb and celebrate the camaraderie of the vertical environment. During the day on Saturday, a beginner's climbing area was available, and Tacoma Mountain Rescue instructed people nearby on self-rescue techniques. A bratwurst and beer feast followed Saturday's climbing adventures. At dusk the real entertainment began. Slide shows by Steve Swenson (AAC) and Wayne Wallace, and more beer, were followed by a raffle of gear donated by over a dozen sponsors. The rain- soaked raffle raised $400 for the Access Fund and the *American Alpine Journal*. A slide show by Erden Eruc (AAC) on his 2003 self-powered expedition from Seattle to the top of Denali and back was the high point of the evening. Climbers awakened Sunday morning to find John Harlin cooking pancakes for everyone, with the assistance of Steve Swenson, while enjoying coffee and a talk from the Forest Service on ways climbers can minimize impact on the environment. A trails project got washed out by all the rain, but many climbers still went climbing. The weekend was a success. The third annual Cascade Climbers Full Moon Ropeup had met its founding objective—'fostering stewardship of the vertical environment.' Look for next year's event during the full moon in October at Bridge Creek Campground outside Leavenworth, Washington." We hope to do more joint events with cascadeclimbers.com and other local climbing groups.

The major mountaineering issue this year was the proposed changes to the Mount Rainier National Park management plan. Lloyd Athearn provided responses on behalf of the AAC with regard to both the proposed fee increases and to the changes to commercial climbing services. We are also monitoring a proposal for an underground science facility in the Alpine Lakes Wilderness area that is currently under consideration.

Congratulations to member Erden Eruc for completing the first part of his self- propelled climbing odyssey by cycling to and climbing Denali and cycling back to Seattle (5,546 miles). The next stages involve rowing, first to South America to climb Aconcagua and then on across the Pacific. For more information see www.around-n-over.org. For climbing exploits of other Section members see the expedition and first ascent notes in this Journal.

Lastly, the Section is pleased to have contributed $1,000 this year to the *AAJ* and would like to thank Craig McKibben, Raymond Huey, and Carlton Swan for their share of that donation. Please visit our Web site at http://cas.alpineclub.org, and if you have questions about the Section contact me at pdack1@attbi.com.

PETER ACKROYD, *Chair*

AAC, OREGON SECTION. Our winter Section expedition was made to Smith Rock to construct an emergency rescue litter shelter. Jeff Alzner, Richard Bence, Bob McGown, Bob Spike, and others participated. The Section has plans for other litter shelters at Smith Rock. The first shelter has an Oregon Section AAC plaque dedicating the shelter to Mike Bearzi, who died climbing in Tibet. Mike's family has assisted the Section.

This year our spring fundraiser was a slide show by Steve Boyer. He is a veteran of six Himalayan expeditions including a successful ascent of the south face of Annapurna. Steve is an accomplished speed climber, having set records on Mt. Hood. Steve is an MD who also holds a masters degree in glaciation. His program covered the highlights of his Himalayan career and he also discussed the major accident on Mt. Hood of May 30, 2002. Recently, Steve continued his glacier research with investigations of the glaciers on Mt. Hood with GPS positioning of the 12 glaciers on the mountain. He compared these present glacier positions with old Mazama photographs supplied by Mazama historian Jeff Thomas.

The Section supported the *Himalayan Bulletin*, Barbra Bower editor, and the Cooper Spur Coalition, a watchdog group on the development on Mt. Hood's Cooper Spur.

Our winter program was a presentation on the traverse of the Southern Picketts by Wayne Wallace. Wayne gave an interesting program on his Cascade climbs of 20+ years, culminating in the traverse of the southern Pickett range with Colin Haley and Mark Bunker. Wayne is a dedicated alpinist who was recently awarded the Section's Fred Becky award for his achievements in Cascade alpinism.

Longtime member, Vera Defoe, was recognized at the Mazama annual banquet for leading Mazama climbs for 37 continuous years through the age of 75. Earlier, the Explorer Scout troop sponsored by the Mazamas climbed a first ascent in British Columbia's Coast Range, naming it Mount Defoe. Vera led several climbs for the Scouts in the Pacific Northwest. She continues to be active in conservation and access issues.

The efforts of Neale Creamer and the Friends of Silcox Hut were noteworthy. This fall the friends along with Timberline Lodge installed a new snow tunnel on Silcox Hut for winter access to the 1933 WPA structure at 7,000 feet on Mt. Hood. This is an excellent base camp for an emergency south side rescue location. Section member Jeff Sheets, of the Friends of Silcox Hut, is also on the safety committee for *Accidents in North American Mountaineering*. Jeff and Bob Speik from Bend, Oregon, promptly reported several notable accidents.

June Hackett (Bill Hackett's widow) and Ric Conrad published Bill's climbing biography including exploits with the 10th Mountain Division and the 1958 K2 expedition. Bill was a longtime Section member and dedicated climber. The book is well laid out as a historical piece with comments by Charlie Shimanski, Dee Molenaar, and Bradford Washburn. The book covers Bill's expedition notes and will be an excellent reference document.

In August, Bob McGown and Steve Holman, President of the Oregon Science Teacher's Association, acted as climbing team support for the four-day experiment for NIAC (NASA Institute for Advanced Concepts) at the Skylight Cave system in Sisters, Oregon. Steve, an alpinist, was so enthused by the success of the CEMSS II biosphere that he plans to help his advanced biology students build several biospheres in the coming year.

The Section's climbing librarian Bob Lockerby created a 47- page index to the *American Alpine Journal* from 1997 to date.

BOB McGOWN, *Chairman*

AAC, SIERRA NEVADA SECTION. The year started with a sometimes-annual Markleeville ski trip. A few hardy souls were out to enjoy the "pow" and soak tired, weary limbs in, where else, but Grover Hot Springs. More people should attend this trip.

We held our spring meeting at John Hart's home in Marin County. Catered food, wine, and beer warmed up a crowd of about 40 people. Greg Couch gave an outrageous slideshow about the first winter ascent of Cerro Torre, in 1999, with three Swiss partners with whom he could barely converse. Our stomachs got pumped from laughing at Greg's epic battles with bad weather, cabin fever, and ... SUPERMICE! Thanks to Greg for sharing this amazing adventure with us and to John for opening his home to us.

In September Royal Robbins hosted his now annual Pinecrest gala with climbing at the Gianelli Edges. Thanks to Royal and Liz for their help in making this our most popular outing. Some 40-50 people attended over the course of the weekend.

Our fall meeting was held at Greg Murphy's house in the hills of Montclair. Some new energetic faces were on hand to liven things up. Climbing tales were told, some true and some embellished by Greg's home brew. Tommy Caldwell and Beth Rodden were on hand to present their "First Couple of Rock," a video of the couple's exploits and misadventures together. In the film the two talk candidly about dating on El Capitan, their epic in Kyrgyzstan, and the pressure of being professional climbers. It was riveting, touching, and funny. Our thanks to them and to Greg and Annie for their hospitality.

In December we held our annual meeting at Berkeley Iron Works. Shawn Chartrand, our Section's events coordinator, arranged for some awesome food that everybody thoroughly enjoyed. We actually had too much; where were the rest of you? Mark Wilford was flown in from Colorado to be our keynote speaker. He delivered in a huge way, as he described the epic tale of the first ascent of Yamandaka in the Indian Karakoram. When he described rappelling off an anchor of slings held in place by rocks stacked on top, the crowd seemed to shiver collectively.

Our hats off to Mark and his partner, AAC President Mark Richey, for this daring ascent made in uncompromising style.

This meeting also marked the end of my tenure as Section Chair. The torch was passed to Ellen Latham of Grass Valley. I had served for three years and had a great time. Thanks to all who helped make it so great and such fun. Let's get out and climb!

STEVE SCHNEIDER, *Chair*

AAC, NORTHERN ROCKIES SECTION. As an AAC representative, a board member of the Boise Climbers Alliance, and an Idaho local, Doug Colwell participated as a member of the Climbing Management Plan (CMP) for Castle Rocks State Park, which adjoins the City of Rocks National Preserve. Over two days the Climbing Management Team developed the CMP, which set forth the rules, recommendations, and guidelines surrounding new route development at Castle Rocks State Park upon opening in May 2003. One provision of the CMP created a lottery whereby 25 people were selected to enter the Park prior to its opening and to establish new routes. The Access Fund facilitated this meeting, and it was a wonderful example of how governmental agencies, non-governmental organizations, and individual climbers can work together for the overall benefit of the climbing community and the public at large. Several of our members were lottery winners, and during two weekends in mid-May helped establish over 40 new routes, which went in with minimal problems or conflicts, despite what the trade rags indicated.

In August, during the official opening of the Park, the AAC and the Access Fund presented Wallace Keck, director of Castle Rocks State Park, with a joint award for his willingness to work with climbers in developing the CMP. Others attending the ceremony were Idaho Governor Dirk Kempthorne, Senator Larry Craig, Rick Colligon, Director of Idaho Parks and Recreation, as well as National Park Service officials. This was a good opportunity to recognize the mutual cooperation of the groups involved.

In April the Boise Chapter of the Northern Rockies Section cosponsored a fund raising slide show by our member Mike Libecki with the Boise Climbers Alliance. Brian Wright has taken over as President of the Boise Chapter from longtime leader Susan Bernatus.

The Section hosted its first event in Salt Lake City with 150+ people attending. Black Diamond graciously sponsored Will Gadd as the speaker. The meeting identified several Salt Lake members interested in increasing the AAC presence in the Wasatch Valley. Mark Holbrook agreed to serve as the Section's Salt Lake City "President." Mark hosted a barbecue for members most desirous of energizing the group and acting on potential issues and projects.

Our fourth "almost annual" Fall Moondance occurred September 6-7 at City of Rocks, with over 45 people reserving space at the group campground, almost double last year's attendance.

DOUG COLWELL, *Chair*

AAC, CENTRAL ROCKIES SECTION. On February 14-17 the Fifth Annual Cody Ice Festival was held in the Shoshone River Valley southwest of Cody, Wyoming. CRS Chair Greg Sievers and AAC Board Member Charlie Mace were on hand to support the popular activity. The Section donated several AAC fleece embroidered jackets for the auction and supplied free AAC mugs to all attendees. This small, quaint event offers everyone a chance to mingle and socialize in the rustic setting of the DDX Ranch. The ice climbing in the area offers over 100 routes, few with grades less than WI3+. For those unfamiliar with the area, it is a world-class destination for ice climbing and a must for your resume. However, be prepared to hike, spend long, full days out, and be self sufficient and exceedingly safe. Treat it like an alpine adventure where your cell phone won't work.

Greg Sievers continued a diligent review of the proposed relocation of the Twin Owls parking lot at the popular Lumpy Ridge climbing area in Estes Park, Colorado. Unfortunately a challenge to the legal access through the MacGregor Ranch, which the public has used for over 40 years, failed. Relocation of the public access will add 1.5 miles to the climber's day if the destination were the "Book" or "Sundance" areas on Lumpy. This has been a 20-year process for the National Park Service, which included three environmental assessments, much public debate, and negative commentary. We will likely see the end of an era in the near future.

The 2003 Lumpy Trails Day on Lumpy Ridge was a commanding success! This is the third year that the AAC has hosted climbers, Club members, locals, and National Park Service employees to collaborate and improve the climber access trails to these highly popular and photogenic rock climbing crags. The narrow single-track access trails leading to the each of the magnificent crags are eroded by summer storms and increasing use. About 35 people showed up on October 18. Over 500 vertical feet of the rugged trail to Batman Rock was given a "complete" face lift, and at the Little Twin Owls bouldering area, 16 additional water bars were placed. The AAC provided donuts in the morning and full lunches delivered to the trail workers in the field. All volunteers received goodies from corporate sponsors, and a raffle was held that included outdoor gear donated by the AAC. Thanks to the vision of the Access Fund and their Adopt-A-Crag program, users and climbers are turning out in their own neighborhoods nationwide to repair trails at climbing crags like Lumpy Ridge.

The Section responded to a recent Environmental Assessment in Rocky Mountain National Park regarding the addition of paved, improved bus stops along the Bear Lake Road. While improvement for visitors is needed, we support vehicular access by the public in the years to come, despite shuttle bus improvement and increased use. With alpinists and climbers often starting their treks in the wee hours of the morning, we feel it is imperative for the NPS to maintain public vehicular access. The Section also responded to Environmental Assessments at Indian Creek and Fisher Towers recreation areas, where the BLM is developing a use plan.

GREG SIEVERS, *Chair*

AAC, NEW YORK SECTION. The New York Section, with membership now exceeding 700 in the Tri-State Area, tries to appeal to a broad cross section of members with a variety of outdoor climbing and indoor social events.

Activities invariably commence in late January with our Annual Adirondack Winter Outing, now entering its second decade. The winter of 2002-03 will be long remembered here in the East as one of the coldest and snowiest on record. As a result a capacity gathering of around 35 members and guests, both old and new members, were on hand to ice climb, snowshoe, and ski in almost ideal conditions in Keene, New York. For many, the chance to be with friends in an isolated, beautiful environment sharing intense experiences followed by a well-deserved cocktail hour and dinner makes it an annual ritual not to be missed. It also provides the opportunity for members to pair up and seek adventures farther afield. Such was the case of Todd Fairbairn and Howard Sebold, who met at the Outing and planned a successful expedition to Katahdin later in March. They recounted their adventure at a slide show co-hosted by the Section in the North Face store in Manhattan a few months later.

In the fall, we once again returned to the Gunks, where Jack Reilly and John Tiernan organized simultaneous outings and, a week later, to the High Peaks area of the Adirondacks for a weekend of climbing and hiking. As in the past, the historic Ausable Club was our base of operations. Despite the area being one of the East's oldest venues, spectacular new routes, such as on the South Face of Gothics (5.9–5.11), are constantly being discovered and opened up.

May and June were busy months. First we began with a party at the Brooklyn Brewery to benefit the Ascent Program, which teaches inner city kids to climb. In June we combined culture with climbing in the Hudson Highlands. After hiking in the Breakneck- Taurus area of Cold Spring, we attended a live, one-man stage show Willi about the life of the legendary climber Willi Unsoeld.

Finally, in November, we held our 24th Annual Black Tie Dinner. As usual, the event draws a capacity crowd of members and guests from around the country drawn by the presence of a celebrity speaker plus the opportunity to renew old friendships and make new ones. This year Peter Hillary was the special guest and spoke about his experiences on K2 in 1995, where good judgment in turning back just short of the summit no doubt saved his life. A riveting speaker, Peter stressed the need to rely on one's informed judgment and not be swayed by group psychology. On that expedition, Peter lost six of his teammates, including Alison Hargreaves, Britain's most successful woman high altitude mountaineer. In a change of pace and mood from Hillary's talk, Mark Richey, new President of the Club, discussed and showed slides of Huayllay, a remarkable, pristine rock climbing area about seven hours from Lima in Peru. Among the new faces were 14 new members who were introduced, gently "roasted," and presented their membership pins. One of these, Britton Keeshan, is close to his goal of being the youngest person, at age 22, to attain the seven summits: only Everest remains.

The dinner benefited the American Alpine Journal and the AAC Library. Over the years, this event has raised well over $100,000 for these and other AAC causes.

Special thanks go to our volunteer hosts, event leaders, and speakers, in particular Vic Benes, Chris Galligan, John Tiernan, Bob Hall, Jack Reilly, Richard Ryan, and Richard Wiese, in addition to others already mentioned above. Vic also doubles as our webmaster. For information on goings-on in the Big Apple, check out http://nysalpineclub.org.

Sadly we mark and mourn the loss of two of our members, David Boyd Brown and Peter Hodgson Wood. David, a member for 22 years, died as the result of injuries suffered in a bicycle accident. Peter, a member since 1951, was the son of former AAC President Walter Wood and served on the AAC Board in the 1980's.

PHILIP ERARD, *Chair*

AAC, NEW ENGLAND SECTION. Owing to the conjunction of the AAC's national meeting in Boston with our Section's Eighth Annual Dinner, we deferred the Eighth Annual for a year, putting our energies into the national gathering.

In June we offered a cookout and social at Nancy Savickas's new place in Albany, NH, which drew seven members.

Rick Merritt and Bill Guida traveled west to bag three state summits: Guadalupe Peak (TX), Wheeler Peak (NM), and Boundary Peak (NV).

In July climbers from New England, known as the "Adamant Eight," enjoyed eight fine days of mountaineering in complete isolation based at the Bill Putnam (Fairy Meadow) Hut in the Northern Selkirks. The weather largely cooperated, the company was great, and some attained eight summits in the eight days. The climbers included Tom Boydston, Tom Carey, Paul Dale (leader), Chris Dame, Richard Doucette, Yuki Fujita, Tom Parker, and Heidi Zinser. We admire the stamina and resolve of the early climbers in the area, such as Bill Putnam, Sterling Hendricks, and Andy Kauffman, and are grateful to Bill for erecting such a wonderful base camp.

Jim St. Jean, Robert Plucenik, and Dale Jancic toured the Santa Cruz Valley in the Cordillera Blanca in Peru. The trio climbed Nevado Alpamayo (5,947m) via the Italian Route after acclimatizing on Nevado Millishraju II (5,500m) and Nevado Loyacjirca (5,600m).

In April, Nancy Savickas with Eric and Zeb Engberg attended the Phoenix Bouldering Competition, where Zeb placed sixth in the elite category. Later in the season Nancy managed two weeks of climbing in the Swiss and Chamonix Alps, doing more rock than snow owing to the unprecedented heat that had effectively closed many of the high alpine routes.

BILL ATKINSON, *Chair, and* NANCY SAVICKAS, *Vice Chair*

THE MOUNTAINEERS. The Mountaineers continues to broaden its offerings of climbing courses, seminars, and programs with a continued commitment to conservation, stewardship, and access that creates a long-standing interest for its members. A growing number of people, currently 232, have been members of The Mountaineers for over 50 years! Donna Price, past Trustee, has organized an annual luncheon to recognize this extraordinary commitment. At this year's luncheon Bob Cram presented an entertaining history of the evolution of illustrations for Mountaineering: The Freedom of the Hills. His illustrations appeared in the first six editions of the text and provided the foundation for the new digitally generated illustrations in the latest edition.

Internationally-acclaimed mountaineering and cultural travel photographer Gordon Wiltsie, introduced by Mountaineers Honorary member Tom Hornbein, was featured at The Mountaineers 2003 Annual Banquet.

The Mountaineers Books was gratified for the enthusiasm and support its 2003 title *Arctic National Wildlife Refuge: Seasons of Life and Land* received from the media, from book buyers, and from the nonprofit community. This conservation title—focused on protecting the refuge from oil commercialization—received broad media attention in newspapers, general interest magazines, and on television. Author/photographer Subhankar Banerjee's images from the book were exhibited at the National Museum of Natural History, Smithsonian Institution in Washington, DC, the American Museum of Natural History in New York City, and the California Academy of Sciences in San Francisco. A generous grant from the Lannan Foundation recreated the photography exhibit into six sets for traveling throughout the country in 2004. *Arctic Refuge* won the 2003 Banff Mountain Book Festival top award for "Mountain Image" and was used as evidence in a U.S. Senate debate on opening the refuge to oil drilling. Conservationists won that debate by a narrow margin, and The Mountaineers Books was proud to have had a role in this important issue.

The publisher's most significant title—*Mountaineering: The Freedom of the Hills*—was released in its seventh edition thanks to the work of approximately 40 Club volunteers who labored for nearly two years on this new edition. [This and select other climbing titles published in 2003 are reviewed in this Journal—Ed.]

The Mountaineers Conservation Division is a major force in the creation of the Wild Sky Wilderness Bill. If signed into law this bill would make 106,000 acres north of Highway 2 near the Washington towns of Index and Skykomish federally designated Wilderness. Division members Harry Romberg and Norm Winn are earnestly lobbying Congress for passage of this important Wilderness Bill. Also, Conservation Chair Nancy Neyenhouse is working with conservation interests on the Mount Rainier National Park boundary extension project known as the Carbon River Valley Conservation Project. The Division graduated 90 students from its 10th annual NW Environmental Issues Course, which aims to inform the average citizen about the key environmental issues of our region including water, wildlife, forestry, global warming, and transportation issues as well as an advocacy session.

The Mountaineers Recreational Resources Division is working to ensure that fee collection under the federal user fee demonstration project is fair and workable, and to influence decisions on the future of the program. The Division has also been a key contributor working toward redistribution of Washington gas tax funds supporting trails and other recreation facilities. The new distribution formula will more accurately reflect the actual contributions of non-motorized trail users. The Division also worked with land managers at Mount Rainier National Park to ensure that climbing fee increases and commercial services adjustments do not inhibit individual climbers. The Division continues to work with Mount St. Helens National Monument to create a workable compromise between users such as skiers/climbers and snowmobilers. In addition to its advocacy work, the Division coordinated successful trail maintenance work parties on National Trails Day and tested the leave-no-trace knowledge of hundreds of boy and girl Scouts.

STEVEN M. COX, *Trustee*

THE MAZAMAS. The many and varied activities of The Mazamas, headquartered in Portland, Oregon, are developed and coordinated by six committees. The Climbing Committee, chaired by Charlene Degener, selects climb leaders, schedules climbs, sets standards, and conducts several levels of training. The Ski Mountaineering Committee, chaired by Wim Arts, encountered strong winds and sleet, which impaired the basic class day at Timberline Lodge and the ski tour planned for the following day. The Trail Trips Committee continued its pattern of expansion with 598 hikes, which attracted 6,217 hikers. The Tuesday and Thursday Street Rambles, which start at the Mazama clubrooms, have become a very popular and important segment of the club's hiking program. The Nordic Committee was hampered by low snow levels at Mt. Hood in January. The Outing Committee, chaired by Kim McClear, fielded nine domestic outings: hiking in Alaska, the Olympic Peninsula, and the North Santiam and Crater Lake areas; rafting in the Grand Canyon, a Lewis and Clark float on the Missouri River; land improvement at the Hart Mountain Antelope Reserve; and kayaking around the San Juan Islands. Foreign outings went to Peru, Switzerland, the Australian Outback, and Pico Aconcagua in Argentina.

The Expedition Committee made six grants totaling $6,700. The projects included climbing in the Zanskar Mountains of India (D. Anderson, A. Chapin, A. Chapman); climbs of Denali's West Buttress (R. & R. Lee, Nancy Miller), Nevado Ulta (T. Josephson, C. Buhler), Huascaran (E. Hoem, B. Wilson, V. Dunn), the North Face of Kalanka (C. Geisler, C. Buhler, R. Slawinski); and a search for the northernmost land on Earth (Lloyd Athearn and eight others).

The new Facility Task Force spent months of fruitless search for a new site for the Mazama clubrooms and offices. The club's rented building at SW 19th and Lovejoy Streets since 1957 will no longer be available after 2005. There is a surprising lack of suitable existing buildings or available land for building. So the search goes diligently onward into 2004. Gary Beck, Harold Crawford, and Eugene Lewins were elected to the nine-person Executive Council. John Youngman was elected President of The Mazamas.

JACK GRAUER, *Historian*

ARIZONA MOUNTAINEERING CLUB. The AzMC is a climbing and mountaineering club with approximately 500 members. In 2003 the club conducted several climbing schools, seminars, and master classes. Over 200 students participated in various training sessions. Two of our members, Richard Horst and Sean Colonello, attempted a new route on the Moose's Tooth in Alaska. They climbed and fixed ropes on the first third of the route but ran out of time due to weather delays. They will be returning in 2005.

The AzMC conducted its annual over-the-rim cleanup at the Grand Canyon. Led by Scott Hoffman, 60 members rappelled over various tourist look-out points and hauled up dozens of bags of trash. We also completed two trash pick-ups in the Queen Creek canyon area. The AzMC continues to be involved in local access issues. We are supporting access efforts of the McDowell Sonoran Land Trust. The Land Trust and the City of Scottsdale are purchasing land for a preserve that, when open, will have non-motorized access to hiking and climbing in the McDowell Mountains in North Scottsdale. In other access concerns, climbing on Mt. Lemmon, near Tucson, has been restricted due to a severe forest fire during summer 2003. Finally, the AzMC celebrated its 40th anniversary in April 2004.

BRUCE MCHENRY, *President*

ALPINE CLUB OF CANADA. Mountains. In addition to copious climbing options from New-foundland to Vancouver Island, Canadians are blessed with vast, unpopulated spaces in-between. But with a relatively small population inhabiting the world's second largest country, it's not easy to maintain a national identity in a social or political sense, not to mention viewing Canada's climbing community as a single cohesive entity. With over 10,000 members, the Alpine Club of Canada includes 18 regional sections.

Every November, the Banff Mountain Film Festival brings ACC members together. They volunteer in Banff at the festival's food concessions, which fund the ACC sponsored prize for Best Climbing Film, then gather in local auditoriums across the country for ACC organized screenings of the festival's best films. Last year the Vancouver section organized a two-week summer climbing camp in the Waddington Range's Upper Tellot Glacier area, the Prince George section embarked on its first international trip to climb warm rock at Joshua Tree in California, and the Ottawa section staged a summer camp at the A.O. Wheeler Hut in Rogers Pass. Volunteer-led mountain outings are the backbone of the ACC, as is a commitment of stewardship toward the places those adventures take place. Across the country, section members collaborate, as the Outaouais, Montreal, and Ottawa sections have, to create the Keane Farm Management Committee. Last August the Manitoba section hosted an invitational climbing weekend for Thunder Bay members, returning Thunder Bay's hospitality during its invitational ice-climbing weekend. Online, the Edmonton section maintains the Alpine Accidents in Canada Website to the benefit of all Canadians.

Along with volunteer-led club outings, ACC membership offers valuable leadership training, from telemark clinics to backcountry orienteering, watercolor painting workshops to writing contests, adventure races to ice climbing festivals. All promote the club's founding objectives: the encouragement and practice of mountaineering and mountain crafts, the education of Canadians in appreciation of their mountaineering heritage, the exploration of alpine and glacial regions, and the preservation of their natural beauties.

Under its new and broader Mountain Culture heading, the publications committee continues to celebrate the people and events that shape Canada's alpine heritage through its ever-expanding library. Three times a year Mountain Culture's volunteers produce the full color *Gazette*, bringing ACC and mountain related news to members across the country. Every year since 1907, climbers in Canada and other alpine nations have looked forward to exploring the pages of the *Canadian Alpine Journal*. Working in partnership with other organizations and individuals, in 2003 Mountain Culture published *Artists of the Rockies: Inspiration of Lake O'Hara*, by Jane Lytton Gooch. Honoring the Association of Canadian Mountain Guides' founding members at the 2003 ACC Mountain Guide's Ball annual fundraiser, Mountain Culture produced the ACMG's only published history, *Route Finding*, by Lynn Martel.

While the past is important to all cultures, so is the present and future. The ACC's Competition Climbing Canada/Compétition d'Escalade Canada encourages Canadian youth to pursue climbing, with over 100 registered athletes competing on a regular basis. Last year 12 climbers traveled to Bulgaria for the World Youth Championships, where Vancouver's Sean McColl won his 17 year-old age category. The Canadian Ski Mountaineering Competition Committee has developed a proposal for a ski mountaineering competition to take place in the Rockies, with plans for a Canadian team for this growing sport. The Huts Committee is planning a new Fay Hut to replace the historic log cabin that was lost to forest fire last August. Honoring the club's past, the Fairy Meadow Hut was renamed the Bill Putnam Hut last summer, while the ACC took over management of the new Kokanee Glacier Trudeau Hut.

While dedicated volunteers put their expertise in areas of access and environment to use for the benefit of club members and all Canadians, the Grants Committee handed out $12,500 last year to worthy mountain related projects, including the Cliff Face Vegetation Communities Project to research and document the impacts of sport climbing on cliff face vegetation in the Niagara Escarpment area, and the Vampire Spires all-woman first-ascent attempt near the NWT's Cirque of the Unclimbables.

Like any organization, the ACC faces unforeseen challenges. Rising liability insurance costs have affected the club's financial picture, as did last year's SARS outbreak, rampant forest fires in B.C., and an unusually high number of avalanche deaths. Such challenges are unavoidable, but serve to highlight the strength of Canada's mountaineering community and its partnerships with related organizations, including the Union Internationale des Associations d'Alpinisme and the American Alpine Club. And at the end of the day, ACC members head to their nearest hills, crags, cliffs and peaks to celebrate the blessing of being able to do so.

LYNN MARTEL

INDEX

COMPILED BY RALPH FERRARA AND EVE TALLMAN

Mountains are listed by their official names and ranges; quotation marks indicate unofficial names. Ranges and geographic locations are also indexed. Unnamed peaks (e.g. Peak 2,340) are listed under P. Abbreviations are used for some states and countries and for the following: Article: art.; Cordillera: C.; Mountains: Mts.; National Park: Nat'l Park; Obituary: obit. Most personnel are listed for major articles. Expedition leaders and persons supplying information in Climbs and Expeditions are also cited here. Indexed photographs are listed in bold type. Reviewed books are listed alphabetically under Book Reviews.

SUBMISSIONS GUIDELINES

The *American Alpine Journal* records the significant climbing accomplishments of the world in an annual volume. We encourage climbers to submit brief (250-500 words) factual accounts of their climbs and expeditions. Accounts should be submitted by e-mail whenever possible. Alternatively, submit accounts by regular post on CD, zip, or floppy disk. Please provide complete contact information, including e-mail address, postal address, fax, and phone. The deadline is December 31, through earlier submissions will be looked on very kindly! For photo guidelines and other information, please see the complete Submissions Guidelines document at the American Alpine Journal section of www.AmericanAlpineClub.org.

Please address all correspondence to:
The American Alpine Journal, 710 Tenth Street, Suite 140, Golden, CO 80401 USA; tel.: (303) 384 0110; fax: (303) 384 0111; aaj@americanalpineclub.org; www.AmericanAlpineClub.org